Portraits of 21st Century Chinese Universities:
In the Move to Mass Higher Education

CERC Studies in Comparative Education

30. Ruth Hayhoe, Jun Li, Jing Lin & Qiang Zha (2011): *Portraits of 21st Century Chinese Universities: In the Move to Mass Higher Education.* ISBN 978-988-17852-3-7. 483pp. HK$300/US$45.

29. Maria Manzon (2011): *Comparative Education: The Construction of a Field.* ISBN 978-988-1785-26-8. 295pp. HK$200/US$32.

28. Kerry J. Kennedy, Wing On Lee & David L. Grossman (eds.) (2010): *Citizenship Pedagogies in Asia and the Pacific.* ISBN 978-988-17852-2-0. 407pp. HK$250/US$38.

27. David Chapman, William K. Cummings & Gerard A. Postiglione (eds.) (2010): *Crossing Borders in East Asian Higher Education.* ISBN 978-962-8093-98-4. 388pp. HK$250/US$38.

26. Ora Kwo (ed.) (2010): *Teachers as Learners: Critical Discourse on Challenges and Opportunities.* ISBN 978-962-8093-55-7. 349pp. HK$250/US$38.

25. Carol K.K. Chan & Nirmala Rao (eds.) (2009): *Revisiting the Chinese Learner: Changing Contexts, Changing Education.* ISBN 978-962-8093-16-8. 360pp. HK$250/US$38.

24. Donald B. Holsinger & W. James Jacob (eds.) (2008): *Inequality in Education: Comparative and International Perspectives.* ISBN 978-962-8093-14-4. 584pp. HK$300/US$45.

23. Nancy Law, Willem J Pelgrum & Tjeerd Plomp (eds.) (2008): *Pedagogy and ICT Use in Schools around the World: Findings from the IEA SITES 2006 Study.* ISBN 978-962-8093-65-6. 296pp. HK$250/US$38.

22. David L. Grossman, Wing On Lee & Kerry J. Kennedy (eds.) (2008): *Citizenship Curriculum in Asia and the Pacific.* ISBN 978-962-8093-69-4. 268pp. HK$200/US$32.

21. Vandra Masemann, Mark Bray & Maria Manzon (eds.) (2007): *Common Interests, Uncommon Goals: Histories of the World Council of Comparative Education Societies and its Members.* ISBN 978-962-8093-10-6. 384pp. HK$250/US$38.

20. Peter D. Hershock, Mark Mason & John N. Hawkins (eds.) (2007): *Changing Education: Leadership, Innovation and Development in a Globalizing Asia Pacific.* ISBN 978-962-8093-54-0. 348pp. HK$200/US$32.

19. Mark Bray, Bob Adamson & Mark Mason (eds.) (2007): *Comparative Education Research: Approaches and Methods.* ISBN 978-962-8093-53-3. 444pp. HK$250/US$38.

18. Aaron Benavot & Cecilia Braslavsky (eds.) (2006): *School Knowledge in Comparative and Historical Perspective: Changing Curricula in Primary and Secondary Education.* ISBN 978-962-8093-52-6. 315pp. HK$200/US$32.

17. Ruth Hayhoe (2006): *Portraits of Influential Chinese Educators.* ISBN 978-962-8093-40-3. 398pp. HK$250/US$38.

16. Peter Ninnes & Meeri Hellstén (eds.) (2005): *Internationalizing Higher Education: Critical Explorations of Pedagogy and Policy.* ISBN 978-962-8093-37-3. 231pp. HK$200/US$32.

15. Alan Rogers (2004): *Non-Formal Education: Flexible Schooling or Participatory Education?* ISBN 978-962-8093-30-4. 316pp. HK$200/US$32.

14. W.O. Lee, David L. Grossman, Kerry J. Kennedy & Gregory P. Fairbrother (eds.) (2004): *Citizenship Education in Asia and the Pacific: Concepts and Issues.* ISBN 978-962-8093-59-5. 313pp. HK$200/US$32.

Earlier titles in the series are listed on the back page of the book.

CERC Studies in Comparative Education 30

Portraits of 21st Century Chinese Universities:
In the Move to Mass Higher Education

Ruth HAYHOE, Jun LI, Jing LIN, Qiang ZHA

SERIES EDITOR
Mark Bray
Director, Comparative Education Research Centre
The University of Hong Kong, China

ASSOCIATE EDITOR
Yang Rui, *Comparative Education Research Centre*
The University of Hong Kong, China

INTERNATIONAL EDITORIAL ADVISORY BOARD
Robert Arnove, *Indiana University, Bloomington*
Beatrice Avalos, *University of Chile, Santiago*
Nina Borevskaya, *Institute of Far Eastern Studies, Moscow*
Michael Crossley, *University of Bristol*
Gui Qin, *Capital Normal University, Beijing*
Gita Steiner-Khamsi, *Teachers College, Columbia University, New York*

PRODUCTION EDITOR
Emily Mang, *Comparative Education Research Centre*
The University of Hong Kong, China

Comparative Education Research Centre
Faculty of Education, The University of Hong Kong,
Pokfulam Road, Hong Kong, China
© Comparative Education Research Centre

First published 2011
ISBN 978-94-007-2788-5   e-ISBN 978-94-007-2789-2
DOI 10.1007/978-94-007-2789-2
Springer Dordrecht Heidelberg London New York

Library of Congress Control Number: 2011941865

© Springer Science+Business Media B.V. 2012
No part of this work may be reproduced, stored in a retrieval system, or transmitted in any form or by any means, electronic, mechanical, photocopying, microfilming, recording or otherwise, without written permission from the Publisher, with the exception of any material supplied specifically for the purpose of being entered and executed on a computer system, for exclusive use by the purchaser of the work.

Printed on acid-free paper

Springer is part of Springer Science+Business Media (www.springer.com)

Contents

List of Abbreviations — vii

List of Figures — ix

List of Tables — ix

List of Photos — x

Foreword — xiii
　Robert F. ARNOVE

Introduction and Acknowledgements — 1
　Ruth HAYHOE

Part I: Overview and Main Themes — 19

1. Understanding China's Move to Mass Higher Education from a Policy Perspective — 20
　Qiang ZHA

2. Equity, Institutional Change and Civil Society – The Student Experience in China's Move to Mass Higher Education — 58
　Jun LI

Part II: Portraits of Three Public Comprehensive Universities — 94

3. Peking University – Icon of Cultural Leadership — 95
　Ruth HAYHOE and Qiang ZHA, with YAN Fengqiao

4. Nanjing University – Redeeming the Past by Academic Merit — 131
　Jun LI and Jing LIN, with GONG Fang

5. Xiamen University – A Southeastern Outlook — 162
　Ruth HAYHOE and Qiang ZHA, with XIE Zuxu

Part III: Portraits of Three Education-Related Universities — 190

6. East China Normal University – Education in the Lead — 192
　Ruth HAYHOE and Qiang ZHA, with LI Mei

7. Southwest University – An Unusual Merger and New Challenges — 221
　Jun LI and Jing LIN, with LIU Yibin

8. Yanbian University – Building a Niche through a Multicultural Identity 244
Jing LIN and Jun LI, with PIAO Taizhu

Part IV: Portraits of Three Science and Technology Universities 270

9. The University of Science and Technology of China – Can the Caltech Model take Root in Chinese Soil? 271
Qiang ZHA and Jun LI, with CHENG Xiaofang

10. Huazhong University of Science and Technology – A Microcosm of New China's Higher Education 307
Ruth HAYHOE and Jun LI, with CHEN Min and ZHOU Guangli

11. Northwest Agricultural and Forestry University – An Agricultural Multiversity? 344
Qiang ZHA and Ruth HAYHOE, with NIU Hongtai

Part V: Portraits of Three Private Universities 372

12. Yellow River University of Science and Technology – Pioneer of Private Higher Education 374
Ruth HAYHOE and Jing LIN, with TANG Baomei

13. Xi'an International University – Transforming Fish into Dragons 400
Jun LI and Jing LIN, with WANG Guan

14. Blue Sky – A University for the Socially Marginalized 422
Jing LIN and Qiang ZHA

Part VI: Conclusion and Future Directions 450

15. Is There an Emerging Chinese Model of the University? 451
Qiang ZHA

Notes on the Authors 472

Index 473

List of Abbreviations

Measures
- Mu (畝): Traditional Chinese unit of area. One Mu is equal to 1/15 of a hectare or 1/6.1 of an acre.
- Yuan (人民幣圓) – Unit of money used in Mainland China. One Yuan was equal to 0.15 of a US Dollar as of March 1, 2011.

AEARU	Association of East Asian Research Universities
APRU	Association of Pacific Rim Universities
BBS	bulletin board system
BCE	Before the Common Era
Beida	Peking University
BK21	Brain Korea 21
BSU	Blue Sky University
CAS	Chinese Academy of Sciences
CE	The Common Era
CMHE	China's Move to Mass Higher Education
CNRS	French National Center for Scientific Research
COE21	Centers of Excellence in the 21st Century
CPC	Communist Party of China
CRC	Canada Research Chair
CSOs	civil society organizations
CUSPEA	China-US Physics Examination and Application
ECNU	East China Normal University
EEG	Electro-Encephalography
ENS	Ecole Normale Supérieure
GONGOs	government-organized non-government organizations
HEEC	Higher Education Evaluation Center
HFNL	the Hefei National Laboratory for Physical Sciences at the Microscale
HHUST	The Yellow River University of Science and Technology

HUST	Huazhong University of Science and Technology
MOE	China's Ministry of Education
Nanda	Nanjing University
NGOs	non-governmental organizations
NNSF	China's National Natural Sciences Foundation
NJU	Nanjing University
NPOs	non-profit organizations
NWAFU	Northwest Agriculture and Forestry University
OISE	Ontario Institute for Studies in Education
OLS	ordinary least squares
PECASE	U.S. Presidential Early Career Award for Scientists and Engineers
PKU	Peking University
PS	political socialization
SCI	The Thomson Scientific's Science Citation Index
SES	socio-economic-status
SWU	Southwest University
TSOs	third sector organizations
USTC	University of Science and Technology of China
WNLO	Wuhan National Laboratory for Optoelectronics
WUR	Wageningen University and Research Center
XAIU	Xi'an International University
Xiada	Xiamen University
XMU	Xiamen University
YBU	Yanbian University

List of Figures

0.1	The Geographical Location of Our 12 Case Study Universities	7
1.1	Higher Education Net Enrollment and Participation Rate Increase: 1990-2008	27
1.2	Three Economic Regions in China	34
2.1	The Conceptual Framework of the Individual Political Socialization Process	73

List of Tables

1.1	Provinces (Municipalities and Autonomous Regions) in Three Economic Regions	33
2.1	Martin Trow's Typology of the Institutional Transformations of Mass Higher Education	71
2.2	Summary of Questionnaires Administered	74
4.1	Statistics on Faculty and Teacher-Student Ratios	154
7.1	Undergraduate Student Enrollment of Southwest University (1990-2005)	225
8.1	Statistics on Undergraduate Student Enrollments from 1990 to 2005	248
8.2	Statistics on Faculty and Teacher-Student Ratios	261
9.1	The USTC's Recruitment Size, 1990-2005	287
9.2	The USTC's Funds under Project 21/1, 1996-2005 (in million *yuan* RMB)	292
9.3	The USTC's Funds under Project 98/5, 1999-2001 (in million *yuan* RMB)	293
10.1	Statistics on Faculty and Teacher-Student Ratios (1990-2005)	333
11.1	The NWAFU Recruitment Size, 1990-2007	352
11.2	Gender and SES Profile of the NWAFU New Enrollment (%), 2005-2007	353
11.3	Disciplinary Patterns of the NWAFU Undergraduate Programs, 2005	355
11.4	The NWAFU's Revenues and Proportion of Budgeted Appropriations, 2000-2007 (in RMB million *yuan*)	356
11.5	The NWAFU Faculty Development, 2000 vs. 2005	357

List of Photos

3.1	The Unnamed Lake	113
3.2	The New Library	117
3.3	The West Gate	122
3.4	The Lang Run Garden	126
4.1	The North Building, designed by American architect A.G. Small as the administration building of the Private University of Nanking in 1919 and still serving as Nanda's administration center nowadays, is widely thought to express Nanda's ethos of "Sincerity with Aspiration, Perseverance with Integrity".	148
4.2	The 25-story Anzhong MBA Building (2007) of the Business School, Nanda's Manhattan, is a new icon of Nanda's spirit in its pursuit of dynamism, excellence and internationalization.	151
4.3	The Flagpole, first erected in 1935 shortly before the Anti-Japanese War and relocated to the South Schoolyard in 1964, is a symbol of freedom and democracy on the Nanda campus.	158
5.1	The Jiannan Auditorium	174
5.2	The Main Administration Building at Xiamen University	181
5.3	The Main Teaching Building on the new Jiageng Campus	182
5.4	The Furong Buildings on the Main Campus of Xiamen University	184
6.1	The Sciences Quadrangle	207
6.2	The Liwa River on ECNU's urban campus	212
6.3	The Minhang Campus with the Yingtao River	216
6.4	The History and Arts Building	217
7.1	Statue of Chairman Mao holding in his hand a blueprint for the new China, erected in 1954, in front of the steps leading up to the original main administration building of Southwest Normal University and representing its ethos of service to the region.	229

7.2	Bust of Wu Mi (1894-1978), an influential scholar in comparative literature who returned from Harvard University in the early 1920s and taught at Southwest Normal College from 1950 up to his death in 1978, in the Wu Mi Garden.	231
7.3	The Great Auditorium, located at the center of the SWU campus in Beipei, symbolizing the university's dynamic spirit and the diversity of the southwest region.	242
8.1	The Logo of Yanbian University – Chinese and English are used in the outer circle, while the inner circle has the Korean word for Yan.	247
8.2	The Main Administrative Building	251
8.3	The Main Teaching Building, recently built, represents YBU's move towards modernity and globalization	252
8.4	The main entrance of the University where its name is written in both Chinese and Korean characters	266
9.1	The Statue of Guo Moruo on the USTC East Campus	281
9.2	A Night View of the USTC's West Campus	282
9.3	The Number One Teaching Building on the USTC East Campus	299
9.4	The Statue of Two Oxen Holding up the Globe on the USTC's East Campus	301
10.1	The South First Building (南一樓) at the Core of the HUST Campus	321
10.2	The Map of the Main Campus shows the Location and Size of the Iconic Nanyi Building, facing the Main Gate, and the Grid-like Pattern of the Overall Campus Layout.	322
10.3	The Wuhan National Laboratory for Optoelectronics (WNLO), the center of Wuhan Optics Valley, located on the east side of HUST main campus in Hankou, is a cutting edge national platform for inter-disciplinary research in opto-electronics.	328
10.4	The outdoor old theatre, located in the central area of the main campus still had a rusted sign on its front en-trance with HUST's original name, the Huazhong Institute of Technology.	338

11.1	The Number Three Teaching Building on the NWAFU's North Campus, Symbolizing Courage and Perseverance.	346
11.2	The International Center on the NWAFU's South Campus	356
11.3	The Long Staircase with 93 Steps in Five Sections in Front of the NWAFU's North Campus Gate, the Original Campus of Northwest Agricultural University	365
11.4	The Historic Library on the NWAFU's North campus	369
12.1	The Library & Information Building on the Fo Gang Campus	379
12.2	The Concert Hall and College of Music on the Urban Campus	385
12.3	The Emblem of the Rising Sun inside the entrance gate to Yellow River's Urban Campus	397
13.1	The Sculpture of A-Fish-Becoming-A-Dragon erected on the Cultural Square of Yuhua campus, symbolizing the XAIU's dynamic ethos inherited from traditional Chinese culture.	409
13.2	The Teaching Building in European Style integrates learning with the school motto "Comprehensiveness with Diversity, Innovation with Self-Strengthening (多元集納，自強創新)."	418
13.3	The Cultural Square with the six sculptures of ancient educators in China and in the West, from Confucius, Laozi and Cai Yuanpei (right), to Plato, Aristotle, and Humboldt (left), symbolizing XAIU as a place where all creative thoughts, traditional or modern, Eastern or Western, are nurtured and encouraged.	420
14.1	An aerial view of the campus of Blue Sky University, with its gourd-like shape expressing the idea of it as a container of miraculous energy.	428
14.2	Main gate to the campus of Blue Sky University	441

Foreword

In his book *River Town*, Peter Hessler describes the changes that have taken place along the Yangtze River with the construction of the Three Gorges Dam. As he notes, "That sense of transformation – constant, relentless, overwhelming change – has been the defining characteristic of China during the past two decades."[1] He contrasts the dramatic changes in China following its opening in 1978 to the outside world and the move to market socialism with the long prevalent notion articulated by eminent historian Leopold von Ranke that the Chinese were "the people of eternal standstill". How the seemingly contradictory forces of change and constancy play out in Chinese higher education is documented in this magisterial book by Ruth Hayhoe, Jun Li, Jing Lin and Qiang Zha.

Portraits of 21st Century Chinese Universities is the most authoritative study to date of the dialectical relationship between globalization and local realities in the particular institutional and regional contexts of China. As such, it is a significant scholarly contribution to the comparative study of higher education systems around the world. The book raises important issues in the field of comparative education concerning the trade-offs between quantity and quality, and between access and equitable outcomes for the increasing numbers of formerly excluded students from rural and lower class backgrounds who now have expanded opportunities to attend both public and private universities. Close collaboration among the contributing authors has resulted in a remarkably consistent set of chapters with regard to the research questions studied, the data gathered, and the ways in which important themes are addressed. These themes relate to institutional mission, vision, governance, finance, curricular emphases, civic education/participation and democratization of Chinese society. Each chapter provides the responses of administrators, faculty, and students to the challenges of globalization and massification.

The authors have judiciously selected 12 universities to represent the range of institutional types that have come into existence since the 1990s: three comprehensive, three education-related, three science and technology, and three private universities. The introduction and first two

---

[1] Peter Hessler, "Return to Fuling," in *River Town: Two Years on the Yangtze* (New York: Harper Paperback, 2006), p.5.

substantive chapters provide historical and conceptual frameworks for understanding the 12 case studies, and a concluding chapter brings all the pieces together by examining whether or not there is an emerging Chinese model of the university. The final chapter's author, Qiang Zha, summarizes what is perhaps the principal finding of the book: "modern Chinese universities [have] emerged between the worlds of European and Chinese culture and epistemology – a place where deep conflicts were inevitable – and they should not be viewed simply as a product of Westernization" (p.460).

Indeed, *Portraits of 21st Century Chinese Universities* is an ideal example of the synergistic relationship that can occur between Western and Chinese epistemologies and research traditions. Not only are the authors from different societal and disciplinary backgrounds, but they took special care to enlist the support of scholars in each of the institutions studied so as to ensure that local realities were reliably documented. In doing so, the authors ensured a more democratic set of institutional descriptions and conclusions.

The most important contribution of this book may reside in its illustrating the "dialogue among civilizations" explored by Hayhoe and Pan.[2] At inter-university and inter-societal levels the dialogue is based on values involving "the melding . . . of Western traditions of university autonomy and academic freedom with Chinese values of self-mastery, social responsibility, and intellectual freedom that has taken shape over a century of modern higher education development in China."[3] This dialogue, characterized by equal status relations that "recognize and value difference", has much to contribute to the worlds of scholarly knowledge and policy analysis. In turn, much in the tradition of comparative education, a firm theoretical understanding of the way things work, and why, is a starting point for reaching more reasonable courses of action that can lead to transformations in education and society.

---

[2] Ruth Hayhoe and Julia Pan (eds.) *Knowledge Across Cultures: A Contribution to Dialogue Among Civilizations*. (Hong Kong: Comparative Education Research Centre, The University of Hong Kong, 2001).

[3] Ruth Hayhoe and Jian Liu. "China's Universities, Cross-Border Education and Dialogue among Civilizations," in David W. Chapman, William K. Cummings and Gerald A. Postiglione. (eds.) *Crossing Borders in East Asian Higher Education* (Hong Kong: Comparative Education Research Centre, The University of Hong Kong and Springer: 2010), pp.96-97.

Readers will find this admirable study of great value for its insights into the transformations in Chinese society and higher education, and as a model of how to conduct cross-cultural research in both the most rigorous and democratic ways. It has been a pleasure and honor for me to have reviewed the manuscript and now written this Foreword.

Robert F. Arnove
Chancellor's Professor Emeritus
Indiana University, Bloomington, USA

Introduction and Acknowledgements

Ruth HAYHOE

This book has been truly a collaborative effort, with four scholars in the inner circle of our efforts to understand China's universities as they have been transformed through the massification process of the early 21st century, and many other scholars contributing in diverse ways. In the autumn of 2005 we made application to the Social Sciences and Humanities Research Council of Canada for funds to enable us to study the changes that had come about in Chinese higher education between 1990 and 2005, and we are most grateful for the support they provided us. As we put together our research proposal, three questions stood out as being of greatest importance, both for China's own socio-political, cultural and economic development, and for a wider global community with which China is interacting in more and more significant ways. It is appropriate to begin this introduction by presenting these questions, since they have shaped the research methods we adopted and the results that are presented in this volume:

1. What kinds of cultural resources are Chinese universities drawing from their own civilization and how do these inform their activities, as they move onto a global stage?
2. How has the move to mass higher education stimulated civil society and the emergence of forms of democracy shaped by Chinese civilization?
3. How has the move to mass higher education affected the diversity of the system and what have been the consequences for equity of access and provision?

These questions immediately tell the reader something about the four co-authors of this book, their background experience and intellectual interests. Ruth Hayhoe has dedicated her scholarly career to researching and reflecting on the cultural values that have undergirded modern Chinese universities, in their evolution over the 20th century. While their development has been strongly influenced by Japanese, German, French, American and Soviet university models at different periods, the heritage of cultural values associated with China's civil service examination system, and with the independent academies or *shuyuan* that flourished between the 9th and 19th centuries, have continued to shape contemporary universities.[1] This has been especially evident in the period of reform and opening up, from 1978 to the rapid move towards mass higher education between 1999 and 2005. As China's economy has grown dramatically, and its leaders have taken new directions in political diplomacy, strengthening their ties with Africa and Latin America, as well as engaging pro-actively with Europe and North America, we felt it was important for us to reflect on the role of her universities. For the first time in the modern period, an active program of cultural diplomacy has been launched, with the establishment of several hundred Confucius Institutes for the dissemination of the Chinese language and culture around the world.[2] Given the unique arms-length arrangement for the management of this program, under the Office of the Chinese Language Council International, universities in China and abroad are playing a significant role in the development of these institutions.[3] This is a minor dimension of the global activity of China's universities in the 21st century, but it leads us to ask what values they will bring to global engagement, and what dimensions of Chinese culture will shape their interactions with universities around the world. Will they be in a position to contribute new ideas or initiate new ways of looking at global issues, given the resources of a civilization that is quite distinct from that of the Western world?

Our second question might be seen as equally important for China itself and for countries around the world seeking to understand and engage with her. In the short span of time from 1990 to 2005, the number of higher education students in China increased from under three million to around 23 million, putting enormous pressures for democratization and the development of civil society on China's highly centralized one-Party political system.[4] Universities are key actors in the democratization

---

[1] Ruth Hayhoe, *China's Universities: 1895-1995: A Century of Cultural Conflict* (Hong Kong: Comparative Education Research Centre, The University of Hong Kong, 1999).
[2] Rui Yang, "China's Soft Power Projection in Higher Education," in *International Higher Education*, No.46, Winter, 2007, pp.23-24.
[3] Ruth Hayhoe and Jian Liu, "China's Universities, Cross-Border Education and the Dialogue among Civilizations," in David W. Chapman, William K. Cummings and Gerard A. Postiglione (eds.), *Crossing Borders in East Asian Higher Education* (Hong Kong: Comparative Education Centre, The University of Hong Kong and Springer, 2010), pp.76-100.
[4] Jun Li and Jing Lin, "China's Move to Mass Higher Education: An Analysis of Policy Making from a Rational Framework," in David P. Baker and Alexander W.

and opening up of society, with a huge number of graduates now seeking employment across all sectors of society, including graduates of newly burgeoning private universities, and an increasingly highly educated population demanding accountability from their government at all levels.

Jing Lin has devoted much of her scholarly career to understanding the contribution of education to the dramatic social changes taking place in China over recent decades, including an important volume entitled *The Opening of the Chinese Mind*,[5] and a series of studies on private schooling and private higher education.[6] She has explored notions of social capital and civil society in a Chinese context and explained some of the unique connotations these terms take on in a society that now defines itself as one of market socialism, yet that is also still profoundly influenced by Confucian familial and social values.

Jun Li has published extensively on classical Chinese educational history, with a first doctorate in this field from China.[7] He also has a second doctorate in international education policy and considerable experience in the study of citizenship education in East Asian contexts.[8] As a postdoctoral fellow working full-time on the project from 2006 to 2008, he has played an important leadership role in our explorations into the first question on the cultural resources Chinese universities are drawing upon as they take up a global role. He also contributed greatly to our reflections on the second question: how are contemporary China's universities, with their hugely increased student numbers, contributing to civil society formation and incipient forms of democratic development?

Our third question brings us into the dimension of comparative studies of the massification of higher education around the world, with its focus on issues of diversification, access and equity in the change process. Qiang Zha developed a strong interest in the comparative theo-

---

Wiseman (eds.), *The Worldwide Transformation of Higher Education* (Oxford: Elsevier Science Ltd., 2008), p.271.

[5] Jing Lin, *The Opening of the Chinese Mind* (New York: Praeger, 1994).

[6] Jing Lin, *Social Transformation and Private Education in China* (New York: Praeger, 1999).

[7] Jun Li, *Xuanrufodao Jiaoyu Lilun Bijiao Yanjiu* (*A Comparative Study of the Educational Theories of the Schools of Metaphysics, Confucianism, Buddhism and Daoism*) (Taipei: Wenjin Press, 1994), 512pp; Jun Li, *Jiaoyuxue Zhi* (*A History of Chinese Thought on Education*) (Shanghai Peoples Press, 1998), 461pp.

[8] Jun Li, "Student Achievement in Social Studies in Urban Public Schools: China and Japan," in *Education and Society* (Australia), Vol.23, No.3, 2005, pp.35-54.

retical exploration of the diversification of higher education systems in his doctoral thesis, putting the Chinese higher education system under the scrutiny of Western theoretical frames, and examining its diversification process through a range of quantitative measures.[9] He has drawn upon perspectives from organizational theory such as population ecology, resource dependency and institutional isomorphism in identifying similarities and differences between the Chinese and the international experience. He is also experienced in the analysis of educational policy making processes, and has applied that skill to an exploration of the policy development process in China's move to mass higher education.

Research Design

Given the breadth of our three research questions, we developed a research design that had three major phases, and would be carried out over a period of three to four years. The first phase involved a careful study of the policy development process for China's move to mass higher education at the national and local levels. Special attention was given to the different roles of senior government figures, scholars, scholarly institutions and regional government offices. Qiang Zha and Jing Lin carried out a series of interviews in Beijing, Shanghai, Xiamen and a minority region of Southeast China in December of 2006, in order to see what could be gleaned from conversations with officials and scholars, that might fill out the analysis of the policy process found in the research literature.

Chapter 1 of this volume, by Qiang Zha, presents various aspects of the policy study. One of its interesting findings is the significant role played by scholars and researchers in the policy process, both as individuals and through major state funded research projects. This indicates the persistence of a pattern long noted in Chinese society of "establishment scholars" offering their knowledge and expertise in direct service to the state, paralleling the role of scholar officials in traditional China. The policy study also uncovers dimensions of the change process

---

[9] Qiang Zha, "Diversification or Homogenization: How Governments and Markets Have Combined to (Re)Shape Chinese Higher Education in Its Recent Massification Process," in *Higher Education: The International Journal of Education Planning*, Vol.58, No.1, 2009, pp.41-58; Qiang Zha, "Diversification or Homogenization in Higher Education: A Global Allomorphism Perspective," in *Higher Education in Europe*, Vol.34, Nos.¾, 2009, pp.459-479.

relating to the structure of the higher education system, access, equity and quality that are illuminated by the comparative literature on higher education massification.[10] At this point we would like to acknowledge the work of five graduate students who contributed significantly to the study through the literature review work that they carried out as graduate assistants at the Ontario Institute for Studies in Education (OISE) of the University of Toronto: Jian Liu, Marina Ma Jinyuan, Yuxin Tu, Lijuan Wang and Xiaoyan Wang.

The second phase of the study involved a series of case studies of different types of universities in different regions of the country. We wished to present a lively picture of how different institutions are dealing with the opportunities, threats and challenges of rapid massification since 1999, also how their visions for the future, strategic planning and key decisions are reflecting different elements of the Chinese context. In choosing the case study institutions, we made a conscious decision to select nine public institutions and three private institutions, since around 12% of enrollments were in private higher education when we began the study, and this percentage increased to increase to 19.4% by 2008.[11] China has a tradition of excellence in private higher education both in the Nationalist period, and over its long history, particularly that of the classical academies or *shuyuan*. Although private higher education was abolished after the revolution of 1949, it re-emerged in the 1980s, and has benefited from the new opportunities provided by the massification policy. A few outstanding institutions show promise for scholarly leadership in the longer term future, even though they are in an entirely different league from the major public universities at the present time. These institutions have tended to draw upon powerful and colorful cultural symbols to raise their profile in Chinese society: "Yellow River," always thought of as the heartland of Chinese civilization, "Turning Fish into Dragons," a phrase associated with the civil service examinations during the Tang dynasty when Xi'an was the imperial capital and "Blue Sky," a concept associated with openness and inclusivity to those suffering social disadvantage.

---

[10] Qiang Zha and Jing Lin, "China's Move to Mass Higher Education: The Policy Process," under review.

[11] Jun Li and Jing Lin, "China's Move to Mass Higher Education," p.272; Jian Liu and Xiaoyan Wang, "Expansion and Diversification in Chinese Higher Education," in *International Higher Education*, No.60, Summer, 2010, p.7.

It will become very evident in the analysis of the policy process and the structural changes in China's higher education over the period of massification that it is the provincial and local level institutions, also private institutions, which have carried the major burden of expansion, while top-tier public universities have seen more modest expansion and in some cases focused on increases only in graduate enrollments. They have also benefited from significant funding from the national government to enable them to maintain their elite standing and strive for world-class quality. Given our interest in the potential cultural contributions which Chinese universities will bring into the global higher education community, as expressed in our first question, we decided that our focus should be on institutions that are in a position to be global actors. Seven of the nine institutions are thus part of the elite 98/5 project, launched at the time of Peking University's centenary in May of 1998, which provides significant additional funding to 43 top institutions, while another two are part of the earlier 21/1 project, launched in 1993, and giving priority funding to about 100 universities nationwide. In selecting the three private universities, we also tried to identify those which have potential for a global role in the longer term future.

A second consideration that influenced our selection of cases was that of geography. We wanted to ensure that the twelve institutions were spread over all major regions of the country. China's rapid economic development has been uneven in terms of region, with the major coastal areas moving ahead most quickly. Thus location has tremendous importance for higher institutions in the Chinese context, and differing regions of the country have different economic conditions, as well as unique elements in their historical experience of higher education development.

Thirdly, we wanted to ensure that all main types of university were represented in the selection of our case studies. Thus we have chosen several major comprehensive universities, as well as two universities of science and technology and one university of agriculture and forestry, both of these being institutional types that emerged with the establishment of the socialist planning system in the early 1950s.[12] We also selected one normal university, with a historic mandate for teacher education, and one university mainly serving a minority population. A further consideration that affected our choice of institutions was the wave of mergers that has been encouraged by the Chinese government in

---

[12] See Ruth Hayhoe, *China's Universities 1895-1995*, pp.77-80.

the process of expansion and the upgrading of an elite group of institutions to global standards. In our choice of institutions we made sure there were some that have embraced a major merger, others that rejected merger entirely and yet others which made their own choice of partners for merger, rather than following Beijing's directives.

The map in Figure 0.1 shows how the twelve universities are distributed throughout China's heartland, and we list them here in the order in which the case studies are presented. Part Two of this volume includes three major comprehensive universities: Peking University (PKU) in Beijing, Nanjing University (NJU) in Nanjing, Jiangsu province and Xiamen University (XMU) in Xiamen, Fujian province. Part Three presents three universities with a strong orientation towards education: the East China Normal University (ECNU) in Shanghai, Southwest University (SWU) in the major city of Chongqing and Yanbian University (YBU) in Yanji, Jilin province, the only institution in China's Northeast, and one that serves a minority Korean population. Part Four sets out case studies of three universities of science and technology: The University of Science and Technology of China (USTC) in Hefei, Anhui province, the Huazhong (Central China) University of Science and Technology (HUST)

Figure 0.1: The Geographical Location of Our 12 Case Study Universities

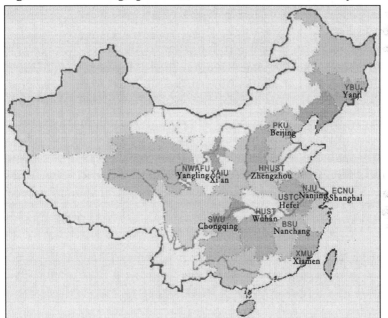

in Wuhan, Hubei Province, and the Northwest Agriculture and Forestry University (NWAFU) in Yangling, Shaanxi province. Finally, Part Five includes the three private universities which we have selected for the study: The Yellow River University of Science and Technology (HHUST) in Zhengzhou, Henan Province, the Xi'an International University (XAIU) in Xi'an, Shaanxi province and the Blue Sky University (BSU) in Nanchang, Jiangxi province.

Willingness to participate was another important factor in our selection process, and a few changes had to be made from the original list of institutions we drew up. Nevertheless, we were able to maintain the principles of selection in terms of types of institution and a broad spread of geographical location. At this point we would like to express appreciation to two academic advisors who were visiting scholars at OISE over the 2006/2007 academic year, attended our project meetings regularly and helped us in important decisions over the selection of institutions. Professor Huang Mingdong of Wuhan University and Professor Zhou Guangli of the Huazhong (Central China) University of Science and Technology in Wuhan also gave advice over the design of a set of base data tables, whereby we gathered information on changes in enrollments, curricular patterns, faculty profiles and finance and budgeting over the period from 1990 to 2005. The collection of this data has served to provide an empirical basis that is roughly comparable for each of the twelve institutions.

Another invaluable advisor and mentor to the project has been Dr. Julia Pan, Senior Coordinator for International Initiatives in the Dean's Office at OISE and a constant encourager to all of us. Some time before the project was born, she assisted in a set of pilot interviews with university leaders in Shanghai and Hangzhou, and she has continued to take a strong interest in the research.[13] We were also privileged to have Dr. Cristina Pinna, a postdoctoral fellow from the University of Cagliari in Sardinia, Italy, spend two autumn terms with our project team, as she carried out research on academic relations between China and Europe.[14]

---

[13] Ruth Hayhoe and Julia Pan, "China's Universities on the Global Stage – Views from University Leaders," in *International Higher Education*, No.39, Spring, 2005, pp.20-21.

[14] Cristina Pinna, "EU-China Relations in Higher Education" (paper presented at an international workshop on "The Dynamics of Transformation in East Asia",

She spent the two spring terms at Peking University, where we linked up with her when doing our case study research there in May of 2008 and our culminating workshop in May of 2009.

Research for the case studies was carried out in the spring of 2007 and 2008, with two members of our core team spending four to six days at each university, interviewing a range of university leaders, and holding focus group meetings with faculty and students. We sought to gain as many insights as possible into the way in which each institution had handled the change process, also to explore their emerging ethos. Gaining institutional permission for these studies and making all the logistical arrangements was a demanding process, and we decided to invite a scholar with experience in higher education research at each university to partner with us. Thus we would like to acknowledge a debt of gratitude to thirteen collaborating scholars from our case institutions, following the order in which the portraits of their universities appear in this volume: Professor Yan Fengqiao of Peking University, Professor Gong Fang of Nanjing University, Professor Xie Zuxu of Xiamen University, Professor Li Mei of East China Normal University, Professor Liu Yibin of Southwest University, Professor Piao Taizhu of Yanbian University, Professor Cheng Xiaofang of the University of Science and Technology of China, Professors Chen Min and Zhou Guangli of the Huazhong (Central China) University of Science and Technology, Professor Niu Hongtai of the Northwest University of Agriculture and Forestry, Ms Tang Baomei of the Yellow River University of Science and Technology, Professor Wang Guan of the Xi'an International University and Professor Xu Xiangyun of Blue Sky University.

The members of our focus group meetings with faculty and students were selected to represent different disciplinary fields in the university: humanities, social sciences and natural sciences and technology. The collaborating scholar from each institution played a key role in selecting individuals who were willing to join a focus group meeting, and comfortable with providing the individual consent necessary in our ethical review process. For faculty members, an effort was made by the collaborating scholar, in cooperation with one of the vice-presidents or the higher education research institute, to select faculty members who would be interested in the questions we wished to discuss,

---

the University of Edinburgh, October 24-26 2007) and published in *The Asia-Europe Journal*, Vol.7, Nos.3-4, December, 1009, pp.505-527.

as these had been provided well in advance. For students, our ethical protocol specified that they would be identified through consultation with the student government, but we imagine our collaborating scholars were also influenced by practical concerns of student availability and political concerns, in some cases, that the students chosen should represent their institution appropriately. Thus there were a few institutions where the student focus group members seemed to be well connected with the Communist Party or the Youth League, but this was not the case for all institutions. We can say that a wide range of disciplines were represented in the members of faculty and student focus groups, and many interesting and candid views were expressed, though we cannot claim these voices to be "representative" in any rigorous sense.

The third phase of our study involved a survey of students in all twelve of the case study institutions. We felt it was important to hear the voices of students in this way, and not only through the focus group meetings. They were asked to respond to questions relating to issues of equity and access, also to give their observations on how the transition to mass higher education affected teaching quality and campus culture, and their ideas on and experiences of civil society and civic participation. In each of our case study institutions we selected three classes of third year students, one from the humanities, one from the social sciences and one from sciences and technologies, with about 60 students in each class. All were invited to fill out a questionnaire which had been developed and pilot tested by the core research team in the early months of our project work. In spite of the sensitivity of the questionnaire, we were pleased that all twelve case study universities gave permission for the survey to be administered, and data collection was completed in the spring and summer of 2007. This made possible the inputting of all the survey data over the summer and autumn of 2007, with significant assistance from our team of graduate students at the University of Toronto.

In Chapter 2 of this volume, Jun Li presents the major findings of the survey and interprets them through a comparative analysis of core concepts in the Chinese and Western literature. We believe this chapter provides a helpful backdrop for the case studies, and particularly for the findings from the student focus group meetings which were held on each of the twelve campuses. I would also note that Dr. Li has written two articles in international refereed journals that go into greater depth on the survey findings, and that two of our graduate students are using the survey data in doctoral theses recently completed.[15]

Portraits of 21st Century Chinese Universities

The main body of this volume is made up of twelve portraits of contemporary Chinese universities in the context of China's move to mass higher education. In crafting these case studies we were inspired by the work of Burton Clark in his influential volume on the entrepreneurial university.[16] Clark selected five institutions in the Northern European countries of Holland, England, Scotland, Finland and Sweden on the basis of their reputation for an entrepreneurial spirit and their success in self-initiated change that took them from being entirely dependent on state funding to a situation where a significant percentage of their funding came from non-governmental sources. He was particularly interested in innovative features of their curricula, research, and service to local and regional economic development.

Clark studied these five institutions through the collection of documents about their development, both historical and contemporary, and through visits which allowed him to carry out interviews with members of the leadership at various levels. He also observed administrative practices, curricular and research innovations and initiatives whereby the institutions were responding to a local and regional public. After immersing himself in the data he had collected, he came up with what might be described as a grounded theory about the conditions that nurtured these entrepreneurial institutions: a strengthened steering core, an enhanced development periphery, a discretionary funding base, a stimulated heartland and an entrepreneurial belief, that had transformed institutional

---

[15] Jun Li, "Fostering Citizenship in China's Move to Mass Higher Education: An Analysis of Students' Political Socialization and Civic Participation," in *International Journal of Educational Development*, Vol.29, No.4, 2009, pp.382-398; Jun Li, "The Student Experience in China's Move to Mass Higher Education: Institutional Challenges and Policy Implications," under review; Ji'an Liu, "Equality of Educational Opportunity in China's Move to Mass Higher Education since the 1990s" (PhD thesis, University of Toronto, 2010); Yuxin Tu, "A Chinese Civil Society in the Making? Civic Perceptions and Civic Participation of University Students in an Era of Massification" (PhD thesis, University of Toronto, 2010).
[16] Burton R. Clark, *Creating Entrepreneurial Universities: Organizational Pathways of Transformation* (Oxford: Elsevier, 1998).

culture towards the valuing of openness and change over tradition.

In Yin's classic work on case study research, he has noted that case studies may be exploratory or explanatory, depending on the situation.[17] Clark's cases demonstrate elements of both, as he explores and defines the emerging concept of an entrepreneurial university, while also explaining the changes in management, organizational structure and financial provisioning that made them possible. He developed a broad theoretical frame applicable to all, yet also identified historical and geographical factors and curricular characteristics in individual cases that made a specific contribution to their entrepreneurial identity.

Thus for Chalmers University in Sweden, the fact that it had been founded in the early 1800s as a private institution dedicated to technical education and only later incorporated into Sweden's public higher education system may have accounted for some aspects of its entrepreneurial success. The fact that Strathclyde University in Scotland had been founded in 1796 in protest against the academicism of the University of Glasgow, with a conscious emphasis on "practical arts for practical students,"[18] was an equally significant element in its history. Geographical factors also played a role, particularly for Twente University in the Netherlands which had been established as a technological university in a remote eastern part of the country in the 1960s, and for Joensuu in Finland, also in a geographically remote area and with a curriculum that focused on teacher education.

In depicting how each of the case universities rose from marginal status within their national systems and became institutions with a high academic standing and innovative orientation, Clark highlighted one or two major initiatives that gave concrete expression to the unique features of each case, while bringing out elements that were common in the transformation of each case. His open-minded exploratory approach reminded us that it was important to listen intently and observe carefully when we carried out our case study visits, and avoid imposing our own pre-conceived theories or hypotheses. His work also reminded us of the importance of institutional history and of geography.

Our core question in studying twelve Chinese universities in the early 21st century was naturally quite different from that of Clark. We wanted to see if the contours of an emerging Chinese model of the

---

[17] Robert Yin, *Case Study Research: Design and Methods* (London: Sage, 1989).
[18] Clark, *Creating Entrepreneurial Universities*, p.61.

university might be found and whether it could be interpreted in relation to persisting elements of China's cultural and scholarly traditions. Our first question focused on the cultural contributions Chinese universities might make to the world community, and led us to a series of questions around vision, mission and strategic planning with leaders at different levels. It also led us to reflect on particular aspects of each institution's history, and to examine recent curricular developments, the organization of teaching and learning as well as research policies and practices, in order to see how the emerging ethos was expressed in these core areas of the university's work. We tried also to discern how far faculty members and students were aware of their institution's vision and mission, and how they related to its history and culture.

In addition to collecting relevant documents, such as mission statements and teaching evaluation reports, developing a set of base data, and collating the information we were able to glean from interviews, we wanted to find visual expression for the university ethos. Therefore we asked leaders, faculty members and students which building or which part of their campus space best expressed its spirit. This has enabled us to include three or four photos from each campus in our portraits, with some comments from university members on why these had become "places of the heart." There were also interesting differences of view in some cases!

Our second question related to the development of civil society in China and how the expansion was affecting relations between the university and government, also the attitudes, expectations and activities of faculty and students, both within the campus and in the wider society. We asked leaders to tell us what it meant for the university to have the status of a legal person, recently enshrined in the 1998 Higher Education Law, and the extent to which there was democratic participation in major decision-making processes. We asked faculty and students about their views of civil society and their opportunities for participation in decision-making processes on campus and in formal and non-formal political or social organizations that linked them to developments in the wider society.

Our third question was the most wide-ranging, covering issues of structure, equity, access and quality. In talking to leaders we were interested in their attitudes towards institutional merger, their approaches to the reconfiguration of campus space, and their decisions regarding whether or not to establish independent second tier colleges as a way of enrolling additional students at higher fees, as well as their views on many other strategic issues. In talking to faculty members and students, we wanted to understand how they perceived these decisions, and how their teaching and learning experiences and their life opportunities were being affected by the move to mass higher education.

Over our four to five days of listening, observing, discussing and debating,[19] we tried to formulate a holistic portrait of each institution, and then encapsulate that in written form at a later point. This involved immersing ourselves in the base data tables that had been provided, the relevant institutional documents and our extensive notes from interviews and focus group meetings. In some cases we listened to tapes of the interviews and meetings in order to recreate the experience of our visit in a vivid way. For each case, we had a lead author, whose name is given first, and who crafted the first draft of the case study, before seeking inputs from the other core member of the research team who had participated. After that the draft was shared with the collaborating scholar of each institution in China, for their feedback and any corrections or amplifications they might with to provide. In addition, we invited all of them to a workshop held at Peking University in May of 2009, so they could offer constructive criticism on the first draft of Chapters 1 to 14 of this volume, and suggestions for the final chapter. We were delighted that ten of the thirteen collaborating scholars were able to come, together with several other scholars doing related work in Beijing. We had three intense days of dialogue, sharing and comparative reflection, with each of the scholars giving detailed attention to two or three of the draft chapters. We have since sought to incorporate their perspectives into the book, as far as has been possible. We have also invited four of them to provide written reflections on our portraits, following the grouping of four distinct types of institutions in the book. We were delighted that all four were able to participate in the Annual Meeting of the Comparative and International Education Society in Chicago in March of 2010, where their papers provided interesting feedback on the findings of the project from the perspective of scholars

---

[19] In many cases institutional members, whether leaders, faculty or students, had studied our questions carefully in advance, and thanked us for stimulating them to think about these issues.

working within Chinese universities. They were published in a special issue of *Frontiers of Education in China* in December of 2010.[20]

Our purpose in presenting these portraits is not to measure Chinese universities against others around the world or to examine how far their patterns conform to international theories, norms or expectations. Rather it is to give them space for a self-depiction of the kind of university they envision themselves becoming in the 21st century. In Western scholarship, criticism is seen as a sine-qua-non of excellence and reliability, and we acknowledge that the way in which we have organized this study may have blunted some of the normal possibilities for critical analysis. However, we have tried to be attentive to the debates and divergent voices that were heard in almost all institutions, and to include them in our portraits. We also believe the pro-active support of university leaders, which was essential to our ethical protocol, and the direct involvement of collaborating scholars in each institution, brings authenticity to the portraits, an advantage that may compensate for the absence of a purely objective external scrutiny.

In the end, it is you the reader who will judge whether these portraits give you insights into an emerging Chinese model of the university in the twenty first century, and whether they succeed in showing the diversity of pathways that have been chosen by institutions with distinctive histories, curricular constellations and geographical settings. We hope you will see these universities as personalities, that share a common source of civilizational values, yet have responded differently to the opportunities, threats and challenges of the massification process.

Not long ago, I published a book entitled *Portraits of Influential Chinese Educators*, which told the stories of eleven influential Chinese educators, and interpreted them in the context of Confucian educational values and ideas, broadly defined.[21] Each of the educators was a unique individual, who had made remarkable contributions in both educational thought and action. They had grown up in different time periods and different regions of China, and had served within different institutions in all the major regions of China. Their lives and educational ideas were thus quite diverse, yet there were certain threads that bound them together, reflecting their shared educational heritage. I hope this book

---

[20] *Frontiers of Education in China*, Vol.5, No.4, December 2010.
[21] Ruth Hayhoe, *Portraits of Influential Chinese Educators* (Hong Kong: Comparative Education Research Centre, The University of Hong Kong and Springer, 2006).

can serve a similar purpose, presenting portraits of twelve contemporary universities, which have certain common features that may be interpreted by reference to their shared heritage in classical Chinese civilization, while also having diverse characteristics that reflect the different visions and strategies that have been adopted in the increasing autonomy from central government control they have enjoyed in recent years.

The use of the word autonomy at this point is almost sure to bring certain questions to the mind of readers of this volume. How much genuine autonomy do Chinese universities have in the contemporary period, and how far are they able to enjoy the kinds of academic freedom that are considered essential to scholarly excellence in the Western context? It has already been noted that Chinese universities were given the status of "legal persons" in the 1998 Higher Education Law,[22] the first to be promulgated in China since 1949. In the same law, the governance system of Chinese universities was defined as "a system of presidential responsibility and accountability under the leadership and guidance of the Chinese Communist Party."[23] While Chinese universities enjoy a growing measure of autonomy over matters such as student enrollment, curricular development, research, international partnerships, mergers and property development, as will be evident in many portraits in this book, there are clearly certain political constraints. These are related to the role of the Communist Party Committee on each campus, with the Party Secretary functioning almost as a Chairman of Council and the President responsible for all major academic decisions. Governance remains a fairly sensitive issue, but readers will find quite a detailed depiction of how this system functions in the portrait of Peking University in Chapter 3.

In my research on Chinese universities over the past twenty five years, I have continued to puzzle over how far the iconic terms "university autonomy" and "academic freedom" from the Western tradition can be used to represent or reflect on the core values of traditional and contemporary Chinese universities. My sense is that it has been important for Chinese universities to gain the protection of law for their action as legal persons, and they have benefited greatly from efforts to introduce the Western principle of autonomy ever since the early

---

[22] "Higher Education Law," *Chinese Education and Society*, Vol.32, No.3, May/June 1999, pp.68-87.
[23] *Ibid.* Article 39, p.78.

experience of Peking University under the influence of Cai Yuanpei, a Chinese scholar who spent many years at the Universities of Leipzig and Berlin. Nevertheless, the Chinese term for autonomy as "self-mastery" (自主) is more often used in discussions about autonomy within China, than the term for autonomy as "self-governance" (自治) which has the connotation of legal or political independence. Chinese universities have always had a closely interactive relation with the state, which arises from the strong tradition of the civil service examinations and the scholar's sense of direct social responsibility. This will be evident in some of the portraits, and will be discussed in greater detail in Chapters 1 and 15 of this volume. Western readers will need to open their minds to grasping some of the subtleties around this term, rather than simply assuming it means subservience to the state.

Similarly the term "academic freedom" (學術自由), which is used to denote a kind of freedom particularly appropriate to the university in the Western context, and which arose from the dominant epistemology of rationalism and dualism in a European context, is not a good fit for China. On the one hand, Chinese scholars enjoy a greater degree of "intellectual authority" (思想權威) than is common in the West, due to the history of the civil service examinations and the close links contemporary universities have with major state projects. On the other hand, there is a strong tradition of "intellectual freedom" (思想自由) in China, which is rooted in an epistemology quite different from that of European rationalism. It requires that knowledge be demonstrated first and foremost through action for the public good, also that knowledge be seen as holistic and inter-connected, rather than organized into narrowly defined separate disciplines. Chinese scholars find it difficult to limit their criticisms to theoretical debates, but feel called upon to demonstrate them in action, and many have paid a high price for this. Similarly they are not likely to stay within the parameters of their particular discipline, but claim a much wider ground in expressing criticism of authority.[24] In this, there are interesting parallels with American pragmatism and the

---

[24] These distinctions have been elaborated in detail elsewhere. See for example Ruth Hayhoe and Jian Liu, "China's Universities, Cross-Border Education and Dialogue among Civilizations," pp.77-100; Jun Li, "World-class Higher Education and the Emerging Chinese Model of the University," *Prospects: Quarterly Review of Comparative Education Quarterly*, forthcoming.

ways in which academic freedom has developed since the statement put forward by the American Association of University Professors in 1916.[25]

I close this introduction with a simpler yet somewhat symbolic aspect of the interaction between Chinese and Western academia – the ordering of personal names. Chinese always places the surname first, and most Chinese show their respect for Western custom by turning their name order around to suit the Western reader. We felt it would be both unnatural and inappropriate to subject all Chinese names in this study to such a distortion, and so have retained the Chinese name order for historical figures and all those living in Mainland China.

Finally, I would like to express sincere thanks to Professor Robert Arnove, who was invited by the Comparative Education Research Centre to review the manuscript before its final acceptance for publication. He read the whole text with great care and gave us detailed comments, chapter by chapter, on points that needed elaboration and clarification. This was a gift beyond compare, that was greatly appreciated by all four authors, as we prepared the final version.

---

[25] Richard Hofstadter and Wilson Smith, *American Higher Education: A Documentary History* (Chicago and London: University of Chicago Press, 1961), Vol. II, p.874.

Part I:
Overview and Main Themes

Part I includes two chapters which provide detailed analyses and insights into important dimensions of China's move to mass higher education at a national level. In Chapter One, Qiang Zha examines the policy process, bringing together findings from interviews held at the national and regional level with key government leaders and scholars involved in decision-making and putting them in the context of the relevant literature. In Chapter Two Jun Li considers the literature on higher education and the development of civil society, in both Chinese and Western contexts, as well as dealing with issues of how equity of access and success has been affected by the move to mass higher education and how students view the changes coming about in this process. This chapter not only draws upon a rich comparative literature but also presents concrete empirical findings arising from a survey of over 2,300 students in our twelve case study universities.

1
Understanding China's Move to Mass Higher Education from a Policy Perspective

Qiang ZHA

The focus of this chapter will be on presenting an analysis of the policy process in the move to mass higher education. It will also provide an empirical overview of the major changes to China's higher education system in the transition to mass higher education, setting this in a comparative framework.

First of all, however, it may be helpful to say something about the persisting core values of Chinese higher education that can be seen in the development of China's universities over the 20th century. While the earliest modern universities were influenced by the Japanese experience, subsequent development reflected European continental models of the university in the period between 1911 and 1921, American influences between 1922 and the early 1930s, then a period in which these external models were adapted to the Chinese context and a uniquely Chinese model of the modern university began to take shape during the second world war and the subsequent civil war.

With the Revolution of 1949, all of the experience and experimentation of these years was set aside, in favor of adopting a Soviet model of higher education, which was close to the continental European model in its main characteristics. Only since the reforms of 1978 has this model given way to forms of experimentation that are once again making possible the emergence of a Chinese model of the university – a process that has been speeded up with the rapid massification since 1999. The case studies that constitute the main body of this book exemplify some common features of this new model. They also illustrate the considerable diversity that has accompanied the greater autonomy experienced by individual institutions, reflecting their geographic settings, curricular characteristics and differing visions and strategic choices.

In her study of modern Chinese higher education development over the 20th century, Hayhoe noted that the European core values of academic freedom and autonomy were never a perfect fit, since persisting values from China's own traditional academic institutions tended to skew these values in one direction or another. Instead of the academic freedom of the medieval European university, which was expressed in debates over theoretical issues in particular disciplinary fields in the modern German context, Chinese scholars were drawn to a broader notion of intellectual freedom. This notion embraced action as well as theory on the one hand, and pointed to an intellectual authority that was closely affiliated with structures of state power on the other. In place of the autonomy which had arisen from the charters given to European medieval universities by Pope or Emperor and which persisted in the modern Anglo-American context, Chinese universities tended to be closely affiliated with the state, and university scholars served in important advisory roles in a kind of scholarly supervision over state power, on the one hand, or took such an independent and critical stance that their very existence was threatened in the face of state power, on the other.[1]

These polarities of value reflected a rich institutional tradition of scholarship in China which went back much earlier in history than that of the medieval university of Europe. Ever since the Han dynasty, formal institutions of scholarship had been a part of the structure of imperial rule, and a system of written examinations was gradually developed, which opened up an opportunity for young men to compete for positions in the imperial bureaucracy. Higher learning was thus a formalized part of the state system of rule, and those selected through these examinations were given positions of great responsibility on a meritocratic basis. While they did not enjoy academic freedom, they did exercise a high degree of intellectual authority, even to the point of admonishing the emperor on the basis of principles in the classical texts.

On the other pole were informal scholarly institutions, which maintained some independence through the ownership of land and through locations that were often geographically remote. A strong tradition of criticism of imperial authority developed in these academies or *shuyuan* (書院), where the same classic texts were debated, critiqued and revitalized over time. While they were characterized by a high degree of intellectual freedom, the academies never received the kind of formal legal protection conferred by the charter in the medieval Euro-

---

[1] Ruth Hayhoe, *China's Universities: 1895-1995: A Century of Cultural Conflict* (Hong Kong: Comparative Education Research Centre, The University of Hong Kong, 1999), pp.10-13.

pean context, and they rose and fell in different historical periods. Thomas Lee suggests that they could be viewed as a kind of embryonic civil society in the Chinese historical context,[2] a theme that has been developed in Chapter Two of this volume.

In the modern period, it has often been said by scholars such as Philip Altbach, that there is only one fundamental model of the university, that of medieval Europe, which has been universally adopted through processes of colonization, modernization and more recently globalization.[3] If one looks closely at the comparative higher education literature, however, a significant distinction was made by Burton Clark in his early study of *Academic Power* between what he defined as the European continental model and the Anglo-American model of the university.[4] Similarly, Guy Neave has differentiated between the Roman model and the Saxon model. While the Roman model is characterized by a top down integration of the university into the structures of the state, with all professors being civil servants, the Saxon model exemplifies a bottom up approach to knowledge and power with universities maintaining their status as legal persons, continuing to own property, and professors never becoming a part of the civil service.[5] The distinction between these two models seems to suggest two rather different historical traditions that have left their mark on the modern university. In the medieval European university tradition autonomy and academic freedom were protected by a legally recognized charter, while in the Chinese academic tradition, which began to influence Europe in the 18th century, knowledge served state power directly and scholars were granted a high degree of intellectual authority, but autonomy was more a

---

[2] Thomas H.C. Lee, *Education in Traditional China: A History* (Leiden, Boston, Köln: Brill, 2000), p.14.
[3] Philip Altbach, "Globalization and the Universities: Realities in an Unequal World," in James J.F. Forest and Philip G. Altbach (eds.), *International Handbook of Higher Education, Part One: Global Themes and Contemporary Challenges* (Dordecht, The Netherlands: Springer, 2006), pp.121-122.
[4] Burton Clark, "Academic Power: Concepts, Modes and Perspectives," in J.V. de Graff et al. (eds.), *Academic Power: Patterns of Authority in Seven National Systems of Education* (New York: Praeger, 1978), pp.164-189.
[5] Guy Neave, "The European Dimension in Higher Education: An Extension into the Modern Use of Analogues," in Jeroen Huisman, Peter Massen & Guy Neave (eds.), *Higher Education and the Nation State: The International Dimension of Higher Education* (Oxford: Pergamon, 2001), p.42.

matter of self-mastery than of legal protection.

There are also striking contrasts in the knowledge patterns of traditional European and Chinese higher education. Specialization was recognized early in Europe, with the traditional professions of law, medicine and theology playing an important curricular role, alongside of philosophy and the arts, as clearly defined subject areas. By contrast, the four knowledge categories of traditional China – classics, history, philosophy and literature – formed an integrated and inter-connected whole, that focused on the application of knowledge to good governance. Such fields as medicine, law, engineering and agriculture were developed as techniques intended to secure the material and social order needed for a prosperous society. From the Song dynasty onward only the first four were part of the examination system and the main learning focus of imperial higher education institutions. There is thus an orientation towards the primacy of applied social knowledge in the Chinese context, right up to the 19th century. This stands in contrast to the increasingly high status given to basic sciences and humanities in the European context, and the increasing specialization that came with the applied sciences and social sciences needed for nation building and industrialization.

After the Revolution of 1949, the new Chinese leadership decided on a complete reform of higher education along Soviet lines, which meant the full institutionalization of the European continental model, or the Roman model, as it had been adapted to Soviet socialism. The main difference from China's own traditional system lay in the organization of knowledge. An array of narrow specializations were defined within ten categories – science & engineering (理工), medicine & pharmacology (醫藥), agriculture (農業), forestry (林業), education (師範), economics & finance (財經), law & politics (政法), physical culture (體育), fine arts (藝術) and foreign languages (外語). The majority of institutions were managed at the national level by sector, with only comprehensive, polytechnical, education and foreign language institutions under the ministry of higher education and all others under specialized sectoral ministries. Students were selected by unified higher education examinations into narrowly defined specializations which were in turn matched to the socialist macro-planning system. All faculty had the status of state cadres and all students were assigned cadre positions on graduation.

By 1956 there were about 181 higher institutions at the national level, directly serving socialist construction in all main sectors of the economy, with a balanced geographical spread across China's six major regions, and the maintenance of a highly centralized political orthodoxy through the role of People's University (人民大學), which was responsible for fields such as law, politics, finance and economic planning, as well as the training of political educators for the whole system. Not only were all specializations narrowly defined, with firm boundaries delineating them, but research was separated from teaching in the institutes of the Chinese Academy of Sciences (中國科學院) and other research centers affiliated with national ministries.[6]

Much has been written about the political eruptions that challenged this system, beginning with the Great Leap Forward (大躍進) of 1958, when a huge number of local higher institutions were founded, and the Cultural Revolution (文化大革命) of 1966, which caused all universities to be closed for a year or two. They were then taken over by radical elements who abolished the entrance examinations and went on to revolutionize the curricula. While these were primarily political conflicts, reflecting warring factions within the Communist Party, Hayhoe has suggested that there were also underlying cultural elements in these conflicts. The extremely specialized nature of the organization of knowledge and the firm separation between basic and applied fields, teaching and research functions, led to a kind of mechanization and fragmentation of knowledge in the service of a hierarchalized system of power, that was deeply out of sync with Chinese epistemological traditions. The destruction of the system through revolutionary activism, however, only led to a more desperate situation. Many universities were closed for a number of years, and there was considerable violence on the campuses and in the wider society, as many took advantage of the power vacuum to settle old scores.[7]

When Deng Xiaoping (鄧小平) came to power in 1977, after the death of Mao and the fall of his radical supporters, education and science were top priorities on Deng's agenda, and the first step was a restoration of the higher education and research systems, more or less along the lines of the Soviet model of the 1950s. In the reforms that followed, we can see a process something like that of the 1930s and 1940s, as eclectic international influences were absorbed and Chinese universities gained increasing autonomy and a degree of intellectual freedom that enabled them to shape important decisions around student recruitment, curricular devel-

---

[6] Ruth Hayhoe, *China's Universities 1895-1995*, pp.75-89.
[7] *Ibid*, pp.90-104.

opment and research. While the Chinese Academy of Sciences and its research institutes have continued to play a key role, the National Natural Sciences Research Foundation (國家自然科學基金委員會) was founded in 1986 to provide increasing research funding on a competitive basis to universities. A series of reforms beginning in 1985 gave universities legal person status, confirmed in the higher education law of 1998.

Two major projects to stimulate excellence in the top tier of institutions, the Project 21/1 of 1993, and the Project 98/5 of 1998, provided significant additional funding to the best institutions. University leaders were stimulated by these opportunities to develop visions and strategic plans that built upon their historic strengths and focused on specific aspects of curricular reform, teaching, research and faculty upgrading in the effort to reach world-class standing. In the case studies that are sketched out in Chapters three to fourteen, it is clear that the massification process opened up new opportunities in the areas of curricular development, research and governance. China's own cultural traditions are being expressed in some of the curricular reform patterns, in research plans and arrangements and in the area of governance, where university leaders relate to the state more on the basis of a kind of "self-mastery" than of an autonomy that is firmly protected by law. While China's legal system has developed by leaps and bounds in recent decades, the overarching authority of the CPC remains a key factor in governance at all levels. Nevertheless, the Chinese political leadership has to be more and more accountable to an increasingly educated populace, just as university leaders are more and more conscious of the need to be accountable to their faculty and students. The form of civil society development or democratic participation is rather different from that of the West and some aspects of it may be interpreted in light of persisting Confucian values, as suggested in Chapter 2.

The Expansion and Massification of the Chinese System

The initial expansion of higher education in China can be traced back to the early 1990s. On his Southern inspection trip in 1992, Deng Xiaoping asserted that education, science and technology should play a leading role in the country's economic growth. In the very same year, China's second national working conference on education included on its agenda a discussion of expanding the higher education system. Consequently, the milestone 1993 policy paper, *Outline for Educational Reform and Devel-*

opment in China (中國教育改革和發展綱要), clearly set expansion as a goal for the 1990s:

> "In the 1990s, higher education must meet the needs of accelerating reform and [economic] opening up, and of the modernization drive, actively explore a new path of development, in order to achieve a bigger growth in size, better rationalization in structure, and a visible improvement in quality and efficiency."[8]

Three years later in 1996, China's *Ninth Five-Year Plan & Plan for Educational Development by 2010* (全國教育事業"九五"計畫和2010年發展規劃) made this goal explicit, aiming for the aggregate enrollment in all forms of higher education to reach 6.5 million by 2000, when the participation rate for the 18-22 age cohort would rise to 8%, from 6.5% in 1995. The enrollment size was to continue to grow to 9.5 million by 2010, with the gross participation rate raised to 11%.[9] Only two years later, the Chinese government raised the bar for the expansion, bringing the goal of an 11% participation rate forward to the year 2000, as stated in the *Action Plan for Vitalizing Education for the Twenty-first Century* (面向21世紀教育振興行動計畫).[10] The 1999 *Decision on Deepening Educational Reform and Pressing Ahead Quality Education in an All-Around Way* (關於深化教育改革, 全面推進素質教育的決定) then set forth a new goal of expansion for 2010, that 15% of the relevant age cohort would be participating in some form of post-secondary education.[11] With this goal set, China's ambition

---

[8] *Zhongguo Jiaoyu Gaige He Fazhan Gangyao* (*The Outline for Educational Reform and Development in China*) (China: State Council of China, 1993), accessed November 12, 2007, http://www.moe.edu.cn/edoas/website18/level3.jsp?tablename=208&infoid=3334.

[9] *Quanguo Jiaoyu Shiye Jiuwu Jihua He 2010 Nian Fazhan Guihua* (*The Ninth Five-Year Plan & Plan for Educational Development by 2010*) (China: Ministry of Education of China, 1996), accessed November 12, 2007, http://www.moe.edu.cn/edoas/website18/level3.jsp?tablename=208&infoid=3335.

[10] State Council and Ministry of Education of China, "Mianxiang 21 Shiji Jiaoyu Zhengxing Xingdong Jihua," (Action Plan for Vitalizing Education for the Twenty-First Century) in Ministry of Education of China (ed.), *Zhongguo Jiaoyu Nianjian* (*China Education Yearbook*) (Beijing: Renmin jiaoyu chubanshe (People's Education Press), 1999), pp.107-116.

[11] *Guanyu Shenhua Jiaoyu Gaige, Quanmian Tuijin Sushi Jiaoyu De Queding* (*The Decision on Deepening Educational Reform and Pressing Ahead Quality Education in an All-around Way*) (State Council of China, 1999), accessed November 12, 2007, http://www.moe.edu.cn/edoas/website18/level3.jsp?tablename=208&infoid=3314.

to achieve mass higher education became deliberate, as they clearly understood that a 15% participation rate was an internationally acknowledged threshold of mass higher education.[12]

As the expansion picked up speed, the 15% goal was re-set for 2005 in the *Tenth Five-Year Plan for Educational Development* (全國教育事業第十個五年計劃),[13] and it was actually met in 2002! China thus embraced mass higher education in less than a decade from the time when it had been vaguely expressed as a goal. If the provision for students in non-formal and private institutions is factored into the statistics, China's tertiary student population reached 29 million in 2008, accounting for 23.3% of the 18-22 age cohort, making China's higher education system the world's largest in absolute numbers. Figure 1.1 below provides a visual

Figure 1.1 Higher Education Net Enrollment[1] and Participation Rate[2] Increase: 1990-2008

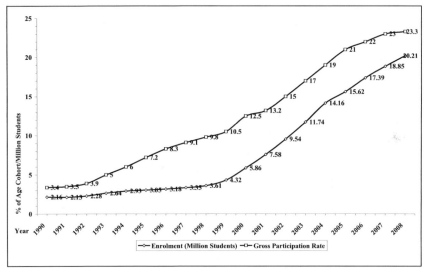

Notes:
1. Enrollments in regular higher education institutions, including postgraduate students.
2. Gross participation rate of the 18-22 age group in all forms of higher education.

---

[12] Martin A. Trow, *Problems in the Transition from Elite to Mass Higher Education* (Berkeley, California: Carnegie Commission on Higher Education, 1973).
[13] *Quanguo Jiaoyu Shiye Di Shi Ge Wunian Jihua* (*The Tenth Five-Year Plan for National Educational Development*) (China: Ministry of Education of China, 2001), accessed November 12, 2007, http://www.moe.edu.cn/edoas/website18/level3.jsp?tablename=208&infoid=3336.

of this extraordinary expansion. The participation rate was raised by close to 15% in 10 years, from around 9% in 1998 to 23.3% in 2008. By contrast, it took the United States 30 years (1911-1941), Japan 23 years (1947-1970), and many European countries 25 years to make the same journey.[14]

The year 1999 witnessed an abrupt jump in new enrollments, with 1.59 million new students, up from 1.08 million in the previous year, or an annual increase of 47.2%![15] The fast expansion continued until 2004, when higher education enrollment at all levels reached 20 million, literally double that of 1998! After 2004 enrollments continued to rise, but at a relatively slower pace. The number of regular higher education institutions also increased dramatically over the same period of time, from 1,022 in 1998 to 2,263 in 2008, an increase of 121.4%.

The Changing Landscape of the Chinese System

A Decentralized Structure to Support the World's Largest System

The expansion ushered in not only an explosion in size but also a completely changed landscape of higher education in China. The 1993 *Outline for Educational Reform and Development in China* spelled out certain strategies for higher education development, including decentralization of the administrative structure and expansion of university autonomy; a reorganization of universities for efficiency, effectiveness, and reasonable expansion; and a diversification of the sources of funding for higher education institutions. It aimed at institutionalizing a two-tiered structure of governance of higher education. The central government would directly administer only a small number of "backbone" institutions that would serve national development and function as models for the rest.

---

[14] Task Force on Issues of Education and Human Resources in China, *Cong Renkou Daguo Mai Xiang Renli Ziyuan Qiangguo* (*Stride from a Country of Tremendous Population to One of Profound Human Resources*) (Beijing: Higher Education Press, 2003), p.23; Martin A. Trow, "Reflections on the Transition from Elite to Mass to Universal Access: Forms and Phases of Higher Education in Modern Societies since WWII," in James J.F. Forest and Philip G. Altbach (eds.), *International Handbook of Higher Education* (Dordrecht, The Netherlands: Springer, 2006), p.245.

[15] Kang Ning, "Dangqian Woguo Gaodeng Jiaoyu Tizhi Gaige Yu Jiegou Tiaozhen De Lilun Jichu," (On the Theoretical Basis for the Structural Reform and Readjustment of Higher Education in China) in *Jiaoyu Yanjiu* (*Educational Research*) Vol.21, No.10, 2000, pp.9-14.

Many responsibilities and powers were to be delegated to provincial governments, which are expected to coordinate higher education growth to meet their own needs at the provincial level. Universities themselves would gradually gain autonomy over decisions regarding admission size, the establishment of programs, staff appointments, professional development, compensation standards, and the expenditure of funds. Since the mid-1990s, the Chinese government has gradually installed and institutionalized an employee system of civil service, which excluded the faculty and staff in universities and colleges from the rank of "state cadres."

The full-scale restructuring began in 1998 when a push came from the government reorganization and adaptation to the market economy. Some of the central ministries were dismantled while others were reduced in size to enhance efficiency. Except for the Ministry of Education, central ministries were now no longer permitted to run higher education institutions. Most formerly ministry-run institutions were transferred to provincial administration. The adverse effects of the disparate administrative mechanisms, the overlap of narrow specializations, the overly small scale of institutions, and the mono-disciplinary character of institutions under central ministries were thus rectified. This was done through such means as joint construction by the central and provincial governments, the forming of consortia among institutions to share their resources, and a large number of mergers that resulted in many more broadly comprehensive institutions.

The 1998 *Action Plan for Vitalizing Education for the Twenty-first Century* set up a timeline of 3-5 years in which the two-tiered governance structure would take shape, and provincial governments would take on the major role of coordinating higher education development in their jurisdictions. The 1999 *Decision on Deepening Educational Reform and Pressing Ahead Quality Education in an All-Around Way* endorsed decentralization as a major goal of higher education reform, and called for a closer integration of higher education with the local and regional economy. It moved the authority for the development of higher vocational education to the provincial level, with provincial governments taking responsibility for approving the establishment of new institutions, and managing their admission plans.

Recognizing that the state alone could never meet the exploding demand for higher education, the Chinese leadership deliberately made a policy of encouraging non-state sectors to engage in educational development. The 1993 *Outline for Educational Reform and Development in China* stated for the first time the national policy of "active encouragement, strong support, proper guidelines, and sound management" for non-state bodies engaged in educational work.[16] In 1995, China's *Education Law* (中華人民共和國教育法) was promulgated, with the 25th article confirming that the state would give full support to enterprises, social forces, local communities and individuals to establish schools under the legal framework of the People's Republic of China. On October 1, 1997, the State Council officially enacted the *Regulations on Social Forces Running Educational Establishments* (社會力量辦學條例), which put the governance of private higher education on a firm legal basis. The *Regulations* evolved into China's private education law, which took effect on December 28, 2002.

In addition Chinese education authorities have encouraged public universities to run second-tier colleges since 1999. These colleges are operated as private institutions which supplement the income of the sponsoring public university. The intention has been to increase higher education capacity by combining public and private resources. Given the advantages that public institutions have in conferring legitimacy and assuring quality, this trend has been criticized by fully private institutions, which see it as unfair competition. After 2003, the second-tier colleges were thus required to become independent from the public universities that spawned them, and now are called independent colleges. Private higher education enjoyed dramatic growth over this period of expansion as well. In 1999, only 37 private universities, with a total enrollment of 46,000 students,[17] were fully recognized by the Ministry of Education and granted authority to confer their own graduation diplomas.[18] By 2008, the number of approved private universities had grown to 640, including 322 independent colleges, with an enrollment of 4 million students, among whom over 2.2 million or 55.6% were pursuing

---

[16] Hu Wei, *Zhongguo Minban Jiaoyu Fazhan Xianzhuang Ji Celue Kuangjia* (*China's Non-governmental Education Development and The Strategic Framework*) *Zhongguo jiaoyu rexian* (*China Education Online*), 1999, accessed November 19, 2000, http://www.eol.com.cn/privateschool/private_school_expert_bbs/psl_gejia_0020.html.

[17] Qiang Zha, "The Resurgence and Growth of Private Higher Education in China" in *Higher Education Perspectives*, Vol.2, No.1, 2006, pp.54-68.

[18] Among the 37 officially recognized private institutions, only one, Yellow River University of Science & Technology had the status to award baccalaureate degrees, gained in 1999, while the others provided only two- or three-year sub-degree programs.

degree programs.[19] They thus constituted almost 20% of the entire enrollment in the formal higher education sector.

All these changes were aimed at rationalizing and optimizing the structure of Chinese higher education. The intention was to improve China's global competitiveness, a role assigned to the national elite universities, while at the same time meeting domestic social demand, a role undertaken mostly by local universities and newly developing higher vocational colleges. The 1993 *Outline for Educational Reform and Development in China*, which first revealed the intention to lift the nation's global competitiveness, gave legal sanction to a new elite university scheme – Project 21/1. Officially launched in 1995, it was to identify and give special financial support to 100 top universities, so that they could reach "world standards" in the 21st century. These universities were selected through a rigorous process, whereby each institution had to demonstrate its strengths and potential. Once enlisted, it could benefit from extra resources provided by both national and provincial governments. As it turned out, most of the graduate education programs and research activities across the country were concentrated in these institutions.

In 1998 the *Action Plan for Vitalizing Education for the Twenty-first Century* announced an even bolder scheme, Project 98/5, which took its name from the celebration of the centennial of Peking University in May of 1998. The then President of China, Jiang Zemin (江澤民), attended the ceremony and announced that China would make a further major effort to create world-class universities. The universities selected were initially nine in number but have now expanded to 43. Two top universities in the country, Peking University and Tsinghua University, have been exclusively funded by the central government (getting 1.8 billion *yuan* RMB each for the first three-year cycle), while the rest have had to gain matching funds from multiple sources at lower levels.

Thus an increasingly stratified and hierarchical system of higher education has emerged, with the top echelon universities aiming for global excellence, and expansion mainly taking place in the lower echelons. Provincial institutions and higher vocational colleges have absorbed most of the increased enrollment, while the elite national universities

---

[19] *2008 Nian Quanguo Jiaoyu Shiye Fazhan Tongji Gongbao* (*National Education Development Statistics Bulletin 2008*) (China: Ministry of Education of China, 2009), accessed August 15, 2009, http://www.edu.cn/jiao_yu_fa_zhan_498/20090720/t20090720_392038_2.shtml.

have experienced much more restrained expansion. Their enrollment grew from 1.36 million in 1997 to 1.63 million in 2005, while provincial and local institutions increased their enrollment from 1.79 million to 11.89 million over the same period.[20] Of course this needs to be understood in light of the decentralization process, which brought some 200 former national universities, affiliated with various specialist ministries, under provincial jurisdiction. Overall, the number of institutions increased 2.5 times, including higher vocational colleges and private universities, while enrollment size increased 7.7 times.[21]

Thus a pyramid has taken shape: at the top are the Project 98/5 universities aiming at improving quality and becoming global players, at the bottom are the higher vocational colleges. Their number has grown from under 100 in the 1990s to 1,184 in 2008, after the central government delegated the authority for approving the creation of such colleges to provincial governments in 2000. In the middle are provincial universities, independent colleges and some private universities that are permitted to offer degree programs. Clearly, institutional stratification is one of the most striking characteristics of the massification of higher education in China. It has made it possible for China to establish and maintain the world's largest higher education system while at the same time nurturing several dozen players at a global level.

Issues of Regional Disparity, Quality & Equality, and Employment

The expansion has resulted in many unanticipated problems along the way. In the process of decentralizing the system and diversifying the funding sources it soon became evident that there were significant regional disparities in the financial capacity to invest in higher education. China is divided into three major economic development zones: the highly developed region includes the East coast municipalities and provinces; the medium-developed region is comprised mainly of the central provinces; and the West is a less-developed region. Table 1.1 details the grouping of the provinces and municipalities in the three

---

[20] Ma Luting, "Zhidu Baozhang Xia De Gaodeng Xuexiao Wei Difang Fazhan Fuwu" (Higher Education Institutions provide Services for Local Development under Institutional Safeguard) in Fan Wenyao and David Watson (eds.), *Gaodeng Jiaoyu Zhili De Guojia Zhengce* (*National Policy of Higher Education Governance*) (Beijing: Higher Education Press, 2009), pp.279-284.
[21] *Ibid*.

development zones, and their geographic positions are demonstrated in Figure 1.2. Our case study universities were deliberately selected to approximate a balance across these development zones. Among the 12 cases, four – Peking University, Nanjing University, Xiamen University, East China Normal University – are located in the East Coastal Developed Region, five – Huazhong University of Science and Technology, the University of Science and Technology of China, Yanbian University, Blue Sky University and Yellow River University of Science and Technology – are in the Central Medium-Developed Region, and three – Southwest University, Northwest Agricultural and Forestry University and Xi'an International Studies University – are in the less-developed West Region. As higher education institutions rely increasingly on the provincial and local economy for resources, those located in less developed areas are disadvantaged in terms of available financial resources. The case studies in this book will illustrate some of the related problems.

Table 1.1 Provinces (Municipalities and Autonomous Regions) in Three Economic Regions

East Coastal Developed Region (9 provinces & municipalities)	Central Medium-Developed Region (13 provinces & autonomous regions)	West Underdeveloped Region (9 provinces & autonomous regions)
Beijing	Heilongjiang	Ningxia
Tianjin	Jilin	Qinghai
Shanghai	Hebei	Gansu
Liaoning	Shanxi	Shaanxi
Shandong	Inner Mongolia	Sichuan
Jiangsu	Henan	Guizhou
Zhejiang	Anhui	Yunnan
Fujian	Hubei	Tibet
Guangdong	Hunan	Xinjiang
	Jiangxi	
	Guangxi	
	Hainan	
	Chongqing	

Source: Tan, S., Wang, R., & Wang, J., "Zhongguo quyu jiaoyu xiandaihua yanjiu," (Studies for Modernization of Regional Education in China) in *Zhongguo jiaoyu: yanjiu yu pinglun* (*China's Education: Research & Review*), No.2, 2002, pp.1-100.

Another serious issue arising in the expansion process is that of quality. A 2005 survey of 1,110 students, faculty and administrators in 15 universities across 9 provinces found the students complaining about a shortage of teachers, and particularly the lack of well qualified teachers. There were also complaints about traditional delivery methods in the

Figure 1.2: Three Economic Regions in China

classroom that failed to foster student/teacher interaction. A majority of students (60.6%) reported they would turn to peers, instead of teachers (!), when addressing problems in learning. Ironically, a majority of the teachers surveyed complained, for their part, about the low level of student preparedness, in comparison to the cohorts they had taught prior to expansion. A good proportion of them (40.4%) reported they had to reduce course content and difficulty levels to accommodate students' learning abilities.[22] This indicates a decline in educational quality with expansion, and the mutual complaints by students and teachers imply that both sides have been affected by the over speedy expansion. A later study based on a survey of 5,953 students in three types of institutions in Beijing, national, local and private, identified even more worrisome quality problems in the local institutions. It used two types of indicators,

---

[22] Xie Anbang, Han Yingxiong, Xun Yuan, Luo Yaocheng and Wang Daohong, "Kuo Zhao Hou Jiaoxue Zhiliang Diaocha Yu Fenxi" (A Study and Analysis of Teaching Quality in the Higher Education Institutions after Enrollment Expansion) in *Jiaoyu Fazhan Yanjiu* (*Educational Development and Research*), No.15, 2005. pp.94-99.

pertaining to knowledge transmission and skills training respectively, to study the students' satisfaction with their educational experience, and found that local institutions lag far behind national universities in knowledge transmission, and behind private institutions in skills training.[23] Considering that local institutions have absorbed most of the increased enrollment, it might be hard to deny some overall decline in higher education quality in China.[24]

A related problem is the gloomy employment situation now facing university graduates. In 2003, 35.38% of the 2.12 million graduates were unable to secure a job at the point of graduation. This rate stayed at 35.36% in 2004 (out of 2.80 million graduates) and 35.29% in 2005 (out of 3.40 million). This reality has disappointed public expectations for higher education expansion, and escalated competition for admission into elite universities, since their students are favored in the job market. While university graduate employment has become a priority concern for governments at all levels in recent years, about 32% of the 6.11 million new graduates in 2009 had not yet landed on any jobs by July of 2009.[25] This can be compared with the situation in the US, at a time of economic recession, with an unemployment rate of 4.8% for college graduates over the age of 25 in June 2009, up from around 2% in 2002.[26] In Western Europe, universities experienced a substantial expansion in the 1970s and 1980s, and by 1990 more than 30% of the age group was enrolled, on

---

[23] Bao Wei, "Xuesheng Yan Zhong De Gaodeng Yuanxiao Jiaoxue Zhiliang," (Higher Education Teaching Quality in Students' Eyes) in *Economics of Education Research* (Beida), Vol.5, No.2, 2007, accessed November 24, 2009.

[24] A striking article appeared recently in *People's Daily*, the mouthpiece of the ruling Communist Party of China, which openly attributed a declining quality of higher education to the over speedy expansion and, in particular, the fact that some universities blindly expanded the enrollment size and curricular offerings without giving serious consideration to their capacities and abilities. For more details, please read "Kuo Zhao Zhi Jiaoyu Ziyuan Zhuo Jin Jian Zhou Jiaoyu Zhiliang Bao Shou Gou Bing," (Higher education expansion resulting in intensified resource constraints and increasing complaints about quality) *People's Daily*, October 30, 2009, accessed October 31, 2009, http://edu.people.com.cn/GB/10286752.html.

[25] "Gaoxiao Biyesheng Jiuye Lv Yi Da 68%," (University graduate employment rate reached 68%) in *People's Daily*, July 9, 2009, A-01.

[26] Sheila J. Curran, "Why Higher Education can't Ignore Graduate Unemployment," July 2, 2009, accessed on July 20, 2009, http://curranoncareers.com/higher-education-ignore-graduate-unemployment.

average, up from under five percent in 1950.[27] As it turned out, most graduates were absorbed by the employment system "taking over positions and tasks traditionally perceived as graduate assignments." Surveys show that "about three fifths of the graduates consider themselves invariably to be in graduate jobs ... and one fifth at most noted considerable limitations and disappointments".[28] These comparative statistics raise questions about the deeper reasons behind the gloomy employment situation in China. Has this been a result of over-rapid expansion, compared to most other jurisdictions?

The employment situation leads in turn to questions of equality and equity. Students from high socioeconomic backgrounds tend to be favored for access to elite universities. The research of Xie Zuoxu at Xiamen University, one of the scholars who initiated research on mass higher education in China, has confirmed this tendency empirically. His survey of 14,500 students from various socioeconomic backgrounds at 50 institutions across 10 provinces found that students who were from the families of government officials were18 times as likely as those with jobless or laid-off parents to get access to national elite universities. The only institution type that showed no significant difference in accessibility among various socioeconomic groups was the newly emerging higher vocational colleges, which cluster at the bottom of the hierarchy. This is where those from low SES families would most likely be concentrated.[29] In 2009, for the very first time since the higher education entrance examination was resumed in 1977, there was a large group of high school leavers – as many as 840,000 – who refused to participate in the examination. Though access has broadened greatly, the higher education experience is now seen to have a declining impact on young people's life chances, often not even leading to a job, especially for the lower socioeconomic group whose members have access only to local institutions and higher vocational colleges.

The Normative Basis of China's Policy for Mass Higher Education

The expansion decision in the late 1990s came rather abruptly, as evident in the fact that the goal for 15% participation rate was repeatedly moved

---

[27] Ulrich Teichler, *Higher Education and Graduate Employment in Europe* (Universität Gesamthochschule Kassel, 1996), p.105.
[28] *Ibid*, p.107.
[29] Interview with Xie Zuoxu, 17 December 2007.

forward, from the earliest target year of 2010 to 2005. Then it was actually met in 2002. The decision was officially announced on June 25, 1999, less than two weeks before the national entrance examinations took place. Even insiders in the policy making circle conceded this to be an unexpected move.[30] Though the expansion decision was abrupt, it is notable that the public cheered this move and leaders of higher education institutions embraced it quickly. Without a strong normative foundation, it is hard to imagine that such a policy could be smoothly implemented within four months of it being initially announced.

Attaching High Value to Education

The foremost normative factor was probably the high value attached to education in Chinese society. Ever since the institutionalization of the imperial examination system some 1,400 years ago, higher education had been associated with power, wealth, respect and opportunities. Stories abound as to how people changed their lives overnight through passing the imperial exam, and higher learning was almost a secular religion. This is evident in many Chinese proverbs. One of the most colorful goes as follows: "to be better-off you need not invest in fertile lands, for books will promise a bumper harvest; to own a home you need not collect huge logs, for books will build a luxurious mansion at your nearest convenience; to find a wife you need not seek a professional matchmaker, for books will pair you with the fairest ... if one wishes to realize these life goals, one had better pore over Confucian books with great interest".[31] This deeply rooted Chinese tradition seems to have smoothed the way for the government's expansion initiative and public expectations at large.[32]

---

[30] Kang Ning, *On the Area of Institutional Innovation in Higher Education Resource Distribution in a Transitional Economy* (Beijing: Jiaoyu Kexue Chubanshe (Educational science publisher), 2005).

[31] Excerpts from the *Poem to Urge Study* (勸學詩) in the Song Dynasty. The original version in Chinese goes as "富家不用買良田, 書中自有千鐘粟; 安房不用架高梁, 書中自有黃金屋; 娶妻莫恨無良媒, 書中自有顏如玉 ... 男兒欲遂平生志, 六經勤向窗前讀。

[32] In an interview with Min Weifang, Party Secretary of Peking University, on 22 December 2006, he asserted that the Confucian tradition had been an important factor in pushing social demand for expansion, and that the ensuing tension had helped to build the momentum for expansion.

This tradition may even have triggered the higher education expansion. A commonly cited story is that an economist couple working at the Asian Development Bank, Tang Min (湯敏) and Zuo Xiaolei (左小蕾), wrote to then Premier of China's State Council Zhu Rongji (朱鎔基) in 1998, suggesting to expand higher education enrollment in order to stimulate domestic consumption as a counter-strategy to the Asian financial crisis, since a shrinking demand in international markets had caused China's export-oriented economy to suffer, and slowed down China's GDP growth considerably. To a large extent, they were betting on the Confucian tradition, anticipating that Chinese parents would be more than willing to invest in their children's education when they had the opportunity. In this sense, the enrollment expansion would not only divert huge amounts of family savings from the banks to higher education growth, but also serve the purpose of stimulating investment in infrastructure, services and other related sectors. Tang and Zuo estimated this would increase consumption by 100 billion *yuan* RMB or so, which could stimulate growth of China's GDP by 0.5%. Their suggestion was said to have been taken seriously by top Chinese leaders, and to have triggered the expansion decision.[33]

Pursuing Optimal Efficiency and Curricular Integration as the Goal

With respect to the normative basis for the process of higher education expansion, there are certain evident links between this policy initiative and certain long-held or recently formed institutional values: economies of scale, comprehensiveness of curricular offering, and the tiered structure. Chinese universities now commonly accept the notion of economy of scale and the benefit of curricular comprehensiveness. Chinese universities used to be small in size and extremely narrow in program offering, with a very high degree of specialization, as a result of the Soviet model adopted in the early 1950s. In the late 1980s a World Bank mission found substantial room for economies of scale in university operations in China, and suggested that there would be significant savings if Chinese univer-

---

[33] (China) National Center for Education Development Research, "Zhong Guo Jiaoyu Chanye De Chulu" (The way to China's educational industry) in *2000 Nian Zhongguo Jiaoyu Lv Pi Shu* (*2000 Green Paper on Education in China*) (Beijing: Educational Sciences Press, 2000), pp.63-83; Wan Yinmei, "Expansion of Chinese Higher Education since 1998: Its Causes and Outcomes," in *Asia Pacific Education Review*, Vol.7, No.1, 2006, pp.19-31.

sities were to expand to an average size of about 8,000 to 10,000 students. So the mission recommended that smaller institutions operating in close proximity should consider the possibility of consolidation under a single administration.[34] Since the early 1990s, some Chinese scholars started to look at the issue of scale efficiency as well. They found all Chinese higher learning institutions tended to be isomorphic in terms of their management style; no matter how small they were, they had to maintain a considerable size of teaching and support staff, as well as research and teaching facilities. Therefore, "without changing the specialization and curricular arrangement, institutional management efficiency could only be increased when enrollment expanded".[35]

This scale efficiency perspective helped to determine an expansion pattern that stressed increasing institutional size, rather than the more common pattern of aggregate expansion. It resulted in the policy of various forms of consolidation among the institutions, formally termed as "coalition, adjustment, cooperation and amalgamation".[36] With this policy, the central government sent a clear message to the higher education sector that encouragement would be given to achieving enrollment expansion through tapping existent resources and extending the capacity of existing institutions. "Big" was thus viewed as analogous to efficient. The 1990s were thus characterized by an emphasis on achieving efficiency through stretching the enrollment capacity of existing institutions, with the regular higher education enrollment increasing from 2.06 million in 1990 to 5.56 million in 2000, while the total number of institutions actually declined from 1,075 to 1,041 over the same period. Only in the early 2000s did this policy give way to the creation of higher vocational colleges, which aimed at meeting social demand more efficiently, while also forming a binary system to prevent academic drift.

---

[34] The World Bank, *China: Management and Finance of Higher Education* (USA: Washington, D.C., 1987).

[35] Ding Xiaohao and Min Weifang, "Guimo Xiaoyi Lilun Yu Gaodeng Jiaoyu Jiegou Tiaozheng" (Theory of Scale Economy and Higher Education Structural Adjustment) in Chen Xuefei (ed.), *Zhongguo Gaodeng Jiaoyu Yanjiu 50 Nian: 1949-1999 (Higher Education Research in China for 50 Years: 1949-1999)* (Beijing: Educational Science Publishing House, 1999), pp.1074-1079.

[36] Kang Ning, "Dangqian Woguo Gaodeng Jiaoyu Tizhi Gaige Yu Jiegou Tiaozhen De Lilun Jichu," (On the Theoretical Basis for the Structural Reform and Readjustment of Higher Education in China) in *Jiaoyu yanjiu (Educational Research)*, Vol.21, No.10, 2000, pp.9-14.

At the same time, Chinese universities were also motivated to broaden their curricular coverage amid the expansion, since comprehensiveness in curricular offering had been associated with the cross-fertilization of knowledge in different disciplines, a characteristic feature of traditional Chinese epistemology.

The *Provisional Regulations on Establishing Higher Education Institutions* (普通高等學校設置暫行條例) issued in 1986 defined for the first time the distinction among universities, specialized institutes and colleges. It set minimum enrollment requirements of 5,000 for a university, 3,000 for a specialized institute, and 1,500 for a college. It also stipulated that an institution must cover at least three disciplinary areas in its curricular offerings, in order to qualify for university status. The newly issued *Provisional Regulations on Establishing Degree-Level Institutions* (普通本科學校設置暫行規定) in 2006 raised the enrollment bar to 8,000 for a university (with a graduate enrollment of no less than 5% of the total), and 5,000 for a university college. Furthermore, this time an institution must not only cover at least three major disciplinary areas, but also offer at least three programs in each of the areas, with a total of no less than 20 programs, in order to have the rank of university. The new phenomenon of university ranking has added fuel to the fire, as the large comprehensive universities often appear in top positions in the league tables. It is thus not surprising to find the average enrollment size of Chinese higher education institutions has soared from 1,919 in 1990 to 8,679 in 2008. The university sector has a much higher average, and there have emerged "multiversities" (巨型大學) in terms of enrollment size in China. For instance, Jilin University, which resulted from the amalgamation of 6 previously independent universities, now has an enrollment of close to 60,000. The Huazhong University of Science and Technology, profiled in Chapter Eight of this volume, is a similar size.

As a matter of fact, the scale efficiency perspective became so popular, particularly among provincial institutions and governments, that the expansion after 2002 was mainly driven by this rationale. By 2002, the central government was clearly aware of the resource deficiency that resulted from expansion at an annual rate of 49% between 1998 and 2001, and decided to reduce the pace to 5-10% annually. Yet, local institutions simply couldn't stop the pace, in many cases with encouragement from local governments at provincial or even lower levels. On the basis of a new enrollment of 2.68 million in 2001, the Ministry of Education planned to enroll 2.75 million for 2002, but ended up witnessing an actual intake of 3.20 million; it adjusted the 2003 plan to 3.35 million, but again saw a much increased intake of 3.82 million; it modified the 2004 plan to 4 million, but eventually had to admit 4.2 million.[37] By this process the number of new entrants hit 6 million by 2008. Although the Ministry of Education had intended to curb the pace of expansion at under 10% annually, it ended up with an annual rate close to 20%. Many local governments are motivated to use the size of higher education as an indicator for local economic and social development, with many institutions aspiring to become "universities enrolling 10,000 students" or "萬人大學" in Chinese.

Some universities have embraced a speed of expansion too rapid to be supported by available resources. They had to rely heavily on bank loans, and some have even come close to bankruptcy. For instance, Jilin University has borrowed 5.4 billion *yuan* RMB since 2000 to facilitate its merger and expansion, and found itself with a debt of over 3 billion *yuan* RMB by 2005. Compared to its less than one billion *yuan* RMB in annual revenue, the university came literally to the verge of bankruptcy. As a result, it became the most expensive university in the province in 2006, charging fees that were 2,500 *yuan* RMB higher than the average tuition fees in Jilin province.[38] It simply couldn't afford to limit enrollment growth, since it was dependent on fee income for survival. A study by the Chinese Academy of Social Sciences revealed that, by 2005, almost all Chinese higher institutions were dependent on loans, which amounted in total to 150-200 billion *yuan* RMB.[39] Banks have tightened their policies towards loaning to universities, and some universities have started to sell parts of their property to pay back the debt. Eventually, central and provincial governments will have to step in to move the universities out of this dilemma. In the rather affluent coastal province of Jiangsu, the provincial government has made a start by providing 3-4 billion *yuan*

---

[37] "Difang Zhengfu Weishenme Hui Bei Kuo Zhao Chong Hun Le Tou," (Why were Local Governments Crazy in Expanding Higher Education Enrollment?) in *China Youth Daily*, May 18, 2006, C-02.

[38] "Zhongguo Zuida Daxue De Kuozhang Yu Fuzhai Zhi Lu," (The Trajectory of Expanding and Going into Debt of China's Largest University) in *Nan Fang Daily*, April 9, 2007, accessed August 15, 2009, http://finance.21cn.com/news/cjzw/2007/04/09/3169695.shtml.

[39] *Ibid*. These figures are pretty striking, if compared to the 466.6 billion *yuan* RMB budgetary appropriation to the Chinese education as a whole in 2005.

RMB to their heavily indebted universities.[40]

If expansion of enrollment size reflects a search for efficiency on the quantitative dimension, the hierarchalization of the system aims at efficiency on the quality dimension. In the higher education pyramid, top-echelon national universities are taking a shrinking proportion of enrollment, while forming an elite sector aimed at world-class standing. Most recently the first nine universities to be included Project 98/5 formed a consortium named "C9",[41] which aims to create what might be called a Chinese version of the Ivy League.[42] By contrast provincial and local institutions absorb 95.3% of all enrollments, and carry out most of the tasks of transmission of knowledge and skills featured by a mass higher education system. This stratification, combined with the integration of curricular offerings, fits with the trends of globalization as well. One aspect of the global economy is the focus on research based knowledge. Consequently, this development implies a move away from a functionally specialized system towards a more hierarchical and horizontally permeable system. There are two important political-economic concerns that may push such a development worldwide. The first concern is that the level of education in the population affects the competitiveness of a nation. Prevailing beliefs seem to indicate that in order to elevate the level of education one must raise academic standards, which are embodied in the most prestigious research universities. The second concern is that higher education systems need to be flexible in order to be efficient. In addition to offering the possibility of specialization in specific disciplines, students should have the opportunity to combine a wide array of subjects from different disciplines as this will make the institutions more efficient and the students they produce better adjusted to the needs of the labor market.

---

[40] *Ibid*.

[41] The nine universities are Peking University (profiled in our Chapter 3), Tsinghua University, Zhejiang University, Harbin Institute of Technology, Fudan University, Shanghai Jiao Tong University, Nanjing University (profiled in our Chapter 4), University of Science and Technology of China (profiled in our Chapter 9), and Xi'an Jiao Tong University.

[42] "Shenme Dou Yao You Zhongguo Tece" (The Chinese style: whatever others have, we must have it). *Lianhe Zaobao* (Singapore), October 23, 2009, accessed October 30, 2009, http://www.zaobao.com/special/china/zaodian/pages2/zaodian_jx091023.shtml.

The Implementation of the Expansion Policy: The Role of Government and the Role of Scholars

In the international context of higher education expansion since 1945, Peter Scott has identified a tendency for this to be intimately linked with the extension of the power and influence of the state.[43] This is particularly true in China's case, where the government initiated and has dominated the entire process. Nevertheless, Chinese educational scholars and researchers have also played a significant role in this process, This is in striking contrast to the wave of expansion during the Great Leap Forward of 1958, when scholars were largely marginalized. In this section, the major policy instruments adopted for the expansion and the role played by scholars in the process will be considered.

Scholars Involvement in Strategic Planning and Public Communication

Compared to the Great Leap Forward, which happened in the context of a planned economy, the recent expansion has taken place against the backdrop of a market economy. It has thus been necessary to create a common ideology, and the communication of information has been crucial, in order to create an impetus and mobilize all available resources. Institutional economists believe a common ideology is a mechanism for saving or reducing costs. When people perceive and understand the environment in a common way, this in turn simplifies the policy implementation process. Over the decades, the Chinese government has accumulated a tremendous propaganda capacity, which was brought into full play to prepare for this wave of higher education expansion, and scholars have played a significant role. Three nationwide theoretical debates on the future of higher education since the early 1990s may exemplify this point. The Chinese government deliberately engaged scholars in an effort to sort out the pattern and path for higher education growth. The first debate in 1992 focused on relations between higher education and the market economy; the second in 1998 concerned the marketization of higher education; and the last one around 2001 pertained to the impact of globalization on higher education.

The first scholarly debate on the relations between higher education and the market economy focused on infusing market mechanisms into

---

[43] Peter Scott, "Massification, Internationalization and Globalization," in Peter Scott (ed.), *The Globalization of Higher Education* (Buckingham, UK: Open University Press, 1998).

the management of higher education. At around the same time a group of scholars at Peking University, who studied economies of scale in Chinese higher education, found that the system as a whole could have saved 20-25% of operating costs, if the higher education growth of the 1980s had chosen a pattern of increasing the average institutional size. Based on this finding, they suggested mechanisms of "coalition, cooperation and amalgamation" for further expansion in the 1990s.[44] This idea was incorporated into the 1993 policy paper, *Outline for Educational Reform and Development in China*, and clearly communicated to the higher education sector and the general public through the Second National Working Conference on Education held in June of 1994.

The second round of scholarly debate centered on the marketization of higher education or an entrepreneurial approach to higher education growth. The significance of this round of debate lay in closely linking higher education growth to the marketplace. This time many more scholars contributed to this controversial debate, and they were roughly split into three groups. The first group fully embraced the notion of treating higher education as an industry. A second group of scholars asserted that education should reconcile the features of both public good and private interest. The third group of scholars insisted that education should only be seen as public or semi-public good. In spite of these differences of view, all agreed that higher education could actively contribute to economic growth.[45] It is thus not surprising that Tang and Zuo proposed to use higher education expansion as an instrument to stimulate consumption. Against this backdrop, the Third National Working Conference on Education took place from June 15-18, 1999, which gave birth to the expansion policy.

The latest round of scholarly debate on higher education and globalization was set against China's entry into the WTO. This debate featured benchmarking China's standards and strategy of human resources development in a global context. It included a formal and systemic introduction of the Western concept of mass higher education. While some scholars argued that mass higher education meant shifting the focus from serving a small number of elites to attending to the

---

[44] Ding Xiaohao and Min Weifang, *op. cit.*

[45] Kang Ning, *On the Area of Institutional Innovation in Higher Education Resource Distribution in a Transitional Economy* (Beijing: Jiaoyu Kexue Chubanshe (Educational science publisher), 2005).

majority of the population, and thus democratizing higher education, others argued that an elite part of higher education must be strengthened in the process of massification. The latter perspective maintained that elite higher education had been far from adequately mature and sufficiently strong to fulfill the leading role in China, compared to other developed systems, and thus the move towards mass higher education shouldn't rely on elite universities, but on community-college type institutions. These opinions were well documented in the *Tenth Five-Year Plan for Educational Development* promulgated in June 2002, which clearly set the 15% participation rate as a goal for 2005, and the tasks of both expanding higher vocational education and creating world-class universities.

The scholars' role has been played out not only through their individual research efforts, but also through major government-sponsored research projects. To give an example, the Institute of Higher Education Studies at Peking University is a national key research base in educational economics, which has pooled a group of educational economists whose research on economies of scale has influenced the higher education expansion policy. Similarly, Xiamen University's Research Institute in Higher Education is another national key research base in higher education studies, focusing on studies of mass higher education, private higher education and the history of China's civil service examinations. In 1999, scholars at Xiamen University translated Martin Trow's widely cited paper *Problems in the Transition from Elite to Mass Higher Education*, which aroused great interest among Chinese scholars. In 2002, the Shanghai Institute of Human Resource Development within the Shanghai Academy of Educational Sciences undertook a large-scale research project investigating China's *status quo* of education and human resource development. The project yielded a 700-page long policy advisory report, *Stride from a Country of Tremendous Population to a Country of Profound Human Resources*, which recommended prioritizing human resource development in the next two decades. As a result, human resource development is almost a buzzword in the *Tenth Five-Year Plan for Educational Development*, and is clearly reflected in the *2003-2007 Action Plan of Revitalizing Education* (2003-2007 年教育振興行動計畫) promulgated in February 2007.

In face of the escalating tension between equality and efficiency in the expansion process, Xiamen University hosted an international symposium on this theme in September 2002. Scholars critiqued the principle of "prioritizing efficiency while attending to equality at the same time," which had been adopted for China's higher education growth to press for greater attention to equity. Another example is that, when the quality and equality issues came to the fore, scholars were consulted by China's Premier Wen Jiabao (溫家寶) at a series of seminars that took place in his office in 2006. Gu Mingyuan (顧明遠), a renowned comparativist and one of our interviewees, was among those who were invited. The discussions of scholars with Wen covered such topics as expanding higher education in a steady and reasonable manner, optimizing curricular coverage and program offerings, quality assurance, innovative teaching, and equity issues. Not coincidently, these topics have become themes of the *Eleventh Five-Year Plan for Educational Development* (全國教育事業第十一個五年計劃), promulgated on May 2007, and the upcoming *Outline of National Medium- and Long-Term Education Reform and Development Plan* (國家中長期教育改革和發展規劃綱要). In short, Chinese scholars have been actively involved in policy formulation and implementation. They play a key role in introducing new theories and ideas aimed at fostering China's human resource development.

Government Policy Papers Having Legislative Power

In this government-initiated expansion process, the Chinese government took advantage of its "visible hand" and issued a series of policy papers to propel the growth of higher education. In spite of the fact that a market economy has gradually come to regulate social life, the patterns of policy making and execution in China to a large extent remain centralized up to the present. Therefore policy papers possess almost the same binding power as law. The aforementioned policy papers set out clear and specific goals for expanding the enrollment, and guiding the patterns of expansion through three stages, from achieving aggregate expansion to expanding the size of existing institutions, then to a combined model of expanding the existing universities while also establishing new institutions.

The State also used its legislative power to create mechanisms that motivated the institutions to expand. Under the planned economy, Chinese higher education institutions were subject to highly centralized decision-making and detailed resource allocation and administration; they were essentially an arm of the government. Over time, they lost any impetus to innovate or shape their own institutional development. Now, the *Higher Education Law* (中華人民共和國高等教育法) of 1999 has granted higher education institutions the status of legal persons.[46] The *Law* details the autonomy that the institutions are entitled to in seven major domains: student admission, new program development, teaching affairs, research and service, international exchange and cooperation, arrangement of internal structure and personnel management, and property management.[47] These new spheres of autonomy provide both motivation and pressure for higher education institutions to plan strategically for themselves, and to grow in most cases.

Adoption of an Enrollment-Based Financing Mechanism and a Fee-Charging Policy

A crucial move in reforming higher education finance in China, along with the massification of access, has been the adoption of a fee-charging policy. From the 1950s up to the early 1990s, university admissions were tightly controlled with quotas set by the State; students paid no fees and were assigned jobs upon graduation. From 1997 all higher education institutions have started charging student fees, in accordance with official policy, and the fee levels have seen a dramatic tendency to rise ever since. This policy change had strong implications for enrollment. Previously, the rationale for setting enrollment quotas was to ensure that needed personnel were trained and the State had the financial capability to finance their training. Once tuition fees were charged to all students, the justification for setting enrollment quotas effectively disappeared. Instead, enrollment would be driven by the social demand for education. Shortly before this policy change, there was another change in the governmental approach to allocating recurrent funds. The amount of funds for each institution for the current year used to be determined by an "incremental approach," which was based on what the institution got in the previous year. The government would make some incremental adjustment according to the development needs of the institution and its own budget for higher education. Since the early1990s, the incremental approach has been replaced by a formula-based approach, which is comprised of two parts – a block appropriation based on enrollment and

---

[46] Higher Education Law in its "Article 30, Chapter IV Organization and Activities of Higher Education Institutions," in Ministry of Education of China, *The Laws on Education of the People's Republic of China* (Beijing: Foreign Languages Press, 1999), p.101.

[47] *Ibid*; see Articles 32 through 38 in Higher Education Law, pp.101-103.

the appropriation for special items, with the former accounting for the largest share. The major allocation parameter is now the number of full-time equivalent students. The enrollment-based approach is thought to improve transparency in resource allocation, and foster competition among institutions over quantitative aspects of development.

The new policy is characterized by cost-sharing and cost-recovery, diversifying the traditional mode of higher education finance in which the state was the sole patron. In general, Chinese universities today must raise an increasing proportion of their operating funds from such non-governmental sources as tuition fees, research grants, sales of services, and endowment gifts. It is notable that the ratio of fiscal appropriation in the aggregate institutional revenue kept declining from 69.3% for national universities and 72.6% for local institutions in 1995 to 51.6% and 44.5% respectively in 2004. This decline is more striking if illustrated in per student budgetary appropriation, which went down from 7,309 *yuan* RMB in 2000 to 5,552 *yuan* RMB in 2004, or by 24%.[48] Meanwhile, the ratio of the contribution made by student fees has been rising, from 10.3% in national universities and 17.2% in local institutions in 1995 to 19.2% and 40.1% respectively in 2004.[49] This change shows that a broad pattern of diversification of funding sources hasn't yet come into being. Rather, a kind of dichotomous pattern has developed in which State appropriations and tuition fees are the two main sources of revenue.

With the overall State investment in education declining since 2004,[50] the drift towards fee-based funding essentially conditions institutions' survival, in particular that of local institutions. Such a move seems to be consistent with the global tendency. In Canada, for example, universities and colleges in Ontario – a leading province in terms of higher learning – also have to rely increasingly on student tuition and fees to support their operations, due to declining government investment. In

---

[48] Li Wenli, *Cong Xique Zou Xiang Chongzu: Gaodeng Jiaoyu De Xuqiu Yu Gongji Yanjiu* (*From Scarcity towards Adequacy: A Study on the Demand and Supply of Higher Education*) (Beijing: Educational Science Publishing House, 2008).
[49] Kang Xiaoming, "Cong Jiegou Xing Yuesu Kan Dazhonghua Jieduan Woguo Gaodeng Jiaoyu Gonggong Zhengce De Xuanze," (A Perspective of Structural Restriction on Public Policy Option in the Stage of Mass Higher Education) in *Higher Education Studies* (China), No.2, 2007, pp.11-16.
[50] Mok Ka Ho and Lo Yat Wai, "The Impacts of Neo-Liberalism on China's Higher Education," in *Journal for Critical Education Policy Studies*, Vol.5, No.1, 2007, accessed September 29, 2008, http://www.jceps.com/?pageID=article&articleID=93.

2002/3, student tuition and fees contributed 25% of the operating budget for colleges, and 39% for universities.[51] In the United States, higher education tuition soared approximately by 250% between 1996 and 2006.[52] However, China's situation is more serious, in terms of its placing a much heavier financial burden on the lowest SES families. In the United States, the net costs for attending a public institution as a percentage of the poorest families' median income rose from 39% in 1999 to 55% in 2008.[53] In China, a 2004 survey found that to support a university student one year would cost 186.9% of the per capita income of the poorest families.[54]

A Systematic Decentralization Pushing the Institutions to Strategically Plan for Their Future

The 1993 *Outline for Educational Reform and Development in China* aimed, for the first time, at institutionalizing a two-tiered structure of higher education governance. The central government was to directly administer a number of so-called "backbone" universities that would have an impact on national development and serve as models for the rest. Many responsibilities and powers were then delegated to provincial governments, which now had to coordinate higher education growth in their jurisdictions, and some were given to the institutions themselves. The full-scale restructuring commenced in the late 1990s, driven by the nationwide restructuring of government. Some of the central ministries were dismantled due to this administrative restructuring and many others were reduced in size to enhance efficiency. Except for the Ministry of Education, central ministries are no longer permitted to run higher education institutions. Most former ministry-run institutions have been transferred to provincial administration and have to find their own means of survival. Higher education institutions have therefore become closer to the provinces and more active in serving local interests, while the financial burden of the central government has been relieved.

The 1998 *Action Plan for Vitalizing Education for the Twenty-first Century* set up a timeline of 3-5 years for creating the two-tiered governance

---

[51] Bob Rae, *Ontario: A Leader in Learning* (Government of Ontario, 2005), p.103.
[52] National Center for Public Policy and Higher Education, *Measuring Up 2008* (San Jose, California: NCPPHE, 2008), p.8.
[53] *Ibid.*
[54] Li Wenli, *op. cit.*

structure, in which the provincial governments would play a leading role in coordinating higher education development in their jurisdictions. The 1999 *Decision on Deepening Educational Reform and Pressing Ahead Quality Education in an All-Around Way* reiterated decentralization as a major goal of higher education reform, and called for a closer integration of higher education and the local economy. As a specific step towards decentralization, this policy paper moved the locus of approving authority for new higher vocational college down to the provincial governments. Such a policy environment rewards those institutions that are large in size and comprehensive in curricular coverage, as they offer more opportunities of connecting to the local economy. It also encourages the creation of new higher vocational colleges, following the same rationale.

Discussion & Conclusion: Theorizing Patterns of Policy Making in China

When theorizing policy decisions, two alternative models are often referred to: the rational model and the incremental model. The former emphasizes the full command of policy knowledge and information on the side of the policy maker, who is seen to choose the optimum policy after scientific and rational analysis. The second model suggests that policy-makers do not have sufficient time, funds or information to control all policy variables so that a new policy is likely to be based on the previous policy. In a context where norms and values conflict, the rational model is less likely than the incremental model.

With respect to policy evaluation, several perspectives are recommended: "explicit articulation of the objectives, efficiency, effectiveness, adequacy, fairness, responsiveness and adaptability."[55] To evaluate a policy, often the "evaluation can be centered on how much the policy objective is achieved rather than on the merit or fault of the policy."[56] In this sense, China's expansion policy underpinning a rapid move to mass higher education appears to be a success. However, given its enormous and long-lasting impact on Chinese people and China's social progress, the policy objectives should also stand the test of equity. In Trow's terms, these objectives imply a policy orientation towards a "mixed-phase"

---

[55] Dong Jingyi, "A Policy Study of the Position of Rural Students in the Transition from Elite to Mass Higher Education in China" (MPhil Dissertation, University of Oslo, 2004), p.50.
[56] *Ibid*.

system, with both elite and mass higher education characteristics. Put explicitly, the elite functions continue to exist or even are reinvigorated when the national system as a whole moves towards massification. As Trow claimed later, "the higher the proportion of the relevant age group going on to higher education, the more the democratic and egalitarian concerns for equality of opportunities come to center on the increasingly important sector of tertiary education."[57]

Embracing the Market Economy: An Efficiency-Driven Rationale Emerging

Given its nature as a government-initiated and dominated process, China's policy formation over higher education expansion seems to have followed a rational model in its initial stage, though it may have over-emphasized efficiency and aligned with a utilitarian approach. The rationale stemmed from the awareness of the crucial importance of higher education in a knowledge-based economy, and escalating social demand for higher education opportunities. This rationale grew also out of the fact that higher education expansion had been curbed in the early and mid-1990s as consequence of the pro-democracy movement of Spring 1989, which started on university campuses. It used such positive sounding terms as efficiency, productivity and excellence, and mobilized market and private resources to expand higher education provision and diversify higher education providers. Such a rationale appeared to warrant a fast track to mass higher education in face of resource constraints, a notion expressed in most of the policy papers. When scrutinizing these policy papers, a recurring theme identified is the need to create a higher education system that gets along with and is responsive to the booming market economy. Above all, it fits well with the little disguised neo-liberal agenda that has been claiming credit for China's success in economic reform and growth. This has involved introducing competition into the public sphere, and offloading some of the costs of public services, such as education, housing, health care, onto the individual. While the Chinese higher education system experienced an unprecedented expansion between 1998 and 2001, the ratio of government fiscal appropriation in higher education revenue actually dropped

---

[57] Martin A. Trow, "Reflections on the Transition from Elite to Mass to Universal Access: Forms and Phases of Higher Education in Modern Societies since WWII," *op. cit.*, p.246.

from 50.9% to 47.4%.[58]

In general, this rationale was effective in terms of linking China's higher education expansion to the "tides" of a rapid transition to the market economy in the country, and the prevalence of a neo-liberal ideology in higher education in global circles. The globalization process has ushered in a convergence trend, characterized by the ideal of universities as market or quasi-market organizations striving to become entrepreneurial in their approach to teaching and research.[59] The last two decades have witnessed the emergence of powerful, unrelenting pressures for change in higher education. Arguably, strongest of all the forces for change has been the growing influence of market forces and competition within higher education.

Higher education institutions, for their part, may turn away from a path of dependence on government authority in their expansion, and choose to seek their own interests. This is evident to some degree in their over-response to government's call for seeking economies of scale and the blind expansion of enrollments and facilities, which has led to debt and serious management problems. The evidence can also be seen in approaches to broadening curricular offerings. Many institutions have chosen to take an easy way through adding "soft" programs, which require fewer resources and promise immediate employment prospects, such as foreign languages, finance, accounting and business administration.[60] In the longer term, the proliferation of these programs doesn't create genuine comprehensive universities, but may intensify employment problems, as supply soon overtakes demand in these fields. This is certainly one factor in the problem of graduate unemployment. In fact, research has also pointed to the phenomenon of over-education or qualification inflation in China's job market. This shows, even among those who have found employment, in that many are still underused for

---

[58] Li Wenli, *op. cit.*

[59] Burton Clark, *Creating Entrepreneurial Universities: Organizational Pathways of Transformation* (Oxford: Pergamon Press, 1998); Sheila Slaughter and Larry L. Leslie, *Academic Capitalism: Politics, Policies, and the Entrepreneurial University* (Baltimore: The Johns Hopkins University Press, 1997).

[60] Qiang Zha, "Diversification or Homogenization: How Governments and Markets have Combined to (Re)Shape Chinese Higher Education in Its Recent Massification Process," in *Higher Education*, Vol.58, No.1, 2009, pp.41-58.

their knowledge and skills.[61] In light of an efficiency-driven rationale, both the management deficiency and educated un-employment or under-employment could hardly be denied as a failure.

"Walking on Two Legs": Quality and Equality Issues Coming to the Center

At the beginning of the rapid growth era in other jurisdictions around the world, the steady expansion of higher education has tended to constitute a threat to academic standards and place an intolerable burden on governmental budgets that have also to cope with growing demands from other public service agencies, such as primary and secondary school systems, social welfare, public health, housing and transportation. The solution everywhere has tended to be a combination of the creation of cheaper alternatives to the elite universities, plus a reduction in per capita support for these institutions. A similar pattern can be seen with China, which is evident in its adoption of the strategy of "Walking on Two Legs." "Walking on Two Legs" as a strategy for educational expansion can be traced back to the Great Leap Forward period in the late 1950s, which advocated expanding both the formal and non-formal education sectors to achieve an accelerated universalization of education. Such a strategy has been revived in face of concerns about quality, but with a different meaning. That is to maintain a small number of elite universities as centers of excellence while developing a vast number of local institutions and letting them grow on their own in response to the demand for mass higher education.

While the Chinese higher education system has become increasingly hierarchical during this wave of expansion, Chinese society has been becoming increasingly democratic and egalitarian. Tensions thus emerge, and the central one is around the quality of higher education provided by the local institutions as well as the pressures for greater equality of provision under conditions of quality assurance. When complaints about quality escalated, the Chinese Ministry of Education launched a "College Undergraduate Teaching Quality and Teaching Reform Project" (高等學校本科教學品質與教學改革工程) in 2003, which not only puts quality monitoring and improvement on the top of its agenda, but also specifically regulates a five-year cycle of program evaluation. All universities

---

[61] Li Fengliang, W. John Morgan and Ding Xiaohao, "The Expansion of Higher Education, Employment and Over-education in China," in *International Journal of Educational Development*, No.28, 2008, pp.687-697.

must pass this evaluation in order not to have their programs shut down. The Higher Education Evaluation Center (HEEC), established 2004 within the Ministry of Education, is mandated to implement the evaluation. During the first five-year cycle, HEEC evaluated undergraduate teaching in 589 colleges and universities. Among them, more than 80% received a score of "A" in the first-cycle evaluation.[62]

The evaluation includes three stages: the institutions make a self-evaluation; external experts conduct investigations; and the institutions are subject to rectification and reform upon feedback.[63] HEEC developed a sophisticated indicator system for the evaluation, which includes 7 first-level indicators and 19 second-level indicators. Adopting the same evaluation instrument and indicator system, provincial education authorities have implemented sub-baccalaureate teaching evaluation on higher vocational colleges with a respective scope. The teaching at most private higher education institutions was later included in the evaluation programs of either HEEC or provincial education authorities, depending on the level of their programs.

---

[62] Jiang Kai, "Undergraduate Teaching Evaluation in China: Progress and Debate," in *International Higher Education*, No.58, 2010, pp.15-17.
[63] *Ibid*.

A Shift in the Policy Formation Model?[64] *What More Can Scholars Do?*

At present, it appears that policy formation is shifting towards an incremental model, with a lot of adjustment or correction measures being taken to address the emerging issues related to quality and equality and employment. This shift may be attributed to at least three reasons. The first and foremost is a reduced pressure for further expansion. The expansion has apparently slowed down since 2006, and is projected to slow down further, if not to stagnate. The force behind this is not so much governmental effort to curb expansion, as a shrinking demand. Research shows the relevant age group (18-22 years old) in the Chinese population should have reached its peak size in 2008, and then started to shrink. In ten years time, its size would become 35% smaller.[65] Once the pressure for expansion is eased, it would be easier to direct resources and attention to aspects of quality and issues of equality. This in turn leads to policy changes and corrective actions.

Second, there are three types of ideologies co-existing in Chinese society: a meritocratic and hierarchical one rooted in the Confucian tradition, an egalitarian one resulted from the first 30 revolutionary years of the People's Republic of China (1949-1979) and the market-oriented

---

[64] Precisely when we were completing this chapter, the news came that China's Minister of Education, Zhou Ji, was removed from his post on 31 October 2009 at a meeting of the standing committee of China's legislature, the People's Congress. It is implied that he was somehow held accountable for public complaints about over speedy marketization and expansion of Chinese education, in particular in the higher education sector, and many concomitant issues pertaining to the falling quality, equity as well as integrity in the sector. He is succeeded by Yuan Guiren, a veteran educator who started his career as a rural school teacher in the under-developed province of Anhui and rose to be the President of China's flagship educational university, Beijing Normal University, and then the Vice Minister of Education. What is really notable is his education background in philosophy, which is significantly different from most other Ministers of Education, who landed this job after fulfilling a leading role in such prestigious institutions as Peking University or Tsinghus University and almost exclusively with engineering education backgrounds. For us, this seems to signal a possible switch in the pattern of educational policy formation, from a pattern driven by scientific rationality to one with more humanistic considerations that is likely to stress balanced growth among various sectors within China's education system. It might be premature to draw any conclusion at this point, but this expectation is certainly reasonable.

[65] Li Wenli, *ibid.*

one taking shape in the recent three decades of the economic reform era. The interplay or conflict among these three ideologies would inevitably swing public policy. Last but not least, by policy design, China's move to mass higher education intended to follow the American model. The American model is attractive not only because it is the first mass system but also it is well adapted, normatively and structurally, to the requirements of a post-industrial age. Yet, one unique feature that has conditioned the success of the American model is that "the United States had the organizational and structural framework for a system of mass higher education long before it had mass enrolments."[66] Given that the Chinese case started almost from the opposite position, a rigidly structured Soviet or continental European model, the explosive enrollment expansion could be expected to trigger numerous problems.

The tackling of these problems, in turn, will stimulate a series of further policies, rather than simply putting an end to the expansion. In this sense, the incremental model might serve the policy objectives better, as it not only offers the possibility of a smooth policy transition, but also echoes the Chinese wisdom of "groping for stones to cross the river," which has become a doctrine for the entire reform era. As a matter of fact, China is also unique in educational history in terms of simultaneously pushing for rapid enrollment growth, instituting new governance structures, and seeking to build world-class universities. Down this road, and interwoven with the interplay among the different ideologies, the conflict of norms and values seems to be inevitable. Reforms may thus only succeed if they carefully detect the broader trends in society and public policy, and try to change institutions in ways that are consistent with them.

It is in this process that Chinese education scholars may play a crucial role. So far, they have become increasingly active in the policy formation process, yet mostly in the sense of offering professional advice, following a "constructive criticism" path at maximum. Such a pattern, however, may not be enough to offset governmental power and market forces in policy making. Burton Clark once uses his famous "triangle" to indicate the equilibrium in higher education coordination, which may also be applicable in the context of higher education policy formation.

---

[66] Martin A. Trow, "Reflections on the Transition from Elite to Mass to Universal Access: Forms and Phases of Higher Education in Modern Societies since WWII", *ibid.*, p.270.

Then what seems to be weak is perhaps the intellectual authority for a policy equilibrium. Compared to academic freedom in the Western tradition, in which criticism can be for its own sake, intellectual authority in the Confucian tradition often requires a unity of knowledge and action, and is possibly more delicate and complex. What kind of mass higher education system China will eventually embrace is thus, to certain extent, dependent on the kind and quality of intellectual authority that can be established by scholars, and how well their role is played out. The case studies that form the main body of this volume provide interesting examples of the ideas and actions of Chinese scholars who hold leadership positions in twelve different university environments in the present period of significantly enhanced autonomy for Chinese higher education.

2
Equity, Institutional Change and Civil Society – The Student Experience in China's Move to Mass Higher Education

Jun Li

Introduction

In China's rapid move from elite to mass higher education, students have experienced dramatic changes. How have they been affected by the expansion process? How do they view the radical institutional changes? And how are they being nurtured to act as dynamic citizens?

In this chapter, we will examine three major aspects of how students have been affected by China's move to mass higher education, based on an analysis of our survey data: their attitudes towards access, their perceptions of institutional changes, and their experience of civic learning and participation. The first section of the chapter provides a comparative overview of higher education and civil society. A historical review of Western and Eastern traditions shows how different cultures have shaped the values of higher learning differently. The second section introduces two analytical frameworks for the analysis of the student survey. The third section describes how the student survey was carried out in 12 Chinese universities in the summer of 2007, and how the data have been analyzed. The fourth section then details the findings, while the fifth section interprets these findings and reflects on issues of equity of access and success in the expansion, institutional transformations, and the role of universities in nurturing civil society. The final section identifies implications for policy.

Higher Education and Civil Society

Universities as Civic Actors

In the Western world, the *idea* of a university was probably first elaborated by John Henry Newman in the mid-nineteenth century. In his *Discourse Seven: Knowledge Viewed in Relation to Professional Skill*, Cardinal Newman stated that the fundamental mission of a university should be centered on philosophical or liberal education for the formation of citizens.[1] He further added that higher education should aim at "raising the intellectual tone of society, at cultivating the public mind, ... at giving enlargement and sobriety to the ideas of the age", and "at facilitating the exercise of political power."[2] Newman firmly rejected any practical aim for higher education, and asserted that "if ... a practical end must be assigned to a University course, I say it is that of training good members of society. Its art is the art of social life, and its end is fitness for the world."[3] Newman's vision placed a high priority on the role of higher education in civil society.

Newman's idea of higher education was later challenged by the emergence of the Humboldtian model of elite universities which should educate scientists (*Wissenschaftler*).[4] However, Wilhelm von Humboldt believed that *Wissenschaft* (science and scholarship) encompassed "the harmonious development of all the capacities" of students, including "the elaboration of the uncontrived substance of intellectual and moral culture."[5] While his emphasis was on the unity of scientific research and teaching in university life,[6] Humboldt had a deep belief in the necessity of facilitating students' civic learning in universities. In addition, he insisted that autonomy and academic freedom[7] should enable them to play a dynamic and independent role in society as civic actors.

In the American context, John Dewey later stated that educational institutions should be a place where students experience being "a member of a community life," in which they feel that they can participate and contribute.[8] In his later years, he further emphasized "education as a necessary condition for creation of the kind of citizenship indispensable

---

[1] John H. Newman, *The Idea of a University* (London: Longmans, Green, & Co., 1907, originally published in 1852), p.167.
[2] *Idid*, pp.177-178.
[3] *Idid*, p.177.
[4] D.F.S. Scott, *Wilhelm von Humboldt and the Idea of a University* (Durham: University of Durham, 1960), pp.12-13.
[5] Wilhelm von Humboldt, "On the Spirit and the Organizational Framework of Intellectual Institutions in Berlin", in *Minerva*, Vol.8, No.2, April 1970, pp.247, 243.
[6] *Idid*, p.243.
[7] *Idid*, p.246.
[8] John Dewey, "Plan of Organization of the University Primary School", in Jo Ann Boydston (ed.), *The Early Works of John Dewey 1882-1898: Early Essays* (Carbondale, IL: Southern Illinois University Press, 1972), Vol.5, p.224.

to the success of democracy."⁹ The tenor of Dewey's progressive views on the role of education in a democratic society has laid a philosophical foundation for American universities, as civic actors, responsible for students' political socialization and civic participation.

The ideals of Newman and Dewey, however, have not always squared with the development of higher education, particularly in the U.S. context. Although Clark Kerr felt it was important to protect the "non-market" functions of higher education, such as "involvement in the life of society" and "training for good citizenship,"[10] he turned the single *idea* of a university into the plural and practical *uses* of the multiversity, with a new emphasis on such utilitarian roles as training professionals, serving national needs, and catering for industrial and business interests. The role of higher education in nurturing responsible citizens was not enhanced, even though it may not have been undermined.

The civic role of higher education has also been emphasized in other cultures. One of China's most deep-rooted normative values is the belief in higher education and learning as a major instrument for achieving the highest good for both individuals and society. The purpose of higher education and learning was defined as "to let one's inborn virtue shine forth, to renew the people, and to rest in the highest good," as stated in *The Great Learning* (《大學》) two thousand years ago. This suggests a harmonious integration between the individual good and the benefit of society,[11] which may have some parallels with Newman's vision. A striking example from early Chinese history is the Jixia Academy (稷下學宮) established in the third century BCE. At one time it had a population of more than ten thousand students and numerous prominent scholars. As an effectively private institution, it provided space for many different schools to debate freely, without any intervention from government. It was self-administered, with teachers and students who adhered to Confucianism, Daoism, the Huanglao School (黃老學), the Yinyang School (陰陽學) and other schools. Students and teachers came and went as they pleased, and the teaching was open to all, regardless of their

---

⁹ John Dewey, "The Social Significance of Academic Freedom", in Jo Ann Boydston (ed.), *The Later Works of John Dewey 1925-1953: Essays and Liberalism and Social Action* (Carbondale, IL: Southern Illinois University Press, 1987), Vol.11, p.378.
[10] Clark Kerr, *The Uses of the University* (Cambridge, MA: Harvard University Press, 5th ed., 2001), p.86, 192.
[11] Thomas H.C. Lee, *Education in Traditional China: A History* (Leiden: Brill, 2000), pp.10-11.

academic background. In short, the Jixia Academy embodied some embryonic elements of a civil society organization.[12]

The *shuyuan* (書院), or traditional Chinese academies, which first emerged in the 8th century CE, are often seen as inheritors of the spirit of the Jixia Academy. Over a period of 1200 years they developed a rich heritage of teaching and learning practices, with a high degree of autonomy in governance and intellectual freedom in teaching. This was due to their independent funding through the ownership of land or through donations. They served as a public sphere and a locus of associational life for the intellectual community, where political issues could be discussed and sometimes acted upon.[13]

After the collapse of the Qing Dynasty in 1911, Western ideals of the university and its role in society were gradually accepted by Chinese educators, who cautiously synthesized them with traditional Chinese concepts of higher education. Cai Yuanpei (蔡元培), Hu Shi (胡適) and Guo Bingwen (郭秉文) were among the pioneers who passionately advocated autonomy and academic freedom, equal opportunity for women and men, and citizenship and moral education in the university. Cai Yuanpei, a returnee from Germany and France, was appointed the Republic's first Minister of Education in 1912 and President of Peking University in 1916. Shortly after taking office as Minister of Education, Cai published his *Opinions on the New Education,* setting up Five Cardinal Principles as the foundation for Republican education. One of them was Citizenship and Moral Education, which drew on the ideas of liberty, equality and fraternity of the French Revolution of 1789, and incorpo-

---

[12] Jun Li, "Jixia Xuegong De Banxue Tedian Jiqi Qishi" (Thoughts on the Characteristics of Jixia Academy and its Modern Implications), in *Gaodeng Jiaoyu Yanjiu (Higher Education Research)*, Vol.34, No.4, 1988, pp.100-105; Ruth Hayhoe and Jun Li, "The Idea of a Normal University in the 21st Century," in *Frontiers of Education in China*, Vol.5, No.1, 2010, pp.74-103; Joseph Needham, *Science and Civilisation in China*, Vol.1 (Cambridge, UK: University Press, 1954), pp.95-96; Denis Twitchett and Michael Loewe (eds.), *The Cambridge History of China*, Vol.1 (New York, NY: Cambridge University Press, 1986), p.73.

[13] Li Guojun, *Zhongguo Shuyuan Shi (A History of China's Academies)* (2nd ed., Changsha: Hunan Educational Press, 1998); Sun Peiqing (ed.), *Zhongguo Jiaoyu Shi (A History of China's Education)* (3rd ed., Shanghai: East China Normal University Press, 2009).

rated traditional Confucian moral values.[14] In addition, he firmly upheld academic freedom, institutional autonomy and educational independence. Hu Shi, who had studied under John Dewey from 1915 to 1917, also advocated these values and helped Cai Yuanpei to enroll women students at Peking University in 1921. Hu helped drafting the 1922 national legislation for China's modern school system, setting "adaptation to the evolution of society" and "citizenship education and life education" as two of the Seven Basic Guidelines for Republic education.

Not only did Cai Yuanpei and Hu Shi's efforts turn Peking University into China's first real modern university, in terms of the defining values of autonomy, academic freedom, the unity of research and teaching, and citizenship and moral education, but their ideas of higher education set the overall tone for modern Chinese universities during the Nationalist period. These ideas inspired Peking University, among others, to become a dynamic civic actor that has always been a pioneer in student-led political movements, from the May Fourth Movement of 1919, to the June Fourth Movement of 1989. This can also been seen in the outpouring of a strong civic spirit by contemporary university students in response to the Sichuan Earthquake and the Beijing Olympic Games in 2008.

This overview of higher education institutions as civic actors has given us a contextual understanding in both the Western and Chinese traditions of how the vision of higher education has nurtured citizenship and the growth of civil society. The two cultural traditions have contrasting views of citizenship and civil society, however, and these will be explored in the next section.

Citizenship and Civil Society

In the Western world, the concept of citizenship originated from the Mediterranean tradition, as developed in many Greek city states. Plato in his *Statesman* and *Laws*, and Aristotle in his *Politics* and *Ethics*, began to theorize the role of citizenship in the sociopolitical advancement of small-scale political systems. For example, based on the belief that "man is born for citizenship,"[15] Aristotle defined citizens as those who are "eligible to

---

[14] Cai Yuanpei, "Duiyu Xin Jiaoyu Zhi Yijian" (Opinions on the New Education), in Gao Pingshu (ed.), *Cai Yuanpei Quanji* (*The Complete Works of Cai Yuanpei*) (Beijing: Zhonghua Book Company, 1984), Vol.2, p.131.
[15] Aristotle, *Ethics*, 1.7.

participate in deliberative and judicial office."[16] The eligibility condition of this definition shows that the Western tradition of citizenship put notable emphasis on citizens' innate rights and responsibilities in their sociopolitical community. For Plato, citizenship was highly related to education. Generally, citizenship was conceived by these early European philosophers in a restricted sense based on descent and property, rather than as a universal category. Their normative ideas of citizenship have had a profound influence on Western societies, though these early ideas developed in diverse ways in later history.

The East Asian tradition, especially the Chinese tradition, has developed the concept of citizenship in quite different ways. Early Chinese philosophers, such as Confucius in *The Analects*, Laozi in *The Dao De Jing*, Mencius in his *Works of Mencius*, and Xun Kuang (荀况) in his *Works of Xunzi*, have devoted considerable attention to intellectuals (*shi* or 士) and common people (*min* or 民), the terms for *citizens* within a traditional Chinese polity and society. In the Confucian view, *shi* and *min* were the foundations of a political community and they should be respected and empowered in political life. This was explained by Mencius in the following way: "the common people are the most valuable in a nation; the land and grain are the next; and the sovereign is the lightest. Therefore, to gain people's support is the way to become sage-king of a state."[17] Xun Kuang further theorized the relationship of *min* and the destiny of a polity in the following way:

> It is said: "The sage-king is like the boat and the people are just like the water. Water supports the boat but also sinks it." Hence if the sage-king wishes to be secure, there is nothing as good as a just government and love for his people. If he wishes to have glory, there is nothing better than exalting rites and respecting intellectuals. If he wishes to have achievement and fame, there is nothing as good as honoring the talented.[18]

In classical Confucianism, the core of an ideal political system lies with *shi* and *min*, who must be respected and accorded their rights and responsibilities of political involvement. A well-known Confucian saying, "everybody has an obligation for the well-being under Heaven" has been commonly accepted as a key civic value in Chinese history.[19]

---

[16] Aristotle, *Politics*, 3.1.
[17] *The Works of Mencius*, 14.14.
[18] *The Works of Xunzi*, 9.4.
[19] Gu Yanwu, *Rizhi Lu*, 13.

This Chinese tradition, however, is often misunderstood by Western scholars. For example, Samuel Huntington argued that Confucianism is "inhospitable to democracy,"[20] and Shils contended that "Confucius is entirely silent regarding the institution of civil society."[21] By contrast, Fukuyama makes the point that at least some dimensions of Confucianism are compatible with the Western model of democracy.[22] Recent scholarship also suggests that the idea of social rights emerged first in China, not in Europe, as has often been assumed.[23] In the Confucian view, both *the intellectuals* and *the common people* are expected to participate in political life in various ways, particularly through individual learning, personal self-cultivation and public engagement.[24] Confucius also made the explicit point that "in education there should be no discrimination on the basis of class."[25] Based on these normative ideas, Mencius developed his conviction that "every human being is able to become a sage-king."[26] This doctrine of universal accessibility to sagehood is a teaching of human equality,[27] and of what may be called "the equal opportunity of citizenship" in modern terms. Many scholars thus believe that Confucianism has something to contribute to global citizenship.[28]

Many influential Western theorists have also presumed that civil society does not exist in China, particularly in contemporary China with its one-party political system, whereas some refute such a presumption,

---

[20] Samuel P. Huntington, "Democracy's Third Wave," in *Journal of Democracy*, Vol.2, No.2, 1991, p.24.

[21] Edward Shils, "Reflections on Civil Society and Civility in the Chinese Intellectual Tradition," in Tu Weiming (ed.), *Confucian Traditions in East Asian Modernity: Moral Education and Economic Culture in Japan and the Four Mini-Dragons* (Cambridge: Harvard University Press, 1996), p.71.

[22] Francis Fukuyama, "Confucianism and Democracy," in *Journal of Democracy*, Vol.6, No.2, 1995, p.25.

[23] Roy Bin Wong, *China Transformed: Historical Change and the Limits of European experience* (Ithaca: Cornell University Press, 1997), p.101.

[24] *The Great Learning*, 1.

[25] *The Analects*, 15.39.

[26] *The Works of Mencius*, 12.2.

[27] Julia Ching, "Human Rights: A Valid Chinese Concept?" in Wm. Theodore de Bary and Tu Weiming (eds.), *Confucianism and Human Rights* (New York: Columbia University Press, 1998), p.72.

[28] Tu Weiming, "Global Citizenship in a Dialogical Civilization and the Language of Confucianism," 2005, accessed February 14, 2008, http://www.beijingforum.org/en/ShowArticle.asp?ArticleID=236.

with historical evidence that some concepts from the Western discourse can be also found in classical Asian works.²⁹ The real issue here, however, may be how the concept of civil society is defined and measured.

The concept of civil society is rooted in Christian speculation around natural law, which was articulated first in the Scottish Enlightenment of the 18th century and later revived by Tocqueville in his romantic narration of his travels to the U.S. in the 1830s. It became prominent again after the fall of the Berlin Wall in 1989. Since its contemporary revitalization in the late 1980s, this ambiguous and contested "big idea" has come to mean different things to different people. It has resonated differently in differing sociopolitical contexts, cultures and traditions. Despite this diversity, there have been several major strands of thought which have made the idea of civil society so attractive. One of these is the notion of civil society as associational life.³⁰

In classical thought, civil society usually referred to a type of political association in which citizens were restrained and protected. In his *Politics*, Aristotle made clear the concept of associations as the coalescence of families and villages to form a polis.³¹ Alexis de Tocqueville extended Aristotle's idea in his observations in the U.S., classifying associations into two major types, political and civil. By political associations, he meant those where "a number of individuals give (assent) to certain doctrines and in the engagement which they contract to promote in a certain manner the spread of those doctrines ... an association unites into one channel the efforts of divergent minds .... ."³²

The other type is civil associations without reference to political purposes. This type of association consists of "not only commercial and

---

²⁹ For discussions of Chinese civil society, see Timothy Brook and B. Michael Frolic (eds.), *Civil Society in China* (New York: M.E. Sharpe, 1997); Randy Kluver and John H. Powers (eds.), *Civic Discourse, Civil Society, and Chinese Communities* (Stamford, CT: Ablex, 1999); Yu Keping, "Ideological change and incremental democracy in reform-era China," in Cheng Li (ed.), *China's Changing Political Landscape: Prospects for Democracy* (Washington, D.C.: Brookings Institution Press, 2008), pp.44-58; and Amartya Sen, *Development as Freedom* (New York: Alfred A. Knopf, 2000), pp.227-248.

³⁰ Michael Edwards, *Civil Society* (Cambridge: Polity Press, 2004).

³¹ Aristotle, *Politics*, 1.2.

³² Alexis de Tocqueville, *Democracy in America*, trans. Henry Reeve, corr. and rev. Francis Bowen and Phillips Bradley (New York: Alfred A. Knopf, Inc., 1966), Vol.1, p.192.

manufacturing companies, in which all take part, but a thousand other kinds, religious, moral, serious, futile, general or restricted, enormous or diminutive" that form a society.[33] According to Tocqueville, more attention should be paid to intellectual and moral associations which are not commonly noted.[34] Neo-Tocquevillians have further developed these ideas, referring to these associations as civil society organizations (CSOs), non-governmental organizations (NGOs), non-profit organizations (NPOs), or third sector organizations (TSOs).[35] This is "the space of uncoerced human association and also the set of relational networks – formed for the sake of family, faith, interest, and ideology – that fill this space."[36] For neo-Tocquevillians, civil society as associational life unites the democratic power of independent yet powerless civilians and prevents the unlimited expansion and intervention of state power, in the name of social justice and equality. This overlaps with Robert Bellah et al's perception of civil society as the good society,[37] Robert Putnam's definition of civil society as social capital,[38] Jürgen Habermas's concept of civil society as the public sphere,[39] and Jeffrey Alexander's new suggestion of

---

[33] See Alexis de Tocqueville, *Democracy in America*, Vol.2, p.106.
[34] *Idid*, p.110.
[35] Please see Lester M. Salamon and Helmut K. Anheier, *The Emerging Nonprofit Sector: An Overview* (Manchester & New York: Manchester University Press, 1996); *Defining the Nonprofit Sector: A Cross-National Analysis* (Manchester & New York: Manchester University Press, 1997); Samiul Hasan and Jenny Onyx, *Comparative Third Sector Governance in Asia: Structure, Process, and Political Economy* (New York: Springer, 2008).
[36] Michael Walzer, "The Idea of Civil Society: A Path to Social Reconstruction," in E.J. Dionne Jr. (ed.), *Community Works: The Revival of Civil Society in America* (Washington, D.C.: Brookings Institution Press, 1998), pp.123-124.
[37] Robert N. Bellah, Richard Madsen, William M. Sullivan, Ann Swidler and Steven M. Tipton, *The Good Society* (New York: Alfred A. Knopf, 1991); Amitai Etzioni, "Why the Civil Society is Not Good Enough?" (paper presented at X Congreso Internacional del CLAD sobre la Reforma del Estado y de la Administración Pública, Santiago, Chile, October 18-21, 2005).
[38] Robert D. Putnam, *Bowling alone: The Collapse and Revival of American Community* (New York: Simon & Schuster, 2000); Robert D. Putnam, "Bowling alone: America's Declining Social Capital," in *Journal of Democracy*, Vol.6, No.1, 1995, pp.65-78.
[39] Jürgen Habermas, *The Structural Transformation of the Public Sphere: An Inquiry into a Category of Bourgeois Society*, trans. Thomas Burger (Cambridge, MA: The MIT Press, 1989); Jürgen Habermas, "Further Reflections on the Public Sphere," in Craig Calhoun (ed.), *Habermas and the Public Sphere*, trans. Thomas Burger (Cambridge, MA: The MIT Press, 1992), pp.421-461.

civil society as the civic sphere.⁴⁰

While many Western scholars continue to doubt whether civil society exists in China in any form,⁴¹ most Chinese people have grown up with a Confucian concept which highly values the associational life among families and local communities, that is regulated by ritual. For example, Confucius viewed dignity without being combative and sociability for justice and equity as the basic requirements for a gentleman.⁴² In this way, a great harmony is to be shared by all:

> When the perfect order prevails, the world is like a home shared by all....Peace and trust among all men are the maxims of living. All men love and respect their own parents and children, as well as the parents and children of others. There is caring for the old; there are jobs for the adults; there are nourishment and education for the children. There is a means of support for the widows and the widowers, for all who find themselves alone in the world, and for the disabled .... A sense of sharing displaces the effects of selfishness and materialism. A devotion to public duty leaves no room for idleness .... This is called the

---

⁴⁰ Jeffrey C. Alexander, *The Civil Sphere* (Oxford: Oxford University Press, 2006); Jeffrey C. Alexander, "Civil society I, II, III: Constructing an Empirical Concept from Normative Controversies and Historical Transformations," in Jeffrey C. Alexander (ed.), *Real Civil Societies: Dilemmas of Institutionalization* (London: Sage, 1998), pp.1-19.

⁴¹ Please see Larry Diamond, "Toward Democratic Consolidation," in *Journal of Democracy*, Vol.5, No.3, 1994, pp.4-17; Thomas B. Gold, "The Resurgence of Civil Society in China," in *Journal of Democracy*, Vol.1, No.1, 1990, pp.18-31; Kristina Gough, *Emerging Civil Society in China: An Overview Assessment of Conditions and Possibilities Available to Civil Society and Its Organizations to Act in China* (Stockholm: SIDA 2004), accessed August 6, 2008, http://www.sida.se/sida/jsp/sida.jsp?d= 118&a=3163&language=en_US; Baogang He, *The Democratic Implications of Civil Society in China* (New York: St. Martin's Press, 1997); R. Madsen, "Confucian Conceptions of Civil Society," in Simone Chambers and Will Kymlicka (eds.), *Alternative Conceptions of Civil Society* (New Jersey: Princeton University Press, 2002), pp.190-204; Edward Shils, "Reflections on Civil Society and Civility in the Chinese Intellectual Tradition," in Tu Weiming (ed.), *Confucian Traditions in East Asian Modernity: Moral Education and Economic Culture in Japan and the Four Mini-Dragons* (Cambridge: Harvard University Press, 1996), pp.38-71; David Dahua Yang, "Civil Society as an Analytic Lens for Contemporary China," in *China: An International Journal*, Vol.2, No.1, 2004, pp.1-27.

⁴² *The Analects*, 15.22.

commonwealth state.[43]

While recent scholarship affirms that central to the Confucian tradition is the idea of humaneness with ritual to guarantee it,[44] few scholars have realized that associational life is one of the major purposes of Confucian ritual. This was true in Chinese history when social justice was threatened by corrupt governments. The student movement in the Eastern Han Dynasty (25-220 CE)[45] and the activism of the Donglin Academy (東林書院) in the 17th century[46] may serve as typical examples of the functioning of civil society in Chinese history. There have also been numerous other civil associations in Chinese history, such as the vibrancy of associational life in the Jixia Academy mentioned earlier, and in the Chinese ancient city of Hangzhou in the late 13th century observed by Marco Polo.[47]

Such associational life was revitalized gradually in the post-Mao era, especially after the Chinese government adopted decentralization and deregulation, along with the open door policy, in the 1980s.[48] This sociopolitical transformation has created space for CSOs or TSOs, or *social organizations* (社會團體) in Chinese terminology. As a recent comparative study shows, civil society in contemporary China "is multifaceted, ranging from government-controlled, government-organized non-government organizations (GONGOs) to a growing number of inde-

---

[43] *The Records of Rites*, 9.1.
[44] Robert C. Neville, *Ritual and Deference: Extending Chinese Philosophy in a Comparative Context* (Albany: State University of New York Press, 2008).
[45] Ying-shih Yu, "Student Movements in Chinese History and the Future of Democracy in China," in Peter Li, Marjorie H. Li, and Steven Mark (eds.), *Culture and Politics in China: An Anatomy of Tiananmen Square* (New Brunswick, NJ: Transaction Publishers, 1991), pp.243-257.
[46] Sun Peiqing (ed.), *Zhongguo Jiaoyu Shi* (*A History of China's Education*) (3rd ed., Shanghai: East China Normal University Press, 2009), pp.251-253.
[47] Arthur Christopher Moule, "Marco Polo's Description of Quinsai," pp.124-126, as cited in Etienne Balazs, "The Birth of Capitalism in China," in Arthur F. Wright (ed.), *Chinese Civilization and Bureaucracy: Variations on a Theme*, tran. Hope M. Wright (New Haven: Yale University Press, 1964), p.99.
[48] Yuanzhu Ding, "Third Sector Governance in China: Structure, Process and Relationships," in Samiul Hasan and Jenny Onyx (eds.), *Comparative Third Sector Governance in Asia: Structure, Process, and Political Economy* (New York: Springer, 2008), pp.207-226.

pendent NGOs and informal grassroots initiatives."[49] According to the statistics of the Chinese government, the number of officially registered non-governmental organizations jumped from 129,000 in 2001 to 425,000 in 2009.[50] In addition, there are many CSOs unable to register officially for various reasons.[51] Meanwhile, as a recent survey uncovers, the private sector has contributed to a variety of community projects, and "private entrepreneurs are involved in their communities, not just by providing jobs and tax revenue, but also by helping provide collective goods."[52]

In the centuries-old discourse of various civilizations, there are no single, universally accepted definitions for citizenship, nor for civil society, as evident in both Western and Chinese traditions briefly outlined above. However, it is clear that the two notions have a complementary relationship in which "citizenship concerns the relationship of the state and the citizen" and civil society "provides the context or 'mediating institutions' between the citizen and the state."[53] And it is equally clear that education, especially formal school education, plays an important role in nurturing citizenship and expanding participation in civil society by young people.

The modern university has seen the nurturing of citizenship and civil society as a major institutional aim, especially in its elite phase, if we recall Newman's discourse, where he said that all branches of knowledge provided by a university are "of great secular utility, as constituting the best and highest formation of the intellect for social and political life."[54]

---

[49] V. Finn Heinrich, *Civicus Global Survey of the State of Civil Society* (Bloomfield, CT: Kumarian Press, 2007), p.57.
[50] Ministry of Civil Affairs, *Zhongguo Minzheng Tongji Nianjian 2005 (China Civil Affairs' Statistical Yearbook 2005)* (Beijing: China Statistics Press, 2005), p.6; Ministry of Civil Affairs, *2009 Nian Minzhen Shiye Fazhan Tongji Gongbao (Annual Statistical Communiqué of Civil Affairs and Development 2009)*, 2010, accessed Feb 16, 2011, http://www.gov.cn/gzdt/2010-02/03/content_1527088.htm.
[51] V. Finn Heinrich, *Civicus Global Survey of the State of Civil Society* (Bloomfield, CT: Kumarian Press, 2007), p.57.
[52] Bruce Dickson, "Do Good Businessmen Make Good Citizens? An Emerging Collective Identity among China's Private Entrepreneurs," in Merle Goldman and Elizabeth J. Perry (eds.), *Changing Meanings of Citizenship in Modern China* (Cambridge: Harvard University Press, 2002), p.277.
[53] Thomas Janoski, *Citizenship and Civil Society: A Framework of Rights and Obligations in Liberal, Traditional, and Social Democratic Regimes* (Cambridge: Cambridge University Press, 1998), p.12.
[54] See John H. Newman, *The Idea of a University*, p.214.

With the intensification of globalization, marketization and privatization of higher education in many countries nowadays, understanding how citizenship education is offered by higher education institutions to young people in different contexts and how students' civic participation is associated with their civic awareness, knowledge, values, skills and feelings has been an important issue for building a vibrant civil society. With China's revolutionary transformation from elite to mass higher education over the last decade, these issues become particularly urgent.

Analytical Frameworks

The radical transformation of universities in the move to mass higher education has drawn the attention of many theorists since the beginning of the expansion process. Among them were George Bereday, Edward Shils, and Martin Trow, all of whom have provided powerful analytical frameworks to look into various aspects of the process. George Bereday proposed the use of inductive method to examine various phenomena that have occurred in the expansion of higher education, focusing on the experience of North America, Japan and the former Soviet Union.[55] Edward Shils compared the Humboltian elite university and the mass university by considering the following key aspects: the increased demand to provide public services; the growing intrusion of govern-mental constraints; the expansion of bureaucratic administration; the reduction in public financial support; obsessive assessment of academic performance; the disaggregation of universities as communities; and the demoralization of intellectual life.[56]

Martin Trow has probably been the most influential writer on higher education expansion. His *Problems in the Transition from Elite to Mass Higher Education* published in 1973, has shaped the ways in which many policymakers, education practitioners and scholars understand the process of higher education expansion in many countries. He has adopted the Weberian approach of abstracting ideal types from empirical reality and emphasizing the functional relationships among the several common components of institutional systems. His theory continues to serve as a powerful lens to examine the key issues arising from higher

---

[55] George Z.F. Bereday, *Universities for All: International Perspectives on Mass Higher Education* (San Francisco, CA: Jossey-Bass Publishers, 1973).

[56] Edward Shils, *The Calling of Education: The Academic Ethic and Other Essays on Higher Education* (Chicago: Chicago University Press, 1997).

education expansion.[57]

In his two benchmark pieces, Trow clearly made the distinction between elite, mass and universal phases and forms of higher education, and laid out a map to clarify the key issues in the expansion and transformation of higher education systems. Recently he reexamined this framework with updated empirical data, giving greater attention to the changing nature of the elite form and more consideration of the dilemmas around controlling educational quality in the system. Trow's typology of the institutional transformations in the phase of mass higher education is summarized in Table 2.1.

Table 2.1: Martin Trow's Typology of the Institutional Transformations of Mass Higher Education

Aspects of Higher Education System	Descriptors of Mass Higher Education
1. Size of the system	15-49% of the relevant age group
2. Attitudes toward access	A right for those with certain formal qualifications
3. Functions of higher education	Preparation for a broader range of technical and economic elites
4. The curriculum and forms of instruction	Modular, semi-structured, flexible courses or programs
5. The student "career"	Higher wastage rates of graduates
6. Institutional diversity, characteristics and boundaries	More comprehensive with more diverse standards; a city of the intellect; boundaries blurred and permeable
7. The locus of power and decision-making	More democratic political processes with more attentive audiences
8. Academic standards	Variable in different parts of the system or institution
9. Access and selection	Meritocratic with compensation for equality of educational opportunity
10. Forms of academic administration	Fulltime administrators/professionals with a large and growing bureaucracy
11. Internal governance	Shared with broader participants such as junior professors and students

Source: Martin A. Trow, *Problems in the Transition from Elite to Mass Higher Education* (reprint) (Berkeley, CA: Carnegie Commission on Higher Education, 1973), pp.7-18; "Reflections on the Transition from Elite to Mass to Universal Access: Forms and Phases of Higher Education in Modern Society since WWII," in James J.F. Forest and Philip G. Altbach (Eds.), *International Handbook of Higher Education* (Dordrecht: Springer, 2006), pp.252-263.

---

[57] John Brennan, "The Social Role of the Contemporary University: Contradictions, Boundaries and Change," in *Ten Years on: Changing Education in a Changing World* (Buckingham: Center for Higher Education Research & Information (CHERI), The Open University, 2004), pp.22-26.

Martin Trow's theory serves the purpose of this chapter well, since we are looking into the complex transition process from elite to mass higher education from the perspective of students. This chapter adapts his framework, while downsizing its scope somewhat. The adapted analytical framework starts from an investigation of students' experiences of access and success in higher education in terms of financial support, then looks into how they perceive and experience the institutional changes brought about by the expansion, with an additional dimension of institutional internationalization which was originally not addressed by Trow.

The second framework is abstracted from the classical Confucian theory of learning focusing on the individual cultivation process and the lifelong pursuit of moral perfection. It has been found that the success of Chinese learners can not easily be understood within Western frameworks.[58] This chapter establishes an indigenous framework for the study of students' civic learning and participation in the Chinese context, distilled from the Three Principles and Eight Guidelines (三綱領八條目) of *The Great Learning*:

> The guiding principle of higher learning is to let one's innate virtue shine forth, to renew the people, and to rest in the highest good....only when things are investigated is knowledge extended; only when knowledge is extended are feelings sincere; only when feelings are sincere are hearts rectified; only when hearts are rectified is morality cultivated; only when morality is cultivated are families in right order; only when families are in right order are states well governed; and only when states are well governed can the world be at peace.

The Confucian framework has been an integral part of Chinese culture and education over two thousand years, with its official adoption as a part of the compulsory curriculum found in *The Four Books* (《四書》) from the Song to the Qing Dynasties (960-1911 CE). It has had a profound influence on Chinese ways of thinking about learning, teaching and schooling,[59] and is still widely used in day-to-day moral and civic education by families, communities and schools not only in the greater China region, but also in Japan, Korea, Vietnam, Singapore and overseas Chi-

---

[58] David A. Watkins and John B. Biggs, *The Chinese Learner: Cultural, Psychological and Contextual Influences* (Hong Kong/Victoria: Comparative Education Research Centre/Australian Council for Educational Research ltd, 1996).

[59] Jun Li, *Jiaoyuxue Zhi* (*A History of Chinese Thought on Education*) (Shanghai: Shanghai People's Press, 1998).

nese communities in other countries.

As shown in Figure 2.1, this analytical framework reflects the classical Confucian theory of learning for the expression and analysis of students' political socialization process in a Chinese socio-cultural context. The Confucian model locates moral cultivation at the center of individual learning process, starts from individual knowing, and extends spirally to integrate personal self-development and social action, but the boundaries among civic knowing, wisdom and action are blurred within a trilateral integration. In addition, this analytical framework covers various measures and dimensions of students' civic learning and participation for this study. Within this framework, we will examine a number of interrelated variables identified from the following four categories of measures: the civic knowing (cognitive) scale (concepts, beliefs and values), the civic wisdom (affective and evaluative) scale (feelings, attitudes and judgments), the civic action scale, and the relationship scale. Using this indigenous framework, we will examine

Figure 2.1: The Conceptual Framework of the Individual Political Socialization Process

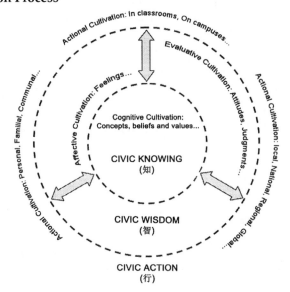

Source: Adapted from Jun Li, "Fostering Citizenship and Civil Society in China's Move to Mass Higher Education", in *International Journal of Educational Development*, 29(4), 2009, pp.382-398; and from Jun Li, "Gongmin Jiaoyu Yanjiu de Lilun Jiagou: Tansuo Yige Rujia Wenhua de Bentu Moshi (Reflections on the Frameworks of Citizenship Education Studies: Exploring an Indigenous Confucian Model)", in *Zhongguo Deyu (Chinese Journal of Moral Education)*, 5(12), 2010, pp.26-33.

students' civic cultivation in their political socialization, particularly focusing on how students' concepts of citizenship and civil society are developed through their associational life on campus and in the wider community. Traditional views of political socialization view the process as a matter of compliance, which does not allow for individuals to refuse indoctrination into a given political culture. We will test this assumption in the Chinese sociopolitical context.

Methods

The data analyzed in this chapter were collected in May and June of 2007 through a nationwide questionnaire survey administered in 12 case study universities, including 9 public and 3 private institutions, which has been introduced in Chapter 1 of this volume. Like many international surveys, a purposive sampling strategy was employed. The student samples in each of the twelve universities consisted of three classes in each of three broad disciplinary areas: the natural sciences and technologies, social sciences, and humanities. Respondents to this survey were largely third year undergraduate students, with a few classes being in their second year. The questionnaire had a total of 70 questions, and was designed specifically for the project. It was finalized after considering feedback from a pilot survey conducted in two case study universities in December 2006.

All questionnaires were distributed to the entire classes. The total questionnaires disseminated for this research were 2,332, and a total

Table 2.2: Summary of Questionnaires Administered

Category	Sub-categories	Number of Participants	Percentage
Institutional type	Private	480	20.7
	Public	1841	79.3
Discipline	Natural sciences/ technologies	871	37.3
	Social sciences	787	33.7
	Humanities	639	27.4
Gender	Female	1237	53.5
	Male	1073	46.5
Geographic background	Rural area (township/village)	1194	52.9
	Urban area (city/county)	1064	47.1
Total	Returned	2332	100
	Valid	2321	99.5

Source: China's Move to Mass Higher Education (CMHE) Project Database (2007).

number of 2,321 valid copies were returned. The valid return rate was 99.5%, as shown in Table 2.2. The data entry work using the SPSS format was verified by a procedure of cross-random checking. The data accuracy rate reached 99.91%, very close to the industrial standard for information capture accuracy.

Limitations

There are several limitations associated with the database and its analysis. Firstly, the samples selected for this study are relatively small, given it was a nationwide survey. However, the samples are sufficient to conduct statistical analysis, as theorized by Gall et al.[60] In addition, a more rigorous threshold of statistical significance ($p<.001$, rather than $p<.01$) is used to interpret the results of the statistical analyses throughout the chapter unless indicated in certain specific occasions.[61]

Secondly, as our student survey was linked to the case study universities selected for the project, and not originally designed for a random sampling, the samples were skewed to those studying in top-level Chinese universities, with the exception of students in the three private universities. We realize that our findings are not generalizable to all Chinese university students. Rather, we aim at offering a "snapshot" of student perspectives on the radical transition from elite to mass higher education in 12 Chinese universities.

Finally, because the database is based on non-random sampling and there are no comparable national statistics available, the variables in the CMHE database are not weighted for analysis. There is also no procedure for missing data analysis as the database is virtually complete.

Results of the Survey

The findings of the student survey are grouped into three themes: students' experiences of access and success in higher education, their perceptions of the institutional changes that accompanied higher education expansion, and their political socialization in terms of civic knowing, wisdom and action. Descriptive statistics, two-way contingency table

---

[60] Meredith D. Gall, Joyce P. Gall, and Walter R. Borg, *Educational Research: An Introduction* (7th ed. Boston, MA: Pearson/Allyn & Bacon, 2003).
[61] Scott L. Thomas and Ronald H. Heck, "Analysis of Large-scale Secondary Data in Higher Education Research: Potential Perils Associated with Complex Sampling Design," in *Research in Higher Education*, Vol. 42, No.5, 2001, pp.517-540.

analyses, and bivariate and multiple linear regression models with the method of ordinary least squares (OLS) were performed to provide snapshots of various dimensions of students' experiences of and perspectives on China's move from elite to mass higher education.

Experiences of Access and Success in Higher Education

Access

The following survey question was designed to examine what experiences students had in terms of access to higher education:

- If it were not for higher education expansion, I would not have been admitted into my university.

Only 10.6% of respondents reported that they would not have been admitted into university if it were not for higher education expansion and 70.6% of students felt the opposite, while 18.8% did not take a position on the statement. When the patterns of students' experiences of access in higher education were examined with their background characteristics, it was found that their experiences were all statistically significant by institutional types, disciplinary areas, father's educational attainment and family economic status, but not by gender. In addition, the probability of agreeing with the statement was about 3.94 times more likely for students in private institutions and about 1.39 times more likely for students from rural as opposed to urban areas, respectively.

Follow-up tests were conducted to examine particular relationships among students from different disciplinary areas, family educational and socioeconomic backgrounds. The LSD method was used to control for Type I error across all the three comparisons. The results show that a pairwise difference was statistically significant between students in social sciences and natural sciences/technology, and the probability of being admitted to university due to the expansion was about 1.29 times more likely for students from social sciences as opposed to natural sciences/technology. Meanwhile, a similar pairwise difference was found between students whose fathers held a primary school diploma or less and students whose fathers held a college degree or above, and between students with a gross family annual income less than 25,000 *yuan* and above 60,000 *yuan*, respectively. The probability of being admitted to university due to the expansion was about 2.09 times and 1.92 more likely for the former as opposed to the latter, respectively.

Affordability

The following survey question was designed to examine what experiences students had in their access in higher education in terms of affordability:

- Overall, I feel that university tuition is too expensive for most families.

Eighty-two percent of respondents reported that tuition was too expensive for most families and only 3.7% of students felt the opposite, while 14.5% did not take a position on the statement. Students' experiences were all statistically significant by institutional types, gender, father's educational attainment and family economic status, but not by disciplinary areas. In addition, the probability of agreeing with the statement was about 1.21 times more likely for students in private universities as opposed to public institutions, about 1.07 times more likely for students who were male as opposed to female, and about 1.18 times more likely for students from rural as opposed to urban areas, respectively.

It was further confirmed that the probability of less affordability was about 1.28 times more likely when a student's father held a primary school diploma or less as opposed to a college degree or above, and about 1.39 times more likely when a student's family gross annual income was below the lowest level (25,000 *yuan*) as opposed to above the highest level (60,000 *yuan*), respectively.

Success

The following survey question was designed to examine what experiences students have in terms of ongoing financial support from their families for their success in terms of survival on campus:

- My family can afford to support me to finish my four years of university study.

In general, 48.4% of respondents reported that their families could afford to support their four years of university study and 35.1% of students experienced the opposite, while 16.5% did not take a position on the statement. When the patterns of students' experiences of success in higher education were examined with their background characteristics, it was found that their experiences were all statistically significant by institutional types, gender, father's educational attainment and family economic status, but not by disciplinary areas. The probability of insufficient family financial support for four years of university study was about 1.66 times more likely for students in private universities as opposed to public institutions, about 1.27 times more likely for students who were male as opposed to female, and about 3.82 times more likely for students from rural as opposed to urban areas, respectively.

It is further confirmed that the probability of insufficient financial support for four-years of university study was about 7.02 times more likely when a student's father held a primary school diploma or less as opposed to a college degree or above, and about 17.96 times more likely when a student's family gross annual income was below the lowest level (25,000 *yuan*) as opposed to above the highest level (60,000 *yuan*), respectively.

Perceptions and Experiences of Institutional Change

Feelings toward the changes

The following survey question was designed to investigate into how students feel about the institutional change that accompanied expansion:

- Overall, I have a positive feeling about the changes in my university after China's move to mass higher education.

While 41.7% of students showed a positive feeling about the change taking place in their universities in the move to mass higher education, 23.3% took the opposite position, and more than one-third of them had neutral feelings. No statistically significant difference in students' feelings toward institutional change was evident by institutional type, disciplinary area, father's educational attainment or family economic status.

Students' feelings toward the institutional changes were statistically different, however, between female and male students, and between students from rural and urban areas. The probability of having positive feelings was 1.1 times more likely when a student was female and 1.2 times more likely when a student was from a rural area.

Views on the role of the expansion in socioeconomic development

The following survey question was designed to investigate students' views on the importance of mass higher education for socioeconomic progress:

- The move to mass higher education produces more qualified

talent for China's socioeconomic development.

Nearly half of the students agreed with this statement while nearly one-fifth disagreed, and one-third were neutral. There was no significant difference in students by disciplinary field, geographic areas, father's educational attainment or family economic status, but there was a statistically significant relationship between students from private and public higher education institutions, and between female and male students. The probability of having a positive view was about 1.03 times more likely when a student was female, and about 1.28 times more likely when a student was from a private institution.

Flexibility in the selection of courses or programs

The following survey question was designed to investigate students' experiences in course or program selection in the expansion:

- I am able to select whatever courses or programs I have an interest in studying.

There were 56.4% of students who responded negatively to this question, and only 22.7% had positive experiences, while more than one-fifth did not take a position. The only significant difference by background variables was that between female and male students, with the probability of male students having positive experiences being about 1.26 times more likely than female.

Teaching quality

The following survey question was designed to investigate teaching quality in higher institutions as experienced by students:

- My professors teach us with up-to-date content.

More than one-third of students responded negatively to this question, while less than one-third of students had a positive sense, and more than one-third took no position. There was no statistically significant difference in their experiences by all the six independent variables.

Institutional internationalization

The following survey question was designed to examine students' experiences of institutional internationalization:

- I notice that there are quite a few foreign students who are studying the Chinese language and other subjects in my university.

There were 41.9% of students who noticed the present of foreign students at their universities, and 26.7% who did not, while 31.3% were neutral. Students' experiences of this aspect of institutional internationalization were statistically significant by all of the six independent variables.

The probability of experiencing institutional internationalization was about 2.73 times more likely when a student was from a public university, about 1.26 times more likely when a student was female, about 1.29 times more likely when a student was in the humanities as opposed to the natural sciences, about 1.20 times more likely when a student is from an urban area , about 1.38 times more likely when a student's father held a college degree or above as opposed to a primary school diploma or less, and about 1.32 times more likely when a student's family gross annual income is above 60,000 *yuan* as opposed to below 25,000 *yuan*, respectively.

Political Socialization toward Citizenship and Civil Society
Civic knowing and wisdom

To investigate students' cognitive cultivation toward citizenship and civil society, the following survey question was chosen:

- As a university student, I have a clear understanding of the concept of civil society.

There were 52.9% of respondents who thought they had a clear understanding of the concept of civil society and 15.8% of students who took the opposite position, while nearly one-third were neutral.

The only statistically significant differences by background variable related to the three disciplinary areas where students were registered. A statistically significant difference was found through follow-up tests between students studying the natural sciences or technologies and those studying the social sciences, with the probability of having a clear understanding of the concept of civil society being about 1.21 times more likely among the latter.

The affective cultivation is defined as students' feelings about their national identity. The following question was designed to examine this:

- Everybody should be patriotic and loyal to her/his country.

The majority of students (82.4%) supported this statement, with 46.5% and 35.2% of male students and 42.3% and 40.6% of female students giving a strong or moderately positive response respectively. Only 3.2% of respondents were negative while 14.4% had neutral feelings, with a few more female than male students in this group. The findings suggest that Chinese students overall have a very strong affection toward their national identity.

To understand students' evaluative cultivation with regard to their individual civil rights and responsibilities, the following statement was used:

- As a university student, I have an obligation to actively participate in activities that benefit the community and society.

Most students (87.5%) supported the statement, while 10.5% took a neutral position, and 2.0% opposed it. The only background variables of statistical significance here were gender differences, the rural/urban gap, and differences relating to father's educational attainment. The findings indicate that female students were somewhat more likely to commit to active participation in their community and society while students from rural areas were 2.7 times more likely. Differences relating to father's educational attainment of course were inter-related with the urban/rural differences.

Associational life as civic action

Five survey questions were designed to help us understand what associational life students have in the process of political socialization. The first was about the ways students learn about social events. Six options were given to measure their personal learning experiences. The results showed that the mass media, including the internet, newspapers, magazines and TV programs were powerful in shaping students' learning in relation to civic engagement, and male students were more likely to acknowledge this influence (75.6%). Both female and male students agreed that weekly political study meetings officially provided by universities were the least preferred channel of learning among the six options (5.4%). The findings also show that students' personal communications with professors, advisors, classmates or friends, and their personal observations were the next two most effective ways of learning.

The second survey question asked what kinds of associations or organizations students had been involved in. Results show that students were most active in the Chinese Communist Youth League (85.9%) and the student council/class parliament (65.7%), and there was no significant difference between female and male students in these choices. By contrast, only 17.7% of students were active in environmental organizations, with male students less likely to be involved than female. Nevertheless, nearly one-third of students took up opportunities for involvement in NGOs or NPOs.

The third survey question asked what kind of voting activities students were most likely to participate in. More than half of male students wanted to participate in voting for representatives of the People's Congress, compared to one-third of female students. Interestingly, the findings suggest that female students (23.0%) were more likely than male students (15.6) to be involved in local voting activities (voting for representatives of student councils).

The fourth survey question related to the voluntary work students may have organized or participated in, including campaigns for protecting the environment, support for education in rural areas, support for the disadvantaged or discussions of social issues. Then the question asked students why they participated in such voluntary activities. Both female and male students rated their obligation to participate in such activities as the most frequent choice, as high as 85.1% and 75.6%, respectively. They also viewed these voluntary activities as a mutually beneficial process both for themselves and society, with 81.4% and 72.0% of positive responses for society, and 80.8% and 69.0% for themselves. The findings suggest that the majority of students took their civic responsibility seriously.

The fifth question asked students how they benefitted from the memberships they held or associations they belonged to. More than 91.4% of students viewed networking as their major benefit out of civic engagement. This was true for both female students (93.3%) and male students (89.3%). Next to networking was social learning, with an average response rate of 76.4%. Leadership ability development was the lowest among the four options, but still constituted 70.9%. The findings indicate that students' political socialization mainly took place through associational life, which was motivated by their sense of civic responsibility, as seen in their responses to the fourth question.

The interplay among civic knowing, wisdom and action

Up to this point, students' civic knowing, wisdom and action have been examined separately, but further effort is needed to identify the interplay among the three trilaterally integrated aspects, as shown in Figure 2.1. A bivariate linear regression model and multiple regression models with the method of ordinary least squares (OLS) were used to explore how students' civic knowing and wisdom can possibly predict their civic action.

All the models employed for analysis show that students' cognitive, affective and evaluative cultivations accounted for a significant amount of their political socialization (PS index), indicating that students with higher cognitive, affective and evaluative cultivations tended to be more engaged in civic action. On the basis of these multiple regression models and the correlational analyses, we tentatively conclude that students' civic knowing and wisdom were statistically significant in predicting their civic action, with limited effect sizes (the magnitude of the effect) ranging from about 3% for the first equation to 7% for the third equation. Moreover, the measures of students' cognitive, affective and evaluative cultivations accounted for 2.8%, 2.6% and 5.4% of the variance in students' civic action, respectively. Clearly students' evaluative cultivation, i.e., their values and judgments toward citizenship and civil society, played the most important role in the process of political socialization, while students' affective cultivation played the least role.[62]

Discussion of Findings

In the section above, we have presented our survey findings in the three main areas of concern to our study: equity issues, institutional change, and political socialization through associational life. It is now time to revisit Martin Trow's framework for understanding higher education expansion, and reflect on the broader meaning of these findings in relation to China's rapid transition from elite to mass higher education.

Martin Trow's Framework Revisited

Since the early 1970s, Martin Trow's framework has served as a powerful instrument to examine various phenomena in the transition from elite to

---

[62] For detailed statistical techniques and analyses with these models, please refer to: Jun Li, "Fostering Citizenship in China's Move from Elite to Mass Higher Education: An Analysis of Students' Political Socialization and Civic Participation," in *International Journal of Educational Development*, Vol.29, No. 4, 2008, pp.382-398.

mass higher education in North America, Europe and Asia, and has particularly attracted the serious attention and interest of Chinese policy makers. In many countries, educational leaders and analysts have applied his theory as a kind of policy goal for the expansion and development of their higher education systems, with little critical reflection.

It is not surprising that our findings confirm and support most points in his assumptions. For example, more than 41% of Chinese students showed a positive feeling about the transition that had taken place in their universities after China's move to mass higher education, while less than one-third of them had negative feelings. Nearly half of the students surveyed were able to afford study in higher education institutions when China moved into mass higher education, thus demonstrating that the expansion process of higher education has been largely in line with China's socioeconomic development. In addition, nearly half of the students believed that the move to mass higher education was preparing more qualified talent for China's socioeconomic development. All these findings are consistent with Trow's conceptualization of higher education expansion at the massification phase.

On the other hand, the findings from this study do not support all of Trow's key assumptions. For example, Trow anticipated that "education becomes more modular, marked by semistructured sequences of courses....allowing more flexible combinations of courses ...."[63] However, we found that only around one-fifth of students were able to select whatever courses or programs interested them, showing that Chinese curricular reforms have not kept up with what is needed in a mass system. This finding shows that in China's astonishingly rapid expansion of higher education, responsive curricular and teaching reforms have lagged behind, creating a situation where students are less engaged and able to follow their interests than would be ideal.

In addition, as China's higher education is moving toward a mass system under conditions of intensified globalization, how the internationalization process affects the institutional transition from elite to mass higher education is a significant issue. Our findings show that, 41.9% of students observed the presence of international students while less than one-third of them did not. Although this single measure cannot capture all aspects of the internationalization process, it nevertheless represents

---

[63] Martin Trow, *Problems in the Transition from Elite to Mass Higher Education* (reprint) (Berkeley, CA: Carnegie Commission on Higher Education, 1973), p.8.

one noticeable impact on Chinese university campuses and this differs by university type and disciplinary area. Given that there were many more women registered in the social sciences and humanities, where international students were also likely to be, it is not surprising that they reported more experiences of this aspect of internationalization. Also private universities and universities in hinterland regions had far fewer international students. Martin Trow did not originally focus on the aspect of internationalization in the transition from elite to mass higher education in the 1960s, but it has become one of the key dimensions to look into the transformation of higher education nowadays.

Reflections on Equal Opportunity in China's Move to Mass Higher Education

Since the classic study led by James Samuel Colman on equality of educational opportunity,[64] quantitative approaches have been widely applied to test whether education is a sorter that legitimatizes, reproduces or enhances the existing socioeconomic stratification, or an equalizer that relieves the tension of class conflict.[65] There have been some empirical studies on the access to higher education in China's transition to a mass system,[66] but the present study is probably the first to

---

[64] James S. Coleman, *Equality of Educational Opportunity (Coleman) Study (OOES)* (Washington, D.C.: U.S. Dept. of Health, Education, & Welfare, Office of Education, 1966).

[65] The notion of "equalizer" used here is based on the so-called "horizontal equity" theory which commits to "the equal treatment of equals," a long-standing and fundamental type of equity framework with Aristotelian origins. Please see David H. Monk, *Educational Finance: An Economic Approach* (New York: McGraw Hill, 1990).

[66] For example, Ding Xiaohao, "Guimo Kuoda Yu Gaodeng Jiaoyu Ruxue Jihui Jun-denghuw" (Expansion and equality in Chinese higher education), *Peking University Education Review*, Vol.4, No.2, 2006, pp.24-33; Fan Mingcheng, "Woguo Gaodeng Jiaoyu Ruxue Jihui De Chengxiang Chayi Yanjiu" (Research on the Urban-rural Difference in the Chance of Receiving Higher Education in China), *Education Science*, Vol.24, No.1, 2008, pp.63-67; Xie Zuoxu and Chen Xiaowei, "Zhongguo Dalu Gaoxiao Xuefei Dui Butong Shehui Jieceng Zinü De Yingxiang" (National Survey and Analysis: The Effect of College Tuition on College Students from Advantageous and Fundamental Strata in Mainland China), *Education and Economy*, No.2, 2007, pp.12-15; Xie Zuoxu and Wang Weiyi, "Gaodeng Jiaoyu Dazhonghua Shiye Xia Woguo Shehui Gejieceng Zinü Gaodeng Jiaoyu Ruxue Jihui Chayi De Yanjiu (The Difference in Higher Education access Opportunity of the Children in Different Strata in China in the Context of the Popularization of

employ the quantitative measurement of affordability based on self-evaluated family financial resources to examine students' opportunities of access and success in China's higher education institutions.

Our findings show that students generally had positive experiences in access to the extended opportunities of higher learning, yet there were significant variations based on dissimilar background characteristics. For example, with regard to students' success in completing four years of university studies, there were serious concerns about family financial support among different student groups. If there were three students in public universities who were worried about ongoing financial support from their families, there would be five peers in private institutions facing this worry. Similarly, if one student was worried for this reason from an urban area or high family income, there would be four students sharing the same concern from a rural area, and eighteen from those in the lowest family income group, respectively. In addition, nearly three quarters of students felt that their admission to universities was not necessarily a result of the expansion of higher education, probably reflecting the fact that nine of our twelve case universities are top-tier institutions in the Chinese system.

The above result may be explained by the unique Chinese sociocultural context, as it is widely observed that students from lower social status – usually from rural areas – have much less access to advantageous educational resources from kindergarten, elementary and secondary school all the way to higher education. At the same time these families have traditionally favored boys over girls, and thus it is rural boys who are most affected by problems of affordability and sustainability. Our findings imply that the expansion of higher education has not really served as an equalizer that relieves the tension of social stratification. Rather more learning opportunities are available for those who are already able to enjoy higher education but there has been a limited increase in learning opportunities for those who can not afford it. While public educational institutions are crucial to achieving equity, at the same time they may also reinforce and even widen the gaps in access to higher

---

Higher Education)", *Journal of Educational Studies*, Vol.2, No.2, 2006, pp.65-74, 96; Yang Dongping, "Gaodeng Jiaoyu Ruxue Jihui: Kuoda Zhizhong De Jieceng Chaju" (Access to Higher Education: Widening Social Class Disparities), *Tsinghua Journal of Education*, Vol.27, No.1, 2006, pp.19-25.

education on class lines.[67]

When higher education moves to the mass phase, as theorized by Trow in 1973 and 2006, the access to and success in the system becomes a right for those with certain formal qualifications. Accordingly, students in private institutions should also have an equal right to benefit from public financial support, such as scholarships or loans. However, private institutions have so far been treated with prejudice by the Chinese government, and financial assistance from the government has only been provided for students in public universities. In our survey, conducted in 2007, one student in a private institution made a strong appeal in responding to an open question: "the government should also provide funding to private universities to relieve the tuition pressure for us."[68] Now the national policy has changed in response to this problem and some government funding is also available for private university students. Based on our findings, financial assistance from the government for disadvantaged groups should be available to students from rural areas, to students from families with limited educational backgrounds, and to students from families with a gross annual income below 25,000 *yuan*. Since there tend to be more male students from rural backgrounds, and more female students from urban backgrounds, we found male students were also relatively disadvantaged. This reflects a continuing tendency for rural families to support sons over daughters for higher education, as explained earlier when the Chinese socio-cultural context was discussed. Although the Chinese government and public universities have taken substantial steps to provide financial resources for student scholarships and loans to close the gap among different student groups, our findings have revealed persisting inequalities in learning opportunities.

Reflections on the Role of Mass Higher Education in Nurturing a Civil Society

Firstly, there were 52.9%, 82.4% and 87.5% of students who believed themselves to have a clear idea about the concept of civil society, to be patriotic and loyal to China, and to have an obligation to actively participate in activities that benefit their community and society, respec-

---

[67] Peter Sacks, *Tearing down the Gates: Confronting the Class Divide in American Education* (Berkley & Los Angeles: University of California Press, 2007).
[68] A student response to open question No.68.

tively. However, if the three variables are compared with one another, a striking question emerges: why did fewer students show a positive cognitive cultivation with regard to civil society, while their affective and evaluative cultivations shared a similar pattern of much higher frequencies of positive responses? This may be explained by the still strong ideological-political education dominating course offerings and campus culture in Chinese universities. Consequently, students may be exposed more to ideological-political education than citizenship education in terms of broader concepts of citizenship and civil society. This explanation is also supported by other findings which will be summarized and discussed later.

Students' cognitive cultivation is positive by and large. Lee shows that Hong Kong students fare very well in citizenship knowledge,[69] and our findings confirm that students in the Mainland have a similarly high awareness and knowledge about citizenship. Moreover, there is a difference in the degree of clarity about the concept of civil society between students studying in natural sciences or technologies and those in social sciences. This fits the commonly recognized view that exposure to the social sciences is likely to have an impact on students' civic understanding.

It is also found that students shared a strongly similar pattern in their affective cultivation with regard to Chinese nationality. In relevant comparative studies Fairbrother has found that Mainland Chinese students show a higher emotional attachment to the nation than Hong Kong students do,[70] and Li has concluded that Chinese students at elementary, lower and upper secondary schools had stronger feelings toward the nation than their Japanese peers.[71] Students in Li's Chinese samples from the fifth grade in elementary schools in 1999 would be second year students in universities in 2007, if they had passed the

---

[69] Lee Wing On, "Students' Concepts and Attitudes toward Citizenship: The Case of Hong Kong," in *International Journal of Educational Research*, Vol.39, No.6, 2003, p.603.

[70] Greg P. Fairbrother, *Toward Critical Patriotism: Student Resistance to Political Education in Hong Kong and China* (Hong Kong: Hong Kong University Press, 2003), p.83.

[71] Jun Li, "Nibbon to Chyugoku Niokeru Gakkou Koumin Kyuoiku No Jiddai Niken-suru Jishyou Dekina Genkyou" (A Comparative Study on Civic Education in Japanese and Chinese Schools), *Bulletin of the Graduate School of Education of Tokyo University*, No.40, 2000, pp.123-124.

National College Entrance Examination in 2005. The coincidentally overlapping samples over time could be seen as a kind of longitudinal research. The very similar findings of the current study and Li's study in 1999, together with Fairbrother's evidence, support the findings that Chinese students generally have very strong and firm feelings toward their nationality.

Among many factors that can explain this phenomenon, ongoing political campaigns for patriotic education centered on nationalism in formal and informal schooling mandated by the Chinese government might be the most obvious. On the other hand, much of the patriotism has also come from independent grass roots movements in China, as evidenced in the fluctuating political relationships of China with Japan and the United States, and recently with the U.K., France and Germany with regard to the Olympic Torch relay. Ironically, patriotism is usually narrowed and blurred by nationalism, and this has become a double-edged sword for the stability and legitimacy of the Communist Party of China. While patriotism is sometimes manipulated as an alternative political source of regime stability and legitimacy, many popular nationalist groups actually use it in ways that detract from or even threaten the CPC's legitimacy.[72]

In addition, a vast majority of students had a generally positive evaluative stance with regard to civil society. Such a sense of obligation toward civil society in large part originates from influential Confucian values about the civil rights and responsibilities of intellectuals (*shi*) and/or the common people (*min*), such as the maxim that "everybody has an obligation for the well-being under Heaven," which was mentioned earlier in this chapter. Even Edward Shils, who was skeptical about the Confucian civil society, admitted that the Confucian tradition can contribute to civil society: "When we turn to the obligation of the highly educated to serve society through civil service, Confucius emerges as a point of departure for a Chinese tradition that is indispensable to civil society."[73] Shu further demonstrated a comprehensive framework for

---

[72] Robert Weatherley, *Politics in China since 1949: Legitimizing Authoritarian Rule* (New York: Routledge, 2006), p.157.
[73] Edward Shils, "Reflections on Civil Society and Civility in the Chinese Intellectual Tradition," in Tu Weiming (ed.), *Confucian Traditions in East Asian Modernity: Moral Education and Economic Culture in Japan and the Four Mini-Dragons* (Cambridge: Harvard University Press, 1996), p.71.

modern citizenship education from a Confucian view.[74] Our empirical evidence also sheds new light on policy initiatives in the international community that might look for cultural sources to enhance citizenship, citizenship education and civil society in diverse civilizations.

Secondly, when students' political socialization is examined in terms of their associational life on campus and in the wider society, some patterns are notable, such as the ways they learned of civic engagement, their motivations and their sense of the benefits of associational life. The findings disclose that the officially organized political study programs have played a minor role in shaping students' political socialization, though these programs are still viewed as a major channel of political propaganda. But it is clear that Chinese students nowadays are heavily involved with organizations officially sponsored by the CPC, while at the same time they are actively involved in CSOs.

More than half of male respondents in our survey indicated they would like to vote for representatives of the People's Congress while only around one-third of females expressed an interest in this. The gender difference of students' political engagement reflects the status quo of a male-dominant Chinese society, mirrored by the imbalance and inequality of gender in Chinese political life. For example, there is not a single woman elected as one of the nine members of the Standing Committee of the Political Bureau of the 17th CPC's Central Committee and there is only one woman among the 25 members of the Political Bureau. Meanwhile, the 11th National Committee of the Chinese People's Political Consultative Conference, the top political advisory body in China, elected its new leadership on March 13, 2008. Among its 24 vice-chairpersons there are only four females, and its chairperson is of course male. This is a taken-for-granted pattern in China's patriarchal political system.

While motivations have been widely recognized as having a special role in political socialization, Almond and Verba did not go in-depth into this dimension in their classic study, nor did Torney-Purta et al., Li or

---

[74] Sinn Whor Shu, "Rujia Daode Sixiang Dui Xiandai Gongmin Jiaoyu De Qishi" (Implications of Confucian thought on Morality for Modern Citizenship Education), in Lau Kwok Keung and Lee Shui Chuen (eds.), *Daode Yu Gongmin Jiaoyu: Dongya Jingyan Yu Qianzhan (Morality and Citizenship Education: Experiences and Prospects from the East Asia)* (Hong Kong: Hong Kong Institute of Educational Research, 1996), pp.147-155.

Fairbrother focus on it.[75] Our findings show that Chinese students tended to see their civic commitment as the most important motivation for civic participation, while most of them benefited from their associational life, with special appreciation of networking and personal socialization opportunities. Together with our previous findings about Chinese students' strong feelings toward patriotism, there is solid evidence that political socialization is a compliance process in which normative values, no matter whether they are from political propaganda or cultural genes, are indoctrinated as a part of students' political learning.

Finally, the role of students' civic cultivations in their political socialization is obvious. Students' cognitive, affective and evaluative cultivation experiences accounted for a significant amount of their PS index, whereas students' feelings toward their Chinese nationality had the least important role in contributing to their political socialization among the three kinds of cultivation. The disconnection is surprising if we recall the previous findings that Chinese students had a robust sense of patriotism. This discrepancy poses a great challenge to Chinese policymakers and educational practitioners. While huge educational resources are invested in encouraging students' patriotic or nationalistic feelings, the outcome does not really account for students' political socialization, if students' cognitive, affective and evaluative cultivations are considered together. Moreover, our findings show that students' awareness and knowledge toward civil society were negatively skewed toward patriotism, which means that students were not really exposed to broader concepts of civil society but only to the official curriculum of ideological-political education.

---

[75] Please see Gabriel A. Almond and Sidney Verba, *The Civic Culture: Political Attitudes and Democracy in Five Nations* (Princeton, NJ: Princeton University Press, 1963); Judith Torney-Purta, Rainer Lehmann, Hans Oswald and Wolfram Schulz, *Citizenship and Education in Twenty-Eight Countries: Civic Knowledge and Engagement at Age Fourteen* (Amsterdam: The International Association for the Evaluation of Educational Achievement, 2001); Jun Li, "Nibbon to Chyugoku Niokeru Gakkou Koumin Kyuoiku No Jiddai Nikensuru Jishyou Dekina Genkyou" (A Comparative Study on Civic Education in Japan and China), *Bulletin of the Graduate School of Education of Tokyo University*, No.40, 2000, pp.117-130; Jun Li, "Student Achievement in Social Studies in Urban Public Schools: China and Japan," in *Education and Society*, Vol.23, No.3, 2005, pp.35-54; Greg P. Fairbrother, *Toward Critical Patriotism: Student Resistance to Political Education in Hong Kong and China* (Hong Kong: Hong Kong University Press, 2003).

Conclusions

This chapter has employed an analytical framework adapted from Martin Trow's theory of the transition from elite to mass higher education and establish an indigenous Confucian framework, respectively, to examine three major aspects of how students have been affected by China's move to mass higher education: their experiences of increasing access, their perceptions and experiences of institutional change, and their political socialization in civic knowing, wisdom and action.

The findings of this study have confirmed most but not all points of Martin Trow's theory about institutional changes in the expansion of higher education. Trow's framework has helped this study to uncover significant inequalities of learning opportunities in Chinese universities. It is astonishing that success on the university campus was above seven times more likely when a student's father held a college degree or above as opposed to a primary school diploma or less, and nearly eighteen times more likely when a student came from a high income family as opposed to a lower income family, respectively. There is also strong evidence that the expansion policy has not necessarily brought about equal opportunities of access and retention in higher education for the relevant age group, with more learning opportunities available for those who were already able to enjoy higher education but with a limited increase in learning opportunities for those who could not afford it.

Using the indigenous Confucian framework, we have found that students' civic cultivation plays a significant role in the process of their political socialization. We have further discovered that Chinese students may have an imbalanced political exposure to citizenship and civil society, show strong gender differences in the exercise of civic participation, and may have been exposed too much to ideological-political education instead of citizenship education. They may also tend towards an overcharged patriotism, or distorted nationalistic affective cultivation. The findings have shown the need to reexamine the role of higher educational institutions as civic actors, noting that the "making of citizens" depends largely on how higher education systems nurture their "apprentice citizens".

This study presents a unique snapshot of the assertion that the process of political socialization can be best understood in terms of "cultural transmission."[76] It offers a great opportunity to better under-

---

[76] Richard E. Dawson and Kenneth Prewitt, *Political Socialization: An Analytic Study* (Boston, MA: Little, Brown & Company, 1969), p.6.

stand the concept of citizenship and civil society in a Chinese sociopolitical context, with its unique Confucian heritage regarding civil rights and social responsibilities. Probably it would go too far to accept Daniel Patrick Moynihan's aphorism that "it is culture, not politics, that determines the success of a society."[77] Nevertheless, we believe that "culture matters,"[78] and cultural factors play an important role in fostering democracy.[79] The Confucian version of civil society, if depicted here appropriately, illuminates a concept of citizenship and civil society that is different from dominant European or American concepts. It enables us to draw valuable ways of thinking about education and development of both individuals and society from China's traditional heritage, such as the purpose of education expressed in *The Great Learning*.[80] When cultural factors are counted, one can rediscover the value of educational wisdom from various traditional cultural heritages as we build new concepts of citizenship and civil society in the global village. If we define Confucian values of learning as a perfection of moral self-cultivation and a process of public engagement,[81] and the Deweyan view of education as "a civic function," and a democratic way of "social life" and "associated living,"[82] we will have an alternative, richer understanding of the role of higher education in nurturing citizenship and civil society.

In sum, we have explored the ways in which students have been affected by China's move to mass higher education and reflected on how the role of higher education can be redefined for civil society, based on the data analyses of our student survey. The findings and conclusions of this chapter provide a background for readers to better understand the twelve case studies that make up the main body of this volume, particularly the responses of students who participated in our student focus group meetings in each of the case study institutions.

---

[77] As cited in Samuel P. Huntington, "Cultures Count," in Lawrence E. Harrison and Samuel P. Huntington (eds.), *Culture Matters: How Values Shape Human Progress* (New York: Basic Books, 2000), p.xiv.
[78] Lawrence E. Harrison, "Why Culture Matters," *op. cit.*, pp.xvii-xxxiv; David Landes, "Culture makes almost all the Difference," *op. cit.*, pp.2-13.
[79] R. Inglehart, "Culture and Democracy," *op. cit.*, pp.80-97.
[80] *The Great Learning*, 1.
[81] *Ibid*.
[82] John Dewey, *Democracy and Education* (New York: The Free Press, 1916), p. 93, 87.

Part II:
Portraits of Three Public Comprehensive Universities

The three public comprehensive universities that are profiled in part two of this volume present an interesting contrast to each other. Peking University (Beida) has been an unrivalled leader in scholarship since 1949, when the national capital moved from Nanjing to Beijing, with the successful Communist Revolution. Nanjing University (Nanda) had been the national flagship of higher education during the Nationalist period, under the title of National Central University, and has had to overcome the disadvantage of its historical affiliation with the rival Guomindang Party before 1949, as well as its geographical location in what is now a provincial capital. Both universities were founded as public institutions near the turn of the century, Beida in 1898, Nanda in 1902, and both have histories closely intertwined with the destiny of the Chinese nation over the 20th century. By contrast, Xiamen University on the Southeast coast in China's Fujian province, opposite Taiwan, was founded in 1921 as a private university. It became a public institution during the Sino-Japanese War, and has experienced both disadvantages and advantages associated with its unique geographical location in the period since 1949. We believe these three portraits will bring out different facets of the experience of major comprehensive universities in China's move to mass higher education.

3
Peking University – Icon of Cultural Leadership

Ruth HAYHOE and Qiang ZHA, with YAN Fengqiao

It is fitting that Peking University (affectionately known as Beida for short) should be first of the portraits of China's universities in the move to mass higher education because of its unique role in modern Chinese history. In our talks with its leaders, faculty and students, we caught the sense of an institution that is constantly under observation as a kind of cultural icon. From the national leadership down to the families of ordinary people in all parts of China, Beida is always being watched for its response to opportunities, challenges, problems and crises. One of its influential educators, Professor Wang Yongquan, described it as "the conscience of the nation."[1]

While Beida has had many illustrious leaders, two have been most widely recognized as defining its spirit, Cai Yuanpei (蔡元培) and Ma Yinchu (馬寅初). The brief historical overview that starts this chapter will therefore reflect on their legacy. We also wish to acknowledge that this book owes a great deal to Beida's contemporary Party Secretary, Professor Min Weifang. A well recognized scholar in comparative higher education, with a PhD from Stanford in the economics of education, Professor Min has served as Director of its Institute for Higher Education Research from 1992, Executive Vice-President from 1993, and Party Secretary and Chairman of Council since 2002. Other aspects of Min's background include five years working in a coalmine during the Cultural Revolution, and his decision to enter Beijing Normal University in 1977. This reflected a strong commitment to education, after the devastating losses of the Cultural Revolution decade, that has shaped his career up to now.

Min was first interviewed for our study of the policy process in the move to mass higher education, which appears in Chapter One of this volume. At that time he agreed that Beida should be included as one of the twelve case universities and signed our ethical protocol. His support

---

[1] Ruth Hayhoe, *Portraits of Influential Chinese Educators* (Hong Kong: Comparative Education Research Centre, The University of Hong Kong and Springer, 2006), p.260.

for the project was important to us, and may well have given confidence to the leaders of some of our other case universities, as they considered our request to include them in this book. Thus we too experienced the sense of Beida as an institution that others look to, when they may hesitate over stepping into unknown territory.

This chapter begins with a brief overview of Beida's history and context, then considers the changes in student numbers, finance and curriculum that constitute the empirical face of the move to mass higher education. From there we reflect on the university's new vision and mission, its governance structure and strategic decision-making processes. Finally views from faculty and students on various dimensions of the move to mass higher education are presented.

History and Context

The Imperial University and the Early Republic

Founded in 1898, as part of an important but largely unsuccessful reform movement, the Imperial University (京師大學堂) is often considered China's first public university, although two major engineering universities had preceded it: Tianjin University in 1896 and Shanghai Jiaotong University in 1897. Under Japanese influence, the Imperial University was originally intended to head up an entire modern education system, as specified in legislation of 1902.[2] After a ministry of education was established in 1904, it continued to serve as the pre-eminent national university, educating the majority of those destined for leadership. With the Revolution of 1911, the Imperial University was renamed Peking University, and was led by a series of prominent scholars, including Yan Fu (嚴復), Ma Xiangbo (馬相伯), He Yushi (何燏時) and Hu Renyuan (胡仁源). Nevertheless, it struggled with inadequate funding and the vagaries of an uncertain political context. Only with the appointment of Cai Yuanpei towards the end of 1916, did Peking University become an intellectual force that was to shape the destiny of modern China.

Cai Yuanpei and the Spirit of Peking University

Cai Yuanpei had served briefly as Minister of Education for the new republic in 1911-12, but returned Europe, when it became clear that

---

[2] Douglas Reynolds, *China 1898-1912: The Xinzheng Revolution and Japan* (Cambridge, Mass.: Council on East Asian Studies, Harvard University, 1993).

President Yuan Shikai (袁世凱) was seeking to restore facets of the old imperial system. Born in 1868, Cai had gained a thorough grounding in classical Chinese scholarship through studies in a traditional *shuyuan* (書院), then had taken the civil service examinations and passed with the highest honor, becoming a Hanlin (翰林) Academician in 1892. His first mentor in the Western academic tradition was Ma Xiangbo, with whom he studied Latin and philosophy. Subsequently he studied in France and Germany, from 1906 to 1911, then returned in 1911 to serve briefly as minister of education and establish a Sino-French University. He also was occupied with translating into Chinese the work of such leading German scholars as Wilhelm Wundt and Friederich Paulsen at this time.

While Cai attempted to introduce the principle of university autonomy in legislation he drafted for the new republic in 1912, it was only when he returned again from Europe in 1916 to become Chancellor of Peking University that he was able to institute forms of university governance that ensured some distance between the university and the national government. On the principle that "professors should rule the school" (教授治校) he strengthened the academic senate, which was composed of all deans and representatives of the professorial faculty. He also instituted a rule that faculty members could not hold concurrent positions in government. His extraordinary efforts to attract leading scholars of diverse academic and political persuasions in all major fields created conditions for lively debate and discussion.

Cai's personal statement on academic freedom has become one of the classics of modern Chinese higher education, because of the way in which it integrates values of scholarship from Europe and China: "I am open to all schools of thought; according to the general standards of the universities of all nations and the principle of freedom of thought, I believe we should be inclusive of diverse viewpoints. Regardless of which school of thought, if their words are logical, those who maintain them have reason, and they have not yet met the fate of being eliminated by natural selection, indeed even if they are mutually contradictory, I will allow them to develop freely."[3]

The notion of tolerating mutually contradictory ideas is probably rooted in Chinese thought, yet Cai's view on academic freedom was otherwise rather European, with a focus on basic theoretical knowledge.

---

[3] Xiao Chaoran et al. *Beijing Daxue Xiaoshi 1898-1949* (*The History of Peking University 1898-1949*) (Beijing: Beijing daxue chubanshe, 1988), p.65. (Author's translation)

He made sure that the curriculum of Peking University was composed of basic sciences and humanities, with applied fields such as engineering moved elsewhere. When the May 4th Movement broke out in 1919, there was little question that it had been nurtured by the atmosphere of free debate that Cai had introduced, yet he himself was concerned that faculty and students should not get directly involved in anti-government activism, following the German principles of *Lehr* and *Lernfreiheit*. He resigned his presidency in protest against the government's crackdown on students and faculty, while at the same time making the following plea to students: "You have the opportunity of receiving education and the chance to take part in pure scientific research, so that you can lay the foundation for a new national culture for China and participate in world scholarly activities."[4] It was striking to find the ideas expressed here continuing to reverberate in the interviews we held with students and faculty members nearly 90 years later.

Peking University in War-time Circumstances

Once China's national capital moved to Nanjing in 1927, Peking University had a less prominent role on the national scene, though it remained a leading centre of scholarship throughout the Nationalist period.[5] In 1937, after the Japanese invasion, it moved to Kunming to share a campus with Tsinghua and Nankai universities. The geographical remoteness of this location made possible considerable autonomy from the beleaguered Nationalist government, and John Israel's well researched history of the Southwest Associated University, known as Lianda, describes its spirit in the following way: "In sharing poverty for the sake of education, faculty members and students felt drawn to each other and a sense of community emerged. It was more akin to that of the traditional *shuyuan* than to that of the status-conscious universities of pre-war days. The existence of

---

[4] Cai Yuanpei, *Cai Yuanpei Xuanji* (*Selections from Cai Yuanpei*) (Beijing: Zhonghua Shuju, 1959), p.98. (Author's translation). In the end Cai was persuaded to stay on as president until around 1927.

[5] Two excellent histories of Beida's early years have been published recently: Timothy Weston, *The Power of Position: Beijing University, Intellectuals and Chinese Political Culture 1898-1929* (Berkeley: University of California Press, 2004); and Xiaoqing Diana Lin, *Peking University: Chinese Scholarship and Intellectuals 1898-1937* (Albany: State University of New York Press, 2005). For an essay review on these two volumes, see Ruth Hayhoe, "Peking University and the Spirit of Chinese Scholarship," in *Comparative Education Review*, Vol.49, No.4, 2005, pp.575-583.

a 'vital, upbeat, creative spiritual life' was a matter of pride and satisfaction .... "⁶ There were effective protests, yet there was also remarkable scholarship and excellent teaching in the harshest of conditions, with two later Nobel Prize winners, C.T. Lee (李政道) and C.N. Yang (楊振寧), among the students.

Beida moved back to Beijing in 1945 and its curriculum was broadened under the presidency of the American-educated philosopher Hu Shi (胡適). Faculties of engineering, medicine and agriculture were added to its three original faculties of humanities, sciences and law. With the success of the Communist Revolution of 1949, however, it reverted to the curricular patterns that had been advocated by Cai Yuanpei. Soviet higher education had been strongly influenced by 19th century Germany and France, and under Soviet influence Beida was defined as a new-style comprehensive university, having programs in basic sciences and humanities only. The medical, engineering and agriculture faculties moved out to become specialist universities in the reorganized system. However this was a small loss, compared to the gains brought by leading scholars and whole departments in the humanities and basic sciences that came to Beida from Tsinghua, Catholic Furen and Protestant Yenching universities. Beida also was given Yenching's beautiful campus, which had originally been a royal garden of the Qing emperors.

Ma Yinchu and the Spirit of Peking University

The second president who contributed greatly to shaping the Beida spirit was Ma Yinchu, a leading economist and demographer, with a PhD from Columbia University. He became president in 1952, at the time of the reorganization of colleges and departments along Soviet lines. As a widely respected progressive thinker, he played an active advisory role in the new government, until his theory on population growth fell afoul of Mao Zedong's ideas in 1957. Reprimanded and later exiled for expressing views that he believed to be soundly based and vitally important for China's future, he held firm. Even the persuasion of Zhou Enlai could not move him to retract the essay he published in his own defense, "My Philosophical Thought and Economic Theories." His parting words before going into exile were as follows: "After writing articles, one should be brave enough to correct mistakes, but one must adhere to the truth

---

⁶ John Israel, *Lianda: A Chinese University in War and Revolution* (Stanford: Stanford University Press, 1996) pp.331-332.

and bear all consequences, even if they are disadvantageous to his private interests or his life. I do not teach and have no direct contact with students, but I always want to educate them by means of action."[7]

Both Cai and Ma embodied a spirit of intellectual freedom and independence, for which Beida is justly proud. Its curricular focus has meant that many of its graduates became scientists, scholars, writers and thinkers. By contrast, its famed rival, Tsinghua, was turned into an engineering university in 1952 and graduated many who became government officials in the period of socialist macro-planning. While Beida could not avoid being caught up in the turmoil of the Cultural Revolution, and influenced by the political movements of the 1960s and 1970s, it retained a sense of calling as the "conscience of the nation" and a sense of responsibility to advise and critique successive governments. This became evident in the student movement that followed upon the 70th anniversary of May 4th in 1989. There is still a sense of the significance of Beida's role in that movement, as became clear when students commented on the administration's plan to re-develop Triangle Place (三角地), a corner of the campus which had been a focal point for student meetings in the fateful spring of 1989.

The anniversary of Beida's 100 years of history was held on May 4th of 1998, in a national ceremony held in the Great Hall of the People, with all of China's top political leadership present. Jiang Zemin, then Party Secretary and President, launched the slogan "Education and Science to Revitalize the Nation" and Beida's leaders joined forces with those of Tsinghua in asking the government for significant funding to support stronger and more focused university development at the highest level. The resulting 98/5 Project, named after this anniversary, has provided substantial amounts of special funding to a total of 43 leading universities throughout the country, with the name of the project as a constant reminder of Beida's unique status.

Peking University's Move to Mass Higher Education: An Empirical Overview

Before considering the vision that has been developed and the strategic decisions that have been taken in the years since Beida's centenary in

---

[7] Howard Boorman, *Biographical Dictionary of Republican China*, Vol.2, (New York: Columbia University Press, 1968), p.478. See also Ronald Hsia, "The Intellectual and Public Life of Ma Yin-ch'u" in *China Quarterly* No.6, April-June, 1961, pp.54-63.

1998, we will present some base data that show the dramatic changes which have taken place in student numbers, finance and curricular development in the context of rapid massification since 1999. With this empirical picture of change in mind, we then turn to the views and reflections of leaders, faculty and students.

Growth in Student Enrollments

The figures Beida provided on student enrollments run from 1995 to 2005, and we can see a clear decision against expansion of Beida's core undergraduate programs over this period, with the main changes reflecting the merger of Beijing Medical University with Beida in April of 2000, and the subsequent development of a small number of engineering programs in new areas that build upon strong Departments of Mechanics, Biology and Physics. Thus undergraduate enrollments increased from 9,280 in 1995, to 13,328 in 2000, and 15,125 in 2005. However numbers of students in the humanities and social sciences changed little, with 4,276 in 1995, 4,484 in 2000 and 4,914 in 2005. Similarly, students enrolled in basic sciences numbered 4,247 in 1995, 4,380 in 2000, with a slight jump to 5,449 in 2005. The increase in undergraduate numbers between 1995 and 2000 was mainly due to the merger with Beijing Medical University, with 3,818 students in medical programs by the autumn of 2000. The further increase in enrollments between 2000 and 2005 reflected new programs in engineering, with the number of engineering students increasing from 550 in 2000 to 1,787 in 2005.

Beida students are recruited from every province throughout the country, and by national policy under ten percent of places are given to Beijing residents. We were not provided with information on the family background or residential status of students, but we understand from ongoing research by scholars of education and sociology at Beida that the percentage of young people from rural and disadvantaged families has gone down.[8] By contrast, the participation of women has increased con-

---

[8] Liu, Yunshan and Wang, Zhiming, "Nüxing Jinru Jingying Jiti: Youxian De Jinbu," (Women enter the elite group: limited progress) in *Gaodeng Jiaoyu Yanjiu* (*Journal of Higher Education*) Vol.29, No.2, 2008, pp.49-61 (in Chinese). According to the researchers, the percentage of Beida entrants from urban backgrounds has always been high over the years, but increased from 76.6% in 1990 to 79.3% in 1996, 81.9% in 2000 and 85.7% in 2005. In the mean time, the rural entrants have been on a continuous decline from 24.2% in 1990 to 20.7% in 1996, 18.1% in 2000 and 14.3% in 2005.

siderably, from 35% of undergraduate enrollments in 1995, to 46% in 2000 and 48% in 2005. This may be partially accounted for by the tendency for high female enrollments in medicine, but this could not be the whole story, since enrollments in engineering had also increased considerably by 2005.

While undergraduate enrollments have largely been kept stable, except for the fields of medicine and engineering, tremendous growth has taken place in graduate enrollments, with a near quadrupling of numbers, from 4,055 in 1995, to 15,229 in 2005. Female participation has also increased dramatically at the graduate level, from 29% in 1995 to 43% in 2005. There has been real concern about preserving standards of academic quality in this rapid expansion process, and a clear differentiation has been made between professional masters degrees of two year duration in fields such as law, business and education and academic masters degrees of three year duration in basic academic disciplines. This distinction is expressed also in campus spatial arrangements, with new high rise buildings for some professional areas being erected in a newly developed part of the campus, close to the subway, where study programs for part-time students can be facilitated. Meanwhile full-time programs in basic fields remain on the traditional part of the campus, with its classical low-rise buildings.

Numbers of international students have increased from 599 in 1990, to 1,011 in 1995, 1,177 in 2000 and 1,790 in 2005, with the percentage of these students studying for degrees increasing from 30% in 1990 to 66% by 2005. These numbers are still relatively low, and there are plans for recruiting much larger numbers of international students in future, as well as for more and more bi-lingual and English medium teaching. By 2007, Beida's report to the teaching evaluation team indicated an enrollment of 2,587 international students. [9]

Overall, we can see a stable situation for undergraduate enrollments in contrast to dramatic growth in graduate enrollments, with professional programs that have relatively high fees making up about one half of the total, and considerable expansion in core academic programs.

---

[9] *Beijing Daxue Benke Jiaoxue Gongzuo Shuiping Pingu Ziping Baogao* (*Self-evaluation Report for the Beijing University Undergraduate Teaching Standards Evaluative Review*), Internal document, November, 2007, p.3.

Beida's Changing Financial Profile

The figures provided by Beida's finance office give a dramatic picture of change, from an overall income in 1990 of 115 million RMB to 2.634 billion in 2005. While 33.9 million came in through student fees in 1990, this figure rose to 48.5 million in 1995, 298 million in 2000 and 744.6 million in 2005. It should be noted that the cost sharing policy began formally in 1997. Since then, both the absolute amount and the relative share of students' fees have increased significantly. Students in professional programs are charged significantly higher fees than those in academic programs. By 2005 student fees constituted 28% of income, up from 14% in 1995 and 13% in 2000. Government direct allocations rose from 44.7 million in 1990 to 97 million in 1995, 209 million in 2000 and 357 million in 2005. Proportionately, however, they constituted 29% of income in 1995, but only 9% in 2000 and 14% in 2005. This shows how crucial has been the government's special project funding, which constituted 29% of income in 2000 and 11% in 2005.

Research funding, much of which comes from government through processes of competitive bidding, is also an important part of income. From research funds of 31.9 million in 1990, the number had risen to 62.9 million in 1995, 371.7 million in 2000 and 630.3 million in 2005. The percentage of this funding coming from prestigious national sources has increased dramatically, from 28% in 1990 to 80% in 2005. As a percentage of overall income, research funds now make up 24%, up from 17% in 2000.

The other major change has been in the scale of donations, and various forms of income generation. Whereas donations constituted only 250,000 in 1990, by 1995, there was 34 million in donations, 77.4 million by 2000 and 176.5 million by 2005, constituting 7% of income. Other forms of income generation, such as Beida's multi-national company, Fang Zheng (方正), contributed 431.3 million or 16% of income in 2005, up from 310.4 million in 2000 and 109 million in 1995. Beida's 2005 profile thus shows an institution that gains 28% of income from student fees, 25% from governmental sources, including general and special project, 24% from research, 7% from donations and 16% from its own efforts at resource generation.

On the budget side there have also been interesting changes. While faculty salaries constituted 17% of a budget of 316.3 million in 1995, this rose to 34% of a budget of 1.441 billion in 2000 and 22% of a budget of 2.710 billion in 2005. Assistance for students has remained about the same, 5% of budget in 1995, 4% in both 2000 and 2005. Teaching affairs made up 78% of the budget in 1995, 55% in 2000 and 71% in 2005. Clearly the major change in 2000 focused on upgrading faculty salaries, while by 2005 it was possible once again to give highest priority to teaching and research needs. We interpret these changes over financial priorities as Beida's endeavor to recruit the best possible talent to fill its faculty positions. This is crucial to its ambition to stand next to such world-class institutions as Harvard and Yale, which often spend close to half of their budgets to attract and maintain a top level faculty.

Curricular Evolution

As noted in the history above, Beida's curriculum has always focused on basic disciplines of the humanities, social sciences and natural sciences, with profound historical roots in the early influence of Cai Yuanpei. While its curriculum had been broadened to include medicine, agriculture and engineering in the later 1940s, its profile returned to a strong focus on basic fields in the 1950s, after the reorganization of colleges and departments under Soviet influence. Thus in 1958 there were Departments of Mathematics and Mechanics, Physics, Chemistry, Biology and Geology in the sciences; in the humanities, there were Departments of History, Philosophy, Chinese Language and Literature, Oriental Languages and Literatures, Western Languages and Literatures, Russian Language and Literature; in the social sciences, there were Departments of Economics, Law and Library Science. While psychology had originally been a strength at Beida, it had been placed within the Department of Philosophy.[10]

An overview of the present curricular provision gives a vivid picture of the dramatic changes that have taken place in the curriculum, mostly since the reforms of 1978 and in recent years. At present there are five main academic sections (*xuebu* 學部) in the areas of humanities, social sciences, natural sciences, information and engineering sciences and medicine. While the first four are regarded as part of the main campus (*benbu* 本部), the medical section retains an independent status, and is headed by a highly respected medical scholar, Professor Han Qide, who is also a Vice-Chairman of the National People's Congress. The merger of the Beijing Medical University and Beida in 2000, which

---

[10] Du Qin and Wei Xingyan, *Beijing Daxue Xuezhi Yange 1949-1998* (*The Evolution of Peking University's Academic System 1949-1998*) (Beijing: Beijing Daxue Chubanshe, 2000), pp.41-43.

strongly encouraged by Vice Premier Li Lanqing, has led to some curricular and research integration but not a complete administrative integration of the two institutions. While medicine functions as a separate administrative unit, the other four teaching sections are headed by scholars whose main responsibility is to see that appropriate criteria are applied for academic decisions relating to faculty promotions and curricular development – they do not function as administrative units. Nevertheless, they may help us to understand the shape and logic of Beida's current curricular provisions.

The other explanatory note that is needed at this point relates to the status of departments and colleges. Up until the mid-eighties, departments were the major academic units in Chinese universities, and the establishment of colleges bringing together several departments has been a gradual process. One of our interviewees pointed out that the merger issue has not only been at the level of universities, but also within the university, at the level of the college.[11] Thus Beida's most illustrious core humanities departments have elected to keep the status and title of department – Chinese literature, history and philosophy. They refused to merge into a College of Arts, since this would raise serious questions of academic leadership. Nevertheless, they hold the same status as colleges within the administrative system.

The other academic units within the humanities section have all become colleges, and include the College of Archaeology (1998), the College of Foreign Languages (1999) and the College of Fine Arts (2006). Of particular note is the College of Foreign Languages, which has programs in 19 different languages and literatures, and has particular strength in the area of oriental languages.

In the social sciences, the earliest department to blossom into a college was economics in 1985; the Guanghua School of Management was separately established on the basis of strengths in economics and management in 1993. By 1998 there was a College of International Relations, based on early strengths in this area, and by 2001 there were Colleges of Journalism and Broadcasting, Government, Law and Information Management. There was also a School of Marxism, and a graduate school of education, developed on the basis of the institute for higher education research established in 1979.

---

[11] Interview with Wu Baoke, Vice Provost, Professor of Sociology and Party Secretary of the Department of Sociology, 12 May 2008.

The one department in the social sciences which refused to be merged into a college was sociology. It had been founded in 1982, after a long neglect of the field of sociology under Soviet influence and the radical politics of the Cultural Revolution. Its members are proud of the work they have developed in sociology, demography and social work, and prefer to maintain their status as a department.

The natural sciences section has seven colleges and one department, again reflecting both tradition and change. The College of Life Sciences was founded in 1993, on the basis of a strong biology department and has developed new bio-technology programs as well as collaboration with the medical section. The College of Chemistry and Molecular Engineering was founded in 1994 and has programs in materials chemistry, nuclear chemistry and nuclear fuels, as well as basic chemistry. The College of Mathematical Sciences was founded in 1995, and has programs in statistics and information science as well as pure and applied mathematics. The College of Physics was founded in 2001, and has Departments of Astronomy, Atmospheric Sciences, Nuclear Physics and Nuclear Technology as well as Basic Physics. Also founded in 2001, the College of Geology and space science has Departments of Space Science and Technology as well as Geology, Geo-physics and Geo-chemistry. In 2007 a College of Urban and Environmental Sciences was established, bringing together programs in geography, the management of resources and the natural environment, geographic information systems, ecology and urban planning.

Meanwhile a Department of Psychology was established in 1977, separating itself from the Department of Philosophy and choosing to be placed within the natural sciences section rather than that of the social sciences. It traces its history back to Cai Yuanpei and his efforts to introduce the scientific psychology of Wilhelm Wundt to China in 1917. It has a strong tradition in experimental psychology and has remained an independent department, similar to sociology, Chinese literature, philosophy and history.

The engineering section is entirely new at Beida, with a College of Information Science and Technology founded in 2002 and a College of Engineering founded in 2005. The College of Information Science and Technology reflects the remarkable success of Beida scholars in physics and mechanics, as they turned their attention to information processing, microelectronics and computer science and technology in the 1980s. Their discoveries relating to the processing of Chinese language materials spurred the success of Beida's fabled company, Fang Zheng, which is now an independently owned multi-national, whose stock provides a significant source of income for Beida. The College of Engineering is newer, and is developing programs in applied mechanics and the analysis of engineering construction, energy and resource engineering, biomedical engineering, and new materials and nanometer technology. A conscious decision was made not to develop more traditional engineering fields.

Finally, the medical section stands alone, maintaining the integrity of its medical departments and programs while cooperating in the teaching of basic sciences and in research. The medical section has departments in basic medicine, clinical medicine, preventive medicine, dentistry, dental technology, medical experimentation, pharmacy, applied pharmacy and nursing.

This overview of the curriculum has been taken from the teaching evaluation report prepared by the university in 2007, and reflects mainly Beida's undergraduate programs.[12] Not mentioned here is the School of Software and Microelectronics, established off campus in 2002, and mainly serving working adults, also the Shenzhen Graduate School, which offers Beida MBAs to executives, and advanced degrees in law, sociology, sciences and engineering, in Shenzhen and South China. Students of these two schools are not counted as part of Beida's formal enrollment numbers.

In the above overview, we can see a blending of tradition and innovation, a building upon strengths in basic fields of knowledge while responding to new demands. There are also contradictions between the determination to maintain high standards of excellence in basic academic fields and programs and the pull to respond to newly emerging professional and technical fields of knowledge, and new kinds of clientele in a dynamic market economy.

Vision and Strategic Direction

We were fortunate to be able to spend a week on Beida's beautiful campus in May of 2008, and hold interviews with a wide range of university leaders, including the Party Secretary, the Head of the Planning

---

[12] *Beijing Daxue Benke Jiaoxue Gongzuo Shuiping Pingu Ziping Baogao* (*Self-evaluation Report for the Beijing University Undergraduate Teaching Standards Evaluative Review*), Internal document, November 2007, p.47.

Section, two Vice-Provosts and the head of the Provost's Office, the Deputy Director of Personnel, the Deputy Director of the International Office, the Director of Student Affairs and the Deputy Director of the Finance Office. Much was learned in these meetings about the process of developing a new vision and mission, curricular decision making, governance patterns, research and personnel issues, also Beida's internationalization process. Over and again we sensed a certain tension, in university leaders, faculty and students, as they felt the responsibilities that went along with Beida's name and reputation. The pressure of high expectations from government, from educational circles and from China's millions of ordinary citizens was intense. "Many Chinese tourists who come to Beijing bring their children to the Beida campus, knowing that the chances of enrollment there are one in a hundred thousand, yet Beida still belongs to them and is accountable to them."[13]

Vision and Mission

Beida's 100th anniversary in 1998, and the government's decision to provide significant funds for a small number of top universities to achieve world class status in the 98/5 project, was a turning point for the university. This was just before the national policy decision on massive expansion in 1999. Many crucial decisions relating to curricular development, research emphasis and faculty upgrading had to be made, in order to deal with the tension between quality and quantity inherent in this process. This caused much reflection on Beida's core mission.

Li Qiang, Head of the Planning Department and President's assistant, also a professor in the School of Government and Public Policy, explained that the decision to formalize a new mission statement was made early in 2005, with the intention of having it complete for Beida's 110th anniversary in 2008. Many meetings of academic leaders, professors, alumni and students were held and a website was established, with the result that over 1,000 comments and suggestions were received.[14] The final draft of the mission statement has four short phrases, which have been drawn from different periods of the university's history.

The first phrase, "mould and cast a broad range of talents" (陶鑄群才), goes back to the first President of the Imperial University, Sun Jianai

---

[13] Member of Beida's Faculty Focus Group, 9 May 2008.
[14] Interview with Li Qiang, President's Assistant and Head of the Planning Section, 14 May 2008.

(孫家鼐), in the early years of the 20th century, and emphasizes Beida's responsibility to educate people at a high level in all important fields of knowledge. Images of the potter and the casting of bronze are used to depict the all round development of every kind of talent, in moral as well as intellectual areas.

The second phrase, "discover new principles of knowledge" (發明新理), is found in Beida's first charter, and clearly refers to the university's research mandate, its responsibility to extend the frontiers of knowledge in ways that benefit the nation and open up new future directions. This is interpreted as producing innovative findings in science, technology and culture that make possible the nation's renaissance and contribute to world peace and development.

The third phrase, "lead culture" (引領文化), goes back to Beida's role in the May 4th Movement, as the institution that did most to build a new national culture based on critical reflection on the past and the selective absorption of ideas from abroad. At present Beida still sees itself as responsible for cultural renewal and for establishing Chinese culture within a global context of multiculturalism.

The fourth phrase of the mission statement, "serve society" (服務社會) is viewed as deriving from Cai Yuanpei's concept of benefiting the nation through innovative scholarship in the humanities and social policy as well as the natural sciences.

While all four phrases that constitute this new vision statement carry the flavor of Beida's history, the goals of nurturing talent, focusing on fundamental research and serving society are common to most research universities. It is the third goal, that of "leading culture," which may be unique to the Beida spirit. We had a sense that Beida somehow embodies Chinese culture in the contemporary period, in the combination of old and new seen in its campus space and architecture, and in the sense of responsibility to nation and world that we found in many of its members.[15]

Li Qiang took the example of Beida economist, Lin Yifu, who heads up Beida's Economic Research Centre and has recently been appointed as

---

[15] This summary is based on both our interview with Li Qiang and a draft internal document he provided, which is entitled *"The Mission of Peking University."* (*Beijing Daxue De Shiming*). See also an interview with Beida President Xu Zhihong, in *Kexue Shibao* (Science Times), 17 April 2008, where the new mission statement is elucidated.

chief economist to the World Bank. In explaining elements of China's economic development to the world, Lin will enrich and broaden economic theory in the West, suggests Li. As a scholar of government with a PhD from the London School of Economics, Li works on state building and faces a parallel challenge to explain China's political development to the world. He remarked that he finds himself constantly in dialogue with such classical economists as Hobbes, Locke and Smith, rather than theorists who deal with contemporary social development issues. "China's changes have been so dramatic, they relate best to the ideas of Western classical theorists of an earlier period," he commented.

We found evidence in our interviews with leaders in the provost's office, student affairs and the international office that the new mission statement is seen as a helpful document. However, the development of a new charter is a somewhat different matter. Given his background in political science, Li Qiang's comments on creating a "constitution" for the university, as he viewed the charter, were thought-provoking.

He began by calling our attention to a recent speech of the President, who identified four important moments in Beida's history. The first was the period of Cai Yuanpei's leadership, the second was the Lianda period during the anti-Japanese war, the third was the period after 1952, when Beida gained top scholars in all basic fields of knowledge from other universities. The fourth has been the period since 2005, when the new mission statement has been formulated and Beida has moved forward in new ways. From 1978 up to the 1990s, Beida had had a very difficult time, due to the shortage of resources, and the necessity of seeking income from research activities that created significant profit but detracted from its academic mission. Now the new mission statement places emphasis on basic theoretical knowledge, and only those applied fields that are closely related, that respond to urgent societal needs or where there is potential for excellence within a short time frame.

Li Qiang explained that one of Beida's vice presidents is responsible for drafting the new charter, and this is much more complex than a mission statement since it is a matter of Beida's relations with government. Even though the higher education law of 1998 stipulates that universities have the status of legal persons, Li believes this status cannot yet be realized. However, he pointed to a document recently released by the Chinese Communist Party which speaks of "four divisions" that are to be accomplished by the year 2020: the division between government and enterprises (政企), between government and social organizations (政事),

between government and capital management (政資), and between government and professional associations (政介). Once these "four divisions" have been accomplished, the Chinese political structure will have changed significantly. Beida is responsible to see that the government goes forward with this plan, in Li's view, and that it meets the time goal of 2020. Only then will it be possible to enjoy real independence from government as a legal person.

Governance and Strategic Direction

This brings us to the question of Beida present governance structure, and we were privileged to have a one hour interview with Party Secretary Min Weifang on this topic. He began by stating that Beida is the most liberal campus in China with academic freedom given highest importance, and all decision-making in the arenas of policy, personnel and finance in the public domain. "We have no secrets of any kind," he stated. At the same time he gave vivid expression to his sense of his own position as one of mediating between the pressures coming from government and those coming from students and faculty. "I constantly need a kind of political wisdom to explain to top government leaders how essential it is to protect liberalism and academic freedom, on the one hand, and to request faculty and students to reflect on the constraints of the context in which they live and modify their demands accordingly, on the other hand." [16]

There has been no real change so far in the governance structure of higher education as a result of the move to mass higher education, in Min's view. The higher education law of 1998 specified a presidential responsibility system under the leadership of the Party Committee. In the case of Beida, as Party Secretary he chairs the Party Committee, which meets every Tuesday afternoon, and includes four vice-secretaries and all vice-presidents, including any who may not be Party members. The much larger Council of the university has deans, faculty and student representatives in addition, but meets less frequently. The Party standing committee makes final decisions in three major areas: personnel appointments at dean and director of office or above, budget decisions and such major projects as new buildings. He and the President work very closely on all matters – "we communicate every day and are like one person." While he has been appointed by the Party Central Committee and is at

---

[16] Interview with Min Weifang, 12 May 2008.

the same level as a vice-minister, the President's appointment is made by the State Council.

The overall structure of the university has three main parts – the provost's office, with the provost being the first of the vice-presidents, a vice-president for administration and a vice-president for logistics and plant.[17] Most academic decision making is made at the level of a committee chaired by the provost, dealing with research, curricular development, and all other academic decisions.

While there has been little change in the governance structure, one of the reforms for which Beida has been most closely watched is that of faculty appointments. Min made the point that he and his colleagues had initiated this reform on the simple principle that it was important for faculty to show they could perform, before being given permanent status. As a result of the reforms, those who are unlikely to be promoted now tend to leave of their own volition, allowing the university to bring in excellent scholars from all over the world. Clearly the appointment and recognition of outstanding faculty is a crucial issue for reaching world-class status, and university leaders were determined to bring about this reform, in spite of the backlash and criticism it called forth.[18]

We could also see the crucial importance of Min's role as chair of the standing committee, where all leadership appointments were made, in the academic sophistication and scholarly excellence of the various administrative leaders we talked with. Min made the point that Party Secretaries of Chinese universities are usually "political figures," while his appointment to this position as a scholar was unusual. It is a highly stressful position, but he has managed to hold it for more than six years, in contrast to the six party secretaries who preceded him in the period since the reforms of the early eighties, with an average tenure of three years each.

When asked about the achievements he was most proud of, Min mentioned two things. The first was campus development. Almost all of the land acquisition and new buildings have been supported through active fund-raising, and the campus will soon have a completely new look. In a new area in the North, a series of buildings in royal garden style are being built for core curricular areas. The first is the famous

---

[17] Interview with Wu Baoke, 12 May 2008.
[18] See *Chinese Education and Society*, Vol.37, No.6, 2004, and Vol.38, Nos.1 & 2, 2005, for translations of many key articles debating the reforms and related commentary.

China Center for Economic Research, headed by Lin Yifu. In another new area in the Northeast, higher rise buildings are under construction for colleges in professional fields of knowledge, which enroll many part-time masters degree students and are accessible to the subway. Another piece of land has been acquired on the East side of the campus where new faculty housing is going up, and a new international centre is under construction with a capacity to house 4000 international students. Thus, the lovely classical buildings at the heart of the campus are being protected and extended, while new areas are being developed contiguous to the campus in response to new programs and demands. The intention is to reduce traffic and maintain a tranquil atmosphere in the core, while ensuring that the new areas are accessible to public transportation.

This determination to protect and further develop classical buildings in royal garden style, in spite of the expense involved, reflected a widely held view that the most symbolic space on the Beida campus was the Unnamed Lake, with its lovely pagoda and tranquil surroundings.[19] The phrase *"yita hutu"* (一塔湖圖) includes the Chinese words for one pagoda, a lake and a library, yet is also a pun that might be humorously translated as "a confused mess." Somehow this quiet classical space embodies the elusive yet deeply felt vocation to be a leader in culture that is embraced by so many at Beida.

Photo 3.1: The Unnamed Lake

---

[19] This came up in our Faculty Focus Group meetings, as well as several interviews with academic leaders.

The second major achievement Min spoke about was the recruitment of outstanding academic leaders to head Beida's various colleges – including three deans who had originally been recruited to another famous university in Beijing, and had been inclined to return to North America, until they were offered positions at Beida. Min attributed it to Beida's reputation for academic freedom and spirit of liberalism. Another element that has facilitated Beida's ability to recruit and hold outstanding academic leaders has been a policy of giving high levels of autonomy to certain units, such as the China Center for Economic Research and the Guanghua School of Management. Under this policy, academic salaries and research funding are under their direct control.[20]

Curricular Innovation

An overview of Beida's unique curricular constellation and its evolution in recent years has been presented earlier in this chapter. With the nurturing of creative talent as a kind of summation of Beida's four phrase mission statement, curricular reform has been seen as a crucial element of change in the move to mass higher education. A core principle has been the strengthening of basic knowledge, while attention has also been given to processes of integration – to foster creativity, and processes of diversification – to cater to different kinds of talent.[21]

On the undergraduate level a number of measures have been taken. All students are now recruited into colleges or departments, rather than specific programs and encouraged to select a certain number of electives. A new summer teaching term has been added to those of autumn and winter/spring, in order to provide opportunities for students to be exposed to visiting international scholars as well as giving them greater flexibility for electives. Students in the Medical College are given one or two years of exposure to basic sciences and other general areas on the main campus before beginning their medical programs on the branch campus, depending on whether they are in eight year programs in clinical medicine or five year programs in pharmacy and nursing. Funding is provided for undergraduate students to participate in faculty guided research on a competitive basis, with independent research projects counting for credit in some programs.

---

[20] Interview with Wu Baoke, 12 May 2008.
[21] Interview with Jin Dingbing, Vice-Dean, Office of Educational Administration, 13 May 2008.

Most radical of all has been the establishment of the Yuanpei Program, an integrated undergraduate program for outstanding undergraduates to experience a broad based curriculum, considerable choice of courses and individual guidance from a professorial tutor. Named after Cai Yuanpei, it began as an experimental program in 2001 with 80 top students being selected. It now recruits about 180 students each year, for a total size of 500 students. In 2007 when the preparation of suitable courses had matured and there were appropriate conditions for student life, it took the name Yuanpei College.[22] Many other universities in China have followed this initiative, in some cases moving much more quickly, but its careful and deliberate development has provided a national model for curricular reform.

Generally, Beida has been cautious about the establishment of new programs, departments or schools, with a strong determination to build upon its historic areas of excellence. Thus its highly successful College of Information Science and Technology, which enrolls the largest number of undergraduates at 2600, arose from its traditional strengths in mechanics and electronics. The only other College of Engineering Sciences avoids such traditional areas as construction and civil engineering to focus on new areas such as nanometers, new materials and bio-medical engineering. "While advances in information science have been remarkable and contributed to Beida's prosperity, the new biological sciences and biotechnology may be even more important for the future, with the advances they promise for human life and cancer research," noted one of the Vice-Provosts.[23] He also emphasized the development of areas like medical sociology and social work, which benefited greatly from the merger with the medical university.

At the graduate level, curricular diversification has been the emphasis, with many new professional masters programs being developed, that require two rather than three years of study. In addition, many colleges are offering high level training programs to professionals in areas such as politics and business, whereby they pay fees as graduate students, but only earn a degree if they write a thesis. Many are satisfied to take courses without going on to the degree. This kind of program gives the expertise of Beida professors considerable influence.

---

[22] *Ibid.*
[23] Interview with Wu Baoke, 12 May 2008.

Internationalization

Beida's international status makes possible some remarkable opportunities for its students in the non-formal curriculum. The Deputy Director of the International Office noted that over 50 national leaders have given lectures at Beida in recent years, and students are often given the opportunity to attend and raise questions. Most recently, the new Prime Minister of Australia dazzled students with a lecture given in fluent Mandarin! Frequent visits from seasoned diplomats, such as Henry Kissinger, often include consultation with students in small group meetings.

Recent efforts to recruit larger numbers of international students also have implications for Beida's students. Thus 30 students from Yale College are now spending one term at the Yuanpei Program, sharing rooms with Beida students, and similar programs are being planned with Harvard and Stanford. Waseda University has a joint program with Beida whereby students spend two years at Waseda and another two years at Beida, for a degree in international relations. Other programs that bring international students to the Beida campus include a one year Masters of Public Administration, oriented towards leaders in developing countries, a Masters in Chinese Philosophy, a joint Master of Law with the University of Missouri, a Summer Institute of Economics, in cooperation with the London School of Economics, and a Summer Institute in Social Statistics, in cooperation with the University of Michigan. All of these programs are given in English.

At the moment, Beida undergraduates do not have many opportunities for study abroad within their programs, though these are under development. Some are able to participate in summer schools abroad. For graduate students, particularly those in the doctorate, about 300 each year have managed to gain an opportunity for a doctoral year abroad, sponsored by the China Scholarship Council, in recent years.

What is evident in this overview of curricular innovation is that Beida sees itself in a global context, with a responsibility not only to nurture creative students within China but to draw students from around the world and create a campus culture where global issues and problems are debated, and where Chinese culture and Chinese economic and socio-political development experience can be interpreted for a wider world. One of its innovative informal programs has been sponsoring the Beijing Forum every year, with financial support from a Korean Organization. Prominent scholars are invited from all over the world to enter into an inter-civilizational dialogue, with a specific theme identified each year. The long-term goal is for this to become a kind of "Davos Summit" that can have a significant influence in global circles.[24]

One of the most important ways of stimulating curricular change has been through the appointment of high level scholars from all parts of the world, many of whom may bring graduate students with them when they take up their posts.[25] This further encourages a wider use of English or other languages in graduate programs. It was mentioned that every doctoral supervisor hopes to have one international student under supervision, to encourage discussion and communication in English.

Overall, curricular integrity, cohesion and coherence is maintained through the all-important Provostial committee, which has as its members the five vice-provosts, representing each teaching section including one from the medical section, the deans of all colleges and the heads of research in natural and social sciences. All major academic decisions go through this body, and every effort is made to ensure that teaching and curriculum development closely adhere to the Beida mission.[26]

Photo 3.2: The New Library

[24] Interview with Hongwei Xia, Executive Deputy Director, Office of International Relations, 16 May 2008.
[25] In the teaching evaluation document, *Beijing Daxue Benke Jiaoxue Gongzuo Shui-Ping Pingu Ziping Baogao (Self-evaluation Report for the Beijing University Undergraduate Teaching Standards Evaluative Review)*, November 2007, p.27, it was reported that there were 120 faculty members appointed from abroad.
[26] Interview with Li Ke'An, Vice-Provost, 13 May 2008.

When asked about buildings or campus spaces that might be seen to represent the Beida spirit, one academic leader spoke movingly about the new library. "It is now the largest library of any Chinese university, with over five million volumes, and it has been closely linked to the history of Beida and of China."[27] Mention was made of the fact that Mao Zedong once worked in this library, and that national leaders from Deng Xiaoping to Jiang Zemin and Hu Jintao have visited the library when coming to campus. The new library building, which was completed in time for the 100th anniversary, combines features of classical Chinese architecture with an ultra modern and high tech interior.

Faculty and Issues of Teaching and Research

We have noted earlier that one of the two achievements of which Min Weifang was most proud was the recruitment of highly qualified faculty members and academic leaders. From 2005, Beida made a policy that no new faculty would be recruited among their own graduating doctoral students – a highly controversial decision to break the patterns of the past, whereby China's top universities tended to recruit faculty largely from among their own graduates. The second controversial policy was to stipulate that faculty members would be required to meet the standards for promotion within a specified period of time, and if unsuccessful, they would be required to leave – there would be no permanent tenure for Beida faculty until they achieved full professor status. Somewhat longer time periods for the promotion process were given for faculty in the humanities and social sciences than the natural sciences.[28]

In this section we will look at the changing profile of Beida faculty, to give a picture of the present situation, then report on the findings of our faculty focus group, and highlight the views of faculty members on the Beida ethos.

The Faculty Profile

There has been no growth in Beida faculty over the period of the move to mass higher education, rather a significant number of faculty retired over the later 1990s, being replaced by young faculty with higher qualifications. The faculty student ratio has therefore risen from 1:3.5 in 1995, to 1:9.8 in 2000, and stabilized at around 1:15 by 2005. Faculty numbers for

---

[27] Interview with Wu Baoke, Vice-Provost, 12 May 2008.
[28] *Chinese Education and Society*, Vol.37, No.6, 2004.

1990 were reported as 2,438, falling to 2,296 by 2000 and 2,212 by 2005. The proportion of faculty in full and associate professor positions rose, however, from 28% full professor and 33% associate in 1990, to 33% full and 35% associate in 2000, 37% full and 42% associate in 2005. Meanwhile those in lecturer level positions dropped from 26% in 1990 to 20% in 2005, and assistant teachers dropped from 13% in 1990 to 1% by 2005. The faculty qualification profile also improved greatly, from 38% of faculty holding doctoral degrees in 2000 to 66% in 2005.

The most telling figures on the faculty profile have been provided in a recent report from the personnel office, which shows the changing pattern of qualifications. Of 1,882 faculty members with doctorates in 2007, 45.7% were Beida graduates, 23.2 graduates of other universities in China and 31.1% graduates who had returned from abroad. For faculty members who had been appointed since 2000, the picture had changed considerably, reflecting the reformed appointment policies. Only 34% held Beida doctorates, while 25.9% held doctorates from other universities in China and 39.9% held doctorates earned abroad.[29] The Deputy Director of the Personnel Office informed us that recruitment of top-level faculty at full and associate professor level continued to be a high priority, and that the third round of government funds for the 21/1 project would be dedicated mainly to these efforts.[30]

Beida faculty members are expected to be highly productive in both teaching and research. The recently implemented undergraduate teaching evaluation was seen as a useful exercise to ensure that due importance to upholding high standards of teaching. At the same time it was felt the university should be able to take responsibility for teaching quality, and it would be wasteful of time to go through such an exercise again.

On the research side, Beida faculty are very successful in competing for prestigious national research funding, with a total of 800 million in research grants won in 2007, up from 630 million in 2005. Of the 800 million, 20% came from the National Natural Sciences Foundation and another 30-40% from the 86/3 Fund of the Ministry of Technology, with some coming from international sources. Faculty publications are carefully monitored, and the yearly output has been around 2000, since 2005.

---

[29] *Yuanshan Jizhi Baozhang Youhuazhizi Peizhi (Improving the mechanisms for ensuring faculty upgrading)*, Internal document from the Personnel Office of Peking University, provided by Liu Bo, Vice-Director of the Personnel Office, 14 May 2008.
[30] Interview with Liu Bo, Deputy Director, Personnel Office, 14 May 2008.

Citations and influence factor are considered in evaluating these publications. Beida's Medical Section has contributed significantly to the attracttion of research funds and to the number and quality of publications, with their share of publications rising from 100 to 300 over recent years.[31]

Perspectives from Faculty

Eleven professors took part in the faculty focus group meeting, two from history, two from sociology, two from international relations, two from mathematics, two from information technology and one from engineering. There were six women and five men. One of the sociology professors was reluctant to sign the consent form, preferring to observe the discussion at first, yet later become one of the most active participants and agreed to sign before departing.

The conversation ranged widely, beginning with reflections on their identity and responsibilities as Beida professors, and going on to issues of the merger, curricular change and the opportunities of their new community-oriented programs. Views on civil society and issues of equity were also shared.

An older history professor began the discussion with the comment that Beida's mission had linked the university to China's destiny in profound ways. From the May 4th Movement of 1919 onwards, it had been involved in every significant cultural and political movement. "In its teaching and research Beida has a very special responsibility for the areas of history, literature and philosophy and it should be a treasure store of ideas for society. It is also an institution that belongs to the world, not only to China, and that is called upon to create a platform where China and the world can meet …. For these reasons, Beida professors must be clear-minded in their thinking, and seek the truth above all. Colleagues from other universities, in China and abroad, look to us to be guardians and developers of the culture. If Beida should take the wrong direction, the consequences for the whole country would be serious."

A younger international relations scholar spoke about the pressure of being a "Beida teacher" that came from the high expectations. "This is true not only within China but when we are presenting a paper at an international conference in Japan or other parts of the world. If it is

---

[31] Interview with Liu Bo, Deputy Director of the Personnel Office, 14 May 2008. Dr. Liu had worked in the research office from 2002 to 2006, before moving to Personnel.

known that we are Beida professors, we are likely to be asked to give the first word or make the first comment." "Any reform at Beida is likely to become a model for others – since we are seen as setting a standard. On the other hand, if we do not meet people's hopes and expectations, we will be the first to be criticized. In the problem of commercialization of education, for example, Beida is likely to be criticized much more severely than other universities, because expectations of us are so high."

Another professor said that Beida scholars traditionally feel a sense of responsibility for the great problems of the country, and that they tend to form students who are independent in character and thinking. This is something much deeper than the phrase about "nurturing creative talent" in the mission statement, which faculty see as a mere political slogan. Others then commented that students had been genuinely independent in thinking and concerned for the country at the time of the events of 1989, while now they have become more pragmatic. Nevertheless, Beida has kept its tradition of a very strong political culture, oriented towards democracy and science. Faculty and students share a fundamental mindset – that of questioning everything, and casting doubt on all orthodoxies. "Beida students are much more outspoken in challenging their professors and asserting divergent viewpoints than is the norm for university students in other parts of East Asia," commented one professor, who had observed classrooms in Hong Kong, South Korea, Japan and Singapore.

A theme that recurred through this discussion was the need for Beida to keep a certain distance from society, and research problems in a deep way for the long term. Beida professors have to be clear minded and extremely careful about what they say, since the influence may be long lasting. "We do not need people to like us, so we can afford to take a different line on issues, and to think for the long term." "We also have to be solid and principled, not frivolous or easily changing."

The two names which came to the fore in this discussion were Cai Yuanpei and Ma Yinchu. All agreed that no later president ever reached the depth of Cai's scholarship or the strength of his cultural leadership. As for Ma Yinchu, one professor remembered meeting him in the 1950s, and commented on how modest he was in some ways. "I remember him telling students that they should take a cold shower every morning for the sake of their health." "At the same time, no-one could forget the stand he took, holding to the truth and refusing to retreat, at the cost of having to step down and suffer a long exile."

When asked about architecture, and which buildings or spaces best expressed the Beida spirit, mention was made of the Unnamed Lake and the pagoda scene depicted earlier. (see Photo 3.1) "Water is very important for Beida, and the lake, pagoda and surroundings are its most important symbol." Beida's famous West gate was also mentioned by several, as a historic place on the campus that evokes the Beida spirit in important ways. (See Photo 3.3) However, the space which aroused the most vehement discussion was the new library. One scholar said he had been determined to stay long enough to voice his dislike of the new library building, though he had to leave early. "It has filled the beautiful grassy space in front of the old library where students and faculty used to enjoy quiet conversations and lively dialogue and debate. Both the architecture of the new library and that of the Guanghua School of Management are sudden and disruptive; they do not fit harmoniously into the campus environment, in spite of superficial elements of Chinese tradition in their style. They were designed by an architect who does not understand the Beida spirit." (See Photo 3.2)

Photo 3.3: The West Gate

Merger Issues

Several members of the faculty focus group raised the issue of the merger with Beijing Medical University. There was a strong consensus that this had been beneficial for both sides. For the medical university, it became possible to recruit students at a higher level, and for all students to have their courses in the basic sciences and some electives in social sciences and humanities on the Beida campus. One of the professors in information science noted how she had begun teaching medical students in 2001, shortly after the merger, and found their ways of thinking about problems and their learning styles were quite different from the norm of Beida students. However, they quickly adapted and benefited from the more critical attitudes and diverse views that they found in the Beida culture.

In terms of curricular development, there were considerable benefits for Beida also in the merger. One of the engineering professors talked about the cooperation between the new Engineering College and the Medical School, with programs in the basic sciences as a kind of bridge between them. New programs in biotechnology are one example. Also the Sociology Department is developing a program in medical sociology, which has only become possible since the merger. The social work program within sociology is now active in liaison with the network of hospitals around the medical section, with opportunities for student placements and for cooperation in research.

Beida has also benefited greatly in its research profile from having the medical section, since its faculty are able to bring in significant research funding, and their contribution to research publications has increased substantially over recent years. Thus faculty saw the merger as bringing considerable benefits to both sides, while no negative implications or outcomes were mentioned.

Curricular Change and Adult Education

When asked what they were most proud of in recent reforms, faculty mentioned the efforts to provide bilingual programs, embracing areas such as history, social statistics and international relations, as well as many science programs. While this put considerable pressure on them, it was regarded by most as a positive trend, facilitating greater integration into the world community, and providing opportunities for Beida students to interact with international students. One professor from sociology expressed strong objections, however, saying that sociology students don't have a strong enough basic understanding of the field in Chinese, so that teaching some courses in English can only undermine their grasp of the field.

The other point raised by faculty was Beida's outreach beyond its formal student body, with programs at both undergraduate and graduate level for the community. Typically these programs are managed at the department or college level, bring in considerable funding, and make Beida's expertise in various fields accessible to the wider community. Undergraduate students are likely to be working adults in a wide range of fields who are seeking to upgrade their qualifications. Graduate students are often administrative or political leaders, who find it atttracttive to enroll in graduate programs that relate to their professional field, and are more interested in the learning experiences than the qualifications. Thus only about one third of those enrolled in community oriented masters program in sociology ever complete a thesis and get a degree, yet many benefit from the affiliation with Beida.

Views on Civil Society and Equity

Focus group members welcomed the chance to talk about the concept of civil society. Even though Beida has a centre for research on civil society, they expressed fundamental doubts as to how the concept could be translated into Chinese and whether it is appropriate for describing Chinese society. "Civil society is a Western concept with a strong association with human rights, and it can be questioned whether China has human rights as such." "China certainly has a society, if not a civil society, and Chinese leaders have launched the idea of a harmonious society in order to avoid sensitive issues and encourage people to accept their place in a docile way." "China does have a notion of citizenship, and a concept of the courageous citizen who is willing to speak out. Can Chinese universities fulfill the mission of nurturing courageous citizens?" This ideal seemed to faculty members a better fit with the Chinese conception of a continuous interaction among different polarities, as against the western concept of a firm line that separates civil from governmental institutions.

The intriguing discussion of civil society led on to some consideration of issues of equity. Faculty felt that higher education still remains rather elite, and economic background tends to be the most important factor affecting access for young people. Thus rural girls are still disadvantaged, and there are growing gaps between their opportunities for education and those of urban girls. Generally the level of economic prosperity of various regions determines the opportunities of their young people in education; while national programs address some of these inequities they are not able to reach all students. There is also a skewing of disciplines, with areas such as law and management having become very popular and attracting top students, while traditionally prestigious areas such as philosophy, literature and history are struggling to attract good students. The job market has become an all-important factor.

Finally, faculty members commented on Beida's personnel reforms which have aroused so much controversy on the national scene. Some felt that Beida cannot maintain some of its famous "scholarly brands" in a situation where it is not allowed to recruit its own doctoral graduates as young faculty. This puts it at a disadvantage in comparison to other Chinese universities which are not so constrained. The fact that most of the new appointments are coming from other institutions, often with postdoctoral experience abroad, means it takes them time to adapt to the Beida environment. However, the reforms have been implemented in a more flexible way than the debates would suggest, and most faculty seem to have come to terms with them.[32]

Perspectives from Beida students

The student focus group meeting involved eleven students, from the fields of mathematics, mechanics, sociology, history, international relations and information science, five men and six women. Students wanted to talk about the Beida spirit and Chinese culture, also the theme of civic responsibility and participation.

The Beida Spirit and Chinese Culture

In the first comment on the Beida spirit mention was made of Cai Yuanpei, his support for intellectual freedom and the inclusion of diverse viewpoints, also the lively debates among figures such as Hu Shi, Li Dazhao (李大釗) and other luminaries at Beida in the 1920s. "This is something I was aware of long before coming to Beida," stated this student. A second student followed up by saying this had established the Beida spirit and continued to give students and faculty a sense of mission up to the present time. A third student spoke of Beida as a platform for free exchange, with students and faculty having a sense of responsibility to lead in thinking through major problems for the nation, and so opening up a way into the future.

Students also mentioned their sense of being linked to a world community, through the opportunities of attending lectures by visiting

---

[32] All of the quotations and viewpoints expressed in this section come from the Faculty Focus Group Meeting, 9 May 2008.

national leaders as well as outstanding scholars from around the world. "What amazes us most is the fact that visiting presidents want to hear from us and get our views, not only speak to us! We treasure these opportunities for interaction, and the sense that even while we are still students our ideas may have an influence beyond China."

This comment led on to a discussion of the role of Chinese culture in the world. Can it be regarded as a "missionizing culture" and do Chinese people have a responsibility to present it on an international stage? Several students made the point that Chinese culture is actually rather introspective, and that it does not have an impulse to dominate or even influence the world. "China's culture will flow out into the world in a natural way, less through the efforts of Chinese people to assert or explain it, than in response to those who may come and ask what lies behind our recent economic and social developments. The Confucius Institutes and the Chinese diaspora will all play a part in this, but Chinese culture will never seek to dominate the world."

"More than anything else Beida is a place where great scholars have congregated, and formed the heart of the university and society." Students expressed great affection for the Unnamed Lake, and several commented on the library as a symbol of the way in which Beida brought together old and new, past and future. The classical architecture reminded them of the past, while the internal facilities, which are extremely modern and futuristic, give them a sense of being on the cutting edge of knowledge. At the same time, the part of the campus which students felt touched them most deeply was the Lang Run Garden (朗潤園), where

Photo 3.4: The Lang Run Garden

famous scholars have had their residences up till now. "This quiet and peaceful place is the most important part of the campus, since so many great teachers and great scholars have lived here, and some still live here now." Students commented on how the Beida campus made them feel a great sense of responsibility to carry forward the achievements of past members of Beida, a sense of the power to serve and change society. These reflections led naturally into the topic of civil society and civic participation.

Civic Responsibility and Participation

One student commented that on his way to the focus group meeting, he had seen a group of students fundraising for victims of the Sichuan earthquake. "It is natural for Beida students to show this kind of concern," he commented. Most of the students were involved both in various formal student bodies, as well non-formal associations of various kinds. One student noted that he represented the university's student association on a number of university bodies, and felt it was his responsibility to supervise the administration from the perspective of students' rights and interests. Several had served in responsible positions of the student associations at college and department level, while others were involved in the university's Communist Youth League. One who was secretary of the college level student association said she felt this was a significant position from which to represent student demands and expectations to academic and administrative leaders. She was proud that she had been able to stimulate leaders of the College of International Relations to organize a visit to the Ministry of External Affairs, which made it possible for students to have a memorable and exciting meeting with Minister Li Zhaoxing.

Some students made the point that they preferred to engage only with the non-official associations and groups, including those relating to their professional field and those organized to offer educational or social assistance. A number of students made reference to a recent decision of the university administration to close down the well-known Triangle Place, and re-develop the area. This has been a focal point for student meetings on campus for decades, and was the centre of the student movement in 1989. The student who brought up the topic said that students now exchange information with each other through the BBS (university website for students) and no longer need Triangle Place. Several other students took the opposing view. "We care a lot about this place and do not want to see it closed down – it is part of the Beida spirit." "Beida's leaders did not consult us about this, and when we have sent letters to ask for an explanation, they have not replied."[33]

In these views of students, it was interesting to see considerable consonance with faculty views, as well as a perspective on the global role of Chinese culture that had its own unique flavor. It was also notable to see evidence of the continuing outspokenness and independence of thought, which has characterized the Beida spirit since the time of Cai Yuanpei.

Conclusion: Cultural Leadership and the Beida Spirit

This picture of Beida gives some interesting insights into the experience of one of China's top universities in the move to mass higher education. Perhaps most striking is the sense of a strong and persistent identity, as an institution whose destiny has been to take the lead in China' cultural development over the 20th century. While the reform period, between 1978 and 1998 had been a difficult one for Beida, due to inadequate resources and enormous pressures to raise funds through entrepreneurial activity, the infusion of government funding through the 98/5 Project opened up a whole new phase of development, a phase that coincided precisely with the nation's move to mass higher education. Beida's approach to that move was to expand and diversify its graduate programs, to integrate its newly merged medical section with its other programs, and to build upon its historic curricular strengths in the humanities, social sciences and basic sciences.

Leaders, faculty and students all shared a strong sense of identity, relating to Beida's tradition of liberalism, of intellectual freedom, and of the responsibility to speak out and be critical, even when such criticism was costly. All agreed on the continuing importance of the spirit of Cai Yuanpei and Ma Yinchu, leaders who had left their imprint in critical periods of the university's development. Yet this sense of identity and call to cultural leadership was expressed differently by different groups.

In Beida's leaders, we could see remarkable qualities of scholarly sophistication combined with a commitment to maintaining the university's autonomy and pressing for wider changes in national political governance that would make it possible to realize the legal person status

---

[33] All quotations and viewpoints found in this section were garnered from the student focus group meeting held on 13 May 2008.

provided for in legislation. There was also a determination to encourage and protect scholarship in fields such as economics, politics and sociology that would address sensitive yet vital questions of national development. This was just as important as the cutting edge research in basic sciences, medicine and new fields of engineering. There was no hesitation about taking steps to reform the faculty appointment system in such a way as to attract top talent from within China and around the world, and prevent the kinds of inbreeding that had been common in Chinese universities since the 1950s. The fact that this policy sparked nation-wide controversy did not result in any significant retreat.

In the faculty group whom we talked to, there was a sense of how heavy was the responsibility of being a Beida teacher – not only within China, but in the wider East Asian region. They felt much was expected of them and they had much to live up to. They must nurture students to be critical thinkers and to think deeply for the long term, if Beida was to retain its cultural leadership. This in turn made it necessary to keep some distance from the immediate demands of society and government. They did not hesitate to express critical views, including fundamental questioning of the concept of civil society in a Chinese context, and a strongly negative opinion about the library building, which both students and leaders felt was a symbol of identity and progress. Overall, there was a clear sense that they would inhabit the space which university leaders carved out for them in ways that were responsible but not necessarily either predictable or comfortable.

In the student group, there was a surprising diffidence about the role of Chinese culture in the world, and a conviction that China would never seek to dominate global circles. At the same time there was a lively awareness of Beida being on a global stage, with the visits of many national leaders, and opportunities for students not only to learn but to express their views to these leaders. There was also a profound appreciation of the Beida heritage, of the great scholars past and present, who had lived on campus and made this the place that it was. There was further a strong sense of civic identity and responsibility, and divergent views on how far this should be exercised within the frame of officially established organizations or in non-official or even dissident settings.

Perhaps we could conclude this chapter with some reflections on the spatial configuration of Beida's campus in the move to mass higher education. In a sense one can see a core tension in the decision to protect and further sequester the classical low rise buildings that form the heart of the campus, on the one hand, while developing whole new campus areas that connect to public transport and have high rise buildings for new professional programs, on the other hand. While the aura of mystery and distance emanating from the Unnamed Lake and the surrounding architecture in Royal Palace style is maintained and enhanced, the periphery of the campus is more firmly connected to the main arteries of the city and the dynamic changes that have overtaken it. There is thus a balancing act between opposed polarities that expresses a fundamental dimension of Chinese culture in these campus developments.

4
Nanjing University – Redeeming the Past by Academic Merit

Jun LI and Jing LIN, with GONG Fang

In the first half of the 20th century, Nanjing University (Nanda) once had a similar national leading status to that of Peking University.[1] Its history is almost as long, but its location in the former capital of the Nationalist regime, and its position as the successor to the National Central University, the leading higher institution of the Nationalist period, have given it certain disadvantages in the new China, established under the Communist Party of China (CPC) in 1949. This chapter illustrates how Nanda has sought to overcome these disadvantages through a determined commitment to academic excellence and through strategic efforts to raise the profile of its published research and engage in significant and long standing international partnerships, such as the Hopkins-Nanjing Centre, which was established in the early 1980s.

History and Context

Nanjing and the East China Region

The city of Nanjing has a history going back over 2500 years. It is located in the upper Yangtze Delta, where agricultural and aquacultural products have long been prolific, with the Yangtze River flowing through. Since the Song Dynasty (960-1279 CE), the greater Nanjing area has been famous for its dynamism in commerce, transportation and handicrafts; it is regarded as the first area where early capitalism emerged in China. Politically, Nanjing was the capital of many dynasties in ancient times, and it was the modern capital during the Nationalist period (1927-1949), except for some years of the Anti-Japanese War.

After 1949 when the CPC took over China, Beijing became the capital and Nanjing was downgraded to the provincial capital of Jiangsu. However, Nanjing and Jiangsu province, together with their neighbors in

---

[1] Meng Xiancheng, *Daxue Jiaoyu (University Education)* (Hong Kong: Commercial Press, 1933), p.70.

the Greater Yangtze Delta Region, such as Shanghai, also Zhejiang and Shandong provinces, have seen the fastest rate of economic growth among China's major economic regions since the late 1970s, with Jiangsu province alone accounting for 10.26% of GDP in 2006.[2] Nanjing has thus been revitalized as one of China's largest commercial, industrial and cultural metropolises.

Nanjing has its own rich history of higher education. In the late fourth century (384 CE), the Guozixue (國子學), an important imperial institution of higher education, was established in Nanjing with 155 rooms on its campus. There were also four kinds of specialized institutions set up independently in Nanjing in subsequent centuries.[3] In the late fifteenth century, the Guozijian (國子監), which also served as a ministry of education, enrolled more than ten thousand students. It could be regarded as the largest imperial university in the world, surpassing the enrollment of Oxford and Cambridge Universities and the University of Paris at the time.[4] In addition, Nanjing was the main center of the Imperial Civil Service Examinations (科舉) during the Ming and Qing Dynasties (1368-1911 CE), with more than twenty thousand cubicles built for examinees. Even after the destruction of the city by the Taiping Uprising (太平天國起義) in the mid-1860s, Nanjing was able to restore and expand its higher educational institutions within a short time.[5] Today Nanjing has 41 higher education institutions, with nearly 621,000 undergraduate students and 64,000 graduate students enrolled in 2006.[6]

The Tradition and Early History of Nanda

Nanda dates back to the Sanjiang Normal School (三江師範學堂) initi-

---

[2] National Bureau of Statistics of China (ed.), *China Statistical Yearbook 2007* (Beijing: China Statistics Press, 2007), pp. 57, 67.

[3] Sun Peiqing (ed.), *Zhongguo Jiaoyu Shi (A History of China's Education)* (3rd ed., Shanghai: East China Normal University Press, 2009), p.132.

[4] Yang Zhishui, et al. (eds.), *Nanjing* (Beijing: China Architecture and Building Press, 1989), p.59, as cited in Wang Dezi, Gong Fang and Mao Rong (eds.), *Nanjing Daxue Bainian Shi (The Centennial History of Nanjing University)* (Nanjing: Nanjing University Press, 2002), p.2.

[5] Barry C. Keenan, *Imperial China's Last Classical Academies: Social Change in the Lower Yangtze, 1864-1911* (Berkeley, CA: Institute of East Asian Studies, University of California, Berkeley, 1994), pp.11-19.

[6] Data from the Nanjing Bureau of Statistics website, accessed September 28, 2008, http://www.njtj.gov.cn/2004/2007/keji/index.htm.

ated in 1902 by Liu Kunyi, Zhang Zhidong and Wei Guangtao.[7] At that time, the Qing Empire was declining in the face of serious internal social problems and the increasing inroads of foreign imperialism. A number of politicians and educators saw that a modern school system was crucial for the nation to survive, and the Sanjiang Normal School was therefore created to train teachers for this system.

Sanjing Normal was upgraded to Nanjing Higher Normal School in 1915. Its President, Jiang Qian, together with its Provost, Guo Bingwen (郭秉文) who earned his PhD from Teachers College Columbia University in 1914, launched several pioneering initiatives. For example, they laid out rigorous procedures for civic and moral education, along with intellectual education and physical education. Sincerity (誠) was adopted as its first motto, drawing on *The Great Learning* and *The Doctrine of the Mean* (《中庸》), two of the *Four Books* (《四書》).[8] In 1918, Guo Bingwen became President and advocated the idea of democracy and science, establishing various committees to facilitate participation by administrators, faculty and students, respectively. During this time, the U.S.-based Chinese Society of Science[9] was moved to the Nanjing Higher Normal School, where it became a center of science education in China and the first higher education summer schools for lifelong learning in China were offered,[10] with more than 100 courses that integrated knowl-

---

[7] Wang Dezi, Gong Fang and Mao Rong (eds.), *Nanjing Daxue Bainian Shi* (*The Centennial History of Nanjing University*) (Nanjing: Nanjing University Press, 2002), p.4.

[8] *Daxue* (*The Great Learning*) and *Zhongyong* (*The Doctrine of the Mean*), were both from *Liji* (*The Record of Rites*) compiled by early Confucians around fifth century BCE. The two classics have had a profound influence on Chinese higher learning and education for over thousands of years.

[9] The Chinese Society of Science (中國科學社) was initially established in 1915 by a group of Chinese oversea students in the United States. It was the first Chinese society of science organized by Chinese scientists and later became the most authoritative institute for the development of science in China, with some parallels to the British Royal Society. The society had a profound impact on the May Fourth Movement in 1919, and significantly shaped Chinese concepts of science and democracy thereafter.

[10] Gong Fang, "Nangaoshi De Shuqi Xuexiao (The Summer School of Nanjing Higher Normal School)", in *Gaojiao Yanjiu Yu Tansuo* (*Research on Higher Education*), 1987, Vol.12, No.2, pp.71-75.

edge with practice and application.¹¹

In 1920 Nanjing Higher Normal School formed an important part of the newly established National Southeast University, under the continuing presidency of Guo Bingwen. As a strong advocate of institutional autonomy and academic freedom, Guo promoted a democratic and scientific spirit on campus, with the help of Provost Tao Xingzhi (陶行知) who was also a returnee from Teachers College Columbia. The influence of the American model of higher education can be seen clearly in this decision to abandon the identity of the normal school or university for that of a comprehensive university.¹²

Under the leadership of Guo and Tao, Southeast University opened its door to women in 1920, becoming China's first public university to register female students.¹³ Southeast University was also among the first universities to adopt an American-style credit system which allowed students to select courses and follow their own pace of learning. In addition, Southeast University hosted two flagship magazines of the New Culture and New Education Movements, advocating a blend of Chinese tradition, Western democracy and science: *The Critical Review* (《學衡》) and *New Education* (《新教育》).

Guo's presidency laid a solid foundation for the development of Southeast University, and he has therefore been regarded as the father of Southwest University. Paul Monroe, then Director of the International Institute of Teachers College Columbia University, commented that Southeast University was "the first promising modern university estab-

---

¹¹ Tao Xingzhi, "Chuangzao Yige Sitongbada De Shehui (Creating a Society that Extends in All Directions)", in the Institute of Educational Sciences Research of Huazhong Normal College (ed.), *Tao Xingzhi Quanji* (*The Complete Works of Tao Xingzhi*) (Changsha: Hunan Educational Science Publishing House, 1985), Vol.5, pp.54-56.

¹² Ruth Hayhoe and Jun Li, "The Idea of a Normal University in the 21st Century," in *Frontiers of Education in China*, Vol.5, No.1, 2010, p.90.

¹³ While both Southeast and Peking Universities were China's first public higher institutions to open their doors to female students in 1920, Southeast allowed women to register formally, while Peking University only allowed them to audit courses. See Zhang Beiheng, "Wo Chengwei Zhongguo Shoujie Nannu Tongxiao Nusheng Zhi Zhuiyi (A Reminiscence of My Experience of Being the First Female Student in China's Co-educational Institutions)", *Gaojiao Yanjiu Yu Tansuo* (*Research on Higher Education*), 1987, Vol.12, No.2, pp.19-21.

lished by the Chinese government,"[14] after his visits to many Chinese universities in the early 1920s. The ethos of "sincerity" and "resting in the highest good," another phrase from the Confucian Classics selected as a motto during Guo's presidency, still serves as a unique aspect of Nanda's spirit today.

When Nanjing became the capital of the new Nationalist government established by the Guomindang Party in 1927, Southeast University was merged with nine other higher educational institutions into a major regional university known as the Fourth Zhongshan University. It was China's largest public university and in 1928, it was renamed Jiangsu University and then National Central University (國立中央大學). The continental European model of the university had some influence on its subsequent development since Luo Jialun, its president from 1932 to 1941, had studied in the universities of Paris, Berlin and London, as well as Princeton and Columbia. He put forward the idea of the university creating an organic culture which would serve national strengthening. The new motto he established, "sincerity with aspiration," was based on four classical concepts: sincerity (誠), simplicity (樸), sublimity (雄) and greatness (偉). He advocated this spirit in pursuing knowledge, learning and scientific research, and he believed that nurturing students' character was the foundation of higher education.

Luo made the recruitment of highly qualified faculty to spur the development of academic disciplines and excellence in research his highest priorities. At the same time, he paid special attention to enhancing teaching quality by passing guidelines for the reform of teaching plans. He also established and chaired a graduate school, and promoted the publishing of academic journals. With his efforts, National Central University developed a total of seven schools with more than 40 departments. Luo had hoped to recruit over 10,000 students, but the Japanese invasion of 1937 brought an end to this dream.

National Central University was moved to Chongqing during the Anti-Japanese War (1937-1945), and Chiang Kai-shek himself was named president from 1943 to 1944 and then president emeritus afterwards. The university moved back to Nanjing in 1946 and was headed by Dr. Wu Youxun, who had a PhD in physics from the University of Chicago (1926). In rebuilding the university after the war, Wu focused on teaching and

---

[14] Wang Dezi, Gong Fang and Mao Rong (eds.), *Nanjing Daxue Bainian Shi* (*The Centennial History of Nanjing University*) (Nanjing: Nanjing University Press, 2002), p.73.

academic research, and was viewed as a president who was close to faculty and students. By 1947, National Central University had the reputation of being China's most prestigious comprehensive university, with 7 schools and 37 departments.[15] After the Nationalist leaders moved to Taiwan in 1949 National Central University was renamed Nanjing University (Nanda for short).

With the reorganization of colleges and departments under Soviet influence in 1952, Nanda was left with 13 departments in basic sciences and humanities. It had lost its schools of medicine, engineering, agriculture and education, but gained some renowned scholars from the University of Nanking, a famous Christian institution that had been founded in 1888, as well as universities such as Zhejiang, Tongji and Zhongshan. Political education was a high priority in the early fifties and students were recruited to rather narrow specializations within each academic department. Nanda experienced the same political campaigns as other universities from the late 1950s to the late 1970s, including the Anti-Rightist Movement of 1957 and the Cultural Revolution of 1966. However, Nanda probably suffered even greater political disadvantages due to its close historical association with Chiang Kai-shek and the Nationalist regime. It was only after Mao's death in 1976 and the launching of Deng Xiaoping's modernization program in 1978 that Nanda was able to gradually restore its status as a leading comprehensive university in China. This took focused effort, over several decades, as we will see in the following sections.

The Redemption of Nanda: From Kuang Yaming to Qu Qinyue

Nanda's early history, prestigious status and location in the capital of the Nationalist regime, and most particularly the presidency of Chiang Kai-shek, were seen as a kind of "original sin" after the Communist Party came to power in China in 1949. In the forty years from 1949 up to the 1990s, Nanda did not receive any major priority funding from the central government, as did Peking, Tsinghua and Fudan Universities, nor was it possible to maintain a status in line with the reputation it had developed before 1949. When the first six key universities were selected by the central government in 1954 and another twenty key universities were

---

[15] Please see Educational news, *Shenbao* (*Shanghai Journal*), March 10, 1947, in Wang Dezi, Gong Fang and Mao Rong (eds.), *Nanjing Daxue Bainian Shi* (*The Centennial History of Nanjing University*) (Nanjing: Nanjing University Press, 2002), p.261.

added in 1959, Nanda was not included on either list. Only in1960 when the list was extended to include sixty-four institutions was Nanda able to join this prestigious club. For this reason, Nanda's leaders and faculty members made the issue of how to redeem their past in the new political environment their first priority. The two presidents who are seen as most influential in this effort were Kuang Yaming (匡亞明) (1963-1966; 1978-1982) and Qu Qinyue (曲欽嶽) (1984-1997).

Kuang Yaming had been a student at Shanghai University, a well-known progressive institution and a Communist activist during the Nationalist period. After 1949, his interests turned to the study of traditional Chinese culture and his *Biography of Confucius* (《孔子評傳》) has been widely used as a textbook for graduate studies in Chinese culture and philosophy. From 1955 to 1963 he served as President of Jilin University, the major comprehensive university of the Northeast, before being appointed President of Nanda. Kuang attached great importance to teaching and research, developing ten year plans for research and for faculty upgrading, also seeking to improve the quality of Nanda's academic journals. He suggested establishing committees to enhance the quality of research in the sciences and humanities, even though this was a period when Chinese universities were mandated mainly to teach, with major national research projects assigned to the Chinese Academy of Sciences. Kuang's early reforms were interrupted by the Cultural Revolution (1966-1976) and only after 1978 was he able to regain his leadership at Nanda and pursue his unique vision.

Kuang wanted to focus on nothing other than teaching and research.[16] He reflected on the various political movements after 1949, especially the Cultural Revolution, and insisted that proactive involvement in political campaigns could only damage a university. He promoted a learning spirit, a working spirit and a campus spirit as the ethos for a revived Nanda.[17] He also reflected seriously on the impact of the Soviet Model with its emphasis on narrow specialization,[18] and advocated general education as a way of bringing greater breadth to the nurturing of students. Nanda was thus among the first universities to

---

[16] The Nanjing University Institute of Higher Educational Research (ed.), *Kuang Yaming Jiaoyu Wenxuan* (*Selected Educational Works of Kuang Yaming*) (Nanjing: The Nanjing University Institute of Higher Educational Research, 1998), pp.253-254.
[17] *Ibid.*, pp.92-94.
[18] *Ibid.*, pp.255-259.

restore the credit system in 1978. In addition, Nanda soon gained a high profile for its research in the natural sciences, social sciences and humanities. In 1978 it was awarded a total of 54 national awards of achievements in the natural sciences, ranking first among all Chinese universities that year. In the same year, an influential article entitled "Practice Is the Sole Criterion for Testing Truth (實踐是檢驗真理的唯一標準)", by Hu Fuming, the then vice-chairperson of Nanda's Philosophy Department, was published in the *Guangming Daily*, the national newspaper for intellectuals. It has been seen as a milestone in rebutting the "two whatevers" doctrine (兩個"凡是") of Mao Zedong's successor, Hua Guofeng, and a rallying cry for Deng Xiaoping's return to power.[19]

As China started opening up in 1978, Kuang opened Nanda's door to the international community. He visited many top universities in Japan and the United States in the late 1970s, and was very impressed by the high degree of autonomy they enjoyed, and the ways in which they linked teaching and scientific research.[20] Realizing that Chinese universities had fallen far behind during the Cultural Revolution, he could see that Nanda's revitalization would require international exchange and collaboration.

From 1954 China had adopted a key school system as a way of dealing with budget shortages for public education, at all levels. In higher education there were 96 national key universities by 1981; even though they were given priority funding and academic resources, they were still very limited in what they could do. In May of 1983 Kuang wrote a letter to Deng Xiaoping, suggesting that higher education be treated in the same way as key economic projects which were given high priority in the reform and opening up, and that 50 of China's 700 universities be given greatly enhanced financial support.[21] Kuang's proposal drew serious attention from the central government as well as from the

---

[19] Roderick MacFarquhar, "The Succession to Mao and the End of Maoism," in Denis Twitchett and John K. Fairbank (eds.), *The Cambridge History of China* (Cambridge: Cambridge University Press, 1991), pp.305-401, Vol.15, Pt.2, p.378. The "two whatevers" refer to Hua Guofeng's statement that "we must support whatever decisions were made by Chairman Mao, follow whatever instructions were given by Chairman Mao."

[20] See The Nanjing University Institute of Higher Educational Research (ed.), *Kuang Yaming Jiaoyu Wenxuan (Selected Educational Works of Kuang Yaming)*, pp.157-163.

[21] *Ibid.*, pp.255-261.

public, with the result that the original key school system was developed in a new way, with some key higher education projects. The State Council originally planned to support around fifteen national universities with priority funding, but this led eventually to Project 21/1 in 1993, which supported 100 institutions and Project 98/5 in 1998, which further enhanced support for 39 top universities.

Kuang's persistent effort was not, however, able to redeem Nanda in the way he hoped. Nanda was not selected as one of the 15 key universities in the initial plan, although Kuang's proposal had been adopted by the Chinese leaders in the mid-1980s. When Kuang retired in 1984, his successor, Qu Qinyue, faced great difficulties. The fact that he was not a CPC member, but a non-Party intellectual, may have reflected a certain attitude towards Nanda on the part of the central government, while most presidents of top national universities were CPC members at the time.

Qu Qinyue, served as Nanda's President for three consecutive terms from 1984 to 1997. In response to the radical socioeconomic changes of the time, he reflected on the nationwide reorganization of colleges and departments that had taken place along Soviet lines in 1952 and decided that the "comprehensive university" of that time, which was limited to programs in natural sciences and humanities, was inadequate. He envisioned a much broader comprehensive university with programs in the humanities, natural sciences, social sciences and areas such as agriculture, medicine, and engineering.[22] With this vision in mind, Qu charted a development plan for the period 1984-1990 immediately after becoming president, with the aim of building a leading national center for teaching and research with multi-disciplinary programs, its own institutional characteristics and an international reputation.[23] This plan has been seen as a turning point in Nanda's transformation into a genuinely comprehensive university.

Nanda's comprehensive reform initiated by Qu in the late 1980s, became one of five national experiments approved by the State Education Commission of the time. Qu's bold approach focused on three urgent tasks: upgrading teaching and research, enhancing the quality of faculty, and improving the facilities for learning and teaching, including campus

---

[22] Qu Qinyue, *Qu Qinyue Jiaoyu Wenxuan (Selected Educational Works of Qu Qinyue)* (Nanjing University Press, 2002), pp.66-88.
[23] *Ibid.*, pp.5-18.

expansion.[24]

The first and highest priority was on teaching and research. Undergraduate programs were fundamentally revised, with new applied content in the social and natural sciences, updated teaching plans for each program, and the editing and publishing of more than 420 textbooks. Certain key disciplines were identified and promoted. New approaches to teaching were introduced, including a model targeted at students who were interested in academic research. A School of Graduate Studies was set up in 1984, which was among the earliest graduate schools reestablished after 1976. In addition, Nanda's Medical School was reestablished in 1987, the first medical school in a national comprehensive university after 1952.

At the same time, Nanda's research moved to a new stage, spurred by several of Qu's strategies. These included the construction of the National Laboratory of Solid State Microstructures, one of the first ten national key laboratories established in 1984, careful organization of applications for key research projects, and the reform of research management in ways that motivated professors to become more active.

Qu's second priority was enhancing the quality of Nanda's faculty.[25] He established a committee of 25 professors who worked closely with the office of teaching affairs, to ensure excellence in teaching. Also, he set up special teaching professor positions which were conferred on faculty who had a high profile in both teaching and research, as well as providing special subsidies to reward excellent professors. Moreover, a tenure system was resumed after 1986 to ensure the recruitment and retention of excellent faculty.

Finally, Qu realized that Nanda's revival depended on obtaining funding from the government in order to overcome the shortage of campus space in the rather small campus in downtown Nanjing. In 1990, the government began to draft the eighth five-year plan (1991-1995) and the blueprint for the next ten years. Qu saw it as a critical opportunity to lobby for Nanda's further development. On Sept. 18, 1990, Qu drafted and co-signed a letter, together with the presidents of Peking, Tsinghua, People's, Beijing Normal and Zhejiang Universities, to the then Prime Minister Li Peng, appealing for support for comprehensive universities in the hope that Nanda could be made one of the key projects of the

---

[24] *Ibid.*, pp.1-4.
[25] *Ibid.*, pp.255-256, pp.257-258.

eighth five-year plan.[26] The co-signed letter of appeal led to a national policy in response, but unfortunately, Nanda was not among those institutions given priority funding in the first instance. His effort seemed to have failed again, just as had the effort made by his predecessor Kuang Yaming. Nevertheless, in late 1994, Nanda was finally recognized as one of the first seven universities to be included in Project 21/1.

Qu Qinyue was still not relieved. The annual budget from the central government provided for only around 40% of Nanda's total expenditures, which meant he had to look for significant additional financial resources by himself. One of his biggest concerns was the small size of the main campus in the downtown area, which confined Nanda's further development. In 1987, he had decided to work with the provincial government to gain support for a new campus in the Pukou District, across the Yangtze River. The following year, the State Education Commission approved Nanda's plan for campus expansion with a special budget of 9.45 million *yuan*. The construction of the new campus went ahead, yet the promised funds were never received. Qu had to borrow money from banks, putting Nanda into a debt crisis in the third term of his presidency, something he regarded as a great embarrassment.

Although the new campus was successfully created and has provided an excellent educational environment for Nanda's expansion, Qu decided to resign from the president's office in late 1995. This was an unprecedented act for a Chinese university president, but he chose it as a way of expressing his disappointment and frustration over the government's response to his efforts. He wanted to show that it was simply too difficult for him to restore Nanda's past excellence, since its history had always caused it to be disadvantaged in both its status and the funding it received from the central government. These were the words used in his official statement about his resignation on March 5 1996: "If the government does not change its lip service into taking real responsibility, it will be very difficult for the development of education to meet the needs of social change, and the morale of university leaders and faculty and staff will be inevitably affected."[27] No university president had ever addressed the Chinese government in this way since 1949, and Qu gained widespread fame for his courage in speaking out. His resignation triggered the reconsideration of Nanda's status by the then State Commission of

---

[26] *Ibid.*, pp.93-95.
[27] *Ibid.*, p.277.

Education, and in fact served as a turning point for the next step of Nanda's development under the leadership of his successor, Jiang Shusheng. In 1999, Nanda was among the first nine universities enlisted in Project 98/5.

Nanda's Move to Mass Higher Education: An Empirical Overview (1990-2005)

Growth in Student Enrollments

The radical expansion of higher education began in Jiangsu province in 1997, two years earlier than in other regions. Nanda has responded to the expansion policy with modest increases in undergraduate student enrollments but a rapid growth in the graduate student body, as shown by the following official statistics for 1990, 1995, 2000 and 2005. While the population of undergraduate students slightly increased from a total of 6,030 in 1990 to 6,796 in 1995, it jumped to 11,205 in 2000 and 13,250 in 2005, with new enrollments of 1755, 2,104, 2,924 and 3,215 in these years respectively. The average growth rate of student enrollments was 32% every five years, much lower than the 104.4% national average growth rate of student enrollments in regular higher educational institutions over the same period. Student numbers in the natural sciences and technologies increased from 3,832 in 1990 and 4,094 in 1995 to 6,342 in 2000 and 6,096 in 2005, with an average growth rate of 28.8% over these years which is marginally lower than that of the overall undergraduate enrollment over the same period. Students registered in social sciences grew from 1,267 in 1990, 1,761 in 1995 to 3,521 in 2000 and 4,696 in 2005, with an average growth rate of 57.4%, nearly double the overall growth rate of the student population. Students in the humanities experienced a temporary increase from 920 in 1990 and 941 in 1995 to 1,342 in 2000, but a sharp cutback to 633 in 2005. In 2005, female students were dominant in the humanities (58%), underrepresented in the natural sciences and technologies (23%), while keeping an almost balanced proportion with their male counterparts in the social sciences.

The enrollments of graduate students almost doubled from a total of 1,266 in 1990 to 2,409 in 1995, and then doubled again, from 4,466 in 2000 to 9,964 in 2005. The average growth rate was 99.6% over these three periods, indicating that graduate enrollments nearly doubled every five years. Graduate students in different disciplinary areas shared a similar pattern of growth with undergraduate students, except in the humanities.

For example, graduate students in the natural sciences and technologies increased from 749 in 1990 and 1,280 in 1995 to 2,181 in 2000 and 4,767 in 2005, with an average growth rate of 86.6% over these years. Students registered in social sciences jumped from 81 in 1990 to 581 in 1995, and then from 1,351 in 2000 to 3,384 in 2005, with an average growth rate of 300.1%. Students in humanities doubled from 279 in 1990 to 548 in 1995, then from 937 in 2000 to 1,813 in 2005. The representation of female graduate students increased significantly over these years, from 22.1% and 23.8%, in 1990 and 1995 respectively, to 32.3% and 43.3% of the graduate student population in 2000 and 2005, respectively.

The Changing Financial Profile

Since 1995, Nanda has seen an accelerating and diversifying increase in funding. Student fees grew moderately from 12.2 million in 1990 to 16.7 million in 1995, but soared to 101.8 million in 2000 and then to 286.4 million in 2005, with an average growth rate of 242.9% every five years. Funding from the central government's budgets increased from 26.6 million in 1990 to 58.7 million in 1995, and jumped to 174.8 million in 2000 and to 213.5 million in 2005, with an average growth rate of 113.7%, which was less than half of the growth in student tuition over the same period. Special funds from Projects 21/1 and 98/5's budgets significantly enhanced Nanda's revenue with an additional 399.7 million in 2000 and 261.1 million in 2005. Tuition fees accounted for around 20.1% and 24.9% of Nanda's total income in 1990 and 2005, respectively. Meanwhile, research grants from governmental funding sources and contracts with industry surged from 10.2 and 11.9 million in 1990 to 203.1 and 91.1 million in 2005, with dramatic growth rates of 1,897% and 665%, respectively. Comparatively, research funding from the government at national, provincial and local levels grew much faster than that from industry. In 2007, the proportion between the two funding sources was 2.3:1.[28] In total, research funds constituted 36.3%, 34.8%, 12.4% and 25.6% of Nanda's income in 1990, 1995, 2000 and 2005, respectively. Nanda's income from all sources grew dramatically from a total of 60.9, 167.1 and 926.4 million in 1990, 1995 and 2000, respectively, to 1.1 billion in 2005, with an average growth rate of 217.6%. The most recent growth in income is particularly associated with its status in Project 98/5.

Additionally, Nanda's income has become increasingly diversified.

---

[28] Interview with Sheng Xiaoqing, Director of Nanda's Financial Office, 24 May 2007.

For example, endowments from alumni or other donors accounted for only 2.8% of the total income in 1995 but reached 5.3% in 2005 with a sum of 60.5 million. Other forms of income generation (創收) also more than doubled from 29 million in 1995 to 80.4 million in 2000, then dropped to 33.1 million in 2005. Unlike the response of many other universities to the national expansion policy, Nanda has been very conservative in establishing its second-tier college and kept the enrollments small. It has thus not become a major source of income.

With rapidly growing revenue in recent decades, Nanda's expenditures have also skyrocketed, for faculty and staff salaries and benefits, teaching, financial assistance for students, and the construction of infrastructure. For example, the expenditures for faculty and staff salaries and benefits rose from 11.6 million in 1990 to 42.4 million in 1995, and again from 191.8 million in 2000 to 291.8 million in 2005. The cost for the construction of infrastructure burgeoned from 6.1 million in 1995 to 193.9 million in 2005, with a growth of 31 times over the ten years. The significant growth in both income and expenditure has provided an unprecedented opportunity for Nanda's revival in recent years, compared to the difficulties it faced in the early years after 1949. Inclusion in Projects 21/1 and 98/5 have been particularly significant for Nanda.

Curricular Change

As mentioned earlier, both Kuang Yaming and Qu Qinyue had worked hard to broaden Nanda's programs, which had focused solely on the humanities and natural sciences after the reorganization along Soviet lines in 1952. Their persistent efforts laid a solid foundation for their successors to continue in developing a greatly broadened curriculum.

Since the early 1990s Nanda has established 19 more schools, including the Schools of Liberal Arts, Foreign Studies, Law, Public Management, Journalism and Communication, Natural Sciences, Geosciences, Geographic and Oceanographic Sciences, Technological Sciences, Chemistry and Chemical Engineering, Environment, and Architecture. By 2008 there were a total of 21 schools, with the Medical School and the Business School having opened earliest in the late 1980s.

In 1990, Nanda had 26 departments with 64 undergraduate programs. Fifteen years later, it had 74 programs and by 2008, there were 80 undergraduate programs in 64 departments, all within the various schools. Undergraduate programs in natural sciences and technologies, social sciences and humanities accounted for 59.4%, 23.4% and 17.2% of the total programs in 1990s, but this proportion had changed to 40.5%, 41.9% and 17.6% in 2005, respectively. The pattern of change reflects the growth of students registered in these programs over the same period, with social sciences having the highest average growth rate, i.e., 57.4%, as noted earlier in the data on student enrollments. For example, the Business School had programs in economics, domestic economic management, international trade, business management, and econometrics in 1990. Additional programs in international finance, tourism management, and accounting had been developed by the mid-1990s, then business administration, finance administration, cameralistics, finance, and marketing by 2000, and e-commerce, and insurance in 2005. By 2005, social work and international politics had been added into the Departments of Sociology and Politics and Administration, respectively.

There have also been significant developments at the graduate level. For example, Nanda had 80 Master's program, 43 doctoral programs, and 18 national key disciplines in 1990. The numbers of these programs and national key disciplines had surged to 186, 122, and 28 by 2005, respectively. By 2008, the numbers of Masters' and doctoral programs had reached 213 and 147. This has been brought about by integrating old programs and setting up new programs in response to China's socio-economic change.

Vision and Strategic Directions

Vision and Mission

After twenty years of struggle to gain the national status of a leading comprehensive university between 1976 and 1997, Nanda's new leaders have set forth a clear vision for the institution to transform itself in response to the challenges of radical socio-economic change, including the national policy of expansion. This vision focuses on three dimensions: comprehensiveness, research, and internationalization. Central to this vision is a determined pursuit of academic excellence in teaching and research.[29]

Zhang Yibin, Nanda's Vice-President, mentioned that Kuang Yaming, Qu Qinyue and Jiang Shusheng have all played a crucial role in shaping Nanda's mission and making possible sustainable development. Meanwhile, Projects 21/1 and 98/5 served as key instruments that gave it the opportunity to actualize this mission. In 1994, Nanda laid out its

---

[29] Interview with Zhang Yibin, Vice-President, 22 May 2007.

concrete mission for Project 21/1 in the following way:

> With around 20 years' endeavor and in the early 21st century, Nanjing University will be established as a leading university in China and a world-class comprehensive research university in educational quality, scientific research, and governance, with its own uniqueness, international influence, and the concerted development of multiple disciplines in humanities, social sciences, natural sciences, life sciences, management sciences, modern engineering and technologies; as an important base for educating high-level specialists and resolving theoretical and practical issues in China's economic construction, technological advancement and societal development; ... as a key international center for research.[30]

This mission statement was revised in 1999 for Project 98/5, setting its long-term goal as to construct a world-class university with high quality by 2012 and a leading world-class university by 2020 or later.[31]

In 2007, Chen Jun, the newly appointed President of Nanda, stated the updated mission in the following appealing way:

> Our mission is to build this university into a world renowned institution enjoying an international reputation and maintaining our own academic characteristics. We aim to be a cradle, preparing innovative talent for the future, a frontier for activities giving insight to the unknown world, seeking truth, providing scientific grounds for solving important problems encountered by humanity; we aim to be an important source of innovation and technology transfer and a bridge for cooperation and exchange between different cultures and civilizations.[32]

The latest mission has thus been broadened and focuses on Nanda's ultimate role in bringing into the international community excellent scholarship based on its high quality services in teaching and research.

---

[30] Wang Dezi, Gong Fang and Mao Rong (eds.), *Nanjing Daxue Bainian Shi* (*The Centennial History of Nanjing University*) (Nanjing: Nanjing University Press, 2002), pp.445-446.
[31] *Ibid.*, p.529.
[32] See Chen Jun's presidential message on the Nanjing University website, accessed September 28, 2008, www.nju.edu.cn/cps/site/njueweb/fg/index.php?ifshow=boutnju&id=157.

Strategic Directions

Our interview with Zhang Yibin showed a clear road map by which Nanda has moved forward to achieving its goals in the recent decade. He explained that Nanda had gone through a bumpy and sometimes awkward path after 1949, but it had held firmly to its own tradition, that of the National Central University, developed in the Nationalist period, which regarded scholarship as the core of its institutional ethos, and which represents a perfect integration of the spirit of Chinese universities and the characteristics of traditional Chinese culture. Zhang repeatedly pointed out that Nanda's revitalization had had to rely entirely on itself, and he was very proud that Nanda had succeeded through the persisting endeavors made by previous presidents, though the road had often been extremely difficult and challenging.[33]

One strategic direction of Nanda's development had been to enhance its institutional ethos by integrating new meanings within it. From 1949 to 2002, Nanda's historic motto, "sincerity with aspiration (誠樸雄偉)", was given up due to political reasons, particularly during the ordeal of such political campaigns as the Anti-Rightist Movement and the Cultural Revolution. In 2002 when Nanda celebrated its 90th anniversary, campus-wide participation was solicited for the making of a new motto, with three guidelines provided: reflecting both the institutional tradition and a new mission, identifying institutional uniqueness and ideals, and expressing the democratic voices of Nanda people. After much careful deliberation, the new motto finally took form in time for the 90th anniversary, and it was interesting to see the revival of Nanda's pre-1949 motto, "sincerity with aspiration" with the added phrase "perseverance with integrity (勵學敦行)", which comes from Confucian heritage and emphasizes the integration of learning and practice.[34] Zhang Yibin judged that the combination of these two phrases rightly reflects Nanda's traditional ethos and uniqueness, as well as the pursuit and realization of its ambitious mission.[35] In his eyes, Nanda's leaders, from

---

[33] Interview with Zhang Yibin, Vice-President, 22 May 2007.

[34] Part of the new motto originated from *Liji* (*The Record of Rites*), one of the Confucian classics that emerged around the 3rd century BCE.

[35] Jiang Shusheng, "Chengpu Xiongwei, Lixue Dunxing: Bainian Chuantong Yu Nanda Xiaoxun (Sincerity with Aspiration, Perseverance with Integrity: Tradition of a Century and Nanda's Motto)", in Wang Dezi, Gong Fang and Mao Rong

Kuang Yaming and Qu Qinyue to Jiang Shusheng, have worked hard to strengthen Nanda's tradition and have managed to integrate it with Chinese culture.[36]

Zhang felt that the North Building (北大樓) is one of the most symbolic and expressive buildings on campus and is widely seen to represent Nanda's ethos, history and culture. In his view, it stands for richness in simplicity and also inspiration with endurance, and it has witnessed the history of Nanda's development over a long period of time. Many of our other interviewees, including faculty members and students, also agreed on this. It is interesting and perhaps ironic that this building was designed by an American architect, who greatly admired Chinese traditional architecture, and that it belonged to the Private University of Nanking, a Christian institution originally founded by American missionaries in 1888.

Photo 4.1: The North Building, designed by American architect A.G. Small as the administration building of the Private University of Nanking in 1919 and still serving as Nanda's administration center nowadays, is widely thought to express Nanda's ethos of "Sincerity with Aspiration, Perseverance with Integrity".

(eds.), *Nanjing Daxue Bainian Shi* (*The Centennial History of Nanjing University*) (Nanjing: Nanjing University Press, 2002), pp.1-5.
[36] Interview with Zhang Yibin, Vice-President, 22 May 2007.

Another strategic direction has been to promote and strengthen Nanda's research profile through strategies that would give it a high profile. Zhang Yibin highlighted two such strategies, of which he was very proud, one in the humanities and the other in the natural sciences. Research in areas such as Chinese literature, philosophy, history and culture, has been one of Nanda's traditional strengths. In 1986, the Chinese Thinkers Research Center was set up, led by Kuang Yaming himself, to provide a platform for a systematic and wide-ranging study of influential Chinese thinkers for the first time in modern history. By 2006, the project had completed the publication of more than 200 biographies of Chinese philosophers, politicians, educators and religious thinkers, written by hundreds of leading scholars in the relevant fields. The series has received several top national awards since 2006. Recently, around 50 volumes from this series have been selected for publication of a bilingual version in Chinese and English. The Nanda Chinese Thinkers Research Center is thus becoming an influential international base for research on traditional Chinese culture.

In the natural sciences, the special strategy which Zhang Yibin spoke about, was one of encouraging faculty to publish their academic papers in the world's leading science and technological journals which have been selected by the Philadelphia-based Thomson Scientific's Science Citation Index (SCI). As a result, Nanda became number one among Chinese universities in the Mainland, for seven consecutive years from 1992 to 1999, in the total number of scientific journal papers internationally published and for eight consecutive years, from 1994 to 2002, in the total number of scientific journal papers internationally cited, as calculated in the SCI. Since the SCI is commonly viewed as a fairly accurate index for measuring an institution's capacity in scientific research, the number one status among Chinese universities in the 1990s symbolized a remarkable upward spiral in Nanda's development at a time when universities such as Peking, Tsinghua and Fudan were all left behind.[37] Nowadays, when Chinese researchers talk about the SCI and excellence in science, almost everybody will immediately recall Nanda's unique role.

The third strategic direction has been to learn from the international community in a rather unique way – by establishing the Johns Hopkins-Nanjing Center for Chinese and American Studies, an early and pioneer-

---

[37] Interview with Gong Fang, Director of Nanda's Institute of Higher Educational Research, 24 May 2007.

ing project of international cooperation and exchange. In November of 1979, Kuang Yaming visited the Johns Hopkins University and discussed collaborative initiatives with then President Steven Muller. Two years later, the Johns Hopkins-Nanjing Center for Chinese and American Studies was already being planned with strong support from national leaders of both China and the U.S. In 1986, the Center began to enroll Chinese and international students for one-year graduate programs in history, culture, and contemporary social and political issues, and it has the distinction of being the earliest sustained international collaborative project in China after 1976. With a U.S. $21 million campus expansion completed in 2006, that added state-of-the-art learning facilities and a two-story library, the Hopkins-Nanjing Center has now introduced a two-year Master of Arts in International Studies to complement its existing certificate program. The Hopkins-Nanjing Center is the pioneer of the earliest joint academic programs approved to offer a master's degree that are fully accredited in China and in the United States. According to Huang Chengfeng, the Chinese Co-director, the Hopkins-Nanjing Center aims at providing an international learning environment where advanced academic study is enriched and expanded to promote the mutual understanding, appreciation and exchange of Chinese and American students, whether in the studies of culture, political science, economics, history or business. She also commented on the contribution of the Hopkins-Nanjing Center to Nanda's campus culture and institutional ethos in the following way:

> As Vice-President Zhang has noted, the Hopkins-Nanjing Center is a key project of Nanda's internationally coordinated education .... The Center has rigorous requirements for the Nanda professors who are recruited through an open competition. They have to work seriously and diligently to pass students' reviews on their teaching. They will bring this kind of working spirit back to their own departments as well .... At the same time, the Johns Hopkins's professors often give public lectures on campus, which brings their perspectives and the Johns Hopkins's teaching style to the Nanda community.[38]

The Hopkins-Nanjing Center serves as a unique example of international cooperation between two universities in very different sociocultural contexts. Its inclusion of the areas of economics and business has

---

[38] Interview with Huang Chengfeng, Chinese Co-Director of the Hopkins-Nanjing Center, 22 May 2007.

also highlighted an important aspect of Chinese-American relations in recent years. When asked about symbolic architecture on campus, Huang Chengfeng pointed to the newly completed Anzhong MBA Building, which has been nicknamed Nanda's Manhatten, and is seen to represent some of the stunning outcomes of Nanda's pursuit of both excellence and openness.

Photo 4.2: The 25-story Anzhong MBA Building (2007) of the Business School, Nanda's Manhattan, is a new icon of Nanda's spirit in its pursuit of dynamism, excellence and internationalization.

The Decision on Merger and Second-tier Colleges

In China's move to mass higher education, most universities have been urged to consider institutional mergers and the establishment of one or more second-tier colleges which would both open up opportunities for local students of relatively modest academic standing and provide another income stream. Nanda was no exception in terms of the initial intentions of its leaders, but Nanda's experience has turned out to be somewhat different than that of most other universities. [39]

---

[39] Interview with Zhang Yibin, Vice-President, 22 May 2007.

A hot debate broke out in around 2000 over whether Nanda should adopt the strategy of merger in response to the massification policy as encouraged by the central government. One faction took the perspective that there were various models for higher educational development, and merger was not necessarily the best. Nanda should enhance its strength by optimizing the management of its resources and recruiting talented professors who could further raise its scholarly status. The other faction critically examined Nanda's situation and made the point that it would be very difficult to develop successful programs in such important areas as engineering, new technologies and life sciences, without a merger, given Nanda's traditional curricular focus on humanities and basic sciences.

Nanda's leaders then proposed a basic principle for making the decision on merger: whether Nanda should go with a merger or not would depend on whether this would be beneficial to the goal of becoming a highly qualified world-class university. Specifically, it was a question of whether merger would benefit the optimization of programs and the development of cross-disciplinary cooperation, the enhancement of teaching and research, and both efficiency of scale and societal contribution. Based on these guidelines, Nanda decided to merge with the Southeast University, a major polytechnic university that had been established in 1952 on the basis of Nanda's original Faculty of Engineering. As it turned out, Southeast University rejected the merger in the end, after some teaching staff wrote a letter of protest. The reason for their protest was both practical, the desire to keep their independent status, and also political – an unwillingness to become a part of Nanda. Decision-makers in both universities had to be careful and maintain the stability of their institutions. Nanda thus became the only university among the first nine top institutions in the Project 98/5 that has not gone through a merger.[40]

The story of establishing a second-tier college is also complicated. As explained by Qian Zhong, the Vice-Dean of Nanda's Jinling College, second-tier colleges were established in Chinese universities for two major reasons. On the one hand, the Ministry of Education called on universities to establish second-tier colleges to meet the sudden demand for higher education expansion. On the other hand, setting up second-tier colleges enabled universities to earn additional student fees and sub-

---

[40] Wang Dezi, Gong Fang and Mao Rong (eds.), *Nanjing Daxue Bainian Shi* (*The Centennial History of Nanjing University*) (Nanjing: Nanjing University Press, 2002), pp.534-535.

sidize the tight annual budget provided by the government. Nanda's leaders felt they had to respond to this official call from the government, and they established the Jinling College (金陵學院) in 1999 but soon suspended it, due to limited learning facilities. It was reopened and developed as an independent college in 2004. Unlike many other leading universities such as the Huazhong University of Science and Technology (Chapter 8) and Xiamen University (Chapter 5), and the Huazhong University of Science and Technology (Chapter 8), Nanda adopted a conservative approach from the very beginning. One main reason was that Nanda's leaders wanted to focus on the promotion and enhancement of its core teaching and research, rather than the expansion of the student population on campus. Another reason was fear of the workload implications and of losing control of teaching quality.[41]

Given these concerns, the Jinling College has strictly limited its student recruitment. There were only 500 students enrolled in 1999, and then after a five year hiatus 300 were enrolled in 2004, 700 in 2005 and 1000 in 2006. In 2008, the Jinling College planned to recruit 2000 new students, with 1600 of them from Jiangsu Province. Although the student body has been increasing in recent years, it remains small compared to most other second-tier colleges. According to Qian Zhong, the Vice-Dean of Jinling College, Nanda did not plan to make much money through this initiative but rather to allow it gradually to become an independent institution.[42] His concerns, which reflected those of the Nanda leadership, were over the possible loss of control over teaching quality, in a situation of investment by a third party outside of the university, and the inequity of enrolling students at Nanda who had far lower marks on the National Higher Education Entrance Examinations than the regular Nanda students.

Faculty and Issues of Teaching and Research

The Faculty Profile

Alongside the changing curricula, Nanda's faculty has also changed dramatically since the early 1990s. Most striking in terms of the changes in the structure of Nanda's faculty contingent was the rapid growth of the number of full professors, as shown in Table 4.1.

---

[41] Interview with Qian Zhong, the Vice-Dean of Nanda's Jinling College, 23 May 2007.
[42] *Ibid.*

Table 4.1: Statistics on Faculty and Teacher-Student Ratios

	1990	1995	2000	2005
Full professors	123	295	397	654
Associate professors	446	645	494	592
Assistant professors	698	234	174	339
Teaching assistants	354	146	132	140
Teacher-student ratio	1:4.5	1:7.0	1:13.1	1:13.5

The average growth rate of full professors was 79.7% while the period from 2000 to 2005 saw the fastest increase of full professors in terms of numbers. This was partly due to many recent openings for full professors who have been recruited as leading scholars in new cross-disciplinary programs spurred by Nanda's new mission. The numbers of associate professors experienced an increase from 1990 to 1995, but a cutback from 1995 to 2000, and a moderate growth from 2000 to 2005. A similar trend was found for the changes in the numbers of assistant professors, while teaching assistants saw a continuous decline over this period, showing the overall upgrading of the faculty contingent. In addition, the student-faculty ratio rose from 1:4.5 in 1990 to 1:7.0 in 1995, then increased dramatically to 1:13.1 in 2000 when the massification took place, but remained at the same level in 2005. These statistics show that Nanda has a strong commitment to building a high profile for its faculty and this is also evidenced by the rapid growth of PhD holders, from 110 in 1995 to 390 in 2000, and 946 or 55% of all faculty in 2005. While there has been a significant rise in the student-faculty ratio, it remains low compared to most other universities in our study, showing the strong commitment of Nanda's leaders to academic excellence.

Issues of Teaching and Research

The focus group meeting with six faculty members and a separate interview with a full professor gave insight into their perspectives on Nanda's institutional transformation, particularly on the changes in teaching and research, in the context of China's move to mass higher education.

Since the radical expansion policy implemented in 1999, some critics have asserted that almost all Chinese universities have lost control of their teaching quality due to the radical growth in the student population. Nanda serves as an exception, with its determination to control the growth rate in enrollment of undergraduate students.[43] To give a vivid example, one professor mentioned that the Department of Computer Science and Technology decreased its admission of students after the expansion policy had been implemented in 1999. It preferred to keep a reasonably sized student body within the capacity that its faculty contingent could handle in order to maintain teaching quality. The class sizes were kept to a maximum of 80 students by this department.[44] This was not an easy decision since the department would have benefited from the additional tuition fees of an expanded student body, at a time when the demand for IT specialists in China's job market was particularly high. Several professors in the focus group took themselves as personal examples, noting that they had not experienced a higher teaching workload after the expansion. Rather, they had been given considerable pressure to get involved in research and publish their findings.[45]

Another good example of Nanda's elite model can be seen in the importance attached to general education. This reflects the vision of Nanda's leaders, and it was mentioned by several professors. Nanda's general education was pioneered by Kuang Yaming who established a core required course in Chinese language which incorporated the learning of literature, culture and morality. With the continued efforts of later Presidents, Qu Qinyue and Jiang Shusheng, Nanda has been very proactive in general education which aims at providing a broad and stimulating learning environment for students.

A committee was established in the 1990s by Nanda's leaders, including the Director of the Office of Teaching Affairs and four leading professors in the humanities, to plan, organize and supervise the overall activities of general education on campus. Since the 1990s, the proportion of elective courses has made up a growing share in Nanda's teaching plan for students, from 31% in 1990, to 33% in 1995, 35% in 2000 and 38% in 2005. A strong foundation in general education has been guaranteed by a registration requirement for all students. They have to complete at least four courses in the humanities, four courses in social or natural sciences, and one more course in any one of these three broad areas

---

[43] Meeting with Faculty Focus Group, 24 May 2007; Also, this assertion was consonant with that of our interview with Zhang Yibin, Nanda's Vice-President, 22 May 2007.
[44] Meeting with Faculty Focus Group, 24 May 2007.
[45] Ibid.

before graduation.[46] In 1996, the Art and Culture Education Center was founded as an independent teaching unit to enhance Nanda's general education. This center has offered more than 40 courses in the liberal arts to Nanda's students over a decade. Additionally, a regular academic forum for general education has been offered for more than a decade, and a total of 348 university-wide lectures have been organized for undergraduate students from 1996 to 2006. Several professors commented on the value of these efforts to promote general education through electives and the ongoing academic forum, noting that it had broken down the narrowly specialist character of traditional subject areas and widened students' perspectives.[47]

Students' Experiences

The focus group interview with six students gave some insight into their perspectives on Nanda's institutional transformation, particularly the changes in their learning experiences and civic participation on campus and in the wider society. All of the six students were in the final year of their studies, with a female student who majored in public administration, two females in educational technology and a fourth in mathematics, also one male student from geography and another from business management.

Learning Experiences under Nanda's Ethos and Tradition

Most of the students were familiar with Nanda's motto of "sincerity with aspiration, perseverance with integrity". Two students noted that Nanda's campus was a very quiet and reflective learning environment where students could focus on their studies. Professors worked diligently but in a low key way, and this style had a great influence on students' learning spirit. One of the women students spoke of how she has been able to study with a calm and focused heart, without distraction or negative influences from the outside, and she felt that this was largely because of Nanda's traditional learning spirit and culture. Another added that the reason for students and teachers being able to focus on study or research may have been linked to its location in Nanjing which was neither a

---

[46]Gong Fang (ed.), *Suzhi Jiaoyu: Nanjing Daxue De Sikao Yu Shijian* (*Quality Education: Ideas and Practices of Nanjing University*) (Nanjing: Nanjing University Press, 2005), pp.61-66.

[47] Meeting with faculty focus group, 24 May 2007.

political center like Beijing nor an economic center like Shanghai.[48]

While some students were concerned about what they saw as the rather conservative character of Nanda's campus culture, other students had different perspectives. A male student who majored in business management shared some examples of his personal learning experiences in the Business School. There were many opportunities for communication with the wider world and most of the teaching content involved case studies from the business world, something that kept his eyes open all the time. Another woman student who majored in mathematics supported his view, and added that she benefited more from Nanda's general education programs than from what she had learnt in her specific area of mathematics.[49]

These views from students offer a kind of confirmation of Nanda's success in enhancing its institutional ethos, by linking tradition and culture to new ideas, as explained in our interview with Vice-President Zhang Yibin.

Participation in Civil Society

There were some students who believed that Nanda's ethos and tradition gave them a unique experience of freedom and democracy. A woman student from the Department of Administration talked about how greatly she had been impressed by Nanda's freedom of speech. This was something she had never encountered before she came to study at Nanda. After a few years on the Nanda campus as a student majoring in political science, she observed proudly that her professors often spoke out freely in class, expressing opinions that were highly sensitive about reforms needed in the current political system.[50] Her experiences may reflect an atmosphere going back to the time shortly after the Cultural Revolution when an influential article, which stirred up a hot nationwide debate on "Practice as the Sole Criterion for Assessing Truth", was written by a Nanda professor, to challenge the doctrine of the "two whatevers", as noted earlier.

Some students also expressed appreciation for how Nanda's leaders allowed them to participate in institutional governance. For example, Nanda provides an official online platform, the bulletin board system

---

[48] *Ibid.*
[49] *Ibid.*
[50] *Ibid.*

(BBS), for students to practice democratic participation conveniently, and the administration is committed to listening to their voices on issues related to Nanda's reform and development. Both the student focus group and the faculty focus group identified the Flagpole as a symbol of Nanda's spirit of freedom and democracy.

Students are passionate and even aggressive about civic participation on campus and in the wider community. Nanda provides various channels and opportunities to encourage student civic participation, while students have also created some autonomous organizations of their own. Basically, there are three types of activity relating to civic participation, according to the student focus group. The first type can be characterized as official activities organized by the Nanda leadership or the Chinese government and attracting broad student participation, such as blood donation, and social service for disadvantaged groups. The

Photo 4.3: The Flagpole, first erected in 1935 shortly before the Anti-Japanese War and relocated to the South Schoolyard in 1964, is a symbol of freedom and democracy on the Nanda campus.

second type is participation in activities organized by professors and student counselors, usually special social projects which are led by professors. The third type is activities organized by groups of students who share the same interest, such as social investigation, sports clubs or other special interests groups. These student-organized activities usually take place in the summer or winter vacation seasons.[51]

When asked how popular these activities are among students, most of those in the student focus group observed that many students have had some experience of participation. Moreover, there is plenty of information available on Nanda's student BBS about these activities, so that students can easily make decisions about participation.

The motivations for student participation are multiple. One major reason is that most students have a high sense of social responsibility and a passion for civic participation. Some explained that this was the best and most direct way to contribute to society drawing on their specialized knowledge, while others saw it as a practical way to accumulate social experience or to develop their personal interests. The student from the Department of Administration gave an example of her personal experience in co-organizing a project involving social investigation in an inland rural area together with four other classmates. It turned out that the business world had a high demand for this kind of social skill when recruiting new employees, and she benefited a lot personally from that activity when hunting for a job.[52]

Nanda's students also show considerable interest in getting familiar with the concept of civil society, and most of the focus group recognized that civil society has been unfolding and developing in the Chinese context, although the concept originally came from the West. One student reported how she got to gradually understand the concept of civil society through investigating the development of associations of professionals that had emerged in China's marketization and privatization process. Other students also indentified many types of civil society organization in Chinese society, such as teachers' associations, professional organizations, environmental organizations and sports clubs. It was obvious these students had been doing a lot of thinking about this concept.

---

[51] *Ibid.*
[52] *Ibid.*

Experiences in the Expansion

Students had dissimilar and sometimes contradictory perspectives on the issue of how Nanda's expansion had affected their lives, depending on the different situations in their respective departments. The student from the Department of Mathematics reported that she was in a class of 80, and communication with faculty was very limited. When giving courses in a big classroom, professors had to use a microphone, and they usually left immediately after the class was finished. Furthermore, they did not personally know many students in their department. The student from the Business School had a similar experience of large classes and little access to faculty. But the other four students in the focus group had a completely different sense of the situation. They felt there had been very little change since the expansion in 1999, and they had individualized guidance from and plenty of communication with their professors. It is obvious that the expansion policy did not affect all the programs at Nanda in the same way.

Conclusion

With a unique tradition and an ethos that has been thoughtfully and consciously developed, Nanda has shown how it was possible to overcome the political disadvantages of its history and achieve a high national status, through the persisting efforts of its leaders and faculty over the recent three decades. With a vision that linked the past to the future and critical strategies for the promotion of excellence in scholarship and teaching, as well as early internationalization, Nanda was able to regain its status as a leading comprehensive university. The Nanda story vividly illustrates how an outstanding institution was put into a disadvantaged political position for around thirty years, and how it finally redeemed its past through an intense focus on striving for academic excellence on the basis of its own strengths. Today, Nanda is aiming to become a world-class comprehensive research university with a global vision for academic innovation. The fact that it has been able to reach its present status also indicates the revival of values from China's traditional civil service examination system in contemporary China, with proven academic excellence being given respect in a new kind of meritocracy.

Nanda people, however, are not satisfied with the striking achievements made so far, as became evident in one of our interviews. Presidents such as Kuang Yaming and Qu Qinyue proposed a three-phase path for Nanda to achieve academic excellence. The first step was to provide evidence of high quality in scholarship, as indicated by academic papers published in the SCI journals, something achieved in the 1990s when Nanda led Chinese higher education for seven consecutive years. The second step was to move further upward to a level of superior scholarship. The third step was to make a great leap with influential scholarship and nurture master faculty who would become China's first winners of the Nobel Prize.[53] Nanda has set its sights on nothing less than this hoped for future achievement, with the view that only then will it have redeemed its past.

---

[53] Interview with Gong Fang, Director of Nanda's Institute of Higher Educational Research, 24 May 2007.

5
Xiamen University – A Southeastern Outlook

Ruth HAYHOE and Qiang ZHA, with XIE Zuxu

Xiamen University (Xiada for short) is located on the Southeastern coast of China, looking out towards Taiwan to the east and the Philippines, Malaysia and Indonesia to the south. While this is an open coastal city, there is a sense of geographical isolation from the rest of China, due to the mountainous terrain of Fujian province. Geography has thus been an important factor in shaping its history. In this chapter we will begin with an overview of its historical development, then sketch out the main changes that have taken place in student numbers and curricular development over the period from 1995 to the present. From there we consider the vision of its leaders and their strategic decisions relating to internationalization, merger and the establishment of a second-tier college. This is followed by a discussion of financial issues, and then the views of faculty members and students on the experience of the move to mass higher education are presented. The chapter closes with an attempt to define the new ethos that is emerging.

In our talks with two vice presidents and with the faculty and student focus groups, we found there was a strong sense of history, and frequent references were made to past presidents of Xiamen University, and to the many crises and struggles it had been through in its history. These were clearly inspirational for current members of the university. Thus it is appropriate to begin this chapter with a brief overview of the university's history as a reference point for understanding its present ethos.

History and Context
The one person who has done most to nurture the spirit of Xiada was Chen Jiageng (Tan Kah Kee 陳嘉庚), the adventurous and inspiring entrepreneur who created Fujian province's first modern university in 1921. He had been born in Jimei, a small town near Xiamen, in 1874, and followed his father to Singapore at the age of ten, becoming a successful businessman by the age of 30. He could not forget the ongoing poverty

and isolation of his home province, and came to believe education was the answer to bringing prosperity. Beginning in 1904, he established a system of schools from kindergarten through primary to secondary, as well as libraries and science centres. He particularly emphasized the education of girls and insisted on full co-education in all of his schools. It soon became evident to him that without a university, there would never be enough qualified teachers for the schools he was founding. Thus he made a public commitment of one million *yuan* for the creation of Xiamen University in 1919 – on a large campus overlooking the Pacific Ocean. The foundation stone was laid on May 9, 1921, a day known as National Shame Day in memory of the indignities imposed by Japan's 21 Demands of 1915. Patriotism and national self strengthening were thus core goals of the new university.[1] Chen remained chairman of the university's board for many years, and it became a respected private university with Colleges of Arts, Sciences, Law, Commerce and Education.

A War-time Campus

With Japan's full-scale invasion of China beginning in 1937, Xiamen University had to move to Changting, a village in the hinterland of Fujian province where it was able to avoid interference from the invading Japanese army. However, finances were a problem, since Chen's business interests had suffered during this period, and he was unable to continue his support. Under these circumstances, Xiada accepted the opportunity of becoming publicly funded by the Nationalist government. A new president, Sa Bendong (薩本棟), appointed by the government, supervised the move inland and kept teaching and research alive over the difficult years from 1937 to 1945.

This was the only public university which remained open east of the main rail line between Canton and Beijing; thus many displaced students came from nearby provinces and new programs were developed in response to war-time needs in areas such as electrical engineering, aeronautics and accounting. After the war ended in 1945, Xiada moved back to its ocean-side campus in Xiamen and Wang Deyao (汪德耀), a biologist who had been dean of science, took up the presidency. With Colleges of Arts, Sciences, Engineering, Law and Commerce, and a

---

[1] Ruth Hayhoe, *Portraits of Influential Chinese Educators* (Hong Kong: Comparative Education Research Centre, The University of Hong Kong and Springer, 2006), pp.146-147.

student body of 1,350 by 1947, Xiada had become an established public university. Its two programs of greatest strength reflected both its history and its geographical location – marine biology and economics.[2]

New Directions after 1949

With the total reorganization of higher education that took place after the Communist Revolution, Xiada found itself disadvantaged in a number of ways. From the perspective of geographical location, the new Communist government had reorganized higher education along the lines of the six major military regions, and Xiamen found itself in the southern part of the East China region, distinctly separate from sister institutions in neighboring Guangdong province, which had been incorporated into the Central South region. As Guangdong was required to look north to Wuhan for direction, Fujian looked to Shanghai, and Xiada was the only comprehensive university south of Shanghai and Nanjing in the region. Given the hostilities over Taiwan, and the insecurities of the Cold War, the new government was focusing its attention on central and northern China, and no funding was available for developing Xiamen University. Rather, many of its most attractive programs, especially the programs in engineering which had been built up with great difficulty during the war, were moved north to be combined with newly established engineering universities in Nanjing and Beijing.

Its location close to Taiwan, and its geographical isolation, gave it a low profile in the new Soviet-influenced higher education system of the 1950s. Fortunately, however, a dynamic new president, Wang Yanan (王亞南), was appointed. Wang was an economist who was determined to maintain and build upon Xiada's strengths, particularly in the fields of economics, marine biology and education. There was great pressure for economics to be moved into a specialist institute of finance and economics, as happened in most other parts of the country, but Wang succeeded in keeping this field at Xiada and building upon it. The programs in economics and finance from the two former missionary universities in the provincial capital of Fuzhou were combined with Xiada in 1953.

While the Faculty of Education was moved to Fuzhou to form the basis for a new normal university under the reorganization of faculties and departments, Wang still insisted on Xiada maintaining a strong educational mandate and kept enough courses and education specialists to

---

[2] *Ibid.* pp.148-149.

prepare students of the sciences and humanities for careers in secondary school teaching. This was unique among China's comprehensive universities of the time, which had departments only in basic sciences and humanities, along Soviet lines, and no education programs. Wang also gave support to the development of higher education as a new field of study, under Professor Pan Maoyuan, with the result that Xiada is now a national leader in higher education research.[3]

Xiamen University was also in a position to reconnect to its founder, Chen Jiageng, during the 1950s. Chen was invited by Mao Zedong to attend the inauguration of the new government on Tiananmen Square in October of 1949 and returned to live in Xiamen in 1952, subsequently serving in several honorary posts, including Chairman of the Overseas Chinese Affairs Committee and Member of the Central People's Government Committee (中央人民政府委員). He died in Beijing in 1961, and his grave is on the Xiada campus, close to the ocean.

Given this important historical link to Southeast Asia, President Wang Yanan supported ongoing links with Southeast Asian countries, nurtured research related to the region, and built upon the university's traditional strengths in economics and marine studies. Xiamen University was thus able to survive and quietly build its academic reputation as a comprehensive university. Being geographically remote from Shanghai and Beijing may have been disadvantageous in terms of attracting financial support, but it was beneficial in times of intense political struggle, such as the Great Leap Forward period of 1958 and the Cultural Revolution of 1966 to 1976. While Xiada suffered setbacks during these periods, they were relatively minor compared to what was happening to universities in Beijing and Shanghai.

Only after Deng Xiaoping came to power, however, did Xiada begin to experience its geographical location as a beneficial factor in its development. In 1984, Xiamen was made one of four open cities, with special conditions to encourage foreign investment, and its economy began to develop rapidly. In 1986, Xiada was able to establish a School of Graduate Studies. In 1993 it gained support from the Ministry of Education in Beijing and the city of Xiamen to be included in Project 21/1, and subsequently to become a member of Project 98/5 in 2001. With the dynamics of the open door and China's emerging role as a global superpower, Xiada is well situated to embrace the opportunities of massifi-

---

[3] *Ibid.* pp.157-160.

cation, and to build upon the strengths of its own unique traditions.

Curricular Development and the Growth of Student Enrollment

Students and Faculty

In 1995, Xiamen University had a modest enrollment of 7,714 undergraduate students, which grew to 10,141 by 2000 and 17,797 by 2005. Over this period, female representation increased from 34% in 1995, to 42% in 2000 and 44% in 2005. The balance of subject areas changed in favor of science and engineering, with 36% of students in 1995, growing to 43% by 2005. The percentage of enrollments in social sciences dropped from 41% to 35%, and in humanities from 22% to 17% over the same period. Meanwhile the increase in graduate students was even more rapid, from 1,269 in 1995, to 2,730 in 2000 and 14,236 in 2005. International student numbers grew from 161 in 1995 to 314 in 2000 and about 1000 in 2005, including students from Taiwan, Hong Kong and Macao. Thus by 2005, there were over 33,000 students in regular programs, plus another 8000 students in the Jiageng College, the second-tier college which had been established on a new suburban campus in 2003. In 2007, the university's published recruitment plan offered 2,623 places to undergraduate students from all provinces of China, while reserving 1,760 or 40% of the 4,383 places for local students from Fujian province.[4]

Faculty numbers grew also, with 2,282 teaching faculty by 2005, and a teacher student ratio in regular programs of around 1:15, higher if one considers that forty percent of the teaching at the second-tier college is done by core faculty. Fifty eight percent of the teaching faculty held the title of associate professor or above in 2005, and there were 458 faculty members qualified to supervise doctoral students. It was clearly a very rapid process of expansion, accompanied by an upgrading of faculty qualifications and a reasonable increase in faculty student ratios.

Curricular Change

The story of curricular change over this period illustrates the transition from the Soviet model of the comprehensive university, limited to basic disciplines in the pure sciences and arts, to a multiversity, with a broad range of applied fields, relating to the new areas of employment that

---

[4] *2007 Nian Benkesheng Baokao Zhinan* (*2007 Guide for Undergraduate Student Enrollment*) (Xiamen University, 2007) pp.4-6.

have burgeoned in recent years. Thus the College of Science and Mechanical/Electrical Engineering has a Department of Physics, which includes also physics education, plus Departments of Mechanical Design, Manufacture and Automation, Measurement Technology and Instrumentation, Electronic Information, Micro-electronics (est. 2002) and Aeronautical Engineering (est. 2004). The College of Mathematics has a Department of Pure and Applied Mathematics as well as a Department of Information and Computing. The College of Chemistry has a Department of Chemistry and Chemistry Education, as well as Departments of Chemical Engineering, Materials Science (est. 2001), Biological Engineering (est. 2002) and Biochemistry (est. 2003). The College of Biology has Departments of Biology, Biotechnology, Ecology (est. 2002) and Biological Informatics (est. 2004). One can see here the development of a wide range of applied fields on the basis of historically strong Departments of Physics, Mathematics, Chemistry and Biology.

In addition, there is a newly developed College of Civil Engineering, with Departments of Civil Engineering (est. 2000) and Construction (est. 2004). There is also a College of Information Science and Technology with Departments of Automation, Communications Engineering, Computer Science and Technology and Electronic Information Engineering. Xiada's original strength in marine studies has blossomed into a College of Oceanic and Environmental Science, with Departments of Marine Science, Marine Technology and Environmental Studies. There is also a College of Medicine, with Departments of Clinical Medicine, Pharmacy, Chinese Medicine (est. 2004) and Preventive Medicine (est. 2004). Given this array of applied scientific and professional areas, it is not surprising to see the number of undergraduate students in the sciences increasing from 2,808 in 1995, or 36% of all enrollments, to 8061, or 43% in 2005.

Changes in the social science curricula reflected a similar orientation towards applied fields with the College of Economics having Departments of Economics, Banking, Statistics, Public Finance, International Economics and Trade, Urban Management, Financial Engineering (est. 2002) and Insurance (est. 2002) and the College of Management Science having seven departments, from human resources management to accounting, tourism management and electronic commerce (est. 2001). There is also a College of Public Administration with four departments, including a newly established Department of Sociology (est. 2003), and a College of Law. These are all areas which either were not taught before the period of reform and opening up, or were limited to centrally controlled institutes of finance and politics.

Similar patterns of innovation can be seen in the College of Humanities, with traditional Departments of History, Archaeology, Philosophy and Chinese Language and Literature (including education) being joined by newer Departments of Journalism, Advertising, Broadcasting, Chinese as a Foreign Language (est. 2002) and Drama and Filmmaking (est. 2004). In the College of Foreign Languages, German was added to Departments of English, Japanese, French and Russian in 2006.

Overall, one can see a notable diversification of subject areas towards new applied fields. One can also see the persistence of patterns put in place in 1952, with core strengths in the basic disciplines of knowledge, and with the particular contribution made by the first post-revolution president, Wang Yanan, who insisted on maintaining and developing the field of economics, in face of a national policy that put all economic studies under central political control in institutes of finance and economics administered by the Ministry of Finance. Wang also had the vision to maintain educational studies for students of physics, chemistry and Chinese language and literature, in order that they might be prepared for secondary school teaching. There is now additionally a Graduate School of Education Science, which has higher education as its leading field, with the only national key program in higher education in the whole country located here, as well as programs in examination studies, educational psychology, and private education.

Vision and Strategic Direction

Vision and Mission

From our interviews with Xiada leaders, we did not get the sense of a focused process of vision and mission building so much as the emergence of new directions on the basis of a deeply rooted historical self understanding. Thus the motto selected for the university by its founder, Chen Jiageng, in 1921, was restored in recent years, reflecting both the idealism and the patriotism of its early history: "Tireless self-strengthening and a commitment to the highest excellence" (自強不息，止於至善).

In a recent speech about the Xiada spirit, President Zhu Chongshi, a prominent economist, made the point that Xiamen University must choose an elite path to excellence, adapting to the requirements of the market economy yet at the same time deliberately selecting a higher path than that of the market. President Zhu's definition of elite was of a group with lofty ideals, a commitment to social progress, and a wide range of expertise and knowledge.[5]

While Xiada had been a national university throughout the period from the early 1950s to the 1980s, with all of its funding coming from the Ministry of Education, it had begun to pay attention to local concerns and needs early and so developed good relations with the provincial government of Fujian, doing a lot of training in economics and law on a commissioned basis. When Project 21/1 was launched in 1993, the city of Xiamen provided all of the needed funds for Xiada to enter the project, a reflection of its early prosperity and its pride in having a major national university. When Project 98/5 was launched, Xiada was admitted into the second round in 2001, and again the Xiamen city government provided the funding to make this possible.

Strategic Decisions on Merger and Expansion

Two of the important decisions that had to be made by university leaders related to the question of merger, and the establishment of a second-tier college. On merger, several leaders told us that this was not a practical possibility for Xiada. As the only major university in the city of Xiamen, there was no suitable partner to merge with. The main merger that did take place was between Jimei University, a low key local institution and several other sub-degree institutions. In retrospect, university leaders were proud of the fact that they had an unbroken history and identity, and were glad to have avoided the many difficult adjustments that went along with the mergers that happened elsewhere.

The direction of development for Xiada has nevertheless been towards becoming a fully comprehensive university. While most other major universities gained their medical schools through a merger, Xiada launched its own College of Medicine in 1996, with funding from the Xiamen city government, which felt the need for a local medical school. The other field which had been missing in Xiada's curriculum since the 1950s was engineering, and through the 1990s, a whole range of engineering fields were launched, as seen in the curricular overview above. Generally, the principle was to build applied fields on the basis of strong disciplinary areas. Thus engineering was established on the basis of physics and chemistry and management on the basis of economics. Also there was a focused effort to raise the quality of selected disciplines to the

---

[5] *China Youth Daily*, 28 September 2007.

status of "key fields" recognized by the national ministry of education. In the first instance, Xiada was able to get recognition for seven key fields, including higher education, and the numbers have now grown to 13, with five in economics and management, one in education, one in history, one in international law, and five in science fields.[6]

Another significant curricular development area has been the revival of a cross-disciplinary Research Institute for National Studies (國學院). It had a history going back to the 1920s, when a number of famous intellectuals were associated with it, including Lu Xun (魯迅), Lin Yutang (林語堂) and Gu Jiegang (顧頡剛). Its restoration in recent years has signaled a wish on the university's part to develop significant research into Chinese history and culture, as a way of balancing the increasing emphasis on international engagement. One of the figures who has much to contribute to this effort is the Dean of Education, Professor Liu Haifeng, an educational historian who has focused his research on the history of China's imperial examination system. With the recent 30 year anniversary of the restoration of national entrance examinations after the end of the Cultural Revolution, Professor Liu has been extremely active in speaking and writing on lessons that can be learned from China's traditional civil service examination system.

Setting up a Second-tier College

If Xiada was able to avoid merger and broader its curriculum through a more gradual and generic route, the possibility of establishing a second-tier college was viewed positively, and considerable energy and planning went into the development of the Jiageng College, named after Chen Jiageng, on its new suburban campus. Land for the new campus was donated by the town of Zhangzhou, where it is located, a distance of several hours travel by boat and road from the main campus. The buildings were built with bank loans, and there was a sense of pride that the whole project had been efficiently managed under the supervision of the President, who is an economist. In the eyes of the vice-president for finance, the development of this new campus was one of the two greatest achievements of the university in recent years, the second being avoidance of a merger![7]

The second-tier college has a total of 8,000 students, with an intake

---

[6] Interview with Liu Haifeng, Dean of Education, Xiamen University, 23 May 2007.
[7] Interview with Li Jianyou, Vice President, 28 May 2007.

of 2,000 each year,[8] and is financially independent but does not contribute to the university's overall income at present. It is permitted to charge fees of 18,000 *yuan* per year to the local students it attracts, in contrast to fees that range between 5,600 and 8,000 *yuan* for regular undergraduate students. The college facilities, including classrooms, sport and administrative buildings as well as hostels, are purpose built for the college, while they share the library with regular undergraduate students of Xiada, who spend the first two of their four years on the new campus, and then move to the central campus for years three and four.

While many people have interpreted the development of second-tier colleges as a revenue generating step, Xiada leaders insisted that their motive was not financial, but rather a sense of responsibility to Fujian province and their local community. It would be some time before there would be any financial benefit to the university from this development, but they felt it was incumbent on them to contribute to major efforts being made by the province to expand higher education access to students who are not qualified for entry to its regular programs. This is an expression of Xiada's increased sense of connection to the local community, which balances their role as a public university recruiting students nationwide.

Teaching and Learning Issues

If localization has been an element in Xiada's development in recent years, so has internationalization, and the vice-president responsible for this area, Professor Wu Shinong, had been in charge of teaching and learning until he took up this role late in 2006. In his responsibility for teaching and learning, he expressed concern about the decision of having undergraduate students spend their first two years on a remote campus, since he felt it was important to the development of the university's culture to have students of all four years interacting with one another.

Other points he made relating to teaching and learning issues were a strongly expressed criticism of the trend towards a general education curriculum in Chinese universities. He felt this was not appropriate to China's level of industrialization and had been based on ill-considered efforts to copy American undergraduate curricular patterns. At most, not

---

[8] By 2007 enrollments were already rising, with a planned total of 10,800 students for the autumn of that year. Interview with Gao Zhonghua, Student Affairs Office, Zhang Zhou campus, 27 May 2007.

more than 25% of China's universities should move in this direction, since employment opportunities required graduates with well developed profiles in specialist fields of knowledge, particularly in areas such as engineering and management, in his view.

When asked what he thought about China's Ministry of Education policy of encouraging universities to find one close partner to emulate abroad, he replied that it would be inappropriate for a Chinese university to model itself after any Western model. Rather they needed to make their own curricular development decisions, based on their strengths and capabilities, also on the needs of Chinese society.[9]

Internationalization Efforts

On Xiada's international profile, and internationalization efforts, Vice President Wu began by noting that Xiada had many, many agreements with universities around the world, but most of them were simply pieces of paper, with little concrete activity. There was thus an effort to identify a small number of regions, countries and institutions where they could develop worthwhile cooperative activities, and move beyond their historic focus on Southeast Asia. Universities where they have concrete cooperation include Cornell, where they have a collaborative research centre in economics and two doctoral students are accepted every year. This relationship had been fostered by a Xiada graduate now teaching at Cornell. Another significant relationship is with the Ecole Normal Supérieure in Paris, where there is a key laboratory in chemistry, supported by the governments of both China and France, with research faculty going back and forth on a regular basis. These two relationships exemplify their policy of careful selection of appropriate partnerships which will be beneficial to both sides.

A significant initiative at the university level has been the creation of a network of seven research universities in 2004, the Global U7 Consortium, with all located on the ocean or a major sea, including two American universities, the University of Washington, Seattle and the University of Rhode Island, the University of Haifa in Israel, Inha University in Korea, the Royal Melbourne Institute of Technology in Australia, the University of Le Havre in France together with Xiamen University. The idea is to participate in a small and flexible network of universities internationally where they could learn from the experience

---

[9] Interview with Wu Shinong, Vice President, 24 May 2007.

of others and gain international exposure.

On the question of international influences on curricular development, Wu felt that three distinct approaches were called for. In the sciences, it was essential to meet international standards and contribute to global research efforts. He felt chemistry at Xiada is already a strong area, which is benefiting from the research collaboration with France, and marine biology also has considerable strengths, based on its long history. Much more effort is needed in physics and various fields of engineering to reach world standards. In fields such as economics, management and law, however, he saw it as a matter of balancing the attempt to reach world standards with equal attention to indigenous perspectives and content. In areas such as Chinese history, literature and philosophy, they must set their own indigenous standards and seek to present aspects of Chinese civilization to the global community. One of the modalities for this is the establishment of Confucius Institutes around the world. Xiada already has partnerships with ten universities that are hosting Confucius Institutes, including Cardiff University (UK), l'Université de Paris X-Nanterre (France), the University of Trier (Germany), the University of Wrocław (Poland), San Diego State University (USA), Mae Fah Luang University (Thailand), the Middle East Technical University (Turkey), Stellenbosch University (South Africa), Nnamdi Azikiwe University (Nigeria), and the University of Malta (Malta). A few more are in the planning, including sites in Australia, Canada and Europe.

With regard to international students, the majority are still coming for short term non-credit learning experiences, but about 500 are spending more than a year, and doing courses for credit. They have also launched six new masters programs to attract international students, in Chinese studies, history, economics, law, marine management, and chemical engineering. The Ministry of Education gives them forty scholarships each year, to attract excellent international students, and others come on self-paying terms. Most of the six new masters programs are taught in English.

Ethos

When asked about the university's ethos, and the building which represents this best, Vice President Wu had little hesitation in replying that it was the Jiannan Auditorium, a huge structure that seats 4,000, constructed in the 1950s with funding from Chen Jiageng, in typical Southern Fujian or *Minnan* (閩南) style of architecture. The Vice President responsible for finance agreed with this view, also seeing the Jiannan Auditorium as the signature building of the main campus. The building of this structure at a time when there were only about 1,000 students on the campus was a remarkable gesture of faith in the future. Its architectural style gives the whole campus the flavor of a local culture that was always open to the outside world.

Some faculty members at the focus group meeting highlighted the point that the Jiannan Auditorium combines both Western and Chinese architectural styles, and used the metaphor of wearing a Western suit but a Chinese hat. To be specific, the main structural features are Western in style, with large windows, arched doors, and Graeco-Roman pillars. Yet, these features are harmoniously integrated with the upturned roofs and eaves of Chinese palace-style, notably a southern version of that style. Furthermore, the Jiannan Auditorium is linked to four other buildings to form the Jiannan Complex, which has a curved shape and faces the South China Sea. This complex is viewed as embodying a spirit of embracing and holding the world.

Photo 5.1: The Jiannan Auditorium

Financial Profile

Over the decade from 1995 to 2005, Xiada's annual budget had grown from around 90 million to 1.1 billion *yuan*, we were told by the vice president for finance, who had headed the finance office since 1995.[10] One

---

[10] Interview with Li Jianfa, Vice President, 28 May 2007.

of the reasons for this ten-fold expansion has been the move from a line budgeting system, controlled from the Ministry of Education, to a much more autonomous system, in which all aspects of development, including building projects, are included in the budgeting process.

In terms of budget inputs, there have also been dramatic changes. In 1995, 82% of all funding came from the central government, and about 18% from sources such as commissioned training for local organizations and very modest student fees. By 2006, only 55% of Xiada's budget came from government, about half of that from Beijing, and the rest from Fujian province or the city of Xiamen. Student fees, at about 200 million made up close 20% of income, while research funding and training contracts of about 220-300 million made up another 20-25%. A relatively new source of funding has been donations from alumni, and this reached 50 million or 5% of overall income in 2006, an 85th anniversary year for Xiada. Traditions of alumni giving were rooted in Xiada's status as a private university before 1949, and have been revived quite successfully.

This rough sketch of Xiada's financial profile, shows the diversification of income sources that has taken place and the university's greatly increased financial autonomy. At the same time, university leaders emphasized the difficulties they faced in seeking to upgrade the quality of teaching and research and attract excellent faculty, while at the same time dealing with the huge costs of a three fold expansion in undergraduate enrollment over the decade, and an even more dramatic rise in the number of graduate students. While student fees had become an important source of income, there was also a responsibility to ensure that all students who qualified for entry were able to come, and approximately 10% of the yearly budget goes to student aid. About 15% of all students enrolled receive direct financial assistance, and 20% of those coming from inland provinces are given assistance, because of the greater need among these students.

Faculty Perspectives on the Move to Mass Higher Education

Our focus group meeting with faculty members at Xiada lasted for a full morning, and was divided into two parts, with six professors from various fields of the social sciences and humanities meeting with us first, including three women, followed by three professors from mathematics and natural sciences, one of whom was a woman. The fields represented on the social science side were journalism, economics, management, law sociology and Chinese, while on the science side they were chemistry, mathematics and information technology. Our discussions were relatively open-ended, and covered issues of Xiada's mission and vision, teaching and research, participation in decision making, equity issues for students and faculty, and the effects of internationalization.[11]

Core Mission, Research and Teaching

On university mission, most faculty members saw it as a good thing that university leaders were pursuing world class educational quality and status, though they recognized that this would require a long-term process of development. They embraced the kinds of competitive spirit that went along with this pursuit, yet also felt it was important that the university should seek to solve important social problems at the local and national levels. For students, they felt the goal should be to nurture innovative thinkers with creative ability, while they recognized that creativity took different forms in different knowledge areas. It was also important to nurture students who would have a collaborative spirit and the ability to work well with others.

As for themselves as faculty members, they hoped to have the space and time to pursue independent knowledge and research agendas, and to experience the personal enjoyment of scholarship. Several said they were inspired by the stories and the spirit of older professors at Xiada who had left memorable examples of scholarship, such as Chen Jianlong, outstanding mathematician and former president. All expressed their appreciation that the leaders had ensured Xiada's participation in Projects 21/1 and 98/5, which were essential for it to have the resources to move forward. They were also proud that it had managed to do so without a merger.

Of the nine professors, three had come to Xiada relatively recently, from institutions in northern cities of China, while most had been on faculty for a relatively long time, and were from Fujian. One woman professor told her story of growing up in Changting, the county town where Xiada had been during the war, and attending primary and secondary school in the buildings it had left behind when it returned to its ocean-side campus in 1946. She felt she had grown up with the Xiada spirit of resistance and resilience in face of all odds, and could recognize how Xiada's older professors, many of whom had studied or taught in Changting, had kept this spirit alive and created a remarkable legacy that

---

[11] Faculty Focus Group Meeting, 26 May 2007.

was felt by all.

The faculty members who had come to Xiada from northern universities had their own interesting perspectives on the local culture and the Xiada spirit. They felt that university administrators paid much more respect to faculty and students than in the North, where there was a much stronger spirit of bureaucratism and control. At Xiada, there was space for individuality of spirit, and university administrators were seen as seeking to serve faculty rather than dominate them. Research was an increasingly important part of their work, yet they felt they were given time to develop it in a serious way, and publish the results only when they were mature, unlike the situation elsewhere where there was intense pressure for rapid publication of results. They gave the example of a research work conference held by the university leaders in 2005, when a particular project in the sciences was criticized for not getting its results out in a timely manner. The decision was to give them more time, and in the end this project was awarded a high level prize.

At the same time, there were many pressures relating to teaching and research. One younger faculty noted how all new appointments in the College of Economics are scholars with doctoral degrees from abroad, and this puts a natural pressure on scholars with local qualifications to measure up. With regard to teaching loads, the main complaint was over the imbalance of student numbers in different knowledge areas, resulting in very large classes and heavy work pressures in certain highly popular areas. Thus while faculty student ratios in the College of Law were about 1:20, professors in the College of Management functioned with a faculty student ratio of 1:50, and found class size and work pressures a problem. In the College of Mathematics, faculty student ratios were very low, with a small number of students who had a strong interest in the subject making for enjoyable classes. However, mathematics faculty also had to teach general courses for students in the sciences and engineering. Here numbers had risen to such a degree that they had up to 200 students in a class. Multi-media approaches were not felt to be suitable for these basic math courses, yet students in these large classes were not able to see the blackboard and follow the reasoning processes in the traditional pedagogy which they judged to be most appropriate to the subject.

All of the faculty members in the focus group were aware of the development of the second-tier college, though only one or two had taught classes there. They felt it was an important aspect of service to local society, as well as a practical conduit whereby funds from the local community could flow into the university. Would Xiada's founder, Chen Jiageng, have approved of such a venture, given the fact that it is essentially a private arm of the university? They felt he would and that its openness to the concerns of local society expressed his spirit. The one faculty who had taught some courses there said it had been a pleasant experience, and the administrative and support staff had a remarkable attitude of service. The fact that faculty had the opportunity to take on teaching duties there if they wished, but were not pressed to do so, was appreciated by all.

Participation in Decision-making

Faculty felt it was not up to them to participate directly in activities such as the determination of the university's mission and strategy, yet they appreciated the fact that the president has a letterbox, inviting suggestions and comments from faculty, and there is also an electronic bulletin where they can register complaints or ask questions. They also noted that the president had visited every college in order to solicit views from faculty, and this had been a positive process. In most cases faculty met in advance to discuss and consolidate their views and concerns, then selected representatives to sit down with the president for a meeting.

While they did not take part in the university's strategic efforts for inclusion in the 21/1 and 98/5 projects, they had been consulted on the university's early draft of the recent 11th five year plan, and later got feedback before it was submitted to the Ministry of Education in Beijing. One of the strengths of *Minnan* culture, which they saw at work in this effort, was the tendency to give attention to the main lines of national policy while being extremely flexible in its application at the local level.

They mentioned that they have a faculty union, but it plays a minimal role in university decision making. Generally they felt the major way in which their voices could be heard was faculty meetings at department or college levels, where issues such as the imbalance in student numbers in different programs or the competing demands of teaching and research were discussed. As for broader issues of the university's role in society, they felt that certain rights and conditions must exist before universities could be proactive – at present most decisions and directions are set in Beijing. At the same time, they emphasized the strength of faculty student relations in Chinese culture, and the fact that this relationship becomes a channel whereby graduates who rise to leadership positions in society continue to be deeply influenced by their professors.

Equity Issues

One new organization that has had some impact on the campus is a recently established association of women faculty and administrative staff, who are concerned to monitor and promote gender equity on the campus. A particular concern of the association is the employment of women graduates, many of whom face discrimination in the job market. They wish to find ways to counter this, as they feel the law does not give adequate protection to women graduates. They are also monitoring gender representation on the campus, and noted that 41% of all faculty and administrative staff are female at the moment. Generally, female administrative staff are well represented in leadership, with 52% of all section heads being women. By contrast, only 16% of full professors and 10.8% of doctoral supervisors are women, yet these figures are improving every year.

On equity issues for students, faculty felt that enrollment is managed in as equitable a way as possible, with quotas for each province, and the same entry standards for all students. Any student who is able to gain entry will be given assistance, if they are in financial need, so no-one is prevented from taking up their studies for financial reasons. Also students are given greater freedom than in the past, with fewer compulsory activities and more opportunities to take initiatives and manage their own lives on campus. However, the real inequity lies at the earlier levels of education, with enormous gaps between the quality of provision in urban and rural schools, and in coastal and hinterland areas. Faculty felt the most important contribution to equity in recent years was the decision of the central government to invest more in basic education, and seek to improve educational standards throughout the country.

Internationalization and Localization

Faculty members were appreciative of the university leadership's efforts to reach out internationally and create opportunities for their involvement in international activities. They noted that any faculty member wishing to take part in an international conference abroad may apply for up to 20,000 *yuan* each year from university funds to cover the costs, while 5,000 *yuan* is available for conferences within China. Through Xiamen University's participation in the Global U7 Consortium, there are many opportunities for both faculty and student participation, to the degree that graduate students often feel under pressure to go abroad, when some would rather stay at Xiada where they are confident that can complete their research work on time. Faculty also feel under pressure to take up opportunities for international experience, such as a recent program of study in England intended to equip them for teaching in English in the new masters programs for international students. Generally younger faculty take up these opportunities with enthusiasm, and are open to adopting new teaching methods and new approaches to research, whereas older faculty are more set in their ways and somewhat reluctant to disrupt their settled patterns of teaching and research. All appreciated the university's recent policy of providing a sabbatical for faculty every five years, but none of those in the focus group had yet taken this up.

Generally, one felt a strong sense of local identity and even passion among this group of Xiada faculty members. Their lives as faculty on the Xiada campus were such that they did not have a strong pull to go abroad, though they recognized the value of international linkages and cooperation. They had strong attachments to the university's history and a high degree of awareness of influential scholars and leaders of the past, with figures such as Chen Jiageng, Sa Bendong, Wang Yanan, Chen Jianlong, Lu Jiaxi[12] and Cai Chiren[13] being mentioned during our conversation. There was also a strong sense of the value of Chinese traditions, particular aesthetic traditions of art, literature and music.

Students should be taught to appreciate Confucian values of education but also learn to be critical in thinking through the relevance of Confucianism to the present times. The re-establishment of an Institute for National Studies was regarded very positively by faculty, as a centre for critical reflection on the traditions. They also felt that more attention should be paid to the history of science in China, since traditional science had never been a part of the imperial examination system, but had developed to a high level through the creativity of ordinary people.

The liveliest part of the focus group meeting came when Xiada's campus architecture was discussed. Science Faculty made the point that the main administration building, with its five sections, beautifully illustrated the idea of a comprehensive university, and was an exemplary piece of *Minnan* architecture in the harmonious way in which it integrated Western and Chinese values and ideas. This ability to integrate Western and Chinese features effectively was attributed to the long

---

[12] Lu Jiaxi was a professor of chemistry at Xiada, who later became President of the Chinese Academy of Sciences and had a nationwide influence on the field.

[13] Cai Chiren was a professor of chemistry and former dean of the College of Chemistry who had returned from the United States.

emigration history of the region, which goes back to the 16th century. In addition, most buildings on the Xiada campus do not stand alone, but several tend to form a complex, connected by long covered corridors. This was originally for the sake of convenience in the often wet weather in the region, but it is also interpreted as a sign of cooperation and teamwork. In the case of the main administration building, it is a complex of five buildings facing a lake on the campus.

Photo 5.2: The Main Administration Building at Xiamen University

Student Perspectives on the Move to Mass Higher Education

The student focus group we met with was made up of six undergraduate students, in their third year, three men and three women, from the fields of economics, marine biology, management, English, chemical engineering and communications. In addition we had a lengthy conversation with a Counselor and Youth League leader who worked on the new campus and was responsible for student organizations. During our half day visit to the new campus, we were impressed by the teaching buildings, the library, the sports facilities, including a large swimming pool, and the student dormitories, which were formed into a kind of student village. On another side of the campus were the teaching buildings and dormitories of the Jiageng campus, close enough that students from the two institutions could intermingle, but still keep their own separate identity. Only the library was fully shared by students and faculty from Xiada and the Jiageng College. Even on a Sunday, the campus was a lively spot with many students strolling around, and various activities underway. We saw a group of Indian students, and learned that a cohort of sixty is following a program in Chinese traditional medicine on the new campus. We also ran into several Tibetan students and learned that there is a government secondary school nearby providing education for Tibetan students, and supporting their entry into higher education within a special quota set by the national government. A number of them were in the first and second year undergraduate cohort.

Photo 5.3: The Main Teaching Building on the new Jiageng Campus

A Student Counselor's Perspective

From the counselor we learned that there are 92 different student groups and organizations on campus, involving 9,900 of the 10,500 first and second year undergraduates who live and study there. These organizations fall into four major types: social service, scholarship, physical education and arts and aesthetics. In the area of social service, students are involved in various kinds of rural education work with children, including participation in programs that the university has with Guizhou Normal University in Guiyang, and with Ningxia University in the Northwest. Students accepted for a Masters program may apply to teach for a year in Guizhou Normal before taking up their studies, and students in the Masters of Social work have the opportunity for a field work practicum there. There are also student organizations promoting traditional Chinese opera, drama and music, and one of the concerns of faculty and counselors is that these should provide opportunities for students to work together collaboratively. Most of the students come from one child families, and their upper secondary years were spent in intensive examination preparation, so they tend to be very individually oriented.

Employment opportunities are a major concern for students, and the counselor acknowledged that there are particular problems for women, with some employers explicitly rejecting female applicants even though it is against the law. Students in literature, philosophy and history also have greater difficulty in the job search that those in economics, management and the various science and engineering fields.[14]

Information on employment issues in the university's 2007 Guide for undergraduate students gave a more rosy picture. This booklet claimed that 95% of Xiada's 2006 graduates had found jobs or taken up graduate studies, with the two main groups being 47% who found positions in enterprises and 22.8% who went on for further study. This source also indicated that 50% stayed in Fujian province, including 38% in the city of Xiamen, while 6.6% moved to neighboring Guangdong province, half of those being in the city of Shenzhen, another 2.3% found jobs in Shanghai, 3.6% in Jiangsu province, and 2% in Beijing.[15] These are very attractive locations for the students who come to Xiada from all parts of China.

Xiada's Ethos and Mission in the Eyes of Students

Members of the student focus group saw Xiada's mission as becoming a world class research oriented university, and were very proud of its profile. They felt this ambition to achieve world class quality stimulated them to work hard and prepare themselves for the demands of a globalized world. In the past, they had felt university students were responsible to contribute to the nation and nation building, but now they felt the demands were even higher – to contribute to the world. "We feel international," they said, "and we especially feel closely connected to Taiwan, Singapore and Southeast Asia." The celebration of Xiada's 85th anniver-

---

[14] Interview with Gao Zhonghua, Youth League official and student counselor on the new campus, 27 May 2007.
[15] *2007 Nian Benkesheng Baokao Zhinan* (*2007 Guide for Undergraduate Student Enrollment*) (Xiamen University, 2007), p.16.

sary in 2006 had been a particularly stimulating event for students, and they mentioned the many public lectures by outstanding scholars from around the world, including several Nobel Prize Winners, which they had been able to attend. They understood that it would be a long and demanding road for the university, and felt it would have to be done one stage at a time, but it was definitely the right direction. As students, they felt a strong sense of responsibility to study hard in order to be able to contribute, and they also felt included in the new international ethos, through the contacts they were able to have with visiting professors and international students.[16]

Students also felt quite a strong sense of local identity, and were familiar with some of the great names associated with the university's history – Chen Jiageng for his spirit of patriotism, Sa Bendong for his example of resistance and struggle during war-time, Wang Yanan for his scholarship and his determination to save and built up the field of economics as a scholarly discipline. All of the students had spent their first two years on the new campus, and loved what they saw as an integration of Chinese and Western ideas and values in the buildings there. They also shared the view of faculty members that the main administration building (Photo 5.2), with its five sections and its *Minnan* cultural influences was truly a world-class building, that expresses the strength and the international spirit of Xiada. This building represented the ethos

Photo 5.4: The Furong Buildings on the Main Campus of Xiamen University

---

[16] Student Focus Group Meeting, 27 May 2007.

of Xiada most compellingly, while the Jiannan Auditorium, which was selected by the two vice presidents, came a close second for students. They saw its shape and location, looking out over the ocean, as an expression of openness to the world. Finally, students also appreciated the Furong Buildings around the lake on the main campus, which they felt expressed the sense of harmony, integrity and wholeness of the campus environment. (Photo 5.4) Most touching of all to them was the grave of Chen Jiageng, on the ocean side, giving a sense of history to the campus, and expressing the *Minnan* spirit and local culture. They had a strong feeling of belonging to the university, which was partially inspired by the campus environment.

Issues of Equity

One of the issues students raised with relation to equity was the opportunity structure of the university entrance examinations. A student from Shandong remarked that it was unfair that nearly half of the places were reserved for students from Fujian province, and the quotas allocated to all the rest of the country were relatively small. Several students noted the much greater difficulties that faced rural students in seeking entry to higher education than urban students, and the urgent need for more attention to rural development and rural education, in order to enable rural students to have equal opportunities for higher education. At present, it was felt the gap between rural and urban students was far greater than it had been in the 1950s and 1960s. Students also commented on the requirement of the university entry process that students give three choices of field of study, in order of their priority, and how often students have to be satisfied with their second or third choice, rather than being able to pursue the field that interests them most.

The biggest problem in terms of higher education entry, they felt, was China's huge population and the fact that competition is extremely intense, given the numbers. With the dramatic expansion of recent years, it has become a common expectation of many young people that they will be able to attend university, but the issue of getting into a famous university puts great pressure on secondary school students. Everyone wants to get into Beida or Tsinghua, which is impossible. It is nevertheless quite unfair that students from outside of Beijing have to achieve much higher marks on the entrance examinations than Beijing residents in order to be considered. Chinese culture has a strong orientation towards "face" and everyone wants to enter top-level universities, while there is actually a great need for people educated in lower level institutions, where they learn the practical knowledge and skills needed for society's development, they commented.

On employment, several of the students mentioned that one of the problems was that of graduates having over high expectations. Students are not simply looking for jobs; they are looking for positions with high status and remuneration rather than for opportunities to work hard and make a contribution. In fact, they said they themselves were quite hopeful, as many Xiada graduates had found positions with multinational companies or foreign joint ventures. Also the university had helpful connections with employing units and organized job fairs every year, where students could learn about various kinds of employment opportunity. Students felt that it was important for them to be rational and realistic in facing the job market. Counseling could be helpful for those who had particular worries, but given the fact there was only one counselor for four hundred students, not everyone could get help that way. Students thus mainly tended to talk these problems over among themselves, they said.

The New Campus and the Second-tier College

All members of the focus group had spent their first two years on the new campus. They enjoyed this experience, yet felt classes tended to be very large and it was not possible to develop close relationships with their teachers. However their first two years were a time of relaxation, after the intense efforts to pass the entrance examinations, and the quiet ambience of the new campus provided an ideal place to adjust to university life. Now that they had moved to the urban campus for their third and fourth years, they felt it was important that they concentrate hard on their studies, in order to prepare for graduation and employment.

While on the new campus, they had had opportunities to mingle with the students of the Jiageng second-tier college. They felt these students were bright and hardworking, in fact "just the same as us." They also noted that quite a number of the Xiada professors taught also at the second-tier college, and the teaching standards were quite good. They felt it was important for higher education to be opened up to more young people through these new colleges. Yet they noted it was unfortunate that the Jiageng students did not seem to feel any connection to Xiamen University, and when invited to attend some of the 85th anniversary seminars and lectures, they did not want to join in. Another comment about the second-tier college students was that the girls were more likely to dress well and wear make-up, compared to the Xiada students, who were characterized as "bookworms."

Civil Society and Social Participation

Students were enthusiastic about their opportunities for participation in campus life and in the various social organizations on campus. A student of economics explained how she belonged to a study group on economics which enabled her to improve her knowledge in the field, but also to do work for rural schools. All of the students in the group said they participated in at least one social organization, most in more than one. They also said they were often asked for their opinions by teachers and felt free to make complaints or give suggestions. One had had the experience of posting a complaint about service in the university hospital on the internet, and had been given a resolution to the issue. Students also appreciated the fact that they could elect their class monitors. Generally students said they felt respected and appreciated all of the opportunities for social participation that university life provided.

The internet expanded their opportunities for some kinds of participation and students spoke of it as a way of "going abroad" while still in China. It was possible to see much of the world through news reports, video etc. They also felt they needed to develop self-discipline, so as not to spend too much time at the computer screen. On average, students said they spent about two hours a day on-line, and were appreciative of the university's facilities for this.

This group of third year students gave a positive and mature assessment of their study experiences and the campus atmosphere they had experienced, both on the new suburban campus and on the main campus where they had moved for their third and fourth years. Overall, one got the sense that they were satisfied with the opportunities and benefits they enjoyed at Xiada, yet also aware of continuing problems and inequities in Chinese society, particularly the gap between rural and urban young people. They had a strong feeling of local identity and belonging, yet also a sense of international connection, particularly to Southeast Asia.

Conclusion

Our overall impression of Xiamen University was of an institution with a high level of independence, that was consciously building upon strengths related to its unique history as a privately founded university, and its geographical location on the Southeastern coast of China. There was a strong sense of local identity and connection to *Minnan* culture, expressed in the consistency of architectural style on its ocean-side campus, and in the constant reference to its founder, Chen Jiageng, who had established a business empire in Southeast Asia yet devoted enormous efforts to educational and economic development in southern Fujian province. Many of the buildings on the Xiada campus have come from donations, rather than government investment, as many alumni and faculty continue to be inspired by Chen Jiageng's spirit and give generously. Students, for their part, have an extraordinary sense of gratitude and appreciation at being able to benefit from this atmosphere, which is unlike that of most other campuses, and which connects them directly to the history of the university and the region.

In terms of academic development, university leaders recognized that they would not be able to reach world-class standards quickly, so they focused on areas of historic strength, such as economics, chemistry and marine studies, and made strategic decisions on international collaboration that would be supportive of these areas. They also chose to join a consortium of seven universities with similar geographic and regional orientations in order to nurture opportunities for international involvement of both faculty members and students. At the same time they have tried to create a humane campus culture, whereby faculty are able to enjoy the pursuit of research, without feeling the intense competitive pressures that are common elsewhere. Distance from Beijing, and a degree of geographical isolation seems to have contributed to this atmosphere.

Their leadership in higher education research, with this field being developed by Professor Pan Maoyuan in the 1950s, has given a focus to their commitment to a revival of Chinese culture, expressed in the establishment of the "Institute of National Studies." Thus the higher education research centre, which is the only key national centre in higher education recognized by the Ministry of Education, has wide ranging research on Chinese higher education traditions, as well as on many dimensions of the recent move to mass higher education. It regularly holds conferences with international participation, and sees itself as having an important contribution to make to global scholarship in higher education. There are three reasons for this, in the view of Professor Pan

Maoyuan: first, the historical influence of China's ancient scholarly culture, particularly in East Asia, but also more widely; second, the fact that China now has the largest higher education system in the world, and many lessons can be learned from its experience; third, the large number of researchers in higher education in China, and the fact that the field has developed in a bottom-up manner through the initiatives of scholars and local institutions, rather than in a top-down way.[17]

---

[17] See Ruth Hayhoe, *Portraits of Influential Chinese Educators*, pp.167-168.

Part III:
Portraits of Three
Education-Related Universities

The three education-related universities profiled in this section reflect an interesting geographic spread, with East China Normal University in Shanghai on China's East Coast, Southwest University in Chongqing, a major centre of the Southwest and Yanbian University in Yanji, a Korean minority region in Northeast China. Teacher education was given considerable importance in the reorganization of higher education that took place in the early 1950s, with the decision to establish a major normal university in each of China's six geographical regions. East China Normal University was an entirely new institution, while Southwest Normal University was established on the basis of a normal college that went back to the 1930s, and originally had agricultural as well as educational programs. Yanbian University was founded in 1949, reflecting the commitment of the new Communist government to make special provision for the needs of China's many minority groups. Although it was not called a normal university, a major part of its responsibility was the formation of teachers for Korean language schools, as well as government cadres for the Korean minority region.

Given the emphasis on education in China's classical knowledge tradition, one would expect normal universities and the field of education to have a high standing in China.[1] While education has formally been given considerable respect in recent years, these chapters give a vivid depiction of the struggle undertaken by these education universities to gain access to the elite projects of recent years, with ECNU being the last of 39th of 43 universities accepted into Project 98/5, and both Southwest and Yanbian exerting tremendous efforts to find their way into Project 21/1. The issues of merger and expansion, and how they affected education-related institutions, are also a fascinating and unique story for each of these three institutions. While ECNU reflects an important national decision to maintain the status and profile of normal universities, the story of Southwest shows how there can always be

---

[1] Ruth Hayhoe and Jun Li, "The Idea of a Normal University in the 21st Century," in *Frontiers of Education in China*, Vol.4, No.1, March, 2010.

exceptions to the firmest of policies in the Chinese context. Yanbian, for its part, has been able to take advantage of the economic and geopolitical dynamism of its region as well as national policies for support of Western development.

6
East China Normal University – Education in the Lead

Ruth HAYHOE and Qiang ZHA, with LI Mei

East China Normal University (ECNU) is unique among our twelve case institutions as the only normal university, also the only university in the major coastal metropolis of Shanghai. This chapter thus begins with a brief historical overview as a background for understanding ECNU's role in the move to mass higher education. From there it looks at the changes in student numbers, curricula, finance and governance over the period from 1990 to 2005. Next some views of the leaders on vision and strategic direction are presented, also a discussion of the major decisions around merger, expansion and international orientation. Finally the perspectives of faculty and students on key issues of concern are summarized. The conclusion seeks to identify the new ethos of the normal university that is being developed in the Chinese context, and the challenges it faces.

History and Context

In order to understand the background of the East China Normal University in Shanghai, two distinct historical topics need to be addressed – the history of an idea and the history of a city. Shanghai played a unique role in the history of Chinese higher education, as an open and cosmopolitan metropolis, with a large international settlement, a French concession and a major port. It had often been a place of experimentation and refuge during the early years of the republic and the Nationalist regime.

The idea of the normal university was born with the French Revolution, and the first Ecole Normale Supérieure opened in 1794, recruiting 1,400 prospective teachers for the new central schools that were to popularize education for all.[1] Subsequently, under Napoleon, the Ecole Normal Supérieure was re-established as a highly elite institution, "a centre of official pedagogical orthodoxy which would provide a pipeline

---

[1] Robert Smith, *The Ecole Normale Supérieure and the Third Republic* (Albany: State University of New York, 1982), p.9.

for the transmission of approved educational policies and methods."[2] Not long after, normal schools were founded in each of France's educational districts to train elementary school teachers, and the model became influential internationally.

Teacher Education in China's Modern History

The education of teachers was a major concern in China's modern development, with the first normal schools and higher normal schools being established before the Revolution of 1911, to train teachers needed for newly developing modern primary schools. The latter were the first public higher institutions open to women in the Chinese context. In 1922 the Beijing Higher Normal School for men was upgraded to university status, followed by the Beijing Women's Higher Normal School in 1924. The two were merged in 1931, and Beijing Normal University has had an unbroken history since then. In Southern China, however, the Nanjing Higher Normal School was merged with other institutions to form Dongnan University in 1922, later to become the National Central University in Nanjing, China's capital during the Nationalist regime. It had an outstanding Faculty of Education, a model that reflected dominant American influences of the time.[3]

Only in the early years of the new Communist regime was the normal university given an important place in China's higher education system, reflecting the Soviet patterns adopted in the early 1950s, which in turn had been influenced by France. Six national normal universities were established in the six major geographic regions of China, with East China Normal University in Shanghai as the leading institution for teachers in the East China region. The model was precisely that of 19th century France – a highly selective university, with departments in all the major subject areas taught in secondary schools – mathematics, physics, chemistry and biology, history, geography, literature and languages, fine arts and music as well as educational theory, psychology and physical education. All students were to be educated in one major discipline as well as gaining the educational knowledge necessary for teaching at the secondary or tertiary level. Graduates were assigned teaching jobs in the

---

[2] Andy Green, *Education and State Formation: The Rise of Education Systems in England, France and the USA* (New York: St. Martin's Press, 1990), p.151.
[3] See Ruth Hayhoe and Jun Li, "The Idea of a Normal University in the 21st Century," in *Frontiers of Education in China*, Vol.4, No.4, 2009, pp.357-358.

upper echelons of the education system, and expected to nurture a unified national ideology of socialist construction.

The Founding of ECNU

Since pre-1949 Shanghai had not had such an institution, East China Normal was established in 1951 on the basis of two patriotic private universities which had formed an interesting part of Shanghai's educational history. In 1924, a group of students and faculty at Xiamen University left the university in protest over actions of its leadership and founded Utopia (大夏) University in Shanghai, building it up over the years into a respected private university with a strong college of education and attached primary and secondary schools. In 1925, at the time of the May 30th incident, a large group of scholars and students stormed out of St. John's University, a renowned Christian university established by the American Episcopal church in Shanghai, because university authorities refused to support student participation in the massive strikes and protest actions against Japanese and British imperialist interests that were shaking the city. They established Guanghua (光華) University, a private and patriotic institution which developed along similar lines to Utopia, with a Faculty of Education and attached schools.[4]

East China Normal University was established in 1951, on the beautiful garden campus of Utopia University, with the Liwa (麗娃) River running through it. All of the academic resources that had been built up in the two private universities were absorbed into the new institution. In addition, the education departments of most other Shanghai universities were consolidated at East China Normal, as well as major disciplinary departments from other excellent universities. While East China Normal's formal history goes back only to 1951, the history of many of its departments and subject areas is thus much longer.[5]

Influential Leaders of ECNU

East China Normal's first president, Meng Xiancheng (孟憲成), was a

---

[4] For brief histories of these two universities, see Yuan Yunkai and Wang Tiexian (eds.), *Huadong Shifan Daxue Xiaoshi 1951-2001* (*An Institutional History of East China Normal University 1951-2001*) (Shanghai: Huadong Shifan Daxue Chubanshe, 2001), pp.348-360.

[5] *Ibid.* See p.393 for a table that shows all the different departments of distinguished universities that were integrated into ECNU in its first few years of history.

noted educational theorist, who had studied in the United States and England in the early part of the century and translated a number of John Dewey's works into Chinese. He had been one of the leaders in the establishment of Guanghua University, and was respected for his patriotism, as well as his scholarship. Even more influential in nurturing East China Normal's early ethos as a normal university was Liu Fonian (劉佛年), who served as provost from 1951 to 1957, vice president from 1957 to the eve of the Cultural Revolution, and President from 1978 to 1984, the period of opening up and reform under Deng Xiaoping. Liu had studied philosophy at Cambridge University, the University of Paris and the Ecole Normale Supérieure in the late 1930s, returning to China in 1939. He had taught in a number of different universities and developed a strongly critical philosophical response to the Deweyan educational theories which were widely influential in China over those years.[6]

It was thus not surprising that Liu should become an important voice in the new Soviet influenced pedagogy of the 1950s, and work closely with the six Soviet scholars who were stationed at ECNU from 1952 to 1957. Liu also developed his own critical views on the ideas of Soviet theorist Ivan Kairov, which dominated educational texts of the time. His textbook on pedagogy, which has had nation-wide influence, presented an approach to education theory that was less linear and rationalist than that of Kairov, while being also critical of the pragmatism underlying Dewey's work. It was rooted in Chinese philosophical views about the unfolding of a series of contradictions in the process of social change, between knowledge and action, unified truth and diverse perspectives, specialist and general education, individual and collective.[7]

During the Cultural Revolution, Liu was nevertheless attacked and reviled as "China's Kairov" and East China Normal University was forced into a merger with the local Shanghai Normal University. Only in 1978 was it able to recover its identity as a national normal university, after Deng Xiaoping had come to power. Appointed president that year, Liu saw one of the main tasks of his presidency as to conceptualize the role a normal university should play. His vision included strengthening foundation programs in the disciplines and building up graduate pro-

---

[6] Ruth Hayhoe, *Portraits of Influential Chinese Educators* (Hong Kong: Comparative Education Research Centre, The University of Hong Kong and Springer, 2006), pp.326-330.
[7] *Ibid.* pp.331-332.

grams, also ensuring the integration of research into all aspects of the university's work. He believed that a normal university should lead in all dimensions of education, including administration and planning as well as teacher education. He had a particular commitment to mentoring young faculty, and nurturing a new generation of scholars.[8]

While the number of undergraduate students remained at about 5,000 over these years, a similar number to that of the early 1960s, graduate student numbers grew steadily after 1978, reaching about 1,200 in 1985. Also the first three non-education related departments were established, as the university extended its programs into areas outside the education of future teachers. After stepping down as President, Liu Fonian continued to be involved in teaching and research up to his death in 2001, and his educational vision and leadership have remained a kind of reference point for subsequent university leaders, as well as faculty members. More than any other scholar, he had embodied the spirit of East China Normal University.

Liu remained a much beloved presence on campus over the years that ECNU transformed itself, from a small elite institution serving the whole nation, to a much larger university that made a renewed commitment to education as it expanded and embraced other fields and took up a stronger local role. The next section of this chapter provides an overview of the changes in enrollments, curricular provision, finance and governance over the period from 1990 to 2005,

ECNU Moves to Mass Higher Education: An Empirical Overview 1990-2005
Student Enrollment Growth

In 1990, East China Normal University had an enrollment of 5,318 undergraduate students, showing only modest growth since the mid-1980s. By 1995, undergraduate enrollments reached 5,913, then 9,913 in 2000 and a total of 12,256 in 2005. Meanwhile graduate enrollments went from 1,088 in 1990 to 1,320 in 1995, 2,415 in 2000 and 6,898 in 2005, almost a seven fold increase. An interesting characteristic of the student population at ECNU is the dominance of women students, which many would explain by reference to the attraction of teaching careers for women. However, this was the period when a large number of new programs were developed which did not lead to teaching careers. In spite of this new

---

[8] Ibid. p.334.

orientation, women continued to dominate enrollments, constituting 52% of undergraduate students in 1995, 60% in 2000 and 65% in 2005. Parallel figures at the graduate level are 33% in 1995, 49% in 2000 and 60% in 2005. Over the same period, international student numbers had grown from 655 in 1995 to 1,941 in 2005.

One of the Vice Presidents explained how this expansion affected campus development, and required the creation of an entirely new campus in the Minhang (閔行) District, southwest of Shanghai. Government regulations specified 10 students per *mu* of land, which meant their urban campus of 850 *mu* could accommodate 8,500 students at most.[9] Raising funds for the new campus, which has 1,800 *mu* (and therefore can accommodate another 18,000 students), also making decisions about which programs would stay on the historic urban campus and which would move to the new campus have thus been matters of intense concern and interest over recent years. In the university's recently developed vision one can see how these issues were resolved, and the profile which ECNU is presenting to the global higher education community as a new-style Chinese normal university.

Curricular Development

With the enrollment growth depicted above has come a dramatic expansion in programs, departments and faculties. Under the Soviet model, universities recruited students by program, and there were only two levels of administration – department and central authority. From the late 1980s, schools or colleges have been established to group departments, and one can see in the present 19 schools how the traditional departments have created a foundation for new broadened fields. One can also see how many entirely new fields have been established. Thus the School of Humanities (est. 1994) has original Departments of History and Chinese, as well as a Department of Philosophy opened in 1986. The School of Foreign Languages (est. 1993) has original departments in the major language areas, and the School of Arts (est. 2004) has original Departments of Fine Arts and Music. The School of Resources and Environmental Sciences (est. 1993) was built upon a historically strong Department of Geography, while having new Departments of Urban and Regional Economy and Environmental Science and Technology. Likewise the School of Life Sciences (est. 2001) is built on a strong biology

---

[9] Interview with Zhuang Huiming, Vice President, 1 June 2007.

department, and the School of Sciences and Engineering (est. 1994) includes original Departments of Mathematics, Physics and Chemistry as well as newly developed Department of Statistics. The School of Education Science (est. 1981) has Departments of Curriculum and Teaching, Educational Information and Technology, Education Theory and Psychology, while the Department of Educational Administration has blossomed into a new School of Public Administration. New Schools of Preschool and Special Education (est. 1997) and Physical Education and Health (est. 2001) have also come into being. Entirely new curricular areas include a School of Business (est. 1993), the Orient Real Estate College (est. 1995), a School of Information Science and Technology (est. 2001), a School of Law and Politics (est. 2001), a School of Software Engineering (est.2002), a School of Communications (est. 2004), a School of Design (est. 2004) and a School of Advanced International and Area studies (est. 2004).[10] A School of Psychology and Cognitive Science was established in 2008, bringing to five the number of education related schools, out of a total of 19 schools.

With this dramatic expansion and diversification of the curriculum the student body has changed also, with a declining percentage of students in teacher education programs, and all students free to seek their own jobs on graduation. The former job assignment system, whereby students had been assigned teaching positions, either in Shanghai or in the geographical region where they had come from, was phased out in the early 1990s. Likewise, with increasing support from the Shanghai municipal government for ECNU, the percentage of students recruited from Shanghai rose. Before 1995, 70-80% of students came from all different parts of the country, and only 20-30% were local students. Now the Shanghai Municipal Government requires that the university recruit at least 49% of its students from Shanghai, a condition for the substantive matching funding the city provides for prestigious national project participation.[11] Many of the new curricular areas have thus been developed in response to new employment needs in Shanghai and the nearby region.

---

[10] Annual Report, East China Normal University 2006, pp.10-37.
[11] It was made clear in an interview with Zhang Minxuan, Vice Commissioner of Education for Shanghai, 12 December 2006 that the condition for the Shanghai government giving substantive support to its national universities was that they are expected to serve the local economy and meet local needs for human resources. However, this percentage was speculated to decline after the new round of negotiations between MoE and Shanghai in 2008.

In 2007, the government introduced a policy whereby all students in teacher education programs in the six national-level normal universities would have their fees waived, on condition that they were willing to accept teaching positions in rural areas for a certain number of years after graduation. Special efforts are being made to attract students from the central and western regions of China, and a strong emphasis is being placed on professional development and the nurturing of a sense of mission and social responsibility.[12] For students from rural areas or lower income families, this constitutes a very important new career opportunity, and demonstrates the government's commitment to the teaching profession. For ECNU, however, there are some concerns about the educational quality of the students recruited under this plan, since their marks on the unified national entrance examinations tend to be less competitive than those recruited for all other programs.

This overview of the changes in student numbers at ECNU, and the expansion and diversification of the curriculum shows an institution that has sought to balance its identity as a normal university, with the challenges of developing many new areas unrelated to teacher education. The leadership considered seriously the option of becoming a comprehensive university in the later 1990s, and this was an important consideration in the dramatic curricular diversification that was undertaken.[13] However, the decision to retain its title and identity as a normal university meshed with national policy on teacher education institutions, which strongly discouraged them from merging with other types of university.[14]

---

[12] *Xinwen Wanbao* (*Shanghai Evening Post*), 7 March 2007.

[13] Interview with Ren Youqun, Assistant Vice-president, 3 May 2008.

[14] There were widespread debates in the mid to late 1990s as to whether normal universities should abandon this designation and become comprehensive universities or maintain their historic identity. The final result of these debates was a national policy decision that normal universities should be maintained, and mergers with other types of university would not be encouraged. For details, please see Liu Haifeng, "Yuanxiao Hebing Shengge Yu Fazhan Zhong De Gengming Wenti (The Name Changing of Higher Institutions in the Process of Institutional Merger and Development)," in *Gaodeng Jiaoyu Yanjiu* (*Journal of Higher Education*). Vol.26, No.11, 2005, pp.21-26; Zhang, Jinfu, "Gaoshi Yuanxiao Fenliu De Xian-Zhuang Yu Qianzhan," (The Status Quo and the Prospects of Diversification for Higher Teacher Education Institutions), 2001, accessed 12 April 2008, http://www.edu.cn/gao_shi_402/20060323/t20060323_13172.shtml.

Clearly, ECNU increased enrollments significantly, in response to the move to mass higher education, with a particularly strong focus on graduate enrollments. Also, it agreed to a series of mergers that would strengthen its leadership over the field of education, rather than seeking the kinds of high profile mergers with medical or engineering universities that have proven attractive to major comprehensive universities. This was the cost of gaining significant support from the Shanghai municipal government. Finally, it gave careful consideration to the establishment of a second-tier college, as an addition to its core programs which would generate income, but decided against it, preferring rather to launch a new program of international outreach. Before turning to the vision and strategic decision making process, a brief overview of the governance patterns and major changes in finance is provided.

Finance and Governance

President Yu began his discussion with us by saying that patterns of governance within the university clearly reflect the wider society, and the degree to which they can move to more democratic management is constrained by the character of the broader political system. He also noted that presidential terms in Chinese universities tend to be somewhat shorter than is common internationally, typically periods of four to five years. The Party Secretary holds the more important leadership role, though both work together very closely, with the president responsible for the overall academic leadership.

The most significant changes that have come about in the move to mass higher education relate to the university's sources of funding. In 1990, nearly 100% of the funding came from the central government in Beijing, while funding sources are now highly diversified. Forty percent of regular operating costs of about 997 million came from the government in 2007, with a 60/40 ration between the central government and the Shanghai government. Other funding comes from major projects such as 21/1 and 98/5, from various kinds of training and consultancy activity, that bring in about 100 million a year, and from research contracts, which amounted to about 150 million a year. Student fee income makes up about 10% of total funding, with all students paying annual fees of about 5,000 *yuan* in 2006.[15] There is beginning to be a culture of fundraising and

---

[15] Beginning from the autumn of 2007, teacher education students are exempt from fees, and the shortfall to the university is made up by the Ministry of Education.

donations, but so far this has contributed only in a minimal way with a total of ten million in donations in 2006. The university plans to set up a foundation that would stimulate greater contributions from alumni and society, but so far the tax system does not provide a favorable environment.[16]

Vision and Strategic Directions in the Move to Mass Higher Education
Deciding on a Vision and Mission

President Yu Lizhong came to ECNU from being president of Shanghai Normal University on January 4, 2006; before taking the leadership at Shanghai Normal University, he had served as Vice President at ECNU for six years (1997-2002). One of his first priorities was developing a vision and set of strategic directions for ECNU. Seminars were held with students and faculty to gather views, and a drafting committee chaired by a vice president included former university leaders and outstanding professors. Once an initial draft was ready it was presented to three university level committees, the university management committee, the university senate or academic board and the committee for approving new programs. All of them added comments and suggestions before the document was accepted by the President and Party Secretary.

The core vision statement calls for the university to be a comprehensive research university with teacher education as its leading knowledge area, with a number of world-class fields of scholarship and with excellent standards overall. Given the lowly status of teacher education in universities around the world it is striking to see this ongoing commitment to teacher education as a leading arena of knowledge, a decision that reflects ECNU's history. The President went on to say that the vision statement called for a central focus on nurturing creative talent, and had two areas of particular emphasis: cross-disciplinary and integrative scholarship, as an essential condition for creativity, and an international outlook, whereby all teaching, learning and research is enacted within a global context. The first of these emphases expresses the deep orientation of traditional Chinese knowledge patterns, while the second reflects the Shanghai context, as China's most internationalized metropolis and window on the world.

---

[16] Interview with Yu Lizhong, President, 31 May 2007.

In presenting this vision statement, President Yu talked about ECNU's motto, which had been adopted in the 1960s: seeking practical truth, innovating, and setting a model for teaching in service of the people (求實創造,爲人師表). He felt that ECNU was best understood through the character of its graduates over the years, and that this motto expressed their reputation very well. It was low key, practical, intellectually strong, yet never trumpeting their achievements.[17]

Joining the 98/5 Project and the Issue of Merger

Although ECNU had been included in the Project 21/1, President Yu noted that it had received far less financial support than Fudan or Jiaotong Universities, the two other major national comprehensive and engineering universities in Shanghai – only about 80 million *yuan*, as compared to the national government's investment of 500 million each for Fudan and Jiaotong universities. Thus when President Yu took up the leadership of ECNU, his most pressing and immediate challenge was to get ECNU included on the list of Project 98/5 universities. There were already 38 universities on the list, with only one teacher education institution, Beijing Normal University. Through persistent efforts going back to 2001, ECNU finally succeeded in being accepted as the 39th in 2006. The importance lay not only in the significant funding that would be available from the central government, but also the opportunity to participate in high profile national programs, such as the new China Scholarship fund which provides significant support for doctoral students to spend a year abroad. Without being included on the 98/5 list, President Yu was aware that it would be difficult for ECNU to keep its most outstanding faculty, since they would easily be attracted to better endowed institutions. As it turned out, the Shanghai Municipal Government provided an investment of 500 million to match the 100 million provided by the national government.

This strong support from Shanghai was linked in turn to a decision made by President Yu's predecessor, President Wang Jianpan, on the crucial issue of merger. While national attention was being given to high profile mergers that involved medical universities and specialist engineering institutions being integrated into comprehensive or polytechnical universities, ECNU was requested by the Shanghai government to take on a very different type of merger – one that would involve the

---

[17] Interview with Yu Lizhong, President, 31 May 2007.

integration of two sub-degree schools at the local level for training preschool and special education teachers, also two colleges of education which had offered in-service courses to upgrade teacher qualifications for many years. Shanghai municipal education authorities wanted to upgrade teacher education for the whole city, and to ensure that the education of teachers at all levels was undergirded by research. They asked ECNU to take on responsibility for this.

There was considerable reluctance initially on the ECNU side, as some were hoping for a higher profile merger that might boost their research and publication profile. President Wang had to hold numerous campus wide meetings to persuade faculty to agree. In the end, the two colleges of education were dissolved and many of their faculty were integrated into appropriate departments of ECNU. The addition of so many lower level professionals brought down the scholarly profile of the departments in question, a matter of great concern to faculty who opposed the merger. As for the Schools of Preschool and Special Education, these were to form the basis for an entirely new school within ECNU, which was founded in 1997, with a new dean appointed in 1999 to implement the integration. It was a difficult yet rewarding task, since he was able to raise funds from Hong Kong's Tin Ka Ping Foundation, as well as from the Shanghai government, to build excellent facilities and equip them with the latest experimental equipment. ECNU's School of Preschool and Special Education now has both a national and an international reputation, with many linkages to excellent universities in North America, Britain and Japan, as well as 119 school partners within Shanghai, which are used for experimental programs and research.[18]

The broader benefit for ECNU itself was the urban property which came with the four institutions that were merged in. Some of the sites were prime real estate, and their sale was one element in the funding package that made possible the purchase of a new campus in Minhang, and the creation of a purpose-fit set of teaching and administration buildings, a library and student dormitories. Other sources of funding that contributed to this were bank loans of 80 million, support from enterprises in Minhang, and the significant investment committed by the Shanghai Municipal government as a condition of ECNU's acceptance into the 98/5 Project.

---

[18] Interview with Fang Junming, Dean of the School of Preschool and Special Education, and Party Secretary Wang Haiping, 30 May 2007.

A Second-tier College for Local Students or an International Student Focus?

If merger has been one of the strategic decisions facing university leaders in the move to mass higher education, the possibility of establishing a second-tier college with a large enrollment of students whose fees would generate significant income for the university was another. After careful consideration, the ECNU leaders decided against this step, feeling that their focus should be on academic quality, and that other institutions could respond to the demands for enrollment expansion in the lower levels of the higher education system.

Their vision for expansion beyond the regular undergraduate and graduate students lay rather in the idea of attracting an increasing number of international students to their beautiful urban campus in Shanghai. They thus made a strategic decision to expand the enrollment of international students, with a goal of having 5,000 students from all parts of the world resident on their urban campus, and 10% of their courses taught bilingually. To accommodate this expanded number of international students, they decided that all programs except education and foreign languages would move to the new Minhang campus. This included the president's office, the whole senior administration team, with the exception of one vice president responsible for international programs, also all other schools and departments, including the School of Graduate Studies. It was a dramatic decision, and one that has not been popular with faculty, given the distance of the new campus, and the relative inconvenience of travel. However, in this decision could be seen the logical outworking of two focal points in the vision statement.

The first was that education and the nurturing of teachers would remain the leading field of ECNU as a normal university and so it will be a dominant presence on the main urban campus. The second was that all students and faculty should carry out their teaching and learning in a broadly international and global frame of reference, reflecting Shanghai's ethos as a major international metropolis. ECNU's internationalization plan included the intention of providing opportunities for 20% of all undergraduate students to spend a semester abroad, opening up the campus to large numbers of international students so it would become a kind of "international student city" within Shanghai, and nurturing a number of high level cooperative programs in graduate teaching and research with appropriate partners. A third consideration lay in the fact that ECNU's five Schools of Education run a large number of part-time programs for Shanghai teachers and other professionals, bringing in considerable income, and thus they needed to stay on the urban campus.

There were also important consequences of this decision for the new campus in Minhang. Many Chinese universities have created suburban campuses as part of their move to mass higher education, and one of the common problems on these campuses is the sense of isolation, as large numbers of undergraduate students live and study in a situation that is remote from graduate programs, research institutes, and the offices of faculty and administrators at all levels. Faculty members come by bus for their classes and leave immediately after, with the only consistent presence on campus, outside of the students, being that of the student counselors, who are responsible to advise students in all aspects of their lives, including the political studies that are still an important part of the common curriculum for all higher education students. ECNU's President has set an example for all schools of the university by moving his own office and the administrative units to the new campus, encouraging them to fully ensconce themselves there and settle into its spacious environment. In this way it should become a genuine community of scholarship rather than a mere extension for the overflow of undergraduate students. Also a conscious decision was made when the land was purchased, to locate themselves adjacent to the campus already established by Shanghai Jiaotong University rather than in the more remote suburb of Song Jiang, where some other Shanghai universities have set up campuses.

When looking at the highlights of ECNU's international cooperation, one can see the seriousness with which they are taking their identity as a normal university. One of their most prominent partners is the Ecole Normale Supérieure (ENS) in Paris, a relationship first nurtured by former President Liu Fonian, who had been there in the 1930s. With the support of the Government of France, they have a collaborative masters program in the sciences, with some teaching done by visiting French professors, and a joint doctoral program, whereby about twelve masters graduates are selected each year for doctoral work and are slated to earn a double doctorate from the two institutions in their chosen fields. These are mainly basic sciences, but also including international relations and European studies. There are now about 40 students in the program, with scholarships provided by the French government, by ENS and by ECNU. There is also considerable research cooperation among professors in the basic sciences on both sides who are guiding the graduate training.

Other collaborative programs involve exchanges of students with

Grandes Ecoles in Lyons and Montpellier, and with a number of American universities, including New York University, whereby its students will spend one year or one term on the ECNU campus, and some collaborative degree programs will be developed. The vision is for a wide range of courses to be offered on Chinese culture, literature, economics, society and history. Longer term, the intention is to develop as many as 100 courses offered in English, and to have some courses taught by visiting faculty from partner universities. Already the dormitories that had been used by ECNU's own undergraduate students are being renovated for international students. In 2006, ECNU launched a Center of International Education to coordinate all of these international activities, and a professor of curriculum studies was appointed its inaugural director.

Another ambitious element in ECNU's international outreach program is the support for Confucius Institutes. The VP responsible for teaching and learning explained that ECNU was responsible for sponsoring three of them, through working with three different types of partners, including the University of Iowa, the Chicago School Board, and the China Institute, an NGO based in New York City. ECNU has long experience in the teaching of Chinese to non-Chinese speakers, and is now hosting a research centre established by the Ministry of Education to prepare materials for the teaching of Chinese in international contexts. They are also doing a lot of training for teachers from various parts of the world who will be teaching in the Confucius Institutes.[19] Over time, ECNU aimed to set up several more Confucius Institutes, in an effort to catch up with such rivals as Fudan University, which has already sponsored nine. To help realize this ambition, the Department of Teaching Chinese as a Foreign Language was taken out of the School of Humanities and expanded into an International College of Chinese Studies in 2002.

Campus Spaces and the University's Ethos

When asked about the special architectural features of the ECNU campus, the President noted that the History and Arts building, which had been built in the 1930s as the signature building of Utopia University, was still regarded as ECNU's most symbolic building. There is a sense of stability and solidity in its form, also an aura of grandeur and solemnity, with Chinese and Western architectural ideas integrated within its conception.

---

[19] Interview with Zhuang Huiming, Vice-President for Teaching and Learning, 1 June 2007.

(See Photo 6.4). President Yu also commented on the set of buildings created under Soviet influence in the 1950s, set in a rectangular shape, with the Departments of Biology, Geography and Physics in the imposing central building that looks East, flanked on each side by two buildings facing each other cross the quadrangle and housing mathematics on the South side and chemistry on the North side. For science students, this has been the heart of the campus, and science graduates like himself are still deeply attached to this complex. Now two modern buildings for sciences, built in 2003, tower over this graceful rectangle, with the Mao statue, and ECNU's logo on its central lawn. (Photo 6.1)

Photo 6.1: The Sciences Quadrangle

The two vice presidents who were interviewed were both reluctant to identify any one building on campus. Rather each separately pointed to the Liwa River, which runs through the campus, as embodying the spirit of ECNU. One of them noted that the most important feature of the new campus is the Yingtao (櫻桃) River, which reminds everyone of the Liwa River and helps them to feel at home in the suburbs.[20] The other vice president told his own personal story of having done his Masters degree at Nanjing University and then having moved to ECNU for doctoral work. He talked about how he had come to love the beautiful surroundings of the ECNU campus and felt the river expressed the uni-

---

[20] Ibid.

versity's spirit – always gentle and graceful, never aggressive, arrogant or self-promoting.[21]

Faculty and Issues of Teaching and Research

Faculty Growth and Development

We have noted the rapid growth of student enrollments earlier, from a total of 7,233 students in 1995, to 12,328 in 2000 and 19,424 in 2005. Growth in faculty numbers has been much slower, reflecting the extremely low faculty student ratios that existed before the move to mass higher education. Thus there were 1,532 full-time faculty in 1995, and a faculty student ratio of 1:4.7, 1,473 faculty in 2000 and a faculty student ratio of 1:8.4, and 1,730 full-time faculty in 2005, for a faculty student ratio of 1:11.2. What did change significantly in the period between 1995 and 2000 was the percentage of full professors in the faculty contingent, from 15% in 1995, to 20% in 2005. Likewise associate professors grew as a proportion of the faculty contingent, from 25% in 1995, to 35% in 2005. Lecturers grew from 34% in 1995, to 37% in 2005, while assistant teachers dropped from 26% in 1995 to 8% in 2005. Overall this reflected the higher qualifications of teaching faculty, and the promotion of well qualified younger faculty members. The total faculty contingent of 1,473 had only 270 members or 18% holding PhD degrees in 2000, but by 2005, the number of PhD holders had risen to 649, 38% of all teaching faculty.

Faculty Perspectives on The Move to Mass Higher Education

Two hours in a faculty focus group meeting with nine faculty members gave us some interesting insights into faculty perspectives on the move to mass higher education. Among the nine faculty meeting with us, two were women and seven were men; two came from the Department of Physical Education, two from the Biology department, one from sociology, one from Chinese, one from higher education and two from educational administration. One was a department chair and another had a post in the Provost's office, while most were mid-level or younger faculty members. All seemed to welcome the opportunity to have their views heard.

On the ECNU visioning process several responded that they had participated and found it to be a positive process. ECNU was finally on the road to establishing its profile as a comprehensive university with

---

[21] Interview with Chen Qun, Vice President for International Affairs, 31 May 2007.

education in a leading position, they felt. Several noted that ECNU had a strong base, but had lost ground in the later 1980s, after Liu Fonian's retirement, due to the fact that all of its graduates became teachers and did not have a social standing that could match that of the graduates of major engineering or comprehensive universities. The teacher education orientation meant they were almost entirely dependent on central government funding, and had little possibility of horizontal projects with industry, which was an important source of funding for other institutions.

One of the institutions they compared themselves to was Tongji University, a major engineering university in Shanghai. They felt that ECNU had originally been in the same league as Fudan, one of China's leading comprehensive universities, and Jiaotong, a major national polytechnical university, and somewhat ahead of Tongji. However, Tongji had benefited from the opportunity to make major contributions to Shanghai's transformation through its expertise in bridge and tunnel building, urban planning and subways. ECNU had not had a parallel opportunity and so had fallen behind. For this reason, faculty had hoped for a merger with a specialist engineering university or one of the medical universities, rather than taking on lower level educational institutions, as the city had called upon them to do.

Balancing this sense of disappointment was appreciation that ECNU had been included in the 21/1 Project, and had recently managed to get into the 98/5 Project, which opened up opportunities for both graduate students and faculty to participate in international scholarly collaboration. Without the funding and profile of the 98/5 Project they felt ECNU could not have developed its emerging international profile, and would not have been in a position to attract so many international students. With its critical mass of excellence in education and teaching, it was in a position to take leadership in programs for international students. Faculty were especially proud of the policy of bilingual teaching which had been adopted in 2003, and implemented in 2005.

Several of them made the point that education was one of the greatest strengths of traditional Chinese culture, and that it encouraged the kinds of cross-disciplinary integration of specialist subject areas which was a core focus of the new vision statement. "Education is in the souls of Chinese people," they said, "and thus there is a strong orienttation towards self-discipline and hard work." However, this was also a double-edged sword, since education had always been closely linked to politics in the Chinese context. In spite of the higher education law passed in 1998 and its specification that universities are legal persons, Chinese universities remained under close and direct political control, with the Party Secretary having the top leadership position, even in private universities. From this perspective faculty members questioned whether universities could be in a position to lead society in the emerging changes, or whether they tended to lag behind, while private enterprises forged ahead. To some degree, the university had a fortress mentality, and was not responding adequately to the emergence of civil society and the opportunities and pressures of globalization, they felt.

In reflecting on this problem, they noted that students were really the ones leading the way in social change, with many of them initiating new kinds of social organizations and participating actively in the new and relatively unregulated arenas of private enterprise and non-governmental activity. Students understood better than professors the reality that they needed broader knowledge and social experience, also the ability to innovate and take initiatives on their own, if they were to find attractive employment opportunities. Thus it was important for faculty to give them maximum autonomy, and allow them to make their own study and self-development plans. In the past, students were guaranteed favorable job assignments if they studied hard and got top marks, whereas now social experience and a range of practical and adaptive skills tended to count for much more in the job market. This was something that students understand better than their professors, in their view.

Issues of Teaching & Research

Generally, faculty did not feel overworked in their teaching, given that undergraduate enrollments had not spiraled, but they did find their advising responsibility for graduate students extremely heavy, and also felt the pressure to be productive in research. They were proud, however, of the new courses emerging, the reform of course content in response to social demands, the greater orientation towards cross-disciplinary work and the opportunities for collaboration in research among departments. Overall, they felt the experience they had had of undergoing the first national teaching evaluation process had been positive and valuable, although there were severe time pressures and other demands upon them in the process.[22]

---

[22] For details on the establishment of the Higher Education Evaluation Centre (HEEC) in 2004, and the national teaching assessment process, see Chapter 1.

Other insights into teaching and research issues came from the two vice presidents interviewed. Vice President Zhuang, who is responsible for teaching and learning, noted how ECNU's strength lay in the basic fields of knowledge, but that great emphasis has been put on giving students more breadth and choice in recent years. The teaching program breaks down into three main parts – foundation courses, specialist courses and courses in education, with a third being foundation courses, somewhat more than a third being specialist courses and a little less than a third in education. There has been a huge increase in elective courses in both the education and foundation areas, as well as a lively development of extra curricular learning activities, which are called "the second classroom" and given considerable support. Many are student-initiated activities such as clubs in the areas of arts, calligraphy, drama, acrobatics and sports, also social service of all kinds, including educational services for the children of migrant workers and children in rural areas. Students are aware that involvement in these kinds of activities may be as important to their job search as academic results.

Vice President Zhuang also noted how ECNU's first experience of a comprehensive assessment of teaching quality at the undergraduate level had been a main focus of attention for the 2005-6 academic year. They had organized groups of senior professors to observe classes and give advice on improving teaching, and particularly focused on support for younger teachers. An on-line system of student evaluation of teaching quality had been put in place, and also a system whereby senior professors were required to do a certain amount of undergraduate teaching as well as their research and graduate teaching. It had been a strenuous exercise, demanding a lot of time, but one that was felt to be very worthwhile.[23]

On research Vice President Chen noted that the university had only begun to place a strong emphasis on research in the 1990s, seeing it as essential to its reputation and also an important social responsibility. Research funds had grown every year in recent years, but ECNU was still far behind universities such as Tongji in Shanghai, he noted. In 2006 it received 150 million *yuan*, with 70% of that coming from governmental sources, more from Shanghai than the national government, and 30% from industry. In future they hope to develop more industry funded

---

[23] Interview with Zhuang Huiming, Vice President for Teaching and Learning, 1 June 2007.

research, and reach a level of 50%, since government funding had limits.

In seeking research funding, they encourage bottom up initiatives from individual faculty and departments, while selecting a few key areas at the university level for priority development. One of the new areas they had recently developed was cognitive science, a multi-disciplinary field that builds on their strengths in psychology, education, early childhood education and genomics. A second area of priority development was Functional Magnetic Resonance Imaging, for measuring activities of the brain, including chemical changes in the thinking process, a field based on theoretical physics and mathematics. With the new equipment they had recently purchased, they considered their centre to be the strongest in China. Funding from the 98/5 Project contributed to this strategic research development, and they were hoping to recruit excellent scholars internationally and build a platform for research in these two areas.[24] It is significant that both areas are closely linked to broad understandings of education.

When faculty members were asked about their feeling for the campus architecture, one of the biology professors noted that many people point to the History and Arts building (Photo 6.4), but he was attached to the science buildings at the heart of the campus, including the twin towers that look over the traditional quadrangle. (Photo 6.1) A faculty member from the Department of Chinese literature expressed a view similar to that of the two vice-presidents, that the most important

Photo 6.2: The Liwa River on ECNU's urban campus

---

[24] Interview with Chen Qun, Vice President, 31 May 2007.

symbol of the ECNU spirit on campus was the Liwa River. (Photo 6.2) She noted that the Chinese department had four typical kinds of graduates: writers, scholars, publishers and teachers. For all four, the expanse of the campus, from the front gate, across the bridge over the Liwa River up to the quadrangle, had been a space of tranquility, free from political control or intrusion, where they could develop their thinking at a deep level.[25]

Student Perspectives and Concerns

The student focus group whom we met with was made up of ten students, eight women and two men, from the fields of chemistry, law and politics, software, public management, early childhood education, arts and media. All were third and fourth year undergraduate students, and three had come from rural areas, while the rest were from urban areas. The discussion was free flowing, but a number of broad concerns came to the fore – equity issues, the quality of teaching and learning in the move to mass higher education and issues of employment.

Equity Issues

On equity, students felt that generally more opportunities had been opened up to everyone in the rapid massification of higher education. Nevertheless, the implementation had been so sudden and rapid that many problems had arisen. It was clear that students from middle class families and from cadre families were benefiting more, in terms of access to higher quality institutions, than students from working class or rural families. The examination system ensured a certain kind of equality of opportunity, but there were huge gaps in the quality of secondary education that made for very different levels of preparation and life chances for young people from different social groups and regions. Of particular concern to these students was the fact that many new higher institutions had sprung up which are of questionable quality and have a far lower level of resources than institutions such as ECNU.

Nevertheless, some students from rural areas were able to get into ECNU, and one of the young women who came from a very poor village in Zhejiang province shared her story. Her parents wanted her to go to a vocational secondary school, and never encouraged her to consider

---

[25] Faculty Focus Group Meeting, 1 June 2007.

university, nor did the family have a single relative with a university degree. However, she had made friends with a university student who encouraged her to try, and she therefore managed to enroll in an academic secondary school and get into the best upper secondary school in the county. This in turn enabled her to get high enough marks on the entry examinations for ECNU. She was happy with this achievement and with her program at ECNU, but concerned about employment opportunities on graduation. She made the comment that male students from Shanghai would have the best job opportunities, followed by female Shanghai students, then male students from outside Shanghai and last of all female students from outside Shanghai like herself.

Student Concerns about Employment

Generally students were concerned about employment prospects on graduation and this theme took up a considerable proportion of the focus group time. One of the major inequalities arises from the residential permit system, whereby local students with Shanghai residential permits tend to be favored in the job market. While it used to be that acceptance in a major national university guaranteed a Shanghai residential permit, this is no longer the case. Thus government bureaus and schools within Shanghai municipality will only hire graduates with Shanghai residential permits, although schools in the nearby counties are more open to graduates from outside Shanghai. Local companies, such as software companies, are sometimes keen to get graduates without Shanghai residential permits as they can pay them lower salaries. Generally non-Shanghai graduates are paid 1,000-2,000 *yuan* less per month, and this makes it very difficult for them to stay, since they do not have families nearby who can help them to make ends meet. They saw these as inequities that required government intervention.

There were different views about employment opportunities, with those in teacher education and those in software feeling confident that they would find suitable jobs, others less optimistic. Those in teacher education spoke of how they had internship opportunities which enabled them to get to know the schools, and that the university helped them in the job search process. Students also mentioned the university's effort in organizing a job fair every year, to enable contact between hiring agencies and students.

Students made the point that they need to think differently about employment than in the past. With a mass higher education system, university graduation meant something very different than in the past, and they needed to change their own attitudes and expectations. Instead of looking for one job they would hold lifelong, they should think about a series of jobs that would enable them to develop their own potential and direction. They should also explore different working experiences, and learn to be self-reliant and flexible, able to gain new skills in response to newly developing areas.

The main problem, they concluded, was not employment itself, but overly high expectations about the kind of employment students wanted. One way round the job search was to apply for graduate study opportunities, and this made sense if one was really interested, but students were aware that master's degree graduates might have just as much difficulty in finding appropriate employment as undergraduates – so it would only be a matter of deferring the problem. In spite of the concerns they expressed, students seemed overall to be quite mature in their thoughts and expectations about employment, and fairly optimistic that things would work out well for them, as long as they were willing to adapt to changing needs and circumstances.

Students on the Learning Experience

How did students feel about their learning experiences and the quality of the education they were receiving under the new conditions of massification? Some students immediately mentioned the problem of isolation and remoteness on the new Minhang campus, with teaching faculty coming by bus to teach and leaving immediately afterwards. They also noted that class sizes were getting larger and larger, and the intimate seminars of 15 students that were common in the past had given way to a typical class size of forty to fifty students. Teachers were not able to give as much individual attention to students as had been customary in the past, and students in turn were less serious about their academic studies and more preoccupied with employment concerns.

At the same time, students expressed satisfaction with many dimensions of their university life. They felt they were respected and listened to as members of the campus community and every week there was a students' advisory committee meeting where they could air their views and concerns to university leaders, and give their inputs on major decisions. They were also able to participate in many different social groupings on campus and felt this was as important a self-development exercise as their formal studies. They mentioned their work for underprivileged children of migrant workers, also some involvement in the collaborative links which ECNU had with Xinjiang University and Xinjiang Normal University in the Northwest and with rural schools in Yunnan province in the Southwest. They valued the opportunities for graduates to go for one year of teaching, before beginning masters degrees, although this was a very competitive program, with only three to four students being accepted each year. Overall there was a high degree of interest and engagement in themes around student involvement in social service.

Photo 6.3: The Minhang Campus with the Yingtao River

Identity and Ethos from the Student Perspective

Finally, we found students had a strong sense of identity with ECNU's history and spirit. When we asked them about their feelings for the university, they immediately mentioned influential figures of the past, whom they were proud to be associated with – Meng Xiancheng, the first president, Liu Fonian, the leading educational theorist, Jin Litong, a highly respected chemistry professor, and a famous graduate of the management school, who founded a successful company and has become a benefactor of the university. They were excited by ECNU's international profile and outreach, and one was thrilled to take part in an international conference on teacher education, organized by Professor Zhou Nanzhao who had long worked in UNESCO's Bangkok office. As this conversation on international activity unfolded, students from the Minhang campus expressed once again their sense of isolation, with information not so readily available to them and fewer opportunities for international contacts.

On architecture, students all agreed that the History and Arts building from the 1930s was the one they loved best. For them, it represented a place of history and a place of many stories – stories of writers such as Lu Xun, who had once taught in that building and Wang Xiaoying, a contemporary female novelist, also stories of successful entrepreneurs, such as Jiang Nanchun, who had graduated from the Chinese department and created a high profile advertising company. By contrast, students felt the buildings on the new Minhang campus were generally too Westernized, even though their quality and facilities were excellent.[26]

Photo 6.4: The History and Arts Building

Conclusion: A New Type of Normal University for the 21st Century

This chapter has allowed us to see how the leaders of East China Normal University have made a series of strategic decisions, arising out of a new vision statement, in which they have not only maintained their status and title as a normal university, but given education a leading role in the university's strategic direction and broadened their educational mandate to include all levels and aspects of education, from early childhood and special education through primary and secondary, physical and health education to adult and higher education, also educational leadership and

---

[26] Student Focus Group Meeting, 30 May 2007.

its relation to public administration. Thus their five education-related schools are remaining on the university's urban campus, along with the School of Foreign Languages, where students and faculty will interact on a daily basis with the large community of international students and faculty coming from other parts of the world. Meanwhile a spacious and well developed suburban campus is becoming a new centre of scholarship in the sciences, humanities and a whole range of newly developing inter-disciplinary schools.

The Faculty of Education Sciences has recently developed a new internet based platform with video conferencing facility which creates a wide range of possibilities for classroom observation, problem solving and consultation at a regional, national and global level. This technology is seen as making possible an integration of educational theory and new developments in the various disciplines of knowledge, as all kinds of direct observations and interactions are made possible, among teachers and between teachers and university scholars, irrespective of distance.[27] At a national level, one of China's most prominent educational theorists, Professor Ye Lan, is leading an extensive school improvement project, involving hundreds of schools in many provinces, which emphasizes a holistic approach that stimulates change based on a deep inner understanding of conditions within each school, including those in poor and remote areas. Some have labeled her work an indigenous Chinese school of educational thoughts.[28] At an international level, there is a vision for developing new global standards of teacher education, in connection with a UNESCO project on teacher education in the Asia Pacific, at a time when many parts of the world are seeking to understand some of the notable achievements of education in Asia.

Given that education is one of the most multi-disciplinary of the university's fields of knowledge, the leading role that it has at East China Normal University should support and facilitate the goal of nurturing an integrative and inter-disciplinary approach to knowledge, while the new technology can further extend modalities that support the second goal of ensuring that all teaching, learning and research be experienced within

---

[27] Shen Zuyun and Jin Zhiming, "Huadong Shifan Daxue Lizhu Jiaoyu Shishi Jiaoshi Jiaoyu Chuangxin Jihua (ECNU Establishes an Innovative Plan for Educational Practice in Teacher Education)," in *Zhongguo Qingnian Bao (China Youth Daily)*, November 19, 2007.

[28] See Ruth Hayhoe, *Portraits of Influential Chinese Educators*, pp.353-358.

an international context and with a global mindset. For ECNU, the move to mass higher education has thus stimulated a rethinking and reclaiming of its identity as a normal university, the creation of an entirely new campus for its expanded student body, and a focused approach to international outreach through the redesign of its urban campus and its active support of the Confucius Institute movement overseas.

Nevertheless, we observe emerging tensions confronting ECNU down the road: between upholding its identity as a teacher education university and the external pressure pushing it towards a comprehensive university; between its endeavor to strengthen its status as a national university and the inevitable localization brought about by its increasing dependence on resources from Shanghai; between its international outreach strategy and the constraints of its human resources.

Over the past decade, ECNU saw its undergraduate enrollment more than double in size, and its graduate student body increase to five times its original size. Over the same period, the percentage of students in teacher education programs has dropped, with an in-take of around 1,300, or 30% of the total at undergraduate level in 2005, down from almost 100% in the early 1990s. Most of the new programs and schools added in the 1990s are not in education, but in areas such as information science, design, software engineering and international studies, although the five education schools that have emerged have strong graduate programs. Thus it will be a challenge for the leadership to maintain the leading role it has given to education and teachers in the coming years, and avoid becoming just one more comprehensive university with education as one of its strengths.

ECNU has also been struggling to balance its status as a major national university and its tendency to depend increasingly on local sources of funding. It requires a national vision and mission to maintain its reputation and to sharpen its competitive edge, yet it has to rely more and more on local resources for this endeavor. Clearly it would have been impossible for ECNU to make its way into the 98/5 Project without the full support of the Shanghai government. This has led to a controversy among some peers over ECNU's participation in the Project. ECNU must also cater more to local needs, which raises the issue of how to balance its national mission and local service.

ECNU's plan for international outreach appears to be an effective counter-strategy, which should serve to benchmark it at a higher level and in a wider context, and to reflect Shanghai's image as China's most international metropolis. Yet, it still faces many challenges, such as the relatively low percentage of PhD holders among its faculty and constraints on its plan of offering bilingual courses. Put in another way, internationalization could provide a good solution to the dilemma of increasing localization. However it needs to be worked into all aspects of its core functions.

With the resources of traditional Chinese culture and scholarship, where education always held high respect and there was a strong emphasis on integrated knowledge and its social applications, ECNU should be in a position to develop the idea of the normal university in new ways, which could have a global impact. A recent encouraging example is the creation of the Meng Xiancheng College, named after its first president, in September of 2007. This is a boarding college especially for the new cohort of teacher candidates whose fees have been waived under national policy. It follows closely the patterns of traditional Chinese *shuyuan* (書院), aiming to integrate educational activities into the students' lives and into the formation of their character and professional beliefs in a coherent manner. With this holistic experience, the students are expected to become teachers with a strong sense of mission and responsibility as well as good teaching abilities and skills. Fittingly, Professor Ye Lan, China's most influential theorist in basic education, has been named Dean of this new college. It is still too early to judge how successful this model can be, but it does suggest a new vision and energy for teacher education within a broader concept of the normal university than the original model from 19th century France.

7
Southwest University – An Unusual Merger and New Challenges

Jun LI and Jing LIN, with LIU Yibing

Southwest University (SWU) in Chongqing presents an interesting contrast to East China Normal University. Originally one of the six national key normal universities established in the early 1950s as Southwest Normal, it is the only one which was given permission by the Ministry of Education to enter into a major merger and give up the title of normal university. This chapter recounts its merger with Southwest Agricultural University, and the ways in which the recently merged institution has responded to the opportunities and challenges associated with the move to mass higher education. This is one of two public institutions in our study which were accepted into Project 21/1, that supports 100 leading universities, but not into the more elite Project 98/5. The other case is Yanbian University which will be profiled in the next chapter.

History and Context
Chongqing and the Southwest Region

Located in the upper reaches of the Yangtze River, Chongqing is currently the largest metropolitan city in China with a population of more than 32 million people. In ancient history, Chongqing was known as the capital of the semi-mythical State of Ba (巴國) as early as in the eleventh century BCE, and has been one of only two or three political and economic centers in the southwest region of China. In modern times, it served as the war-time capital of the Nationalist government from 1937 to 1946, becoming a national political and educational center as many governmental institutions and elite universities were forced to move to the southwest from Nanjing, Shanghai, Beijing and other major cities as a result of the Anti-Japanese War.

Chongqing served as a political and educational centre for the southwest region, after the reorganization of higher education in 1952. Then in 1997 it was upgraded to become one of four municipalities directly under the central government, along side of Beijing, Tianjin and

Shanghai. This separated it from Sichuan province, which had originally been the most populous province in China. The southwest region, including Chongqing, Sichuan, Yunnan, Guizhou and Tibet, has a total of more than 30 minority groups. Such a diverse multicultural context has created a particularly complex and difficult situation for education, from elementary schools to higher education.

In addition, the Sichuan Basin, the Tibetan Plateau and the Yunnan-Guizhou Plateau are all situated in the southwest region, with the Yangtze River, the longest in China and the third longest in the world, having its source in the Nyainqentanglha Range and meandering through Chongqing down to Wuhan, Nanjing and Shanghai. The uniqueness and diversity of natural resources mean that the region has historically relied on agriculture. Agricultural technologies have traditionally played a dominant role in the development of the regional economy, and agricultural science and education have been crucial for local communities.

The Early History and Traditions of Southwest University

SWU came into being through a recent merger, approved by the Ministry of Education on December 16, 2004 and formally announced on July 16, 2005, between Southwest Normal University and Southwest Agricultural University. In 1950 Southwest Agricultural University had been separated out from the Sichuan Provincial College of Education, established in 1937. At the same time the Sichuan Provincial College of Education was merged with the National Women's Normal College, established in 1940, to become Southwest Normal University. The Sichuan Provincial College of Education in turn had been upgraded from the Sichuan Rural Reconstruction Institute (四川鄉村建設學院) in 1933. The latter can be dated back to the East Sichuan Teachers College (川東師範學堂) established in 1906 by Zhang Zhenzi, as a regional teacher education institution.[1]

The traditional strength of Southwest Normal University made it the center of teacher education for the whole southwest region of China, while Southwest Agricultural University, which was administered by the Ministry of Agriculture, became the center of agricultural higher learning in the region. Both were national-level institutions with a high profile in the areas of teacher education and agriculture, and a non-interrupted

---

[1] The Editorial Board (eds.), *Xinan Shifan Daxue Xiaoshi* (*The History of Southwest Normal University*) (Chongqing: Southwest Normal University Press, 2000), p.2.

tradition that has been focusing on service for the local and regional communities.

The Story of the Merger

SWU's recent merger is an unusual case in China's move to mass higher education for two reasons. Firstly, it took place only in 2005, much later than the nationwide movement towards major mergers. Secondly, teacher education and agriculture had been officially designated as areas of key importance where mergers with other types of institutions would normally not be allowed by the central government.

In the early 1990s, the Chinese government realized that the highly specialized and sectoralized model of higher education system, developed under the Soviet influence in the 1950s, was no longer working efficiently and had failed to respond to the social changes brought about by the burgeoning of the socialist market system. Merger was adopted as a strategy to optimize institutional resources in higher education in the mid-1990s, resulting in a nationwide reorganization and re-adjustment of public universities and programs. By 2000, a total of 490 institutions had taken part in mergers and 204 much larger universities emerged, including such giant institutions as Jilin University in the Northeast and Zhejiang University in East China. Few new mergers took place after that time. This was the largest nationwide organizational change in higher education since the 1950s, and it has played a critical role in shaping China's move to mass higher education.

In the radical amalgamation process, higher education institutions for teachers were not allowed to be merged with or into other types of universities, since the education of teachers was seen as a national priority and normal universities were to keep their independent identity and role. The only choice for them was a merger involving the bringing in of lower level teacher education institutions, as in the case of East China Normal University, which has been depicted in Chapter 6.

This national policy prevented Southwest Normal University and Southwest Agricultural University from being amalgamated into one institution at the beginning of the merger movement. In fact, the two universities, both key national universities, had fallen in love and had been hoping for a merger ever since 1993, we were told by the top leaders.[2]

---

[2] Interview with Wang Xiaojia, President of Southwest University and former president of Southwest Agricultural University, and Executive Vice-President

First and foremost, the two universities shared the same origin, developing out of the Sichuan Provincial College of Education, established in 1937, which in turn went back to the East Sichuan Teachers College, founded in 1906. In Chinese terminology, they had close family ties (同根同源), and they had built a strongly collaborative relationship over a period of decades. It was a natural desire for both of them to get back together as one single institution. Secondly, the programs of the two universities complemented each other perfectly, and there would be no redundant or duplicate programs if merged. Thirdly, there were no other higher education institutions at the same level in the greater Chongqing area that could be considered suitable for a merger with either of them. And lastly, the campuses of the two universities stood side by side, separated only by a wall. Interestingly, more than a dozen families in the two universities had conjugal relationships across the wall, with husbands serving in one institution and wives in the other.[3]

While Southwest Normal and Southwest Agricultural both saw a merger as desirable and put forth good reasons to merge into one institution, their attempt to get permission was thwarted in both 1995 and 1999, mainly due to the national policy mentioned earlier. Another critical issue was that the local government did not support their bid, since Chongqing was absorbed with its own struggle to be upgraded to a municipality directly under the central government and having the status of a province.[4]

The turning point came in 2003, when the Chongqing government finally realized that the merger of Southwest Normal and Southwest Agricultural would have a lot of benefits for the local community. Practically, it would also make it possible for one more major university in Chongqing to be included in Project 21/1, while it was very unlikely, if not impossible, that either Southwest Normal or Southwest Agricultural could make it onto the list alone. The outcome would thus raise the status of local higher education, and this, in turn, would greatly benefit the development of the local economy and society. With the strong support of the Chongqing government, that by now had provincial-level

---

Song Naiqing, who had formerly served as President of Southwest Normal, 30 May 2008.

[3] Interview with Wang Xiaojia and Song Naiqing, President and Executive Vice-President, 30 May 2008.

[4] Interview with Song Naiqing, Executive Vice-President, 31 May 2008.

status, the merger was finally approved by the Ministry of Education on December 16, 2004, and Southwest University was formally established as a union of the former agricultural and normal universities on July 16, 2005. President Wang joked at how long the journey had been: "After a ten-year love affair the marriage finally took place between the two institutions".[5] While most other mergers were orchestrated from above, with considerable pressure to move quickly, this was a case of a merger entirely initiated at the institutional level, with nearly a decade of effort before approval was given at the national and local levels.

Southwest's Move to Mass Higher Education: An Empirical Overview (1990-2005)

Growth in Student Enrollments

SWU has experienced an uneven growth of expansion since the late 1990s, in terms of the change in undergraduate student enrollments. The undergraduate student population in the two former institutions did not change much in the early 1990s, from 6,040 in 1990 to 6,071 in 1995, but radically jumped to 11,996 in 2000, and soared to 38,689 in 2005 after the merger, as shown in Table 7.1. The growth rate in the undergraduate student enrollment remained steady in the early 1990s, but almost doubled up 97.6% from 1995 to 2000. Between 2000 and 2005, it soared by 222.5%, the most striking growth since the early 1990s. SWU's recent merger and status in Project 21/1 greatly contributed as key factors in this fast changing landscape, allowing it accommodate more talented students who were recruited from all over the country.

Table 7.1: Undergraduate Student Enrollment of Southwest University (1990-2005)

	1990	1995	2000	2005
Male	4,100	4,111	8,159	23,287
Female	1,940	1,960	3,837	15,402
Total	6,040	6,071	11,996	38,689
Growth rate	-	0.5%	97.6%	222.5%
Female : Male	1:2.11	1:2.10	1:2.13	1:1.51
Urban : Rural	1:3.57	1:3.59	1:2.36	1:2.67
Minority : Han	1:12.16	1:11.97	1:8.71	1:8.80
Teacher : Student	1:3.4	1:3.5	1:7.2	1:16.0

---

[5] Interview with Wang Xiaojia, President, 30 May 2008.

The ratio of female to male students on the SWU campus shared the same pattern with the enrollment changes, with the ratio of 1:2.11, 1:2.10 and 1:2.13 in 1990, 1995 and 2000, respectively, but significantly increased to 1:1.51 in 2005. The change in the ratio between female and male students showed that SWU's expansion and merger had a significant positive impact on females' opportunities of higher learning. By contrast, the ratio of students from urban and rural areas remained unchanged at around 1:3.57 in the early 1990s, but the gap was widened from 1:3.59 in 1995, to 1:2.36 in 2000, and 1:2.67 in 2005. While both institutions had traditionally been dominated by rural students, the ratio of urban students increased in the final stage, indicating the university's higher status nationwide and possibly also China's rapid urbanization.

In addition, there were more than 3,948 students from 38 minority groups in 2005, accounting for nearly one-tenth of the whole student body on campus. The growth in the number and ratio of minority students changed the character of SWU's student population between 1995 and 2005, with a dramatic rise from 468 in 1995 to 3,948 in 2005, and a ratio of one minority to nearly nine Han students in 2005, up from one minority to around twelve Han students in 1990. Without doubt, minority students benefited significantly from the expansion policy, as the university had put forth even greater effort at serving the needs of the region in recent years.

The Changing Financial Profile

SWU's financial situation has changed significantly within the fifteen years, in terms of student fees, funding from central and local governments, research grants, and other sources, with the income of both institutions combined for the years before the merger. Its overall income increased from 42.3 million in 1990, to 110 million in 1995, 410 million in 2000, and 1.14 billion in 2005, with growth rates of 148.7%, 272.5% and 180.4%, respectively. The fastest growing periods, from 1995 to 2000 and from 2000 to 2005, were largely the result of significantly increased funding from the local government, student fees, income-generating projects and the special government grants associated with Project 21/1.

Student tuition surged at an average rate of 360.9%, from 2.8 million in 1990 and 15.45 million in 1995 to 96.1 million in 2000, and 200 million in 2005. The most rapid growth in student tuition took place from 1995 to 2000 when the radical expansion policy was adopted, with a growth rate of 521.8%. Student tuition constituted 6.6%, 14.1%, 23.6% and 17.6% of

SWU's total income in 1990, 1995, 2000 and 2005, respectively. It constituted the largest proportion of the total income during the radical expansion period from 1995 to 2000.

Research grants also saw a rapid growth in recent decades, from a total of 3.6 million in 1990 and 6.0 million in 1995 to 20.4 million in 2000 and 81.6 million in 2005, with the ratio of direct governmental and nongovernmental sources of funding, changing from 1:0.89 in 1990 and 1995 to 1:0.43 in 2000 and to 1:0.45 in 2005. In other words, direct governmental grants grew much faster than nongovernmental funding, particularly from 1995 through 2000, reflecting the greater difficulty that educational and agricultural institutions have in gaining contract research opportunities compared to engineering institutions. In general, the growth in research grants was slower than that of other income over these years.

Naturally, expenditures also soared significantly over these years, for faculty and staff salaries and benefits, teaching, student aid, and the construction of infrastructure. The budget for payroll and benefits of faculty and staff jumped from 14.3 million in 1990, to 44.5 million in 1995, 97.4 million in 2000 and 340 million in 2005, with the fastest growth rate between 2000 and 2005. Teaching expenses surged from 13.1 million in 1990, to 29.3 million in 1995, 90.0 million in 2000 to 280 million in 2005, with a similar growth pattern. A striking expenditure over these years was in the construction of infrastructure which soared from 7.4 million in 1995 to 90.9 million in 2000, and again to 189.0 million in 2005, reflecting the radical expansion of the student body that took place after 1999 and up to the time when the merger was formally approved in 2005. Comparatively, there was limited growth in student aid over these fifteen years, from 2.6 million in 1990, to 7.4 million in 1995, 11.8 million in 2000, and 31.8 million in 2005.

Curricular Change

The structure of the curriculum and its scope has changed remarkably since the early 1990s, particularly at the time of the radical expansion in 1999 and the merger in 2005 but also earlier. For example, Southwest Normal had a total of 26 undergraduate programs in 1990, mainly focusing on areas of teacher education and professional studies in education and psychology. In 1993, it set up new programs in national economic management, law, applied physics, visual communication design, economic geography and urban and rural planning. Thus by 1998 it had a total of 8 colleges and 34 undergraduate programs, with many new programs that were not connected with teacher education, such as applied chemistry, applied mathematics, pharmaceutical engineering, accounting, environmental sciences, information and management. It is obvious that Southwest Normal tried to adapt its programs to newly developing applied areas in order to meet the need of socioeconomic development and the expansion policy in the late 1990s. By 2000, it had also set up new programs in philosophy, human resources management, journalism and applied psychology. It had a total of 17 colleges in 2005 before the merger, including the College of Historic Culture and Tourism, the College of Chemistry and Chemical Engineering, the College of Material Science and Engineering, the College of Resources and Environmental Science and the College of Law.

Southwest Agricultural University had focused on its traditional areas before the merger, with 54 undergraduate programs in 15 colleges, including the College of Agronomy and Biotechnology, the College of Horticulture and Landscape Architecture, the School of Fish Production, the College of Animal Science and Technology, the College of Food Science, the College of Textile and Garments and the College of Engineering and Technology.

After the merger in 2005, SWU became a much stronger comprehensive university with a total of 95 undergraduate programs in 31 colleges, almost doubling the number in the two institutions before the merger. So far, most programs and colleges in the pre-merger institutions have remained unchanged, as the curricular areas on the two former campuses were complementary. Of course there has been some integration of programs and colleges. For example, the new College of Resources and Environmental Science was formed by an integration of the program in Land Management in Southwest Agriculture's College of Economics and Management, the program in Water Resources Engineering in Southwest Agriculture's College of Fish Production and the program in Land Management in Southwest Normal's College of Geographical Sciences into Southwest Normal's original College by this name. Other colleges, such as the College of Political Science and Public Management and the College of Computer and Information Science, have also experienced similar integration in the process of merger.

Vision and Strategic Directions

Vision and Mission

As a newly merged institution, SWU has naturally developed a new vision and mission based on the traditions of both institutions. The new vision is stated in eight Chinese characters: "uniquely established in the southwest (特立西南), our learning and practice embrace the world (學行天下)." The phrase *teli* (特立) originates from *The Record of Rites* (《禮記》), and refers to a gentleman's unique life pursuit and independent moral stance.⁶ This vision has multiple meanings for SWU, including encouraging a unique mission of education that can serve the diverse communities of the region, and a distinct ethos of teachers and learners who have a high level of moral self-cultivation. The phrase *xuexing* (學行) was adopted from *The Works of Xunzi* (《荀子》), designating an integration of learning into real social action for the local community, the wider society and the public good more generally.⁷ SWU has also kept its historic original motto, which was first adopted by the East Sichuan

Photo 7.1: Statue of Chairman Mao holding in his hand a blueprint for the new China, erected in 1954, in front of the steps leading up to the original main administration building of Southwest Normal University and representing its ethos of service to the region.

---

⁶ *The Records of Rites*, 57.41.
⁷ *The Works of Xunzi*, 8.

Normal School in 1928. It goes as follows: "With a breadth of understanding and brightness of vision, carrying forward the cause of our predecessors and forging ahead into future (含弘光大，既往開來)."

The new institution has set forth a mission of becoming a top research-oriented comprehensive university, featuring a unique emphasis on educational science, agricultural science, life science and management science. SWU clearly values quality in teaching and research, with its focus on teacher education and agricultural education that can serve the southwestern multicultural context. When asked what might symbolize SWU's vision and mission, several of the university leaders pointed to the Mao Statue inside SWU's front entrance, which gives a sense of the university's mission of service. This statue was erected in 1954, on the former Southwest Normal campus. Mao is seen holding a scroll with the blueprint for new China's development in his hand, and the impression is quite different from the radical revolutionary statues erected on many university campuses in the late sixties during the Cultural Revolution.

Strategic Directions

For the newly merged institution, SWU's leaders have endeavored to set forth clear strategic directions, and the first priority relates to the integration of the two former institutions. Though they had collaborated in many areas over several decades, the challenging task of bringing about full integration has been a major concern for both President Wang Xiaojia and Executive Vice-President Song Naiqing.

This must involve administration, finance, the working style of university members and the campus culture. Many conflicts have arisen in the process of university mergers, such as the conflict over the appropriate allocation of leaders' and administrators' positions in the newly merged institution. In the SWU case, Wang Xiaojia, former Executive Vice-President of Southwest Agricultural University, took the SWU's presidency, while Song Naiqing, former President of Southwest Normal University, was appointed as SWU's Executive Vice-President. This was an interesting reversal of roles, which seemed to be working harmoniously. The practical problems emerged gradually, including the conflict among campus cultures and the conflict among time allocation and working schedules in the two original institutions. For example, classes originally lasted for 50 minutes in Southwest Agriculture University but 40 minutes in Southwest Normal University. Now SWU has adopted 40 minutes for each class as a standard across the merged institution.[8]

There were also problems of administrative integration. In his Report on the Work of the Administration at the Second Session of the First SWU Congress on January 4th, 2008, President Wang paid serious attention to the challenges of the current administrative mode, expressing dissatisfaction with its inefficiency, the unclear allocation of responsibilities among individual administrative offices, and what he described as a "closely guarded localism".[9] An example of this which our project team experienced related to the collection of base data for our study. It took much more time for SWU's several administrative offices to complete the compilation of the base data tables for our project than was the case in most other universities in our study. While these problems are common to newly merged institutions, they have posed great challenges to SWU's new leaders. But it seemed that they were working on this, with the current stage of "deep integration" expected to be finished by 2010.[10]

Photo 7.2: Bust of Wu Mi (1894-1978), an influential scholar in comparative literature who returned from Harvard University in the early 1920s and taught at Southwest Normal College from 1950 up to his death in 1978, in the Wu Mi Garden.

---

[8] Interview with Zhou Guangming, Director of the Academic Affairs Office, 2 June 2008.
[9] Wang Xiaojia, *Xinan Daxue 2007 Niandu Xingzhen Gongzuo Baogao (Report on the Work of the Administration Southwest University 2007)*, 4 January 2008, pp.11-12.
[10] Interview with Yang Weiguang and Zhang Daiping, Director and Associate Director of the Development and Planning Office, 2 June 2008.

The second strategic direction is to promote high standards of scholarship by recruiting and retaining an excellent faculty contingent. President Wang emphasized the point that SWU has to establish itself by the excellence of its scholarship, and this is widely agreed among all of SWU's members. This was confirmed for us by the fact that almost everybody interviewed during our case study visit, including leaders and administrators, faculty members and students, pointed to the Wu Mi Garden as a symbol of SWU's tradition of academic excellence. The Wu Mi Garden opened in May of 2007 as an important memorial site on the SWU campus.

Since SWU finished the merger process in 2005, its leaders and administrators have shifted their priority to boosting the quality of teaching and research, which must be built around a highly qualified faculty. Several strategies have been adopted for this task, as introduced by Vice-President Song.[11] For example, SWU requires all new faculty members to hold a doctoral degree, while still making an exception for unusual talents in needed areas. It warmly welcomes scholars returning from abroad, especially those who have earned a tenured position at a university of standing. To stimulate current faculty members and ensure that they perform well, SWU sets strict measures of accountability relating to their teaching and research outcomes, with some flexibility and a recognition that teaching needs to be rewarded, and not only research. In addition, SWU has also launched a project entitled "Teaching Masters" (名師), which gives a high-profile appointment to well-established scholars, selected through a rigorous screening process, usually individuals with more than 20 years of professional experience in their field.

The third strategic direction is to enhance SWU's traditional strengths in agricultural education and teacher education both in service of diverse local communities, and with the idea of developing new programs with extensive international outreach. For example, in the field of agriculture and agronomy, there are certain traditionally strong programs that go back to the 1930s, such as sericulture and biotechnology. The silkworm genome research led by Xiang Zhonghuai and Xia Qingyou in the College of Agronomy and Biotechnology has been recognized internationally. SWU has two national key laboratories – the Key Sericultural Laboratory under the Ministry of Agriculture and the Key Sericultural and Genome Laboratory under the Ministry of Education, which

---

[11] Interview with Song Naiqing, Executive Vice-President, 1 June 2008.

have published several refereed papers in internationally leading journals, such as *Science* and *Genome Biology*.[12]

Another traditionally strong field is teacher education and research on education and psychology.[13] The former Southwest Normal University had been one of the six national key normal universities since the 1950s, and a center in educational and psychological research and teacher education in the southwest region. For example, Professor Zhang Furong, a returnee from Stanford University in 1936, had served as a leading scholar in the Southwest Normal for over 50 years until he passed away in 1998. In the mid-1980s, he was the first doctoral supervisor to be appointed in the area of curriculum and teaching in China.

The newly merged SWU continues to focus on teacher education, and has joined the new initiative of the Ministry of Education to waive fees for pre-service teachers, along with the five key normal universities at the national level, even though it is no longer identified as a normal university. Moreover, SWU has developed a unique approach to teacher education, which involves internships for all students as substitute teachers in rural schools. This initiative has been recognized by the Ministry of Education as an effective way to provide intensive opportunities for teaching practice in rural schools, which in turn benefit greatly from the input of these young teacher interns from a major university. SWU's pioneering approach has been gradually popularized in other parts of China, particularly in rural areas of the Northwest. Furthermore, SWU has taken the initiative to establish a new teachers college to optimize its teaching and learning resources in the field for the southwest region, authorized by the Ministry of Education in 2008.

Research on minority education is also a focus at SWU and it is mainly conducted by the Center for Studies of the Education and Psychology of Ethnic Minorities, one of the key research institutes funded by the Ministry of Education in the area of humanities and social sciences. The Center recently hosted a conference on Research Methods in Minority Education, in cooperation with Northwest Normal University's Center for the Educational Development of Minorities.

Another strategic direction of SWU in recent years has been the de-

---

[12] See Xia Qingyou, Zhou Zeyang, Lu Cheng, Cheng Daojun, et al. "A Draft Sequence for the Genome of the Domesticated Silkworm (*Bombyx Mori*)," in *Science*, Vol.306, No.5703, 2004, pp.1937-1940.

[13] Interview with Song Naiqing, Executive Vice-President, 1 June 2008.

velopment of international exchange programs. SWU used to have very small international education program, with a total of 70 international students at the two previous universities in 2003. This number grew to 186 in 2005, 239 in 2006, and 393 in 2007. The plan is for it to reach 1,500 by 2010. Three types of international education programs are offered: undergraduate or graduate degree-granting programs, programs for visiting students (non-degree granting) and short term language or cultural programs.[14] Another form of outreach is collaboration with foreign universities to establish Confucius Institutes. SWU has taken a first experimental step in this direction through establishing a Confucius Institute in Thailand in 2006, in collaboration with Khon Kaen University there.

The strategic direction in the international arena is of course very important for SWU, but a couple of factors have constrained the efforts that are being made.[15] As one of the most inland universities in China, SWU's outreach is significantly hindered by its geographic location, which makes it difficult to compete with many other Chinese universities. Another prohibitive factor is the lack of qualified teachers who are able to teach courses in English. But the most challenging problem may be the way in which international education programs are managed within SWU's administrative system. In the opinion of the Director of the International Education and Exchange Program, there is a need for much greater acceptance of the program by leaders of SWU's colleges or centers. This is a problem that needs the attention of SWU's top leadership.

The strategic directions outlined above have set forth a clear path for SWU to work towards achieving its mission to become a research-oriented comprehensive university, with a unique focus on education and psychology, agriculture, life sciences and related areas. In the next section we will explore how faculty members felt about the recent transition of the university in terms of both merger and massive expansion.

Faculty and Issues of Teaching and Research

The Faculty Profile

After the merger had taken place in 2005, SWU found itself with a much stronger faculty contingent than either of its predecessors. By 2005, SWU had a total of 2,413 teaching staff, a rise from 1,784 in 1990, 1,718 in 1995

---

[14] Interview with Wang Jing, Director of the International Education and Exchange Centre, 1 June 2008.
[15] *Ibid.*

and 1,677 in 2000. Among the current teaching contingent are 930 females and 169 returnees from oversea studies, and 414 teachers who hold a PhD. The percentage of women teaching staff remained almost unchanged from 1990 to 2000, accounting for around 35.5% of the whole faculty, but increased to 38.5% in 2005. The percentage of overseas returnees increased from 0.9% in 1990, to 3.1% in 1995, and 8.2% in 2000, but could not keep pace with the growth rate of the faculty body and dropped back to 7.0% in 2005. Generally speaking, the percentage of PhD holders grew much faster, from 0.6% in 1990, to 3.0% in 1995, 8.8% in 2000, and 17.2% in 2005. For SWU, it has been rather difficult to recruit PhD holders, particularly overseas returnees, due to its geographic disadvantages. But this focus has remained as one of the top priorities for its development. SWU has worked hard to recruit more than one hundred new teachers every year, with 123 new faculty members joining SWU in 2007.

Issues of Teaching and Research

Four faculty members joined our focus group meeting on June 3, 2008, with two more intending to come but finding themselves unable to make it due to timing. They were in their 40s or 50s and came from the College of Economics and Management, the School of Journalism and Communication, the School of Psychology and the College of Agronomy and Biotechnology, respectively. In addition, the Directors of the Academic Affairs Office and the Social Science Department, responsible respectively for the management of teaching and of research in the social sciences, provided further detailed information about teaching and research.

Three of the professors who participated in our focus group meeting showed a very positive attitude toward the merger. They viewed the merger as a win-win situation, since the two universities genuinely complemented each other, and they believed both sides benefitted significantly, in terms of both a stronger faculty contingent and stronger programs. The students have also benefited significantly from the merger. The university's new name gives it a higher profile and students feel there will be greater flexibility and competitiveness in the job market, than if they graduated from a normal or an agricultural university. The university's new status as a member of Project 21/1 is also a factor in attracting academically excellent students.

The other professor, however, expressed serious concerns about the merger. He felt it was still too early to say whether it was a success, since the new university would be just in its infant stage for a few years. The merger has had multiple impacts on the functions of the university, but a critical issue was how the university could maintain and enhance the quality of its education for the greatly enlarged student body, and how the different administrative offices could work together more smoothly and effectively. This professor did not seem to have confidence in the various strategies that SWU's leaders had talked about.

The faculty members in the focus group also showed serious concerns about their work situation after the merger and expansion. To them, the requirements for teaching and research, as well as the processes of evaluation, had become very demanding, and the pressures on them were overwhelming. The reason was that the increase in the faculty contingent had by no means kept pace with the radical growth in student numbers, which meant many large classes for teaching, at the very time when the quality requirements for teachers were constantly being elevated. As a result, class sizes tended to be constantly increasing, and sometimes several classes were combined into one for teaching. As professors had to manage their teaching for much larger numbers of students, many unique teaching strategies and approaches had to be abandoned. This was particularly the case for the general core courses, which are intended to nurture the overall quality of students.

In addition, as part of the preparation for MOE's Evaluation of Undergraduate Teaching Quality (本科教學水平評估),[16] which was launched in 2003 and continued until 2007, SWU has gradually developed various quantitative measurements to evaluate faculty teaching and research. For example, classroom teaching must pass at least four types of assessment: a regular check-up in the beginning, middle and end of each semester; irregular inspection of classrooms by the University Committee of Teaching Inspection or by observers sent by the respective schools, colleges, or centers; student evaluation at the end of every

---

[16] The National Undergraduate Teaching Quality Evaluation was originally initiated by the Ministry of Education (MOE) in 1993, and major indicators adopted for assessment include school mission, faculty, teaching facilities and their utilization, program construction and teaching reform, teaching administration, teaching and learning style, and teaching effectiveness. Since it is compulsory and its results are publicized on the MOE's official website, every university has to make a critical effort, including taking on the political dimensions of this process, in order to earn and maintain an excellent reputation. See Chapter 1 for further details on this.

semester; and the regular monitoring of teaching activities through a 24-hour feedback system. In case of any teaching mishap for which the instructor was responsible, there would be a penalty, which varied accordingly to how the mishap affected the teaching quality.[17] Many professors felt that such rigorous, quantified forms of evaluation had caused them severe stress and added greatly to their workload. Others appreciated these controls, saying they may have helped their growth and the improvement of their teaching.[18]

In terms of research, the requirements have also become extremely demanding. For example, there used to be some teaching professors who were not required to do any research, but this policy was changed in 1999 and now research is a must for everybody.[19] It appeared professors still enjoyed some freedom in choosing whether to focus on teaching or research, according to members of the faculty focus group. Some professors may have over 80% of their time dedicated to research, but other professors may spend that percentage of their time on teaching. No matter what type of positions they had, all of them still felt they were pushed very hard to do research, either through the stimulus of various awards or the sense that gaining no award was a kind of penalty.[20]

Two of our four faculty focus group members were women and we asked them if female faculty members experienced any disadvantages in their careers and whether the university had any supportive strategies to encourage their success. They felt that there were no special policies to support their development. Furthermore, they experienced many obstacles on the road to academic achievement, mainly from the fact that they had heavier responsibilities for supporting their families than did their husbands.

In addition to the above themes, some professors mentioned that they had made real efforts to serve SWU's vision in their teaching and research. The professor from the School of Psychology put it in this way:

> We have a lot of students from the southwest region, so our teaching and research projects have echoed the vision and mission of our university, "uniquely established in the Southwest, our learning and prac-

---

[17] Interview with Zhou Guangming, Director of the Academic Affairs Office, 2 June 2008.
[18] Interview with Faculty Focus Group, 3 June 2008.
[19] Interview with Xu Hui, Director of the Social Science Department, 2 June 2008.
[20] Interview with the Faculty Focus Group, 3 June 2008.

tice embrace the world." For example, I have been involved in some psychological research projects for minority groups in the region, and I have edited some textbooks for them.[21]

It is obvious that although many teachers in SWU have mixed feelings toward the merger and expansion, and toward the imposition of rigorous quality control processes in recent years, they have a strong sense of responsibility for the university and for its wider communities in the Southwest region.

Students' Experiences

A total of nine students participated in our two-hour focus group meeting on June 2, 2008. Among them, five students were in the fourth year and the other four students in the third year, with four male students from the College of Foreign Languages, the College of Chinese Language and Literature, the College of Computer and Information Science and the College of Political Science and Public Management, respectively, and five female students from the College of Foreign Languages, the College of Horticulture and Landscape Architecture, the College of Mathematics and Statistics, the College of Education and the College of Agronomy and Biotechnology, respectively. In addition, we also talked with the Director of the Student Affairs Office for further information about student life. The topics were mainly centered on their experiences and participation in civil society, and their views on SWU's merger and massive expansion.

Equity Issues in the Expansion and Merger

Compared with other economic regions in China, the southwest region has been traditionally disadvantaged due to the inconvenience of transportation and communication with the outside world. SWU's students are mainly from the local area, and financial issues for students have become critical in the move to a mass system. In response to this specific situation, SWU has made this a key policy concern and its Students' Affairs Office has created an independent administrative unit, the Student Loan and Scholarship Office, to address the issue. In 2007, there were a total of 13,000 students from low income families, which accounted for one-third of the student population. SWU has provided

---

[21] *ibid.*

student loans, scholarships and assistantships for 12,000 students, and additional assistantships for another 5,000 students who have to work on campus as research or teaching assistants. There are three major types of financial assistance that students can enjoy: governmental student loans, non-governmental student scholarships and SWU's student scholarships and assistantships. The university has tried its best to guarantee that no student is excluded due to the cost of tuition, following the policy of a green pass for all students who are qualified and selected to register as new students.[22]

Our meeting with student focus group members confirmed this claim made by the Director of the Student Affairs Office. One student observed that her university has paid serious attention to the national policy of supporting students from poor family backgrounds. One of her classmates has successfully applied for a student loan since his second year, and six of her 34 classmates were also able to do so, with a success rate of 20%, which is fairly standard according to our interviewees. Students from the College of Chinese Language and Literature and the College of Agronomy and Biotechnology estimated that there were around 30% of students who were able to get student loans in their respective colleges. For the College of Agronomy and Biotechnology, probably more students have a low-income family background. A student from the college noted that there were 8 students who applied for student loans in the first year, out of a class of 28. The student loans, which provided up to 6,000 *yuan* a year, were mainly used by them to pay for tuition fees, which amounted to 3,500 *yuan* a year.

Students also confirmed that the Green Pass policy has served as a guarantee for those students who have severe financial problems, and they are not aware of any students who have dropped out due to the problem. SWU's assistantship is another great help for needy students, with a monthly salary of 400 *yuan* which would basically cover their living expenses. In addition, there were some special subsidies for ethnic minority groups, and subsidies for all students who may need emergency help for a personal or family accident. According to the student focus group, around 60% of students in the university were able to afford all of the costs through the support of their families.

But students also mentioned that female students tend to have more serious financial problems, due to the traditional family preference for

---

[22] Interview with Li Ronghua, Director of the Students' Affairs Office, 2 June 2008.

boys over girls in rural areas. In the southwest region, where agriculture is the main source of livelihood, people mainly depend on physical labor for survival, and these prejudices persist. Girls are thus much more likely to suffer from unequal learning opportunities than boys, if their families have the same limited financial resources.

Participation in Civil Society

Some basic information about students' participation in civil society was provided by the Students' Affairs Office. There are about 100 student organizations on campus, with some hosted by the university but most organized by students themselves. In terms of administration, SWU has assigned responsibility for student organizations on campus to the Communist Youth League (共青團), and it is also supposed to guide and encourage students to get involved in numerous associational activities. Although most student organizations are officially registered with the university's administration, there are still some that are not and they function as informal groupings organized through independent student initiative. Among many official organizations and activities which enable students to participate in local community life, the Social Practice of Intellectual Support for Rural Society (智力支鄉社會實踐) is one worthy of being highlighted. Every year in the summer vacation, SWU's Student Union [23] recruits volunteers to join social practice teams that offer intellectual support to rural society. What happens is that students go back to their home towns for around two weeks, and offer their professional services to the local community. This activity has gone on for more than twenty years and has been widely acclaimed in the region.[24]

According to the interview with the student focus group, students were generally very active in civic participation in their local communities and in the wider society. There were basically two types of student voluntary activities, which they differentiated on the basis of the organizers. One type was the semi-official voluntary activities regularly associated with a student organization or in response to an ad hoc social cause, administered by either the Student Union or the Communist Youth League. Some official activities were combined with teaching and professional learning, such as the internship program for student

---

[23] The Student Union is an official student organization which is commonly found in Chinese universities, usually under the supervision of the Communist Youth League.
[24] Interview with Li Ronghua, Director of the Students' Affairs Office, 2 June 2008.

teachers to teach in rural schools. This was the most popular form of student civic participation because it was usually well organized and backed up by official funding and official guidance. However, it may not have always served students' individual interests.

The other type was the highly autonomous, voluntary activities organized by students themselves, such as the associations of fellow villagers or townspersons (同鄉會). Some of these types of activities still needed funding from the university, at least partly, but most of them were self-funded or funded by third parties for commercial purposes. This type of activity was less controlled by the university but by the same token it got very limited support from the university.

Students gave some comments and criticisms with particular reference to the latter type of civic participation. One point they made was that this type of unofficial activity appeared sometimes to be poorly organized and too informal, but it may have served students' individual interests quite well. Moreover, it was often rather ad hoc and not sustainable, with some activities being simply for the purpose of "show". The focus group also concluded that there were two major motivations of the organizers: shared personal interests or preferences, and the social need for communication and sharing resources that could result in self-improvement. Students made an interesting observation that more female students tended to act as the leaders of these informal civic groupings than male. They felt female leaders had superior organizational abilities and were able to develop a stronger affinity among group members and a wider appeal.

No matter what type of group or what motivation, it appeared that SWU's students were very active in civic participation. A good example was the outpouring of civic spirit in response to the Sichuan Earthquake in May of 2008. Chongqing was close to the epicenter and many SWU students witnessed the sufferings of local people. There were many officially organized voluntary activities for students to help these people shortly after the earthquake took place, while numerous self-organized student groups rushed to the area to provide voluntary help and support.[25]

When asked what space on the campus best symbolized the spirit of Southwest University, members of the student focus group pointed to the Great Auditorium that had originally been on the campus of Southwest Normal University. Students felt that it somehow represented SWU's

---

[25] Interview with the Student Focus Group, 2 June 2008.

dynamic spirit and also its diversity, as they had lots of memories about it as a venue for major celebrations, graduation ceremonies, and so on.

Based on students' experiences in SWU's move to a mass stage the strategies it has taken to relieve students' financial burdens seem to have been critical. In addition, the officially organized activities that complemented SWU's ethos and mission provided significant opportunities for its students to actively participate in their local communities and the wider society, while the more autonomous forms of associational life seemed to be nurtured in ways that served their individual interests.

Photo 7.3: The Great Auditorium, located at the center of the SWU campus in Beipei, symbolizing the university's dynamic spirit and the diversity of the southwest region.

Conclusion

Southwest University is an unusual case of merger in China's move to mass higher education. After a long journey of courtship that was twice thwarted, Southwest Normal University and Southwest Agriculture University finally won support for a merger from the local government, and successfully obtained approval from the Ministry of Education for a re-union that took place in 2005. The merger has brought about significant institutional changes in the two former universities, with a new vision and mission, diversified funding, an enhanced faculty contingent, a greatly enlarged student population on campus, and a higher academic status in the nation. It also has posed great challenges to the new leaders and administrators, in terms of the efficiency of administration, deep integration among the many individual administrative offices, the collaboration among programs in cross-disciplinary areas at different levels, the heavier workload of staff and faculty, and the creation of learning opportunities in civic participation for students.

In the SWU case, we can see how an ethos rooted in an institutional tradition going back many decades played a critical role in the transformative change of the university. We can also see how a clearly articulated vision and mission have been crucially important in leading the university in a new direction. More importantly, while SWU is located in the southwest region of China, which is commonly viewed as a disadvantage in terms of competition with other national key universities for public funding and status and the recruitment of academic staff, SWU's leaders have endeavored to turn this into an advantage, by building on its unique traditions and providing its services to the development of the local and regional community. At the same time, it has also reached out to the nation and the international community. The radical expansion of student enrollment since 1999 and the final approval of the merger in 2005 have served as two key steps in enabling SWU to become a more fully comprehensive university, in terms of stronger and more diverse programs, a more qualified teaching force, and a higher level of student intake. Success in being included within Project 21/1, with support from both Chongqing and Beijing, made a huge difference to the financial resources and the quality of student enrollments that became possible after 2004.

SWU's expansion and merger illustrate a different pathway from that of East China Normal University which is profiled in the previous chapter, and also that of Yanbian University which will be introduced in the next chapter. Its vision, innovations and endeavors shed light on how two geographically disadvantaged universities managed to integrate their complementary areas of strength and become a comprehensive institution by building upon a tradition that goes back to the early part of the 20th century.

8
Yanbian University – Building a Niche through a Multicultural Identity

Jing LIN and Jun LI, with PIAO Taizhu

Yanbian University (YBU) is the only university among our twelve case studies that has as its main mission serving Korean minority students in China. It has played a critical role in the development of the Yanbian autonomous prefecture, and in many ways reflects the history of ethnic minority development in China over the past sixty years. In recent years, YBU joined the ranks of Project 21/1, a national project aimed at enabling 100 universities to become comprehensive research universities in the 21st century. Being in a marginal position both geographically, in Northeastern China, and ethnically, as a minority institution, YBU has striven to build a unique niche for itself through a focus on multiculturalism. It is gradually becoming a "center in the margins," both academically and politically. Geographically, Yanbian University is in the margins, located in a small town bordering North Korea. However, it is also in the center due to the tensions over North Korea's nuclear program, and its proximity to both North and South Korea, as well as Japan and Russia. The resource-rich Changbai mountain (長白山) area has given it some remarkable opportunities. Overall, there are interesting dynamics at play in the region and within the university itself, which makes it a unique case study and gives us some new thoughts as to what comprises a first class national university or even a world-class university.

History of the Korean Minority in China

Korean Chinese (朝鮮族) are an ethnic minority group in China. Their population reached 2.5 million by 2005.[1] Most of them live in Jilin province, and there is a relatively high concentration in the Yanbian Korean Autonomous Prefecture (延邊朝鮮民族自治區 the Changbai Korean autonomous county. The area where many Koreans live is along

---

[1] "Koreans in China," Wikipedia, accessed April 16, 2009, http://en.wikipedia.org/wiki/Koreans_in_China.

the edge of the Changbai Mountains, in the southeastern part of Jilin, bordering on North Korea, with 80.3% of all land covered by forests. It is rich with herbal medicines, such as ginseng, and has a great variety of plants. It is also known for the many species of wild animals. As this mountain range connects Jilin province and North Korea, it is militarily and politically an important place as well. Yanbian prefecture has a major river flowing through it, the Tumen River (圖們江), which is shared with North Korea for a length of 510 kilometers. The river also has several branches flowing into the different parts of the region. Hence Yanbian and North Korea are closely linked geographically.

There has been a Korean minority group living in China for a long period of time, due to the geographical proximity of the two countries. Migration from the Korean peninsula to Northeastern China has been going on since the end of the 17th century. In 1869, a major natural disaster caused a large number of Koreans to immigrate to Yanbian, and after Japan annexed the Korean peninsula in 1910, another wave of immigrants came to settle down in various parts of Northeastern China.

Before 1945, the Yanbian region was a rice producing area in a situation where 50% of the peasants had to rent land from landlords in order to survive. In 1945, after the end of the Second World War, Japan was driven out of China, and Yanbian came under the control of the Chinese Communist Party. On September 3, 1952, the Yanbian Korean Autonomous Prefecture was established. In 1958, the Changbai Korean Autonomous County was formed and several dozen Korean Autonomous villages were established in various parts of the province.

Koreans have their own language, and it is often noted that the Confucian tradition has remained particularly strong among Koreans, with filial piety and respect for elders being upheld as values of utmost importance. The Korean people have a tradition of respecting teachers as well, and education is given extremely high importance. This cultural tradition is reflected in a popular saying: "no matter how hard our life is, we will support our children to go to school." There are six universities, five adult learning universities, and several dozen post-secondary vocational technical schools in Yanbian. More than 1,000 primary and lower secondary schools carry out compulsory education, upper secondary schooling is almost universal, and there are virtually no illiterate people. The Koreans people are hence often called the "model minority" in China.

The Yanbian Korean Autonomous Prefecture is the region with the greatest concentration of the Chinese Korean population. The Prefecture had 2.17 million people in 2005; of them 820,000 were Koreans, comprising 37.7% of the total population. The university is located in Yanji City, which is the capital of the prefecture. The city has a population of nearly 400,000 people, with Koreans, Han Chinese, Manchurians, Hui Muslims and 16 other ethnic groups living together. The street signs are mostly in Korean, with some being bilingual Chinese and Korean. The overwhelming presence of the Korean language on street signs, stores, and newspapers and in other venues makes one feel one is in South or North Korea.

YBU's Founding and Experience of Merger

Yanbian University was founded in 1949, mainly in response to the fact that secondary school graduates in Yanji did not have a university to attend and many felt they had to go to Korea for higher education. The other main reason was the need, as perceived by the new Communist government, to train leaders who could cooperate in governing the Korean nationality region and to prepare teachers for the primary and secondary schools. The university was initially under the administration of the Ministry of Higher Education until September of 1957, when it was handed over to the educational authorities of Jilin province. In 1958, under the influence of the Soviet model, which featured narrowly specialized institutions, YBU was divided into four institutions, which were named Yanbian University, Yanbian Medical College, Yanbian Agricultural College, and Yanbian Engineering College. The engineering college was re-integrated with Yanbian University in 1959.

Originally, Yanbian had only Korean faculty and students, and teaching was conducted in the Korean language only. However, beginning in 1958, its mandate changed, from being a university training talent only for the Korean population to one that enrolled students from Han and other ethnic groups as well. With this change it started to hire some teachers from well known universities around the country, and the Korean faculty began to improve their knowledge of the Chinese language. Some were sent for in-service study programs in domestic universities, such as Peking University and Jilin University, or to universities in the Soviet Union, North Korea, and Romania. Beginning in 1959, after the admission of a significant number of students from Han and other ethnic minority groups, teaching became bilingual, in Korean and Chinese. This was the beginning of Yanbian University trying to construct an environment for multicultural learning and integration.

Photo 8.1: The Logo of Yanbian University – Chinese and English are used in the outer circle, while the inner circle has the Korean word for Yan.

In the 1950s, YBU was under heavy Soviet influence, with most of the textbooks written by Soviet scholars, and many faculty receiving training in the Soviet Union. During the Cultural Revolution, many school leaders and faculty were denounced and persecuted. In the 1980s, it underwent revitalization, adding new programs and areas. In 1996, when there was strong encouragement from Beijing for the amalgamation of universities, YBU officially merged with the two colleges that had been split off in the 1950s, namely the Yanbian Medical College, and the Yanbian Agricultural College, as well as absorbing Yanbian Teacher Training Postsecondary School and the Yanbian campus of the Jilin Arts College.[2] This merger enabled it to be accepted as one of the 100 universities in Project 21/1, with the central government giving them special funding for research and development and many other advantages, such as the right to enroll students nationwide, in the first round, with the top range of scores on the unified national entrance examinations. Currently, Yanbian has the status of a university that is given priority for development by both Jilin province and the Ministry of Education in Beijing.

YBU's Move to Mass Higher Education: An Empirical Overview (1990-2005)

Growth in Student Enrollments

In the early 1990s, YBU experienced a slight drop of undergraduate stu-

---

[2] Piao Wenyi and Sun Dongzhi, *History of Yanbian University 1949-2004* (Yanji: Yanbian University Press, 2004), p.350.

dent enrollments, from 1,939 in 1990 to 1,890 in 1995. But the numbers soon surged to 8,451 in 2000 with a growth rate of 347.1%, partly due to the merger of five institutes taking place in 1996, and again to 15,485 in 2005 with a growth rate of 83.2%. Table 8.1 shows the trends of these changes in the three broad disciplinary areas, i.e., natural sciences/ technologies, social sciences, and humanities. It is clear that students enrolled in natural sciences and social sciences grew much faster than those in the humanities.

Table 8.1: Statistics on Undergraduate Student Enrollments from 1990 to 2005

	1990	1995	2000	2005
Natural sciences/ technologies	525	659	5,008	8,025
Social sciences	389	488	1,263	3,796
Humanities	1,025	743	2,180	3,664
Total	1,939	1,890	8,451	15,485

Before 1999, Yanbian was a provincial level university and had authority only to recruit students from the Northern provinces of Jilin, Liaoning and Heilongjiang, also from the Inner Mongolian Autonomous Region. With expansion in higher education, and with the new Project 21/1 status Yanbian became a national level university being able to admit students at much higher admission scores. This has allowed it to reconfigure itself in terms of the composition of students. It hopes to have a balance of students in terms of their ethnicity, region, learning styles, etc.[3] However, the impact is not obvious yet. Currently, the university enrolls 4,000 new undergraduates each year, of whom 1,000 are recruited from all parts of China.

YBU used to have a very small graduate student body in the early 1990s, but the number grew rapidly alongside the national expansion policy, particularly in the early 2000s. In 1990, there were only 48 graduate students in the university, but they grew to 184 in 1995, 562 in 2000, and 1,902 in 2005, with a growth rate of 283.3%, 205.4% and 238.4%, every five years respectively. Over 60 years of its history, YBU has graduated 100,000 students, with half of them being from the Korean minority.

The Financial Profile

As the financial data for analysis are limited to the four years between

---

[3] Interview with Gai Tongxiang, Vice President, 22 May 2008.

2004 and 2007, the historical trends of YBU's financial profile are unavailable for the fifteen-year period from 1990 to 2005; however, we can get a rough picture from the data available for the four years.

Students pay from 3,800 RMB (for teacher education students) to 10,000 RMB (for students in arts) for tuition annually.[4] From 2004 to 2007, student fees increased from 82.2 million to 114.3 million RMB at a growth rate of 39.1%, and their proportion in YBU's total revenue grew slightly from 35.4% to 38.6%. Direct funding from government grew from 113.6 million to 160.3 million at a growth rate of 41.1%, and its proportion in the total revenue grew noticeably from 48.9% to 54.2%. Special public funding from the Project 21/1 soared from 1.6 million to 10.7 million at a growth rate of 578.6%, and its proportion in the total revenue increased from 0.7% to 3.6%. The funding from the 21/1 project in YBU's annual budget also surged from 1.4% in 2004 to 6.7% in 2007, with an increase of 380.6%. Direct public funding for research, however, dropped significantly from 12.5 million to 6.3 million, and its proportion in the total revenue also significantly dropped from 5.4% to 2.1%. By contrast, funding from non-governmental sources doubled from 1.3 million to 2.6 million, an increase from 0.6% to 0.9% in the university's total income. Through these trends, we can see that the growth of direct governmental funding was obviously faster than that of student fees, and that YBU's research was more and more oriented towards serving the local community.

On the other hand, YBU's budget also experienced dramatic changes, growing from 155.1 million in 2004 to 219.9 million RMB in 2007 with a growth rate of 41.8% during the four years. Budget for total salaries and benefits jumped from 60.7 million in 2004 to 91.2 million RMB in 2007, with a growth of more than 50%. At the same time, the proportions of budget for teachers' salaries and benefits increased marginally from 39.1% in 2004 to 41.5% in 2007. Expenditures for teaching increased by 15.8%, from 69.7 million in 2004 to 80.8 million RMB in 2007, but its proportion in the overall budget significantly dropped from 44.9% in 2004 to 36.7% in 2007. Student aid increased by 40.9%, from 24.7 million in 2004 to 34.8 million RMB in 2007, but its weight in YBU's whole budget remained almost the same (16%) during these years.

In the spring of 2008, there was a nationwide rise in food prices. Like other universities, Yanbian gave each student 80 RMB per month to offset the rise in prices. The very poor students were permitted to delay

---

[4] Interview with Yang Yueyou, the Associate Director of Finance Office, 23 May 2008.

their payment of tuition. Around 200 students were taking part in work study programs, earning 8 RMB an hour, which translated into 320 RMB a month, enough to cover their living costs.[5]

Curricular Changes

In 1990, Yanbian had a total of 14 undergraduate programs, with 12 of them being for teacher education. In 1995, six additional non-teacher education programs were set up to cater for the socioeconomic development of the local region. After the 1996 merger, the non-teacher education programs were significantly expanded. By 2003, Yanbian had a total of 12 colleges, including the College of Teacher Education, the College of Foreign Languages the College of Law, the Medical School, the Agricultural School, the College of Physical Education and the College of Economics and Management, with a total of 65 undergraduate programs.[6] In 2008, Yanbian had 19 colleges, with 69 undergraduate degree programs, 78 MA degree programs, 8 doctoral degree programs, and one postdoctoral station. Its curriculum covered the broad areas of science, engineering, agriculture, medicine, social science, history, economics, law and teacher education. In terms of these curricular changes, YBU has become a comprehensive university, covering a broad range of disciplines and interdisciplinary areas.

Mission of the University: Commitment to Multiculturalism and Striving to Move from the Margins to the Center

In 1996, in order to be included in Project 21/1 and to become competitive with other universities nationwide, Yanbian underwent an amalgamation with several other institutions, as noted earlier. That same year, the university had a major discussion involving all faculty and students. The question was not whether or not to merge, but how to combine effectively with the other colleges and institutions. In 1997, the university further underwent two major periods of discussion, on what type of university Yanbian should become, and how it could become a great university. A total of six major debates took place in the period up to 2007. On the basis of these discussions, the university set its goal as to "become a national first rate comprehensive university with Korean ethnic charac-

---

[5] Interview with Yang Yueyou, the Associate Director of Finance, 23 May 2008.
[6] See Piao Wenyi and Sun Dongzhi, *History of Yanbian University 1949-2004*, pp.375- 377.

teristics." They aimed to achieve the goal by training students to "have a solid foundation, specialized expertise, practical ability and adaptability, and versatile talents."[7]

In 2002, in the process of the fourth "great discussion," the university decided its features were to pursue multiculturalism and integration, and in 2004, the fifth "great discussion" pushed this further to establish the core values of the university as "seeking truth, perfecting wisdom, and integration." The sixth round of discussion in 2007 resulted in a more clarified vision of "training talent who have a creative spirit, practical ability and cross cultural dispositions."[8]

The current administration came on board in 2003. Under the leadership of President Jin Bingmin, they set their goals to strengthen multicultural education and train talent with cross-cultural competence. The president was well aware that as a university located in a minority region serving mostly minority students, it was hard to avoid being marginalized. "We need an awakening from the margins," he said. He believed that Yanbian needed to maintain its Korean characteristics, while it should also be integrated with mainstream [Han] culture and with the world. "Our goal is to move from the margin to the center and eventually become a center ourselves."[9]

YBU's motto is set as "Seeking truth, perfecting wisdom and embracing integration." The university leaders, faculty and staff were proud

Photo 8.2: The Main Administrative Building

---

[7] Interview with Jin Bingmin, President of Yanbian University, 22 May 2008.
[8] *Ibid.*
[9] *Ibid.*

that they had a long history – by 2009, the university was 60 years old – and that it had added a lot of new features to its old campus and buildings. "Quality in the inside" was their comment on the main administration building, seen below in Photo 8.2. Even though Yanbian had been labeled as a "minority" university, remote from the center of China, it was proud of its tradition and multiculturalism. When asked about which building on campus best represents YBU's ethos, President Jin and his colleagues pointed both to the main administrative building (Photo 8.2) and the main teaching building. (Photo 8.3)

To the administrators and the faculty, the main administrative building, constructed during the 1950s under Soviet influence, with strong Soviet and European features in its architectural style, represented YBU's history and culture. They were particularly proud that they had played a key role for the region and the country, having trained a large number of leaders, teachers and professionals working in the Yanbian region, as well as having sent Korean language and history experts to all parts of the country working in universities and government offices.

Meanwhile, the new teaching building was chosen because it represented modernity and YBU's drive to be an outstanding university on the national and international stage. The leaders and faculty were proud that they had a building with modern facilities standing side by side with the older main administrative building, which to them symbolized a connection between their glorious past and a leap toward a bright future.

How can Yanbian promote "multicultural co-existence and integration while embracing innovation, and multi-ethnic culture?" The

Photo 8.3: The Main Teaching Building, recently built, represents YBU's move towards modernity and globalization

president noted this required establishing certain niches, such as focusing on high quality education and innovation in research. "We need to be moving from the margin to the center, and become a center ourselves eventually" is what we heard repeatedly. The president commented that there were people who resisted such policies, however, and that is why so many debates were needed.

One way to implement multicultural and cross-cultural education was through emphasizing the importance of multi-language acquisition. "To master a new language allows one to know a whole new world," the president said.[10] Hence, while the university's Korean students were studying in Chinese, more than 2,000 Han majority students were studying Korean. The university provided courses free of charge for students to learn the Korean language, and study modern literature in North and South Korea to cultivate an understanding of the Korean culture. Meanwhile, all the students were required to learn English, and many students also learned Japanese.

In our interview with the Director of Teaching Affairs, we learned that the Korean language was the most popular major in YBU. More than 70 universities in China had Korean as a major, yet YBU's Korean major was the most famous and popular. Most of the faculty now working in these 70 universities had graduated from Yanbian and were now teaching the Korean language and literature, ancient Korean, music and dancing in many of those institutions.[11]

While trying to be integrated into the mainstream trends and culture, Yanbian also insisted that it needed to serve local economic and socio-political needs. The key mission of the university has been, and continues to be, training teachers for Korean schools, and training government officials, media personnel, and researchers in charge of Korean ethnic minority affairs in "the three provinces and one region," meaning the Northeastern provinces of Jilin, Heilongjiang, Liaoning, and the Inner Mongolia Autonomous Region. We were told that Yanbian was responsible for training 80% of the teachers for Korean schools, 80% of government officials, newspaper/TV/radio personnel, and research personnel in charge of Korean affairs around the nation, also 80% of government officials in Yanji itself, from the county level and above.[12] Hence teacher

---

[10] Interview with Gai Tongxiang, Vice President, 22 May 2008.
[11] Interview with Yu Aizong, Director of Teaching Affairs, 22 May 2008.
[12] Interview with Gai Tongxiang, Vice President, 22 May 2008.

education was a key responsibility for Yanbian, and it offered many courses on ethnic psychology and related areas. Research and teaching in agriculture were also important, with a focus on developing the Changbai Mountain region in areas such as herbal medicine and animal protection.

While remaining committed to its core feature of serving the Korean minority, Yanbian has also striven to become mainstream. It offers most subject areas found in a typical comprehensive university, and since 2002, has gradually added new programs, such as Teaching Chinese to Non-Native Speakers, Bio-technology, Educational Technology, Pharmacology, International Politics and Geographic Information Systems.

Serving the Korean Population and Maintaining a Korean Identity

As a Korean university, YBU used to have a mandate to keep 50% of its places for Korean students. However, in recent years, there has been a trend for Korean rural and urban residents to migrate out of the Yanji region in search of jobs and higher pay elsewhere. As a result, local Korean schools in Yanji have decreased from 1,000 to 300. Schools in the Yanji region teach all subject areas from grade one to senior high school in Korean. But the decrease in student population has led to a revised ratio of Korean students that the university must fulfill. Currently, 40 percent of the students are required to be ethnic Korean students.[13] The rest of the students come from other nationalities, including the majority Han. As a reflection of the government's minority policy, preference is given to Korean students, who get 10 points added to their total score in higher education admission.

Since becoming a Project 21/1 university, Yanbian has been given the authority to enroll students from all over the country, which gives it a much higher profile. Every year, it now admits 1,000 students from the other 29 provinces. The students are of very high quality, we were told,[14] as they are admitted under the criteria for elite Project 21/1 universities. Being higher achievers and having "more advanced" habits of learning than the local students (such as being more creative and reflective), these students have significantly improved the overall quality of the student population at Yanbian, we were told. In assigning students to a dormi-

---

[13] Interview with Jin Bingmin, President of Yanbian University, 22 May 2008.
[14] Interview with Gai Tongxiang, Vice President, 22 May, and with Faculty on 23 May 2008.

tory, the university tried to match Korean students with Han students, so that by the time the Han students graduated, they had mostly become fluent in Korean and vice versa.

Being fluent in Korean and knowing the habits and culture of the Korean people gives Yanbian graduates a big advantage in finding jobs. There are many businesses owned by South Korean companies in coastal and southern China. They prefer hiring students who know the Korean language and culture. Hence, by the time students graduate, more than 80% have already found a job.

Seventy percent of Yanbian's faculty members are Koreans and it tries to establish its Korean identity in many ways. It has programs that are related to Korean language and literature, and offers courses on Korean ethnic history and psychology. Courses in tourism administration and economics also try to highlight Korean characteristics. Also, Yanbian caters to regional needs in its programs; for example, its agricultural programs center their courses on resources exploration and the management of the Changbai Mountains.

Becoming a National Research University by Strengthening its Core Features

As a "university in the margins,"[15] it is a great source of pride that the university belongs to the rank of Project 21/1 universities. While focusing on serving local economic needs and striving to meet the demand for teachers and cadres for the Korean community, Yanbian nevertheless defines itself as a teaching and research university that has a national and international role to play. It aims to become a comprehensive university with "a certain impact abroad, with an important position in the country, with strong ethnic characteristics and with a high quality of education."[16]

One key feature of a Project 21/1 university is that it produces research. YBU is taking advantage of its geographic location to builds some unique niches in this regard. Yanbian is called the "Golden Triangle" in Northeast Asia since it connects Northeastern China (Jilin, Heilongjiang and Liaoning provinces) and North and East Asia (Russia, Japan and South and North Korea). This location gives it strategic importance, and in turn it takes advantage of its location in three particular ways.

First, Yanbian conducts research on the Changbai mountain area. It has an allocation of 30 million RMB per year for research on exploration

---

[15] Interview with Jin Bingmin, President, 22 May 2008.
[16] YBU's Self Evaluation Report 2008, p.7.

and protection of the resources in this area, such as minerals, plants, herbal medicines and rare animals.[17] Faculty study the economic values of these resources and research topics such as extracting bear's bile, a precious material for Chinese medicine, and raising yellow cows, a particular type of cow which is known for its delicious beef and can cost as much as 300 RMB per pound in the market.

The region is also known as one of the five treasure houses of natural herbal medicine in the country. Of the 3,119 kinds of plants in the Changbai mountain area, about 862 can be used as herbal medicine. There are also approximately 1,200 animal species. It is known for ginseng, velvet, and marten skin. Rice, apple, and yellow cow are also the region's well known products. In 2001 Yanbian requested and was approved by the Ministry of Education to be a university for key development and reconstruction under the government's "Great West Development Project."[18] This means it receives funding from the central government and the province to enable it to take advantage of these regional resources. It is very interesting that although Yanbian does not qualify to be a part of Western China (it is in the Northeast) it has been able to benefit from the Western China Development initiative. This is because of its high concentration of Koreans and other minorities, which enables it to benefit from the funding given specially to universities in minority and underdeveloped Western and Southwestern provinces.

Yanbian hence has a Ministry of Education Key Lab of Factors of Biological Function of the Changbai Mountain, and a Medicinal Research Center. It has received funding from the National Natural Science Foundation, the National Social Science Foundation, and research grants from provincial level government offices. It can boast about faculty publishing in high visibility journals and receiving awards and patents of all kinds.

---

[17] Interview with Piao Cankui, Director of Social Sciences Research, 22 May 2008.

[18] This is a national strategic project that began in 2000 and aimed at developing the underdeveloped areas in Western China, with 12 provinces in Western and Southwestern China covered. Projects include building a gas pipeline to transport gas from Xinjiang to mainland, building the world-famous railroad to Tibet, returning farmland to forestry, among others. The region has a significant number of minorities living in it, and economically has only one third of the GDP of the more developed Eastern part of China. In higher education, the universities covered by the Great West Development Project can receive certain amounts of funding from the central and local governments, and can be upgraded to higher categories of universities with lower criteria.

Secondly, Yanbian has become a place for strategic research. It takes advantage of the tension between the United States and North Korea, and cultivates certain important opportunities associated with its location at the intersection of China, Russia and North Korea in Northeast Asia (東北亞). It connects with South Korea through the southern part of the Tumen River, and it faces Japan across the Japan Sea. It has a shared border with North Korea of 522.5 kilometers and with Russia of 246 kilometers. Five counties, 18 villages and 10 ports have the capacity to receive 2.9 million people each year from these neighboring countries. Hence, Yanbian is considered an important window of Northeastern China, a frontier for Jilin province to trade and do business with other countries, and a stronghold for Chinese businesses wishing to venture into Russia and North Korea. In sum, the region's unique location is considered to have strong advantages and great potential for development.

Yanbian has several institutes studying policy issues and political and diplomatic strategies relating to this region. Their research focuses on North and South Korean history, culture, and economics; also the relationship between North and South Korea and between those two countries and Japan and Russia. They also research refugee problems (there are between 200,000 and 300,000 refugees from North Korea in China), nuclear problems, and the investment environment in South Korea.[19]

Thirdly, Yanbian has become a center for studying ethnic minority history and culture. It has a College of South Korean and North Korean Studies, offering programs in Korean Language and Literature, Korean Media, and Korean Language. Besides, its College of Foreign Languages offers programs in English, Russian, Japanese and German. Overall, it has offered 106 courses with multicultural features, cutting across 60 majors. Clusters of courses are offered, such as the cluster on Chinese Korean cultures, the cluster on social and economic development in the Korean minority region, and the cluster on Northeast Asia (東北亞). Korean language and animal science, and another five programs are recognized as "minority nationality specialized programs."

In research, Yanbian has recently completed a national key research project entitled "Research on Korean national arts and culture." It publishes books on the history of Koreans in China and leads all other universities in research on Korean language and literature, Korean education, Korean arts and physical education. As national unity is

---

[19] Interview with Piao Cankui, the Director of Social Science Research, 22 May 2008.

considered of utmost importance in China, and the Korean minority group is considered to have exemplified a harmonious and collaborative relationship with the Han majority, the role YBU has played is viewed very positively by the government. Hence in 2005, the Ministry of Education named Yanbian University as one which should be given strategic priority for development.

Furthermore, Yanbian has a Ministry of Education affiliated Research Center of Comparative Chinese, North Korean, South Korean and Japanese Culture. It also has the Northeast Asia Research Institute, and an Ethnicity Research Institute. Provincially backed institutes include North Korean and South Korean Research Centers, and the Asia Research Center. It is also the host to professional associations such as the Chinese and Japanese Research Association, and the Chinese Korean History Research Association. YBU takes advantage of its connections with North and South Korea and Japan to send many faculty members, about 100 each year, to study, conduct scholarly exchange or joint research in these countries.

As a result of the focused development of these three research areas, faculty have received more and more grants over the years. The Director of Social Science Research informed us that in the past, most research projects got only 20,000 RMB; now the projects are mostly funded at 70,000 to 120,000 RMB each. As mentioned earlier, YBU's research funding from non-governmental sources doubled from 1.3 million in 2004 to 2.6 million in 2007, with a change of its proportion in YBU's whole income from 0.6% to 0.9%. Faculty have great freedom in using the grants. The grants help with improving faculty's life, since part of the grant can be used to supplement their salaries.[20]

It has been quite a transition for Yanbian to move from being traditionally a teaching university to one combining teaching and research. A mechanism has been set up to evaluate the faculty based on their research output: at the top is a special category, followed by categories 1, 2, and 3. Professors in the various categories get very different salaries. The faculty has a basic teaching load: 160 hours a year, which translates into three courses a semester. On top of teaching is a research requirement. Hence faculty feel a lot of pressure. Every three years, the faculty are evaluated on the quantity and quality of their work, and if they fail to reach the criteria, they can be demoted, for example,

---

[20] *Ibid.*

from a full professor to an associate professor. With this kind of pressure, grant applications have increased and the success rate has also increased. In 2001, the university had one to two research grants from national level competitions. From 2004 on, this has increased to seven to eight projects a year. There are also provincial and foreign-funded grants. While grants received in the social sciences are mainly related to the Korean language, culture and history, and refugee problems, in the natural sciences, the main grants the university receives are related to the development and protection of resources in the Changbai mountain region, and they cover research on plants and animals in the Changbai Mountain.[21]

Meanwhile, there are funds to help students to become creative learners and researchers. Half a million RMB is allocated each year for students. Usually, about 100 projects by students are funded every year, mainly for third and fourth year undergraduate students and for graduate students, with faculty's supervision to learn how to conduct research.

Teacher Education

We interviewed Professor Jin Changlu, Dean of the College of Teacher Education. Jin informed us that one key role YBU has played in its history of 50 years is to provide teacher education for China's minority schools providing basic education in the three provinces (Jilin, Liaoning, and Heilongjiang) and one region (Inner Mongolia Autonomous Region). Meanwhile, it has conducted research on Korean language teaching and played a role in maintaining Korean language and literature.

There used to be 1,000 schools that used Korean in classroom teaching. This practice is encouraged by the government and schools can choose to do so or not. In recent years, as a large number of Korean people have migrated to other parts of China for jobs, there are only 300 primary and secondary schools left that teach in Korean. Of these minority schools, more than 75% of the teachers are graduates from YBU.[22]

In 2008, the College of Teacher Education had 800 students studying in 9 programs. There were eight other teacher education programs provided by other colleges such as those in music, dance, and physical education, totaling 1,200 students. In order to train "cross-cultural integrated talents," starting in 2005 Yanbian dropped its practice of admitting students directly into the College of Teacher Education. Instead, the

---

[21] *Ibid.*
[22] Interview with Jin Changlu, Dean of College of Teacher Education, 23 May 2008.

students study general subjects in the first two years and indicate in the first semester of the third year whether they choose to major in teacher education or not. If so, they take four basic courses in teacher education, and other courses on pedagogy, plus electives and an internship. The teacher education students enjoy low tuition (3,800 RMB a year). We were told that the employment ratio for teacher education graduates was 80%.[23]

Strategies of Internationalization

Although Yanbian has signed intentions of collaboration with 113 universities, it has mainly interacted with South Korean and Japanese universities in exchanges of faculty and students. It knows it cannot compete with other famous universities in the country which focus mainly on collaboration with North American and European universities. However, since 2003, the current president has increased its efforts to develop exchanges with universities in these regions, and in 2005 signed an agreement to co-sponsor faculty to study abroad with the National Foundation for Studying Abroad, a subdivision of the Ministry of Education. In 2005 it also formed a plan for comprehensive collaboration with South Korean universities which included the following measures: 1) sending faculty to do PhD or postdoctoral study programs; 2) sending students to get MA degrees; 3) conducting collaborative research; 4) inviting visiting scholars from South Korea; 5) importing resources, such as books and equipment, from South Korea; 6) enrolling South Korean students. In 2006, it formulated a similar plan for exchanges with universities in Europe and North America.

Since 2003, Yanbian has also actively launched some new programs for student exchange with other countries, e.g., "3+1" or "2+2" programs which allow students in more than 20 majors to study at Yanbian for 3 years, and go abroad for another year, or to study at Yanbian for 2 years, and study in a foreign university for 2 years. Yanbian has collaborations with 52 Korean higher education institutions, including Kim Il Sung Comprehensive University of North Korea and Seoul National University. Since 2006, Yanbian has sent out MA students to 6 Korean universities, with a new "2+1" program. Each year, more than 300 undergraduate students, as well as several dozen MA and doctoral students are sent abroad for further study.[24] On the other hand, Yanbian also

---

[23] *Ibid.*
[24] Interview with Huang Jian, Director of International Exchange Office, 22 May 2008.

recruits international students, mainly from South Korea, Japan and Russia. Currently, there are around 500 international students studying on YBU's campus.

In training its faculty, YBU does not have the advantages of top universities like Peking and Tsinghua Universities. However, because of their minority status, they do enjoy favorable treatment in certain ways. As previously mentioned, Yanbian is counted as a "Western university" under the "Western China Development Project, which has allowed it to be promoted into a higher category of university with lower criteria, This ensures favorable treatment in terms of the allocation of resources and opportunities for sending faculty and students abroad. Having said this, of the 121 faculty who hold doctoral degrees, 56% obtained their degrees in South Korea, with full tuition and other costs paid by YBU.

Faculty: Maintaining Teaching Quality and Cultivating a Culture of Research

By 2008, YBU had 1,273 faculty members, of whom 723 were professors and associate professors, and the total number of faculty, staff and personnel in supporting units added up to 2,621. Over the period from 1990 to 2005, YBU's faculty profile has changed considerably, as shown in Table 8.2.

Table 8.2: Statistics on Faculty and Teacher-Student Ratios

	1990	1995	2000	2005
Full professors	20	42	117	209
Associate professors	141	128	330	406
Assistant professors	170	254	570	399
Teaching assistants	172	143	431	264
Teacher-student ratio	1:3.9	1:3.3	1:5.8	1:12.1

On average, YBU's teaching force had experienced the fastest growth between 1995 and 2000, during which period expansion was taking place in most higher education institutions. During these five years from 1995 to 2000, the number of full professors, associate professors, assistant professors and teaching assistants increased by 178.6%, 157.8%, 124.4% and 201.4%, respectively. Another significant change in the faculty contingent can be seen in the proportion of faculty at different academic levels. In 1990, only 3.9% of all faculty were full professors, whilst 28.0% were associate professors, 33.8% were assistant professors and 34.2% assistant teachers. By 1995, these ratios had changed to 7.4%

for full professors, 22.6% for associate professors, 44.8% for assistant professors and 25.2% for assistant teachers. By 2000, 8.1% were full professors, 22.8% associate professors, 39.4% assistant professors and 29.8% assistant teachers. The change was even more significant in 2005, 16.4% of the faculty were full professors, 31.8 % associate professors, 31.2% assistant professors and 20.7% assistant teachers. Full professors have seen a steady growth in the fifteen-year period, partly due to the dramatic growth of graduate student enrollments and graduate programs in the recent decade. By 2005, 16.7% of all faculty were doctoral degree holders, as compared to 3.1% in 2000, 1.4% in 1995 and a mere 0.2% in 1990.

The teacher-student ratio has also seen significant changes since 1990s, growing from 1:3.9 in 1990, to 1:12.1 in 2005. The significant rise in the teacher-student ratio, shows a considerable increase in the teaching workload and higher pressure on the YBU's teaching staff, but it is still not that steep, if compared with that in other major comprehensive universities in the move to mass higher education.

Yanbian has set up various mechanisms to improve the quality of teaching. A supervisory team of experienced scholars or retired teachers (who are rehired by the university) constantly goes to classes and collects feedback. Also, in each grade, students are selected to report on any cases of poor quality of teaching to the Office of Academic Affairs. Teachers being reported will be investigated and if the report of the students is verified they will be required to improve their teaching methods.[25] Furthermore, in May and October of every year, ten weeks into the fall and spring semesters, the students will provide online comments on their teachers. Teachers with poor ratings will be inspected by the supervisory team, and if it confirms that a particular teacher's teaching quality is low, the year-end evaluation of this faculty member will be affected, as well as the bonus and other kinds of benefits that make up a significant portion of the faculty's total annual income. The faculty will be asked to make improvements and will be assigned a mentor who can assist student.

We conducted a focus group meeting with 8 faculty members. Half of them were from the Department of Education and the other half from Psychology, with six of them being female and two male. These faculty members told us that it was hard to maintain a high quality of education, since the best Korean students tended to be recruited by top universities

---

[25] Interview with Yu Aizong, Director of Teaching Affairs, 22 May 2008.

outside the region, and the requirement to keep the ratio of Korean students at 50% (although recently this has dropped to 40%) tended to hamper the overall quality of education at Yanbian. Many Korean students had difficulty learning in Chinese, as they attended schools where Korean was the language of instruction at the primary and secondary level. Hence, teachers often resorted to using Korean to explain concepts in class and switched between Chinese (Putonghua) and Korean.[26]

The faculty in the focus group informed us that in the past they could teach in a traditional teacher-dominated manner, with the primary method being lecturing, but now they had to find ways to improve their teaching, as the students have become much more active and creative. One faculty member was in the field of psychology and explained that he needed to use three languages to explain concepts in psychology – Chinese, Korean and English, since many concepts originated from Western theories. It was important to be considerate of the level and characteristics of the students in their teaching, we were told by several.

The faculty felt they were under tremendous pressure to produce research. There were requirements for the publication of articles in various levels of journals, in addition to teaching requirements. For lecturers, they were required to have one publication in provincial level journals each year; for associate professors and professors, the publication requirements were higher, including publishing at the national and international levels and their income and research output were connected. Those publishing in the highest level journals got handsomely rewarded, and those who produced little would suffer a loss in income. Faculty members felt that administrative personnel had too much power in deciding how much the professors should produce, without understanding the nature of intellectual work and the fact that it could sometimes take a long time to bear fruit.[27]

Students' Voices

Four Korean students, three Han students, and one Hui minority student participated in our focus group meeting. Our talk with these students confirmed the fact that a lot of preferential treatment is available for minority students. There are subsidies of 44 RMB a month for minority students, and 40 RMB for Han students, which comprises about 8% of the

---

[26] Meeting with the Faculty Focus Group, 23 May 2008.
[27] *Ibid.*

students' spending each month.

The monthly cost of living is at least 500 RMB, which is considered very high in the region. Yanji has many people going to South Korea to work and they make more money than people in other regions, which has driven up the cost of living. And many goods shipped from big cities cost quite a bit. Hence the cost of living is similar to that in major cities. A female student commented that the Koreans in Yanji liked to spend money, as many had made money in South Korea.

A student who grew up in Yanji, said he had no financial problem. He observed that other students were in a similar situation. Tuition was 3,850 a year in general, while some programs had higher fees. Adding up the cost of living and tuition, over four years of study, the parents would need to come up with as much as 100,000 RMB or possibly somewhat less. The students were heavily dependent on their parents. Nevertheless Yanbian had 140 different kinds of scholarships, which helped to offset the cost of higher education. The students mentioned they had all obtained some sort of aid or scholarship. Students who averaged 70% (out of 100) in their course grades were eligible for scholarships, and the students who were most outstanding could get higher amounts.

Students in very dire financial situations relied on work and loans. Most students did some part-time jobs to supplement the cost of their tuition. One outstanding student had the highest level of scholarship but also worked during his spare time. Hence he was able to cover his own living costs and also support his younger brother in his studies.

We asked the students, whether the equality of education opportunities had increased or decreased after the expansion of higher education? One student said it had increased, since now 20 out 40 high school graduates could get into a university. Another student said it had decreased, citing the fact that students in different provinces can enroll in different categories of universities with widely different scores. In some provinces students can easily get into national-level comprehensive research universities, while students with much higher scores in other provinces can only get into second-tier teaching universities.

Regarding employment, we asked whether the university has helped students to find jobs, and the students said that the career counseling provided has been helpful. Teachers offered their help, and job fairs were helpful. The students also can go to other universities for job fairs as well. One student said confidently: "If one wants to work, one can always find something." Another student disagreed: "there are not so many jobs out there as a matter of fact." On the other hand, the university reported its graduate employment rate to be 92% in 2007,[28] which included students who reported they intended to continue onto graduate study, or do study abroad. To increase the chance of employment for their students, the university adopted measures such as focusing on training students' abilities, providing career counseling, and job information to students and providing platforms for students to connect with businesses.

On the amalgamation of 5 colleges into the current YBU, one student thought this had been helpful in providing cross-disciplinary study opportunities. Originally, he had no interest in learning Korean, or in business administration, but now he had the opportunity for study in these two areas as well as his main field.

What is Yanbian's position among the more than 1000 universities in China? We asked. Well, the students said, in terms of equipment and facilities, it is below average, but in terms of teacher quality, it is above average. "After all, we are a Project 21/1 university."

> "We have minority culture as an advantage, and we can learn Korean and other languages. This will give us a lot of opportunities."[29]

A teacher education student said that her teachers were very concerned for them. The teachers knew all of their names. A psychology student said they can always go to the teachers to discuss issues and consult them. "It is a mutual relationship."

On whether Korean culture can contribute to the world, the students stated that Confucianism can contribute to the world. One student mentioned that she heard that the United States and Canada are becoming interested in the *Analects*, especially the idea of Grand Unity in Confucianism. They mentioned that they have friends in the U.S., who are helping to promote Chinese culture over there. Chinese culture has influenced Korean and Japanese culture as well, the students commented. Further, the students mentioned that China is learning from other countries as well. Chinese need to change their rote learning methods, and integrate what is valuable in other cultures, so that it will become even stronger.

On internationalization, there are a lot of exchanges with South

---

[28] Interview with Gai Tongxiang, Vice President, 22 May 2008.
[29] Interview with the Focus Group Students, 23 May 2008.

Korea and Japan. Many scholarships are set up by South Koreans. Students go to study or do exchange in South Korea. There are also South Korean students coming to study at Yanbian. These are mainly exchange students, but not all YBU students have had the opportunity to get to know a foreign student. One student indicated she enjoyed the experience of interacting with foreign students as she could get to learn about another culture by talking with them about culture and personal interests. Yet, another student said he did not enjoy this, as they did not have a common language.

When asked which architecture on campus best represented the university, nearly all the students mentioned the front entrance, noting that the name of Yanbian University was written in both Chinese and Korean, giving it a Korean identity. (Photo 8.4) The students also mentioned the main teaching building. (Photo 8.3) One student said the building's size, its interior and its external appearance were the best on campus. "When you take pictures from the front gate of the campus, our university looks great." The Administrative Building was also mentioned, where the president's office is; it has an historic look and is a witness to YBU's history. The new sports center was also mentioned, as a symbol pointing to Yanbian's famous soccer team, which was ranked third in Jilin province in 2008, and had been first in 2005, as well as back in 1992.

Photo 8.4: The main entrance of the University where its name is written in both Chinese and Korean characters

We asked the students if they had participated in student groups or societies and the unanimous answer was yes. The Red Cross, collecting donations for poor people, serving as volunteers in all kinds of activities, joining book clubs, were among some of the activities they mentioned. What they liked to do the most were activities that helped and served society. For the May 2008 earthquake victims they donated money, and 2,000 students held condolence rituals by forming a heart shape. This was organized by the students themselves.

One student mentioned she has organized students to visit a very poor family that has been taking care of more than 10 children who were deserted or orphaned. The students collected clothing for them, and visited the kids once in a while. These were all voluntary activities. The university usually only organized major activities, the students said, and the smaller ones were organized by students. Their understanding of civil society was as follows: "civil society to me is to do our due for the society;" "civil society should focus on equality and unity;" "there would be no laws needed as people would all have moral integrity."[30]

In terms of having a voice in the university's policy making, the students said that they felt they were heard by the school leaders, and some of their suggestions were reflected in policies of the university. However, the Korean students said:

> We have suggestions, but sometimes the university does not have the conditions to meet them. For example, [the Korean] students studied in Korean during their primary and secondary education, but now we are studying entirely in Chinese, so we hope the university can translate textbooks into Korean for us. But we are only 20% of the students so we cannot expect the university to translate all textbooks.[31]

In terms of political education, the students told us they had three years of courses in this subject, with different content each semester, including ideology, cultivation and personal quality, Marxist philosophy and political economics, law, international trends and situations, and history. "Are they helpful? Are you interested?" we asked. The response was that this depended on the teachers. Some teachers used case studies and gave objective analyses with their own interpretations, not like the teachers in primary and secondary schools, who just used cramming

---

[30] *Ibid.*
[31] *Ibid.*

methods. Some teachers collected a lot of information and had their own analyses. "We like this kind of teacher," students commented. One teacher in international politics invited outside speakers or successful people from the community to share their experience and broaden the students' views. However, another student said: "this also depends on the students' motive in learning. I am not interested in political economy but because I have to take the graduate entrance exam, I have to be very attentive. Another teacher is great, who is very talented and touched us in our hearts, so I study very hard in her class."[32]

Challenges and the Future

YBU is located in a town where the majority of the residents are Korean. This is a part of China where one may feel one is in a foreign land when visiting. The street signs are prominently Korean, and only some are bilingual, with Korean written ahead of Chinese, as required by the government. Newspapers are mostly in Korean, and so are TV programs.

All the schools in the Yanji region teach all subject areas from grade one to upper secondary school in Korean. However, when the students attend YBU, almost all the courses are taught in Chinese. Many students fall behind as a result. The university offers courses to help students improve their Chinese, but many still have difficulty. The dilemma is that the best Korean students have all left for better universities in other parts of the country and those students YBU admits are mostly second tier local students. Hence the university needs to make great efforts to help the students. Fortunately, the university belongs to Project 21/1, which allows it to accept students from other parts of the country (mainly Han students) who have higher scores.

This is a rather ironic dilemma, as Yanbian specializes in teaching Korean students yet it needs Han students to boost the overall quality of the student population. On the other hand, Yanbian sees this as an opportunity, which allows it to move closer to the mainstream. Yanbian very much wants to be a center in the margin, and "awakening from the margin" has been repeatedly mentioned, indicating their sense of urgency to pursue national first class and world-class university status. Can YBU become a national center of higher education? Can it rise from the margins?

---

[32] *Ibid.*

A multicultural approach is the direction the university is pursuing which seems to us to be a good idea. This approach posits Korean culture as enriching to Chinese culture, while at the same time needing to take nutrients from the mainstream Han culture. Furthermore, Yanbian's focus on cultivating and developing local resources, such as those of the Changbai Mountains, is a smart move. No other institution can take the place of a university which has the advantage of rich opportunities in research funding by serving the local economy. Another well-aligned move, it seems to the authors, is that of placing itself strategically into the space created by the political and international wrangling among China, the United States, Russia, South Korea, North Korea, and Japan. Its proximity to South and North Korea, as well as to Russia and Japan, is its niche and advantage. Hence, in "rising from the margin," Yanbian University has been smart in placing itself in the center of the world educationally and policy-wise. The case of Yanbian University may thus call for a new definition of what comprises a world-class university, or a national top rated university. We feel that a university that best plays its role for the students it serves, that best serves the needs of the local economy, and that has an important part to play in terms of mediating conflicts for the nation and the world should be viewed as first class or world-class.

Part IV:
Portraits of Three Science and Technology Universities

Universities of science and technology have played a special role in China's development since 1949, and their high profile is evident in the fact that six of the nine leading universities first selected for the 98/5 project had originally been shaped to some degree by the famous model of France's école polytechnique and the Soviet polytechnical university. While China has largely repudiated the high degree of specialization, sectoralism and tendency to a separation between pure and applied sciences that characterized the Soviet model, there is still a strong determination to maintain the diversity of the higher education system in face of globalization pressures that favor the comprehensive research university. Thus present policy encourages institutions focusing on science and technology, agriculture and education to build on the identities they have developed in their own unique ways over the decades since 1949.

The three institutions profiled in this third part of the volume illustrate both the varieties of historical experience and the different strategies being adopted by contemporary leaders of universities of science and technology. The University of Science and Technology of China was a maverick from its origins, in 1958, as a university created by the Chinese Academy of Sciences in a determined effort to integrate research and teaching, basic theory and applied knowledge at the highest levels. The Huazhong University of Science and Technology was founded in 1952, on the standard Soviet polytechnical model, and found its own way, after the Cultural Revolution, to the integration of basic sciences and research that was essential to excellent scholarship. The Northwest University of Agriculture and Forestry has roots in the 1930s but has recently added "science and technology" to its title and become a new kind of multiversity in the merger it embraced as part of the move to mass higher education.

9
The University of Science and Technology of China – Can the Caltech Model take Root in Chinese Soil?

Qiang ZHA and Jun LI, with CHENG Xiaofang

The University of Science and Technology of China (中國科學技術大學) has a relatively short but remarkable history. If Peking University is commonly viewed as a national higher education icon, the University of Science and Technology of China, for its part, might be regarded a landmark in terms of higher education development after the founding of People's Republic of China in 1949. It is one of a very few universities that have "China" in their names, and its leaders have mandated the use of USTC as its English name due to its significant national reputation.

In a deliberate decision by the Chinese leadership to integrate basic and applied sciences in a high level university administered by the Chinese Academy of Sciences (CAS) (中國科學院), the USTC was launched in 1958 in Beijing. It was consciously designed to supersede the then prevailing Soviet model of the polytechnical university, which had had a strongly applied orientation to its curriculum and relatively less emphasis on the basic sciences. It was also intended to create a strong link between teaching and research at a time when all major national research projects were assigned to the Chinese Academy of Sciences and higher education functioned as a separate system mandated to focus mainly on teaching. In the Cultural Revolution, the USTC was forced to move out of Beijing, and finally settled down in Hefei, the capital city of the relatively underdeveloped Central China province of Anhui. Since then it has been a national leader in science education and its response to massification has been deliberate and interesting. Convinced that neither merger nor expansion of the student body were appropriate, it is perhaps the only Chinese university that didn't increase its enrollment in the recent expansion of the Chinese higher education system. Rather, its leaders have forged an identity that emphasizes regional and international leadership in the sciences and leading-edge technologies.

In this chapter, we will begin with a brief overview of USTC's history and context, and then consider the changes in student numbers, finance and curriculum that constitute the empirical face of the move to mass higher education. From there we consider the university's new vision and mission, its strategic direction, and finally views from faculty and students on various dimensions of the move to mass higher education. This chapter draws mainly on data obtained from interviews and focus group meetings. We carried out an intensive case study visit on the USTC campus from May 17 to 22, 2007. During this visit, we interviewed a number of university leaders, including Lu Ming, Vice Party Secretary (student affairs), Zhu Canping, Director of the Office of Student Affairs (who has now become Secretary-General of USTC), Cui Xianying, Deputy Director of Student Affairs, Liu Bin, Director of the Office of Teaching Affairs, Tang Jiajun, Deputy Director of Teaching Affairs, Zhang Mengping, Director of the Foreign Affairs Office, and Zhou Zhengkai, Deputy Director of the Foreign Affairs Office. We also conducted two focus group meetings respectively with faculty members and students. In addition, as part of the pilot study for this project, one of the authors did an interview on July 5, 2006 with Chen Yi, Director of Anhui Province's Department of Education, who had been USTC's Vice President 1999-2004.

History and Context

"A Cradle of Scientists" at Birth

The USTC was established at a significant time in Chinese history, some years after the reorganization of colleges and departments that set in place a new system of higher education in 1952. In 1956, China launched the *Long Range Plan on Science and Technology Development (1956-1967)* (1956-1967 年科學技術發展遠景規劃), which outlined a number of priority areas. They included launching China's man-made satellite, producing artificial synthetic crystalline bovine insulin, and developing atomic bombs and missiles. These ambitious goals made it clear that a new type of talent was needed with excellent training in both basic and applied sciences. It was probably coincidental that a group of top Chinese scientists visited the New Siberia branch of the Soviet Academy of Sciences and the New Siberia University in 1957. They were both surprised and impressed by the University-Academy articulation arrangement they saw there, which promised the University smooth access to the Academy's research facilities, and guaranteed the Academy a reliable supply of talent from the University. Inspired by this marriage between research and education functions, the CAS proposed the idea of launching a new type of university to the Chinese leadership. This new-style university was to overcome the then common pattern that placed basic science programs in comprehensive universities and applied science programs in polytechnical universities, by offering an integrative curriculum that brought together pure and applied sciences. On another level, it was also intended to supersede the structural divide between teaching in higher education institutions and research in the institutes of the Chinese Academy of Sciences and research institutions under various ministries.

On May 9, 1958, the Chinese Academy of Sciences officially submitted its proposal for creating the University of Science and Technology of China to the State Council. On June 2, 1958, the Secretariat of the Central Committee of the Chinese Communist Party (中共中央書記處) approved it. On June 8, 1958, a preparatory committee was formed, which made decisions with respect to the academic structure, the proposed departments and specializations and the admission plan. Between July and August 1958, the department chairs were appointed, and the teaching plans were reviewed and approved. Most importantly, a strategic plan was developed for the USTC's future development, which involved laying a foundation in the first three years and then stepping into the top ranks of higher education in five years. On September 20, 1958, the USTC had its launching ceremony, witnessed by its first cohort of 1,634 students. In an amazingly brief 100 days, the USTC went through the whole process from initial paperwork to full establishment. This fact clearly indicated its important position in China's blueprint for science and technology modernization.[1] Guo Moruo (郭沫若), a high profile lit-

---

[1] The year 1958 marked the launch of the Great Leap Forward movement, which represented a bold and idealistic attempt to achieve an accelerated move towards communism. The promotion of social equality became a key national development goal, which was to be achieved through a rapid expansion of education at all levels. On average there emerged three regular higher education institutions every day in 1958, which resulted in a near six-fold increase in the aggregate total of Chinese higher education institutions between 1958 and 1960. In this scheme, the polytechnical and specialized institutions were to serve the three unities of education and politics, education and productive labor, and theory and practice at the tertiary level. Most of the new institutions were of such types as engineering, teacher training, agriculture, and medicine (traditional Chinese medicine in particular). Many new polytechnics and engineering colleges were hastily estab-

erary figure and early Communist activist who was then President of the CAS, served as its founding president.[2]

In its early days, the USTC designed all of its 13 departments[3] and 41 teaching specializations around the technology required to fulfill the nation's ambition to have "two bombs and one star" (兩彈一星), that is both atomic and hydrogen bombs, and an artificial satellite. Since then, the USTC has developed a broader mission: to forge a vision ahead of the times, aim at frontier science and leading technology, foster state-of-the-art research, and closely serve the nation's immediate and long-range strategic needs. The USTC's first cohort of students graduated in 1963; in the period since then, it has graduated 50,000 undergraduate students, among whom about 5,000 are working in various fields of national defence. The CAS provided full support to the USTC by creating close links between its institutes and the relevant departments of the university. As a result, many well established researchers at the CAS held concurrent positions as department chairs and faculty members at the USTC.[4] They have made a crucial contribution to raising teaching quality

---

lished and had inadequate equipment and facilities. There can be no doubt that the USTC was an exception.

[2] Guo Moruo (16 November 1892-12 June 1978) was a prolific Chinese writer of poetry, fiction, plays, biographies, translations, and historical and philosophical treatises – for which he was awarded the Lenin Peace Prize in 1951 – along with holding important government offices in China. He joined the Communist Party of China in 1927. He was involved in the Communist Nanchang Uprising and fled to Japan after its failure. He stayed there for 10 years studying Chinese ancient history. In the summer of 1937, soon after the Marco Polo Bridge incident, Guo returned to China to join the anti-Japanese resistance. After the founding of the People's Republic of China, Guo Moruo was the first President of the Chinese Academy of Sciences and remained in this position from its founding in 1949 until his death in 1978.

[3] The initial 13 Departments were Nuclear Physics and Engineering, Technical Physics, Chemical physics, Thermal Physics, Radio Electronics, Automation, Mechanics and Mechanical Engineering, Radio and Nuclear Chemistry, Geochemistry and Rare Elements, Polymer Chemistry and Physics, Applied Mathematics and Computer Technology, Biophysics, Geophysics.

[4] For instance, Zhao Zhongyao (趙忠堯), then Deputy Director of the CAS' Nuclear Energy Institute was made Chair of the Atomic Physics and Engineering Department; Shi Ruwei (施汝爲), then Director of the Physics Institute as Chair of the Technical Physics Department; Guo Yonghui (郭永懷), then Deputy Director of the Mechanics Institute as Chair of the Chemical Physics Department, Wu Zhonghua (吳仲華), then CAS Fellow at the Dynamics Research Unit as Chair of

and to connecting teaching with research, enabling students to be exposed to state-of-the-art research in their fields.

Relocation to Central China in the Early 1970s

In the beginning of 1970, at the height of the Cultural Revolution, there was a strong emphasis on students' exposure to practice and revolutionary activism as well as serious preparations against a possible war with the Soviet Union. Under these circumstances the USTC was moved to Hefei,[5] the capital city of Anhui province in the Central Region of

---

the Thermal Physics Department, Gu Dehuan (顧德歡), then Director of the Electronics Institute as Chair of Radio Electronics Department, Wu Ruyang (武汝揚), then Director of the Automation Institute as Chair of the Automation Department, Qian Xueshen (錢學森), then Director of the Mechanics Institute as Chair of the Mechanics and Mechanical Engineering Department, Yang Cheng-zong (杨承宗), then CAS Fellow at the Geology Institute as Chair of the Radio and Nuclear Chemistry Department, Hou Defeng (侯德封), then Director of the Geology Institute as Chair of the Geochemistry and Rare Elements Department, Hua Shoujun (華壽俊), then Deputy Director of Chemistry Institute as Chair of the Polymer Chemistry and Physics Department, Hua Luogeng (華羅庚), then Director of the Mathematics Institute as Chair of the Applied Mathematics and Computer Technology Department, Pei Shizhang (貝時璋), then Director of the Biophysics Institute as Chair of the Biophysics Department, and Zhao Jiuzhang (趙九章), then Director of the Geophysics Institute as Chair of the Geophysics Department.

[5] The USTC's relocation to Hefei should be understood in relation to two political documents of the Cultural Revolution period: Chairman Mao Zedong's "Directive of 7 May, 1966" and Deputy Chairman Lin Biao's "No. 1 Order in 1969." Mao's "Directive of 7 May, 1966" specified that students should undertake industrial, agricultural and military work in addition to their academic course work, the length of the period of formal education should be shortened, and in general "education should be revolutionized." In the light of this directive, the USTC decided in October 1969 to set up an experimental base in Nanyang Prefecture, Henan Province, for the purpose of revolutionizing its educational programs, and planned to move the entire university there in 2-3 years. Meanwhile, the Chinese and Soviet armies entered into border combat in March of 1969, and this situation worsened in Fall 1969, when China started to prepare itself for a possible full scale hit by the Soviet Union. On 18 October 1969, Lin Biao issued his "No. 1 Order" which put China essentially in a state of war. Under this circumstance, the CPC sent out the "Circular of Decentralizing Higher Education Institutions" on 26 October 1969 aiming to move most universities out of Beijing. At that point, Henan wasn't ready to host the USTC, and so it was temporally moved to the small city of Anqing, in the neighboring Anhui Province, with its first batch of

China.⁶ In the current Chinese context, the concept of region is based partly on geographic considerations and partly on economic implications. The Eastern Region represents the country's most developed part, the Central Region is viewed as still developing, while the hinterland or Western Region is another name for China's least developed area. In the era of the planned economy, however, there were six major regions, based originally on military districts and used for macro-planning purposes. While Anhui was part of the East China region in this early period, it has now been placed within the Central Region, reflecting its relatively disadvantaged economic position. Since the reform towards a market economy was launched in the late 1970s, the differences among regions have widened into large gaps. Between 1981 and 1998, the Eastern Region increased its share in China's GDP by 7%, while the Central and Western regions suffered a drop of 2.8 and 4.2% respectively. Anhui, where the USTC is located now, is not even ranked top in the Central Region. Its per capita GDP was below the national average until 2000.⁷

In the relocation process, USTC lost two thirds of its equipment and instrumentation but what was far worse was the loss of highly valuable teaching and research personnel. As noted earlier, the USTC had benefitted in unique ways from the special arrangement that linked its departments with the research institutes of the CAS. Thus many renowned researchers had served concurrently as department chairs and professors at the USTC. It was this high profile faculty that enabled the USTC to find its way into the nation's top rank only a couple of years after it was founded. When it moved to Hefei, it lost more than half of its faculty members, and basically had to start again from scratch, since many more chose to leave even after settling down in Hefei. This pain and loss has

---

900 faculty, staff and students left stranded in the humble three-storey building of the local party school. By a coincidence, Anhui Province had decided to dismantle the then Hefei Teachers Training College just at that time, and thus the USTC could finally settle down on its campus in January of 1970. When it settled down in Hefei, the USTC had 798 faculty (including 23 full and associate professors) and 1,278 students.

⁶ China's Central Region comprises nine provinces: Heilongjiang, Jilin, Inner Mongolia, Shanxi, Henan, Anhui, Hubei, Hunan and Jiangxi.

⁷ Wang, Aolan, "Lue Lun Zhongbu Fazhan Zhanlue De Jiben Quxiang," (A Brief Account of Strategic Direction for the Development of the Central Region), *Working Paper Series of the Development and Research Center of Anhui Province*, 2000, accessed December 5, 2000, http://ahdrc.ah.gov.cn/cghj/cg23.htm.

been a recurring one for the USTC, since the disadvantage of its location has continued to make it difficult to attract and keep the best talent.

The location disadvantage has had an impact on its revenue as well. Against the backdrop of China's market economy, most universities are engaged in revenue generating activities, ranging from selling their auxiliary services to running high-tech enterprises, such as the Founder's Group (方正集團) in the case of Peking University. Obviously those located in the more prosperous Eastern Region are greatly advantaged in launching this type of activity, while those in the Central and Western regions, like the USTC, suffer from the economic disadvantages of their localities. Therefore, the USTC has largely functioned as a self-enclosed society, isolated from its local environment. A symbol of this separate status is the fact that most people speak Chinese with a northern accent on the USTC campus, something that is not often heard even steps away from the campus.

A Unique Culture and Ethos

From its first day, the USTC blew some fresh air to China's higher education sector. In many ways it deviated from the then dominant Soviet patterns representing a bold experiment in search of a new university model that would nurture scientists, rather than engineers. Given this unique mandate, the USTC naturally embraced quite a different culture and ethos from that of most other campuses visited in this book. Such a mandate might be best summarized by Nie Rongzhen (聶榮臻), then Chinese Vice Premier responsible for education and the sciences, in his speech at the USTC's launching ceremony on September 20, 1958:

> "We propose to launch a new type of university, which is in close proximity to major research establishments, offers a core curriculum based on the world's most leading science and technology, recruits the most promising among high school leavers, and provides them with a rigorous training in the basic sciences and operational technology; in their third and fourth year, the students are to participate in real research in the relevant research institutes of the CAS, in order to gain professional experience quickly and to accelerate the nurturing of professionals in the new science and technology areas. This should enable our nation to catch up with the advanced countries on a short timeline, as we build our strengths in the emerging disciplinary areas that are most needed but have remained gaps."

This quotation reveals the USTC's original mission, which has determined its innovation-based culture and ethos. Also, during our case study visit on its campus, we could easily identify a down-to-earth manner and low-key style that was shared by faculty, administrators and students. We became aware that many happenings of an innovative nature on that campus have been controversial in the currents of the time, e.g., spearheading the offering of cross-disciplinary specializations/courses and creating the Special Class for the Gifted Young (少年班), two initiatives which are discussed in more detail later in this chapter, and thus there was almost an agreement that they shouldn't be given high publicity. If one deals with things that are controversial, the best way is to do it quietly but steadily, in order to survive the controversy and eventually gain acceptance for change. In 1958, the USTC came to life with no history or burden of heritage, which essentially allowed all kinds of experimentation and innovation to take place. Probably two are of the greatest importance. One was the peculiar policy of "the whole academy running the university and the (research) institutes being paired with (university) departments" (全院辦校, 所系結合). The other was the policy of setting up programs and specializations around the rationale of filling the nation's gaps in emerging disciplinary areas.

A Unique Policy for Running the University

The deliberate policy that linked the USTC's departments to the research institutes of the CAS was absolutely unique in China's higher education community. Not only did it promote an efficient mode of resource sharing but more importantly it articulated teaching with research. In the then context of absolute functional separation between the higher education and research systems in China, the USTC set an unprecedented and pioneering example, which has proven to be successful in nurturing creative minds, and effective in practice.

For its part, the CAS made full use of its advantage in research personnel and facilities to support the USTC, and fostered strong co-operation between the paired institutes and departments. With such an arrangement, a large number of the CAS scientists gave lectures and conducted research at the USTC. In the early years when it was located in Beijing, the USTC would have an annual average of 300 visits of CAS scientists, who came to its campus and lectured to students, which gave them exposure to state-of-the-art research in their fields. In addition to lecturing, the CAS scientists also helped to set up new specializations and compile teaching outlines and syllabuses as well as course materials. Many of these scientists were Western educated, and so their approaches were essentially different from the then prevailing Soviet patterns.

The articulation arrangement with the CAS greatly enabled research at the USTC. Only two years after its founding, the USTC joined efforts with the CAS' institute of computer science, and successfully made China's first electronic computer in 1960. Zhao Zhongyao (趙忠堯), a famed physicist at the CAS and Chair of the Atomic Physics and Engineering Department at the USTC generously donated an accelerator to the USTC, which he had taken enormous trouble in bringing back from the West, and supervised students' experiments on it. This perhaps led to the USTC being chosen in the 1980s to house a national megaresearch project, the National Synchrotron Radiation Lab. Because of its promising research performance, the USTC was designated to offer graduate programs in 1963, in the same year that its first cohort of students graduated. In 1978, the USTC established its School of Graduate Studies in Beijing, the first among all Chinese universities to have a graduate school.

The CAS patronage together with the peculiar articulation arrangement contributed not only to the USTC's strength in research and teaching but also to its unique culture and ethos. The USTC was intended to nurture future scientists for research institutes of the CAS. Over the years, it has been proud of its identity as a "cradle of scientists," and spared no efforts to turn itself into "a top-level university offering an elite education" (精品辦學, 英才教育). For its part the CAS has granted the USTC a high degree of autonomy in order to create a "relaxed environment" in which effective means can be developed for nurturing the most elite talent. This would not have been possible to the same degree, if the USTC had been administered by China's Ministry of Education like most other national universities.[8] The agreement endorsing the USTC's participation in Project 98/5, reached on July 25, 1999 among three parties—the CAS, the Ministry of Education and Anhui Province—carries a commitment to respecting and fostering the USTC's autonomy, in an effort to "establish an operating mechanism that combines autonomy and self-mastery," the latter being a core value of traditional scholarship in China.[9]

---

[8] Interview with Lu Ming, Deputy Party Secretary of the USTC, 22 May 2007.
[9] CAS, Ministry of Education of China and Anhui Province, "Guanyu Zhongdian Gong Jian Zhongguo Keji Daxue De Jueding," (A Decision on Prioritizing the

Integrative Curricular Coverage

A pivotal reason behind the founding of the USTC was to fill certain evident gaps in new and emerging disciplinary areas in the Chinese context. This was clearly evident in the establishment of the initial 13 departments and 41 specializations at the USTC, with areas such as nuclear physics, space technology, computer science, automation, chemical physics and modern mechanics being new to China at the time. The departments underwent some adjustments later, but this rationale continued to guide all developments, in ways that would cater to the CAS' human resource needs. The students enrolled in all specializations studied for 5 years at the USTC, while their peers in other universities often studied only for four years.[10] The extended program length was meant to accommodate the intensified course content, as most of the specializations had a full array of foundational courses, and incorporated content in both basic sciences and applied sciences.

The integration of basic and applied sciences in the curricular offerings constituted a major innovation with the USTC. In the 1950s, the prevailing curricular patterns separated the basic and applied sciences, and emphasized students' acquisition of highly specialized applied knowledge and professional skills in polytechnical universities, without exposing them to basic science foundations. This model aimed at turning the students into engineers in a range of highly specialized fields that matched the employment needs of different sectors of the planned economy. Yet, at the launching ceremony of the USTC, its inaugural president, Guo Moruo, expressed his expectations of the USTC students into the following way: "[I] hope our students ... not only master the state-of-the-art [specialized knowledge] but also have a solid and wide

---

Joint Efforts to Support the USTC), July 25, 1999, accessed May 22, 2000, http://www.ustc.edu.cn/chinese/ustcnews/mzdt/first_class/gjjueding.html.

[10] In October 1951, the Chinese State Council issued "Guanyu Gaige Xuezhi De Jueding" (A Decision on Schooling Reform), which stipulated that the university programs ranged from 4 to 5 years. In this policy context, there were a proportion of engineering, polytechnical and in particular medical universities that offered 5-year programs, while others adopted 4-year programs. In May 1959, with the mentality of the Great Leap Forward, the Chinese leadership promulgated "Guanyu Shiyan Gaige Xuezhi De Jueding" (A Decision on Piloting Reform of Schooling). This document was more concerned with elementary and secondary schooling, though, the universities were inevitably influenced, and increasingly adopted 4-year programs.

[knowledge] base, and a wide array of skills." His inscription for the USTC, "fostering redness and expertise equally, integrating basic sciences and applied sciences fundamentally" (紅專並進, 理實交融) has become motto of the USTC. If the first half of this motto is stamped with the revolutionary spirit of the times, the second half has underscored the USTC's ethos ever since.

Photo 9.1: The Statue of Guo Moruo on the USTC East Campus

As a result, from its early days, the USTC has tried to make sure that students have a solid science and mathematics foundation, a good mastery of laboratory skills and a strong spirit of innovation, with a tendency to emphasize the science and mathematics foundation above all. Lu Ming, the Deputy Party Secretary of the USTC, illustrated this by using the metaphor of two "legs" that underpin the USTC's curriculum: the USTC has a longer "science leg" than a "technology leg".[11] From a curricular perspective, the USTC resembles neither a typical polytechnical university nor a comprehensive university in the Chinese system – it is a kind of maverick. The USTC also pioneered the offering of cross-

---

[11] Interview with Lu Ming, Deputy Party Secretary of the USTC, 22 May 2007.

disciplinary specializations. Lu Ming used her own major (when studying at the USTC) as an example: Chemical Physics, which didn't even exist in the Ministry of Education's Catalogue when established.[12]

To complete the sophisticated and demanding study programs offered at the USTC could have taken as long as 7 years, but students had to complete them in 5 years. The first three and a half years were taken up with foundational courses, and then students participated in research projects and completed theses in their senior year at various CAS' institutes. When all the programs were shortened to 4 years in 2003, most foundational courses remained untouched, leaving the students with less time for working in laboratories. In addition, the USTC was also the first Chinese university that incorporated foreign language courses into the core curriculum, ever since its early years.

This curriculum left the USTC's students with no choice but to study very hard. Over the years, this has become an integral part of the USTC's ethos, resulting in the high quality of its graduates, many of whom earned their university an excellent reputation overseas with their extraordinary academic records when studying abroad. It is also reflected in a much celebrated saying: "only those who devote their life to the pursuit of knowledge should come to study at the USTC."[13] In this study, we have tried to link the campus buildings or space to each university's culture and ethos. When asked which building on the USTC campus

Photo 9.2: A Night View of the USTC's West Campus

Note: Courtesy of the USTC website

---

[12] *Ibid.*
[13] *Ibid.*

could embody its ethos, quite to our surprise, some interviewees responded by calling attention to the lit-up classrooms during the night, which are packed with USTC students who study extremely hard and often forget time.[14]

With this fresh approach to knowledge and these remarkable achievements in both teaching and research, the USTC was included in the nation's first group of "key-point" universities in 1959, and was ranked 4th among the 16 universities in that first group. The USTC was also the youngest one among them, only one year old at the time when it was selected. Innovation was its core value, as evident in Guo Moruo's expectations for research: "aggressively pursuing innovations while seeking truth from facts; seeking the truth from facts while aggressively pursuing innovations."[15] Almost 50 years later, the current President of the CAS, Lu Yongxiang (路甬祥), challenged the USTC and its faculty and students with the following phrase: "I innovate, therefore I am",[16] which is clearly borrowed from René Descartes' famous phrase, "Cogito, ergo sum."

The Trajectory of the USTC's Revival

After the remarkable achievements of its early years, the USTC suffered huge losses during the Cultural Revolution. Only after 1978, when the "Spring of Science" finally arrived, in the words of Guo Moruo,[17] could it begin its journey back to becoming one of China's top ranking universities. Although only 20 years old, the USTC played a leading role among Chinese universities in terms of reaching out to the world higher education and academic community. It began sending its junior faculty and promising students to pursue advanced studies in the West at an early point. Perhaps due to this early and wide exposure to the West, the USTC has cultivated a kind of atmosphere of democracy on the campus, and is often viewed as a major initiator of the student pro-democracy

---

[14] The USTC Students Focus Group Meeting on 19 May 2007.

[15] The USTC, "Xiaoshi Gai Lan," (A Glimpse of the USTC History), n.d., accessed November 18, 2008, http://www.ustc.edu.cn/zh_CN/column/000015.

[16] *Ibid*.

[17] At the first National Science and Technology Convention in Beijing in March 1978, Guo Moruo, then-President of both CAS & USTC, delivered a speech under this title, which poetically pronounced that the "Spring of Science" had arrived. Thereafter this milestone conference has been nicknamed the Spring of Science conference, and seen to mark a new era of revitalized scientific research.

movement in China, despite its science and technology-focused curriculum.[18] It also took a bold step in March of 1978 to create a Special Class for the Gifted Young, adopting an innovative way of nurturing the minds of highly promising young people. Also in 1978, the USTC established China's first School of Graduate Studies, placing it in Beijing and so enabling a new generation of students to benefit from close ties with the CAS. In 2001, it was converted into the CAS' School of Graduate Studies.

In 1984, as part of a national key-point infrastructure development scheme, the State Synchrotron Radiation Laboratory was established and housed in the USTC. It is the first and insofar the only state mega-research facility on a university campus.[19] It came to the USTC with a

---

[18] The USTC is commonly regarded as the initiator of the student pro-democracy movement at the end of 1986 and in early 1987. This is somewhat puzzling given its focus on science and technology in the curriculum and its location, far from Beijing or any other major cities. One of the authors happened to meet the former Deputy Party Secretary of the CPC Anhui Provincial Committee, Xu Leyi (徐樂儀), on 19 December 2009. He was in charge of educational affairs at the time and helped to handle the situation, and thus shared the first-hand story behind the scene. In the second half of 1986, the *People's Daily* carried six opinion articles on democratic governance within the university, and the USTC was cited as a positive example of "professorial rule." At the end of the year, Wan Li (萬裏), then member of CPC Polibureau and Vice Premier of the State Council, came to Hefei and organized a seminar on this theme, with all the university leaders in Anhui participating and a significant visibility of the USTC – 20 participants from this single institution. Unfortunately, a debate occurred between Wan Li and Fang Lizhi (方勵之) (then VP of the USTC) over the topic of whether democracy could be conferred from above, which led to termination of the seminar without any conclusion reached. Shortly after, in the neighboring Anhui University, a few students and staff started a campaign to run for seats in the local chambers of the People's Congress, which was highly controversial at the time and opposed by the authorities. When asked about his opinion about this phenomenon, Fang Lizhi burst into a provocative speech, which led to the students' quitting of classes in protest. This action was immediately echoed by students in Shanghai Jiao Tong University as well as others in Shanghai and Beijing, and spread nationwide. In January 1987, Hu Yaobang (胡耀邦), then CPC General Secretary, was held accountable for this movement, and was forced to resign from his post. His death from a heart attack on 15 April 1989 triggered what ended up as the "June Fourth" tragedy. Fang Lizhi was expelled from the CPC in January 1987, and has been exiled to the US ever since 1990.

[19] There are up to date three such state mega-research facilities, which were listed in the "five-year plan" for national development, and supported by state financ-

budget of 59.9 million *yuan* RMB, which was 5 times as much as the USTC's own operating budget in 1983. In 1995, the USTC was included in Project 21/1, among the first group of 15 universities; in 1999, it was selected for Project 98/5, as one of the initial 9 universities. In 1998, at the recommendation of the Chinese government, then-President of the USTC, Zhu Qingshi (朱清時), made a presentation on reforming university curriculum and teaching in China at UNECSO's World Conference on Higher Education.[20]

Having just celebrated its 50th birthday, the USTC is now proud of the fact that one out of every 1,000 alumni are elected to the Chinese Academy of Sciences or the Chinese Engineering Academy, a rate that hasn't yet been beaten by any other universities in China. Between 1998 and 2007, the USTC faculty published 7,521 SCI (Science Citation Index) indexed papers, which had been cumulatively cited 61,919 times. These statistics rank the USTC the highest among all the Chinese universities in terms of its academic standards and research impact,[21] and indicate that USTC overtook the leadership that had been established by Nanda in the earlier 1990s (see Chapter 4, p.131). The USTC is also ranked among the top Chinese universities, in terms of research productivity, by such internationally prestigious journals as *Science* and *Research*.

In recent years, the USTC has taken part in a number of major national science advancement programs, such as the second phase of the State Synchrotron Radiation Laboratory, and the HT-7U Superconducting Tokmak. In 2003, the USTC reorganized its CAS key laboratories of Structure Analysis, Bond-Selective Chemistry, Quantum Information, Structural Biology with a few other university-wide laboratories of Atomic and Molecular Physics, Physical and Chemical Analysis, and Low Temperature and High Magnetic Field, and formed a multidisciplinary National Laboratory, the Hefei National Laboratory for

---

ing: the State Synchrotron Radiation Laboratory (launched in 1984, operated by the USTC), Beijing State Laboratory of Electron Positron Collider (1988, the Institute of High Energy of the CAS), and Lanzhou State Laboratory of Heavy Ion Accelerator (1988, the Institute of Modern Physics of the CAS).

[20] The USTC Chronicle of Events, http://arch.ustc.edu.cn/memorabilia.htm.

[21] The USTC, "2007 Niandu Woxiao Guoji Lunwen Shuliang He Zhiliang Jixu Baochi Quanguo Gaoxiao Qianlie," (The Quantity and Quality of Our University's International Publications continue to Lead Universities Nationwide in 2007), December 14, 2008, accessed December 15, 2008, http://news.ustc.edu.cn/zh_CN/?article=00017657.

Physical Sciences at the Microscale (HFNL). This move has led to the USTC being the only university in China that has one state mega-research facility and one national laboratory.[22]

The USTC's Move to Mass Higher Education: An Empirical Overview
Stable Undergraduate Recruitment since 2000

The figures the USTC provided on undergraduate enrollment run from 1990 to 2005, and we can see a clear decision against any further expansion after 2000, just the period when enrollments exploded nationally. There had been an increasing trajectory before that, from 3,646 in 1990 to 4,685 in 1995, and 7,126 in 2000, with little change thereafter and a total of 7,394 in 2005. Table 9.1 below shows the USTC increased its undergraduate recruitment by only 393 in 1999 and then maintained a constant intake figure from 2000 on, in sharp contrast to what happened in most other Chinese universities over the same period. Over the same period the USTC increased its graduate enrollment substantially, from 906 in 1990 to 1,464 in 1995, 7,171 in 2000, and 8,697 in 2005. Between 1998 and 2005, undergraduate recruitment grew by only 27.7%, while graduate recruitment increased nearly three-fold. Today, the USTC has 7,473 undergraduates, 9,483 master's students, and 2,604 doctoral students. This is a very rare case of a university whose graduate enrollment is nearly double the size of the undergraduate population.

As a result of this firm commitment to elitism, the USTC's then-President, Zhu Qingshi, was widely viewed as a hard-headed figure who took a strong stand against expansion. He argued for a functional differentiation, in which the central mission for elite universities like the USTC

---

[22] There are so far 6 national laboratories in China, sponsored by the Ministry of Science and Technology (MOST): Shenyang National Laboratory for Materials Science (founded in 2001, and operated by the Institute of Metal Research of the CAS), Beijing National Laboratory for Molecular Sciences (2003, Peking University and the Institute of Chemistry of the CAS), Beijing National Laboratory of Condensed Matter Physics (2003, the Institute of Physics of the CAS), Tsinghua National Laboratory for Information Science and Technology (2003, Tsinghua University), Wuhan National Laboratory for Optoelectronics (2003, the HUST), and Hefei National Laboratory for Physical Sciences at the Microscale (2003, the USTC). More details can be obtained from the MOST website at http://www.chinalab.gov.cn/labsite/Site/LabList_all.aspx?kind=2&dep=&field=&cyear=&region=&search=0.

Table 9.1: The USTC's Recruitment Size, 1990-2005

	Sub-degree	Undergraduate	Master's	Doctoral
1990		664	345	
1995	498	1123	404	114
1998	140	1449	460	194
1999	140	1842	555	247
2000	140	1902	906	329
2001	180	1826	1025	400
2002		1863	1222	500
2003		1862	1580	650
2004		1848	1709	648
2005		1851	1735	680

was to raise the bar of quality, not to contribute to growth in quantity When he stepped down in 2008, he spoke of his decision against enrollment expansion and the creation of a new campus as a major merit of his presidency, which saved the faculty from the distractions caused by heavy teaching loads and daily transportation among disparate campuses, and secured their time and energy for research. He was proud not to have followed others blindly, but to have stuck to a principled vision based on scientific considerations. While he wished his successor could carry forward this vision, he revealed the enormous pressure he was subject to when fighting against the expansion policy:

> "Expansion was not only something wanted by the authorities from the top but also by the local government, who wished to have more students recruited from this province, since this was taken as an indicator of local government performance. The general public would also like to see their kids to go to our university. The pres-sure was never made public, but there were many implications. For instance, if you expanded the enrollment, you would be given more matching funds. The higher authorities and local government would pay more attention to you. If not, they tended to ignore you. We knew that, but we didn't expand, though we were indeed affected in these respects."[23]

If the enrollment size showed little change, then what about the family background of students? The issue of equity has been widely de-

---

[23] "Zhong Keda Yuan Xiaozhang Zhu Qingshi: Xuexiao Shi Jing Tu Shehui Cai You Xiwang," (Former President of the USTC Zhu Qiangshi: Only When the School is kept as Sacred Land, is there Hope for Society), *China Youth Daily*, November 6, 2008, accessed November 18, 2008, http://zqb.cyol.com/content/2008-11/06/content_2420041.htm.

bated in the massification of Chinese higher education. On this question we were able to interview Zhu Canping, who was then Director of Student Affairs and has now become Secretary-General of the USTC, a very senior administrative position under the President. He responded that the USTC had traditionally recruited 70-80% of its entrants from urban areas, that is, county towns and above; this percentage had risen slightly in favour of urban students over recent years. He saw this as related to the designation of "key-point" schools in the Chinese education system, leading to a concentration of students in such schools, which are normally located in urban areas. Consequently, elite universities like the USTC increasingly recruit the majority of students from urban areas.[24]

Modest Changes in Curricular Coverage

Paralleling its rejection of expansion, the USTC has maintained the core of its curricular coverage unchanged over the years, only grouping the departments into schools in recent years. The School of Chemistry and Materials Science was formed the earliest in 1996, followed by the School of Life Sciences and the School of Engineering Sciences both formed in 1998, the School of Information Science and Technology in 1999, the School of Sciences in 2000, and finally the School of Earth and Space Science in 2002. These schools and the departments within them represent the core curricular offerings at the USTC, and its historical areas of strength. Most can be traced back to the 13 departments and 41 specializations established at the birth of the USTC.

However, two new schools have been founded. The School of Management came into being in 1995, initially called the School of Business but adopting its current name in 2005. It now has three departments: the Department of Information Management and Decision Science, the Department of Management Science, and the Department of Statistics and Finance. The School of Humanities & Social Sciences was formed in 2000, on the basis of the existing Department of Foreign Languages, Department of the History of Science and Archaeometry, and Department of Scientific Communication and Policy, with the Director of the CAS Institute of the History of Chinese Science & Technology appointed as its dean. This school is expected to add some flavour from the humanities to the USTC's culture and ethos, and its component departments indicate USTC's unique way of doing this. This effort goes back to the early 1980s

---

[24] Interview with Zhu Canping, Director of Student Affairs of the USTC, 18 May 2007.

when the USTC proposed to launch a number of specializations in humanities and social sciences. This was not approved by the education authorities at the time, and ever since the USTC has been seeking an appropriate way to add humanities and social sciences specializations, rather than following the patterns of comprehensive universities.[25]

In addition, a Special Class for the Gifted Young (少年班) was established in March 1978, the first of its kind in China and a major innovation in China's higher education sector. The intention was to find the most effective way of nurturing gifted youth. Upholding the principle of "selecting talents despite their age and catering to their individual potential," the program adopts a curriculum focusing on foundation courses in the sciences and provides an all-round education in the first two years. Students have enjoyed wide latitude in developing according to their potential and interests in the later years. The students are encouraged to attend seminars, and sign up for various "student research schemes," which allow them to participate in faculty research projects. This kind of involvement in a real research environment is supposed to provide opportunities for them to apply the knowledge gained in the classroom and develop initiative and creativity, also raise their ability in teamwork and cultivate their personal integrity. Since 2002, some practices developed for this Special Class are now widely used. For instance, all students now have a second chance to decide on their major in the second year, instead of only once at admission.[26] Since 2008, China's Ministry of Education has designated this program as a model for exploring effective patterns for fostering cross-disciplinary talent.

The idea of creating the Special Class for the Gifted Young was suggested by such renowned scientists as T.D. Lee (李政道), C.N. Yang (楊振寧), and Samuel C.C. Ting (丁肇中), and supported by the then Vice Premier of the State Council, Fang Yi (方毅). As of 2008, it has enrolled a total of 1,220 exceptionally gifted youth, 1,027 of whom have already graduated. Its students have won numerous prizes in such international contests as the American Mathematical Modeling Contest, and such national contests as the Chinese Mathematical Modeling Contest, and parallel contests in physics, chemistry and other areas. Ninety percent of

---

[25] Sun Xianyuan, "Women Shizhong Zai Zuiqiu Wenli Jiaorong," (We've been always Seeking an Integration of Humanities and Sciences) in *Zhongguo Keda Bao* (*USTC Newsletter*), No.589, 2006.
[26] Interview with Liu Bing, Director of Teaching Affairs of the USTC, 21 May 2007.

its graduates have been enrolled in postgraduate programs at home and abroad, one third of whom have obtained doctoral degrees. These include a 24-year-old assistant professor and a 34-year-old full professor at Harvard University, a 31-year-old IEEE Fellow and Vice President of Microsoft, and the winner of the U.S. Presidential Early Career Award for Scientists and Engineers (PECASE), to name a few.

The Changing Financial Profile

The USTC wasn't ready to provide detailed financial data when this case study was carried out on the campus in May of 2007. Yet, with data later obtained from public sources, we can discern three tendencies with respect to the USTC's financial profile. First, along with its participation in Project 21/1 and Project 98/5, the USTC has seen a dramatic increase in its revenue. Second, the USTC's income is primarily dependent on budgetary appropriations from the national government. Last but not least, the USTC now turns increasingly to local sources or additional funds generated through its own efforts.

In 1983, as China's educational reform began, the USTC's budget was 11.78 million *yuan* RMB.[27] In 1999, when the USTC had nearly completed its first phase in Project 21/1 and just joined Project 98/5, its revenue had grown to 179.65 million. This number nearly doubled to 348.34 million in 2000, and grew further to 601.16 million in 2001.[28] Apparently, inclusion in Projects 21/1 and 98/5 has made for a significant leap in revenue. The increased revenue has come primarily from the state, including sources from CAS and local governments. If we can assume that the USTC relied 100% on state appropriations in the 1980s, this percentage dropped to 74% in 1999, and 72% in 2000, and then climbed back to 84% in 2001, due to enhanced governmental support under Project 98/5. Notably, the USTC's level of dependency on state appropriations is significantly higher than most of its peers under consideration in

---

[27] The USTC Chronicle of Events, http://arch.ustc.edu.cn/memorabilia.htm.
[28] Department of Finance of Ministry of Education of China & Department of Social and Science & Technology Statistics of China State Statistics Bureau, *Zhongguo Jiaoyu Jingfei Tongji Nianjian 1999* (*China Educational Finance Statistical Yearbook 1999*) (Beijing: China Statistics Press, 2000); *Zhongguo Jiaoyu Jingfei Tongji Nianjian 2000* (*China Educational Finance Statistical Yearbook 2000*) (Beijing: China Statistics Press, 2001); *Zhongguo Jiaoyu Jingfei Tongji Nianjian 2001* (*China Educational Finance Statistical Yearbook 2001*) (Beijing: China Statistics Press, 2002).

this study, over the same period.[29] We assume this has to do with its geographic location, which doesn't provide favourable opportunities for revenue generation.

The USTC has also been attracting more research grants from the state and CAS, than from contracts with industry. In its 1999 pool of 95.32 million *yuan* RMB for research, 36% came from national grants, another 14% from the CAS, and only 18% from contracts.[30] This pattern continued in 2000, with 55% from state or vertical sources, 14% from the CAS, and 21% from horizontal sources in a pool of 117.2 million.[31] Although there is clearly a trend for research funding to increase, with the pool reaching 373.6 million in 2005,[32] the USTC's rank among peers in terms of research funding has moved down over the years. While it was the 2nd in 2000, next only to Tsinghua University which had 413.4 million,[33] it dropped to 20th in 2005, far behind such peers as Peking University (685.5 million) and HUST (595.5 million).[34] We assume the booming market economy has greatly favoured universities located in more prosperous areas, which normally have much better opportunities for research contracts.

---

[29] *Ibid*. In 1999, 2000 and 2001, Peking University was 55%, 58% and 69% dependent on state appropriations. Similar was Nanjing University (68%, 72% and 74%), ECNU (48%, 56% and 46%), Xiamen University (62%, 66% and 59%), and particularly HUST (44%, 43% and 40%). Only NWAFU shows an even higher dependency, which averaged above 80%, as its students enjoy almost full subsidy from the government. Even though ECNU students enjoy a similar level of subsidy, yet it exhibits a much lower level of dependency on appropriations. We conclude this pertains to the institutions' efficiency and capacity of generating additional revenue, and in particular to their locations which, in turn, provide quite different opportunities for revenue generation.

[30] The USTC Chronicle of Events, http://arch.ustc.edu.cn/memorabilia.htm.

[31] *Ibid*.

[32] *Ibid*.

[33] China Education and Research Network, "Gaoxiao Keyan Jingfei Paihangbang (A Rank of Research Funds of Higher Education Institutions)," January 1, 2001, accessed November 18, 2008, http://www.edu.cn/shu_ju_pai_hang_1088/20060323/t20060323_3546.shtml. Notably, the USTC is far behind Tsinghua in terms of contract funds, with its 13.98 million compared to Tsinghua's 197.39 million in 2000.

[34] China Education and Research Network, "2005 Nian Quanguo Zhongdian Gaodeng Xuexiao Keji Yanjiu Zong Jingfei Paixu Biao (A Rank of Scientific and Technological Research Funds of the 'Key-point' Institutions Nationwide in 2005)," December 4, 2007, accessed November 18, 2008, http://www.edu.cn/shu_ju_pai_ hang_1088/20071204/t20071204_268646.shtml.

Perhaps for this reason, the USTC formed a special committee in 2000 that aims at promoting cooperation with local industries, with then-president, Zhu Qingshi, serving as its inaugural chair.[35]

Table 9.2: The USTC's Funds under Project 21/1, 1996-2005 (in million *yuan* RMB)

	Phase I (1996-2000)	Phase II (2001-2005)	Total
State Planning Commission/ (after 2003) Development & Reform Commission	41.00	35.00	76.00
Ministry of Finance	19.00	43.00	62.00
CAS	40.00	73.78	113.78
Self-Generated	23.62	78.01	101.63

Source: Zhu Qingshi, "Guanyu Zhongguo Keji Daxue '211 Gongcheng' 'Jiuwu' Qijian Jianshe Gongzuo De Baogao" (A report on the USTC's Project 21/1 progress in the "ninth five-year plan" period), 9 May 2001; the USTC, "Zhongguo Keji Daxue 'Shiwu' '211 Gongcheng' Jianshe Zhongqi Jiancha Baogao" (The USTC's mid-term report on Project 21/1 progress in the "tenth five-year plan" period), 2004.

We also noted a tendency for the USTC to draw increasingly on local sources and self-generated revenue to meet the resource needs for its strategic development. It accomplished two phases of Project 21/1, primarily with central government resources, despite the increasing contributions from its self-generated funds in Phase II, as shown in Table 9.2. By contrast, the USTC gained equal contributions from the central government, the CAS and the local government for its participation in Project 98/5, as seen in Table 9.3, since central government funding alone was not adequate. In the long run, the USTC may have to match external resources with self-generated funds, which would usher in a challenge to its own capacity for revenue generation. For years, the USTC has had a policy of not running enterprises, for the sake of maintaining a quiet and purely academic environment. This policy must now stand the test of a booming market economy in which many of its peers have brought in a huge amount of revenue through their affiliated enterprises. For instance, in 2005, Peking University's enterprises made a profit of 785 million *yuan*

---

[35] The USTC Chronicle of Events, http://arch.ustc.edu.cn/memorabilia.htm.

RMB.³⁶ The enterprises affiliated to HUST and Nanjing University also made 55 million and 20 million respectively in 2005.³⁷ In most cases, a substantial part of these profits would go to institutional support.³⁸

Table 9.3: The USTC's Funds under Project 98/5, 1999-2001 (in million *yuan* RMB)

	1999	2000	2001
Ministry of Education	60.00	100.00	140.00
CAS	60.00	80.00	160.00
Anhui Province	60.00	100.00	140.00

Source: The USTC, "Zhongguo Kexue Jishu Daxue Jianshe Shijie Zhiming De Gao Shuiping Daxue Guihua" (University of Science and Technology of China plan for becoming a world renowned high standard university), 2000; CAS, Ministry of Education of China and Anhui Province, "Guanyu Zhongdian Gong Jian Zhongguo Keji Daxue De Jueding" (A decision on prioritizing the joint efforts to support the USTC), 25 July 1999.

Vision and Strategic Direction

The USTC seems to have benefitted from a vision that was unique and might even be seen as maverick in the Chinese context. Upholding the principle of "establishing the university through innovation and advancing the university through quantum leaps," (創新立校, 跨越發展) it managed to rise to the top rank within a very few years of its founding. After being relocated to Hefei in 1970, it has overcome the major difficulties of this new location and regained its status as a top-tier university in China. Now, in the face of its third phase of development aimed at world-class standing, it appears to be once again forging a unique path. In addition to its strategy of maintaining an elite profile and redefining its articulation with the research institutes of the CAS in the new context, the USTC has also turned to internationalization as a core strategy.

---

³⁶ China Education and Research Network, "Quanguo Gaoxiao Xiaoban Chanye Shouru Zhaoguo Shi Yi Yu Xuexiao Paixubiao (A Ranking Table of Nationwide Higher Learning Institutions whose affiliated Enterprises generated more than 1 billion *yuan* RMB)," August 18, 2005, accessed November 18, 2008, http://www.edu.cn/shu_ju_pai_hang_1088/20060323/t20060323_135850.shtml.
³⁷ *Ibid.*
³⁸ The amount reported to us by Peking University for 2005 was some 450 million *yuan* RMB.

Vision and Strategic Planning

In 1998, when Project 98/5 emerged, the USTC approached the CAS and the Ministry of Education with its aspiration to become a world-class university in the 21st century. Specifically, it aimed to reach this goal by 2018 for its 60th anniversary. Its new vision is to become a high standard research intensive university of an appropriate size and extraordinary quality, with a suitable structure and unique features. It seeks to maintain its traditional relationship with the CAS as well as its research institutes and hi-tech industries, and rise even higher to be one of China's major education and research bases with a strong capacity to foster knowledge and technology innovation.

In order to achieve this goal, the USTC first of all benchmarked itself with a few dozen top universities in the world, through a careful study of their teaching and research practises. It then identified its own advantages, including its ability to attract the most talented students in China, full state patronage as well as the experience derived from 40 years of innovative practice. It identified its own weaknesses as well, in terms of deficiencies in teaching and research infrastructure, in revenue and the remuneration offered to faculty, also in outdated teaching content and pedagogy. From there, the USTC has come up with a multi-phased strategic plan to reach its ultimate goal of achieving world standing.

Phase I (2000-2002) focused on optimizing curricular structure, and upgrading infrastructure. In this phrase, the USTC gives priority to enhancing its strengths in such disciplinary areas as information science, life science, engineering and materials science, while endeavouring to maintain its traditional strengths in mathematics, physics and chemistry. The guiding principle was to map the USTC's frontier disciplines, instead of pursuing an even growth across the board. Phase II (2003-2007) pertained to soft power enhancement. In this phase, the USTC has worked hard to pull a body of top talent in teaching and research, and to develop state-of-the-art teaching outlines, textbooks and pedagogy. On the basis of the first two phases, Phase III (2008-2018) will launch the USTC's full scale march towards world-class standing, fulfilling all the major objectives set up in the strategic plan.[39]

---

[39] The USTC, "Zhongguo Kexue Jishu Daxue Jianshe Shijie Zhiming De Gao Shuiping Daxue Guihua" (University of Science and Technology of China Plan for turning into a World Renowned High Standard University), 2000.

Fostering International Exposure to Nurture Talent

The USTC has benefitted from an effective internationalization strategy. As mentioned above, it was among the earliest Chinese universities to have exposure to the international higher education and academic community. At the very beginning of the open door policy, the USTC selected some 200 of its faculty members and sent them for advanced study in the West. Shortly after, it selected students from its first post-Cultural Revolution cohort, the class of 1977, and sent them for doctoral study in Western universities. Later on, many came back and became backbone teachers. Others stayed abroad, and the USTC is known for having the most alumni in North America, along with Peking and Tsinghua universities.

The CUSPEA (China-US Physics Examination and Application) is another example of the USTC's pioneering role in internationalization. CUSPEA was an examination and admission system used by the physics departments of some American and Canadian universities for graduate school admission from China between 1979 and 1989. It was created by the Nobel Prize winning physicist T.D. Lee and the Chinese physics community as an alternative graduate school admission procedure at a time when it was difficult for Western universities to evaluate Chinese physics graduates. About 100 Chinese students went to North America every year through the CUSPEA exams, with a total number of 918. Over the years, the three universities with the most students passing the exam were the USTC (237), Peking University (206) and Fudan University (127). When taking our interview, Zhang Mengping, the Director of the International Affairs Office, told us an interesting story. In early 2000, the USTC sent a delegation to visit a dozen top universities in the USA, and in all cases it was met by the top leaders in the American universities. Coincidently, China's Ministry of Education sent another high profile university leaders' delegation to the USA at the same time, with a similar agenda. This group was not given the same level of treatment. Zhang concluded it was the USTC's alumni who had earned its delegation the respect they received.[40]

Employing International Benchmarks in Strategic Planning

As the USTC is determined to find its own unique path to world-class

---

[40] Interview with Zhang Mengping, Director of International Affairs Office, 20 May 2007. Zhang is also a professor of computing mathematics.

standing, it has no intention of following its Chinese peers. Instead, it looks to the world community, and benchmarks itself to a number of institutions it most admires. Since 2000, it has sent three delegations to North America and Europe to observe and study mission formation and strategic planning in these institutions. In January of 2000, the first delegation visited MIT, Harvard, Cornell, Purdue, Notre Dame, Wisconsin-Madison, Southern California, University of California at Santa Barbara, Stanford, and California Institute of Technology (Caltech) in the USA. In January 2001, another delegation visited Nottingham, Oxford and Cambridge in the UK, Gottingen, Heidelberg and Aachen University of Technology in Germany, École Normale de Musique de Paris, ParisTech, the University of Paris-Sud in France, Rome and Padua in Italy. These two delegations were led by the then President Zhu Qingshi, while in August of 2002, the then Party Secretary, Tang Honggao, led a visiting group to Cambridge, Oxford and Nottingham in the UK, Stuttgart and Technische Universität Berlin in Germany, the French National Center for Scientific Research (CNRS) and University of Paris-Sud in France, and the Abdus Salam International Centre for Theoretical Physics in Italy.

Eventually Caltech was singled out as the most appealing model to the USTC.[41] Just before the USTC's visit in 2000, Caltech was ranked the top national university by the *US News & World Report* in its America's Best Colleges 1999. During the visit, President David Baltimore, a Nobel Laureate in Biology at the age of 37, impressed the visitors with its small size, 900 undergraduates, 1,000 graduate students, and fewer than 300 faculty. He noted that numbers had been stable for over 20 years, and were not likely to grow in the future. More importantly, Baltimore made the point that Caltech was first of all a first-class research institution, and second a teaching institution, making use of its faculty and facilities to educate students.[42]

Inspired by the Caltech model, the USTC initially put in its strategic plan a primary goal of becoming a major science research center in China and a secondary goal of being an education center, which meant a small student body was desirable. It later modified these goals, giving equal

---

[41] Lu Yongxiang, "Zai Zhongguo Kexueyuan Zhongguo Keji Daxue Fazhan Gongzuo Huiyi Shang De Jianghua" (A Speech at the CAS' Working Conference on the USTC's Development), March 3, 2000.
[42] *The USTC Newsletter*, Special Issue 2000.

weight to research and teaching, at the advice of the CAS.[43] Another experience during the trip affected their thinking about their location. The delegation visited Connell in Ithaca, and found Ithaca was even more remote and less accessible than Hefei. This was somewhat incidental, but it gave them confidence that they could reach world-class standing in spite of the disadvantage of their location.[44]

Founding the Association of East Asian Research Universities

As a part of the USTC's internationalization drive, since 1980 it has entered bilateral relations with over 60 universities and research establishments in the USA, UK, France, Germany, Italy, Russia, Australia, Japan and Singapore. Since the mid-1990s, the USTC moved beyond bilateral relations towards the creation of a university alliance, joining efforts with the University of Tokyo and the Hong Kong University of Science and Technology to form the Association of East Asian Research Universities (AEARU) in January of 1996. The AEARU has since grown to 17 members and is being kept at that size.[45] Sharing "common academic and cultural backgrounds," the AEARU member universities interact frequently, with regular annual general meetings, board of director meetings, symposia, workshops and student summer camps. Zhang Mengping told us that the USTC had been working most closely with AEARU members in recent years, as the homogeneity of their standards and commonality of mission and aspiration has led to substantial and effective cooperation. In 2004-2005, the USTC served as AEARU's 5th Chair University, the first mainland China university to take up this responsibility.[46]

---

[43] Lu Yongxiang, *ibid*.
[44] Interview with Cheng Yi on 5 July 2006. Cheng was the Executive Vice-President of the USTC, before he held the position of the Director of Anhui Province's Education Department, when interviewed. He also joined in the visit to the US in January 2000.
[45] Its current membership includes Peking University, Tsinghua University (Beijing), Fudan University, Nanjing University, the USTC, the Hong Kong University of Science and Technology, National Taiwan University, Tsing Hua University (Taiwan), the University of Tokyo, the Tokyo Institute of Technology, Kyoto University, Osaka University, Tohoku University, Tsukuba University, Seoul National University, Pohang University of Science and Technology, and Korea Advanced Institute of Science and Technology.
[46] Interview with Zhang Mengping, Director of International Affairs Office, 20 May 2007.

Precisely for the sake of maintaining the effectiveness of collaboration among the peer members, AEARU made a decision to stabilize its membership size, during the USTC's term as the Chair University, and turned down universities such as Zhejiang and Shanghai Jiaotong in China and Kyushu in Japan. Zhang emphasized the point that an international alliance must ensure the benefits of all participants if it was to remain effective, and keeping it selective would make this possible.[47] The USTC has also joined a much larger consortium, the Association of Pacific Rim Universities (APRU) with 42 member universities, yet it is far less active in this alliance, perhaps due to its size and diversity. We also noticed, somehow to our surprise, that AEARU seems to be the earliest one of its kind, compared to other major international university consortia active today, such as Universitas 21 (established in 1997), APRU (1997), Worldwide Universities Network (2000), League of European Research Universities (2002), Academic Consortium 21 (2004), and International Alliance of Research Universities (2006).

The USTC Campuses and Merger Issues

The USTC has taken a firmly negative stance towards expansion as well as mergers. When there was a strong trend in China for mergers involving medical schools, with the belief that a world-class university must have a medical school, the USTC did not even consider this type of merger. It did, however, merge in a specialized institution run by the National Tobacco Products Administration in 2000, the Hefei Institute of Economics and Technology, which was located not far from the USTC's East Campus. This was not really a merger, but a matter of taking over the campus and facilities of an institution that was part of the planned economy and had no role to play within the market economy. After its current students graduated, all of its programs were closed down. This was also a matter of national policy that central ministries or offices should no longer run higher education institutions.

Now the USTC has four campuses, which are very close to each other. The main campus, the East Campus, was inherited from the former Hefei Teachers Training College, when the USTC moved to Hefei in 1970. The North Campus used to be a provincial banking school. The West Campus was developed on farmers' fields in the 1980s, when the National Synchrotron Radiation Lab was established, and it looks like a

---

[47] Ibid.

typical suburban campus in a North American setting with a pragmatic architectural style, and no buildings that could be termed a landmark. Now, the South Campus is also an inherited one, from the Hefei Institute of Economics and Technology, and it has few special features. We thus noticed that we truly gave our interviewees a headache when asking them to name one or several campus buildings or spaces that could typify the USTC culture and ethos. Some came up with the #1 Teaching Building on the East Campus, as a kind of fallback choice. It is a building that had been there before the USTC moved to Hefei. It seems that the Soviet style of architecture reminded people of the days in Beijing in the late 1950s and 1960s, and the struggle made by faculty and students at various times to move back to Beijing.

Photo 9.3: The Number One Teaching Building on the USTC East Campus

Faculty Perspectives on Teaching and Research

The Faculty Profile

The USTC has experienced a shrinking in its faculty numbers over the period since 1995, as it has greatly reduced the number of lecturers and assistant teachers. In 1990, there were 1,852 full time faculty members, including 114 full professors and 541 associate professors. This number rose slightly to 1,884 in 1995, including 273 full professors and 788 associate professors. By 2000, the USTC had 1,650 full time faculty members, including 377 full professors and 826 associate professors. When it came to 2005, the USTC had 491 full professors and 559 associate professors, but the total had dropped to 1,491. This is perhaps due to a shrinking layer of lecturers at the USTC, given its focus and emphasis on research, and could only be possible at the USTC, which refused to expand the enrollment and thus had no concomitant increase in teaching load. According to the data provided by the USTC, about 33% of the faculty have doctorates. This figure is not really high, compared to its peers in this study, e.g., 66% in Peking University, 55% in Nanjing University, and 38% in ECNU. We speculate it has to do with the USTC's practice of retaining many of its own graduates for teaching positions in the mid- and late 1970s, when it suffered an extreme shortage of teachers. These faculty members may have had masters' degrees, but doctoral programs were not common in China until the mid-1980s.

Given its determination to stabilize the undergraduate enrollment size, the USTC was able to focus on raising the quality of its faculty through professional development, and greatly strengthening the proportion of those in senior positions. Now, around 1,100 full and associate professors constitute the core of the teaching and supervising force at the USTC. For this reason, the USTC tends to excel when benchmarked on per faculty indicators, given the consistently high standards of its faculty. Indeed, we found the frequently cited *THE/QS World University Rankings* had ranked the USTC as China's top university on the indicator of "Citations per Faculty" consistently since 2005.[48]

Perspectives from the Faculty

The faculty focus group meeting took place on May 22, 2007, and turned out to be a demanding session, running for two and a half hours with no break. It involved nine faculty members, among whom were such renowned scholars as Chen Chusheng, then executive dean of the School of Chemistry and Materials Science and now Vice President, Zheng Yongfei,

---

[48] *THE/QS World University Rankings*, 2005, 2006 and 2007, details available at http://www.topuniversities.com/worlduniversityrankings. In 2007, the USTC scored 76 over "Citations per Faculty," way above its peers in this study which managed to enter the list: Peking University (53) and Nanjing University (69). Nevertheless, the USTC was still far behind the universities it has taken as peer models, such as Caltech (100), MIT (98), Cornell (93), Tokyo (89), and Tokyo Institute of Technology (91).

an internationally recognized scientist in geochemistry, and Xin Houwen, a veteran physicist and former VP responsible for the Special Class for the Gifted Young. Five of them preferred to remain anonymous. They all appeared to be very dedicated to the USTC, also rather critical, suggesting a mentality of "love you well and push you hard." As the discussion unfolded, it became more and more focused on the issues of curricular patterns and faculty quality. A view which all shared was that the USTC's reputation should be largely attributed to the quality of its faculty, and its integrated and unique curricular patterns. From its early days, the USTC adopted an "open-door" policy, meaning that it was run in a resource-sharing mode with the CAS' research institutes. Thus it was slow to develop a full scale infrastructure of its own. Even now its campuses are rather modest in size, compared to those of many of its peers. Faculty members thus explained that they sometimes like to compare themselves to an ox, that labors extremely hard but asks for very little![49]

Photo 9.4: The Statue of Two Oxen Holding up the Globe on the USTC's East Campus

The discussion revolved around two of USTC's special characteristics which enabled it to make its initial rise very quickly. One was its unique curriculum. It was launched in 1958 at a time when China had

---

[49] In Chinese culture, an ox is symbolic of bearing hardship and enduring hard work.

vowed to develop its high technology – symbolized by the nuclear bomb and the satellite. A second was its inbuilt tendency to innovate and the expectation that it turn out promising young scientists in a short time, as opposed to the engineers who were being produced by polytechnical universities at the time. The existing universities, basically modeled on Soviet patterns featured a separation of basic and applied sciences, and thus could not meet this challenge. The USTC's integrative and cross-disciplinary curriculum and its unique mandate to fill emerging gaps in China's sciences and technology gave it a special edge in its early years. This is less the case now, since the reforms of the 1980s and 1990s have allowed many former specialized engineering institutions to take advantage of expansion and mergers, and move towards becoming comprehensive universities.

The second period when the USTC was able to make a strategic leap forward came in the mid to late 1970s, according to members of the faculty focus group. When the USTC was relocated to Hefei, it lost many faculty members. In order to re-build its faculty contingent, it managed in 1975 to call back some 300 of its alumni who had graduated between 1967 and 1970, and then put them through a re-training program so they could take up teaching posts. Once the Cultural Revolution was over, it was quick to send some 200 faculty members for advanced study abroad, most of whom returned and became core faculty members. At a time when most other universities were still recovering from the political turmoil, the USTC seized the opportunity to pioneer some exceptional measures to improve its faculty quality. Members of the focus group felt this was due to its short history and the relatively simple nature of personnel relations on the campus.

Nevertheless, many of the USTC's advantages from earlier days no longer exist. For instance, it piloted a direct articulation between undergraduate and postgraduate programs which allowed students to move smoothly from bachelor program to master's and then doctoral programs, without the distraction of preparing for the admission examinations in between. Some at the focus group session pointed out this model had been ideal for nurturing scientists. Yet, in the current context of a market economy, students have a lot more choices, and thus this opportunity is less attractive than it used to be. Even for those who aspire to be scientists, it is more attractive to have exposure to several different campuses and different kinds of ethos. The USTC thus must identify new areas of strength in order to raise its status, Xin Houwen asserted.

One way forward might be to build upon its experience in nurturing innovative minds for the past five decades. If it were possible to identify the essence of this achievement, the USTC might be able to seize the opportunity for a third phase of outstanding development, especially since China is now investing heavily in its innovation system. Unfortunately, focus group members felt this was not yet happening. Rather there is a tendency towards isomorphism, as the USTC becomes more similar to other campuses, and teaching and learning is inevitably influenced by the market economy. For instance, the university administration has become more and more bureaucratic and there have been cases of plagiarism found among the students, though they are still some of China's best.

Perspectives from the USTC Students

The student focus group meeting took place on May 19, 2008, involving six undergraduate students, from the Departments of Precision Mechanics and Instrumentation, Theoretical and Applied Mechanics, Information Management, Communications, Finance, and Foreign Languages. The students shared their understanding of the USTC's mission and aspirations, their thoughts on Chinese culture and their feelings about the impact of mass higher education.

Given the USTC's size, it is not surprising that the students are well informed about what is happening on their campus. They understand well the commitment to elite education, and thus the concomitant higher standards of the study programs, in particular the foundational courses in sciences and mathematics. The students in humanities and social sciences programs, though few in number, have to take some sciences and mathematics courses as well. Consequently, the USTC students have to spend most of their time on study, and have less interest in social engagement, compared to their counterparts in other universities. Also, the students realize they are being nurtured towards research careers, and most will go on to graduate studies. Therefore they don't have to worry too much about employment, or divert their attention to study for various professional certifications that might be useful in the job market.

What was a bit surprising to us was their appreciation of traditional Chinese culture and their longing for a stronger humanistic atmosphere on the campus. They understood the popular undergraduate research scheme, which allows undergraduate students to be engaged in real research projects in the 3rd year and enables them to develop their own research interests, following the traditional notion of "teaching in accordance with students' aptitudes" (因材施教). Students also mentioned how the empirical sciences that emerged in the West are constructed on rationalism and mathematical logic, while there is now an increasing tendency to adopt a broader epistemology that embraces human factors and judgement, where traditional Chinese culture may enjoy an advantage. In this sense, they wish to see more courses in humanities and social sciences available to them. They also wish their campus could be more colorful and dynamic, not only in its learning environment but also in its architectural style.

Finally, they touched upon the impact of mass higher education. Although they felt protected by their university's elite policy, something they repeatedly expressed their appreciation for, they were still affected by what was happening in the larger society. For instance, the USTC traditionally offered 5-year programs, so that the students could have the time to fully absorb the demanding curricular content and research work. For this reason, the USTC students had earned a reputation for having a solid foundation and highly promising potential. While this program length was an advantage in the planned economy, that was not longer the case in the market economy context, as a one year delay in graduation would leave them in a disadvantaged employment situation, compared to peers in other universities. As a result, the USTC had to shorten all its programs to 4 years in 2003, which involved a restructuring of specialized courses, sometimes merging several into one. Now the students have to absorb the same amount of content in foundational courses within a shorter timeline, and suffer from even less time available for specialized and laboratory-based courses. Students thus feel it is increasingly a challenge for the USTC to hold on to its high reputation, and there is a desperate need for it to forge a new kind of competitive advantage.

Concluding Remarks

It is widely acknowledged that the USTC is the only Chinese university that has firmly and successfully resisted the national expansion policy. Since 2000, its undergraduate recruitment size has remained at about 1,860, while graduate intakes have grown dramatically, outpacing undergraduate from 2003 on. Apparently, the USTC has been taking a different path in the massification of Chinese higher education—maintaining a small size and embracing a kind of extreme elitism. It is suggested that expansion and diversification of higher education are twin phenomena that have been associated with the development of higher education in many countries around the world. Martin Trow has thus proposed the concept of "phases of development," maintaining that national systems of higher education do not achieve a complete transition from one phase to another, but exhibit hybrid characteristics, with older institutions created in one phase surviving and adapting in a somewhat different form in later phases. Thus elite functions may continue to exist or even be reinvigorated, when the national system as a whole moves towards massification.

The USTC case shows also that Chinese universities now have a relatively high degree of autonomy with respect to making strategic decisions about their future directions. The USTC seems to stand out, in this regard, for a number of reasons. First and foremost, it is a university born at a particular period of China's history, with a unique mission and mandate. Though its unique advantages have inevitably been diminished over time, it is still able to plot its own path of development. Secondly, it is the only university that belongs to the CAS, and thus it still enjoys the benefits of this special scientific patronage. Furthermore, since the CAS is a national research organization, it naturally focuses mainly on research and pays little attention to other aspects of university administration. This has resulted in a relatively high degree of freedom and autonomy for the USTC. Finally, the USTC is located far from Beijing, which makes it difficult for the CAS, with its modest education arm, to interfere with the USTC's operational details from a distance. As Zhu Qingshi put it, the remote location could sometimes be an asset. The USTC is certainly not the only Chinese university which is enjoying greater autonomy in decision making, but it does benefit from certain unique circumstances that that have allowed it to take a strong stand against national massification policies.

Nevertheless, a relatively elite size may provide favorable conditions for the endeavor to achieve world-class standing, but not sufficient ones. As repeatedly reflected in the faculty and students' discussions, the USTC must take action to reinforce its uniqueness, whether in teaching or in research, and move higher, if it is to keep its current status. This is easier said than done, as there is no existing model to follow in the current Chinese context. To take Caltech for example, though it has been proven to be a successful model in the American context, it cannot easily be reproduced on Chinese soil. It is a private institution with a remarkably high resource base. In recent years it enjoyed a revenue of over 2 billion USD, reaching 2.58 billion USD in 2007, which afforded it a high degree of autonomy and flexibility to do things in its own way and to attract the best students and faculty from around the world. This can only be matched by a few most elite institutions in the world and hardly by a public university in China. Even more unique, the Caltech's world famed Jet Propulsion Laboratory has often contributed two thirds of its revenue with direct grants totaling 1.75 billion USD in 2007, something almost unthinkable elsewhere in the world.

Just as we were concluding this chapter, the USTC launched a new school in January of 2009, the School of Nuclear Science and Engineering, in collaboration with the CAS Hefei Institutes of Physical Science. This School will make full use of the State Synchrotron Radiation Laboratory (housed in the USTC) and the Experimental Advanced Superconducting Tokamak (housed in the Institute), and be responsible for research outcomes and human resources for China's energy strategy. We see the revival of past traits in this move of pairing CAS research institutes with USTC departments (now schools) and catering to the strategic needs of national development. For the USTC, to move ahead at the present time, it needs still to handle a number of tensions, between its aspirations as a university and the diversifying career intentions of its students, between its agenda as a university and changes in the wider environment, and between the internationally successful model it has chosen to emulate and the characteristics of the current Chinese context and of Chinese traditional culture.

10
Huazhong University of Science and Technology – A Microcosm of New China's Higher Education

Ruth HAYHOE and Jun LI, with CHEN Min and ZHOU Guangli

The Huazhong University of Science and Technology (HUST) in Wuhan provides an interesting contrast to the University of Science and Technology of China (USTC), which has been profiled in Chapter 9. While the USTC resisted pressures for both merger and the rapid expansion of undergraduate enrollments, HUST embraced a complex merger and more than tripled its undergraduate enrollments, from 9,000 students in 1990 to 35,500 students in 2005. It also established two second-tier colleges, with enrollments close to 30,000 students by 2005.

HUST was established as a national polytechnical institution in the major industrial city of Wuhan under the Soviet influences of the early 1950s. Its initial curricular emphasis was on such applied fields as mechanical, electrical, power and auto engineering. The USTC was founded in 1958, and might be viewed as a reaction to the polytechnical model in its commitment to integrating basic and applied sciences. Both have had high profile roles since the reforms of 1978, yet the different paths chosen by their leaders illustrate the degree of autonomy they enjoy.

This chapter begins with a brief historical overview, which provides a background for understanding HUST's experience in the move to mass higher education. This is followed by an empirical account of major changes in student numbers, finance and curriculum between 1990 and 2005, then a discussion of major decisions around merger, expansion and campus space from the perspective of contemporary university leaders. Next views from faculty and students are presented and the chapter concludes with reflections on the core values and cultural characteristics of an institution seen by many as a "microcosm" (縮影) of new China's higher education.

History and Context

Wuhan and the Central South Region

After the 1949 Revolution, Wuhan became a major centre for the development of higher education, as the leading city of the Central South region, which stretched from Henan province, directly south of Beijing, down to Guangdong province in the South. One of six major geographical regions, the Central South lines up beside the East China region, which reaches from Shandong on the Coast north of Shanghai, down to Fujian, opposite Taiwan. While the Southwest, Northwest, North China and Northeast regions seem to make geographical sense, one cannot help wondering whether the Central South and East China were defined in this way so as to ensure control over the dynamic southern provinces of Guangdong and Fujian.[1]

As a major industrial city in the middle reaches of the Yangtze River, Wuhan was designated the leader of the Central South region, and a large number of national level universities were located there, including Wuhan University, a national key comprehensive institution, Huazhong Normal University, and the Huazhong Institute of Technology, later retitled the Huazhong University of Science and Technology. HUST was established in 1953, in a reorganization that brought together Engineering Departments from Wuhan University, Hunan University, the Huanan Institute of Technology in Guangzhou, Guangxi University and Nanchang University in Jiangxi. In addition to these three major national institutions under the Ministry of Education, there were many specialized institutions under such national ministries as Metallurgy, Construction, Finance and Health. As a major industrial city with a large steel and auto industry, Wuhan was to educate specialists both for the Central South region and for the nation, while the provinces of Henan, Hunan, Guangdong and Guangxi were dominated by local institutions serving provincial needs.[2]

When HUST was established as a major national polytechnical institution, it was expected to have a parallel role in the Central South to that of Harbin Institute of Technology in the Northeast, Zhejiang University in East China, Jiaotong University in Shanghai and later the North-

---

[1] See the discussion of this issue in Chapter 5 on Xiamen University, p.161.
[2] Ruth Hayhoe, *China's Universities 1895-1995: A Century of Cultural Conflict* (Hong Kong: Comparative Education Research Centre, The University of Hong Kong 1999), pp.149-195.

west, and Chongqing University in the Southwest. Each region was to have at least one major polytechnical university, as well as a comprehensive and a normal university. In spite of all the changes over the half century since the reorganization under Soviet influence, it is interesting to see that HUST leaders still see these institutions as major reference points in their development.

If HUST found itself with all the right geographical and logistic conditions to become a leading technological university in the 1950s, this might never have happened without the leadership of one man, whose spirit continues to inspire its leaders, faculty and students nowadays. That is Professor Zhu Jiusi (朱九思), the vice-chair of HUST's organizing committee in 1953, and subsequently Vice Party Secretary, Vice President, Party Secretary and finally President from 1979 to 1984. The vision Zhu developed for HUST during the dark days of the Cultural Revolution, led to it becoming a nation-wide model in the 1980s. Zhu himself also emerged as an influential higher education thinker on the national scene.

A New Vision for HUST after the Cultural Revolution

In the Great Leap Forward of 1958, when the Chinese Academy of Sciences established the UTSC, with a focus on integrating basic and applied sciences, HUST also established programs in basic mathematics, physics and chemistry for the first time.[3] Unfortunately these were cut back in the retrenchment of the early sixties, and the outbreak of the Cultural Revolution in 1966 left the campus nearly empty, as no new students were recruited and faculty were required to move to the countryside. Zhu was among the first to move back to the campus in 1970, and he found it was being used by local farmers to grow vegetables. In the year before faculty members returned and the first cohort of revolutionary students was recruited, he had time to reflect on the idea of the university. The vision he developed was implemented gradually, as the country recovered from the ravages of the Cultural Revolution.[4]

It arose initially from reflections on his memories of Zhu Kezheng,

---

[3] Yao Qihe (ed.) *Huazhong Ligong Daxue De Sishinian* (*The Forty Years of the Central China University of Science and Technology*) (Wuhan: Huazhong Ligong Daxue Chubanshe, 1993), p.68.

[4] Ruth Hayhoe, *Portraits of Influential Chinese Educators* (Hong Kong: Comparative Education Research Centre, The University of Hong Kong, and Springer, 2006), pp.132-133.

President of Zhejiang University during the 1930s, when he had worked there, as well as his earlier experience of an excellent academic secondary school in Yangzhou. There were several core features to the vision: an emphasis on human talent and the need to attract excellent scholars; an understanding of the vital necessity for research to be integrated with and indeed to lead teaching, a feature absent from the Soviet model; and an awareness that scientific knowledge knows no borders and thus a free flow of knowledge from international sources is essential.

On the basis of this vision, Zhu recruited 600 talented new faculty members, from among scholars of top universities who had been banished to the countryside. He took every opportunity to seek new sources of research funding, long before the establishment of the National Natural Sciences Foundation (in 1985) or the 863 High Technology Fund (in 1986), through linkages with the ministries of Mechanical Industry and Electronics Industry and the establishment of new programs in areas related to laser technology and electronics. He set up a program to ensure that all faculty could raise their standards of English and gain access to international scientific research information. Finally, he determined that it was not enough for HUST to be a university of science and technology, it must move towards a more comprehensive curriculum and include selected areas of the humanities and social sciences. Excellent scholars were thus recruited in philosophy, Chinese, the history of science, journalism and higher education and small programs set up in each of these areas, as well as opportunities for students in basic and applied sciences to have some exposure to the humanities and social sciences.[5]

When the first national science and education conferences were held after Deng Xiaoping came to power in 1978, Zhu contributed a paper on the importance of having scientific research in the forefront of teaching and learning, and in the reform document of 1985, Chinese universities were declared to be centres of research as well as teaching for the first time since 1949.[6] Although Zhu retired from the Presidency of HUST in 1984, he has continued to be an active scholar and commentator on higher education issues up to the present, working in HUST's influential Higher Education Research Centre and nurturing a generation of

---

[5] *Ibid*. pp.133-138.
[6] See Ruth Hayhoe, *China's Universities 1895-1995: A Century of Cultural Conflict*, p.122.

doctoral students in higher education.⁷

The subsequent presidents of HUST have all been HUST graduates except Huang Shuhuai, president from 1984-1993 and a graduate of Harbin Institute of Technology and Tsinghua University. He was succeeded by Yang Shuzi, HUST's first Academician, and a specialist in Information Technology and Manufacturing, 1993-1997, then Zhou Ji, a Computer Science and Manufacturing specialist,⁸ 1997-2001, then Fan Mingwu, an expert in Cyclotron and Magnet theory, 2001-2005 and finally Li Peigen, the current president and an expert in Information Technology and Manufacturing.⁹ Probably the president whose leadership has had the greatest impact in terms of the massive expansion of enrollments was Zhou Ji, who left HUST to become Mayor of Wuhan in 2001, and was subsequently appointed Vice Minister of Education in 2002 and Minister of Education in 2003.

As for the decision to enter into a major merger, this was made in 1998. The story of how it came about illustrates the continuing influence of long-retired president Zhu Jiusi. After the launch of the 98/5 project at the 100ᵗʰ anniversary of Peking University's founding, seven other top institutions were invited to join Beida and Tsinghua in this elite group: Fudan, Nanjing University, Shanghai Jiaotong, Xi'An Jiaotong, Harbin Institute of Technology, Zhejiang University and the USTC. It was widely thought that few other institutions would be allowed in, and a merger between HUST and Wuhan University was suggested as a way in which Wuhan might be able to get the tenth place.¹⁰

Although Zhu Jiusi had been a student at Wuhan University in the

---

⁷ Zhu Jiusi, *Jingzheng yu Zhuanhua* (*Competition and Transformation*) (Wuhan: Huazhong Ligong Daxue Chubanshe, 2001). This volume contains many of the essays Zhu wrote on different facets of higher education, that had a national influence.
⁸ Zhou Ji has a first degree from Tsinghua, a Masters from HUST and a PhD from SUNY Buffalo.
⁹ Li has a first degree from Donghua University, a Masters degree from HUST and a PhD from University of Wisconsin Madison.
¹⁰ Ruth Hayhoe and Julia Pan, "China's Universities on the Global Stage – Views from University Leaders," in *International Higher Education*, No.39, Spring, 2005, pp.20-21, and Ruth Hayhoe and Qiang Zha, "China's polytechnic transformation," in *International Higher Education*, Vol.60, No.2, Summer 2010, pp.11-13. It is interesting to note that six of the original nine top institutions included in this project are technological universities, reflecting the continuing influence of the Soviet patterns of the 1950s.

1930s, his career had been dedicated to creating an institution that distinguished itself by very different standards of excellence than those of Wuhan University. He also had strong views about the lack of unity and cohesion among the leadership at Wuhan University. He thus took the initiative to write to Chen Zhili, then Minister of Education, and express strong objections to the merger idea. He also got in touch with a famous academician at the Tongji Medical University in Wuhan, Professor Qiu Fazu, who was opposed to his institution being merged with Wuhan University. Chen Zhili came to Wuhan and views on merger possibilities were heard from all sides. In the end, a different set of mergers took place, than the one originally envisaged.[11] HUST entered into a merger agreement with the prestigious Tongji Medical University, as well as the Wuhan Urban Construction Institute, originally under the national Ministry of Construction.[12] Wuhan University, for its part, embraced a local medical university and two specialized universities that had been under national ministries.[13] Both universities were ultimately able to join the 98/5 Project.

While Zhu Jiusi had considerable influence in shaping this merger decision more than a decade after his retirement, he was not able to constrain the university's decision to embrace a massive program of expansion, which brought an overall growth in enrollments from around 10,000 in 1990 to over 60,000 by 2005. A combination of financial incentives for growth, an unusually large main campus and continuing close relations with a president who became minister of education over the years when national policy promoted rapid expansion, all played a role. Undaunted by this situation, Zhu has remained vocal in expressing his principled opposition to top-down pressures for merger and "uncontrolled" enrollment expansion. Given the opportunity to attend a meeting called by Premier Wen Jiabao early in 2008, he wrote a paper expressing the reasons for his opposition, and elaborating his own

---

[11] Interview with Zhu Jiusi, 25 May 2008.

[12] The main HUST merger took place on 26 May 2000, but the Wuhan Science & Technology Vocational College, a training college for administrators under the national Ministry of Science and Technology, had been merged in earlier, on 28 February 2000.

[13] These were the Hubei Medical University, the Wuhan University of Hydraulic and Electrical Engineering, and the Wuhan University of Surveying and Mapping.

philosophy for higher education leadership and development.[14]

Critical Perspectives of a Former President

The paper begins by critiquing top-down pressures for merger and questioning to what extent mergers can enhance university quality and how well the multi-campus institutions that result can be managed. It goes on to express strong criticism of the national policy decision for rapid expansion, pointing out problems of teaching quality and student neglect that have resulted, also issues of high unemployment rates for university graduates and the neglect of the mid-level technical education needed for the job market.

Part two of the paper questions the quality of university leadership and makes a plea for university presidents with genuine scholarly qualifications as well as leadership ability and higher education vision. One of the most important responsibilities of a university president is to protect academic freedom, Zhu asserts, giving examples from his own experience and that of Zhang Kaiyuan, a renowned historian and former president of nearby Huazhong Normal University. University presidents should be seen as scholarly leaders rather than administrative appointees, and their terms should not be limited to four or five years; rather they should stay in office as long as they are effective. A list of well-known presidents of famous Western and Japanese universities who served between 15 and 49 years is provided to support this point.

The final section of the paper focuses on faculty and the importance of nurturing strong scholars and researchers as the most essential factor for university excellence. Here a strong case is made for maximum autonomy for scholarship, with Cai Yuanpei's famous phrase "professors rule the school" (教授治校), being highlighted. Professor Zhu was clearly using this paper to call attention to core values of the university which he fears may have been neglected in the scramble for expansion and the flurry to rebuild the campus and integrate the departments and programs of the recently merged institutions.

Against the background of these critical comments from an influential former president, we now turn to a presentation of the data we have

---

[14] This unpublished paper is entitled "Zemoyang Ban Daxue" (How to run Universities) and dated November 2007. He gave a copy of this paper to both authors of the chapter at the beginning of their week of interviews with university leaders, faculty and students, on 25 May 2008.

collected on HUST's enrollment growth, financial profile and curricular development from 1990 to 2005. This historical overview has shown that these decisions were not without contestation or vigorous debate!

HUST Moves to Mass Higher Education: An Empirical Overview

Growth in Student Enrollments, 1990-2005

Growth in student enrollments has been dramatic since the national policy decision of 1999. Figures provided by the university for the years 1990, 1995, 2000 and 2005 give clear picture of this. While total undergraduate enrollments in 1990 were 8,895, rising only to 9,407 in 1995, by 2000 they had jumped to 21,195, and by 2005, to 35,586. Graduate enrollments saw even more striking growth, from 1448 in 1990 and 2434 in 1995, to 6558 in 2000 and 25,484 in 2005. Clearly the huge undergraduate increase between 1995 and 2000 reflected the merger situation, with the addition of students from the medical and construction institutions, while the dramatic increases in both undergraduate and graduate students between 2000 and 2005 were a matter of institutional policy. Further statistics provided by the university show that the percentage of students in social science and humanities areas in undergraduate programs remained nearly constant over this period, with 13% in 1990, 15% in 1995, 15% in 2000 and 14% in 2005. Given that all the students integrated into the merged university from the medical and construction institutions were in basic or applied sciences, this indicates a relative strengthening of humanities and social science areas within the merged institution.

The percentage of female students at the undergraduate level has shown a significant increase over the period, with 20% in 1990, 19% in 1995, then 28% in 2000 and 27% in 2005. At the graduate level, female percentages have increased from 16% in 1990, to 20% in 1995, 25% in 2000 and 26% in 2005. These figures do not reflect a greater enrollment of female students in engineering fields, as much as the tendency for there to be high female enrollments in medicine, and also in social science and humanities programs. Breakdowns on enrollments in social sciences and humanities showed 48% of students in the social sciences were female in 2005, and 71% of students in humanities.

We were only given a very general breakdown of students by family background, with the head of student affairs informing us that about 50% of students came from rural families and that this percentage had remained constant. Minority students constituted a very small percentage of the total in 1995, 447 out of 9,407 (4.7%), dropping to 408 in 2000 (1.9%) but this number rose to 2,337 in 2005 (7%). This reflects deliberate support policies for minority students, including two special classes for Tibetan and Uighur students, as well as those minority students who come in through regular channels but are given some priority in admissions.

About 38% of HUST students come from the province of Hubei, with the remainder being recruited nation-wide. National policy calls for no more than 30% of students being recruited locally, in order to ensure fair opportunity for students nationwide to gain access to popular national institutions. Hubei students generally are of high quality and HUST is very popular with top students locally. Thus this situation is justified in light of modest financial support from Hubei province.

In addition to the 61,070 students enrolled in regular programs in 2005, there were another 29,606 enrolled in Wuchang and Wenhua Colleges, the two second-tier colleges established by HUST between 1999 and 2003.[15] These students receive graduation certificates from the colleges, which are independent legal persons, yet their degrees have been from HUST up till most recently.[16]

Numbers of international students at HUST have been very limited, with only 66 in 1995, 330 in 2000 (57% in degree programs), and 234 in 2005 (74% in degree programs). By 2008, there were reported to be 1,022, with 80% in degree programs and students mainly coming from Korea, India and various countries in Africa.[17] Two programs were being offered in English to international students, one in electronics and information engineering and the other in clinical medicine. Historically HUST had not been well equipped to provide programs in Chinese language and culture that used to attract the majority of international students, but this situation is clearly changing, as more and more international students come for degrees.

This statistical overview of changes in student numbers shows an institution that has undergone dramatic expansion in the period between 1995 and 2005. Both national policy and financial incentives have played into this, and we thus turn next to HUST's changing financial profile.

---

[15] In terms of management and finance these colleges are independent of HUST, though a percentage of their teaching staff are retired or part-time HUST professors.
[16] They will soon be conferring their own degrees, under new national policies for second-tier colleges.
[17] Interview with Yu Hailin, Dean of the College of International Education, 25 May 2008.

The Changing Financial Profile of HUST

The overview of the university's financial situation from 1990 to 2005 shows certain significant trends of change. Most striking in terms of annual income is the rising importance of student fees as base income, with a growth from 6.8 million in 1990, to 23.3 million in 1995, 243 million in 2000 and 603.7 million in 2005. From a mere 7% of income in 1990, student fees have now come to constitute 34% of the university's overall income. Over the same period, direct government grants have grown from 46 million or 48% of income in 1990 to 437.5 million or 25% of income in 2005. Special government grants associated with the national Projects 21/1 and 98/5 constituted about 5% of income in 2000 and 2005. The other major source of income has remained a relatively stable percentage, that of research grants from governmental and non-governmental sources. Over all research funding grew from 26.4 million in 1990 to 479.7 million in 2005, but remained at close to 27% of total income.

Other sources of funding in 2005 included 159 million from various types of income generating projects. One of the most important of these in recent years, we learned, was the running of the two second-tier colleges. HUST claims 20% of all student fees, in return for their advisory and quality assurance services. With nearly 30,000 students paying 10,000 per year in 2005, this adds up to an annual input of 60 million for HUST. By contrast, donations and gifts have remained very modest, 8.9 million in 2000, 7.2 million in 2005, well under one percent of the total income of 1.77 billion in 2005.

With student fees now constituting the largest proportion of the university's income, and each regular undergraduate student attracting 6,600 per year in government grants on top of direct fees of 4,000, one can see what a strong incentive there has been for expansion of student numbers. The reality of a large and commodious campus which has accommodated a major building program in terms of new classrooms, libraries and laboratories, and the addition of the adjacent campus of the Urban Construction Institute, has meant there has been no need to develop a suburban campus.

On the university budget side, information was provided on four main categories: faculty and staff salaries, teaching expenditures, student assistance and basic construction. In these figures, we could see a gradual increase in the percentage of the budget going to salaries, from 26.9 million (31%) in 1990 to 667.2 million (41%) in 2005. The other major item, teaching and research support rose from 43.2 million (50%) in 1990 to

877.4 (53%) in 2005. Student aid increased from 2 million (2%) in 1990 to 65.4 million (4%) in 2005, and constituted a little over 10% of student fee income of 607.2 million. Basic construction fees remained relatively low, 6% of budget in 2000 and 2% in 2005. We understand that some major construction projects are budgeted separately, also that the finances of the two teaching hospitals associated with the former Tongji Medical University have not been included in these figures. They provide only basic insights into the significant changes that have come with the move to mass higher education.

Curricular Change from 1990 to 2005

The third area of change that needs to be profiled here is that of the curriculum. In the early years after the end of the Cultural Revolution, Zhu Jiusi had set HUST on a unique course, that distinguished it from most other technological universities. His intention had been to strengthen the basic sciences, to link science and technology research to international currents in the field, and to build a small but excellent set of social science and humanities programs that would complement the strong focus on engineering. Thus in 1990, HUST had 19 departments in three major areas. Basic Science Departments included mathematics, physics, chemistry and mechanics. Engineering Departments included optical engineering, bio-engineering, mechanical engineering, power engineering, electrical engineering, shipbuilding, electrical and information engineering, solid state electronics, automatic control engineering, computer science, construction and civil engineering. In addition were Departments of Humanities, with programs in Chinese linguistics, journalism, English, Chinese society, higher education administration, and management, with programs in economics, international trade, economic statistics, sociology, patents, engineering management, material management and management information.

Over the 1990s, the curricular profile changed, both in terms of content and organization. As elsewhere in China, departments were grouped into colleges or schools. At first it was proposed that only those departments with doctoral programs could be upgraded into a college, but later it was decided that colleges could be created on the basis of major disciplines or programs.[18]

By 1998, the curriculum had a whole new face – with a College of

---

[18] Interview with Xu Xiaodong, Provost, 25 May 2008.

Economics, having Departments of International Trade, Economics and Finance, a College of Management, having Departments of Finance, Information Management and Information Systems, Business Management, Accounting, Financial Management, a College of Humanities, with Departments of Law and Chinese, a College of Education and a College of Journalism and Media Studies, as well as independent Departments of Foreign Languages, Sociology, Mathematics, Physics, Chemistry and Optical Engineering. In the sciences and engineering were Colleges of Life Sciences and Engineering, Materials Science and Engineering, Mechanical Science and Engineering, Computer Science and Technology, Construction and Communications, as well as independent Departments in Instrumentation Science and Engineering, Power Engineering, Electric Power Engineering, Electronic and Information Engineering, Automatic Control Engineering, Electron Science and Engineering, and Civil Engineering. This was pre-merger, and all the new developments were evolving from the rich curricular base already in place.

By 2000 the curricular profile had been further transformed, with almost all departments now within colleges, and evidence of the new areas in construction, environmental science, medicine, public health, and pharmacy being integrated into the picture. There were now new colleges of law and public administration, in addition to economics, management, humanities and education. The Departments of Mathematics, Physics and Chemistry were grouped within a College of Science and there was a new College of Informatics which grouped together Optics, Electronics and Systems Engineering. There were also new Colleges in Hydroelectric Power and Digitization, Energy and Power Engineering, Electronics and Electrical Engineering, Construction and Urban Planning, Environmental Science and Engineering, Civil Engineering, Transportation Science and Engineering, Public Health, Clinical Medicine, Pharmacy and Health Management. In 2003 a College of Software Engineering was added, and by 2005 the College of Education had developed new Departments in Educational Philosophy, Applied Psychology, Developmental Psychology and Physical Education, all added to the early focus on Higher Education Administration. The only Departments that remained free standing were Sociology, Foreign Languages, Medical Law and Nursing.

This information on curricular change has been gleaned from internal university documentation, which was provided to us. In the next section, we will try to get an inside view of some of the key decisions that lay behind these developments.

Vision and Strategic Direction

We were fortunate to be able to interview two vice presidents as well as leaders responsible for teaching affairs, research, student affairs, finance and the dean of the newly established college of international education. Among them were two individuals who had come from the former Tongji Medical University and the Wuhan Urban Construction Institute. We were thus able to get a multi-dimensional view of core issues such as the university's vision and mission, the merger experience, the spatial reconfiguration of the campus, the decision on second-tier colleges and basic teaching and research concerns.

Vision and Mission

Comments on the university's vision and mission arose in many of our interviews, giving a sense that there was an intense awareness of the important role played by core values in the university's development. The head of student affairs put it this way:

The reason HUST has developed so well is because it has been rich in ideas, the ideas of a series of leaders who have left their mark. Zhu Jiusi gave us the phrases 'daring to compete' and 'excellent in transformative capacity;' Yang Shuzi caused us to focus on the 'cultural and humanistic quality of students' and started a national movement of cultural rejuvenation on Chinese campuses; Zhou Ji emphasized the importance of integrating production, learning and research, enabling us to link our work closely with the changing demands of industry, and Li Peigen has given us the concepts of 'cultivating students as the fundamental focus,' 'creativity as the basic spirit' and 'bearing responsibility for action.[19]

The Provost talked about the process of establishing a mission statement, and described how the mission and vision put forward under current president Li Peigen had been arrived at. First the main outline was discussed by the university's Party Committee, and then delegated to a policy committee to refine the language and concepts and get broad feedback from different sectors of the university committee. After lengthy deliberation of this kind, a revised document was presented to the annual congress of faculty and staff for a formal vote. The Provost

---

[19] Interview with Zhu Xin, Head of the Student Affairs Department, 30 May 2008.

particularly wanted to make the point that no one leader could control this process in spite of a Chinese context where revered scholars and authority figures tend to have a powerful voice in decision-making. He illustrated this by noting that an earlier president had tried to narrow down HUST's curricular focus to emphasize a few specific areas in the natural sciences, engineering and medicine but had failed to gain faculty support for this.[20]

The contemporary mission is succinctly expressed in the following way: "a research-based university with an open-minded spirit and an internationally recognized reputation." The three core phrases constituting the vision are as follows: "cultivating students as the fundamental focus," "creativity as the basic spirit", and "bearing responsibility for action." A new motto has also been recently adopted: upholding morality (明德), advocating learning (厚學), seeking truth (求是), and innovating (創新).

The motto developed under the leadership of Zhu Jiusi in the late 1970s had featured a somewhat different set of values: Unity (團結), Truth (求是), Rigor (嚴謹) and Progress (進取). One leader commented that these concepts, and most particularly unity and rigor, have continued to inspire and guide HUST, whereas the new motto could easily constitute a vision for Chinese civilization more generally.[21] In a certain sense, the two mottos are visually related to two significant buildings on campus, one old and one very new. The South First Building (南一樓) was identified by at least five of those participating in our interviews or focus group meetings, as the building most expressive of the HUST spirit. Built in the 1950s, it typifies the Soviet influences of the time, a rectangular building with vertical and horizontal lines that give one a sense of the linear precision of the engineering profession. It was originally established as the university's main laboratory building. Then in the 1970s it was linked up to two large teaching wings in the shape of rectangular horseshoes to the East and West, making this complex the largest building on the campus. In front, facing the main entry gate to the campus, is a statue of Chairman Mao which is still standing to this day.

---

[20] Interview with Xu Xiaodong, Provost, 25 May 2008.
[21] Interview with Feng Xiangdong, Vice President, 29 May 2008.

Photo 10.1: The South First Building (南一樓) at the Core of the HUST Campus

In addition to mentioning the Nanyi Building, the most common comment of students, faculty and leaders on spatial features that reflect the campus ethos was related to the grid-like character of the campus. All roads are straight and those on the north-south axis are paved with green bricks while those on the east-west axis are paved with red bricks. This means that it is impossible to lose one's way. Unlike the campus of Wuhan University, where there are many winding paths and unexpected turns, the HUST campus expresses the engineering spirit, where everything is clearly laid out and there are no anomalies or puzzles.

By contrast, a huge new teaching building has recently been erected on the East side of the campus, with four rectangular end buildings connected by an elongated main building that curves around the edge of a lake. In front of this building is a newly unveiled bronze statue of Confucius, given to the university by a Hong Kong donor.[22] This building is the pride and joy of the President's assistant, who is responsible for campus spatial development and who noted that it was designed by an architect from the South China University of Technology.[23] However, neither students nor faculty mentioned this building, when asked what architectural features of the campus reflected the HUST ethos. We assume it is still too new to have found roots in their minds and hearts. The overall shape and layout of the campus, however, may express some kind of integration of the revolutionary and engineering spirit that

---

[22] HUST website, accessed July 19, 2008, http://www.hust.edu.cn/english/hustnews/news109.htm, for photos of the unveiling in the presence of HK donor, Dr. Tong Yun Kai.
[23] Interview with Du Zhongxian, Assistant to the President, 26 May 2008.

characterized the university's founding and the more explicitly cultural and holistic spirit expressed in curricular developments since the 1980s.

A graduate of the 1980s, who later wrote his doctoral thesis on HUST, noted parallels between the campus layout and the Beijing Imperial Palace, as both face south, with a hill behind them to the north. There is a kind of axial symmetry in the location of the Nanyi building at the centre front of the campus, dividing it into east and west sections, while a central commercial street divides the front of the campus, where teaching and research occur, from the back, where there are residential and recreational facilities. In his view, "the architects of the HUST campus ... consciously or unconsciously practiced the principles that were used in the palace because these principles represent China's traditional philosophy and aesthetics in architecture. They are the cultural umbilical cord between this new university and traditional China."[24]

Photo 10.2: The Map of the Main Campus shows the Location and Size of the Iconic Nanyi Building, facing the Main Gate, and the Grid-like Pattern of the Overall Campus Layout.

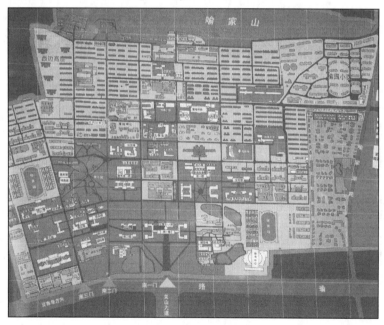

---

[24] Zhao Juming, "The Making of a Chinese University: An Insider's View of an Educational Danwei" (Unpublished book manuscript, 1999, drawn from a PhD thesis, McGill University, 1998), p.44.

Strategic Directions

Our interview with HUST's Executive Vice-President, Ding Hanchu, opened up insights into the university's broad strategic directions and how they had been developed. He explained that HUST leaders were reflecting on the experience of several local peer universities, including Shanghai Jiaotong University and Zhejiang University, also that they had chosen to learn from several American models. Ever since the late 1970s, former President Zhu Jiusi had upheld models such as MIT and Berkeley, noting that when he visited North America in 1979, he did not find a single university of high reputation which was not comprehensive in curricular offerings. Ding explained that President Zhou Ji had led the way in a careful historical study of MIT's development, and concluded that its most important period of flourishing had been between the first and second world wars, when it raised the status of technological research to a leading area of scholarship and spawned many high tech companies on the famous Route 128 around Boston. Stanford's experience with the development of Silicon Valley was also an inspiration to HUST, and more recently the Yale medical school experience.[25]

Ding went on to say that HUST had to take a very different development strategy from that of Peking University, with its focus on basic fields of knowledge. The starting point for HUST is the integration of liberal arts and engineering and its responsibility is to be an industry leader. Ding was proud of the fact that HUST graduates have been involved in a large number of start-up companies, many of them in Shenzhen, the dynamic city that has sprung up next to Hong Kong, including famous brand names such as Huawei (華爲), which is now a major Chinese multinational. HUST itself does not yet benefit greatly in financial terms from Huazhong Keji, the company it started in the mid-1990s, which now carries forward its innovative legacy.[26] Nevertheless, HUST members are proud of the huge number of new jobs that have been created and the tax base enjoyed by government, as a result of their capacity to innovate and start up new areas of industry. Outsiders find the spirit of HUST somewhat of a puzzle, commented Ding, and his best way of explaining this is by contrasting it with the more conservative

---

[25] Interview with Ding Hanchu, Executive Vice-President, 28 May 2008.
[26] In an interview with Nie Ming, Vice-Director of the Finance Department, we learned that HUST shares in Huazhong Keji are worth more than 1 billion *yuan*, but the company does not pay high dividends, since it is investing in its own future.

scholarly ethos of Wuhan University: "Wuda is like England, with a long history, a deep culture and considerable resistance to change ... by contrast HUST is like the USA, open to change, experimental and never held back by history."[27]

HUST has gone through three important phases of change, in Ding's view. The first took place in the 1980s, when its renewed strength in physics and its application to production led to a strong focus on optics. The second took place in the 1990s, as optics was integrated with electronics and information technologies, opening up new areas of high tech industry. The third was linked to the merger with Tongji Medical University and the integration of optical electronics with biology and medicine, leading to many new medical applications of technology.

HUST's proudest achievement has been its success in persuading the national government to establish the "Optics Valley (光穀)," a state laboratory in opto-electronics, close to the HUST campus in Wuhan. This is one of only five such laboratories, the other four being affiliated with the Chinese Academy of Sciences, Tsinghua University, Peking University and the University of Science and Technology of China. The fact that President Li Peigen chairs its Board of Directors makes possible many synergies in research and teaching between the university and this state lab. Ding believes that biotechnology will be the leading area of this century, as the very mysteries of life itself open up some of their secrets in response to the new technologies. This national laboratory is thus a crowning achievement of HUST's development strategy. Ding credits it to the determination of President Zhou Ji, now China's minister of education, to ensure that the university leads industry by integrating production, learning and research.

The Merger Issue
From the main leaders of HUST, we got a sense that the merger with the medical university was a welcome move, one which opened up a whole new set of possibilities in high technology with medical applications, and was a particular stimulus in research. HUST already had a large and commodious campus of 4,000 *mu* in Hankou, while absorbing the Wuhan Urban Construction Institute next door had extended its size by another 3,000 *mu*. So far, Tongji Medical University has remained on its original campus in Wuchang.

---

[27] Interview with Ding Hanchu, Executive Vice-President, 28 May 2008.

The fact that former President Zhu Jiusi had guided HUST towards becoming more and more comprehensive from the late 1970s was also a positive factor in facilitating the merger.[28] There were some among the students and faculty who would have welcomed a merger with Wuhan University, due to its longstanding academic reputation,[29] but the leaders and most faculty agreed with the initiative of Zhu and Qiu Fazu at the Tongji Medical to embrace a merger which allowed HUST to maintain and broaden its own unique ethos.

Once the merger decision had been made, the question of how integration among the three institutions would take place became an important one. Would the medical school remain practically independent, running its programs as usual under a new name, or would it truly integrate? The same question faced the Urban Construction Institute. As it turned out, full integration was to come about under the presidency of Li Peigen, for reasons relating both to his vision for the university and his personal network. Before relating that story, we need first to hear the views on merger from the perspective of Tongji Medical University and the Wuhan Urban Construction Institute.

Dr. Ma Jianhui, formerly a professor of Tongji Medical University and now Vice Provost of HUST, gave his view of the merger from the Tongji perspective. He noted that Tongji Medical University had a long history. Originally founded by German doctors in Shanghai in 1907, it had been a leading faculty of national Tongji University in Shanghai in the Nationalist period. With the reorganization of 1952 under Soviet influence, Tongji's medical faculty was moved to Wuhan, where it was combined with the medical faculty of Wuhan University (founded in 1916) and given a new campus in Wuchang. From 1952 to the mid-1990s, it developed as a strong national medical university, following the Soviet model of a high level of specialization from the beginning of each program, including medical fields, public health, pharmacy and nursing. It also has two teaching hospitals, with a large number of staff.

The merger decision was not highly controversial for Tongji, since most medical school around the country were re-connecting to nearby comprehensive universities, in some cases restoring relationships broken in the reorganization of 1952. Given the support of academician Qiu Fazu, the decision to merge with HUST rather than Wuhan University, was

---

[28] Interview with Xu Xiaodong, Provost, 25 May 2008.
[29] Interview with Zhou Guangli, Higher Education Research Institute, 27 May 2008.

accepted, and Tongji began to revise its programs towards greater breadth. Clinical medicine and basic medicine were linked together, and three types of programs were formed – eight year programs leading to doctoral degrees in specialist medical areas, five year programs in areas such as pharmacy and nursing, leading to Masters level qualifications and three year programs in basic medicine to train assistant doctors. All those enrolled in eight year programs now spend their first two years on the HUST campus, with courses in basic sciences as well as social sciences and humanities. Students in five year programs spend one initial year on the HUST campus.

The first benefit of the merger for Tongji is the ability to attract higher quality students nationwide, due to the reputation of HUST and the synergies of the new programs. The second significant benefit has been in research. Tongji faculty have found the research culture at HUST highly stimulating, and they have become much more active researchers, winning significantly higher levels of research funding from the National Natural Sciences Foundation (NNSF) than before the merger. They have also started to participate in many collaborative research projects, linking medicine to engineering and in some collaborative teaching programs. Finally, the management of Tongji has been improved through integration with a well-managed comprehensive university. However, the distance of Tongji's Wuchang campus from HUST in Hankou still creates some obstacles to cooperation.[30]

The view of merger from the Wuhan Urban Construction Institute, on a campus contiguous to the HUST campus, was shared by Professor Du Zhongxian, a former vice president who now serves as assistant to the President at HUST. He reported that there had been lively debates among the university's leadership over whether or not to agree to merge with HUST, before a decision was made by the Party Committee. The Wuhan Urban Construction Institute was one of seven national institutes administered by the Ministry of Construction, and regarded itself as at least third in ranking after parallel institutions in Harbin and Chongqing. It had moved to a new campus in 1983, and had a strong sense of institutional identity, developed in an energetic struggle for survival after the Cultural Revolution. Since there have been many attractive urban construction jobs in recent years, it had been able to attract high quality students from all over China.

---

[30] Interview with Ma Jianhui, Vice Provost, 27 May 2008.

For these reasons, some leaders and faculty opposed merger, feeling they would lose their distinctive edge. The majority, however, favored merger. They could see that there was little future for universities under national ministries other than the Ministry of Education. The alternative to merging with HUST was a merger with a provincial university or becoming an independent institution under provincial administration. Since funding per student head is lower at the provincial than the national level, the merger with HUST was definitely more attractive and secure.[31]

Another issue in many mergers of Chinese institutions has been how to accommodate multiple sets of university leaders. Du's personal story was quite interesting in this regard. He was offered major leadership positions in two other universities, one in Sanxiang, a smaller city in Hubei province, and another in the Wuhan Conservatory of Music. While he loved music, and was quite attracted to the second option, he felt he did not want to re-locate at age 52. He was attracted by the HUST ethos, which he described as "practical and down to earth" and wanted to work within the merged university. So he contacted then President Zhou Ji, and offered to serve as President's assistant, and contribute his experience and network in the field of urban construction to campus development for the newly merged institution.

This turned out to be a great decision, as he has had the opportunity of overseeing the re-development of one of China's largest urban campuses, with more than 6,000 *mu* of land on the combined campus in Hankou, as well as another 600 on the Wuchang medical campus. He has been responsible for considerable campus expansion, which involved complex negotiations with local farmers. He has also overseen major developments – including a new section of the campus devoted to faculty housing, with high quality apartment buildings available for faculty to purchase. This has made a major contribution to attracting and keeping good scholars. He is particularly proud of the new teaching buildings, made to accommodate 45,000 students, and the huge building for the Opto-electronics Laboratory, which was designed by an architect from Beijing.[32]

---

[31] While the national government provides 6,600 *yuan* per student per year for the institutions under direct MOE administration, the provincial government provides only 3,000 per student head.

[32] Interview with Du Zhongxian, Assistant to the President, 26 May 2008.

Du noted that he originally hoped the Urban Construction Institute could maintain most of its programs on its own campus, but in the end they had been fully integrated with HUST. Only some years after the merger was a road built that conveniently linked the two campuses. In the meantime, the six departments of the original Urban Construction Institute had been successfully merged, with civil engineering, environmental engineering, computer science and urban construction integrated into parallel HUST colleges, and its own unique departments in planning and construction, also Road and Bridge construction finding a place within appropriate HUST colleges. Before merger, the university had 4,000 undergraduate students but only 7 masters programs and no PhD programs. It has benefited greatly from the new research and graduate training opportunities that the HUST environment offered. Meanwhile Du himself enjoyed his job immensely, and felt proud to be able to use his extensive network of graduates in Wuhan and elsewhere to facilitate the many exciting campus developments.

Photo 10.3: The Wuhan National Laboratory for Optoelectronics (WNLO), the center of Wuhan Optics Valley, located on the east side of HUST main campus in Hankou, is a cutting edge national platform for inter-disciplinary research in opto-electronics.

If the merger with the Urban Construction Institute was facilitated by geographical proximity and the many overlaps in subject area between the two institutions, the merger with the Medical University brought considerable excitement because of the new horizons of knowledge that it opened up. Both the Provost and Vice Provost spoke enthusiastically about a new six year program about to begin in bio-medical engineering, with students having one general year, one year in medicine and four years in engineering, and reaching the masters level. There was an awareness of many new job opportunities and developmental areas related to medical technology and hospital equipment which needed this type of personnel.

There was also tremendous enthusiasm about the new areas of research opening up in bio-medical engineering. Vice President Ding told how he had got top level professors from medicine and engineering to sit down and confer with one another at the time of the annual faculty representative council. Out of this had come many new research ideas in areas such as bio-electronics, nuclear medicine and medical instrumentation. HUST has seen a dramatic increase in research funding since the merger, from a total of 253.2 million in 2000 to 479.7 million in 2005, with the balance shifting from 36% in basic funding from prestigious national sources in 2001, to 56% in 2005. The main reason for this change was the research funds obtained from the National Natural Sciences Foundation for medical research projects. In 2007, the medical school received more funds from the NNSF than all other programs at HUST, for the first time. Also HUST's national ranking in terms of NNSF funding moved to No. 4, a significant indicator of the status of its research profile.

The final frontier in terms of the integration of the medical and engineering areas lies with geography. Current HUST President, Li Peigen, grew up on the campus of Tongji Medical University, where both his parents were professors and he had many opportunities for contact with academician Qiu Fazu. This familiarity may have been an important factor in the kinds of integration that have been fostered between the medical and engineering programs, in teaching, research and administration. However, distance between the two main campuses still inhibits full integration.

It was interesting to hear from the Vice-Director of Finance the kinds of consideration under discussion in terms of a merger of the two campuses. He noted that it would be theoretically possible to sell the Tongji campus in Wuchang, for at least 400 million *yuan*, and create an entirely new campus for the medical school on land available to HUST. Since facilities were generally better on the HUST campus than in Wuchang, this would be welcomed by the majority of students and faculty. The main issue was what the city of Wuhan might claim in such a sale, and what support it would offer to facilitate campus integration.

While Hubei province had promised 500 million to match the funding from 98/5 for Wuhan University and HUST, so far none had been received, though 200 million was expected in the following year. By contrast, Guangdong province had given 1.2 billion each to Zhongshan University and South China University of Technology, more than matching what Beijing gave under the 98/5 Project, and the Shanghai government had given 600 million each to Fudan and Shanghai Jiaoda. Nie recognized that Hubei province simply could not afford this level of support. One of its constraints was the fact that it was responsible for a huge number of provincial universities, as a result of the concentration of universities located there in the 1950s, with most former ministry universities now placed under provincial jurisdiction. Even if they could not give adequate financial support, Nie hoped that they would develop policies regarding land sale that would be helpful.[33]

This discussion of the HUST merger experience shows the many dimensions involved in a merger process – curricular, research and administrative integration, campus space considerations, leadership challenges, and the role of personal networks in initial merger decisions and implementation processes. Overall, it seems the HUST merger has been a positive experience, leading to all three major partners being stimulated and extended in both teaching and research. Yet there are continuing challenges of geographical distance and differing campus cultures.

Establishing Second-tier Colleges

Parallel to its positive response to national policy on enrollment expansion, HUST also took a very pro-active role in the establishment of second-tier colleges. Provost Xu Xiaodong noted that it was a policy strongly promoted by HUST's President Zhou Ji, who subsequently became Minister of Education. It was viewed as an important means of stimulating rapid expansion in the private sector of higher education, while ensuring the maintenance of quality standards. For HUST as a top public institution, the main consideration was service to society and the opportunity for their retired faculty to serve.[34] There were economic incentives as well, however.

Vice President Feng Xiangdong noted that there had been intense

---

[33] Interview with Nie Ming, Vice-Director of Finance, 30 May 2008.
[34] Interview with Xu Xiangdong, Provost, 25 May 2008.

debates in China over Trow's 1973 article on the move to mass higher education in the later 1990s, and he saw this as crucial to the firm decision on massive enrollment expansion made in 1999. Recognizing that the whole burden of expansion could not be carried by the public sector, and that private universities in the Chinese context were still relatively inexperienced, the MOE had decided to encourage top universities to establish independent colleges, using private investment but ensuring the quality of programs by deploying some of their own faculty and offering the kinds of academic oversight that would make it possible for degree programs to be accredited quickly. Feng saw this as a win-win situation, in that it expanded opportunities for students, enabled top universities to gain some additional income and also generated a profit for investors. At the same time he hastened to add that he recognized that the policy created an uneven playing field for competition between fully private universities and the independent colleges of top public institutions. This was regrettable, yet unavoidable, in his view.[35]

Why did HUST decide to take up this challenge? They could have refused, but they saw it as an opportunity to make a practical contribution to enrollment expansion locally, as well as generating significant income. The first college established was named the Wuchang Branch College, and three years later Wenhua College was established, close to the HUST campus in Hankou. Both are independent legal persons with their own property, and both have developed well, with total enrollments close to 30,000 students by 2005. Many retired HUST professors have been teaching in the two colleges, but they are also developing their own faculty contingent, and have practical programs related to the local employment market. Students get a graduation certificate from the college but a degree from HUST, something that is most attractive. A small number are able to pass entrance examinations for Masters programs at HUST. One of the controversies that has given rise to serious student activism in recent years is the demarcation of the university degree as linked to a second-tier college, which students see as devaluing the credential.[36] For HUST's two colleges there have been no serious

---

[35] Interview with Feng Xiangdong, Vice President, 29 May 2008.
[36] Student protests took place in several second-tier colleges in recent years. For example, in June of 2006, students in Zhengzhou University's Shengda Economics Trade and Management College protested the fact that their degrees specified that this was the second-tier college of Zhengzhou University, not the university itself. They had serious concern about the value of the degree in the eyes

protests so far, and they expect to be conferring their own degrees very soon. The whole process is regarded as transitional, with an established university supporting the birth of new private institutions.

Finance and Governance

Executive Vice-President Ding Hanchu explained how key reforms of the early 1990s affected the university's finance and governance. It was already noted earlier that only 25% of its budget comes from direct governmental allocations, down from 48% in 1990. While faculty salaries had originally been paid directly out of a government budget line, now universities receive government allocations on the basis of enrollment size, and have to be responsible for their own budget. One of the significant burdens is the high percentage of retired faculty, whose salaries, housing and health care come out of the university budget, with only a small contribution from government. With rising living standards, it is a demanding task to cover the whole range of budgetary areas, including items such as retiree salaries and health care, the costs of attached schools on campus, faculty housing and campus development. Students are fully aware that their fees make up a significant portion of the university's income, and university leaders are concerned about possibilities of student protest, if they feel their fee income is being diverted to subsidize budget items unrelated to teaching and facilities. This sense of accountability to students as primary clients and supporters of the university is something quite new and challenging.

The same thing is true for faculty and issues of governance. The Provost explained the main governance process in the following way. The major decisions on vision and mission are made by the University's Communist Party Committee, while high level committees on finance, policy, curricular development, scholarship and related areas, chaired by vice-presidents, make more specific development decisions. Overall, the style of governance mirrors Chinese tradition, with the following order – heaven (天), earth (地), the ruler (君), parents (親) and teachers (師). First of all, the laws of nature must be respected (heaven and earth), then the ruler – once the emperor, now state leaders, then parents and finally teachers. As provost, he is responsible for the committee on curricular

---

of employers (See news report by BBC on 21 June 2006: http://news.bbc.co.uk/chinese/simp/hi/newsid_5100000/newsid_5100900/5100988.stm). Similar cases were also seen in Shanxi, Anhui, and Jiangxi.

development, and if the responsible vice-president is not available to chair a meeting, he will invite a respected academician to do so.[37] In spite of this traditional authority structure, Xu emphasized the fact that no individual leader can dominate decision-making, and faculty interests and concerns have to be carefully considered. There is clearly a sense of accountability on the part of the leadership not only to students but also to faculty.

Faculty and Issues of Teaching and Research

The Faculty Profile

HUST's faculty profile has changed considerably over the period from 1990 to 2005, as can be seen in Table 10.1 below. Total faculty numbers dropped between 1990 and 1995, rose significantly after the merger in 2000, while falling somewhat again by 2005. The student faculty ratio rose gradually between 1990 and 2000, then reached a high of 1:19.6 in 2005. The huge expansion in graduate enrollments, with self-paying masters' and doctoral students bringing in significant income, led to rising concern over the quality of graduate supervision.[38] As a result, graduate student numbers were cut back from 25,484 in 2005, to 20,044, as reported on the HUST website in 2008.

Table 10.1: Statistics on Faculty and Teacher-Student Ratios (1990-2005)

	1990	1995	2000	2005
Total Number of Faculty	2,604	1,758	3,231	3,081
Faculty-student ratio	1:4	1:6.6	1:8.6	1:19.8
Full professors (%)	7	15	20	24
Associate professors (%)	34	39	34	34
Assistant professors (%)	36	35	27	33
Teaching assistants (%)	24	11	18	9
Faculty with PhD (%)	2	8	13	28
Female Faculty (%)	23	25	25	32

Other significant changes in the faculty contingent can be seen in the proportion of faculty at different academic levels. In 1990, only 7% of

---

[37] Unlike the situation in Western universities, the provost is usually not vice-president, but is responsible for all teaching programs.

[38] Interview with Zhou Guangli, 27 May 2008. Zhou was asked to do a research project on the quality of graduate supervision and discovered one professor who was supervising 47 doctoral students. Since then the university has limited the number of doctoral enrollments.

all faculty were full professors, but this rose to 24% by 2005, while the category of teaching assistants dropped from 24% to 9% over the same period, with a balanced number of faculty in the middle ranks of associate and assistant professor. By 2005, 28% of all faculty were PhD holders, up from a mere 2% in 1990, a significant indicator of a more highly qualified faculty. Female percentages had also increased significantly from 23% in 1990 to 25% in 1995 and 2000, and 32% in 2005.

The hugely expanded graduate programs were clearly important for the development of young faculty, and we were told that their goal was to attract one third of new faculty with doctoral degrees from abroad, one third from other universities and one third from among their own graduates.[39] While they admired the Beida policy of making no appointments from among their own doctoral graduates, this was not practical in the Wuhan context. Even keeping their own excellent graduates was often difficult, given the attraction of job opportunities in coastal cities such as Shenzhen, Guangzhou and Shanghai. One of the factors that was helpful in attracting good faculty was the newly built faculty housing complex, with good quality apartments that could be purchased at a reasonable price.

Issue of Teaching and Research

When asked how the university maintained teaching quality in face of the rapid expansion of enrollments, the Provost first called attention to the three capacious new teaching buildings, which could accommodate 45,000 students, as well as the fact that 60 million had been spent on new laboratories and 80 million on new equipment since 2002. He was concerned about class sizes, and explained that he hope to bring classes of 150 down to 100, and classes of 120 down to 80. However, this meant each faculty had to teach more classes, which reduced their research time.

One of the initiatives of recent years has been the establishment of the Innovation College (創新學院), a special group of 60 outstanding undergraduate students who are given an integrated exposure to the arts and basic sciences with a strong theoretical foundation, such that they can complete their undergraduate courses in three years and spend the fourth year on a special project or begin graduate courses. Another initiative has been the provision of funding for undergraduate students to take part in research. For example, the Department of Electronics has pro-

---

[39] Interview with Feng Xiangdong, Vice President, 29 May 2008.

vided a budget of 300,000 *yuan*, with some additional funding from individual professors, for student research projects. Additionally, since 2006 more than 70 students have succeeded in applying for the research funding sponsored by the MOE's National Program of Undergraduate Innovation Training each year, with an average of 10,000 *yuan* per project.[40]

Perspectives from Faculty and Student Counselors

Our faculty focus group meetings involved three faculty members and three student counselors. Counselors are having more and more professionalized roles, with many having master's degrees in psychology and related areas, rather than being political appointees with responsibility for political education, as in the past. The "second classroom (第二課堂)" is an important new concept, emphasizing the wide range of student learning experiences that take place through activities on campus or in the wider community rather than formal study. Faculty members came from the Departments of Physics, English and Mechanical Engineering, while two of the counselors came from the Optical-electronics Department and one from Mechanical Engineering.[41]

One faculty member started with a lively defense of HUST's role in developing its two second-tier colleges, noting that it was a significant contribution to social change, and there were some parallels with HUST's own development in the early 1950s, on the basis of departments brought in from other universities. Two other faculty members had had experience in teaching in HUST's second-tier colleges, and one commented on the poor quality of the students and the fact that they were passive and did not raise questions. The other argued that some of the students were actually better than the lowest level of student in HUST itself, and some had succeeded in getting into a graduate program at HUST. Wenhua, the second college to develop, had learned important lessons from the Wuchang experience and made improvements, especially in the development of practical programs linked to local employment needs.

A second topic that came up in discussion initiated by two faculty

---

[40] Interview with Xu Xiaodong, Provost, 25 May 2008.

[41] The decision to include three counselors, alongside of three faculty members, in the Faculty Focus Group was made by Professor Chen Min, one of our two collaborating scholars at HUST, on the grounds that it was important for us to learn about informal education and the 'second classroom' as well as the more formal aspects of education under faculty direction.

members was the quality and expectations of contemporary students. Many come from good secondary schools and they put high demands on the faculty. They want to see courses updated each year, the latest technology being used in teaching and the opportunity for questioning and participation in class. One of the counselors agreed that students are now much more active than they were when he graduated in 1999, with a lot of their attention being given to independent study and research projects, also various organizations set up by students themselves.

The professor of English felt that today's students have a sense of world citizenship and are eager to reach out and communicate with the wider world. She sees them as future ambassadors for China, who will bring a positive image of China to the world, and explain its culture and achievements. This awareness inspired her to develop a new approach to teaching English for all students, with three different levels, so that students across all fields can take classes that are appropriate to their level of English ability. Her new English teaching program has now begun to have an influence nationwide. She was also cooperating with the College of International Education to provide a program for 66 undergraduate students who are doing their first two years of study at HUST, and will continue with the second half of their university studies abroad. Students for this program come from mechanical engineering, computer science, electronics, and electrical equipment. Some of these students are expected to stay abroad and create positive linkages for cooperation between China and Western countries.

The three counselors noted that students have a strong sense of responsibility as well as gratitude for the learning opportunities they have and a desire to give back to society. In face of the Wenchuan Earthquake of May 12, 2008, students had organized fund-raising activities and were extremely eager to volunteer practical help. Students were also very active in taking the opportunities provided for research at the undergraduate level and the various networks that have been set up to encourage students to exchange ideas and initiative innovative projects. The other side of this openness to new forms of media and communication was a tendency among some students to become addicted to the internet in ways that interfere with their studies.[42]

Overall, our discussion with faculty members and counselors gave us a sense of a very lively community of learning, in which students are

---

[42] Faculty Focus Group Meeting, 27 May 2008.

more and more pro-active and there are significant pressures for improvement in teaching, both from students and the administration, and for balancing the demands of teaching and research. The role of counselors in promoting informal kinds of learning is significant, but they too feel the stress of numbers, with one counselor responsible for 300-400 students.

Student Perspectives

There were eight students in our student focus group, two from mechanical engineering, two from opto-electronics, one from physics, one from law, one from management and one from foreign languages, with four female students among them, and four from rural family backgrounds. Most were undergraduate students, but there were two in the first year of a masters program. They had received our interview questions ahead, thought about them and had a great deal to say. We will summarize their perspectives under the themes of cultural identity, civil society and civic participation, equity and employment issues.

Cultural Identity

Several students spoke rather passionately on issues of Chinese cultural identity and the university's role. They were aware of the university's mission and felt it was important for the leaders to demand rigorous standards of scholarship and to improve the university's facilities accordingly. It was important for the university to reach international standards and represent Chinese culture on a world stage. It was interesting to see the student from foreign languages, who was studying English, put forward a view that paralleled that of the faculty member who had been developing new approaches to the teaching of English. Here is how she expressed herself: "Until recently, there has been a strong sense of inferiority among Chinese, with a great deal of writing that reflects the attitude that the moon is fuller in the West than in China, the social systems and standards of living are better etc.... But now that the Chinese economy has surged ahead, Chinese people have more confidence in themselves, they are more objective in making comparisons than they used to be and have a greater sense of their own history and the quality of their people."[43] She made the point that learning English well was crucial to being able to communicate aspects of Chinese culture and

---

[43] Student Focus Group Meeting, 26 May 2008.

society to the world.

Other students agreed with this, and there was some discussion about the advantages of comprehensive universities such as Wuhan University and Nankai University having a real history to draw upon and some historic buildings, while they were a young university, without this background. "We long for a sense of history, as a basis from which new ideas can be drawn. At the same time, our shorter history has some advantages. We are more open to reform and it is easier for us to be open and move forward .... We always think of (former president) Zhu Jiusi and his incredible spirit of reform – this is the greatest influence in our university's history."[44]

Photo 10.4: The outdoor old theatre, located in the central area of the main campus still had a rusted sign on its front entrance with HUST's original name, the Huazhong Institute of Technology.

Students went on to speak about university buildings and spaces that expressed their ethos. One spoke of the South First Building with the Mao statue, with a special appreciation, noting that he was from Hunan, the birthplace of Mao Zedong. Several spoke of the character of the campus, with its straight roads going precisely North and South, East and West expressing the engineering mind. "This is our trademark," they said. Another campus space which students identified as very important to them was the outdoor movie theatre, which had been built in the 1950s.

---

[44] *Ibid.*

Recently, university leaders had planned to tear it down for new campus developments, but there was strong student resistance, and the development plans have been cancelled. Students identified this as a place of many meetings, as well as movies and entertainment, a place graduates always visit when they return to campus, an important place in their memories.

Students also made reference to Yang Shuzi, who had been president from 1992 to 1997, and was credited with starting a national movement of cultural enrichment for university students. In 1994, HUST launched a program of humanistic education and made itself the first university that established a research base in humanistic education for all students at the undergraduate level. The student from the Physics Department noted how important he found the general humanities courses he had taken in areas such as history, law and philosophy. All of the students had a sense of the combination of cultural awareness and responsibility with a cutting edge scientific and technological environment that characterized the HUST ethos.

Civil Society and Civic Participation

Students were critical of their university leaders, suggesting that the university's vision and mission largely consisted of "empty words (空話)." They felt they did not have much opportunity to communicate with the leadership, and were not in touch with the strategic directions. For them, it was crucial that facilities should be improved, equipment upgraded and the quality of the learning experience be given importance. They felt the leadership was accountable to deliver a high quality educational experience, given their capabilities and status as students and the fees they were paying. It was interesting to see how different their attitudes were from those of students in the old planned economy, who were more passive and subordinate.

All of the eight students talked enthusiastically about the different societies and social groupings they belonged to. They explained that there were two main types, those officially organized by the Youth League or the student association at university, college or department level, and those which were started up by students' own initiatives. Those formally organized covered many areas, including such social services as visiting the elderly, supporting orphans, helping with rural development projects, and protecting the environment. Most activities were well organized and sometimes even competitive in terms of participation, with first and second year students taking part enthusiastically, but upper year students often less active. Students also mentioned activities closely related to their professional studies, which they particularly appreciated. One was a program organized by students in the college of law, whereby they educated people in rural areas about their rights and the law, to empower them and ensure they were not exploited by local government cadres. Another program was fostered by the Sociology Department, and offered training and internship opportunities in the area of social work.

One of the entirely self-organized activities that students were particularly proud of was a bike ride from Athens to Beijing, which had been led by an alumnus who was good at fund-raising and organizational work, and had attracted a large number of students to participate. Other students mentioned hiking expeditions within China, which had enabled them to get more familiar with the conditions and needs of rural society.

It was clear that students were deeply concerned about social issues, and eager for opportunities to participate and contribute. Nevertheless, they felt constrained by the demands of their studies, limited resources and concerns about the future and preparation for employment.

Equity Issues

Students' comments on issues of equity were particularly striking. Several students from rural backgrounds emphasized how important the expansion and move to mass higher education had been for rural youth. One made the following comment: "Just imagine if only 100 places had been given, instead of 200, how many young people would have been excluded …. All of these young people will become parents and with their own improvement from university study, they will make a huge difference for their children. The whole of society is being uplifted by the move to mass higher education, and people will have a much greater capacity to transform themselves and the younger generation." Another said, "Mass higher education has changed people's ideas about what it means to be a university student. This is no longer a matter of elite status, rather of responsibility as a citizen, where one is expected to make a difference, also of the overall quality of people being improved." A third student made reference to a comment by former President Zhou Ji who clearly influenced HUST's massification policies and decision on second-tier colleges: "If we do not have an increase in numbers, we cannot have quality."[45] The point was that China cannot transform itself by depending on the leadership of a few top people, but the quality of the whole of Chinese society had to be raised.

Generally, students felt the unified national entry examinations were essential to fairness in terms of university entry, yet they noted that the system could not be truly fair until educational opportunities at the basic and secondary level were more equal. Thus it was most important to ensure that economic development reached the more remote and poor parts of the country, and that the quality of education at the basic level be improved.

Employment Issues

One student started this topic by saying that employment should not be seen as a zero-sum game where the elite kept all the best job opportunities to themselves, but an open playing field where all could compete for good jobs. Society needed to have the kind of order that allowed for this competition, and ensured no-one was held back artificially by a refusal to expand higher education enrollments. Students commented that it was relatively easy for graduates of nationally prestigious institutions such as HUST to find suitable jobs, but more difficult for graduates of local and private universities. At the same time, the employment market had changed in recent years, so that qualifications were not the only consideration, but effort, performance and results were rewarded.

"There are many more opportunities for young people to prove themselves in a market oriented society than was the case in the planned society of the past .... The expansion of enrollment has allowed a lot more young people to take part in the competition and it is good for them and for society. There is also greater pressure on young people to compete and make a great effort to show their quality and contribution. This is all for the greater good of society." One student even made the comment that: "I think the devaluation of university degrees is a good thing; as people realize that their efforts can make a difference, a lot of energy has been released and people want to compete .... This is a big change from the old times when everything was planned and effort did not make a difference."[46]

Overall, we found this group of HUST students to be thoughtful,

---

[45] Ibid.
[46] Ibid.

highly motivated, and very conscious of the fact they were living and studying in an era of dramatic change for China – both in its internal socio-economic system and in its international status and role. There was a sense of responsibility to society and the world that paralleled the demands and expectations they put on their institution and its leaders.

Conclusion: HUST as a Microcosm of Higher Education Development in the New China

A number of our interviewees made the comment that HUST was a microcosm of higher educational development in the new China. It was born shortly after the revolution of 1949, and its development and contribution reflected the phases of change in China over a period of nearly sixty years: socialist construction, the cultural revolution, modernization and globalization. In the 1950s, HUST was one of the new polytechnical universities that was to train a large number of engineers who would bring China up to world standards in technology while adhering to the "socialist road." In the Cultural Revolution, HUST saw most of its faculty sent down to learn from the peasants in rural areas, and its leadership under attack. However, it was one of the first institutions to take up Deng Xiaoping's call to serve "modernization, the world and the future" after the end of the Cultural Revolution, with the result that it developed a new model of a comprehensive university in the late 1970s, and pioneered the integration of research and teaching. As China moved onto a world stage in the 1990s, HUST leadership saw the need for an explicit cultural identity, and the potential of broadly based cultural studies for all undergraduates. In the early 21st century, HUST was proud to be a leader in massification of enrollments, and the integration of teaching, research and new technological and industrial developments.

There was a strong sense of its leadership responsibility at each stage of development, and this was a matter of pride among faculty and students. There was a widespread awareness of the innovations brought about by Zhu Jiusi, which pre-dated national university reforms of the mid-1980s, as well as pride in the movement for cultural rejuvenation brought about by Yang Shuzi in the 1990s. This sense of responsibility to lead probably also lay behind the decision on massive expansion of enrollments and the establishment of two leading second-tier colleges. There was further tremendous pride in HUST's successful industrial leadership, in spawning successful high-tech companies, in hosting one of five National Laboratories and in helping to create the Wuhan Optics Valley.

What we see in the HUST ethos is a spirit of realism that embraced both the scientific and political dimensions of new China. It asserted itself and took leadership at every stage of China's development, helping to nurture new and cutting edge scientific and technological knowledge for socialist China. As a microcosm of the development of new China's higher education, HUST showed how necessary was the break with history that came about in the revolution of 1949. At the same time, it has also demonstrated how essential China's traditions had been to the achievements of a new era of globalization and how important it has been to bring them explicitly into curricular development. This balance of innovation and tradition may lie behind the phrase used by both leaders and faculty in describing the Huazhong spirit: "If you want to immerse yourself in learning, come to Huazhong."

11
Northwest Agricultural and Forestry University – An Agricultural Multiversity?

Qiang ZHA and Ruth HAYHOE, with NIU Hongtai

Northwest Agriculture and Forestry University (NWAFU) is the only public university in our study located in the Northwest region of China, an area that has been a considerable focus of development aid and infrastructure investment from the central government in recent years. Located in Yangling, not far from the major city of Xi'An, the NWAFU has a history going back to the 1930s, as a centre of agricultural teaching and research. In recent years, it has embraced a highly complex merger which involved two universities, and a number of research institutes under the Chinese Academy of Sciences (CAS), the Ministry of Water Conservancy and the Shaanxi provincial government. As one of only two agricultural universities to be included in the prestigious Project 98/5,[1] it has an important role nationally and within the Northwest region. This case study gives insights into the ways in which it has responded to the opportunities of massification and the outcomes of its complex process of merger.

We carried out an intensive case study visit on the NWAFU campus from May 18 to 22, 2008. During this time, we interviewed a number of university leaders, including President Sun Wuxue, Vice Presidents Zhao Zhong (executive), Wang Ge (student affairs) and Wu Pute (research), the Director of the Office of Teaching Affairs, Wang Guodong, the Deputy Director of the Office of Student Affairs, Hua Xiaofeng, and the Director of the Finance Department, Liu Zengchao. In addition, we conducted four focus group meetings with faculty members and students from the School of Agronomy, the School of Animal Sciences, the School of Food Sciences and Engineering, and the School of Humanities. We had planned more focus group meetings, which, however, were interrupted by the aftershocks of the catastrophic earthquake which took place on May 12, 2008 in the southwest province of Sichuan.

---

[1] The other one is the China Agricultural University located in Beijing.

The History and Context

The Evolution of the NWAFU

A core constituent of today's NWAFU, the Northwest Agricultural University, originated from the National Northwest Junior College of Agriculture and Forestry, which was founded in 1934 by the respected Nationalist politician and educator, Yu Youren (於右任).[2] It was the earliest special college for agriculture and forestry in the Northwest of China, and is the foremost predecessor of the current NWAFU. In 1938, the Junior College merged with the Agricultural College of the National Northwest Associated University and the Animal Husbandry Department of the Agricultural College of Henan University, to form the National Agricultural College. In 1941, it was approved by the Ministry of Education of the Nationalist government to offer graduate programs.

This happened against the backdrop of the Japanese occupation of Eastern China, when the Chinese government was forced to develop the Northwest. The Wei River valley, where the College was located, became an important military, economic and administrative base for the war effort against Japan. One building remains from that period, namely the Number Three Teaching Building on the NWAFU's North Campus, as seen in Photo 11.1 below. This building, designed by an American architect, served also as a clock tower on the campus. During the anti-Japanese war, this historical building suffered extensive damage from a Japanese attack, and one can still see the bullet marks. However, it was rebuilt and is used regularly for university classes up to the present. Almost all the university leaders, faculty and students whom we met on the campus took it as a symbol of the NWAFU culture and ethos, in particular the spirit of courage (勇) and perseverance (毅), two of the values highlighted in its motto.

The National Agricultural College was renamed Northwest Agricultural College after the founding of the People's Republic of China in 1949. In 1985, it adopted the name of Northwest Agricultural University, with the approval of the Ministry of Agriculture, Animal Husbandry and Fishery, to which it belonged under the sectoral structure that had been modelled after the Soviet system. However, its Department of Forestry

---

[2] Yu Youren (11 April 1879 – 10 November 1964) was a politician and educator of the Republic of China. He was a notable member of the Guomindang or Nationalist Party, then China's ruling party, and was also the first President of Shanghai University in the 1920s.

Photo 11.1: The Number Three Teaching Building on the NWAFU's North Campus, Symbolizing Courage and Perseverance.

had been taken out in 1979, to form an independent Northwest Forestry College under the jurisdiction of the then Ministry of Forestry. In 1999, Northwest Forestry College was re-united with Northwest Agricultural University in a merger that also embraced five independent research institutes located in Yangling, namely the Institute of Soil and Water Conservation of the Chinese Academy of Sciences (CAS), the Northwest Institute of Water Resources Science of the Ministry of Water Conservancy, the Northwest Institute of Botany under the joint administration of the CAS and Shaanxi Province, the Shaanxi Provincial Academy of Agricultural Sciences and the Shaanxi Provincial Academy of Forestry. The new institution is called the Northwest Agricultural and Forestry Science and Technology University, to give its full name.

The NWAFU is now jointly administered by the Ministry of Education and the Shaanxi Province, and it reports to the Ministry of Education on important and strategic issues and to the Shaanxi Provincial Government on operational and routine business, with fiscal appropriations from the Ministry of Education, the Ministry of Science and Technology, the Ministry of Water Conservancy, the State Administration of Forestry, the Chinese Academy of Sciences and Shaanxi Province. In June 2004, the NWAFU was included in Project 98/5, as one of the second group of universities privileged to benefit from this national elite university scheme that aims to raise a small number of China's leading institutions to world-class standing.

The Rural Location

Among all our case study universities, the NWAFU is the only one that is not located in a city, nor even in a suburban area. Rather, it is in a small rural town named Yangling. Yangling is situated on the plains of the Wei River, roughly 80 kilometres to the west of Xi'an, the capital city of Shaanxi Province. As early as 4,000 years ago, Hou Ji (后稷), the first high-ranking official in charge of agriculture in Chinese history, taught people how to grow crops here, giving Yangling the reputation of being the birthplace of China's agricultural civilization. In the years following the establishment of National Northwest Junior College of Agriculture and Forestry in 1934, and especially after 1949, the central and provincial governments established a number of teaching and research institutions in the fields of agriculture, forestry and water conservancy in Yangling. By the late 1990s, there were ten such institutions, including two universities, five research institutes and three junior colleges. This meant there were close to 5,000 teaching faculty and researchers, specializing in nearly 70 disciplinary fields related to agriculture, forestry and water conservancy in this rural town of about 4 square kilometres in size!

Also some important contributions were made by scholars such as Zhao Hongzhang (赵洪章), who worked closely with farmers and developed a new strain of high quality wheat, which doubled productivity. Altogether four of the six new strains of wheat developed since 1949 had been researched here,[3] and there was great pride over this among students, faculty and leaders.

Yangling thus gained the nickname of "City of Agriculture," despite its rural location and poor infrastructure. When one of the authors of this chapter visited Northwest Agricultural University in 1993, it took more than two hours by poorly maintained rural roads to reach the town. For this reason, Yangling suffered severe problems of brain drain after China adopted the policy of reform and opening up, and regional disparities became greater and greater. When Li Lanqing (李岚清), then Vice Premier in charge of science and education, visited Yangling for the first time in 1996, he commented that it could only be called a "Township of Agriculture". Then he started to push for infrastructure development in this place and for mergers among universities, colleges and research

---

[3] Interview with Zhao Zhong, Executive Vice-President, 20 May 2008; Niu, Hongtai, *Hua Shuo Yangling* (*Illustrating Yangling with Pictures*) (Yangling, China: NWAFU Press, 2004).

institutes, such as the one that led to the founding of the NWAFU in 1999.

In 1997 the Yangling High Tech Agriculture Demonstration District was established, as a testing ground for new agriculture technology and techniques. The District is jointly sponsored by 19 central ministries and Shaanxi Province, and now hosts the China Agricultural Fair every year in early November. In 2004, the Chinese Agriculture History Museum broke ground on the NWAFU campus, which has firmly engraved Yangling's name into the history of China's agricultural civilization. As a footnote to this infrastructural development, Yangling now has the appearance of a beautifully maintained modern town, with wide avenues and no traffic jams – it can be reached in forty minutes from the Xi'An airport on a smoothly paved four-lane highway.

The Merger: Successes and Problems

The merger resulting in the NWAFU's establishment was extraordinary, in terms of its scope and complexity. Up to now, this is still the only case of a higher education merger involving universities and research institutes of the Chinese Academy of Sciences. In the Chinese context, such a merger could only be possible with the central government's determined intervention. Indeed, it was initiated, guided and pushed by the government. Prior to, during and after the merger, Li Lanqing paid seven visits to Yangling, and involved himself in even the smallest details of the process.[4] Financial incentives were also offered. When the merger took place, the State Development and Reform Commission established an "appropriation base," in light of the appropriations originally given to the seven independent institutions. The NWAFU's leadership was assured that this "appropriation base" would grow annually at 15% for the first three years after the merger.[5] In addition, they were offered a start-up fund of 600 million *yuan* RMB, over a certain timeline, with 400 million coming from the central government, and the remaining 200 million from the Shaanxi provincial government.[6]

In spite of the fact that the merger was mostly planned from above, most people we talked with during our visit expressed positive feelings about it. The first thing they would mention was the NWAFU's inclusion in Project 98/5, which took place in 2004. This wouldn't have been possi-

---

[4] Interview with Zhao Zhong, Executive Vice-President, 19 May 2008.
[5] *Ibid.*
[6] *Ibid.*; Interview with Wang Ge, Vice President & Vice Party Secretary, 20 May 2008.

ble for either Northwest Agricultural University or Northwest Forestry College, if they had remained stand-alone institutions. Up to the point of merger in 1999, Northwest Forestry College didn't even have a single doctoral program, which meant it was far from being qualified for either of the elite university schemes. In 2005, the NWAFU joined Project 21/1, which makes it the only Chinese university that joined Project 98/5 first and Project 21/1 later. Given that the former is more prestigious and selective than the latter, this was most unusual and is another piece of evidence that the NWAFU benefited fundamentally from the merger. The merger also brought together a large number of research staff, which has greatly strengthened the NWAFU's research capacity, not only in terms of the critical mass of researchers but also the concomitant inter-disciplinary opportunities. This is evident in the more than eight fold increase in research income between 1999 and 2007.

Nevertheless, as one would expect, the merger was not entirely a success story, but had shortcomings and problems as well. To run a university formed by a combination of seven formerly independent institutions certainly brings huge challenges to the leadership. Furthermore, these institutions used to report to very different authorities, and had quite different mandates. Consequently, the Ministry of Education and Shaanxi Province decided to bring in new leaders from outside. A vice governor of Shaanxi Province was appointed the inaugural President of the NWAFU, and a senior official of the CPC Shaanxi Provincial Committee was appointed the Party Secretary.

At the faculty level, the NWAFU has a unique profile, with one half of faculty members teaching courses and the other half expected only to do research and be responsible for knowledge mobility or disseminating agricultural knowledge and research products to famers. When the retirement boom hit a few years after the merger, the NWAFU suffered from a structural shortage of teaching faculty, in particular those who could teach foundation courses. With respect to curricular integration, though some inter-disciplinary opportunities did emerge, as seen in the formation of a School of Life Sciences, genuine integration is still more a matter of rhetoric than reality. This can be clearly seen in the existence of separate schools of agriculture and forestry, which exactly parallel the former stand-alone institutions, Northwest Agricultural University and Northwest Forestry College, and indicates that the a clear segregation in curricular offerings still exists. Vice President Wang Ge explained that the continuity expressed in this arrangement was largely for the sake of accommodating the existing faculty and their knowledge structure. It would take another 20-30 years to truly integrate the faculty and curricular offerings from the two institutions, he asserted.[7]

The "Western China Development" Scheme

The merger also coincided with the central government's "Western China Development" (西部大開發) Scheme and needs to be understood in that context. Under the leadership of Deng Xiaoping, China began to reform its economy in 1978, with a dramatic change from a command economy to a market economy. The coastal regions of Eastern China benefited greatly from these reforms, and their economies quickly raced ahead. The Western half of China, however, lagged seriously behind. Against this backdrop, the Chinese leadership announced in mid-1999 that a campaign to open up the West would start at the beginning of 2000. The stated goals were the social and economic development of the interior and Western regions of China, now seen as having become unacceptably disadvantaged by the growth strategy of the previous 20 years. The main components of the strategy included the development of infrastructure (transport, hydropower plants, energy, and telecommunications), efforts to entice foreign investment, increased attention to ecological protection (such as reforestation), the promotion of education, and the retention of talent that had been flowing out to richer provinces. In April of 2000, shortly after its founding, the NWAFU hosted a Ministry of Education symposium on higher education strategy for "Western China Development," which involved 50 national universities under the direct jurisdiction of the Ministry.

This policy covers 6 provinces (Gansu, Guizhou, Qinghai, Shaanxi, Sichuan, and Yunnan), 5 autonomous regions (Guangxi, Inner Mongolia, Ningxia, Tibet, and Xinjiang), and 1 municipality (Chongqing). If we consider Shaanxi Province alone, it used to benefit from the "Third Front" (三線建設) strategy of the 1960s and 1970s in the command economy,[8] which led to central government investment in coal mining, electricity production, defence industries (particularly aerospace and electronics), precision machinery, building materials and metallurgy.

---

[7] Interview with Wang Ge, Vice President & Vice Party Secretary, 20 May 2008.
[8] "Third Front" regional development policy of the late 1960s and early 1970s sought to develop a military-industrial heartland away from the PRC's Northern borders and Eastern coastline.

However, this tradition of State support for many of Shaanxi's industries had not prepared it for the challenges of a market economy in the 1980s. Shaanxi fell behind the growth experienced elsewhere, particularly that of China's Eastern provinces. Its share in national investments dropped from over 4.5% in the late 1970s to 1.7% in the 1990s. In 1978 and 1990, the per capita disposable net income of its urban residents was 10% below China's average, but by 1998 this gap had more than doubled. The rural income gap widened from parity with the country as a whole in 1978 to 22% lower in 1990 and 35% lower in 1998. Between 1990 and 1998, Shaanxi's industrial output value (in comparable prices) grew at a rate 24% lower than that of the whole country.[9]

From this overview of the context and the NWAFU's own history, we can see how the move to mass higher education coincided with a period of new opportunities in the region, as the central government began its determined effort to improve infrastructure and attract investment to the Northwest region. It also shows the particular attention given to agriculture and higher agricultural education, which has some parallels with the policies on normal universities, which also have not been encouraged to be involved in mergers with other types of institutions.[10] Nevertheless, an increasing number of agricultural institutions, in particular those located in coastal areas, can not resist the benefits coming with comprehensive university status, in terms of raising their profile.[11] With China's progress in industrialization and the advent of a knowledge-based economy, agriculture or farming, the so-called first industry, has little attraction and is often associated with poor technology and productivity. Consequently, agricultural institutions tend to have a lower status and are seen to cater mostly to rural students. This situation presents both opportunities and difficulties for the NWAFU, a theme we will deal with in later sections in this chapter.

---

[9] Eduard B. Vermeer, "Shaanxi: Building a Future on State Support," in *The China Quarterly*, No.178, 2004, pp.400-425.
[10] Liu Haifeng, "Yuanxiao Hebing Shenge Yyu Fazhan Zhong De Gengming Wenti (Name Alterations in the Case of Higher Education Institutional Mergers and Upgrading)," in *Gaodeng Jiaoyu Yanjiu (Journal of Higher Education)*, Vol.26, No.11, 2005, pp.21-26.
[11] *Ibid.*; "Nongye Daxue De Hebing Yu Gengming (Mergers and Name Alterations of agricultural universities)," *Guang Ming Daily*, July 31, 2008.

NWAFU Moves to Mass Higher Education: An Empirical Overview
Growth in Student Enrollments, 1990-2005

In 1990, undergraduate enrollment in both Northwest Agricultural University and Northwest Forestry College totaled less than 4,000. This number grew to 7,442 in 1999, when the merger happened. Afterwards, enrollments started to soar, reaching 12,150 in 2000, and 17,490 in 2005. No wonder when we interviewed Wang Guodong, the Director of Teaching Affairs, he responded that, among the top-ranking universities in China, the NWAFU had been one of the few truly committed to mass higher education.[12] Meanwhile, the NWAFU has also witnessed rapid growth in its graduate enrollment, as a particular result of the merger with five research institutes, some of which had already been enrolling graduate students. Table 11.1 shows that the year 2000 marked a dramatic increase in both undergraduate and graduate recruitment, by 44.3% and 73.6% respectively. Afterwards undergraduate enrollment increased steadily at 5.3% annually, while graduate enrollment rose significantly in 2003 and 2004, around the time when the NWAFU made its way into Project 98/5, and in general at an annual rate of 42.4%, much faster than that of undergraduate enrollment. In 2003, the Ministry of Education approved the establishment of a School of Graduate Studies in the NWAFU.

Table 11.1: The NWAFU Recruitment Size, 1990-2007

Year	Undergraduate Intake	Graduate Intake
1990	804	109
1995	1113	159
1999	2777	280
2000	4008	486
2001	4000	601
2002	4576	723
2003	4633	1043
2004	4932	1440
2005	5106	1569
2006	5374	1814
2007	5485	1929

The NWAFU's pattern of enrollment expansion has a remarkable parallel to China's move to mass higher education as a whole. By 2008, it had an enrollment of 26,885 students, among whom were 20,943 undergraduates, 4,624 master's students, and 1,318 doctoral students. In many

---

[12] Interview with Wang Guodong, Director of Teaching Affairs, 19 May 2008.

ways, the NWAFU reminds us of a multiversity-type approach to mass higher education. It is large in size, has become more and more comprehensive in curricular provision, while retaining its historic focus on agriculture, and provides conditions for the integration of elite and mass higher education. At this point we should point to the university's full name in Chinese, which is difficult to translate smoothly into English: Northwest Agricultural and Forestry Science and Technology University. The addition of *ke ji* (科技), science and technology, to its title in Chinese has expressed the intention of broadening the curriculum that is evident in many of its programs.

The multiversity approach has also had implications for gender and socio-economic-status (SES) as well. Traditionally, agricultural institutions in China have recruited a predominance of male students from rural areas. While this tendency is still evident at the NWAFU, with rural male students constituting 60% of the annual intake, a change can be observed in recent years both in gender and SES profiles. On one hand, the enrollment of female students appears to be on the rise, from 39.4% in 2005 to 42.8% in 2007, as shown in Table 11.2,[13] possibly resulting partly from the addition of some humanities and social sciences programs. On the other, more urban students seem to be attracted to the NWAFU, from 37.9% in 2005 to 40.7% in 2007, due to its rising status, marked in particular by its acceptance into Project 98/5 in 2004.

Table 11.2: Gender and SES Profile of the NWAFU New Enrollment (%), 2005-2007

	Gender Profile		SES Profile	
	Male	Female	Urban	Rural
2005	60.6	39.4	37.9	62.1
2006	59.9	40.1	38.1	61.9
2007	57.2	42.8	40.7	59.3

Given the continuing high enrollment of rural students it was interesting to learn that 46% of students were given some kind of financial assistance and there were also work opportunities on campus for needy students. The Deputy Director of Student Affairs noted that fully 40% of students at the NWAFU came from extremely poor rural family back-

---

[13] In 1990, female enrollment in Northwest Agricultural University had been under 10% – we were told by Hua Xiaofeng, Deputy Director of Student Affairs, interviewed on 19 May 2008.

grounds, while the norm at engineering universities would be around 20%.[14]

The Curricular Profile

When founded on the basis of a major merger, the NWAFU re-organized the existing teaching and research programs across the seven formerly independent institutions, with many overlapping or duplicated programs, into 16 teaching units, namely the School of Agronomy, the School of Plant Protection, the School of Horticulture, the School of Animal Sciences, the School of Food Sciences and Engineering, the School of Enology, the School of Forestry, the School of Water Resources and Architectural Engineering, the School of Resources and Environment, the School of Mechanical and Electrical Engineering, the School of Information Engineering, the School of Life Sciences, the School of Sciences, the School of Economics and Management, the School of Humanities, and the Department of Foreign Languages. It is clear that the NWAFU set up programs initially around its traditional strengths, namely dryland farming, water-saving irrigation, wheat breeding, integrated management of soil and water erosion on the Loess Plateau and biotechnology, and then started to extend its curricular coverage to fields such as mechanical and electrical engineering, information engineering as well as some humanities and social sciences.

The merger apparently opened some multi-disciplinary windows, and the NWAFU has been offering an increasing number of undergraduate programs ever since, 31 programs in 1999, 34 in 2000, 40 in 2001, 49 in 2002, 55 in 2003, and 59 in 2004. Among the 28 undergraduate programs added between 2000 and 2004 are such multi- or inter-disciplinary programs as geographic information system, food quality and safety,[15] enology (wine) engineering, breeding science and engineering, agricultural infrastructure science and engineering, as well as such humanities and social sciences programs as fine arts design, business administration, public administration, tourism management, international economics and trade and electronic commerce. Now, the School of Humanities offers programs in law studies and sociology; the School of Economics and Management offers programs in accounting, finance,

---

[14] *Ibid*.

[15] The need for this kind of program became evident with the tainted milk scandal that broke out in 2008.

land resource management, business administration, public administration and tourism management; and the Department of Foreign Languages offers programs in English and international economics and trade. These new and non-traditional programs in an agricultural university would certainly have some impact on gender and urban/rural diversity in the student population, also on the campus culture and ethos.

By 2005, the NWAFU offered a total of 59 undergraduate programs, covering the broad areas of agriculture, sciences, engineering, economics, management, law and literature, as summarized below in Table 11.3. Executive Vice-President Zhao Zhong explained that there had been a strong intentionality in this development towards comprehensive curriculum. "Without knowledge support from other disciplines, agricultural programs can't excel alone," he commented.[16]

Table 11.3: Disciplinary Patterns of the NWAFU Undergraduate Programs, 2005

Disciplinary Fields	Number	Percentage
Agriculture	13	22.03
Sciences	8	13.56
Engineering	23	39.98
Economics	3	5.08
Management	8	13.56
Law	2	3.39
Literature	2	3.39
Total	59	100.00

The Financial Profile

In many senses, the merger that led to the establishment of the NWAFU was both initiated and pushed by the central government, which provided significant financial incentives. This is evident in the growth of the NWAFU's revenue ever since the merger. Prior to the merger in 1999, the total amount of revenue available to both Northwest Agricultural University and Northwest Forestry College was RMB 101.9 million *yuan*. This number has risen significantly since 2000, as detailed in Table 11.4.

In the eight years following the merger, the NWAFU enjoyed close to an eight-and-a-half fold increase in revenue, a 105.4% annual rate of increase! Table 11.4 also shows that the increased revenue has come largely from enriched governmental support through budgeted appropriations also that a revenue boom in 2004 coincided with the NWAFU's

---

[16] Interview with Zhao Zhong, Executive Vice-President, 19 May 2008.

Table 11.4: The NWAFU's Revenues and Proportion of Budgeted Appropriations, 2000-2007 (in RMB million *yuan*)

Year	Total Revenue	Proportion of Budgeted Appropriations
2000	143.0	80.8
2001	366.9	83.7
2002	540.3	80.0
2003	613.6	78.7
2004	746.1	74.4
2005	573.3	80.5
2006	695.8	78.1
2007	859.3	78.5

entry into Project 98/5. With this increasing financial capacity, the NWAFU could afford some large-scale infrastructure development. In 2004, its International Center was opened, a complex that houses the university administration and a new library, and that cost RMB 600 million *yuan*. It is now a landmark, not only on the NWAFU campus, but also for Yangling as a whole.

Photo 11.2: The International Center on the NWAFU's South Campus

Among the nine public universities profiled in this book, the NWAFU has probably enjoyed the greatest rate of revenue increase in the period under examination, and definitely the highest proportion of governmental support in its revenue. This of course indicates its inability to generate significant revenue from other sources, which may be attributed to its rural location. This funding pattern is also reflected in its profile of research grants. Research funds rose dramatically, from a pre-merger level of 18.4 million *yuan* in 1999 to 36.6 million in 2000, 134.3 million in 2005 and 155.7 million in 2007, an over eight fold increase in eight years. However, this increase reflects an increasing proportion drawn from State research funds, compared to those brought in by contract efforts or horizontal sources, from 52.9% in 2000 to 85.5% in 2005 and 79.6% in 2007.[17]

The Faculty Profile

We can see that the NWAFU has been struggling to develop its faculty, on both dimensions of quantity and quality. On the quantity dimension, faculty numbers grew from 1,013 in 2000 to 1,568 in 2005, a 54.8% increase. This appears to keep pace with the undergraduate enrollment expansion of 44.0% over the same period, yet the fact that many new teachers used to be researchers in the research institutes that were merged into the NWAFU has created a problem. Most of these faculty members can teach specialized courses well, but not necessarily foundation courses. On the quality dimension, we looked at two parameters: the professional rank and the proportion of PhD holders. Table 11.5 shows that, over the years, the NWAFU has maintained an increasingly experienced faculty, with 45.9% of them in the senior professional ranks of full and associate professors by 2005, compared to 41.6% in 2000 when the NWAFU was established.

Table 11.5: The NWAFU Faculty Development, 2000 vs. 2005

		2000	2005
Professional Rank	Full Professor	138 (13.6%)	268 (17.1%)
	Associate Professor	284 (28.0%)	451 (28.8%)
	Lecturer	331 (32.7%)	558 (35.6%)
	Assistant Lecturer	260 (25.7%)	291 (18.6%)
PhD Holder		206 (20.3%)	285 (18.2%)

Yet, the proportion of PhD holders declined over the same period, which indicates the struggle in attracting and keeping talent, mostly caused by the serious disadvantage of location, in the Northwest region and in a rural area. In its first two years, the NWAFU conferred a total of 95 doctoral degrees, yet the majority of degree holders chose to work elsewhere and the few who stayed to teach were faculty members who had pursued in-service doctoral studies.[18] Given this circumstance, the

---

[17] Interview with Wu Pute, Vice President, 20 May 2008.
[18] Zhang Guangqiang, "Quanmian Tuidong Gaoshuiping Daxue Jianshe Jincheng," (Fully push forward the Process of Building a High Profile University), in

NWAFU adopted the policy of encouraging its own junior faculty to pursue doctoral studies. Between 2002 and 2005, a total of 579 current faculty members enrolled in in-service doctoral programs.[19] After the completion of these programs, the NWAFU's ratio of faculty holding PhDs is expected to rise significantly. A downside of this trend, which cannot be avoided, is the problem of inbreeding. Between 80% and 90% of the NWAFU faculty are either its own graduates or local natives.

Vision and Strategic Directions

Vision

Basically, two events have caused the NWAFU's leadership to think through its vision: its inclusion in Project 98/5 in 2004 and its experience with the Ministry of Education's undergraduate program evaluation in 2005. These events required medium- to long-term strategic planning, and stimulated efforts to redefine the university's identity and goals. Both VPs Zhao Zhong and Wu Pute described to us in plain language the NWAFU's vision for the next 15 years: 1) to formulate its own unique niche, 2) to become irreplaceable in certain specific fields, 3) to foster integration among production, learning and research (產學研一體化), and 4) to achieve world-class standing based on comprehensive strengths.

We understand that the first goal focuses on the education programs, that is to nurture high end talent in the agricultural and forestry fields, broadly defined. The second goal relates more to research, with the aim of bringing its research edge up to international standards in the seven areas of soil science, agricultural soil and water engineering, plant pathology, clinical veterinary medicine, genetic crop breeding, animal genetic breeding, and soil and water conservation and desertification control. The third goal stresses service, something closely linked to the NWAFU's tradition and its geographical location. Teaching and research have always been closely linked to the needs for local and regional development, with knowledge mobility and dissemination to the production sector having great importance. Based on these goals, the NWAFU is seeking to become a world-class university.

Sun Wuxue (ed.), *Xibei Nong Lin Keji Daxue Jiaoyu Sixiang Wenxuan* (*An Anthology of Educational Concepts of NWAFU*), Yangling, China: NWAFU Press, 2005.

[19] Zhao Zhong (ed.), *Xibei Nong Lin Keji Daxue Benke Jiaoxue Gongzuo Pinggu Tansuo Yu Shijian* (*NWAFU Undergraduate Program Evaluation Reflection and Practice*), Yangling, China: NWAFU Press, 2007.

The NWAFU has come up with a strategic plan to achieve these goals in two phases. In Phase One (1999-2010), its leaders are seeking to put in place an operational model that fosters a close integration among teaching, research and production, which enables it to excel as China's leading education base for high end agricultural and forestry talent, the leading innovation base for high technology in arid and semi-arid agriculture, the leading dissemination and demonstration base for modern agricultural science and technology products, and also an international exchange and cooperation base for agricultural research and education. In Phase Two (2011-2020), the aim is to benchmark the NWAFU's performance in these four dimensions – education, innovation, dissemination and internationalization – to world-class standards, and become an internationally high profile university featuring a close integration of teaching, research and production.

In the first four years after its founding in 1999, the NWAFU suffered from the lack of a clear strategic direction. The discussions and debates over the model it should aspire to stretched from "a multi-disciplinary teaching-focused university" with a core curricular coverage in the fields of agriculture, forestry and water conservancy to "a comprehensive university" with the same core curricular coverage, then to "one of China's top teaching-research-balanced universities with a high international profile" and offering the same core curriculum, and "a major research university" offering this core curriculum. Finally, in the first assembly of the NWAFU CPC Committee in September 2004, it was announced that the NWAFU would strive to be an internationally renowned research-intensive university featuring a close integration of teaching, research and production by 2020.

So, we can see that the NWAFU's aspirations grew as it explored the strategic directions it might take, from a multi-disciplinary teaching-focused university to a comprehensive research-intensive university. However, there has been a deliberate commitment to maintaining the core curriculum in its traditional areas of disciplinary strength, and use the integration of teaching, research and production as a way of imprinting its traditional disciplinary strengths into its institutional character. This may also turn its disadvantage in location into an advantage, where there are favorable conditions in terms of connecting its teaching and research activities in applied fields of agriculture, forestry and water conservancy to the actual agricultural production needs of the locality, and indeed of rural areas across China, through the Yangling High Tech Agriculture Demonstration District.

The Integration of Production, Learning and Research: Forming the University Character

The NWAFU has been diligently using the process of university character formation as a means of re-organizing its internal structure into an organic one. Prior to the merger, Northwest Agricultural University and Northwest Forestry College represented a typical approach to knowledge modeled on the outdated Soviet patterns adopted in 1952, an approach which not only hindered inter-disciplinary cooperation but also segregated teaching and research. Universities based on this model normally committed to teaching, while research activities were allocated to stand-alone research institutes. The merger provided the NWAFU the opportunity of not only integrating teaching and research but also creating close links between both of these and production. Among the five research institutes that were merged into the NWAFU, the two local ones, namely Shaanxi Provincial Academy of Agricultural Sciences and Shaanxi Provincial Academy of Forestry, were more engaged in the dissemination of agricultural knowledge than pure research. Therefore, the NWAFU faculty can be roughly divided into three streams: teaching, research and knowledge mobility.

As a result, the NWAFU's approach to integrating production, learning and research is quite different from that of other Chinese universities. Many universities interpret this integration as a matter of registering patents and running affiliated enterprises, such as Peking University's Founder Group (方正集團). However, the NWAFU's disciplinary strength and location don't allow for such an approach. Instead, they stress providing services for agricultural production in the broadest sense. Since 2000, the NWAFU has set up 45 rural agricultural knowledge show rooms, 37 agricultural expert centers, and 14 agricultural technology demonstration zones. These show rooms, centers and demonstration zones are all targeted at the major agricultural products in Shaanxi Province and Northwest China, and they have formed a service network that starts from Yangling, covers Shaanxi and the whole Northwest of China, and even extends to the rest of the country in some areas.

Internationalization: Identifying Peer Models

Along with the integration of teaching, research and production, internationalization was announced as a second major development strategy in the NWAFU's first CPC assembly in September 2004. It is quite symbolic that the NWAFU's senior administrative offices are actually housed in the building labeled the International Center. Over the years since 1999, the NWAFU has developed linkages with a couple of dozen counterparts in Europe and North America. Among them, two universities appear to hold the greatest appeal and inspiration: Wageningen University in the Netherlands and Cornell University in the US.

There are many similarities between Wageningen and Yangling. It is a historical town in the central part of the Netherlands. In 1918 the town acquired its first institution of higher education, Landbouwhoge School Wageningen, which later became Wageningen University, an internationally famed university specializing in the life sciences. The university's achievements led to this small historical town developing into a modern technological community, a process which still continues today. Wageningen has become the center of Food Valley, which is commonly regarded as the largest food and nutrition Research & Development cluster in the world. The university and its associated institutes, which have been consolidated into Wageningen University and Research Center (WUR), form the research and higher education core, which consists of Wageningen University, the Van Hall-Larenstein School of Higher Professional Education, and the former agricultural research institutes from the Dutch Ministry of Agriculture. The city has around 35,000 inhabitants, of which many thousands are students; the WUR alone employs about 8,000 people.

Anther peer model for the NWAFU is Cornell University, located in the small town of Ithaca in upper New York State. Agriculture was a major catalyst for Cornell University's creation in 1865. The University's New York State College of Agriculture and Life Sciences is considered by many to be the top school of agriculture-related sciences in the world. With about 3,100 undergraduate and 1,000 graduate students enrolled, it is the second-largest undergraduate college at Cornell, and the only school of agriculture in the Ivy League. Its vision echoes that of the NWAFU in many aspects: "[T]hrough teaching, research, and extension ... we strive to improve the nation's food supply and maintain its safety, to enhance the environment, and to help people improve their lives."

Since 2007, the NWAFU has created a Yangling International Agri-Science Forum as part of the China Agricultural Fair, and as a permanent platform for its international academic exchange and cooperation. Its inaugural forum, held from November 5 to 7, 2007, focused on the theme of "International Agriculture Cooperation, Innovation and Development." It attracted scientists from Australia, USA, Canada, Japan, Hungary and China for in-depth and extensive discussions on dryland farming and water-saving agriculture, high-efficiency animal husbandry and disease prevention and control, food science and safety, environmental protection and sustainable development. The 2007 Forum agreed on a declaration that goes as: "global warming, ecological environment deterioration ... have rendered an increasing intimate interrelationship within agricultural industries worldwide. So it is getting more imperative and beneficial to strengthen international cooperation and exchanges among agricultural scientists and research institutions." "The Yangling International Agri-Science Forum has provided us an ideal platform for our co-operation and exchange in the future."[20] The 2008 and 2009 Forums are respectively entitled "Circular Agriculture: Science, Technology and Policy" and "Rural development: Science and Technology, Finance and Policy."

The Governance Model of the NWAFU

The NWAFU's merger would not have been possible without strong intervention from the central government, as has been noted earlier. The result is a rather unusual governance model. Normally the Party Secretary has the highest authority in Chinese universities under the system known as a "Presidential Responsibility System under the Leadership of the Party Committee." Because so many different authorities were involved in the establishment of the NWAFU it was decided that all leaders of the institutions contributing to the merger would be given early retirement and a high profile figure would be named the first president. This was Chen Zongxing, then Vice Governor of Shaanxi Province. The Party Secretary, Sun Wuxue, was also appointed from outside and took on important academic leadership roles in a situation where the President only came to the campus a few times each year, due to his obligations as Vice Governor. After four years under this arrangement, Party Secretary Sun Wuxue was appointed President in

---

[20] "Declaration of Yangling International Agri-Science Forum," accessed December 10, 2009, http://gjc.nwsuaf.edu.cn/guojihuiyi/yanglingxuanyan.php.

2003, indicating the continuing high status of the Presidency in relation to the university's Party leadership.

In other ways, the governance model was fairly similar to that which has been described in the case of Peking University in Chapter Three. The Party Standing Committee meets twice a month, and is responsible for decisions in the three important areas of budget, personnel and major projects. The Presidential Committee meets once a week, and is responsible for all major academic decisions. Another important academic body now under formation is a committee of senior professors which will oversee the committees already established for decision making on degree granting, curricular development and the appointment of doctoral supervisors.[21]

Faculty and Student Perspectives on Teaching and Learning

We conducted four focus group meetings in total, in the Schools of Agronomy, Animal Science, Food Science and Humanities. Unlike in other case study universities where we did faculty and student focus group meetings separately, we were asked to organize these meetings in the different schools, with a mixture of faculty and students attending in each school. This seemed to reflect considerable interest among faculty and students in taking part in our project. In total, 15 faculty members, 14 graduate students and 15 undergraduates participated in our four focus group meetings, and we will present their perspectives under different headings. In general, all believed that the massification of Chinese higher education was a positive move, benefitting students greatly, though presenting a challenge to the university itself. We believe this has to do with the fact that a majority of students in the NWAFU come from rural backgrounds. Without the policy of massification, many would not have had the chance to come to this campus.

Faculty Perspectives

Most faculty members participating in our focus meetings shared the perspective that the students are the major beneficiary of the mass higher education policy. Now 45% of secondary school leavers have access to higher education nationwide, while this number is even higher, at around 50%, for Shaanxi Province, given the fact that this province had a critical mass of higher institutions established to serve the Northwest

---

[21] Interview with Wang Ge, Vice President & Vice Party Secretary, 21 May 2008.

Region under the planning system of the 1950s. Some viewed this policy as paralleling the one that had restored university entrance examinations some 30 years earlier, another milestone marking the historical development of Chinese higher education. They felt that they themselves owed a huge debt of gratitude to Deng Xiaoping, who had opened up higher education to them in the late 1970s, after the end of the Cultural Revolution decade, while current students should be grateful to this mass higher education policy, they asserted. Nevertheless, they expressed concern over quality issues, while observing that some remedial actions have been taken. In the next paragraph we share some direct quotations from our meetings with them.

> "There is a tension between enrollment expansion and university capacity. The expansion happened too fast, and the university has had to cope with it in a rushed way, without adequate facilities and with enormous pressure being put on teachers. Classes are now scheduled in afternoons, evenings and Saturdays, while in the past they were mainly in the morning."[22] "The State is making constant efforts to solve these problems, for example, by providing loans for the university to expand its facilities and by imposing program evaluations (the monitoring mechanism put in place by the Ministry of Education to halt the decline in the quality of teaching)."[23] "Graduate students now have to work in professors' offices at night, as there is no space provided for them. Fortunately, however, full professors now have private offices, while associate professors and lecturers have shared offices with two and four in each respectively, a change from the past when they did not have offices at all."[24]

Many of the faculty members echoed the NWAFU's motto of honesty (誠), austerity (樸), courage (勇), and perseverance (毅), when describing the university culture and ethos. They attributed the resonance of these values to the NWAFU's location and the composition of the student body: it is close to the rural countryside and a majority of the students come from rural villages. This location adds to the sense of the importance of connecting teaching and research to agricultural production and rural development, and the feeling that they have a real

---

[22] School of Agronomy Faculty & Students Focus Group meeting on 20 May 2008.
[23] School of Animal Sciences Faculty & Students Focus Group meeting on 20 May 2008.
[24] *Ibid.*

influence in the local area. Many students who come from rural areas and understand rural life have a strong sense of purpose regarding the need to improve rural life, and a deep emotional commitment to their studies. They mentioned the huge historic staircase, leading to the gate of the NWAFU's North Campus, the original campus of Northwest Agricultural University which goes back to 1934. This long flight of steps is divided into five parts to match the university's culture and ethos: the 93 small steps represent the 93 counties of Shaanxi province, and the 5 big sections of steps correspond to the five administrative entities (three provinces and two autonomous regions – Shaanxi, Gansu, Qinghai, Ningxia and Xinjiang) of the Northwest China Region. All these steps exemplify the honesty, austerity, courage, and perseverance that are part of an ethos of pursuing knowledge in order to better serve the agricultural production and rural development of Northwest China.

Photo 11.3: The Long Staircase with 93 Steps in Five Sections in Front of the NWAFU's North Campus Gate, the Original Campus of Northwest Agricultural University

Though sharing a sense that their participation in governance is limited to the school/department level in matters of curricular development and reform, most faculty members were aware of the NWAFU's strategic directions, and strongly endorsed the approach of integrating production, learning and research (產學研). They cited it as a strategy that inspires teaching reform, and encourages a lot of experimentation with ongoing changes in the content of teaching that respond to changes in rural society. Related to this strategy, there is a high demand on teachers to really understand basic rural villages and to develop applied knowledge.

Another theme that came up particularly in the focus group discussion with faculty in the School of Agronomy was the learning style of Chinese students, and how the study of agriculture highlighted differences between China and the West in student learning. Chinese students may at first appear to be passive and to lack ideas of their own, but in fact it takes them time to digest new knowledge and to respond with questions and critical comments. Nevertheless, they do have well developed ideas of their own, and in the circumstances of mass higher education they are being given more and more opportunities to take an active role in the learning process. The fact that so much of what they learn has to be tested in practice in rural environments is a positive feature of their campus culture. The discussion with this group of faculty and students on learning styles reflected much of the recent literature on the paradox of the Chinese learner.[25]

A related theme was the applicability of the teaching and research on dryland agriculture in Northwest China to the needs of developing countries. The Associate Dean of the School of Agronomy had spent a year in Ethiopia under a project sponsored by China's Ministry of Agriculture, and he was proud of the fact that a number of faculty and graduate students had had opportunities to serve in both Africa and Latin America. Another faculty member made the point that China is now in a leading position in the world with important discoveries having been made in rice and wheat cultivation which have much to contribute, and this can be seen as a kind of sharing of Chinese civilization on a very practical level. A student commented at this juncture that it was great to meet international students on campus, not only from the West but from other developing countries and that he would particularly like the opportunity to go to a developing country.

Student Perspectives

The generally positive feeling expressed by students towards mass higher education had not erased their sense of struggle in some specific

---

[25] School of Agronomy faculty and students focus group meeting on 20 May 2008; Wing On Lee and Magdalena Mo Ching Mok (eds.), *Construction and Deconstruction of the Chinese Learner: Implications for Learning Theories* (United Kingdom: Routledge, 2008).

areas of concern. Some shared with us their observation of credential inflation. Not long ago, in the context of elite higher education, a university degree was sufficient to open up opportunities for a decent career. With the mass system now in place, a graduate degree has become essential for the same purpose. And even when one catches up with the currents and becomes a doctoral degree holder, one may find dim employment prospect. Unlike in the West, the industry sector in China is not ready to hire a large number of doctoral degree holders. We interpret these student comments as reflecting the over-education phenomenon that has emerged with the massification of Chinese higher education, and a possible concomitant waste of both education and human resources.

The students also expressed their frustration over the mismatch between the rigid study program patterns inherited from the planned economy and an ever changing job market corresponding to economic change and the inroads of globalization:

> "I'd suggest curricular offerings should not focus on nurturing research-type talents only, what I would call bookworms, but on providing appropriate knowledge for those who want other types of jobs in society. A mass higher education institution should prepare talent for all kinds of jobs, and thus a lot more elective courses should be made available to us."[26] "In the context of mass higher education, students should be taught in the light of their aptitudes, and allowed more opportunities to transfer among departments and disciplinary fields, which is not the case at present. Now we students often have to go on to graduate programs, if we wish to transfer to another field, which is very hard. A well-intended policy must pay attention to detail in its implementation."[27]

Some students did mention an initiative that tried to break these barriers, that is the Yu Youren College, which we learnt about also in our interview with Wang Guodong, Director of the Office of Teaching Affairs. It is actually an experiment in nurturing the most creative minds. A certain number of highly promising students, based on the scores they have obtained in the national university entrance examination and personal expressions of intention, are brought in with a special status as members of the elite Yu Youren College, named after the famous educator who founded the university's predecessor in the 1930s. In the first

---

[26] School of Agronomy faculty and students focus group meeting on 20 May 2008.
[27] Ibid.

two years, they take foundational courses only, and in the third year, they begin to be separated into designated groupings. So far, the NWAFU has two such groupings that are included in the State plan: plant science and economics and management. Two more groupings – animal science and food processing – are self-financed. Those who can survive and perform well in these three years will be put on a fast track for graduate studies, while those who do less well will be kept in their chosen field, take specialized courses in the fourth year and graduate with a bachelor's degree. In total, close to 300 students are now enjoying this sort of individualized educational arrangement, which is geared to bringing their full potential into play. The irony that occurs to us lies in the fact that the very flexibility which a majority of mass higher education students are crying out for has been granted only to a small group of the most elite students.

On other aspects of campus life, the students painted us a colourful picture of various theme-oriented and service-oriented volunteer groups on the campus, whose activities occupied a large proportion of their extracurricular time. They acknowledged that participating in student groups had been a good way of getting to know the wider society, and understanding life outside of the university. At the same time they expressed regret over the fact that many such groups and activities remained rather shallow and superficial, and lacked diversity. Only a few activities were regarded as the exceptions, particularly those of the "three rurals" or 三農 society, which pertains to studies about agriculture (農業), rural village development (農村) and peasants' life (農民), and truly helps urban students to get to know rural areas.

Generally, students believe the massification of Chinese higher education has contributed to the improvement of the overall quality of the Chinese population. This was evident in Chinese people's attitudes and behavior in the face of a series of natural disasters such as the snow storms at the end of 2007 and the catastrophic earthquake in Sichuan in May of 2008, they suggested.

When asked about their sense of campus space and architecture, students immediately pointed to the historic Number Three Teaching Building, which was mentioned also by a number of leaders. (See Photo 11.1) They also expressed a deep attachment to the library on the historic north campus, which had been built in the 1950s. They felt the style of the building was symbolic, including both the original structure, which looks a little like the historic Beijing Railway Station, and the new section that had been added later. They were particularly proud of its huge collection, which was crucial for research. A faculty member also noted that the ground in front of the library was a favorite gathering place where students met for quiet conversations, information sharing and relaxation.

Photo 11.4: The Historic Library on the NWAFU's North campus

Concluding Remarks

When reflecting on the NWAFU's profile within the wider picture of China's move to mass higher education, we thought of the idea of the multiversity. It occurred to us that the NWAFU is taking a multiversity approach in the currents of movement towards mass higher education. Clark Kerr characterizes the multiversity as a "city of infinite variety,"[28] a complex, diverse entity with greatly fractionalized power; the multiversity is massive in size, has many levels, serves diverse populations, and feeds into various societal echelons in the graduates' employment. "As a city, there are many separate endeavors under a single rule of law."[29] The NWAFU is indeed such a city, as it covers and overlaps with the town of Yangling. It has grown dramatically in size, and has come to

---

[28] Clark Kerr, "The Idea of a Multiversity," in Clark Kerr, *The Uses of the University* (Cambridge, Mass.: Harvard University Press, 1982), p.41.
[29] *Ibid*.

embrace the formerly separate functions of seven different institutions as a result of the merger. These characteristics of a multiversity mirror to a large extent the three major constituencies now existing within the NWAFU community: teaching, research and knowledge mobility. If research is perceived a more significant or elite function, teaching addresses explicitly the mass role of higher education, while knowledge mobility connects it directly to agricultural production. Put together, the NWAFU now serves various societal sectors and echelons.

The multiversity concept could be adapted to the present Chinese situation in ways that would reflect a transition to mass higher education characterized by a greater concern for social equity. A crucial parameter is the students' socio-economic background, which points to perhaps the most fundamental issue in terms of social equity. At this point, the notion of disciplinary hierarchy may be relevant. In China's context, there was a clearly recognized hierarchy of prestige by subject area with such fields as agriculture, teacher education, geology, and certain kinds of engineering holding little attraction. Thus they tended to enroll a considerable number of rural students who had little hope of competing for entry to fields such as finance, economics, law, management, trade, and basic humanities and sciences, which are popular among the best urban candidates. Geography has been another determining factor in the hierarchy, with a clearly recognized pecking order from such centers as Beijing and Shanghai to the hinterland. In this sense, the NWAFU, though disadvantaged in terms of its core disciplinary fields and location, has stood the test of social equity, and been seeing notable improvements in gender equality.

Nevertheless, the NWAFU is somehow at a crossroad, as its name indicates. Literally, its name is the Northwest Agricultural and Forestry Science and Technology University, as mentioned earlier. Executive Vice-President Zhao Zhong told us that this name was decided by the central government, denoting both the tradition and the future of the NWAFU.[30] Agriculture and forestry are the NWAFU's traditional strength, and science and technology promise the modernization of China's agronomy. Yet, can the NWAFU stand the opposing pressures of becoming a large-scale comprehensive university while also striving to be a research-intensive one? Though agriculture and forestry are kept at the core of the NWAFU's curricular offerings, its curricular coverage has exhibited the

---

[30] Interview with Zhao Zhong, Executive Vice-President, 20 May 2008.

contours of the comprehensive university. Though research remains a relatively small proportion of the NWAFU's function, yet the influence of this elite function can never be underestimated. It may come to dominate all other sections, given its status and prestige. For instance, faculty are said to have been losing their enthusiasm for teaching, but becoming increasingly interested and engaged in research activities.[31]

When describing the process of transition to mass higher education, Bereday makes the following three points. Firstly, open admission and rapid quantitative expansion need not reduce quality, except possibly in the short term. Secondly, it is not necessary to link enrollments closely with the economy's ability to absorb highly educated talent since a continual upgrading of various positions can be expected with the stimulus of mass higher education. Thirdly, openness is the basic principle, along with a belief that everyone is educable.[32] These points are very relevant to the case of the NWAFU, and seem to hold both opportunity and challenge for the NWAFU down the road.

---

[31] Interview with Wang Guodong, Director of Office of Teaching Affairs, 20 May 2008.
[32] George Bereday, "Chapter 8," in George Bereday, *Universities for All: International Perspectives on Mass Higher Education* (San Francisco: Jossey Bass, 1973).

Part V:
Portraits of Three Private Universities

The private universities that are presented in part five of this volume should not be viewed as typical of the recently burgeoning private university movement. Rather we have chosen three rather high profile institutions that have gained considerable national attention for their achievements in recent years. China had a significant tradition of private institutions of higher learning over the nation's long history,[1] and they have played a critical role in the formation of Chinese culture and educational traditions.[2] Thus there was a significant number of outstanding private universities that emerged in the first half of the twentieth century. These were either closed down or merged with public institutions after the 1949 Revolution, however, and it was only in the 1980s that private institutions were once again allowed. Given this short history, none are yet in a position to compete with major public institutions. Nevertheless the policy of massification in higher education has given them an opportunity to develop more rapidly than would otherwise have been the case.

While there are many problems and concerns, relating to the legal framework for private institutions, the management style, issues of finance and ownership and the quality of student intake, significant progress has been made.[3] The three institutions profiled here exemplify three of the different types of private institution that have been identified in the research literature. Yellow River University of Science and Technology has been established and led by a remarkable family team;[4] Xi'an

---

[1] Jun Li, "Lun Zhongguo Gudai Sixue De Chansheng (On the Emergence of Private Education in Ancient China)," in *Jiaoyushi Yanjiu* (*Research on History of Education*), No.3, 1991, pp.14-19.

[2] Jun Li, "Lun Sixue Yu Zhongguo Chuantong Wenhua (On Private Education and Traditional Chinese Culture)," *Jiaoyu Yanjiu* (*Educational Research*), No.12, 1991, pp.70-73.

[3] Yan Fengqiao and Wu Peijuan, "Zhongguo Minban Gaodeng Jiaoyu Yanjiu: Huigu, Bijiao Yu Zhanwang (Private Higher Education Research in China: Retrospect, Comparison and Prospect)," in *Gaojiao Yanjiu* (*Higher Education Research*), No.5, 2005, pp.45-50.

[4] Feng Shujuan and Xu Xuqing, "Guanyu Wuoguo Minban Gaoxiao Jiazuhua Guanli De Ruogan Sikao (Some thoughts on family management of non-

International Studies University is headed by a highly entrepreneurial individual; and Blue Sky University has been inspired by a special interest group, in this case, the handicapped. All three stand out as institutions that hold promise for academic excellence in the longer term future, though at present they still face many challenges.

---

governmental higher Education Institutions)," in *Jiaoyu Fazhan Yanjiu* (*Research in Educational Development*) No.12, 2009, pp.39-43.

12
Yellow River University of Science and Technology – Pioneer of Private Higher Education

Ruth HAYHOE and Jing LIN, with TANG Baomei

This chapter presents a portrait of the Yellow River University of Science and Technology, which is located in Zhengzhou, the capital of Henan province. In some ways it is rather surprising that the first fully fledged private university to develop in post-Deng China should have been founded in this large agricultural province, which is considered a heartland of Chinese culture, yet has not generally been seen as one of the leading provinces or regions in the opening up and reform of recent decades. Henan province is the most populated in China, with around 98 million inhabitants, more than 70% of whom live in rural areas. In the reorganization of colleges and departments that took place in 1952, Henan was a province which failed to gain any national level universities under the Ministry of Education.[1] It experienced the traumatic loss of its most prominent faculties, departments and professors to the city of Wuhan in Hubei, the next province south, which became a regional centre in higher education for the Central South Region under the Soviet influence of the time.[2] Most of Henan's public universities are thus provincial level institutions at present, and the province has put great effort into upgrading and improving them since 1978.

Historically, however, Henan had seen many remarkable educational initiatives. Just a short distance from Zhengzhou stands the

---

[1] There were a number of institutions under other ministries, such as the Zhengzhou Institute of Technology, the Zhengzhou Institute of Aeronautical Industry and the Zhengzhou Institute of Light Industry, but these have now been handed over to provincial authorities or merged with local institutions. Two institutions under the military were merged but still remain under the administration of the People's Liberation Army.

[2] Ruth Hayhoe, *China's Universities: 1895-1995: A Century of Cultural Conflict* (Hong Kong: Comparative Education Research Centre, The University of Hong Kong, 1999), p.155. See also the introduction to Chapter 10 of this volume.

Songyang Academy (嵩陽書院), a traditional shuyuan (書院) founded in 484 CE, and considered one of the four most enduring and influential of China's classical academies. Close by is the Shaolin Monastery (少林寺), founded in 496 CE, one of the world's best known centres of Chan Buddhism (禪宗). It is celebrated for the ways in which it has nurtured martial arts over the centuries. Furthermore, Henan University of the 1920s and 1930s was a well developed academic institution, which was raised to national status during the Sino-Japanese war.[3]

In choosing the name Yellow River College of Science and Technology, the founder of this new-style private university was conscious that she was connecting a commitment to innovation in science and technology, so necessary to the development of this huge province, to the sense of China's ancient cultural traditions evoked by the Yellow River, one of China's longest rivers that flows through its heartland. Herself a graduate in Chinese literature, and teacher of Chinese at secondary school and at Zhengzhou University, her motivation in founding a new institution had elements of both intense patriotism and an ambition to excel in something entirely new. The slogan which she has put at the heart of this new institution and uses to challenge her staff and students is "Dare to be the first under heaven (敢爲天下先)!"

This chapter begins with the founder's account of the creation of the Yellow River University of Science and Technology, and then provides an overview of the university's curricular development, its students and faculty, its financial situation, patterns of governance, and finally some reflections on its ethos.

The Founder's Story

In telling us the story of how she came to found this new-style university, President Hu Dabai (胡大白) began with some comments on the importance of a new awareness of civil society and the role that could be played by independent social organizations in socialist China after Deng Xiaoping came to power in 1978. She recounted how one phrase in the new Chinese constitution of 1982 had opened up space for a new way of thinking: "The State encourages ... social forces to set up educational institutions of various types in accordance with the law."[4] This was a

---

[3] Ruth Hayhoe, *Portraits of Influential Chinese Educators* (Hong Kong: Comparative Education Research Centre, The University of Hong Kong, 2006), pp.77-81.
[4] This phrase is found in Article 19 of the 1982 Constitution. An English copy of the

simple yet dramatically new concept for someone educated under traditional socialist orthodoxy, and at a time when all private endeavors had been banned for over thirty years.

What stimulated her to step into this new space and create a new type of educational institution? In speaking with us, Hu Dabai summed it up in one short phrase: "Sharing the nation's sorrow, and relieving the people's suffering." Clearly this was a retrospective view, which added a sense of drama to an endeavor that actually had rather modest beginnings in the early 1980s.

Hu's biography, published at the time of the university's 20th anniversary, gives further insight into the way the founding story has been communicated. As an educator and professor of Chinese at Zhengzhou University, she was deeply concerned at how far China was behind in education, and how few young people were able to benefit from the educational resources of universities in the public system. She was struck by a set of comparative statistics indicating that 49% of young Americans and 29% of young Soviets enjoyed some access to higher education by the early 1970s. By contrast, fewer than 2% of Chinese young people had such an opportunity ten years later in 1983, putting China second from the bottom among 100 countries globally. Furthermore, Henan province was second to the bottom in higher education access among all of China's provinces and autonomous regions, a reflection of its huge rural population.[5]

These sharp contrasts, and her sense of social responsibility, motivated her to action. A window of opportunity for action had been opened when the national examinations for self-study students, established in 1981, were made available to Henan students for the first time in 1984. However, only 6% of the Henan students taking the examinations were successful in gaining a credential that year. Hu concluded that they lacked appropriate learning materials and she was confident she could fill this gap. She rented facilities in Zhengzhou's city centre and organized evening and weekend classes in Chinese and politics for students preparing for the exams. She hired the best professors she could find,

---

constitution can be found on the Congressional Executive Commission on China at the following website address: http://www.cecc.gov/pages/virtualAcad/gov.

[5] Zhang Qingxian, *Qingshi Danxin Ershi Nian – Huanghe Keji Xueyuan Yuanzhang Hu Dabai* (*A History of Loyalty for 20 years – The President of Yellow River College of Science and Technology*) (Beijing: Zhongyang Minzu Daxue Chubanshe, 2004), p.41.

making teaching excellence the lifeline of her new enterprise. Half a year later, 217 students under her tutelage took the examinations, with an 87% success rate. This surprising result was widely publicized and many young people became interested in this new possibility for higher education certification. By the third term, there were six thousand students taking classes in three subject areas, and parents were clamoring for her to establish a day school for students who had failed to gain access to the regular public higher education system. By 1988, there were 1,800 day students and 6,500 evening students in her school. Many graduates were able to find employment in Zhengzhou, through the Zhengzhou Talent Exchange Center, a government body with which the school formed a collaborative relationship since 1995.

Beginning in 1989, Hu Dabai began to think of establishing a college or university that could have its own independent ethos, create its own programs and gain government approval for its degrees. She and her colleagues began to accumulate capital and acquire land, and finally obtained their own campus, with one major teaching and administration building and some student dormitories and staff housing quarters. Some years of effort were put into building up a team of full-time faculty, vigorous program development and the establishment of laboratories and a library. Then in early 1994 they received approval from the Ministry of Education for the Yellow River College of Science and Technology to run sub-degree programs and grant government recognized diplomas. In that same year three other private colleges were approved: Shanda (杉達) in Shanghai, Shuren (樹人) in Zhejiang and Tianyi (天一) in Sichuan.

Hu's first vice-president for administration, who had partnered with her from the beginning, described how she had had to learn how to drink hard liquor with local peasants, in order to acquire the needed land. This was not easy for someone not even used to drinking wine! She had also had to deal with thirty different government bureaus and offices in order to gain permission to build and develop the campus. While student fees were the main source of income, some development funds also came from the donations of a dedicated staff.[6]

In the years from 1994 to 1999, Yellow River expanded its program offerings from the eight that were initially approved, with engineering as a key focus and a widening range of subject areas relevant to changing employment needs in the province. Hu and her colleagues had at once

---

[6] Interview with the first Vice President for Administration, 4 June 2007, Zhengzhou.

set their sights on the opening of programs at the undergraduate degree level, knowing that it would be a long journey to get government approval. In 1999, an evaluation team was sent from the Ministry of Education, which included a retired president of Wuhan University, a senior leader from the Beijing Municipal People's Congress and other high-level scholars, to evaluate the college for permission to recruit students for degree programs.[7] That year Yellow River became the first private institution in socialist China to gain degree granting status, after meeting the same criteria that had been set for public universities with substantial government support. This was a significant turning point for China's private higher education.

The initial plan was to develop gradually, starting with a recruitment of 600 degree-level students each year, and focusing on quality in the development of degree programs. However, this was the year in which the State Council and the CPC Central Committee held an unprecedented meeting to decide on speeding up higher education development through a rapid expansion of enrollments.[8] In response, Yellow River's leaders set aside their original plan and seized the opportunity to expand rapidly, along with many other public and private universities. By 2007, they had a total student body of around 20,000, with 13,000 in degree programs.

With this remarkable record of vision, effort and a series of serendipitous opportunities to respond to new government initiatives, President Hu became one of the best known leaders of private higher education in China. While many private institutions focused on practical skill training, Yellow River promoted engineering and the arts, broadly defined, and strove to provide the best possible learning facilities and learning environment. We were shown the 1,000 seat concert hall, the largest and one of the best in the province, the excellent technological facilities of the College of Journalism and Broadcasting , and the state of the art library building, located on a recently developed campus in the nearby village of Fo Gang (佛崗), where Hu had grown up, and had taught secondary school in the 1960s.

When asked which piece of architecture best expressed the spirit of

---

[7] Ibid.
[8] Jiao Xin "Jinnian Quanguo Gaodeng Jiaoyu Zhaosheng Dafu Zengjia (This Year the Recruitment of Students for Higher Education will be Greatly Expanded)," in *Zhongguo Jiaoyubao (China Education Daily)*, June 25, 1999, p.1.

Yellow River, Hu had no hesitation in identifying the new library building – which she saw as setting the architectural tone for the whole campus. Simplicity, good taste, usefulness and elegance were the terms she used to describe it.[9] Interestingly, faculty and students immediately pointed to the same building, when asked this question.

Photo 12.1: The Library & Information Building on the Fo Gang Campus

How did Hu Dabai develop the vision and find the resources to create an institution of this size and influence in a brief twenty years? If we reflect on private universities before 1949, some of the same patriotism and passion for education can be seen in figures such as the industrialist Chen Jiageng (Tan Kah Kee), founder of Xiamen University,[10] and Li Denghui, long-time president of Fudan University during its years as a private institution.[11] However, conditions in socialist China were very different from those before 1949, and Hu did not have either private wealth or overseas connections. She had depended entirely on personal entrepreneurship in a country that had long abjured entrepreneurial effort. In our interviews with leaders, faculty, staff and students, reference was often made to this entrepreneurial spirit, as if the greatest lesson each carried in their heart was the remarkable fact of Yellow

---

[9] Interview with Hu Dabai, 4 June 2007, in Zhengzhou.
[10] Ruth Hayhoe, *Portraits of Influential Chinese Educators*, (Hong Kong: Comparative Education Research Centre, The University of Hong Kong and Springer, 2006), pp.146-148. See also Chapter 5 of this volume on Xiamen University.
[11] *Ibid.* pp.177-178.

River's existence. It was a constant reminder that they should be creating opportunities for contributing to the community and the nation, rather than expecting ideal jobs to be awaiting them on graduation.

In order to present a detailed picture of the university's development and present situation, we held interviews with the head of the finance office, the head of the research office, the head of the teaching office, the head of the international office, the vice party secretary, two vice presidents, one responsible for administration and the other for teaching and learning, and the president herself.[12] In addition, we held two focus group meetings with faculty and student representatives. Our observations and experiences in visiting the campus, attending a concert and participating in a public lecture series during the first week of June, 2007, also contributed to the understanding we developed. Furthermore, we wish to acknowledge the contribution of Ms. Tang Baomei of the institute of higher education research, who assisted us by organizing the meetings and providing helpful factual information. Clearly, what we learned from these meetings can provide only a partial view of a complex and dynamic institution. However, we believe it will enable readers to gain some understanding of how private higher education is nurturing civil society in China, of the new ways in which Chinese cultural traditions are being expressed in the private sector of higher education, and of the many practical challenges that are being handled on a daily basis as new private institutions participate in China's move to mass higher education.

Curricular Characteristics

Yellow River made engineering a core focus from its early days, a rather unusual profile for a private university, given the cost of equipment and facilities. President Hu made the point that engineering graduates are most likely to find good jobs, which is one reason she has held firmly to this focus. The Vice President for Teaching and Learning emphasized the fact that there have been two Colleges of Applied Sciences since the mid-1990s, a College of Engineering that has Departments of Civil Engineering, Mechanical Engineering and Construction Engineering, and a Col-

---

[12] This was one of our first case studies, carried out in June of 2007, and we decided to use the title rather than name of university leaders interviewed, with the exception of the president. The same ethical procedures for informed consent were followed as in all the other case studies.

lege of Information Engineering that has Departments of Electronic Information Engineering, Computer Science and Technology, Communications Engineering, Software Engineering and Network Engineering. There is thus good reason for the name Yellow River University of Science and Technology.[13]

The Head of Teaching Affairs had earlier worked in the President's office, and described to us the complex preparations made in the late nineties to get official approval from the Ministry of Education for the launching of the first six bachelor degree programs in computer science and technology, electrical information engineering, English, design, business management and physical education. From these six programs launched in 2000, the number had grown to 37 programs by 2007, organized within eight of the eleven broad disciplines found on the Ministry of Education's official list. Each new program had to be approved by the provincial bureau of education, and certain programs, such as those in medicine, law, finance and martial arts, had to gain approval from the Ministry of Education in Beijing. Plans for curricular development are made by an academic committee that takes account of the needs of social and economic development and then invites appropriate departments or colleges to prepare new program proposals. These are first evaluated by external scholars, then reviewed by Yellow River's academic committee before being submitted to the provincial bureau of education.

While new programs are supposed to be selected from the Ministry's official list, newly developing fields of knowledge are often not found on that list. Yellow River was ahead of public universities in opening one of China's first programs in network technology and information management, for example, and this program has now been replicated elsewhere. Animation was another new program, not on the official list, which they initiated. While the Higher Education Law of 1998 states clearly that universities have autonomy to establish their own programs,[14] in practice this is the case only for top-level public universities; all others have to go through complex approval processes at the provincial and national level. This has slowed their efforts to respond to the

---

[13] Interview with the Vice President for Teaching and Learning, 6 June 2007.
[14] See Article 33, "Law on Higher Education in the People's Republic of China," in *Chinese Education and Society*, May-June, 1999, p.77: "Institutions of higher education shall, in accordance with the law, have the autonomy to establish and internally regulate the structure of curriculum and programs of study."

demands from employers for graduates in newly developing areas.[15]

The program in the martial arts, which enrolls 100 students each year, reflects an interest in building on China's cultural traditions. It was also stimulated by the nearby Shaolin Monastery, which attracts enthusiasts in martial arts nation-wide and from around the world. The program in Chinese and Western Medicine, which ran for several years, was also an expression of efforts to bring Chinese traditions into the curriculum. Unfortunately it had been recently closed, due to Ministry of Education concerns that the three year sub-degree program was too short to provide adequate knowledge in both fields of medicine. They were now hoping to develop a program in Chinese traditional medicine, but it was difficult to get approval for this from the Ministry of Education. There was a new bachelor level program in pharmacy, however, which covered considerable knowledge about traditional Chinese herbs.[16]

In its curricular development, Yellow River has had to establish itself as an institution that focuses on teaching, rather than research. It also had to fit the profile of its students, most of whom come from a third echelon, with the top students entering national universities and the second tier entering public universities at the provincial level. Many students have been traumatized by the examination experience, and lack confidence in themselves. Thus a main concern of curriculum development has been to find out what areas of knowledge and approaches to teaching can arouse students' interest and enable them to develop self confidence. Efforts are being made to give students more freedom and choice in their studies, also to allow for hands-on experience through internships and other opportunities for service in the community.[17]

The most vivid insights into curricular development, teaching and learning came from the faculty focus group meeting. It included the deans of the Colleges of Journalism and Broadcasting, Engineering, Medicine, and Foreign Languages, also a professor from the College of Music. The dean of Engineering commented that Yellow River's President had been very bold in making engineering its leading field, something that not many private universities had done. At the same time Yellow River could not model its programs on those of the leading public universities, since they had neither the caliber of students nor the job

---

[15] Interview with the Head of Teaching Affairs, 5 June 2007.
[16] *Ibid.*
[17] Interview with the Vice President for Teaching and Learning, 6 June 2007.

opportunities for graduates. Thus, after in-depth reflection on their own capacity and on local employment needs, they had decided on various forms of applied engineering suited to the technological and technical needs of county level government organizations and also of newly developing small companies at the local level. Their graduates are above the level of technician, with significant theoretical understanding, yet oriented to basic problem solving at the grassroots. On their new campus, they are now building a huge laboratory building suited to their own programs, after careful study of the equipment and conditions of parallel institutions in Shanghai and Nanjing.

The dean of journalism and broadcasting explained that their program emphasized application and action, and promoted four kinds of linkage: between theory and practice, between major lectures and small group work, between the planned curriculum and extracurricular learning and between study within the college and internship opportunities in the community. He noted many of their students spent lengthy periods of time working with radio and television stations at the local level and gained rich professional experience that way. One graduate got a position as editor in the Central Chinese Television Station and another became a provincial television announcer, in spite of coming from a poor rural area where little Mandarin was spoken.

The dean of medicine noted how different is the field of medicine in the Chinese context, as against in the West, where it has elite status within the university. While medical education programs have to gain approval at the national level in China, there are two levels of qualification, with unified national examinations for each: a three year training period for an assistant doctor at the sub-degree level and a six year training period for a regular doctor. Yellow River has focused on programs for certified assistant doctors who will work at the county level, also programs in nursing and pharmacy at the undergraduate degree level. For those who do not wish to work in rural areas, there are opportunities in businesses developing herbal medication and other drugs, also opportunities for nurses in major cities with aging populations. The College of Medicine has close links with 42 hospitals throughout the province, at the county level and above, and Yellow River is now planning to open its own teaching hospital on the new campus. Their intention is to model new approaches to medical care for rural areas at the county level – an important and neglected arena of medical care in China.

The College of Music has three programs, in piano, voice and dance.

In the voice program, students learned piano as well as singing, and had exposure to three types of music – Western classical music, such as opera and traditional songs, indigenous Chinese music and contemporary popular music. Students concentrate on one of these three areas, while developing a repertoire in all three. On graduation, it has not been easy to find jobs, but many of them had formed their own small music groups and performed within their communities. Of great importance to the music program had been the construction of a magnificent concert hall, seating over 1,000 persons, on the ground floor of a music teaching building that is equipped with the latest in instruments, computer assisted composing facilities and studios of different types. Every year the College of Music had four hundred graduates, and all of those in the voice program were encouraged to give a concert, either solo, or with a group of fellow students. This was their graduation project and great effort was put into making it as professional as possible.[18]

We were invited to attend one of these concerts performed by a graduating student who had come from a rural village three hundred kilometers south. It was a moving experience to see this young woman give solo performances in three different repertoires, with elaborate changes of dress for each, and another student presenting each part of her program with all the aplomb of a professional master of ceremonies. The student's mother had traveled all the way from her village, to attend this important and symbolic event. In the audience were several hundred fellow students and some faculty members from the College of Music, also the elder sister of the President, who served as an advisor to the university, and who conveyed congratulations to the student on behalf of the university leadership. Throughout the evening, there was an overwhelming sense of the disciplined effort and passionate commitment on all sides, that had made it possible for a village girl to achieve this level of performance.

Yellow River's concert hall is the largest and one of the best in the province of Henan, and it has brought much credit to the university. Not only concerts, but important meetings, such as colloquia relating to China's involvement with the World Trade Organization and international conferences have also been held in this venue. It somehow symbolizes the university's vision to bring talented young people from rural

---

[18] Most of the information in this section came from the Faculty Focus Group meeting, 5 June 2007.

areas, who have had to overcome many obstacles, onto a provincial, national and even global stage.

Photo 12.2: The Concert Hall and College of Music on the Urban Campus

Other curricular areas include the College of Commerce, the College of Law, the College of Foreign Languages and the College of Art and Design. All of them have close links with local business and industry, with the College of Art and Design doing cutting edge work in product design, packaging and advertising, and the College of Commerce having programs in accounting, foreign trade and business management. All of the programs had certain core academic elements, yet put a strong emphasis on application and practice, and required a considerable amount of small group work and individual work. Effort, discipline, the building of pragmatic capability and an innovative mentality were seen as the essential qualities that would make it possible for students whose marks on entry examinations had been less than ideal to develop into qualified professionals in a wide range of areas.

Students' Background and Outlook

Students at Yellow River have many difficulties to overcome. Those entering sub-degree diploma programs may have equivalent marks on the unified national entry examinations as their counterparts in the public sector, since Yellow River's focus on practical and applied fields is highly attractive. However, those entering degree programs normally have lower examination results than their counterparts entering public universities. There was a kind of dual, even contradictory, way of thinking about this issue on the part of faculty and university leaders. On the one hand, it was often said that students must discover their own talents and come to enjoy learning. Programs are thus intended to be flexible and give students the chance to discover themselves and gain confidence. On the other hand, there was a sense that firm discipline is more essential for these students than for the more academically qualified students of the public system. Yellow River thus felt it should provide an environment that combined strict discipline with encouragement and confidence building, a characteristic shared by other private universities in China.

Yellow River's overall student body was close to 20,000 in 2007, with 13,000 being enrolled in four-year undergraduate programs, another 5,000 in sub-degree programs and 1,500 in adult education. Over 70% of the students came from Henan province, and this ratio was growing, while the majority were from rural areas, rather than cities. About 55% of students were boys, and 45% girls, probably reflecting the greater willingness of rural parents to pay the rather high private university fees for their sons than daughters. The fees were variable by field, but averaged around 9,000 *yuan* per year, 10,000 for music and design, fields where facilities were rather costly. These figures compared with an average fee of 13,000 for students attending the second-tier affiliated colleges of local public universities and 3,500 per year for students whose examination results gave them places in local public universities. Some students were able to get government loans, for which they needed certification to show the poverty level of their families, and about 30% were awarded scholarships by the university. On graduation, the highest salary they were likely to make was 3,000 *yuan* a month and the lowest was 700. On average they made 1,000 *yuan*, a rather modest level that reflects the provincial economy. About 15% of graduates from some degree programs were able to get into masters degree programs in public universities.[19]

The Vice Party Secretary, who is concurrently head of student affairs, had been educated in a military college at the sub-degree level,

---

[19] Interview with the Vice-Secretary of the Party and Head of Student Affairs, 4 June 2007.

and had come to Yellow River as a student counselor twelve years earlier in 1995. She had continued her studies part-time, first gaining a bachelor degree, then a masters degree from the Central South University of Finance and Economics in Wuhan. She was currently enrolled in a doctoral program at Wuhan University.[20] After nine years as a counselor, she had been appointed Vice Secretary of the university's Communist Party Committee at the age of 32 in 2004. She noted that this kind of rapid career advancement would never have been possible in the public system; only a private university would give someone of her background the chance to develop her talents and gain a leadership position at such a young age.

In her role as Head of Student Affairs, she was responsible for students' overall development, employment opportunities and political development. She and her staff made sure that abundant activities were organized outside of the formal classroom in order to enable the students to discover their interests, participate actively in campus life and serve the community. Much of this was done by students themselves, with support for them to establish their own clubs and associations in areas such as calligraphy, sport, dance, and various types of social service, including small groups contributing to rural development in different ways. Students are allowed to run these organizations independently, but they are required to register them with an internal department of the university. Students were also encouraged to play an active role in social activities and in the student association, where student leaders were nominated and elected by vote of all students. The one constraint here was that nominations had to be approved by the university authorities.

In order to stimulate students' interest and ensure a well rounded education, weekly seminars are organized by the student affairs section on a range of topics, including themes of cultural interest, such as the ideas of Laozi and Zhuangzi, China's famous Daoist philosophers, literature such as the Dream of the Red Chamber, psychological topics relating to youth self-understanding and personal relationships etc. These seminars are open to all, but there is no compulsion to attend, and they are viewed as supplementary to the formal curriculum.

The other side of this impetus to stimulate student interest and initiative is a rigorous system of student supervision and guidance. Most of the students live in dormitories on campus, as only a small number come from the city of Zhengzhou. There is a large number of student

---

[20] These are both national level public universities of high standing in China.

counselors, one for every 194 students, with at least one present in each of the student dormitories.[21] These counselors are typically university graduates, who do not qualify to teach but are responsible for student guidance. After a period of time, some may be allowed to teach classes in politics, if qualified. Gradually the counselors are becoming more and more professional. While they work in a team, they have distinctive specialisms in areas such as educational psychology, career counseling or administration.[22]

The group of eight students we interviewed in the student focus group were all active members of the Communist Youth League, with many holding leadership roles.[23] They informed us how elections had recently been held for membership in the college level Youth League Committees, and many of them had been active in this process. They came from the fields of English, construction engineering, environmental design, commercial management, electrical information engineering, pharmacy and nursing, and were students of second, third and fourth year. One began the discussion by explaining that Yellow River students tended to be very independent and have a high level of autonomy or self-mastery. They have to face a lot of competition in the job market, but good references from the professors and other support from the university helps a lot. They are also pro-active in reaching out to society in different ways. One example they gave was the fact that many students had joined in an essay writing competition sponsored by Henan province, showing their confidence and willingness to compete with students in public higher education institutions.

A second year student in construction engineering expressed his enormous gratitude at being able to get into the program and be trained for kinds of work that would be valued at the county level – a few years earlier he would not have had the opportunity for higher education.[24] A

---

[21] This figure can be compared with 1 counselor for 400 students in a public university such as Xiamen University. See Chapter 5 of this volume. See also Chapter 10, for the views of three counselors participating in the Faculty Focus Group at HUST.

[22] Interview with the Vice-Secretary of the Party and Head of Student Affairs, 4 June 2007.

[23] This may have indicated the university's concern to ensure that we talked with students who were politically "responsible."

[24] The national entrance examinations were being held in the very week we did our interviews at Yellow River, and it was interesting to hear the province's

third year pharmacy student spoke about the high demands her program made upon students, and that it had been rewarding to have a two week internship in a mountainous area high above sea level, where they were collecting new herbs to create samples for the university's collection. She mentioned that the university was planning to develop this area as a base where student interns could be involved in growing various medicinal herbs. A third year nursing student spoke about her sense of calling to serve at the county level in health system reform work, and her excitement at the prospect of the model hospital to be established on campus. She also noted how much the nursing program benefited from having senior experts come to give advice from the top provincial hospital.

A student from the College of Commerce, who was studying business management, talked about how this field is rapidly changing, and curricular materials need to be updated year by year. What was being taught in 2007, he noted, was completely different from what was taught in 2000. The program had been started that year in order to prepare for China's accession to the World Trade Organization, and all the changes this would bring. He also mentioned a new course in micro economics launched in 2007.

Finally, one of the most impressive of the students was in her second year in the College of Design. She was not from a rural area in Henan, as were most others, but from the northeastern province of Shandong. From quite a young age she had had to work to support her family, and was still working part-time while studying at Yellow River. She noted how different her working experience was now, as what she was learning at the university helped her to reflect on the problems faced at work. She compared this with her earlier job in a company, while in upper secondary school, and explained that she had not had the tools or ability at that time to be self-reflective about her working environment.

All of the students agreed enthusiastically that the library building best expressed the ethos of Yellow River. (Photo 12.1) They spoke about their many reasons for loving the building: the feeling that the library was the heart of the campus, a love for some of its special collections, such as China's pharmaceutical classic, the *Bencao gangmu* (《本草綱目》), the fact that many open seminar meetings on general interest topics were

---

statistics. 837,000 students were taking the examinations, and it was expected that 400,000 would be offered higher education places. Private higher education was contributing significantly to this remarkable level of provision.

held there every week for students, and that major exhibitions of design items were also held there, with company sponsorship and high profile opening ceremonies.

It was the design student who had most to say about the building itself. She said that she had recently visited five cities, Shanghai, Suzhou, Zhenjiang, Xi'An and Hangzhou, in order to reflect on urban design and the ways in which Chinese and Western values and concepts become integrated into building designs. She felt that Chinese tradition tended to focus on nature, and the human person in nature, and to be more holistic than the Western tradition. She recounted that many people had taken part in the design of the library building and there had been passionate debates about it. Those responsible for design decisions had traveled as far as Hong Kong in looking for ideas, but in the end had chosen a top architect from Beijing, and everyone had been satisfied with the result.

This design student felt Yellow River's study programs reflected Chinese tradition in their holism and orientation to practice and to action. She particularly appreciated the fact that classes were small in the design school, relations with the professors were close and there were many opportunities to get out into the community and learn, observe and investigate. There was a definite effort to integrate theory and practice in all areas of the curriculum, something she believed was less often seen in public universities.[25]

The students we talked with in the focus group painted a very positive picture of their study experiences at Yellow River. We felt that the information was authentic, and reflected the ethos of the university and the efforts of staff in seeking to help each and every student to grow. It bore out what President Hu told us, that providing quality education was the lifeline of the university. At the same time we were aware of the status of the students chosen to meet with us and guessed there must be some disgruntled students, or students who felt differently about their learning experience. One example of student independence came up in a speech by the Vice-president for Administration. He complained that the university had negotiated job opportunities for several hundred Yellow River graduates with T-mobile, yet most of the students felt the pay was not high enough and did not take the offer.[26]

---

[25] Focus Group Meeting with students, 6 June 2007.
[26] Speech by the Vice President for Administration at the time of our lecture, 7 June 2007.

Faculty and Issues of Teaching and Research

Yellow River had a total teaching staff of 1064 in 2007, with 755 on full-time appointments and another 309 professors cross-appointed from other universities who were teaching part-time. In addition, there were 261 teachers hired from abroad, and an administrative staff of about 200.[27] Government regulations required that at least one third of faculty should be full-time and Yellow River had already long surpassed that requirement. The student-faculty ratio was about 17.5 to 1.

Faculty members came from three different backgrounds. Senior faculty were often recently retired professors from public universities, who brought a life-time of experience and a solid scholarly profile. Younger faculty were being recruited year by year from the ranks of newly graduating Masters degree students, with 130 new faculty of this type being appointed in the autumn of 2006, at a time when a double cohort graduated due to the shortening of the masters program in public universities from three to two years. In addition a certain number of bachelor degree holders were also appointed each year. The third source of faculty was from experienced practitioners and professionals in areas such as design, construction engineering and computer science. Yellow River was permitted to appoint its own faculty up to lecturer and assistant professor level, while those appointed at associate professor level or above, including the university's president and party secretary, had to be approved by the provincial bureau of education.

Generally teaching staff were paid higher salaries than administrative staff.[28] Particular attention was given to the appointment of deans, who were seen as influential scholarly leaders within the institution. Most had been appointed from well known public universities in Henan and other provinces.

Excellence in teaching quality was regarded as the university's "lifeline" and great attention was given to fostering this. Experienced older professors from public universities were invited as consultants, to give guidance and advice to new faculty, both through one-on-one mentoring and short-term training classes. Also Yellow River was one of the first private universities to establish a research section in 1998, and encourage faculty to do research. This was seen as essential for them to maintain a high quality of teaching, and keep up to date with new

---

[27] Interview with the Head of Teaching Affairs, 5 June 2007.
[28] Interview with the Head of the Finance Office, 5 June 2007.

developments in their fields.

The university's first funded research project was a grant of 50,000 *yuan* from the provincial science and technology bureau in 2006. This was a great encouragement. In addition they were allowed to submit projects for approval to the province's education bureau and social science academy, even though funds could not be awarded. A total of 19 projects had recently been approved in science, social sciences and education. This approval from provincial government offices gave legitimacy and recognition to research efforts, even when funding support had to come from the university itself.[29] A total of 46 faculty had been involved in the design of these projects, and once projects were approved, faculty qualified for a lighter teaching load. The norm was 12 class hours a week in most subject areas, a little higher in foreign languages.[30]

While Yellow River did not have extensive international connections, they were able to attract some foreign specialists from Australia, the USA and Japan to teach in the College of Foreign Languages, and the Music College had a number of visiting faculty members from the Belorussian National Academy of Music in Minsk. Also about 20 of Yellow River's music faculty had been sent there for study.[31] The Belorussian professors were glad to have the opportunity to teach in China, since living standards are considerably higher than in Belorussia, and they jokingly reported that they were learning how to reform capitalism at home by studying the way the Chinese are reforming socialism![32]

The demanding challenge that was facing the teaching faculty at the time we visited was the prospect of going through a formal teaching evaluation process under the Ministry of Education's initiative in June of 2008.[33] The vice president for teaching and learning was putting a supervision system in place, whereby older professors from both within and outside would observe classes and write reports. A set of performance indicators was being developed in order to document the management of

---

[29] Only in May of 2009 did we learn from one of the scholars who attended our workshop at Peking University that private institutions were finally being allowed to compete for government research grants at the national and/or provincial levels.

[30] Interview with the Head of the Research Office, 5 June 2007.

[31] Interview with a member of the College of International Studies, 5 June 2007.

[32] Interview with the first Vice President for Administration, 4 June 2007.

[33] See Chapter 1 for details on the national teaching evaluation process, which is being applied to private as well as public universities.

teaching, and everyone was beginning to prepare for the formal visits that would kick off the quality assessment exercise the following year.[34]

Before long Yellow River hoped to be able to launch its own masters programs, but its leaders had been told by the Ministry of Education that only after ten years of successfully running undergraduate degree level programs, would they be permitted to have their own masters programs. In the meantime, they were collaborating with nationally prestigious universities such as Zhejiang University in Hangzhou and the Huazhong University of Science and Technology (HUST) in Wuhan to run some collaborative masters programs in areas where they had recognized curricular strength, including a Master of Business Administration and a Master of Medical Administration.[35]

One vignette from our visit gives some insight into the life of teaching faculty at Yellow River. On the final day of our week of interviews and meetings, faculty were invited to a formal lecture, where each of us was to present a paper. When we entered the small auditorium where the meeting was to be held, we were intrigued to see that every seat in the room was labeled with the name of a particular faculty member, in writing large enough that the names could be easily seen from the front. As faculty gradually assembled, it became clear that the vice president, who was chairing the meeting, would be able to see at a glance who did not show up for the lectures. When we asked him about this, he explained that faculty could put in a formal request to be excused from the lectures, but otherwise they were expected to be there. He then opened the lecture session by saying that the university encouraged a policy of "a hundred flowers blooming and a hundred schools of thought contending" in relation to the exchange of ideas, but this did not mean that disorder or lack of discipline would be tolerated!

The imposition of rather strict discipline upon faculty is not unusual in private universities, and it is fairly common to find the use of all kinds of measures to ensure that faculty comply with the university's standards and rules. At Yellow River, faculty were paid additional bonuses, over and above their salaries, we were told, based on their teaching effectiveness. That in turn was evaluated through a strict yet transparent system. Private universities resort to these measures to ensure that students learn and that faculty are accountable and deliver

---

[34] Interview with the Vice President for Teaching and Learning, 6 June 2007.
[35] Ibid.

the results which parents want to see. Their leaders are aware that they cannot afford to make any major mistakes, since there is still a lack of trust in them on the part of both government officials and parents.

Yellow River's Financial Situation

President Hu Dabai did not have personal wealth or property to put into developing Yellow River, nor was she able to draw upon external sources of support from overseas communities, as had been the situation for many of the pre-1949 private universities. She has mainly relied on student tuition to develop Yellow River. In 1992, the first piece of land 30 *mu* in size was bought, and the first building erected at a cost of 2 million *yuan*. The money came almost entirely from student fees and the profits of service businesses on campus, with a small amount coming as donations from teaching staff.[36] Later two pieces of contiguous land were bought, bringing the size of the urban campus up to 90 *mu*. In 1995, a new piece of land of 500 *mu* was acquired in the village of Fo Gang, south of Zhengzhou. The funds came mainly from the fees of training classes for the self-study examinations. These enrolled over 10,000 students at times and were continued up to the year 2000, providing significant income. By then, permission had been given for a massive expansion of both sub-degree and degree level programs. Student fee income in 2000 amounted to 100 million a year, and by 2007, this figure had reached 200 million a year.

The budget, as of 2007, had the following rough breakdown: 40 million for salaries (20%), 36 million for teaching resources and support, including the library, laboratories and need teaching equipment (18%), 20 million (10%) for logistics and service, 10 million (5%) for student recruitment costs, 10-20 million (5-10%) for scholarships for needy students, leaving between 74 and 84 million for building projects. The plan is to build one building at a time on the new campus, and not go into debt. All past loans had been paid off by 2004. Extra expenditures for teaching improvement and the library were expected in 2008 in preparation for the teaching evaluation by the Ministry of Education.[37]

Governance Structure

In their early stages of development, private universities have been

---

[36] Interview with the first Vice President for Administration, 4 June 2007.
[37] Interview with the Head of the Finance Office, 5 June 2007.

managed somewhat like family businesses in China. The founder and a few co-founders tend to have the final word in all important decisions. As the institutions grow in size, however, more layers of administration are added and an appropriate delegation of power becomes necessary. Another important factor for the administration and structure is the requirement laid out in the Private Higher Education Law of 2003, which states that every private university must have a board of trustees.[38]

In response to this legal requirement, Yellow River had set up a board of trustees, and its membership had already been reported to the provincial bureau of education and the Zhengzhou city office of education. Annual reports on finance, student numbers and other key developments were sent to provincial bureau of education and the Ministry of Education in Beijing each year.[39]

As for the leadership structure of the university, under the president there were five vice presidents, one responsible for administration on each of the two campuses, one responsible for teaching affairs and one specifically focused on the upcoming teaching evaluation by the Ministry of Education. The fifth vice president, who was responsible for the university's logistics and public relations, was the only woman, and the daughter of the president. Recently the president's older son had been appointed chief financial officer for the university. He graduated from Peking University and acquired a doctorate in Chemistry and an MBA in the United States. He returned from a financial career in the United States to help establish high standards of financial regulation for Yellow River. In addition the president's elder sister served as an advisor to the university. This was probably typical of the strong family ties found in the leadership of many private universities.

There were also ongoing efforts to regularize Yellow River's administrative practices and decision-making processes through the establishment of representative internal bodies. A trade union for faculty and staff had recently been formed, and a representative assembly of all academic and administrative staff. The intention was to promote democratic forms of government, and channels for all members of the

---

[38] Zhonghua Renmin Gongheguo Minban Jiaoyu Chujin Fa (Promotion Law of People-Run Education of the People's Republic of China), Articles 46 and 51, http://www.moe.gov.cn/edoas/website18/info1433.htm. This law also makes the point that government allows a reasonable return on private school investment.
[39] Interview with the Head of Institutional Research, 8 June 2007.

university to be able to express their views.[40]

One of the most sensitive aspects of governance relates to the role of the Communist Party on campus. In the president's biography, one whole chapter is devoted to the story of her dream of becoming a Communist Party member, which was fulfilled in 1995, when she was accepted into the Party. She had been offered the opportunity to join one of the democratic parties, which has a consultative role in Chinese politics, but she chose membership in the ruling Communist Party. Two years after she became a Party member, the university was able to establish its own Party Committee, with Hu Dabai as Secretary, a first for private universities.[41] In 2000 she attended a national meeting of university Party Secretaries, as the first and only secretary from a private university. Since 2001 the position of Party Secretary has been held by a senior leader who has had experience in this role in a public university.

In explaining the role of Party organizations in Yellow River, the Vice President for Administration indicated that the university's academic organs and the Party organs were seen as having an equal status, but different responsibilities. The following three points were set forth as guiding principles in the university's literature:

- Putting the improvement of teaching quality at the center
- Improving the quality of management as a means
- Strengthening political education as a guarantee

While academic leaders are seen as responsible for the first two areas, the Party's responsibility is delineated in the third. The strengthening of political education is viewed as a guarantee of conformity to government policy and thus of political stability.[42]

Conclusion: A New Ethos of Academic Entrepreneurism

It is easy to see the important role that Yellow River has played in the massification of Chinese higher education, with its pioneering status as

---

[40] Interview with the first Vice President for Administration, 4 June 2007.
[41] Between 1994 and 1997 Yellow River had had a Party Branch under the direction of the Party Committee of the provincial science bureau.
[42] Wang Gang et al., *Zhongguo Minban Gaoxiao Fazhan De Dianfan – Huanghe Keji Xueyuan Jianxiao Ershinian Congshu* (*A Model for the Development of People-run Higher Institutions in China – a Collection of Material relating to the Twentieth Anniversary of the Establishment of Yellow River College of Science and Technology*) (Beijing: Zhongguo Minzu Daxue Chubanshe, 2004), p.90.

the first private university permitted to run degree programs, and with its decision to expand enrollments massively in 1999, in response to national higher education policy. It has opened up the doors into higher education for young people from rural areas whose past disappointments with the national unified entry examinations had caused them to talk about "black July," the month when many took the examinations and most failed to gain a place. Now, by contrast, about 50% of those taking the examination are admitted to higher education in Henan. Thus the emblem of the rising sun, seen on the top of its new Library and Information science building (Photo 12.1) and at the entry gate of its urban campus (Photo 12.3) expresses this sense of the new hope it has brought to disadvantaged young people.

Photo 12.3: The Emblem of the Rising Sun inside the entrance gate to Yellow River's Urban Campus

All of the staff members we interviewed were profoundly aware of the fact that Yellow River students were different from those who entered the public system buoyed by examination success. They needed to be given an environment where they could gain self confidence, identify their own interests and abilities and prepare for professional work in areas of need at the local level. Thus we saw evidence of many types of student-initiated organization, and of study programs that incorporated internships, opportunities for community service and a deep-level integration of theory and practice, knowledge and action.

Although China's traditional scholarly culture was related to the imperial examinations and a highly hierarchical and meritocratic set of patterns and structures, this was balanced by the role of the informal academies and other local institutions of scholarship and higher learning. Knowledge was always viewed in a holistic way, and great importance was given to the integration of moral discipline and academic learning, of theory and practice, and the application of knowledge to action. It is some of these progressive elements of Chinese scholarly culture that one can see undergirding the programs that have been sketched out earlier in this chapter. Out of their intense concern for community and their commitment to preparing graduates for local development needs, a constant stream of creativity has flowed, evident in new engineering programs such as network engineering and animation, and in the remarkable contributions to product design and wider urban design from the School of Design. At the same time, this creativity has been rooted in aspects of Chinese culture, that has its manifestation in programs such as martial arts, Chinese and Western medicine, pharmacy, and programs for television, video and film that make much of local historical and cultural sites. Yellow River may not be in a position to bring Chinese culture to the world, given its strongly local orientation and the constraints of its position within the higher education system, but no one can deny the authentic ways in which it embodies those traditions.

From the perspective of civil society, perhaps the most fundamental question relates to the degree of independence and autonomy which the university and its students and faculty actually experience. Are they truly independent actors, with a status protected by law, or are they subordinate to the same political and administrative forms of control that are evident in the public system? In answering this question, we can reflect on the remarkable degree of entrepreneurship demonstrated by the President in launching a private institution that has depended entirely on the willingness of students to pay significant fees for the opportunity to learn rather than public funding. However, this does not mean that the President has been seeking to develop an institution whose independence is expressed in opposition to the government, or through efforts to protect itself from government interference. While careful attention has been given to the provisions of the 1998 higher education law and the 2003 private higher education law, one gets the sense that the leadership has cordial relations with both the government and the Communist Party, and that this is seen as more important for its protection than law alone. The president herself is thus proud of her status as a Party member and the university's first Party Secretary.

This might be interpreted in terms of the commonly used Chinese term for autonomy in the context of higher education – self-mastery (自主權) rather than self-governance (自治權), the term used for autonomous regions in the Chinese context.[43] What can be seen in President Hu Dabai's leadership is a remarkable vision that carried her beyond the boundaries of normalcy in creating a new type of institution, able to respond to needs which were as yet barely discerned by the established higher education leaders of the time, or their political masters. She stepped into this space, with her ambitious slogan of "daring to be the first under heaven" and created a precedent that many others have followed. In the process, she did not seek distance from the political leadership, but rather sought to gain their support and approval, as the guarantee of the long-term viability of her enterprise.

---

[43] Ningsha Zhong and Ruth Hayhoe, "University Autonomy in 20th Century China," in Glen Peterson, Ruth Hayhoe and Yongling Lu (eds.) *Education, Culture and Identity in Twentieth Century China* (Ann Arbor: University of Michigan Press, 2001), pp.265-267; See Ruth Hayhoe, *Portraits of Influential Chinese Educators*, pp.140-141.

13
Xi'an International University – Transforming Fish into Dragons

Jun LI and Jing LIN, with WANG Guan

Xi'an International University (XAIU) is another private university that has successfully established its institutional reputation in China. While forging an ethos oriented towards international outreach, it has also nurtured a large private higher education community in the heartland of Northwest China, the major city of Xi'an. This chapter depicts how its founders and faculty members have managed to use traditional cultural symbols, political strategies and a practical administrative model to build a new type of university with a vision of transforming fish into dragons.

History and Context

The City of Xi'an

Xi'an, the capital of Shaanxi Province and the largest city in the northwest region, is one of China's oldest cities, with a history going back to the Western Zhou dynasty (1100 BCE). Many ancient educational initiatives took place here, such as the opening of the Imperial University (太學) in 124 BCE and the adoption of the Imperial Civil Service Examination System (科舉) in 605 BCE. Xi'an also has a strong tradition of private education, that can be traced back to the third century BCE.[1]

Xi'an served as a dynamic hub of international exchange and trade in ancient Chinese history, and was particularly famous as the departure city of the Silk Road to Central Asia and Europe since the Han Dynasty (206 BCE-220 CE). In the Sui and Tang Dynasties (581-907 CE), numerous overseas students from Japan and Korea studied there. With a population of 8.6 million people, Xi'an continues to hold a leading role in socio-economic and educational development in China's northwest region today.

---

[1] Jun Li, "Lun Qinhan Shiqi De Sixue (Private Schools in the Qin and Han Dynasties)," in *Shanghai Shehui Kexueyuan Jikan (Quarterly Journal of the Shanghai Academy of Social Sciences)*, Vol.35, No.3, 1993, pp.166-175.

A Brief History of Xi'an International University

XAIU was established at a time when the Chinese government had begun to encourage private education as a way of supplementing public higher education, which was experiencing serious funding shortages. The situation was favorable to the development of private higher education, yet it was not easy for the pioneers to build their institutions entirely on the basis of private investment, with no public support.

The early 1990s saw private higher education flourish, spurred by Deng Xiaoping's speech on further opening and reform during his trip to Shenzhen in 1992. Xi'an was among three areas which saw the fastest growth of private schools during this critical period, and it was well ahead of Beijing and Shanghai. In 2003, enrollments in private higher education institutions in Shaanxi Province reached 137,000, which was the largest concentration of private higher education students in the nation.[2]

XAIU was established in 1992, as a very small training school for those who were seeking to earn a certificate by self-study. This is a common way in which private educational enterprises have begun in China after 1978, as can also be seen in the case of the Yellow River University of Science and Technology in Chapter 12. The institution was originally named the Xi'an Training School of International Affairs Services, and its original plan was not very ambitious, with an intention of accommodating around three thousand students on its campus.[3] Unexpected radical growth of enrollments in the early years of the new institution forced its founders to look for a new campus in 1995, when a total of 5,600 new students were recruited in a single year. The next year, it was decided to move the main campus to Yuhua (魚化), a small suburban village in southwestern Xi'an, to accommodate the rapidly expanding student body.

In 1997 XAIU was accredited by the government to offer sub-degree programs, which was a significant step in academic recognition. XAIU adopted its current name in 2000. In 2005, after thirteen years of effort, it was one of fifteen private institutions to gain official approval from the

---

[2] Jin Zhongming, Li Ruochi and Wang Guan (eds.), *Zhongguo Minban Jiaoyu Shi* (*A History of Private Education in China*) (Beijing: China Social Science Press, 2003), pp.358-359.
[3] Interview with Huang Teng, President, 28 May 2007.

Ministry of Education,⁴ to offer undergraduate programs at the bachelor degree level. By 2008, XAIU had around 40,000 students enrolled in undergraduate and sub-degree programs in 10 colleges and a total of 2,200 faculty and staff.

The Founder's Story: From 3,000 to 60,000 Students

Before telling the founder's story, it will be helpful first to understand a widely known traditional Chinese folktale. Once upon a time, probably thousands of years ago, something happened in a place called the Dragon Gate on the Luo River near south Luoyang, an ancient city not far from Xi'an, and the story spread rapidly all over the country. It was said that by jumping over the Dragon Gate, an ordinary humble carp was able to transform itself into a noble dragon (鯉魚跳龍門). The gate was high and steep, so that jumping over it for a better future was a big challenge for an ordinary carp. Only a few lucky ones managed to do so.

This folktale has multiple connotations in the Chinese cultural context. The carp is an ordinary yet tough fish, able to resist strong currents in big rivers, persistent in resisting hardship and swimming upstream, able to jump above the water, and over the high gate to become a dragon, the most admired of creatures. The carp thus symbolizes perseverance, determination, luck, and great achievements in one's pursuit of a life goal. Because of this folktale the carp is often regarded as a potent symbol of scholastic success, literary luck, a joyful marriage, and other kinds of fortune and prosperity. It has particular relevance to education and is seen as a charm that can help one pass competitive examinations with flying colors. It is thus used often by Chinese educators and parents to encourage children to strive for success in learning with persistent hard work, and particularly to make every effort to pass the highly competitive National Higher Education Entrance Examinations.

Huang Teng, the main founder of XAIU, might be viewed as such a dragon, who had been transformed from a humble carp. He was born and grew up in an extremely poor family of farmers in the late 1950s and 1960s, losing his mother at nine and his father at twelve. He was lucky to be admitted into a local normal school which enabled him to earn a basic

---

⁴ Zhao Yifeng, "Jiaoyubu Xinpizhun Shezhi Shiwusuo Minban Benke Gaoxiao (Fifteen Degree-granting Private Higher Education Institutions approved by the Ministry of Education)," in *Zhongguo Jiaoyu Bao* (*China Education Daily*), March 25, 2005, p.1.

teaching qualification. But he was not satisfied with this preliminary achievement and later managed to pass the National Higher Education Entrance Examination, and enroll in a bachelor level program in a local vocational college. Huang's effort to get into college and earn a degree was a typical story in China, and many of his peers and students have shared a similar experience. Until recently the majority of high school graduates have failed in the National Higher Education Entrance Examinations since the places in what was long an elite higher education system have been very limited and highly sought after. Huang's experience of success has thus given him a unique perspective in reflecting on how an individual may be able to overcome great difficulties to achieve a life goal, and how a local vocational institution can respond to deeply felt needs.[5]

After he earned a bachelor degree, Huang remained at the vocational college as a young teacher and researcher of higher education. However this position held no real challenge for him and seven years later he left the college and jumped into the sea of business, like many other pioneers in China's transition to a market economy. After two years in the business world, with some international exposure, he was so successful that he was looking for new opportunities. He came up with a plan of running a vocational school together with his partners that could fulfill his dream of contributing to the local community. It was a time when there was a high demand for training young people enrolled in self-study programs.

The rapid development of XAIU demonstrates how Huang Teng achieved his plan, step by step. Originally he intended to open a vocational school able to accommodate around 3,000 students with practical training relating to the job market. He and his co-founders had limited financial resources, and they did not have the ambition to open a large higher education institution. The new school had only one teaching building, one small library, and a narrow schoolyard, with a few associated teachers. Yet this small school was so welcomed by students and their parents that there was an almost immediate need for a rapid expansion of the campus and enrollment capacity. By 1995 Huang set a new goal for 6,000 students on a new campus in Sanqiao (三橋). By 1997 the plan was for 30,000 students on a third campus in Yuhua. Ten years later, there was a plan for a total of 60,000 students. It has been a bumpy

---

[5] Interview with Huang Teng, President, 28 May 2007.

and sometimes awkward road for Huang and his co-founders, as some have withdrawn and there have been arguments and even lawsuits over issues of the development of new campuses, the recruitment of qualified faculty members, student admissions, marketing and financial management. The Yuhua Campus is now the main campus, and the Sanqiao campus continues to be used for some educational activities.

Through this long journey, Huang has continuously reflected on critical issues, such as how to develop a far-reaching vision and how to ensure that his institution responds to the rapid changes in society. He decided to take some time to study educational theories, first at East China Normal University in 1999, then at Peking University in 2002 and at Brunel University in the U.K. in 2006. He felt that these critical issues demanded careful and comprehensive academic consideration.[6]

XAIU's Move to Mass Higher Education: An Empirical Overview

Few of China's new private institutions have kept consistent records on their development in the way their public counterparts have done. XAIU is no exception, and as expected, we were not able to obtain accurate and consistent data about its development over the years since 1992. However, the following descriptions provide some salient facts about how XAIU has responded to the move to mass higher education.

Growth in Student Enrollments

There has been a radical growth in student enrollments since XAIU was founded in 1992. New entrants for self-study qualification doubled from a total of 2,400 students in 1994 to 5,600 in 1995, and increased to 6,000 in 2000. The total enrollment jumped from 12,000 in 1999 to 36,000 in 2007, and 40,000 in 2008. Among them 60% were students from rural areas. After XAIU was accredited as a bachelor degree-granting institution in 2005, it began to recruit students at this level. There were a total of 526 students who enrolled in bachelor degree programs that year, of whom 329 were male and 197 were female. Since then the numbers have grown to 4,473 with 2,951 females and 1,522 males in 2008, and a goal has been set of enrolling 15,000 students in degree programs in the mid-term future. By 2005, there were 28,375 students enrolled in sub-degree programs, with a goal for the mid-term future of a total of 45,000 students on campus at the sub-degree level. The teacher-student ratio was 1:21.7, and

---

[6] *Ibid.*

it continued to grow up to 1:27.0 in 2008 (part-time faculty members are averaged at one half). These ratios may not be accurate, as there were additional part-time teachers associated with XAIU. But it seemed that XAIU had faced a highly pressured teaching workload with this rapid growth in student population.

In terms of expansion, XAIU has adopted a different strategy from many other private higher education institutions. As has been noted earlier in this volume, the Chinese government decided to radically expand the size of its higher education system in 1999, and the nationwide enrollment in higher education institutions jumped from 7.2 million in 1999 to 9.1 million in 2000, 11.8 million in 2001 and 16.0 million in 2002. Most higher education institutions took advantage of this opportunity to radically expand their size. But XAIU did not follow the national trend and kept its enrollment stable at around 12,000 students from 1999 to 2002. There was some internal as well as external criticism of this strategy, as it seemed that XAIU had missed a rare opportunity for further expansion and growth. But Huang gave his explanation of why this had happened.[7] The decision was actually made because XAIU's campus and facilities for teaching and learning were unable to keep up with the pace of the explosion in its student body, after its intensive upgrading of campuses in the three years from 1994 to 1996. As a responsible private higher institution, Huang believed that the first priority should be to meet students' basic learning needs, rather than being opportunistic about rapid expansion. Personally, he felt the need to recharge himself by exposure to educational theory and research at ECNU, so that he could think through a better vision for his institution. It was only in 2002 that XAIU decided on a rapid increase in its enrollment, and in 2005 it set the goal of a total of 60,000 students in the mid-term future.

Curricular Development

In the very beginning, most private higher education institutions focused on vocational training to assist students who were preparing for national self-study examinations, which would give them recognized qualifications at the diploma or sub-degree level. Students were those who had been unable to pass the National Higher Education Entrance Examinations and enter a regular higher education institution. After around three years' study, these students on private university campuses would

---

[7] Ibid.

be conferred a nationally recognized certificate if they managed to pass the national examinations in certain required courses, as well as some examinations at the provincial level and some institutionally required courses. The courses organized for these examinations largely centered on applied sciences, social sciences and humanities, with a direct relevance for the job market rather than strong academic content. Private higher institutions relied heavily on this self-study examination system in their early years before they gained accreditation from the Ministry of Education and were able to confer their own sub-degree diplomas and degrees. Even after they gained accreditation to confer diplomas and degrees, many students still continued to take the self-study examinations, in order to gain these qualifications in addition to the private university's diploma or degree.

XAIU also followed this development path, from a focus on training students for the national self study examinations to the launching of its own diploma programs as of 1997, and its own degree programs from 2005. Currently, XAIU aims at becoming a comprehensive university and it has already established ten colleges: the College of Foreign Languages, the 1st and 2nd Colleges of Economics and Management, the College of Information Engineering, the College of Auto Engineering, the Medical College, the College of Humanities, the College of Cultural Industry, the College of International Cooperation, and the College of Adult Education and On-Line Education. There are 22 departments and 96 programs in the ten colleges, covering economics, literature, management, engineering, agriculture, medicine and law. The College of International Cooperation has set up two collaborative programs with the Sydney Institute of Technical and Further Education in Australia.

Currently, there are more than 35 vocational programs at the sub-degree level offered by the university, and 19 four-year bachelor level programs. The latter include English Literature, Japanese Literature, Journalism, Art and Design, International Economics and Trade, Financial Management, Marketing, Computer Sciences and Technology, Electronic and Information Engineering, Tourism and Management. It is clear that the university has kept and enhanced its original focus on international studies in its curricular development.

In terms of program, all students are required to take a total of 54 hours of general education, which they can select from 15 optional courses, covering areas such as traditional Chinese culture, public relations, social etiquette and the art of leadership.

Other Aspects of Institutional Development

With the increase in student numbers, XAIU twice had to expand its campus between 1992 and 1997. It was originally located at Hongmiaopo, with a very limited number of classrooms and other facilities. In 1995, its main campus was moved to Sanqiao, adding 82.4 acres, with the capacity to accommodate a total of 6,000 students. Due to the radical growth in student numbers, its main campus was moved again to Yuhua in 1997, a small town in the Xi'an Hi-Tech Industry Development Zone in the southwestern suburban area, where it could enjoy a quiet learning environment and convenient access by public transportation.

The Yuhua campus has a total of 332.8 *mu* in space, and its buildings have a total floorage of 685,000 square metres. Its library has 1.4 million books, 0.6 million electronic books, and 2,200 journals. There are also dormitories that that can accommodate more than 5,000 students. Like all private universities, XAIU depends mainly on student fees for its income, with some additional income from various kinds of services. In 2000, its student fee income amounted to 69.2 million *yuan*, while this had risen to 314.1 million *yuan* in 2005, with the huge expansion in student numbers. All other forms of income increased from 0.6 million *yuan* in 2000 to 5.7 million *yuan* in 2006.

Vision and Strategic Directions

Vision and Mission

By the early 1990s, it was clear that public higher education institutions were unable to meet the societal demand for skilled labor in the transition from a planned to a market economy that had begun in the 1980s. XAIU's founders were very sensitive to this situation, and believed that private higher education institutions would be able to provide new and alternative opportunities to meet the rapidly growing social demands as well stimulating reform in the public higher education system. But it was not clear how XAIU should situate itself as a private institution in the Chinese context.

Huang Teng, as a business person and an educator, has been reflecting on one critical issue from the very beginning – that was how to develop a far-reaching vision for his institution. From 1996, when he decided to move XAIU's main campus to Yuhua, he got the idea of drawing on elements from traditional Chinese culture to develop a vision for the future. In October of 2000, Huang expressed his new vision in the following way, using four key Chinese terms: school (校), teaching (教), learning (學) and educating (育):

> In schooling, there should be no difference between large and small institutions (校無大小); In teaching, there should be no difference between upper and lower levels (教無高下); In learning, there should be no difference among different ages (學無長幼); In educating, there should be no boundaries among different nations (育無國界).[8]

This was a vision unlike anything seen in public higher education institutions in China, as it clearly claimed the role of emerging private higher institutions as a powerful dynamic for individual and social development, regardless of issues of size, level, age and national identity. Also it integrated important values from traditional Chinese culture, most notably Confucius' famous slogan for his private school: "in teaching there is no such thing as social classes."[9] This vision has situated XAIU in a position where it can strive to achieve excellence in a form of higher education open to all, and in a setting dominated by major public universities that are much more exclusive in their recruitment of students. Huang's vision was developed on the basis of the motto he had chosen for XAIU in 1996: "Comprehensiveness with Diversity, Innovation with Self-Strengthening."[10] This gives concise expression to his educational philosophy of drawing on multiple sources of learning, self-cultivation and tireless innovation.

Local cultural elements serve as another resource for XAIU. In traditional Chinese culture, the dragon is a symbolic creature, said to be the son of heaven sent to govern and care for people on the earth. The fish, on the other hand, is seen as an ordinary and humble creature,

---

[8] Huang Teng, "Xiaowudaxiao, Jiaowugaoxia, Xuewuzhangyou, Yuwuguojie: Fazhan Minban Gaodeng Jiaoyu De Jiben Silu (No School should be Discriminated against on the Basis of Size, No Teaching on the Basis of Level, No Learning on the Basis of Age, and No Education on the Basis of National Boundaries: Preliminary Reflections on the Development of Private Higher Education)", in Huang Teng, *Minban Jiaoyu Qiusuo* (*Exploration of Private Education*) (Xi'an: Shaanxi People's Press, 2002), pp.64-72.
[9] *The Analects of Confucius*, 15.38.
[10] The original Chinese of the motto is *Duoyuan Jina, Ziqiang Chuangxin* (多元集納，自強創新), and the translation officially used by XAIU is "Comprehend, Creative, Never Yield," but we have tried to paraphrase it here in a way that will be clearer to Western readers.

representing the masses. The ancient Chinese tale of the carp leaping over the dragon gate, introduced earlier, suggests how a fish can transform itself into a dragon by jumping out of the water and over the Dragon Gate. In other words, an ordinary person can climb up to a higher social status through hard study and persistent effort. In ancient times, the process was usually by passing the extremely competitive Imperial Civil Service Examinations, while now it is by success in the highly competitive National Higher Education Entrance Examinations.

The Imperial Civil Service Examinations were first held in Xi'an, then called Chang'an, during the Tang Dynasty. Some examinees traveling to Chang'an found lodging in a small village just outside the city. While staying in this village they studied extremely hard and encouraged each other. Over time, as many of them met with success in the Imperial Civil Service Exams, this small village became known as a place of good fortune – Yuhua, the place where an ordinary humble fish can become a respected dragon. Literally, Yu (魚) means a fish, and Hua (化) means to transform. XAIU's new campus is now located in this same Yuhua village.

Photo 13.1: The Sculpture of A-Fish-Becoming-A-Dragon erected on the Cultural Square of Yuhua campus, symbolizing the XAIU's dynamic ethos inherited from traditional Chinese culture.

Given Huang's own successful career, it was natural for him to adopt the local folktale of a-fish-becoming-a-dragon (魚化龍) as XAIU's core ethos. He wanted his new university to serve as a place that could transform the lives of its students through focused efforts at learning. When asked what campus space or building was most symbolic for XAIU, he immediately pointed to the Sculpture of A-Fish-Becoming-A-Dragon situated on the Cultural Square of the Yuhua campus.

While Huang Teng envisioned XAIU as a place that should transform fish into dragons, he also wanted to transform his school from a vocational institution into a world class comprehensive university. Based on this vision, Huang saw XAIU's mission as sharing China's destiny, as a nation that is fast rising, serving the interests of its people, and becoming a top private university. For this long-term goal Huang went so far as to express his dream that XAIU might someday become a Harvard or a Stanford in China and enjoy that kind of international reputation. However, he knew this would be a very long journey![11]

Strategic Directions

A major public concern about private education in China has been how private higher institutions balance the investment needed for further development and the economic returns expected by their founders and stakeholders. This concern has cast a deep shadow on public confidence in this emerging enterprise.

From the very beginning XAIU has taken the stance that its development should be viewed as a public good, rather than an enterprise for making private profit. To ensure that this principle be maintained, XAIU established a Board of Trustees in 1994, which was later called a Board of Directors. This was done long before it became a requirement laid down by the Law of the People's Republic of China on the Promotion of Privately-Run Schools in 2002.

The Board of Directors mandates that no members of trustees' families are allowed to work in the Finance Office, nor may they inherit the status of trustees. Furthermore, trustees are not allowed to hold XAIU's stocks or shares. Meanwhile, the tenure of most trustees is limited to no more than two terms, or three terms in specific cases. In addition, the Board of Trustees has agreed that 100% of the revenue, including student fees and donations, has to be invested for institutional development. On

---

[11] Interview with Huang Teng, President, 28 May 2007.

the other hand, XAIU's founders are all automatically awarded the status of permanent or life-long trustees in order that their personal benefits can be guaranteed, in terms of the status and privileges they enjoy as trustees. By this system, XAIU protects itself from becoming a profit-oriented institution, while its founders' benefit can also be assured.

This strategy has gradually cleared away doubts about how the university can benefit the local community and the wider society, and has created a positive public image for parents and students. It has also made it possible to attract and retain many talented administrators and faculty members who are devoted to XAIU's development.

Another often voiced public concern has been about the quality of education provided by private higher institutions, since most have very short histories and lack the accumulation of experience and expertise necessary for a sound reputation. Naturally they are thus unable to compete with public universities in attracting new entrants. This is one of the major reasons why the Chinese government has not shown real respect and trust toward them. XAIU's leaders have taken this concern very seriously as is evident in several of their initiatives to promote quality in teaching and learning.

Our interview with Provost Li Rufeng provided many insights into the strategies that XAIU has adopted. One has been to establish a Committee of Teaching Assessment (教學考核領導小組), consisting of administrators from the Research Office, the Human Resources Office, and Deans of the ten colleges, who provide professional evaluation of and supervision over teaching.[12] In addition, the university has adopted several strategies of quality assurance learned from public universities which have accumulated significant experience in this area. Many of their administrators have been hired from among recent retirees of public universities, who are able to draw on their longstanding professional experience in the public sector. For example, before joining XAIU as Vice-President, Li Yuhua had been a Vice-President of Xi'an Jiaotong University, one of a few top leading public universities that are included in the prestigious 98/5 Project. Li Rufeng, Vice-President and Provost of XAIU, used to be a Vice-President of Xidian University, a key national university of electronic technology and informatics. There were also many other administrators in mid-level positions, who had been hired from public universities. They have helped XAIU to develop a systematic model of

---

[12] Interview with Li Rufeng, Provost, 30 May 2007.

quality assurance for private higher institutions in a short period, with the establishment of an academic senate, and institutional level committees responsible for teaching, academic degrees and textbooks.[13]

Another strategy was to recruit students with stronger academic backgrounds for undergraduate programs after XAIU was upgraded to a degree-granting institution in 2005. This made it possible for XAIU to compete with public universities in real terms.[14] With these initiatives relating to student recruitment, teaching supervision, evaluation and academic management, XAIU has created forms of quality assurance suited to its status as a private higher institution, which must protect the interests of students, regulate itself, and assure its public accountability and competitiveness in the market.

The third public concern has been over the research capacity of private higher institutions. As private institutions are reviving yet are still at an infant stage in China, there has been a persistent prejudice in the public arena over their genuine capacity for carrying out academic research, even though observable progress had been made in promoting teaching quality. XAIU's founders and leaders clearly saw this concern as both a challenge and an opportunity to fulfill their vision and mission, and to raise their public image. They also realized that a unique approach must be adopted, given their limitations. The choice they made was to undertake research on private education as a key frontier, and research on humanities and software development as their two key areas of focus.

In 2003, a Research Office was established to administer and support seven research institutes and centers. These include the Qifang Education Research Institute (七方教育研究所), the Traditional Chinese Culture Research Institute, the Foreign Language and Culture Research Institute, the West China Economic Development Research Institute, the Art Research Institute and the Computer Software Research Institute. The Qifang Education Research Institute was first set up as the Research Institute of Private Education in 1996 with President Huang Teng as its director, and it was renamed in 2001. It is the first research institute focusing on private schooling in private higher education institutions in China. It publishes two journals: *Private Education Research* (《民辦教育研究》) and *The Journal of Xi'an International University* (《西安外事學院學報》). By 2007, it had published ten books in its *Private Education Research*

---

[13] *Ibid*.

[14] Interview with Li Yuhua, Vice-President and Deputy to the President, 29 May 2007.

Series, four books in the *Qifang Liberal Arts Education Series*, and 29 books in various areas of the social sciences. It has also undertaken a number of state and provincial research projects. Most of these projects were conducted with the support of internal research grants, and there were a few research projects officially recognized by the Shaanxi government, though funding sources were not available from the government. The institute was awarded the National Excellent University Education Research Institute in 2005, and it has been widely recognized as a leading research institute in private education in China. XAIU has set up other research institutes on campus with the successful model of the Qifang Education Research Institute.[15]

Governance and Administrative Model

Although XAIU has elements of a family-style institution,[16] the founders viewed its development more as a public good, rather than a personal business. The Board of Directors has seven members with three types of memberships: permanent directors, who are the original founders, position directors, who may serve for two or three terms and tenured directors, who have a particularly high social status and so retain their title as director even after stepping down. The Board of Directors is the highest decision-making body for institutional vision and mission, key development plans, budgeting, financial management and strategic initiatives. It appoints the President and supervises the overall administration of the University. The President leads the University Council and presides over the university administration. The Council takes overall responsibility for the administration of the university, with several high level committees responsible for teaching, research, and general advice, respectively.[17]

---

[15] Interview with Wang Guan, Associate Director of the XAIU Qifang Education Research Institute, 31 May 2007.

[16] China has various types of private institutions, such as publicly-owned but privately-aided, privately-run but publicly-aided, and privately-owned and run. Among private institutions in the third type, the family style is usually the dominant model. See Yan Fengqiao and Wu Peijuan, "Zhongguo Minban Gaodeng Jiaoyu Yanjiu: Huigu, Bijiao Yu Zhanwang (Private Higher Education Research in China: Retrospect, Comparison and Prospect)", in *Gaodeng Jiaoyu Yanjiu* (*Higher Education Research*), No.5, 2005, pp.45-50; Philip G. Altbach, "Universities: Family Style," in Philip G. Altbach and Daniel C. Levy (eds.) *Private Higher Education: A Global Revolution* (Qingdao: China Ocean University Press, 2005), pp.29-32.

[17] Interview with Zhou Yanhai, Secretary of the CPC Committee, 28 May 2007.

The commonly followed administrative model of public universities is mandated in China's Higher Education Law of 1998 as a presidential responsibility system under the leadership of the university's Communist Party of China (CPC) Committee,[18] meaning supervisory leadership by the university's CPC Committee and executive leadership by the president of the university. By contrast the model of private universities is a presidential responsibility system under the leadership of the Board of Trustees or Directors. However, the Chinese central government has recently required private schools to set up institutional CPC network organs, and a university CPC Committee if conditions are mature for that. XAIU established the CPC network organs on campus in 2000 and recently the CPC Committee has begun to play a supervisory role, which is defined as ensuring that the CPC's guiding principles for education are implemented, that it adheres to the socialist orientation of education, and that the stability of the university is maintained.[19]

In most private universities the board of trustees or directors is the top policymaking body for institutional development, at least on paper, yet its real governing role and political power may often be in question. Usually the founder or president has a dominant role. We found an opportunity to explore this issue with President Huang Teng during our three hour interview with him. When asked about the relationship between the Board of Directors and the President and who has the final say in institutional decision-making, he explained it in the following way:

> Of course it's the Board of Directors which takes the main responsibility based on the charter of our board, but in the Chinese context, those who take the lead in a particular area have the final say …. for example, with regard to campus construction or the nomination of vice-presidents, I may take the lead in the decision-making process, but these decisions still have to be approved formally by the Board.[20]

The president or founder led administrative model of private universities was confirmed in this case. This model may result in neglect or even manipulation of the administrative power of the board of trustees or directors, but we found that this model has an obvious advantage for the institutional development of private higher education institutions – it

---

[18] "Article 39," in Zhonghua Renmin Gongheguo Gaodeng Jiaoyufa (Higher Education Law of the People's Republic of China), 1998, August 29.
[19] Interview with Zhou Yanhai, Secretary of the CPC Committee, 28 May 2007.
[20] Interview with Huang Teng, President, 28 May 2007.

allows the policymaking process to be very flexible and responsive. This has made it possible for XAIU to recruit experienced administrators and faculty in an effective way, to streamline the policy-making process, and to stimulate excellence in teaching and research. Vice-President Li Yuhua gave a vivid example of such a decision-making process. While XAIU only began looking for partners to establish its College of Auto Engineering in April of 2006, the collaboration with Japanese sponsors was decided on by May 16 of the same year. Such an important decision would have taken at least six months or possibly much longer in public universities.[21]

Faculty and Issues of Teaching and Research

The Faculty Profile

In 2005, XAIU had a total of 1,610 faculty member, of whom 563 were part-timers. Among them were 84 full professors (51 females), 259 associate professors (173 females), 231 assistant professors (127 females) and 473 teaching assistants (296 females), with 19 PhD holders (11 females). The larger proportion of female faculty members reflects a job market in which more male graduates tend to go to public institutions. In addition, there were more than 3,400 part-time teachers associated with XAIU.[22] They were supplemental academic staff to the full and part-time faculty members. Most of the faculty members were recruited from the graduates of public universities, and about 20% were experienced professors, retired from public institutions. For example, two of our four faculty focus group interviewees were in this category, with one having retired from Xi'an International Studies University and another from the Fourth Military Medical University.

By 2008, XAIU had a total of 1,685 faculty, of whom 407 were part-time faculty members. Among the 1,278 fulltime academic and teaching staff, 81 were full professors, 221 associate professors, 242 assistant professors, and 414 teaching assistants. Obviously, the growth of the teaching force at XAIU was unable to keep pace with that of student population on campus.

Issues of Teaching and Research

The faculty focus group meeting involved four faculty members from the

---

[21] Interview with Li Yuhua, Vice-President and Deputy to the President, 29 May 2007.
[22] Interview with Yao Qun, Director of the Human Resources Office, 29 May 2007.

College of Economics and Management, the College of Humanities, and the College of Foreign Languages. Our conversation touched on multiple themes, but two major topics came to the fore. One related generally to how they felt about their work in the university, and the other related to demands by the university in the areas of teaching and research.

Most of our interviewees felt that XAIU's leaders had attached much importance to building up the teaching workforce, in terms of human resources management, facilities and continuing education opportunities provided for faculty members. One professor from the College of Economics and Management put it in the following way:

> I joined XAIU in 2004, and have felt that teachers here are truly valued by the leaders. Every administrator is terribly busy, but still shows a very humane administrative style in relating to teachers. Compared with those in public higher education institutions, XAIU's administration building is not that beautiful, but the teaching buildings and student residences are all gorgeous. Based on our President's vision, XAIU's administration system is very flexible and responsive. And we are given many opportunities to further develop ourselves. I myself have just returned from Macau where I had a ten-month professional training. Overall, I feel that our vision is both new and flexible....

Other faculty members shared similar views, and one added that the cultural spirit of a-fish-becoming-a-dragon had also encouraged her efforts for excellence.[23]

It is commonly observed that faculty and staff in private universities have a highly demanding workload, and we found this was the case for XAIU. Most interviewees felt that the university put high pressure on them. Two professors commented that their workload was too heavy for them, with one of them putting it in the following way: "The most difficult thing I feel here is the heavy workload, and I am always too busy on campus, but such an intensive workload can also give you a special opportunity and a push to develop yourself." Another professor added that he felt the average workload was more than double that in public universities, as he was involved simultaneously in three kinds of work, teaching, student counseling and research, all extremely demanding. One major reason for feeling pressure was that the university had a tough evaluation system for all teachers, with campus-wide, year-round assessment of teachers' work at the end of every semester by

---

[23] Interview with the Faculty Focus Group, 29 May 2007.

the Committee of Teaching Assessment and also by students. Another reason was that the university urged teachers to be actively involved in research, as it has taken the initiative of moving toward a comprehensive university in the future. The interviewees admitted, however, that XAIU had been very supportive of teachers' research, with tangible strategies such as providing funding, and publication opportunities.

In the focus group meeting, we were also told about many critical challenges facing these professors. For example, student quality has been a haunting problem in their teaching, as most of their new entrants have been recruited from student pools with low scores in the National Higher Education Entrance Examinations. Another complaint from them was about their salaries. Whereas we have heard from the Human Resources Office and the Finance Office that the average salary of teachers was higher than that of administrators,[24] our interviewees felt that their salaries did not really match the work they did for the university.[25] Obviously, these are problems that are common for private universities in China, particularly in their early stage of development and expansion.

Students' Experiences

The focus group meeting with seven students provided insights into their learning experiences on the XAIU campus and their perspectives on private universities. The seven students were mainly in their third year of undergraduate studies, with two from the College of Foreign Languages, three from the College of Economics and Management, and two from the College of Humanities. While private higher education institutions are viewed as making a significant contribution in China's move to mass higher education,[26] our major concerns were to learn how students have experienced the expansion process in private universities, how far they have been supported in career development and to what extent they have experienced civic participation.

---

[24] Interview with Yao Qun, Director of the Human Resources Office, 29 May 2007; and Interview with Liu Yajie, Director of the Finance Office, 30 May 2007.
[25] Meeting with the Faculty Focus Group, 29 May 2007.
[26] Jun Li and Jing Lin, "China's Move to Mass Higher Education: An Analysis of Policy Making from a Rational Framework," in David P. Baker and Alexander W. Wiseman (eds.), *The Worldwide Transformation of Higher Education: International Perspectives on Education and Society* (Bingley: JAI Press, 2008), pp.271-272.

Experiences in the Expansion of Higher Education

Students admitted into private universities tend to have feelings of frustration because of their low performance in the National Higher Education Entrance Examinations, and this became evident in the stories of members of the student focus group. One opened his heart in this way: "I felt so depressed when I first registered in XAIU that it seemed all my dreams would be grey forever."[27] But he and a second student who reported similar feelings were strongly encouraged by XAIU's leaders and teachers, and by the ethos of A-Fish-Becoming-A-Dragon inherited from traditional Chinese culture. Both of them appeared to be confident and content during the focus group meeting, and one said that he was indeed very proud of being a student in XAIU and another reported he had already managed to be successfully upgraded to enrollment in a degree level program. Similar comments from other students gave the impression XAIU has created a very supportive, humane learning environment, particularly for new students, and that class counselors have worked very hard to nurture strong motivation for learning and growth. Students identified the Teaching Building with its Western architectural style and the Cultural Square as their favorite symbols of XAIU's institutional ethos and campus culture.

Photo 13.2: The Teaching Building in European Style integrates learning with the school motto "Comprehensiveness with Diversity, Innovation with Self-Strengthening (多元集納，自強創新)."

---

[27] Meeting with the Student Focus Group, 29 May 2007.

In addition, most students felt that learning in private universities was a dynamic process, and they showed a strong sense of confidence in what they were learning. One student noted that she felt XAIU was very modern, and the professors were all real experts in their respective fields. Compared with the situation in public universities, teaching and practice was well integrated at XAIU, students felt, and this served their needs well. However, there were concerns about how the university could provide better services. For example, some students mentioned that they badly need a classroom or a study room in the library that was open 24 hours a day and seven days a week.

Career Development

The students we talked with were appreciative of the career development opportunities provided by XAIU. For example, they were very satisfied with the internship bases established in Dalian, Beijing, Hangzhou, Guangzhou and Shanghai. These internship bases provided a very good service, in terms of broad career opportunities, also nice facilities for room and board. Some students found jobs in these cities immediately after they showed excellent performance during their internships. Students were also happy that their university had provided regular career guidance and consultation, including seminars on career planning. In their third year, they received intensive guidance from professionals about how to get familiar with the job market, which was especially valuable. Obviously, XAIU has put great effort into helping its students find suitable jobs and develop their careers, beginning from an earlier period than is common in public universities.

Of course, our interviewees felt nervous about their career possibilities after graduation, particularly in their final year of study. They worried about the market value of their certificates and degrees, and the reputation of their university, sensing that it would be difficult to compete in the job market with graduates from public universities.[28]

Participation in Civil Society

When asked about how private higher education institutions have contributed to civil society, President Huang Teng gave us some very thoughtful comments. One point he made was that private universities have similar social functions with public universities, but are different in

---

[28] *Ibid.*

many ways. For example, private universities have created more diverse and broad learning opportunities and have contributed to local development by providing job opportunities both on and off the campus.[29]

In the case of XAIU, most of its students would not have been able to gain access to higher learning in the public higher education system In other words, private higher education has made it possible for more youth to be exposed to civic responsibility and rights through their university experience. Our student focus group members reflected a sense that private universities have served the local community and the wider society not only through education but also through stimulating students' sense of social responsibility. For example, in addition to professional knowledge and skills, XAIU has taken practical strategies to encourage students' civic participations since 2002. Under the sponsorship of the university, students voluntarily organized more than 23 student associations. One of them, which deals with the environment, is called the Association of Green Lives. When a fish is transformed into a dragon, the dragon is almost certain to have a stronger sense of responsibility for society, especially in the Chinese context. Students felt that both their academic abilities and their understanding of social responsibility were being nurtured through their participations in these activities.[30]

Photo 13.3: The Cultural Square with the six sculptures of ancient educators in China and in the West, from Confucius, Laozi and Cai Yuanpei (right), to Plato, Aristotle, and Humboldt (left), symbolizing XAIU as a place where all creative thoughts, traditional or modern, Eastern or Western, are nurtured and encouraged.

---

[29] Interview with Huang Teng, President, 28 May 2007.
[30] Interview with the Student Focus Group, 29 May 2007.

Conclusion

Private universities have contributed to the opening up of higher education from an elite to a mass level, providing millions of graduates educated with applied vocational programs, of a kind that used to be very limited in China.[31] As we have seen in XAIU's rapid expansion of enrollment and its ambitious plan to accommodate 60,000 students in the mid-term future, it has significantly contributed to the expansion process in China, bringing to this effort its unique ethos of transforming ordinary fish into respected dragons. Through its fifteen-year journey from a training school to a comprehensive university, we can see how important its ethos has been in an unusual combination of traditional Chinese cultural elements and an active response to changing social demands. The strong leadership, open vision, practical strategies and effective administrative model have propelled its institutional establishment, development and transformation. In this exploratory pathway, private institutions have made mistakes, and experienced ups and downs, as they have faced both market and political risks, and had to deal with many critical comments. However, the functions they serve and the contributions they have made to the higher education system, their local communities and the wider society should be affirmed.

Private education is not something new in China. Before ancient pioneers such as Confucius set up their private schools two thousand and five hundred years ago, education was absolutely and exclusively dominated by a governmental school system. The Confucius-led movement for the privatization of education was dynamic and progressive, greatly challenging the status quo of public schooling, and creating a new model that was complementary to the public system.[32] While this long tradition has been twice suspended in Chinese history, in the Qin Dynasty (201-226 BCE) and in the 1950s after the CPC established its communist regime, the rebirth and blossoming of private education in the late 20th century has much promise for the future. This portrait of Xian International University shows some of the reasons why this is so.

---

[31] Interview with Zhou Yanhai, Secretary of the XAIU's CPC, 28 May 2008.
[32] Jun Li, "Jixia Xuegong De Banxue Tedian Jiqi Qishi (Thoughts on the Characteristics of Jixia Academy and its Modern Implications)", in *Gaodeng Jiaoyu Yanjiu (Higher Education Research)*, Vol.34, No.4, 1988, pp.100-105; also, Jun Li, "Lun Sixue Yu Zhongguo Chuantong Wenhua (On Private Schools and Traditional Chinese Culture)", in *Jiaoyu Yanjiu (Educational Research)*, Vol.143, No.12, 1991, pp.70-73.

14
Blue Sky – A University for the Socially Marginalized

Jing LIN and Qiang ZHA

Blue Sky (*Lantian*) University was founded in 1994 to provide vocational technical education. In 1999, it was approved by the Ministry of Education as a Higher Vocational Education College, and in 2005, it was granted the authority to offer undergraduate degree programs.[1] By 2008, Blue Sky had 57 majors at the undergraduate and postsecondary level, enrolling 21,592 students. It also had about 30,000 students enrolled in the preparatory program for the government-sponsored Self-taught Higher Education Examinations. Hence the total number of students was over 50,000. Blue Sky's chief focus is on engineering, but it also has programs in education, languages, medicine, law, arts, business management and administration. Faculty and staff totaled 3,000 in 2008.

The university is located in Jiangxi, an inland province in Central China, a region that has been economically defined as "developing" in comparison to the more developed Eastern coastal region, along with such provinces as Anhui, where the USTC is located, Henan, with Yellow River University of Science and Technology and Hubei, with the HUST.[2] Jiangxi was a revolutionary stronghold for the Communist Party of China (CPC) in the 1930s. Since it is remote and has a lot of mountainous areas it was a good hiding place at the time. With the economic reform of the late 1970s, however, this remoteness has resulted in neglect and a lack of investment by the central government. As a consequence, Jiangxi has lagged behind eastern provinces, and even some western provinces, where the government has given special support in recent years.[3] Despite this problem, Jiangxi's private higher education development has given it

---

[1] In that same year, 16 other private universities were also given degree-granting status, bringing the total number to 25.
[2] See Chapters 9, 10 and 12 of this volume.
[3] Huang Hui, "Strategy for Development of Central China (Zhongguo Zhongbu Jueqi Moulue)," in *Lianwang Weekly*, March 16, 2005, accessed February 12, 2011, http://www.agri-history.net/news/050316.htm.

a high profile, since a triangle of strong centres for private universities has emerged, involving Xi'an[4] in the West, Beijing in the North and Jiangxi in the central south. This was possible due to a unique set of government policies as well as boldness and commitment by leaders such as Yu Guo, Blue Sky's visionary founder.

Blue Sky has attracted nationwide attention and was rated a top private university in 2008.[5] Firstly, its founder's story has touched and inspired many people. Secondly, it has continuously maintained an employment ratio of about 97% for its graduates. Thirdly, its collective synergy and constant effort to adjust and innovate, in a higher education environment, which is not very friendly for private institutions, has won national and international attention.

In this chapter, we will detail Blue Sky's history, highlighting the role of the founder, Yu Guo, in building its spirit and reputation. We will examine the leadership team, and analyze the strategies it used to build particular niches for the university. Efforts to manage students and recruit and retain faculty are also described, followed by excerpts from the voices of faculty and students at our focus group meetings. Also examined is the effort to build research capacity in an unfavorable environment. Finally, the volatile relationship of the university with the government is discussed.

A Brief History of Blue Sky and its Founder's Story

Yu Guo was born in 1962 into a rural family. His mother was a school teacher and his father was in charge of a long distance bus station. He got polio at a very young age and inappropriate treatment by doctors resulted in one of his legs being slightly crippled. During the Cultural Revolution, his father was locked up, and he had nowhere to study. His mother founded a local elementary school with the help of some villagers. Yu Guo studied in this school and in 1978, he participated in the National University Entrance Examination and achieved a score of 40 points higher than the required acceptance level. Nevertheless, he was turned down since there was a policy of not admitting handicapped students at

---

[4] See Chapter 13 of this volume.
[5] "2008 Ranking of China's Minban University Just Comes Out and Jiangxi Lantian College Ranks at the Top," China Master's and Doctural Web, (Zhonghua Shuobo Wang), April 28, 2008, accessed February 12, 2011, http://www.china-b.com/zixun/bjkjzyxy/zixun_6218.html.

that time.[6] He therefore made it a goal for himself to set up a school one day that would admit students like himself who had been unfairly denied access to higher education.

Yu Guo later found a job in a Jiangxi Opera (*Ganju*) Theater (贛劇團) as a stage and costume designer. This job required a lot of climbing, also the loading and unloading of equipment for the stage. However, Yu Guo did a great job, showing that he was physically as able as anyone else, while also developing good costume design skills. He even won the heart of a beautiful actress. The 1980s saw a decline in the traditional arts in China as popular arts and Western-style performances were revived. Hence, the Jiangxi *Ganju* Opera Theater experienced financial difficulties. Knowing that Yu Guo learned fast and had a spirit of perseverance, the head of the theater sent him to learn a rare form of performance in which the performer changes faces many times during a short time on stage, without the audience being able to detect the process. The technique for doing this art form is known to only a few people and masters performing this art choose their disciples very strictly. Although there was a master performer in Sichuan, where he was sent, he was turned down again and again. With incredible determination, he stood outside the master's house for months, and finally got the master to hint at some basic principles while still revealing no details. Yu Guo returned home, did his own research and eventually mastered the art of "Changing Face." This story illustrates qualities of persistence and quickness in learning that were later vital to Yu Guo's success in building Blue Sky University.

In the end the Jiangxi *Ganju* Opera had to close down, and Yu Guo decided to go to the border between Russia and China to sell clothes. He had a talent for business, and with hard work he earned about 2 million *yuan* in three years. This was a huge sum of money in the early 1990s. Yu Guo decided to use it to fulfill his dream of opening up higher education to those who were unfairly denied entrance. He returned to Jiangxi and set up the Jiangxi Higher Vocational School in 1994.

At the beginning there were only a few programs in areas such as clothing design, computer science and accounting. However, the school attracted many students since there was a great need for vocational technical education in Jiangxi at that time. Many people wanted to learn some specialized skills in order to make a living. Many had left the province

---

[6] Physical fitness was a requirement under the socialist planning system, when no fees were charged and all students were assigned jobs on graduation.

due to its low level of economic development and lack of job opportunities.

By 1995 the school had 500 students and the number had grown to 1,000 by 1996. At that time, only 17-20 % of the upper secondary school graduates in Jiangxi could attend any form of post-secondary education. Meanwhile, the central and local governments were supportive of private post-secondary education, and vocational colleges and adult learning institutions mushroomed. The National Self-taught Higher Education Examinations (高等教育自學考試) were initiated in 1985 to provide an alternative higher education credential for those who failed to enter formal higher education. Yu Guo therefore set up another school called "Jiangxi Southeastern Further Study Institute," to help students pass these examinations and obtain certificates or degrees. The Self-Study Examinations were known for their toughness, with a pass rate under 10%. However, when more than 50% of the examinees in this new institution passed, another 3,000 students were attracted within a short time.

In 1998, another golden opportunity came for private institutions. The government decided to offer degrees and certificates in vocational technical postsecondary education by a new arrangement: one third of the courses, those in general subjects, were to be tested by the Ministry of Education; one third, those in major core courses, by the provincial education authorities; and one third, those in various specializations, by private higher institutions. This arrangement gave private institutions a great advantage, and enabled them to attract many more students. Jiangxi Southeastern Further Study Institute thus had 8,000 applications in 1998 alone.

Yu Guo set up his first campus in 1995, having collected 10 million *yuan* from a variety of sources. This campus has 250 *mu* (about 42 acres) of land and 180,000 square meters of living and teaching space. It provided a stable environment for teaching and learning. By 2008 this was called "the Old Campus," and as a second campus it accommodated 465 full time teachers, 1,070 part time teachers and around 15,000 students.

Opportunity for the construction of a much larger campus came in 2003 when the Jiangxi government decided to create a university town. The provincial government aspired to "develop the province through education" and the original plan was to carve out a significant amount of land for public universities to build large new campuses. However, private universities were not included in the plan. Yu Guo went to the provincial officials and showed the recently passed "Law for the Promotion of Minban (people-run) Education" (民辦教育促進法), which stated that private universities should be treated equally with public universities.[7] The government officials conceded his point, and Blue Sky received equal treatment with public universities, being allocated 2,000 *mu* (357 acres) at 30,000 *yuan* per *mu*, an incredibly low price for today. Within nine months, a new campus was established.

With this new campus, Blue Sky has a total of 1.5 million square meters of space for its teaching buildings, dorms, libraries, labs, scholarly activity rooms, sports facilities and theaters. Most impressively, the university has vast open areas with gardens, water fountains, a lake and spacious sidewalks. This change allows the university to expand its teaching force from only a dozen teachers in 1994 to around 2,000 faculty in 2004, with students now coming from across the country, not only Jiangxi. The new facilities earned the university favorable review when it applied for approval to offer undergraduate degree programs, a privilege tightly controlled by the government.[8] In 2005, Blue Sky received a unanimous vote from the Ministry of Education evaluation committee for its newly developing degree programs.

In the process of developing Blue Sky, Yu Guo has gradually formed his own philosophy of education. Yu had a close relationship with Zhang Qimin, a former president of Jiangxi Vocational and Technical Teaching College, and later the president of Jiangxi Institute of Education. Zhang introduced Yu Guo to the Tao Xingzhi (陶行知) Research Society,[9] inviting him to serve on the society's Board of Directors. Yu Guo

---

[7] The *Law for the Promotion of Minban (people-run) Education* was passed on 28 December 2002, and implemented on 1 September 2003. Its English version is available at http://www.albany.edu/dept/eaps/prophe/data/Country_Law/ChinaPromotionLaw.doc, and an article "China's New Private Education Law" in *International Higher Education*, No.31, Spring 2003, discussed the evolution of this law, which is co-authored by Fengqiao Yan – our collaborating scholar at Beida – and Daniel C. Levy.
[8] Jing Lin, Yu Zhang, Lan Gao and Yan Liu, "Trust, ownership, and autonomy: Challenges facing private higher education in China," in *The China Review*, Vol.5, No.1, Spring, 2005, pp.61-81.
[9] Tao Xingzhi (1891-1946) established several schools and promoted education for ordinary people in the 1930s. He was critical of traditional rote learning and of educational content that was detached from the needs of society. He was a student of John Dewey and promoted the integration of learning and action, and education and society, in an even more radical way than Dewey. See Yusheng Yao, "The Making of a National Hero: Tao Xingzhi's Legacies in the People's Republic of China," in *Review of Education, Pedagogy, and Cultural Studies*, Vol.24, No.2, 2002, pp.251-281.

was struck by Tao Xingzhi's dedication to the education of rural and disadvantaged people and he embraced one of Tao's sayings as his own life's mission: "To come to this world with a loving heart, and to leave this world without taking away a single blade of grass." He decided his goal for running his private university was to serve the country and to help China train human resources for social and economic development. "With this sense of mission, we have never yielded, no matter how great are the difficulties we meet with," Yu Guo says.[10] The name *Lantian* (藍天), meaning blue sky, was chosen by Yu Guo to signify that all students, regardless of their background, will be given an equal opportunity to fulfill their hopes and dreams under the blue sky.

Yu Gu, is the university's undisputable leader. Like other well known private universities such as Yellow River University of Science and Technology and Xi'an International University, the founders often have endured tremendous hardship and demonstrated amazing resilience to make their institutions successful. Their charisma has given them a profound relationship with the faculty and students such that they tend to be equated with the heart and soul of the university.

Yu Guo has also been recognized by the government. The various honors and titles he has been given, such as one of the National Ten Outstanding Young People and a People's Representative to the National People's Congress, now constitute a part of the university's social capital, which in turn enables them to attract students. Yu Guo made use of his position as a representative to the National People's Congress to propose the bill for the "Law of the Promotion of Minban Education".[11]

Yu has galvanized a lot of energy around himself, yet he maintains

---

[10] Interview with Yu Guo, 26 May 2008.

[11] Yu was elected to be a representative to the National People's Congress in 1998, the only one coming from among private school leaders. At that time, there was no law for private educational institutions, only some tentative regulations. In March 1998, Yu joined with 38 representatives nationwide to submit a proposal for promoting private education. This proposal got attention from the National People's Congress, which established a law drafting panel, surveyed private schools and colleges nationwide, and passed the *Law of Promotion of Minban Education* at the 5th meeting of the National People's Congress on 28 December 2002. The law came into effect on 1 September 2003. With this law, private educational institutions have got equal status with public schools. This means private universities are legally exempted from taxes on their profits and can receive preferential treatment for land acquisition from the government.

a low profile, eating with faculty members in their canteen, and refusing to pay himself the highest salary among all his staff. He has spent significant sums of money improving the university, especially establishing its engineering majors. "He truly takes private higher education as a serious public undertaking," we heard from faculty members.[12]

The Campus

Yu Guo sees his university as having a soul. The shape of the campus is designed to look like a gourd or *hulu* (葫蘆), famous in Chinese legends as a container in which alchemists refine and hold the energy (丹), which can bring about miracles and lead a person to immortality. The design of the university also reflects a belief in *fengshui* (風水), the idea of good energy accumulating knowledge, wealth and talent for the university.

Photo 14.1: An aerial view of the campus of Blue Sky University, with its gourd-like shape expressing the idea of it as a container of miraculous energy.

In the center of the campus stands the Blue Sky Pavilion. This is an imitation of the Teng Wang Pavilion (滕王閣), an ancient building in downtown Nanchang, the capital of Jiangxi. It was famous for an essay written by a Tang Dynasty poet, Wang Bo (王勃), who wondered about the universe, marveled at the spectacular beauty of the local scenery, and expressed his ambition to serve society despite the shortness of life. The Blue Sky Pavilion in the center of the campus gives it a sense of history.

---

[12] Interview with Faculty Focus Group, 27 May 2008.

In the central part of the campus, the best location, stands the library. It is shaped like an open book, symbolizing the acquiring of knowledge. In between the Blue Sky Pavilion and the library is a lake. Yu Guo and his architect believed that water will bring a kind of divine energy (靈氣) to the campus. In designing the campus, the architect also placed laboratories and workshops in the most prominent place near the entry to the university. This is to highlight the emphasis on technology and engineering.

The whole campus is like a garden. Flowers blossom in all seasons. The garden-like campus gives the impression this is a wonderful place for study and helps to attract students. Since Blue Sky students are mostly from working class or rural families, this environment is seen as important for fostering good taste and cultivating their character. When we asked who took care of the greenery on campus, we were informed that about 800 peasants who were displaced when the university took over their farmland to build this campus are now employed to tend the gardens and maintain the buildings.

Building a Highly Capable Leadership Team

"Hiring talent without restriction or by any fixed norms" has been a strategy used by many private universities in China to form their leadership teams. Given the fact that they get neither financial nor academic support from the government, founders like Yu Guo make a great effort to hire capable leaders. First, he has hired highly reputable and experienced administrators from public universities. Some of these people came after they had retired, and a few came when still in the prime of their careers. Second, he has hired experienced former managers of companies, factories or hospitals, most of whom had retired from their jobs.[13] Third, he recruits graduates from well known universities and gives them significant responsibilities, also trust and encouragement, so they can use their abilities to the full.

In the first category, the president of the university, Zhang Qimin, used to be the president of the Jiangxi Vocational College, and later he had led the Jiangxi Institute of Education before retirement. Zhang is

---

[13] In China, women retire at 55 and men at 60. Many people after their retirement seek to work more years so that they can earn extra income as well as using their talent to serve society. They also add legitimacy to private universities, as well as bringing social capital in terms of their connections.

thus a highly experienced official in higher vocational education in Jiangxi. Zhang was the one to suggest that Yu Guo should focus on vocational education when he was thinking of setting up his own school. Since then Yu has sought Zhang's advice in many stages of Blue Sky's development. In 1999, after Zhang retired from public office, Yu Guo invited him to be the president of Blue Sky, while he himself held the position of the Chairman of the Board. Zhang had the greatest respect for Yu and has put in all his time into helping Yu develop Blue Sky. He planned to retire at the end of 2008.[14]

Vice President Xu Xiangyun told us he was recruited to Blue Sky by Yu Guo, and was given a high level of trust and considerable freedom to act. He had been a leading scholar at Jiangxi Agricultural University and as provost he had instituted significant changes in that university. When Yu Guo first approached him, he would not consider the prospect of working in a private college, since he felt they had low social prestige and did not open up opportunities for higher governmental positions. But once Xu came to Blue Sky and saw with his own eyes how effective the university was, how dedicated Yu Guo was, and how innovative its leaders were, he felt he could put many of his ideas about higher education into practice there. Defying misunderstanding from his colleagues and the reluctance of his family, he came to Blue Sky, and felt that he could do a lot more than would be possible in a public university. For example, he established an Institute of Research in Educational Science within a month, with four staff working under him. He also made a proposal to Yu Guo to set up a practical training facility for business major students, which would cost 3 million *yuan*. From putting together the proposal to validating the project and building the facility, it took only three months. According to Xu, this kind of project could take months or years for a public university to complete. Xu feels Yu Guo places a lot of trust in his subordinates: "President Yu never interferes with what we do; we need to report to him only about major affairs. As long as our work is good for the students, he will give his full support".[15]

In the second category, Blue Sky has taken advantage of the fact that they can appoint people who may not have the normal academic qualifications or titles. For example, public universities would require faculty to have doctoral degrees and stress their record of publication

---

[14] Interview with Zhang Qimin, President, 26 May 2008.
[15] Interview note, 26 May 2008.

and grants. However, at Blue Sky they hire people who have been managers in the frontline of work, who thus have no publications but rich practical and professional experience. The Director of the Nursing Center had 40 years of experience in nursing in a major public hospital before she was hired. This experience helps students in the nursing program to get first rate training, and be prepared to deal with a wide range of problems. The director of the program of Digital Control used to be a factory manager. He had many years of experience working on site and could tell students exactly how to operate the complicated machinery using digital control technology.

Blue Sky is bold in finding ways to motivate and reward its leaders. For example, all the top-level university leaders have been given a car of some well-known brand for their personal use. The mid-level leaders, who get bonuses from their job, have all purchased their own vehicles. In an economically underdeveloped province, this symbolizes status and respect. Private university leaders worry that their universities may lack an appropriate social status and they want to change this situation as soon as possible. We found that Blue Sky's leaders were fully aware of what was happening in other private universities, as well as in the public sector, and constantly adopted new ideas from what they observed elsewhere.

Management Structure

The university's highest leadership body is the Board of Directors with seven members. It makes all the important administrative and personnel decisions. At the university level, there is an Academic Affairs Committee whose members are comprised of associate professors and above in each department; they are considered academic experts who formulate policies on academic affairs. Under this Committee there is a Curriculum and Instruction Advising Committee and there is also a Program Advising Committee which consists of core teachers of a discipline in each department.

A Presidents' Meeting, involving the president and vice-presidents, is held once a month. The meetings are mainly to discuss school management, teaching and instruction. When it comes to the appointment of the president and deputy presidents, they have to be nominated by the board of directors. They need to have five years or more of working experience in public universities as president or deputy president. Or they must be distinguished scholars with working experience in public universities.

Creating Blue Sky's Niche: Practice-Oriented Education

A distinctive feature of Blue Sky's profile is that it treats student employment as its lifeline. For several consecutive years, the university has boasted an employment record as high as 97% for its graduates. In a national context where only 70% of university graduates have been able to find jobs in recent years, Blue Sky's record is envied by many.

The secret has been the provision of "practice-oriented" education. Blue Sky has built its niche through constant innovation and adjustment to the changing employment situation. Firstly, it pays close attention to students' employment from the day they begin their studies. It has a career counseling center with several dozen employees. Every year, 1,000 graduates are hired by employers who had already made arrangements with the university in advance, since it has built up collaboration with about 2,000 companies. In 2009, the director in charge of student employment was working to extend this to 3,000 companies eventually. Secondly, Blue Sky is careful to avoid the use of inflated promises and false information to recruit students, as happens at some private universities. It gives students information about the limitations as well as the advantages of its programs. It attracts students by emphasizing the governmental and societal recognition won by its founder, also the investment in its campus and facilities, and the employment rate of its graduates over the years. Thirdly, Blue Sky emphasizes the importance of providing excellent conditions for students' learning, as we will see in subsequent sections. Fourthly, the ability to apply what is learned in real work situations is emphasized.

In 2005, the university established its mission as "to build a first-class practice-oriented university providing higher vocational technical education."[16] Its niche area is clearly engineering, with a balanced development of other majors. The decision to select this niche was arrived at through an understanding that China is still undergoing major development, and there is a great need for people in engineering. To be more specific, Blue Sky uses market needs to guide its establishment of majors and specify its goals of education. It also realizes that two critical factors are the quality of education and flexibility in requirements. For example, beyond emphasizing test scores and grades, students are also evaluated on their commitment to their profession, and their problem solving abilities. Blue Sky focuses on training "frontline workers," whose most

---

[16] Interview with Xu Xiangyun, 25 May 2008.

important qualities are commitment and problem solving ability. "Practice-oriented" education makes eminent sense in a situation where many students are not academically strong, but have strong abilities in using their hands.

The set up of the automobile building illustrates practice-oriented education. Inside the building there are lines of cars of all types with their engines open and a full view of the inside, such as the electrical wiring of the whole car. Along side of the display rooms are seminar rooms which are arranged in such a way that students can brain storm right after they have examined the engines, quite different from traditional classrooms with the teacher's platform in the center at the front.

Programs and Curriculum Development

When Blue Sky was first founded, it had only three majors: fashion design, accounting and computers. By1999/2000, it had seven majors: Computer and Internet Technology, Electrical Engineering, Industrial and Business Management, Accounting, Business English, Decorative Art Design, and Computer Assisted Art Design. In 2001 three new majors were added: Electrical Information Technology, Electronic Commerce, and Tourism English.

In 2002, four more majors were added, including Digital Control Technology, Real Estate Management, International Finance, and Movie and Television Animation. In 2003 another nine majors were added, including Software Programming, Automobile Production and Assembly Technology, Music Performance, Dance Performance and Physical Education. The addition of Automobile Production and Assembly Technology was especially important, since it later became the key major at Blue Sky. 2004 saw the addition of 12 more majors, including two relating to Automobile Technology, Legal Affairs and Civil Engineering. In 2005, three more majors related to automobiles were added, plus other five majors including Environmental Art Design, bringing the total to 45. By 2008, there were 57 majors and so the expansion continues.

2005 was the year Blue Sky was formally accredited to admit undergraduate degree students. That year, it admitted 507 students, with 386 male students, and 117 female students. The first batch of undergraduate students was enrolled in the following six programs: Computer Science; Mechanics; Engineering and Automation; Automobile Services; Electrical Information Technology; English; and Arts Design. Subsequent years saw the following undergraduate enrollments:

2006: 11 undergraduate programs admitting 381 students
2007: 14 undergraduate programs admitting 558 students
2008: 18 undergraduate programs, with a plan to enroll 1,000 students

Although the number remains modest, it is a great leap for Blue Sky as it indicates an equal standing with public universities with the presence of degree students on campus.

Finance

In our interview with the Director of Finance, we learned that the university has only once received funding from the government, a grant of 2.2 million *yuan* from the Ministry of Education for building a "Digital Control Laboratory." Generally, 98-99% of Blue Sky's funding is from tuition, with the rest coming from interest and the sale of services. Student enrollment is kept within the range of 50,000, including all types of programs and training for the government's Self-taught Examinations.

Expenditures are mainly on faculty and staff salaries, instruction, and the construction of facilities. The university has a policy of adjusting expenditure according to their revenue. Salaries, including benefits, usually make up 15-22% of total expenditure. In 2007, faculty salaries were increased by 48%, and this sudden rise was mainly intended to improve the quality of teaching and to attract talented faculty from elsewhere. In 2007, salaries made up 22% of the total expenditure. For some years 35-40% of revenue was spent on the construction of new buildings and facilities, but all the buildings have now been completed, and 20% of revenue is spent on the repayment of loans. The remaining expenditures are: Instruction 25%, student financial aid 4.8%, administration costs 20%, and savings 5-10%. Student recruitment costs 10 million *yuan* annually.

We were informed that annual student aid totaled 4 million *yuan* in the form of scholarships, assistantships, and work-study opportunities, from Blue Sky's own budget. For years, private universities were not allowed to receive financial aid or loans from the government, but beginning in 2007, this policy changed and Blue Sky received 10 million *yuan* in loans for student aid since 2007. Blue Sky itself has to pay for the interest on these students loans, which can cost hundred of thousands of *yuan* per year, we were told.

Self Study students have always been a great s in 2008, and tuition was 6,000 *yuan* per student. In terms of success rate, their single subject pass rate is 80-90%. The pass rate for all subjects (to get a credential) is

50-60%. Most Self Study students are not able to get into universities due to their low scores in the National University Entrance Exam. We were told that 85% of the students are from outside Jiangxi Province, while 15% are from Jiangxi. This is considered a major achievement as it indicates the university has a national reputation and is able to compete with other universities in the country for students. Most students are from middle-income families and 15% of the students need to apply for financial aid.

Over the years, the University has established a "Development Foundation" with 600 million *yuan* in it. Each year, 20 million *yuan* will be budgeted for equipment renewal. In the end of 2007, Blue Sky's total assets were estimated at 1.2 billion *yuan*, including the land.[17]

Student Recruitment

Students are the lifelines of private universities and it is often said that it may be difficult to set up a private university, but it is even more difficult to recruit students. Private universities have suffered from a lack of trust from both society and the government. In the early years, Yu Guo and his teachers had to go from one village to another, to schools and townships, "almost to every corner in Jiangxi, and many places in the country," to use his own words, to get students interested in applying to Blue Sky.

Private universities often put a lot of effort into attracting students and Blue Sky is no exception. First of all, it has used Yu Guo's reputation as a charismatic leader. The fact that Yu Guo has been elected ten times as a people's representative to the provincial or national People's Congresses is used to demonstrate that the university can be trusted. Yu Guo is also a member of the executive committee of the National Youth League, and has been named one of the "Ten Outstanding Youth" in the nation. He was also elected as "A National Outstanding Educator" and "A National Labor Model." These honors bring credibility to the university, and hence the admissions team would always stress that the university is being led by a reliable and trustworthy leader, not some unknown person.[18]

Secondly, the university uses exemplary cases among its students and graduates to attract students. For example, Chen Jie, who had lost

---

[17] This information on Blue Sky's financial situation was provided by the Director of Finance, Lan Gongcheng in an interview on 26 May 2008.
[18] Interview with Jiao Kouyun, Director of Student Admissions, on 26 May 2008.

both arms but had obtained high scores in the National University Entrance Exam, was rejected by all other universities except by Blue Sky. She was exempted from tuition and fees and her mom was assisted her move to Jiangxi and settled in an apartment there so that she could help Chen Jie while she was studying. Chen Jie excelled in her major, eventually got a Master's degree and is now a faculty member at Blue Sky. The case of Chen Jie is often cited to convey the university's commitment to equity and to portray it as a caring place.

Thirdly, the arrangement of majors is key. The university offers programs that focus on practical experience and employability, rather than status or high income. This attracts a great number of students from the lower levels of society, as their main goal is to find a job and survival is their first and foremost concern.

Fourthly, a highly capable team of staff works 24 hours a day to provide consultation and recruit students. Jiao Kouyun, Vice President in charge of Student Admissions, impressed us as a highly capable leader. She has more than 50 staff, working on public promotion, and answering call-in and online inquiries. With more than 20 telephone lines, 20 staff work during the day, and another 20 staff work on a night shift. Previously, they sent one representative to every province to recruit students. Now this is no longer necessary, because phones and emails are very efficient for communication.

Jiao Kouyun informed us that in the sequence of admitting university students, Blue Sky is in the third round of admission, after key universities and then regular public universities have picked their students from those qualified in the National University Entrance Examinations. Blue Sky admits their students in this third round, taking the best they can select until they meet their quota for undergraduate degree students, which is set by the government, and their own plan for other types of students such as Diploma or Self Study students. According to Jiao Kouyun, among the students they have accepted, 70-80 percent have put Blue Sky as their first choice.

Faculty Recruitment, Training and Benefits

In our interview with Wei Jianghong, Director of the Personnel Office, she informed us that Blue Sky has 1,248 teachers, of whom 1,035 are full-time and 213 are part-time. Part-time teachers are mostly from nearby universities. Among the 1,248 teachers, 270 are associate professors or above in rank. Ten hold doctoral degrees, and 366 hold Master's degrees.

Among the 366, 318 are under 35 years old. Director Wei noted that Blue Sky aims to develop a balanced age structure in its faculty.[19] To improve the quality of their faculty, Blue Sky has established four programs since 2005:

1) Master's degrees for faculty members. This program encourages teachers to go for Master's degrees, with tuition reimbursement and benefits provided by the university.
2) Educating prospective backbone teachers, or teachers who will form the core of the teaching force, providing exemplary teaching and service. This involved helping selected faculty to obtain higher degrees and gain promotion.
3) Prospective first-class expert-faculty program. This aims to train "master" teachers who will be leaders of teachers.
4) "Double-track" faculty program. This aims to train teachers to be both strong academically and in practical ability. Since Blue Sky specializes in engineering, it encourages teachers to participate in long-distance education programs, or go to factories and enterprises for field study and training.

Over the period 2005-2007, more than 5 million *yuan* was spent on faculty upgrading, with the following breakdown: 1.91 million *yuan* in 2005; 1.71 million *yuan* in 2006, and 2.02 million in 2007.

Faculty with a bachelor's degree generally have to teach 12 hours a week. Those with a graduate degree are encouraged to do research, which can be counted as part of their work load. Wei Jianghong told us frankly that faculty research has just started, and they are trying to attract faculty who can do research. For example, a faculty member with a doctoral degree would be paid 90,000 *yuan* a year, with an additional settlement subsidy of 25,000 *yuan*, and a housing subsidy 300,000 *yuan*. This is much higher than normal faculty or staff salaries.

---

[19] Most private universities have relied on hiring faculty from nearby public universities as part time teachers, or hiring retired faculty. So the faculty tend to be older, with few young or middle aged teachers. With expansion and an increase in assets and revenue, many private universities gradually increase their full-time faculty, especially paying attention to attracting middle aged or young faculty. Now with the expansion in graduate study programs in public universities, they have a much easier time to hire teachers with MA or even PhD degrees. It used to be that the private universities had such low status and poor benefits that they could hardly attract any qualified faculty. But now the benefits and facilities most private universities are able to offer have changed that situation.

Generally, faculty members have felt less secure in private universities, and have had less sense of belonging than in public ones. As private universities have developed, they have started to address this critical issue. In Blue Sky's case, starting from 1999, they have provided retirement insurance, health insurance, maternity leave insurance, injury insurance, unemployment insurance, and a housing accumulation fund. Blue Sky pays 400 *yuan*/month insurance for each faculty member, and another 200 *yuan*/month is paid by faculty themselves. For the housing accumulation fund, Blue Sky pays 120 *yuan*/month, and faculty pay another 120 *yuan*/month. The expenditure on insurance for faculty is 15 million *yuan* per year.

Blue Sky has established a number of mechanisms in order to hear the voices of faculty members: the president's mailbox, mailboxes of each college dean and department head, and an online complaint mailbox. Furthermore, every year a Faculty and Staff Representative Conference is held, hosted by the Faculty Union. Faculty members have proposed suggestions to the university such as providing in-service training, establishing a supervision system to standardize the quality of teaching, and increasing funding for improving faculty teaching ability.

Student Management

The guideline established by Yu Guo for student management is as follows: "Everything is for students; it is for all students; and for all aspects of students' well-being." (一切為了學生；為了一切學生；為了學生一切)

Student management takes place at many levels, by the Office of Student Affairs, the Department of Campus Security, the Department of Ideological Education[20] and by staff in student dormitories. Class directors, non-teaching faculty whose major task is student management, play an especially crucial role.

The daily management of students takes place at the department level. Generally, students in private universities are strictly managed, as they are seen as not having formed good study habits and not being good at managing their time.[21] However, Blue Sky's administrative personnel

---

[20] This is a typical entity in Chinese universities. It reflects the importance of universities maintaining adherence to government ideology among their students. In a way, this reflects the limitations on autonomy for the university.

[21] Jing Lin, "Students and Teachers at Private Universities in China," in *International Higher Education*, No.38, Winter 2005, pp.21-22.

realize that it is counter productive to restrict students too much, and so they spend a lot of time on moral education,[22] and also encourage students to be self-disciplined, independent and self-reliant. Blue Sky sent some staff to learn from other universities and establish a few priorities for moral education. One is love and care education. This is conducted by activities such as visiting elderly homes and providing help to poor people. It is also manifested in students helping each other, and in students writing letters to their parents to express appreciation for their love and care. The younger generation is mostly from single child families, and they have been the center of care by others, so this latter effort is to remind them to reciprocate the love they have received from their parents.

Blue Sky has a tradition of holding a special opening ceremony for their new students every year. It is usually held in the Nanchang Sports Center, which cost 100,000 *yuan* to rent each time. The students walk from the old campus to the Sports Center, a distance that takes one to two hours. While walking, the students talk among themselves and are recognized and cheered by onlookers in an atmosphere that is extremely lively. In the ceremony, there are performances by senior students, and talks given by outstanding alumni about their stories of success. The president, Yu Guo, sings a song he has composed, "Believe in Yourself", which has been adopted as the university's song,

In the daily life of students, there is an advisor in each dormitory, and in every two dormitories there will be a supervisory teacher. These supervisors provide counseling to students, organize clubs and parties and are also responsible for Communist youth league activities. These supervisory teachers do not actually teach, but function as full time administrators.

In the classroom, there are class directors and counselors. For every 100 student there is one class director assigned. The whole university has a total of 500 class directors, who are full time faculty looking after the students, taking care of all kinds of affairs from student activities to problems in learning and emergencies in students' lives. These teachers can also teach but most do not. They are mostly students who have

---

[22] The content of moral education includes discipline, respect for parents and teachers, patriotism, responsibility, collectivism, diligence in academic study, etc. It covers a wide range of topics. In China, students are considered to be unmolded products, and all levels of schools have the moral obligation to mold them in moral terms. Moral education is not seen as a choice but a necessity.

studied at Blue Sky University and are retained to be class directors after they graduate. This is done by most private universities, as they believe their own students know their university best and have a sense of loyalty. For graduates, this is seen as a rather good choice of employment.

Fairly strict management is considered a necessity so that students can form good habits and make up the knowledge they may have not learned earlier. For example, the class director comes to the classroom every day to check if all students are in class. They also organize students to supervise each other.

Perspectives from the Faculty

The faculty we interviewed in our focus group meeting were graduates of a range of universities, mostly from local or nearby provincial universities, including Anhui University, the Huanbei Coal Mining Teachers' College, the University of Science and Technology of China, Nanchang University, and Jiangxi Normal University.

One faculty member made the following point:

> Private universities have a better management system. Public universities' development is restrained by their system. Private universities should keep their flexible system. However, private universities ... and China's higher education as a whole are somehow heading toward the wrong track, mainly oriented towards students' employment. Under this priority, universities look for "short term, easy and quick" forms of education and neglect to foster students with sustainable ability and holistic development.

A second faculty member had come to Blue Sky in 2002. At that time, there was a clear distinction between private and public universities, and people would definitely prefer public universities. He noted that now people from all over the country are coming to Blue Sky, so that is real progress. However, faculty members feel that private universities lack a research environment and culture. He hoped Blue Sky would hire more faculty who did not focus only on teaching. A third member of the faculty focus group was an art teacher. He made the following comments:

Blue Sky has let me do what I like to do. I came here in 2003 and left in 2004, then I came back again in 2005 after comparing different types of institution. I came back because I can recommend and select textbooks, and with the department head's approval I can even compile my own textbooks. We have a lot of flexibility in teaching; for example I can take my students to study outside rather than always staying in the classroom.

A fourth faculty member confirmed the art teacher's view and added that the university encouraged them to compile new books and open new courses, but not on purely theoretically subjects. Courses needed to be connected to the needs of the business world and should focus on cultivating students' practical abilities. The fact that Blue Sky stressed students' practical abilities led some faculty members to observe that there is a lack of emphasis on long term sustainable knowledge and skills.

When we asked them to name a couple of places on Blue Sky's campus that most illustrate its spirit, they mentioned the Front Gate, with its open space and expansive view of the garden-like campus. "This represents the spirit of the ocean into which all streams of water flow, and symbolizes a university spirit that can absorb and attract all kinds of talent." They also mentioned the library building at the centre of the campus, which is shaped as an open book, indicating an aspiration for knowledge.

Photo 14.2: Main gate to the campus of Blue Sky University

Note: Courtesy of the BSU website

When we asked if they have outlets to express their opinions, they said they can express their ideas in the Faculty Representative Conference or they can directly go to Yu Guo. They noted that while a private institution had the advantage of being flexible and efficient, it also had huge pressures, mainly because their social status and benefits still could not be compared with those of faculty in public universities.

Student Perspectives

The students who attended our focus group meeting came from various departments, including the Foreign Languages Department, the Arts Department, the Automobile Department, and the Mechanics Department.

The first questions we posed to the students were as follows: "why did you choose to come to Blue Sky? And what has your experience been like?" Here are some of their responses:

> I came to Blue Sky because I have a classmate studying here; I made a campus visit and decided to come. We are the first batch of students in the undergraduate degree program so we will be given a lot of attention. I'm from a rural area, and I used to be very shy and afraid of public speaking. After coming to Blue Sky, I have put high demands on myself, and through running for the position of class president, I have learned to communicate with people. I have enhanced my practical abilities and become very confident.

> I chose the Automobile Service Program because of the great potential of the automobile industry and the good teaching faculty. I'm from a rural area. Blue Sky, like its President Yu Guo, has great charisma and gives me inspiration. I can learn what I didn't have the chance to learn earlier, and participate in social practice while on campus.

> I'm from Hubei Province. I worship President Yu Guo. We have very close relationships between teachers and students. Our class directors live with us. The class director system is our distinguishing feature. The class directors love us; they visit our dorm 3-5 times a week.

> Coming to Blue Sky was a joke for me. I was in high-track class in secondary school, but didn't do well in the National University Entrance Examinations. I was very desperate, so I came to Blue Sky. In Chinese people's eyes, private universities are not good ones. In the beginning, I was very depressed. I'm from the countryside, and I cannot afford the tuition. In the beginning, I didn't make much effort. Being from the countryside, I was shy. But the English teacher cares about me. I was the only one in the class who passed the English level 4 test, and after that I became very confident. Our class director often talks with me, and appointed me to the Student Steering Committee; I became more confident. Tuition is a big pressure, but I got funding from scholarships.

Students mentioned that Blue Sky had more than 100 student societies. One student said he founded a "Social Dance Club." One indicated he planned to work for the university after graduation. Students noted that Blue Sky teachers were young, and needed to build up more experience and knowledge.[23]

Compassion for the Handicapped

Because of his own experience of being denied higher education due to his physical handicap, Yu Guo tries to open door to students with similar problems. Blue Sky has graduated about 1,000 students with disabilities over the years. Barrier-free paths are available campus-wide for students with physical disabilities. Wheelchairs can be pushed from the ground floor to the second floor, which is not the case in other universities.

In 1995, a fund called "Yu Guo's Fund for Helping the Outstanding Poor Students and Students with Disabilities" was set up. By 2007, a total of 14.93 million *yuan* had been dispersed to more than 10,000 students. Yu Guo hopes to preserve a piece of "blue sky" for these students.

An interesting piece of evidence of Yu Guo's generosity came to one of the authors' attention when she went to the bank to do some personal business. In talking with the driver she learned that Yu Guo had asked him to arrange transfer of a large sum of money to the Sichuan earthquake victims, without letting anyone know. A couple of students we interviewed also noted that Yu Guo exempted their tuition when they could not afford to pay tuition in a certain semester.

The Research Dilemma

Blue Sky has taken the aim of being "an application-oriented university" as its niche. It thus seeks to solve employment problem for its students, and to provide practically qualified graduates for the manufacturing, commercial, and service industries. This is its current mission. However, its leaders also have a long term view. They want to upgrade the university, so that it can eventually gain an equal position with that of reputable comprehensive universities with a research capacity. There is limited funding for research, and also little capacity to attract researchers. Nevertheless, for those who come from prestigious universities and want to settle down at Blue Sky, the university carves out some financial support to enable them to establish their labs.

Zhao Gang, a member of the faculty focus group, is an interesting

---

[23] All the information in this section came from the Student Focus Group meeting, 27 May 2008.

example. He graduated from the University of Science and Technology of China, which has been profiled in Chapter 9 and is one of China's top research universities. After he came to Blue Sky as a young faculty member, he was awarded a research fund 400,000 *yuan*. Currently, he has five full time faculty working with him on research projects, and soon his research staff will grow to eight.

Hu Jianfeng, the Vice President, graduated from the East China Normal University, which has been profiled in Chapter 6, and obtained his doctorate in Neuroscience from an institute of the Chinese Academy of Sciences in Shanghai in 2002. In 2003, he came to Blue Sky first as a full-time faculty member. Two months later he was appointed as Dean, and given supervision over 2,000 students.

Under his leadership, the Computer Science Department was honored as an "Advanced Institute of Jiangxi Province." In 2004 Yu Guo promoted Hu Jianfeng to Assistant President, in charge of accreditation, which was the vital step for Blue Sky to be approved as a university offering undergraduate degrees. In April 2005 Hu Jianfeng proposed to Yu Guo that Blue Sky establish a research program. In 2006, the Brain-Machine Interface program was officially approved. The university has provided 4 million *yuan* in funds for the research institute. Hu was given half a floor in a new building, and was able to purchase equipment and employ personnel. Now the research institute has purchased an Electro-Encephalography (EEG) machine, and has 13 employees, most of whom are Master's graduates. Projects include Neuroeconomics and Brain-Machine Interface. They are studying human volition through detecting electrical currents in the brain. Also, they are studying how the electric currents in the brain can direct a toy car or dial phone numbers.

They mostly do information analysis, models recognition and neuro-networking. By early 2009, they had published 50 articles in journals in China and abroad. However, at first they were not able to apply for funding from the government, as government research funds at national and provincial level were not accessible to private universities. Hu Jianfeng thus resolved to produce results and publish first, with the hope of eventually wining recognition from the government. Things did improve, in 2009, and they can now compete for most grants at the provincial and national levels.[24] Researcher Gao Shangkai who worked in

---

[24] We were informed of this policy change by Hu Jianfeng himself when we met him again at our project workshop at Peking University, 15-18 May 2009.

Hu's lab said:

> We are not sure about what exactly the code in the brain is like. Huge individual differences and environmental interferences exist. Sometimes the accuracy is 100%, sometimes 50%. In our Neuro-economics Research Institute, we are studying people's reaction in the brain when they are engaging in economic activity.[25]

To keep researchers at Blue Sky is not easy, as the academic atomsphere is not as good as in a public university. Some neighboring public universities have tried to recruit Hu Jianfeng, but he didn't want to go. "During the phase of 2008-2012, our research goal is to catch up with international standards," he said.

Now Hu Jianfeng is in charge of the career center, seeking cooperation between the university and enterprises, providing career counseling and connecting with alumni. By the end of 2008 he plans to contact more than 3,000 enterprises to build up collaborative relationship and help students find employment, so he only does research at night.[26]

Blue Sky has several research projects similar to that developed by Hu Jianfeng. Yu Guo's idea is to test the idea of research, be low key and hope some fruit can be born for the long term. "As long as the projects help the researchers themselves and contribute to society, I support them," Yu Guo said to us.

Relationship with the Government

Private universities have had difficult relationships with the government. For example, in terms of student recruitment, private universities have been forced to be the last group to admit students, after elite and regular public universities have chosen the students with the highest scores on the national university entrance examinations. In terms of degree programs, from the beginning, private university development has been relegated to the status of vocational training, and their aspirations to become recognized comprehensive universities offering undergraduate and graduate education have been greatly restricted. A large number of private universities appeared in the early 1990s, and by 2002, there were more than 1,200 private institutions in China. However, only five of them were able to gain accreditation from the Ministry of Education to award

---

[25] Interview with Gao Shangkai, 27 May 2008.
[26] Interview with Hu Jianfeng, 26 May 2008.

bachelor's degrees. Yellow River, which is profiled in Chapter 12 was one of those five. Between 2002 and 2003 seven were approved, and in 2004, no new private institutions were accredited to offer bachelor's degrees. Only in 2005, after much lobbying by private university leaders, were sixteen more private higher education institutions upgraded to that status.

By contrast, the Ministry of Education has allowed public universities to establish many "second-tier colleges" in recent years. These are institutions that capitalize on the teaching resources of the public universities to which they are attached, as in the case of Xiamen University in Chapter 5 and the Huazhong University of Science and Technology in Chapter 10. They offer very similar programs to those of private universities, and the government has given them a beneficial policy by approving them as undergraduate degree granting institutions, on the basis of the experience and academic management of the attached public university. This has edged out the advantages of private universities which have built up their academic experience over many years in order to be able to offer undergraduate degree education. Currently, there are more than 300 second-tier colleges, and many of them are now becoming independent private institutions under recent policies.[27]

Blue Sky has received some support from the government. They got the land for building the campus from the provincial government on beneficial terms. However, as a private university, the relationship with the government has been volatile. For example, some Jiangxi private universities got into trouble by lying to the students about their job prospects on graduation and a riot took place in 2007. As a result all the private universities in Jiangxi have been more closely monitored by the government since then. This is done by sending an inspector to each of the private universities to monitor all of their work. Private universities say that they "seek to survive between the cracks." To adopt a "practice-oriented" approach is one such strategy. Private universities have not been able to compete with public universities in general, but their practice oriented focus has gained them some ground. However, now that some of them are offering undergraduate degrees, they need to undergo the same kind of government controlled accreditation as public universities. Private universities have complained that the government

---

[27] The new policy on establishment and governance of independent colleges, *Duli Xueyuan Shezhi Yu Guanli Banfa*, which took effect on 1 April 2008, has regulated the transition from affiliated second-tier colleges to independent institutions.

uses the same ruler to measure all kinds of institution, treating them in the same way as public universities which have many more resources and opportunities. They are asking for the accreditation process to be independent of government, and for different criteria for private universities. There is no way they can compete in faculty, funding and the background of their students, but they have their own educational goals, their own models and their unique niches.

In another domain, in the government's structure for treatment of businesses, agencies and corporations, private universities like Blue Sky are placed in the category of "private non-enterprise corporations" (similar to unions, or non-governmental agencies where the government does not pay for pensions and any other kinds of benefits), while public universities are "institutional corporations" (parallel to government branches, public organizations and schools, with a full range of benefits which can be transferred among the institutions of like status), and businesses are "enterprise corporations" (with no governmentally paid benefits).

This non-enterprise status is problematic. Blue Sky is not entitled to benefits such as pensions that institutional corporations have. Some provinces even treat private universities as businesses which need to pay 33% income tax but are not allowed to make a profit. Teachers, without being employed in the category of "institutional corporations," cannot transfer to public universities or government agencies and they don't have pensions after retirement. Hence, Yu Guo proposed to the National People's Congress in 2008 to change the status of private universities to that of "institutional corporations," and to divide this category into two sections: one is fully funded by government; the other is self supported until the teachers retire or leave. This would mean teachers in private universities could benefit from government pensions after retirement.

Challenges and Vision for the Future

Blue Sky has built itself up from a very small beginning to a large scale institution by seizing crucial opportunities in various stages of China's historical development. For example, in 1992, after Deng Xiaoping's speech in southern China, economic reform in China was jump-started again, following a difficult period in the wake of the 1989 student movement. Blue Sky was founded just at that time. 1999 was the year of dramatic expansion in higher education and many private universities were approved for establishment. Blue Sky became one of 38 new institutions in Jiangxi which was accredited to issue sub-degree diplomas, and it took the name "Blue Sky Vocational Technology College." In 2005 it was accredited as a comprehensive undergraduate university and stepped into a new stage of development.

In terms of faculty, in 1994 Yu Guo was himself the only full-time teacher, with some part-time teachers from other universities. In 1995, after new buildings were constructed on the old campus it began to have some full-time teachers. After 1999, more full-time teachers were added. After the university was accredited to offer degrees in 2005, full-time faculty members became the majority. These changes, according to Yu Guo, were significant but not enough. It would take many more years for them to move into the mainstream, given their short history and the lack of government support and investment.[28]

In our interview with Vice President Xu Xiangyun, we ask about the limitations of "practiced oriented" education. He mentioned that, for now, this is feasible and effective for private universities, but the importance of liberal arts education cannot be ignored. There needs to be a balance between practical skills and scholarly abilities, specialized and liberal arts education, sustainable skills and more profound knowledge.

Blue Sky's development is certainly tightly linked with Yu Guo, as an entrepreneur, leader, strategist and philosopher. He reflects the qualities of a generation of private university presidents who have had to defy a lot of odds and searched for ways to survive, grow, define a culture and fulfill a mission. In this process, the presidents have acquired a rare combination of qualities as educators, politicians, entrepreneurs and social reformers. Yu Guo himself is rather realistic and humble about his role as a founder of a university.

I am not a businessman, and I am not an educator either. One will not build and run a great university if one runs it only from a business perspective. From the point of view of an educator, I feel I have a lot of catching up in terms of ability. I see myself only as a pioneer and practitioner of people-run education, who dares to face any kind of situation, who has courage and takes action, who is willing to explore and dares to chart a new road for education.[29]

---

[28] Interview with Yu Guo, 26 May 2008.
[29] Zeng Guohuan, "Interview with Yu Guo, Chairman of the Board of Jiang-xi Lantian College, who is also a National Labor Model," July 24, 2006, accessed April 22, 2008, http://www.999edu.cn/web/20060512/999edu/html/news_3378_1.shtml.

When attending a seminar for university presidents at Peking University, one day Yu Guo walked around the campus after class, and saw Beida students studying and walking around. This is the most sacred place for learning in Chinese people's mind. Yu Guo came upon the statue of Cai Yuanpei (蔡元培), and thought of Peking University's 100-year history. He thought about what Blue Sky would be like in 100 years. There, he affirmed his mission in life, which is to build Blue Sky into a higher learning institution that can "empower the nation with science and technology." Cai Yuanpei is remembered for his leadership of Peking University nearly a hundred years ago, and Yu Guo hopes a hundred years later people will remember the name of "Yu Guo." This is what keeps him going, to run a university for the disadvantaged that strives for the highest excellence.

We certainly hope Yu Guo's dream will come true, that is, Blue Sky University will stand and prosper for a hundred years and even longer. On the other hand, this is truly an arduous task, given the fierce competition among Chinese universities nowadays, with all having increased their capacities and believing "big is beautiful." Nevertheless, we don't think this is the fundamental challenge to Blue Sky University, as it has been way ahead of most of its competitors in terms of overall reputation, education quality as well as infrastructure and facilities. Rather, we see the real challenge as coming from the inside, i.e., how to make sure Yu Guo's mission and aspiration will be carried on after him. Most organizations tend to be path dependent, that is, to automatically follow the path of their past growth and success. A shift in the path means transformation, which is often very difficult. For Blue Sky University, there is a high level dependency on Yu Guo's vision and capacity. For example, we noted BSU's new driving school, which is built on a deserted piece of land acquired a couple of years ago. The idea came as kind of spark in Yu Guo's thinking and it is now a leading school in a nation that has embraced the personal automobile over a brief few years. The new school is essentially a cash cow for the university, making something out of an unused piece of land. In this sense, Yu Guo, with his charisma and vision, is certainly an indispensable asset to BSU. The question is who can carry on his role after him. This seems to be the dilemma facing most private universities in China and Blue Sky University seems not yet to have resolved it.

Part VI:
Conclusion and Future Directions

This volume comes to an end with a chapter by Qiang Zha, which explores the Chinese model of the university that is emerging in the 21st century. How is it linked to China's own scholarly traditions? What are its limitations? What contributions may it make to global debates over higher education in the future? These are some of the questions Qiang Zha addresses in his effort to tie together the various threads of the text.

15
Is There an Emerging Chinese Model of the University?

Qiang ZHA

Introduction

In bringing this volume to a close, we feel compelled to consider whether there is an emerging Chinese model of the university. Admittedly, this consideration is influenced, more or less, by China's economic success, which is now viewed by many as a Chinese model for development.[1] This model, characterized by a unique approach to governmentality, social organization, economic management, and outlook on the world, has now won some recognition for its efficiency and effectiveness, in particular in face of the global economic recession. Politically, it may bring into question the Western tendency to emphasize the dichotomy between democracy and authoritarianism. Our question then is whether or not there is also an emerging Chinese model in the cultural and educational sense, and how it relates to this dichotomy.

A model might be defined as a set of instructions for action or a patterned way of doing things. In this case, we are considering the patterns of organizing, governing, steering and operating a university or a university system. We would like to draw on a recent article by Bernasconi who sought to clarify its connotation in relation to Latin America: "It distils the variety of actual forms of the university in an abstract and general construct, a concept of the university as it exists in the minds of faculty, students, administrators, and other constituencies and is expressed in their discourse about the university".[2] Throughout

---

[1] Tianyu Cao (ed.), *The Chinese Model of Modern Development* (Abingdon and New York: Routledge, 2005); Martin Jacques, *When China Rules The World: The End of the Western World and the Birth of a New Global Order* (New York: Penguin Press, 2009); Wei Pan, "The Chinese Model of Development" (an address presented at the seminar on *The China Model-the Chinese Way in World Politics*, London, UK, October 11, 2007), accessed December 10, 2009, http://fpc.org.uk/fsblob/888.pdf.

[2] A. Bernasconi, "Is There a Latin American Model of the University?" *Comparative Education Review*, Vol.52, No.1, 2007, p.29.

this volume we have reported the views of national policy makers, university leaders, faculty and students, giving readers an insight into that discourse within contemporary Chinese universities. We thus resonate with Bernasconi's definition of "a model of the university ... as a culturally embedded idea of the essence, role, and mode of organization of the university and of its relationship to the state and to society at large, which exerts a normative influence over those who are in a position to shape such a role, organization, and relationships".[3]

To consider how national culture and context might influence the university, it may be helpful to explore briefly the ancient historical roots and more recent development of higher education in the Chinese context. Our belief that there is a cultural core informing the emerging Chinese model of the university is first and foremost derived from China's extraordinary higher education tradition. Evolving over more than two millennia, higher education in China is one of the world's oldest systems.[4] By the time of the Tang Dynasty (618-907 C.E.) there was a whole range of higher education institutions, headed by the *Guozijian* (國子監), the School of the Sons of the Empire – sometimes called the Imperial Central School or Imperial Academy – which took major classical texts of the Confucian school as their curricular content.[5] By this period, publicly regulated examinations in classical knowledge areas had already been established, and meritocratic selection for the civil service had been institutionalized.[6] In the subsequent Song Dynasty (960-1279 C.E.), the major Confucian classics were re-ordered into the *Four Books* (四書). Together with the *Five Classics* (五經), these formed a knowledge system that had to be mastered by all students aspiring to become scholar-officials in the imperial civil service. The imperial examination system

---

[3] *Ibid.*

[4] H. Galt, *A History of Chinese Educational Institutions* (London: Arthur Probsthain, 1951); S. Gu, *Zhongguo Lidai Jiaoyu Zhidu* (Education Systems in Chinese Dynasties) (Nanjing, China: Jiangsu People's Publishing House, 1981).

[5] Yuan Zheng, "Local Government Schools in Sung China: A Reassessment," in *History of Education Quarterly*, Vol.34, No.2, Summer 1994, pp.193-213; Ruth Hayhoe and Qiang Zha, "China," in J.F. Forest and P.G. Altbach. (eds.), *International Handbook of Higher Education*, Vol.18, Part Two, (Dordrecht, Netherlands: Springer, 2006), p.667.

[6] Ruth Hayhoe, *China's Universities 1895-1995: A Century of Cultural Conflict* (Hong Kong: Comparative Education Research Centre, The University of Hong Kong, 1999), p.10.

thus dominated traditional higher education, creating a class of intellectuals who climbed the ladder from local to provincial and finally capital and palace examinations.[7]

Alongside the official system of higher education, private academies (*shuyuan* 書院) began to flourish as an alternative system during the Tang Dynasty, a knowledge tradition that encouraged freer discussion and debates over the classical texts and their application to the task of government. Thus China's scholarly tradition manifested a dualism between the highly centralized, control-oriented imperial higher education system and the diffuse and somewhat independent private system of local academies. The latter are often seen as embodying progressive aspects of Chinese scholarship and favoring an ethos and culture that encouraged interdisciplinarity and the integration of theory and practice in a problem-solving approach to knowledge.[8]

Traditional institutions of higher learning gradually lost their legitimacy and viability in the late Qing Dynasty. China suffered humiliation in the face of Japanese and Western military incursions. Reform and self-strengthening was essential. The evolution of modern Chinese higher education was thus deeply interwoven with influences from Japan and the West. In this sense, Chinese higher education has been uniquely experimental in the ways it has adopted elements and influences from most existing models of the university at different time periods.

The Evolution of Modern Chinese Universities: A Century of Experimentation with Western Models

Officials of the late Qing Dynasty launched a self-strengthening movement, which involved the introduction of Western technology for the purpose of national salvation, while seeking to keep the basic character of the Chinese empire intact. Japan was their most important model. The fact that Japan defeated China militarily in 1895 had a devastating psychological impact on China. The Japanese model was believed appropriate in cultural terms, since the two countries shared the Confucian

---

[7] Ichisida Miyazaki, *China's Examination Hell: The Civil Service Examinations of Imperial China* (New York and Tokyo: Weatherhil, 1977).

[8] John Meskill, *Academies in the Ming Dynasty* (Tuscon: University of Arizona Press, 1982); Ruth Hayhoe, *China's Universities and the Open Door* (Armonk, N.Y.: M.E. Sharpe, 1989); Sheng Langxi, *Zhongguo Shuyuan Zhidu* (*China's Academy System*) (Shanghai: Zhonghua shuju, 1934).

tradition.⁹ Convinced that Western techniques could be absorbed into a revitalized Confucian empire, China modeled its educational reform legislation of 1902 and 1903 directly on the Japanese education system as a pathway to modernization with the preservation of Confucian values.¹⁰ The Hundred Day Reform (百日維新) in 1898 was a first step towards radical reform and one of the earliest modern universities in China – the Capital Metropolitan University (京師大學堂), later Peking University – was one of the innovations that lasted. It was patterned after the University of Tokyo.¹¹

With the Revolution of 1911 (辛亥革命), the Republican government decreed a major reform to instil Republican values. As the first Minister of Education, Cai Yuanpei (蔡元培) designed the higher education legislation of 1912, which reflected a European model derived largely from his experience of studying in German and French universities. Later, under his leadership as the chancellor of Peking University, the ideas of university autonomy and "professorial rule" blossomed into a transformative cultural movement, known as the May Fourth Movement (五四運動).¹² The Republican higher education legislation made a clear

---

⁹ P. Chen, *Zhongguo Daxue Shi Jiang (Ten Topics on Chinese Universities)* (Shanghai: Fudan University Press, 2002); Qiang Zha, "Foreign Impacts on Japanese and Chinese Higher Education: A Comparative Analysis," in *Higher Education Perspectives*, Vol.1, No.1, 2004, pp.1-15.
¹⁰ Douglas Reynolds, *China, 1898-1912: The Xinzheng Revolution and Japan* (Cambridge, Mass.: Council on East Asian Studies, Harvard University, 1993).
¹¹ Hayhoe, 1999, *op cit.*, p.19; X. Lin, *Peking University. Chinese Scholarship and Intellectuals, 1898-1937* (Albany, NY: State University of New York Press, 2004), p.11.
¹² The May Fourth Movement is the name given to the collective effort made by intellectuals in China between 1915 and 1923 to cast off traditional Confucian values and undergo a cultural rejuvenation. A milestone of the era occurred on 4 May 1919 when demonstrators protested the treaty that ended World War I. The treaty recognized Japan's claims to territory taken from China. This time – known either as the "May Fourth era" or the "New Culture era" – was a vibrant time for Chinese intellectuals. People called for cultural rejuvenation and a more modern worldview, arguing that without such changes China could not liberate itself from the oppressive forces of imperialism or warlordism or both. Advocates of "new culture" from various groups criticized many of China's philosophical, literary, and social traditions between 1915 and 1923. The May Fourth Movement, with its emphasis on science, democracy, and antitraditionalism, has cast a long shadow over modern Chinese history. (Excerpts from Cheng, L. (ed.), *Berkshire*

distinction between specialist higher education institutions and universities, following the European patterns. Nevertheless, the weakness of China's central government from 1911 to 1927 provided conditions for vigorous experimentation. By 1921, there were 16 missionary colleges and universities in major Chinese cities, mostly chartered with American state governments and headed by American missionary presidents.[13] Educational legislation of 1922 and 1924 opened the way for increasing American influences on China's emerging higher education system. The definition of university was broadened to include most higher education institutions, including specialist professional ones.[14] There was also less emphasis on autonomy, in terms of the rule of professors within the university, and more on social responsibility.

With the accession to power of the Nationalist Party in 1927, the new government proceeded to develop policies and legislation for higher education that put a strong emphasis on practical knowledge and skills. In the education legislation passed in 1928, it was possible to see European and American influences integrated within patterns that served Nationalist educational goals.[15] Chinese universities went through a process of adaptation and indigenization that might be compared to the development of American universities in the 19th and 20th century. In her 1996 study, Hayhoe reached the conclusion that Chinese universities had developed into mature institutions in the Nationalist era, achieving a balance between their Chinese identity and the models and ideas they had adapted from Europe and North America.[16]

At its birth in 1949, the People's Republic of China inherited a higher education system close to the American one in its knowledge patterns. The new government, however, chose to carry out a total reorganization of the higher education system modelled on Soviet patterns of the time (院系調整) and intended to serve a centrally planned economy. The new system took shape between 1952 and 1957, with a complete reorganization of old institutions and the creation of new ones around a national plan. Curricular patterns ensured close coordination with the personnel needs of the State. At the core of the system were

---

Encyclopedia of China. Great Barrington, Massachusetts: Berkshire Publishing Group, 2009)
[13] See Ruth Hayhoe, *China's Universities and the Open Door*, p.15.
[14] *Ibid*, pp.14-15.
[15] *Ibid*, pp.15-16.
[16] Hayhoe, 1999, *op. cit.*, p.59.

three main types of institution: comprehensive universities with programs in the basic arts and sciences, polytechnic universities with a wide range of applied scientific programs, and teacher training universities responsible for setting national standards for education. In addition to these core institutions, there was a large number of sectoral institutions in areas such as agriculture, forestry, medicine, finance, law, language studies, physical culture, fine arts, and minority education. Each institution was narrowly specialized in its programs, and its role was to train personnel for its specific sector.

When China adopted the Open Door policy in the late 1970s, an important part of the re-emerging identity of Chinese universities in the 1980s was the role they played in helping China to re-connect to an international milieu after a decade of isolation during the *Cultural Revolution* (文化大革命). One of the major reasons for considerable support being given to higher education was the leadership's realization of a need for people who could build bridges to the outside world. The international relationships initiated at this time were both multilateral and bilateral, as opposed to learning from one specific foreign model in most of earlier periods. In fact, China has been remarkably open in its approach to internationalizing higher education. The past 30 years witnessed 1.2 million Chinese students and scholars going abroad, among whom nearly 320,000 had completed their study programs and returned by the end of 2007.[17] China has also made itself the world's 5th destination for international students in recent years, only behind the US, the United Kingdom, France and Germany and positioned far above any other developing country.[18] Chinese universities have played a crucial role in this process. Not only are they actively engaged in a kind of brain circulation process, but also in more substantial forms of international cooperation, such as collaborative research programs and international university consortia. Some of them are founding members of such consortia, as can be seen in the portraits of the University of Science and

---

[17] B. Xiang and W. Shen, "International Student Migration and Social Stratification in China," in *International Journal of Educational Development*, Vol.29, Issue 5, September, 2009, pp.513-522.

[18] *Atlas of Student Mobility*, "Global Destinations for International Students at the Post-Secondary (Tertiary) Level, 2007," accessed December 10, 2009, http://www.atlas.iienetwork.org/?p=48027. *Atlas of Student Mobility* data for China is collected in partnership with the China Scholarship Council and uses the OECD definition of "international student".

Technology of China (Chapter 9) and Peking University (Chapter 3). They have also formed partnerships with universities and other educational or cultural institutions worldwide to establish Confucius Institutes, as noted in several portraits within this volume.

With Chinese higher education now increasingly connected with the international community, the reform of the system in the 1990s can be viewed as part of a world phenomenon. The logic underlying the current restructuring of the Chinese higher education system includes decentralization of the administrative structure and the expansion of university autonomy; diversification of the funding sources for higher education institutions; and forms of reorganization intended to increase efficiency and effectiveness, while also supporting expansion. These trends reflect an international context characterized by a rising tide of human capital theory and "efficiency" movements, and they are vigorously pushed by the prevailing processes of globalization.

What Constitutes the Cultural Core that Influences Chinese Universities?

Philip Altbach argues that contemporary higher education systems in all countries, regardless of ideology, economic system, or level of technological development, are based on variations of the 19th century Western university model.[19] Based on this argument and understanding, a center-periphery paradigm has dominated the studies of higher education development worldwide. Universities and academic systems in the developed world – the "centers" – are viewed as the leaders with regard to organizational structure and mission and knowledge dissemination. Academic institutions in the developing world – the "peripheries" – have to take the "centres" as their model for research, the communication of knowledge, and advanced training.

Following this logic and paradigm, it has also been long held that the modern university, as an institutional model, was imported to Chinese soil, and had clear roots in Western social history. We believe, however, modern Chinese universities emerged between the worlds of

---

[19] Philip Altbach, "Twisted Roots: The Western Impact on Asian Higher Education," in *Higher Education*, No.18, 1989, pp.9-29; Philip Altbach, "Globalization and the University: Realities in an Unequal World," in J. Forest & P. Altbach (eds.), *International Handbook of Higher Education. Part One: Global Themes and Contemporary Challenges* (Dordrecht, The Netherlands: Springer, 2006), p.122.

European and Chinese culture and epistemology – a place where deep conflicts were inevitable – and they should not be viewed simply as a product of Westernization. Put in another way, the surface patterns of organization are one story, but the cultural and spiritual connections to China's scholarly tradition and cultural core are another. These connections have been maintained over the years of dramatic change for China. As a matter of fact, China has been noted for its historical-mindedness. "Chinese people have been able to 'look at the past from the present' to judge and shape the present in the light of the ideal past, and to judge the past in the light of the present ideals thus shaped".[20]

What then characterizes the cultural core of Chinese scholarly tradition? First and foremost, the dominant stream of Chinese traditional culture, Confucianism, is secular and fosters an articulation between higher learning and State governance. There was nothing in the early Chinese philosophical visions that suggested Plato's conception of an unseen eternal world of forms, with the actual world as only a pale copy.[21] In Chinese traditional culture there was never the sharp dichotomy of a Christian type between the transcendent world inhabited by God and the human world. As a result of a very different Chinese idea of transcendence going back to the time of Confucius, the all-important idea of the *Dao* (道) or Way emerged as a symbol of the world beyond the actual world of everyday life, yet staying not far from the human world. "The Chinese transcendental world of *Dao* and the actual world of every-day life were conceived from the very beginning to be related to each other in a way different from other ancient cultures undergoing the Axial breakthrough," Ying-shih Yu (余英時) suggested.[22] As best expressed by Confucius himself, "The *Dao* is not far from man. When a man pursues the *Dao* and remains away from man, his course cannot be considered the *Dao*".[23]

In this tradition, the scholars were prompted to realise their ideals through action and a kind of direct responsibility for managing the State. This tradition was best explained by the imperial examination system which selected intellectuals to serve as scholar-officials. Knowledge was

---

[20] C.C. Huang, "The Defining Characters of Chinese Historical Thinking," in *History and Theory*, Vol.46, No.2, 2007, p.180.
[21] Ying-shih Yu, "Address on the occasion of receiving the John W. Kluge Prize," December 5, 2006, accessed December 10, 2009, www.loc.gov/loc/kluge/docs/yu_kluge.pdf.
[22] *Ibid*.
[23] Quoted by Ying-shih Yu, *op. cit.*

less a matter of understanding the world than of changing it and scholars were expected to "cultivate the self, regulate the family, govern the State, and make the whole kingdom tranquil and happy".[24] Put explicitly, they sought a unity of knowledge and action through their roles as scholar-officials. Rather than seeing themselves in the role of independent social critic, they saw themselves as offsetting political authority with intellectual authority and being responsible to "tame" the ruler so that he would be a "Philosopher King." At the same time, the imperial examination system planted and perpetuated a strong tradition of meritocratic and hierarchical values. Though the examinations were abolished in 1905, many aspects of their spirit and influence persist in the unified national university entry examinations that remain in place in China today.

At the other end of the spectrum, there existed an alternative tradition expressed in the private academies (*shuyuan*), which stressed a liberal tradition with an independent ethos that was tolerant of different schools of thought. The academies also promoted a humanistic education that fostered character development, as opposed to the pragmatism of the examination system. "For twelve centuries … China has made literary education the exclusive measure of social esteem; it has done so far more exclusively than Renaissance humanism and, most recently, Germany has done."[25] Indeed, Max Weber explicitly located Chinese literary education as leaning towards the extreme of emphasizing the nurturing of charisma in the spectrum of educational aims he sketched out. The other extreme in this spectrum, he argued, was the transmission of specialized knowledge. Reflecting this tradition, the Chinese are characterized by analogical thinking, which has in turn made literary education essential. "Metaphor is thus an essential part of Chinese thinking … The West inserts metaphor as a feather onto a hat as an adornment, while Chinese thinking employs metaphor as a feather on an arrow."[26]

The *Great Learning* (大學), one of the *Four Books* in Zhu Xi's ordering of the Confucian classical texts was the orthodox doctrine for Chinese higher learning from the late 12th to early 20th century. It stated the Con-

---

[24] Confucius, *Confucian Analects, The Great Learning & The Doctrine of the Mean*. Translated, with critical and exegetical notes, prolegomena, copious indexes, and dictionary of all characters by James Legge (New York, N.Y.: Dover Publications, 1971), p.359. Originally in Chinese, it goes as "修身, 齊家,治國, 平天下。"
[25] Max Weber as cited in Fritz K. Ringer, *Max Weber: An Intellectual Biography* (Chicago: University of Chicago Press, 2004), p.226.
[26] C.C. Huang, *op. cit.*, p.187.

fucian aims and principles for humanistic education in the following explicit way, "What the *Great Learning* teaches, is – to illustrate illustrious virtue; to renovate the people; and to rest in the highest excellence." "Things being investigated, knowledge became complete. Their knowledge being complete, their thoughts were sincere. Their thoughts being sincere, their hearts were then rectified. Their hearts being rectified, their persons were cultivated. Their persons being cultivated, their families were regulated. Their families being regulated, their States were rightly governed. Their States being rightly governed, the whole kingdom was made tranquil and happy."[27] Its pedagogy emphasized an active role for students as well as interaction among students and teachers. This type of humanistic education nurtured a unique class in Chinese society, the scholar-gentlemen or *shi* (士), who embraced a high level of political responsibility, and formed a pool of talent for the imperial system. This might be seen as yet another pole that was in tension with the imperial system, while also stimulating and reinvigorating that system.

It is fascinating to observe how these two poles co-existed throughout Chinese history, and generated a kind of constant tension. This may shed light on a core philosophical notion that is embedded in Chinese scholarly tradition: unity with diversity or "*he er bu tong* (和而不同)."[28] This notion can be seen in the normative values and in the tendency to experimentation that formed the thread of higher education development in modern Chinese history. It is thus not surprising to see a kind of moving back and forth between the European and American models in the 1930s and 1940s. Even in the socialist era when Chinese universities were closely modeled on Soviet patterns, there were at least two large scale attempts in the 1950s and 1960s – the *Great Leap Forward* (大躍進) and the *Cultural Revolution* – that aimed to break the Soviet patterns.

This notion of unity with diversity is also manifested in Chinese scholars' thinking. Here, we'll take Cai Yuanpei and Mei Yiqi (梅貽琦) as examples, since they are perhaps the most influential figures in modern Chinese higher education history. They are viewed as the architects of China's two best known and most reputed universities, Peking and Tsinghua, where they both held leadership roles for a fairly long time.

---

[27] Confucius, *op. cit.*, pp.356-359. Originally in Chinese, it goes as "大學之道，在明明德，在親民，在至於至善。" "物格而後知至。知至而後意誠。意誠而後心正。心正而後身脩。身脩而後家齊。家齊而後國治。國治而後天下平。"

[28] Confucius, *The Analects*, 13: 23.

Cai served as the Chancellor of Peking University from 1916 to 1926, and Mei held the longest presidency in the history of Tsinghua University, from 1931 to 1948. There are some overlaps in their perceived model of the Chinese university, in their shared commitment to university autonomy and professorial governance, also academic freedom, values derived from the European and American models that they were familiar with, yet they clearly had different emphases. Cai gave top priority to research and the advancement of knowledge among all the functions of the university, while believing the teaching function was also important, as it served to nurture research minds. Nevertheless, when conditions did not permit, due to resource constraints or capacity limitations, the university must first function as the center of excellence in research, while leaving education *per se* to other types of higher learning institutions.[29] By contrast, Mei seemed to have been a strong proponent of the educational function of the university, in particular that of general education.[30] There is no doubt their perceptions had a deep impact on the university culture and ethos of the two universities respectively, yet this didn't prevent Peking University and Tsinghua University from uniting with each other, and with the private Nankai University, during the anti-Japanese war period. This was done in such a harmonious way that the consequent institution, Southwest Associated University (西南聯合大學), reached world class standing at the time.[31]

Interrogating the Emerging Chinese Model of the University

If there is an emerging Chinese model of the university, we can certainly cite these traditional roots in Chinese scholarship to characterize many of its aspects. Indeed, during the tenure of this research project, we witnessed certain characteristics of contemporary universities that are clearly connected to traditional roots in one way or another. To a large extent, the Chinese university remains the State's educational and research arm for national development. Compared to their Western counterparts, Chinese universities appear to be more responsive to

---

[29] Li Baocun, *Daxue Linian De Chuantong Yu Bianqe* (*Tradition and Change in the Idea of the University*) (Beijing: Jiaoyu Kexue Chubanshe (Educational Science Press), 2004), p.93.
[30] *Ibid.*, pp.104-105.
[31] John Israel, *A Chinese University in War and Revolution* (Stanford: Stanford University Press, 1996).

national and local development needs, embracing a close articulation between institutional strategic planning and national and local development plans. State control seems to have always had a place, but now it is evident under the guise of something that we might identify as "academic centralization or nationalization (學術機制集權化或國家化)." The State promotes decentralization of steering and management in exchange for institutional performance and accountability on the one hand, and tightens control over normative criteria for knowledge production on the other. State control, which used to reside mainly in the organizational process, has penetrated into the knowledge production process, which is now often driven by a kind of State willpower or managerialism, according to a technical rationale. Put explicitly, knowledge production no longer arises from scholars' individual interest, but has become an integral part of national efforts to fulfill the century-long dream of China's resurgence. In return, the government looks at higher education as a driver of the country's future, and is compelled to give priority to supporting its development.

This helps us to understand much better why the Chinese government likes to label major initiatives aiming to achieve research excellence as this or that "project." Examples include Project 21/1, Project 98/5, and Project 973 or the National Basic Research Project launched in 1997 and implemented by the Ministry of Science and Technology.[32] An overarching rationale behind the scene is that knowledge production is to be managed by the State, functioning like a corporation in this context and setting out goals and conditions for higher performance and efficiency. Thus the elite universities included in Project 21/1 and Project 98/5 benefit enormously from high levels of extra financial support from the State, while never being seriously challenged or required to go through a transparent competition process. This was particularly the case for Project 98/5, while institutions applying to Project 21/1 did have to present carefully developed plans in support of their applications. This phenomenon of direct State support to the elite sector of higher education could be partially attributed to persisting meritocratic and

---

[32] Ministry of Science and Technology of China, *National Basic Research Project of China*, accessed December 10, 2009, http://www.973.gov.cn/English/Index.aspx. The universities included in Project 98/5 have undertaken 40% of the research work funded by Project 973, and 50% of that funded by the National Natural Sciences Research Foundation, which is mentioned in Chapter 1.

hierarchical values,[33] and the legitimacy of these values and of the status of elite institutions is largely dependent on their performance and productivity. This approach appears to be extraordinarily efficient, and has resulted in China being unique in educational history in terms of simultaneously pushing for rapid enrolment growth, instituting new governance structures, and seeking to build world-class universities. It may also have triggered a worldwide race for world-class universities.[34]

Many other countries and systems in both the developed and developing world have chosen to join in this race with similar initiatives. Examples include the "Centers of Excellence in the 21st Century" (COE21) program in Japan, the "Brain Korea 21" (BK21) program in South Korea, the German Initiative for Excellence and the Canada Research Chair (CRC) program in Canada.[35] Notably, systems like Germany and Canada that have historically had non-hierarchical arrangements in which all universities or institutions within given categories were considered

---

[33] Cf. Ezra Vogel, *The Four Little Dragons: The Spread of Industrialization in East Asia*. (Cambridge, Mass., Harvard University Press, 1991). In this book, Vogel identifies four cultural patterns in his analysis of Confucian society: the role of a meritocratic elite, the examination ladder, the importance of the group and echoes of self-cultivation or self-improvement. All of these cultural patterns are closely linked to highly stratified higher education systems. Indeed, the Chinese higher education system has long engaged in a systematic hierarchical ranking, with the institutions being ranked by prestige, level of administration and concomitant resources.

[34] Cf. Jan Sadlak and Liu Nian Cai (eds.), *The World-Class University and Ranking: Aiming Beyond Status* (Bucharest: UNESCO-CEPES, 2007); Philip Altbach and J. Balán (eds.), *World Class Worldwide: Transforming Research Universities in Asia and Latin America* (Baltimore: Johns Hopkins University Press, 2007); Mara Hvistendahl, "Asia Rising: Countries Funnel Billions into Universities," in *The Chronicle of Higher Education*, October 5, 2009, http://chronicle.com/article/Asia-Rising-Countries-Funnel/48682.

[35] B.M. Kehm, "The German 'Initiative for Excellence' and the Issue of Ranking," in *International Higher Education*, No.44, 2006, pp.20-22; A. Labi "Germany Moves Closer to Restructuring Its University System," in *The Chronicle of Higher Education*, Vol.52, No.22, 2006, A47; G.E.J. Lee, "Brain Korea 21: A Development-Oriented National Policy in Korean Higher Education," in *International Higher Education*, No.19, Spring, 2000, pp.24–25; A. Yonezawa, "Making 'World-class Universities': Japan's Experiment," in *Higher Education Management and Policy*, Vol.15, No.2, 2003, pp.9–23; Qiang Zha, "Diversification or Homogenization in Higher Education: A Global Allomorphism Perspective," in *Higher Education in Europe*, Vol.34, No.3, 2009, pp.459-479.

roughly equal in terms of prestige and quality now have gradually embraced this ideology as well. In the context of this competition, the *Academic Ranking of World Universities*, launched by China's Shanghai Jiaotong University in 2003, has quickly gained great international prominence. Despite its neglect of teaching quality and student learning experiences, also its bias against the humanities and most social sciences, there have been few concerted efforts to discredit this ranking process; rather it has been widely cited as providing a legitimate mechanism for the evaluation of universities worldwide.[36]

Internally this pattern has put Chinese faculty members and researchers under enormous evaluative pressure, based on a range of quantitative measures. Once one can excel in terms of productivity and meet the State's criteria for producing valuable and useful knowledge, one may enjoy a high level of intellectual authority. This type of intellectual authority is not identical with academic freedom in the Western context, but in some ways it provides even more flexibility and greater power than does academic freedom. There is certainly some overlap between these two concepts, yet clearly a different emphasis. Westerners focus on restrictions to freedom of choice, whereas Chinese scholars looking at the same situation focus on the responsibility of the persons in authority to use their power wisely in the collective interest.

The planning head of Peking University admitted in 2008 that it was still hard for his university to enjoy real independence from government as a legal person, even though the *Higher Education Law* of 1998 had granted this status to all Chinese universities. Nevertheless, faculty are proud of the close articulation with the government and with national development in certain ways, even though "professorial rule" remains their dream: "*Beida* (the name of Peking University in Chinese) ... should be a treasure store of ideas for society. It is also an institution that belongs to the world, not only to China, and that is called upon to create a platform where China and the world can meet …. Colleagues from other universities, in China and abroad, look to us to be guardians and developers of the culture. If *Beida* should take the wrong direction, the

---

[36] K. Lynch, "Neo-liberalism and Marketisation: the implications for higher education," in *European Educational Research Journal*, Vol.5, No.1, 2006, pp.1-17; M. van der Wende, "Rankings and Classifications in Higher Education: A European Perspective," in J.C. Smart (ed.), *Higher Education: Handbook of Theory and Research*, Vol. XXIII (Dordrecht, London: Springer, 2008), pp.49-71.

consequences for the whole country would be serious".[37] Indeed, there is a fairly widely shared belief that strong government intervention is needed to create good universities. The autocratic government thus has the luxury of planning for the universities two or three decades in advance, in ways that may be unthinkable in the West.

Driven by the very same rationale, the Chinese government is enthusiastic in creating platforms or mechanisms to articulate relations between the university and industry. Most Chinese universities are engaged in a unique industry-university articulation arrangement which is called integration of production, teaching and research (產學研一體化). This is initiated and supported by the government, and enables the universities to play an active role in knowledge mobility and transfer. Many Chinese universities used to be mandated to serve specific sectors of the planned economy. Now delinked from such affiliations, they may still take advantage of this type of historical relationship to work out new forms of articulation framed by the notion of knowledge transfer. Chapter 11 of this volume shows how Northwest Agricultural and Forestry University has put this concept at the core of its mission statement. When discussing it with us, the faculty were not only aware of this strategic direction, but also talked about how valuable it was as a source of inspiration for teaching reforms.[38] It may still be too early to obtain enough empirical data to demonstrate the effectiveness of this approach. However, it is interesting to reflect on the question of whether this kind of systemic articulation might help to address the so-called "European paradox," whereby Europe has the necessary higher education infrastructure, yet fails to transfer it into innovation that can enhance productivity.[39]

When it comes to reforms in curriculum and teaching, there seems to be a renaissance of Confucian humanism on Chinese university campuses. Against the backdrop of an over-rapid and somewhat chaotic massification with some deterioration in quality, the call for a focus on students' character development has become more and more urgent in face of an increasing pragmatism in education. Even in the private

---

[37] Quote from the Faculty Focus Group, Peking University, 9 May 2008.
[38] Focus Group of the School of Agronomy faculty & students, NWAFU, 20 May 2008.
[39] M. van der Wende, "Rankings and Classifications in Higher Education: A European Perspective," in J.C. Smart (ed.), *Higher Education: Handbook of Theory and Research*, Vol.XXIII (Dordrecht, London: Springer, 2008), pp.49-71.

universities which cluster at the bottom of the higher education hierarchy and survive on providing students with an education directly related to the job market, this can be seen. There are strong voices criticizing the tendency to address students' employability only and neglect their holistic development, as evident in the portrait of Blue Sky University in Chapter 14. In other universities portrayed in this volume, the very fact of naming innovative units for curriculum and teaching reform after famous educational figures from the period prior to 1949, who were renowned for traditional scholarship, signals this same tendency. See for example the *Yuanpei Program* (元培計劃) at Peking University described in Chapter 3, the *Meng Xiancheng Shuyuan* (Academy) (孟憲成書院) at East China Normal University portrayed in Chapter 6, and *Yu Youren College* (於右任學院) at Northwest Agriculture and Forestry University depicted in Chapter 11.

East China Normal University launched the *Meng Xiancheng Shuyuan* in 2007 in a deliberate effort to link the traditional values of the *shuyuan*, with their focus on integrating general education into the professional curriculum of teacher preparation. In this way they hoped to foster healthy character formation for their teacher candidates, so that they in turn can become role models for their students. Interestingly, the curriculum and teaching reforms inspired by the *shuyuan* tradition are likely to bring the issues of institutional independence or autonomy and intellectual freedom back into the fore. As a matter of fact, the planning head of Peking University anticipated the realization of "four divisions" in Chinese political life would ultimately lead to an ascendance of university autonomy as well intellectual freedom in China.[40] Therefore, the sense of tension noted earlier is being restored, a tension between the renaissance of Confucian humanism and the aforementioned "academic centralization or nationalization."

It is this pattern of constantly recurring tension that fascinates us, and brings us to consider another characteristic of the Chinese model that may be unique. That is the use of efforts to balance persisting tensions as a way of maintaining both vitality and stability, also of avoiding overly radical changes. This brings us back to the notion of unity with diversity,

---

[40] They refer to the division between government and enterprises (*zhengqi* 政企), between government and social organizations (*zhengshi* 政事), between government and capital management (*zhengzi* 政資), and between government and professional associations (*zhengjie* 政介).

derived from a Chinese epistemological tradition that has always featured pluralism. In many senses, China's traditional epistemology and the core assumptions of European epistemology, which shaped the Western university tradition, are different and complementary. While positivism emerged in the wake of the scientific revolution in Europe and has tended to foster a subject-object dichotomy that has to deal with the question of how the subject is able to know the world, the dichotomy of subject and object does not exist in the Chinese epistemological tradition. This is arguably attributed to the analogical thinking mode noted earlier, which enables the Chinese instinctively to think from one perspective, pick another one and comprehend all – the whole situation. The Western mode, by contrast, tends to disregard analogous effects (argument as midwifery, as persuasion), and thus to be restricted to one aspect of the situation highlighted by one particular perspective. Western scholars thus often take argumentation as "war," and talk about "winning" or "losing" an argument.[41]

There is a sense of immanent transcendence in Chinese thought and a high tolerance of paradox. Put explicitly, the Chinese higher education tradition has transcended time and moved from stage to stage, driven mainly by the internal dynamics generated from constant tensions. Indeed, compared to other civilizations, Chinese civilization is marked by its long historical continuity, but continuity and change often went hand-in-hand in Chinese history. It is this aspect of the Chinese model of the university that may have a significant impact on the world community. This spirit of pluralism and tolerance may enable Chinese universities to contribute in a significant way to global cultural dialogue. The Ming Dynasty neo-Confucian scholars under the influence of Wang Yang-ming (王陽明) (1472-1529) believed that each of the three religions in China captured a vision of the same *Dao* (Way). This Confucian faith in the commonality of the human mind and the universal accessibility of the *Dao* to every human person in every part of the world has also led some Chinese converts to promote a synthesis of Christianity and Confucianism. It was also this Confucian humanism that predisposed the late Qing Dynasty Confucian scholars to be so readily appreciative of the Western theories which were introduced. After all, the recognition of a

---

[41] For more of the discussion along this line, please refer to George Lakoff and Mark Johnson, *Metaphors We Live By* (Chicago: University of Chicago Press, 1980), pp.3-13.

common humanity and a common human dignity is what the Chinese *Dao* has been about. Therefore once Chinese universities bring this core of their culture to the world community and use it to build relationships that flourish, the longstanding problematique of the-East-versus-the-West should also come to an end.

Conclusion: China Must Develop Its Own Unique University Model for the 21st Century

In addition to the persisting influences of traditional Chinese culture, the Western and Soviet models that shaped Chinese higher education at different historical junctures have certainly contributed to some aspects of the Chinese model of the university. Thus the emerging model of the Chinese university is by no means peculiar to the Chinese context, but resembles certain characteristics of other systems or models. Indeed, the centralism or strong federalism can be found in many continental European systems, and general education is deeply embedded in the American model. However, one could argue that it is the combination of these different characteristics that makes the Chinese model unique. As a matter of fact, the Chinese model for development demonstrates a kind of hybridity of political authoritarianism and economic liberalization.

Indeed, we are not trying to argue for a well-established Chinese model of the university, but rather an emerging model, still at the stage of birth and suffering from some shortcomings and pitfalls in its current form. For instance, its close articulation with national development could forge an orientation towards utilitarianism and bureaucratization. In 2008, Chinese universities conferred over 50,000 doctoral degrees, outnumbering those conferred by the American universities and becoming the world's largest system of doctorate education. However, more than half of the Chinese doctoral degree recipients ended up at jobs within the government bureaucracy at national or provincial levels.[42] This has resulted from an explicit or implicit strategy of absorbing academic elites into the polity and bureaucracy in order to heighten the government's legitimacy, given that there are no democratic elections in China. Indeed,

---

[42] Phoenix Satellite Television, "Zhongguo Boshi Chao Meiguo, Yiban Jinru Guanchang (China Outnumbers the US in Conferring Doctoral Degrees, One Half of the Recipients enters Government Bureaucracy)," July 29, 2009, accessed December 10, 2009, http://phtv.ifeng.com/program/zbjsj/200907/0729_6349_1274950.shtml.

this very phenomenon also sheds light on certain dysfunctional aspects of university education in China. The concentration of so much talent in a non-creative sector of employment would inevitably limit the possibilities of social creativity at large. This certainly has some part in the situation that has led to the famous "H.S. Tsien (錢學森) Question": Why couldn't Chinese universities nurture great creative minds?[43] Indeed, it is embarrassing to admit that China has not been a source of ideas for the world community over the past 200 years. Measured by influence on global culture, "China does not even matter," some have argued.[44]

Even worse, academic corruption has become a problem over recent years in China, and this may also be linked to "academic centralization or nationalization." The other side of academic nationalization could be a kind of "academic corporatization," that is leading to an increasing utilitarianism among intellectuals. This, in turn, results in their "alienation" from genuine academic pursuits. Instead of pursuing real academic interests, some tend to target their research at specific projects, in order to secure easy and generous funding. In some cases they also get involved in such academic misbehaviour as manipulating data or plagiarism.[45]

Ultimately, the challenge seems to be whether a model derived from "academic nationalization" and functioning within an authoritarian political regime can contribute to dialogue and harmony among different cultures. Political authoritarianism might serve China's current priorities well, in the achievement of economic efficiency and social stability, yet we doubt it can go on indefinitely.[46] It is common to observe less-

---

[43] "Qian Xuesheng De Zuihou Yici Xitong Tanhua – Tan Keji Chuang-xin Rencai De Peiyang Wenti (H.T. Tsien's Last Systematic Talk on Nurturing Creative Talent in the Sciences and Technology)," in *People's Daily*, November 5, 2009, p.11.
[44] Gerald Segal, "Does China Matter?," in *Foreign Affairs*, Vol.78, No.5, 1999, p.34.
[45] An international scientific journal *Acta Crystallographica* has recently uncovered evidence for an extensive series of scientific frauds involving 70 papers published in this journal, principally by Chinese scholars from Jinggangshan University in Jiangxi Province together with authors from various other institutions in China. Further retractions could result from close examination of 9,204 papers published in the journal between 2001 and 2009 and identified as by Chinese authors from over 500 universities in the country. See details in Harrison *et al.*, "Editorial," in *Crystallographica*, E66, 2010, pp.e1-e2.
[46] Even though some, such as Martin Jacques in his book *When China Rules the World*, argue that most Chinese will back their leaders, with or without democratic reforms, as long as the country keeps getting stronger, we tend to hold a cautious and conservative view, in particular with reference to the increasing

developed countries rely on sound policies under an authoritarian regime to achieve relatively quick economic success, but then they still have to democratize their society.[47] Indeed, many of our portraits have shown the expectations of the hugely increased cohort of students for accountability from their university and government leaders as well as the opportunity to participate actively in local and national affairs. Although the form of democracy that will emerge in China is not yet clear, the trend towards greater accountability and participation is unavoidable, with an increasingly vocal civil society and a rapidly growing middle class. In the same sense, academic excellence will only come with increasing degrees of China's unique form of intellectual freedom, one that integrates values from the *shuyuan* tradition into the concept of academic freedom associated with Western universities.

Nevertheless, we firmly believe China needs to develop its own unique university model for the 21st century. This is because, only when a university model grows out of its own national spirit, can it avoid external manipulation, whether political or economic, and create a spiritual base for the nation's pursuit of knowledge and for the formation of national character. The emergence of the American university model in the early 20th century followed precisely such a path, and has served well to nurture America's own thinkers and scientists. As Charles Eliot,[48] the influential 19th century Harvard president, put it, "[W]hen the American university appears, it will not be a copy of foreign institutions,

---

cases of conflict between the governments and the grassroots in recent years over such issues as corruption of officials, enterprization in educational service, and relocation of displaced people (*chaiqian* 拆遷). Nowadays the Chinese people are increasingly demanding participation in the social transformation, and rigorously guarding their interests and rights in the process, which is particularly voiced out on the Internet. In the past 20 years or so, China's Gini coefficient has got much worse, from 0.28 in 1983 (comparable with that of Sweden, Germany and Japan at the time) to 0.47 in 2007 (closer to Argentina and Mexico). This indicates a dramatically increasing inequality of income or wealth, which will eventually emerge as problems beyond the economic domain that affect the political domain.
[47] Edward Glaeser, Rafael La Porta, Florencio Lopez-de-Silanes, and Andrei Shleifer, "Do Institutions Cause Growth?," in *Journal of Economic Growth*, Vol.9, No.2, 2004, pp.271-303.
[48] Charles William Eliot (20 March 1834 – 22 August 1926) was an American academic who was selected as Harvard's president in 1869. He transformed a local college into America's preeminent research university. Eliot served the longest term as president in the university's history.

or a hot-bed plant, but the slow and natural outgrowth of American social and political habits".[49] While adapting to international intellectual trends, Eliot saw what he was doing as being in continuity with the American religious past and its contemporary political reality.

Only when rooted in its own independent and mature scholarly tradition, can the Chinese university embrace academic inputs from around the world, and provide conditions for Chinese scholars to carry out world-class and groundbreaking research. Otherwise Chinese academia may have to remain peripheral to such existent center systems as the American, for knowledge production and dissemination, being maximally a good follower. One scholar has suggested that China is "better understood as a theoretical power – a country that has promised to deliver for much of the last 150 years but has consistently disappointed."[50] After 30 years of reform, it is time for China to demonstrate what it can do, and it is indeed in a unique position to reconcile its indigenous roots with aspects of the Western model. In particular, such a strategic deliberation should be based on a strong historical consciousness, i.e., using history as an important weathervane and concrete guide. In this way, the Chinese university should be able to make a unique contribution to the world community.

This is our earnest wish and indeed has been the whole point of conducting this research. "The ethos of Chinese universities must find its own expression and identity in the modern world".[51] "Chinese universities will ... not only serve as channels of new knowledge and technology for needed areas of economic and social development within China, but also in introducing to a wider world progressive dimensions of Chinese culture and lessons learned from China's social development over a dramatic century of change".[52] After all, we would like to emphasize the importance of China's traditional scholarship, indigenous and local knowledge in the process of successful institution-building, and argue that participatory democracy is indeed the meta-institution that facilitates such use of indigenous and local knowledge, and promotes the ideal of *"he er bu tong"* or unity with diversity.

---

[49] Charles Eliot as cited in G.M. Marsden *The Soul of the American University: From Protestant Establishment to Established Nonbelief* (New York, NY: Oxford University Press, 1994), p.188.
[50] Gerald Segal, *op. cit.*, p.24.
[51] Hayhoe, 1999, *op. cit.*, p.142.
[52] *Ibid.*, p.272.

Notes on the Authors

Ruth HAYHOE is a professor at the Ontario Institute for Studies in Education of the University of Toronto. Her professional engagements in Asia have spanned 30 years, including foreign expert at Fudan University in Shanghai 1980-82, Head of the Cultural Section of the Canadian Embassy in Beijing, 1989-1991, and Director of the Hong Kong Institute of Education, 1997-2002. She has authored or edited more than a dozen books and about 80 articles in refereed journals.

Jun LI is assistant professor in international education policy at the Hong Kong Institute of Education and served as associated instructor at the University of Toronto from 2007-2010. While gaining wide international experience over several decades, he has published extensively in English, Chinese and Japanese, focusing on Chinese studies in education and culture, comparative and international education, policy studies in education and leadership, citizenship education and civil society, teacher education, and higher education and glocalization.

Jing LIN is professor of international education policy at University of Maryland, College Park. She has done extensive research on Chinese education, culture and society. She is the author of four books on Chinese education: *The Red Guard's Path to Violence* (1991), *Education in Post-Mao China* (1993), *The Opening of the Chinese Mind* (1994), and *Social Transformation and Private Education in China* (1999). Jing Lin has also published three books on peace education, environmental education, and spirituality education.

Qiang ZHA is an assistant professor at York University. His research focus has been on globalization and the internationalization of higher education as well as policy studies in higher education, and he has written and published widely on these topics in journals such as *Higher Education, Higher Education in Europe,* and the *Harvard China Review*. He was a co-recipient of the inaugural UNESCO Palgrave Prize on Higher Education Policy Research in 2004.

Index

A

academic freedom 16-8, 20-2, 57, 59-62, 97, 111, 114, 134, 313, 461, 464, 470
agriculture 6, 9, 23, 99, 104, 222-3, 232, 270, 345, 347-9, 351, 355, 359-61, 366, 370-1
Altbach, Philip 22, 28, 71, 413, 452, 457, 463
Analects, the 63-4, 67, 265, 460
applied sciences 23, 270-3, 280-1, 302, 307, 309-10, 314, 380, 406
Aristotle 62-3, 65, 420
arts 23, 59, 105, 150, 163, 166, 180, 182, 193, 197, 211, 213, 385, 406, 424
autonomy 16-7, 20-2, 25, 29, 47, 59, 62, 114, 279, 305, 307, 381, 388, 398-9, 426

B

basic sciences 23, 98-9, 101, 107, 114, 123, 128-9, 136, 152, 165, 205, 270-1, 277, 280, 317
Beida *see also* Peking University 35, 94-6, 98-116, 118, 120-9, 185, 311, 426, 464
Beijing 4, 7, 14, 26, 37-9, 47-8, 97-9, 131-2, 163-5, 221, 271, 284, 290, 299, 401
Blue Sky University (BSU) 8-9, 33, 373, 422-49, 466

C

Cai Yuanpei 17, 61-2, 95-6, 98-9, 104, 106, 115, 125, 128, 420, 449, 454, 460

Cambridge 60-1, 64-7, 69, 89, 96, 132, 138, 195, 296, 369, 454, 463
Changbai Mountains 245, 254-6, 259, 269
Chen Jiageng 162, 165, 168, 170, 180, 184-5, 188
Chen Min 307-43
Cheng Xiaofang 9, 271-306
China 1-3, 13-7, 25-8, 30-2, 38-41, 45-9, 67-9, 83-7, 95-9, 118-20, 131-6, 218-22, 274-80, 449-56, 466-71
China Education Daily 378, 402
China Quarterly 100, 351
China Youth Daily 41, 169, 218, 287
China's Move to Mass Higher Education 2, 4-5, 11, 19, 21, 23, 25, 27, 29, 31, 55-8, 73-4, 83-5, 92-4, 417
Chinese Academy of Sciences (CAS) 24-5, 137, 180, 270-1, 273-4, 276-80, 283-6, 290-4, 296-7, 301, 305, 309, 324, 344, 346
Chongqing 7, 135, 221-2, 224, 241, 243, 326, 350
citizenship 59, 61-4, 69, 74, 80, 83, 88, 90-3, 124
citizenship education 3, 62, 70, 88, 90, 92
civic
  action 81, 83
  knowing 72, 74, 79, 81-2, 91
  participation 10-1, 60, 70, 83, 91-2, 127, 156, 158-9, 240-1, 243, 337, 339, 420
  wisdom 72

civil society   2-3, 10, 13, 58-9, 61-71, 73-5, 79-81, 83, 87-93, 124, 159, 240, 267, 419
civil society organizations (CSOs)   61, 66, 68-9, 90, 159
colleges   29-30, 32, 40, 48-9, 105-6, 113-5, 227-8, 250, 315, 317-8, 331, 339-40, 377-8, 402-3, 406
community   69-70, 72, 81, 87, 98, 124, 178, 205, 229, 268, 336, 380, 382-4, 387, 390
  local communities   30, 67, 171, 222, 224, 229, 232, 240, 242, 249, 403, 411, 420-1
Communist Youth League   240, 388
Comparative Education Research Centre   2, 15, 18, 21, 72, 95, 163, 195, 308-9, 374-5, 379, 452
Comparative Education Review   98, 451
Confucian/Confucianism/Confucius   3, 15, 60, 63-4, 67, 89-90, 93, 180, 265, 321, 408, 420, 453, 458-60, 467
Confucius Institute(s)   2, 126, 174, 207, 220, 236, 461
construction   113, 115, 140-1, 167, 308, 312, 317-8, 326, 328, 366, 384, 388, 391, 425, 434
context   15, 19, 43, 50, 56, 60, 69-70, 85, 96, 101, 111, 272, 350-1, 367, 399-400
  socio-cultural   73, 86-7, 150
cooperation   9, 39, 44, 47, 116, 123, 146, 180-1, 233, 292, 326, 336, 362, 445
countries/country   2, 5-6, 31, 100-1, 120-1, 245-6, 252, 254-8, 260, 268, 351, 426-7, 435, 462-3, 469

Communist Party of China (CPC)   25, 89-90, 131, 274-5, 284, 414, 421-2
Cultural Revolution   24, 95, 100, 106, 136-8, 147, 157, 165, 170, 195, 230, 247, 270-1, 309, 342
culture   2, 12-3, 58, 60, 65, 68, 93, 109, 148-50, 155-7, 251-3, 255, 257, 265-6, 468-9
  Chinese   2, 72, 109, 126, 128-30, 137, 148, 178, 185, 188, 206, 265, 269, 337, 398
curricular
  development   13, 16, 24, 101, 105, 108, 112, 123, 163, 167, 171, 173-4, 198, 318, 326, 336, 347, 368, 370, 380, 386-7, 410-1
  reform   25, 114-5
curriculum   12, 71, 96, 98-9, 104, 107, 170, 198-9, 227, 233, 250, 271-2, 317, 381-2, 465-6

D

Dao   63, 458, 467
Daoism   3, 60
degree programs   31-2, 250, 315, 331, 378, 386, 394, 397, 404, 406, 418, 445
  bachelor/undergraduate   140, 144, 227-8, 250, 314, 354-5, 368, 381, 402, 404, 412, 422, 426, 437, 442, 444, 446
  masters   150, 173, 180, 182, 328, 331, 335, 337, 391, 393, 436-7
  doctoral   116, 119, 145, 300, 302, 317, 387, 395, 444
  graduate   117, 124, 128, 205, 262, 279, 335, 345, 367

democracy   1, 60, 64-8, 91, 93, 121, 133, 157-8, 283-4, 451, 454, 470
departments   99, 104-7, 114-5, 135-6, 144, 155, 164-5, 167-8, 193-4, 196-8, 203-4, 272-4, 278, 288, 317-8
Dewey, John   59-60, 62, 93, 195, 426
diversification   3-5, 28, 48, 52, 114, 168, 175, 198-9, 304, 457, 463
Donglin Academy   68

E

East China Normal University Press   61, 68, 132
East China Normal University (ECNU)   7, 33, 190, 192-209, 211, 213-21, 223, 243, 291, 300, 404-5, 444, 466
economics   23, 104-5, 116, 150, 164-5, 167-70, 172-3, 183-4, 187-8, 250, 298-9, 317-8, 354-5, 406, 416-7
education   22-8, 44-5, 59-61, 84-8, 93, 155-6, 163-5, 170, 192-201, 203-5, 209, 211-3, 217-20, 222, 425-7
   civic   72, 88, 91
   elite   279, 303
   minister of   61, 97, 312, 324
   ministry of   96, 132
   moral   61-2, 73, 133, 439
   political   88, 91, 136, 267, 335, 396
   private   3, 168, 372, 400-1, 408, 410, 412-3, 421, 427
   quality of   263, 341, 411, 432, 449
   secondary   213, 267
   technical   12, 313, 422, 424, 432
education policy
   higher   363-4
   international   3, 477
educational development   26, 29, 373, 400
   higher   152, 342
educational institutions   59, 209, 375-6
   higher   86, 92, 132, 135, 142
   private   427
   public   86
elite   6, 28, 31, 44-5, 51, 56, 58, 70-2, 75-6, 83-5, 92, 124, 168, 341, 353
engineering   23, 99, 101-2, 106-7, 152, 163-4, 169, 172-3, 228, 273-4, 317-8, 329, 354-5, 380-2, 432-3
English   102, 116-7, 123, 149, 169, 174, 181-2, 207, 236, 250, 256, 260, 266, 275, 314, 319, 321, 339-41, 358, 360, 386, 393, 411, 438, 447
enrollments   5, 8, 27-8, 30-2, 39-40, 42, 46-7, 101-2, 166-7, 196-7, 286-7, 341-2, 352-3, 401, 405
equality   36, 45, 51, 55, 58, 61, 66, 85, 213, 264, 267
equity   1, 3, 5, 10, 13, 19, 36, 46, 50, 55, 58-9, 67, 85-7, 124, 185
Europe   4, 8, 21, 23, 64, 84, 97, 173, 463, 465, 467
evaluation   50, 54, 236-7, 412, 464
examinations   21, 36, 295, 356, 376-7, 389, 397, 406, 425, 434, 459
exchanges   146, 150, 205, 260, 265-6, 362, 393, 462
Executive Vice-President   95, 223-4, 230, 232-3, 323-4, 347-8, 355, 370
expansion   5-7, 25-8, 30-2, 34-5, 37, 40-4, 55-6, 70-2, 76, 78-9, 84-5, 160, 238, 286-8, 312-3

policy   43-4, 92, 142, 155, 160, 226, 228, 287

F

faculty   98-9, 111-2, 118-25, 152-5, 176-81, 201-6, 208-10, 234-6, 250-4, 258, 260-3, 299-302, 331-6, 391-3, 437-8

fields   23-4, 102, 123-5, 164, 168-9, 180-1, 184-5, 189-90, 212-3, 232-3, 358-9, 367-8, 370, 382-3, 386

finance   8, 23-4, 39, 41, 47, 52, 163-4, 168, 174, 200, 307-8, 317-9, 329-30, 332, 434-5

forestry   6, 9, 23, 256, 270, 345-7, 349, 354, 359-60, 370-1, 456

founders   165, 168, 188, 375, 379, 395, 400-1, 410-1, 413-4, 423, 427, 429, 432, 448

Four Books   72, 133, 452, 459

France   61, 89, 97, 99, 172-3, 193, 205, 270, 297, 456

Frontiers of Education in China   15, 61, 134, 190, 193

Fujian province   7, 162-3, 166, 171, 175, 183, 185

funding *see also* grants   6, 11, 25, 28, 87, 103, 143, 169, 175, 200, 209, 226-7, 249, 256, 334-5

G

globalization   22, 42-4, 70, 210, 252, 342-3, 367, 457

Gong Fang   131-61

governance   16, 25, 28, 30, 61, 146, 192, 196, 200, 332, 365, 375, 396, 446

government   3-4, 43, 46-7, 51-2, 87, 100, 103, 108, 110-11, 140-1, 153, 425-7, 434-6, 444-7, 464-6

central   28, 31-2, 39-40, 49, 136, 138-9, 141, 152, 175, 179, 200, 202, 223-4, 348, 350-1

Chinese   6, 26, 29, 43, 46, 68-9, 87, 89, 135, 141, 158, 223, 285, 345, 401

local   40-1, 224, 226, 242, 256, 287, 290, 292, 425

provincial   29, 31-2, 41, 49-50, 141, 169, 327, 344, 347-8, 425, 446

graduates   3, 36, 71, 100, 118-9, 123, 178, 209, 213-4, 216, 341, 368-9, 382-3, 432, 440

grants *see also* funding   258-9, 392, 431, 434

Great Learning, The   60, 64, 72, 93, 133, 459-60

Guo Bingwen   61, 133-4

Guomindang   94, 135, 345

H

Hayhoe, Ruth   1-19, 21, 24, 61, 95-130, 134, 162-89, 192-220, 307-71, 374-99, 452-3, 455

Hefei   7, 271, 275-6, 284, 293, 297-9, 302

Henan   275-6, 308, 374, 384, 389, 391, 397, 422

Henan province   8, 275, 308, 374, 376, 384, 386, 388

higher education   1-4, 19-20, 22-9, 43-53, 56-62, 70-2, 75-8, 83-7, 92-7, 132-5, 221-3, 270-3, 351-3, 369-72, 462-5

comparative   95

development   6, 20, 28-9, 50, 271, 378, 408, 422, 457, 460

expansion   35, 38, 43-4, 51-3, 70-1, 75-6, 83-4, 86, 92, 152, 264, 418
integration of   29, 50
institutions   23, 28-9, 32-4, 37, 40, 46-7, 49, 52, 62, 70, 84, 132, 223-4, 273, 291
law   13, 16, 25, 46-7, 110-1, 209, 381, 398, 414, 464
private   3, 5, 30, 45, 374, 378, 380, 389, 401, 408, 413, 420, 426, 428
quality   35, 53
reform   29, 50
research   9, 61, 75, 95, 105, 165, 188, 372, 380, 413, 421
system   4-5, 20, 25, 27, 42, 51, 53, 71, 84, 193, 204, 214, 270-1, 455, 457
Higher Education Press   28, 32
Hong Kong   2, 15, 21, 88, 90-1, 95, 121, 131, 163, 195, 308-9, 321, 374-5, 379, 452
Hu Shi   61-2, 99, 125
Huazhong   7-9, 343
Huazhong University of Science and Technology (HUST)   7, 33, 40, 153, 270, 286, 291, 307-43, 388, 393
Hubei Province   8, 315, 327, 330, 442
humanities   9-10, 74, 98-9, 104, 136-9, 142-4, 146, 155, 165-6, 248, 288-9, 303-4, 314, 317-8, 353-4

I

Icon of Cultural Leadership   95-130

identity   120, 128-9, 134, 169, 181, 195, 199, 205, 216, 219, 270-1, 279, 399, 471
ideologies   55-6, 66, 457, 464
Influential Chinese Educators   15, 95, 163, 189, 195, 218, 309, 375, 379, 399
institutional development   46, 407, 410, 414
institutions   5-12, 14-5, 29, 31-2, 39-40, 46-50, 52-4, 203-5, 223-6, 228-30, 269-70, 349-51, 372-4, 446-7, 455-6
   local   32, 34-6, 40, 42, 48, 53, 169, 189, 308, 374, 398
   private   5-6, 12, 27, 30, 35, 60, 74, 76, 79, 86-7, 305, 372, 378-9, 412-3, 425
   public   5, 30, 49, 77-8, 94, 221, 330-1, 372, 415
integration   42, 114, 147, 184, 203, 218, 228-30, 243, 246, 251-2, 270, 280, 321, 323-6, 329
intellectual
   authority   17, 21, 57, 459, 464
   freedom   17, 21, 24, 61, 100, 125, 128, 466, 470
international
   cooperation   150, 205, 362, 406, 456
   education   207, 319, 323, 340, 477
   students   84-5, 102, 113, 116-7, 123, 150, 173, 180, 184, 204, 206, 209, 261, 315, 456
International Handbook of Higher Education   22, 28, 71, 452, 457
International Higher Education   2, 5, 8, 54, 295, 311, 426, 438, 463

International Journal of Educational Development 11, 53, 73, 83, 456
International Journal of Educational Research 88
internationalization 43, 85, 116, 145, 151, 162, 171, 176, 179, 220, 260, 265, 293, 295, 361
   institutional 72, 79-80

J

Japan 3, 28, 70, 72, 89, 91, 120-1, 138, 163, 203, 244-5, 255, 269, 297-8, 453
Jiangxi 276, 332, 422-6, 428, 430, 435-6, 446-7
Jixia Academy 60-1, 68, 421
Journal of Higher Education 101, 199, 351

K

Kerr, Clark 60, 369
knowledge 4, 17, 22, 24, 40, 69-70, 72, 109, 168-9, 218, 381-2, 397-8, 440-1, 457-8, 460-1, 471
Kuang Yaming 136-7, 144-5, 148-50, 155, 160

L

law 16, 23-5, 46-7, 163, 173, 227-8, 250, 267, 318, 339-40, 355, 370, 381, 398, 425-7
leaders 2, 13-4, 37, 49, 95-6, 127-9, 252, 271, 307-9, 319-21, 342-3, 378-9, 393-4, 429-31, 435-7
   academic 108, 113-4, 118, 396
   national 116, 118, 126, 129, 150, 165, 271
leadership 11, 16, 96, 111, 134, 137, 142, 179, 188, 199-202, 311-2, 339, 341-3, 349-50, 414

Li, Jun 58-93, 131-61, 221-69, 271-343, 400-21
Li Mei 192-220
library 113, 118, 122, 126, 163, 171, 181, 203, 316, 368-9, 377, 389, 394, 407, 429
Lin, Jing 131-61, 221-43, 244-69, 374-449
literature 22, 104-5, 120, 124, 155, 167, 172, 179, 182, 192, 205, 238-9, 254, 258, 358
   comparative higher education 22
Liu Fonian 194-5, 204, 208, 215
Liu Yibing 221-43
Liwa River 207, 213

M

Ma Yinchu 95, 99, 121, 128
Mainland China *see* China
Mao Zedong 23, 132, 134-5, 138, 146-7, 152, 230, 277
market economy 29, 43, 46, 51-2, 168, 276, 298, 302-3, 350-1, 403, 407
Mass Higher Education 2, 5, 11, 20-1, 23, 25, 27, 29, 35-7, 45, 47-51, 57-8, 70-1, 73-4, 83-5
massification 6, 11, 25, 32, 43, 45, 47, 51, 154, 215, 271, 305, 342, 344, 363
May Fourth Movement 62, 133, 454
Mencius 63-4
Meng Xiancheng 131, 195, 217, 221, 470,
merger 6-7, 101, 122-3, 151-2, 169-70, 202-4, 223-8, 234-6, 242-3, 246-8, 298, 311-3, 324-9, 348-52, 354-5

institutional   13, 151, 200, 356
  major   7, 221, 223, 311, 354
Minister of Education   55, 96, 311-2, 330
Ministry of Education (MoE)   29-30, 40-1, 49, 54, 152, 232-3, 236, 258, 293-5, 345-6, 377-8, 381-2, 392-5, 402, 445-6
Ministry of Education of China   26-7, 31, 47, 165, 178, 247, 279, 293, 381, 395
mission   13, 39, 96, 108, 124-5, 145-6, 168, 183, 199, 219-20, 229-30, 242-3, 319, 412-3, 448-9
  statement   108-10, 121, 146, 319, 465
models   20, 22, 28, 49-50, 83, 121, 140, 193, 220, 305-6, 359-60, 382-3, 413-4, 451-3, 468-9
  American   56, 323, 468
  Chinese   20, 450-1, 466-8
  Emerging Chinese   12, 15, 17, 451-3, 455, 457, 459, 461, 463, 465, 467, 469, 471
motto   135, 168, 202, 229, 281, 320, 345, 408
Move to Mass Higher Education   2, 5, 11, 20-1, 23, 25, 27, 29, 31, 33, 35, 37, 39, 57-8, 73-4
Multicultural Identity   244-269
multiculturalism   109, 244, 250-2

N

Nanchang   8, 278, 312, 433, 444-5
Nanda *see also* Nanjing University   94, 131-2, 136-45, 147, 149-58, 160-1, 285
Nanjing   7, 94, 98, 131-3, 135-7, 146, 148, 152, 156, 164, 221-2, 383, 452

Nanjing Daxue Bainian Shi   132-3, 135-6, 146, 148, 152
Nanjing University (NJU)   7, 33, 42, 94, 131-61, 300
Nanjing University Press   132-3, 135-6, 139, 146, 148, 152, 156
National Central University   94, 131, 135-6, 147
National Higher Education Entrance Examinations   153, 403, 405, 417-18
National People's Congress   104, 427, 447
Newman, John Henry   57-9, 68
Niu Hongtai   9, 344-71
non-profit organizations (NPOs)   65, 81
non-governmental organizations (NGOs)   66, 82, 206
North Korea   244-6, 257, 269
Northwest Agricultural and Forestry University (NWAFU)   8, 33, 291, 344-71, 465-6
Northwest Agricultural University   345-7, 349, 353, 365
Northwest Forestry College   346, 349

O

Ontario   48-9
Ontario Institute for Studies in Education (OISE)   5, 8
Outline for Educational Reform and Development in China   26, 28-9, 31, 44, 49

P

Party Secretary   16, 105, 107, 111, 200-1, 210, 296, 309, 349, 362, 380, 391, 396

patriotism   89, 91, 163, 168, 184, 195, 379, 439
Peking University (PKU)   6-7, 9, 14, 16-7, 44-5, 61-2, 94-130, 291-3, 300, 323-4, 449, 454, 464-6
Piao Taizhu   244-69
Plato   62-3, 420, 458
policy   2, 29, 37, 39, 41, 46, 50, 56, 114, 278, 292, 330-2, 350-1, 362, 434
  educational   4, 193
  national   30, 87, 101, 141, 145, 168, 178, 191, 199, 220, 223-4, 239, 298, 312, 315
political socialization (PS)   60, 74-5, 80-3, 90-2
portraits   9, 11, 13-7, 94-5, 190-1, 270, 372-4, 421, 456-7, 466, 470
president   98-100, 135-7, 178, 195-6, 200-2, 206-7, 253, 311-3, 319-21, 326-7, 380, 395, 398, 412-15, 429-31
  university   141, 313, 449
professors   22, 81, 97, 120-1, 154-7, 159-60, 175-8, 210, 235-7, 261-3, 276, 299-300, 364, 390-2, 415-7
provinces   32-3, 36, 41, 49, 101, 163, 166, 171, 253-4, 256, 264, 350, 374-5, 377-8, 424-5
provost   112, 133, 195, 317, 319-20, 325, 330, 332-5, 411, 430

Q

Qifang Education Research Institute   412-3
Qu Qinyue   136-7, 139, 141, 144, 160
quality   5, 13, 26, 30, 33, 53, 55, 213, 236, 300-1, 335-7, 339-41, 371-2, 448, 464-5
  assurance   46, 53, 411-12
  education   26, 29, 50, 156
  educational   34, 71, 146, 176, 199

R

region   5-6, 15, 24, 142, 164-5, 172, 181, 222, 229, 244-5, 252-3, 256-7, 259-60, 263-4, 276
Republic of China *see also* China   30, 47, 55, 271, 274, 345, 381, 395, 410, 414, 426, 455
research   8-9, 24-5, 117-9, 137-40, 145-6, 152-6, 175-8, 203-4, 210-2, 232-7, 253-5, 257-9, 358-61, 369-71, 415-7
  grants   48, 119, 143, 226-7, 256, 259, 291, 316, 356
  institutes/institutions   25, 205, 273, 276-9, 293-4, 301, 344, 347-8, 357, 360, 362, 412-3, 430, 444
responsibility   29, 49, 63, 81, 89, 100, 108-9, 119-21, 125-9, 171, 237-8, 319-20, 335-6, 339-40, 342
rural areas   74, 78, 81-2, 86-7, 159, 199, 211, 213, 226, 233, 240, 340, 342, 383, 442
Russia   244, 255, 257, 261, 269, 297, 424

S

scholars   1, 4, 8-9, 14, 19, 22, 36, 43-6, 55, 100-1, 126-7, 177, 196, 231-2, 458-9
  Chinese   17, 21, 39, 45-6, 57, 460, 464, 469, 471
scholarship   21, 59, 87, 94, 97-9, 129, 147, 160-1, 173, 176, 182, 184, 205, 232, 264

Science 33, 61, 100, 133, 233, 285, 288, 362, 372, 374-7, 379, 381, 383, 385, 395-7
sciences 6-7, 10, 23-5, 59, 133-4, 163, 165-7, 177, 270-3, 284, 288-9, 303, 346-7, 353-5, 370
Shaanxi 344, 348, 350-1, 360, 365
Shaanxi Province 8, 346-50, 363, 365, 400-1
Shanghai 4, 7-8, 61, 68, 72, 132, 164-5, 192, 194, 197-8, 202-4, 211, 214, 221-2, 453-4
Shuyuan (Academy) 1, 5, 20, 60, 97-8, 221, 380, 457, 463, 470, 474
social capital 3, 66, 427, 429
social sciences 9-10, 23, 41, 74, 76, 80, 85, 88, 104-6, 117-8, 138-9, 142-6, 248, 310, 314
society 3, 16, 59-63, 81-2, 87, 93, 120-1, 133-4, 178, 267, 338-42, 367-8, 426, 428-9, 435-6
  Chinese 4-5, 37, 53, 55, 124, 159, 172, 187, 317, 341, 460
socioeconomic development 78-9, 84, 228, 250
sociology 101, 105-7, 120, 123-5, 129, 145, 167, 208, 317-8, 354
South Korea 121, 257, 260-1, 264, 266, 269, 463
Southeast University 134-5, 152
Southwest Agricultural University 221-3, 228, 230
Southwest Normal University 190, 222, 229-30, 241
Southwest University (SWU) 7, 33, 134, 221-43
Soviet Union 246-7, 275
specializations 23-4, 38-9, 42, 270, 273, 278, 280, 288-9, 325

state 4, 17, 21-2, 25, 29-30, 43, 46-8, 63, 69, 72, 275, 290-1, 364, 375, 458-62
student
  affairs 108, 110, 272, 288, 314, 319, 344, 353, 386-8, 438
  fees 48, 103, 143, 152, 175, 226, 249, 316, 377, 394, 407

T

Taiwan 136, 162, 164, 166, 183, 297
Tang Baomei 374-399
Tao Xingzhi 134, 426
teacher education 6, 12, 190, 193, 196, 199, 201, 203, 214, 218, 222-3, 227-8, 232-3, 250, 259-60
teaching 59-62, 117-20, 139-40, 152-4, 171-2, 175-8, 201-6, 208-11, 232-7, 329-37, 358-60, 363-6, 380-2, 391-3, 415-7
  quality 10, 34, 79, 119, 153-5, 175, 211, 213, 232, 237, 262, 313, 364, 391, 396
  reforms 84, 236, 365, 465-6
technologies/technology 6-7, 9-10, 25, 33, 74, 76, 80, 88, 106, 109, 142-4, 146, 167, 218, 228, 248, 270, 274, 277, 374-5, 381
Third sector organizations (TSOs) 65, 67
Tongji 136, 209, 211, 325-6
Tongji Medical University 324-5, 329
top institutions/universities 6, 31, 108, 138-9, 152, 261-2, 294-5, 310-1, 331
tradition 5, 12, 38, 65, 106-7, 121, 147, 156-7, 180, 222-3, 229, 243, 245, 252, 458-9

Chinese   63-4, 89, 122, 134, 180, 382, 390
transition   10, 20, 27-8, 45, 50-1, 56, 70-1, 83-5, 92, 166, 258, 370-1, 407, 446
Trow, Martin   70, 84-5, 305
Tsinghua   99-100, 140, 149, 185, 291, 311, 460
tuition   77, 239, 249-50, 264, 434, 436, 442-3

U

universities   40-2, 58-61, 74-6, 134-8, 149-54, 170-3, 194-7, 199-202, 234-57, 264-70, 282-7, 386-93, 425-41, 447-53, 461-71
  agricultural   235, 344, 351, 355
  American   60, 172, 206, 295, 455, 468, 470
  Chinese   1, 6, 15-7, 38, 124-5, 137-8, 149, 171-2, 285-6, 304-5, 455-6, 460-1, 464-5, 467-8, 471
  comprehensive   52, 134, 139-40, 165-6, 169, 180, 199, 208-9, 219, 228, 243, 250, 254-5, 273, 371
  elite   31, 35-6, 45, 53, 59, 221, 286, 288, 462
  engineering   100, 200, 202, 209, 354
  leading   100, 146, 153, 221, 270
  (national) key universities   136, 138-9, 243, 436
  national   31, 35, 42, 48, 139, 169, 198, 214, 219, 223, 244, 279, 296, 350, 411
  normal   6, 61, 134, 190, 192-3, 195-7, 199, 204-5, 217, 219-21, 223, 225, 233, 309, 351
  polytechnical   202, 271, 273, 280-1, 302

private   30, 32, 77-8, 194, 331, 372-3, 378-80, 386-7, 393-6, 416-23, 425-7, 434-5, 437-8, 440, 444-8
provincial   32, 327, 330, 440
public   6, 30, 80, 86-7, 381, 386-8, 390-2, 411-2, 414-6, 419, 425-6, 429-31, 437, 440-1, 445-7
Western   261, 295, 333, 470
world-class   31, 45, 56, 146, 152, 244, 269, 294, 298, 359, 463
university leaders   8-9, 15, 25, 107-8, 112, 129, 141, 169, 175-7, 188, 196, 204, 215, 339, 344-5
University of Science and Technology of China (USTC)   7, 9, 33, 42, 270-307, 311, 324, 422, 440, 444
Unnamed Lake   113, 122, 126, 130

V

vice-presidents   170, 172-4, 197, 201, 212, 248, 253-4, 265, 300, 309, 320, 331, 334, 357, 436, 145, 147-8, 151, 206, 411-2, 415, 9, 111-2, 170-1, 212, 332-3, 390, 414, 431
vision   5, 13, 16, 20, 25, 100, 145, 168, 200-1, 229-30, 309-10, 319-20, 378-9, 399-400, 407-8
von Humboldt, Wilhelm   59

W

Wang Guan   400-21
Wu Mi   233-4
Wuhan   8, 164, 222, 307-9, 311-2, 325, 328, 387, 393
Wuhan University   308, 311-2, 321, 324-5, 378, 387

X

Xiada *see also* Xiamen University 162-5, 167, 169-77, 179-81, 183-5, 187
Xiamen   4, 7, 162, 164-5
Xiamen University (XMU)   7, 33, 36, 45, 94, 153, 162-89, 379
Xi'an   5, 8, 344, 347, 372, 390, 400-2, 408-9, 423
Xi'an International University (XAIU)   8-9, 400-21, 427
Xie Zuxu   162-89

Y

Yan Fengqiao   95-130
Yanbian   191, 244-64, 266, 268
Yanbian University (YBU)   7, 33, 190, 221, 243-69
Yangling   8, 344, 346-8, 356, 358, 360-1, 370
Yanji   7, 246-7, 253-4, 264
Yellow River   5, 375, 377-98, 446
Yellow River University of Science and Technology   8-9, 33, 372, 374-99
Yu Youren   345, 367-8, 466

Z

Zha, Qiang   20-57, 95-130, 162-89, 192-220, 271-306, 344-71, 422-49, 451-71
Zhengzhou   8, 374, 377, 379, 387, 394
Zhou Guangli   307-43
Zhu Jiusi   309, 311-2, 317, 319-20, 338, 342
Zhu Xi   459

CERC Studies in Comparative Education (ctd)

13. Mok Ka-Ho (ed.) (2003): *Centralization and Decentralization: Educational Reforms and Changing Governance in Chinese Societies*. ISBN 978-962-8093-58-8. 230pp. HK$200/US$32.

12. Robert A. LeVine (2003, reprinted 2010): *Childhood Socialization: Comparative Studies of Parenting, Learning and Educational Change*. ISBN 978-962-8093-61-8. 299pp.

11. Ruth Hayhoe & Julia Pan (eds.) (2001): *Knowledge Across Cultures: A Contribution to Dialogue Among Civilizations*. ISBN 978-962-8093-73-1. 391pp. [Out of print]

10. William K. Cummings, Maria Teresa Tatto & John Hawkins (eds.) (2001): *Values Education for Dynamic Societies: Individualism or Collectivism*. ISBN 978-962-8093-71-7. 312pp. HK$200/US$32.

9. Gu Mingyuan (2001): *Education in China and Abroad: Perspectives from a Lifetime in Comparative Education*. ISBN 978-962-8093-70-0. 252pp. HK$200/US$32.

8. Thomas Clayton (2000): *Education and the Politics of Language: Hegemony and Pragmatism in Cambodia, 1979-1989*. ISBN 978-962-8093-83-0. 243pp. HK$200/US$32.

7. Mark Bray & Ramsey Koo (eds.) (2004): *Education and Society in Hong Kong and Macao: Comparative Perspectives on Continuity and Change*. Second edition. ISBN 978-962-8093-34-2. 323pp. HK$200/US$32.

6. T. Neville Postlethwaite (1999): *International Studies of Educational Achievement: Methodological Issues*. ISBN 978-962-8093-86-1. 86pp. HK$100/US$20.

5. Harold Noah & Max A. Eckstein (1998): *Doing Comparative Education: Three Decades of Collaboration*. ISBN 978-962-8093-87-8. 356pp. HK$250/US$38.

4. Zhang Weiyuan (1998): *Young People and Careers: A Comparative Study of Careers Guidance in Hong Kong, Shanghai and Edinburgh*. ISBN 978-962-8093-89-2. 160pp. HK$180/US$30.

3. Philip G. Altbach (1998): *Comparative Higher Education: Knowledge, the University, and Development*. ISBN 978-962-8093-88-5. 312pp. HK$180/US$30.

2. Mark Bray & W.O. Lee (eds.) (1997): *Education and Political Transition: Implications of Hong Kong's Change of Sovereignty*. ISBN 978-962-8093-90-8. 169pp. [Out of print]

1. Mark Bray & W.O. Lee (eds.) (2001): *Education and Political Transition: Themes and Experiences in East Asia*. Second edition. ISBN 978-962-8093-84-7. 228pp. HK$200/ US$32.

Order through bookstores or from:

Comparative Education Research Centre
Faculty of Education, The University of Hong Kong, Pokfulam Road, Hong Kong, China.
Fax: (852) 2517 4737
E-mail: cerc@hku.hk
Website: www.hku.hk/cerc

The list prices above are applicable for order from CERC, and include sea mail postage. For air mail postage costs, please contact CERC.

No. 7 in the series and Nos. 13-15 are co-published with Kluwer Academic Publishers and the Comparative Education Research Centre of the University of Hong Kong. Books from No. 16 onwards are co-published with Springer. Springer publishes hardback and electronic versions.

CERC Studies in Comparative Education 17

Portraits of Influential Chinese Educators

Ruth Hayhoe

Publishers: Comparative Education Research Centre and Springer
ISBN: 978-962-8093-40-3
Date: 2006; 398 pages
Price: HK$250/US$38

China's economic rise has surprised the world, and most governments and large corporations feel the need for a China-strategy to shape their relations with this emerging super-power. What do they know, however, about the educational ideas and achievements that have contributed to this economic success? Names of political figures such as Mao Zedong, Deng Xiaoping and Jiang Zemin are household words, yet how many people have heard of Li Bingde, Gu Mingyuan, Lu Jie or Ye Lan?

Substantial research has been done on Chinese educational development by Sinologists and Comparative Educationists, making a wealth of data and analysis available to the specialist reader. Most of these studies have been framed within Western social science parameters, integrating an objectivist assessment of Chinese education into the international research literature.

This book conveys an understanding of China's educational development from within, through portraits of eleven influential educators whose ideas have shaped the educational reforms initiated by Deng Xiaoping in 1978. They are portrayed in the context of their cultural heritage, families, communities and schools, offering their own deeply reflective interpretations of Chinese education. The book is written for the general reader, to provide glimpses into the educational context of China's recent move onto the world stage.

Ruth Hayhoe is Professor at the Ontario Institute for Studies in Education of the University of Toronto, President *Emerita* of the Hong Kong Institute of Education, Past President of the Comparative and International Education Society, and an Associate Member of the Comparative Education Research Centre at the University of Hong Kong. She has written extensively on higher education in China and on educational relations between China and the West. She is an Honorary Fellow of the University of London Institute of Education, and was awarded the Silver Bauhinia Star by the Hong Kong SAR Government and the title of Commandeur dans l'ordre des Palmes Académiques by the Government of France in 2002. In the same year she was also awarded an honorary Doctorate of Education by the Hong Kong Institute of Education.

More details: www.hku.hk/cerc/Publications/publications.htm

CERC Studies in Comparative Education 27

Crossing Borders in East Asian Higher Education

Edited by
David W. Chapman, William K. Cummings & Gerard A. Postiglione

Publishers: Comparative Education Research Centre and Springer
ISBN 978-962-8093-98-4
June 2010; 388 pages
Price: HK$250/US$38

This book examines issues that have emerged as higher education systems and individual institutions across East Asia confront and adapt to the changing economic, social, and educational environments in which they now operate. The book's focus is on how higher education systems learn from each other and on the ways in which they collaborate to address new challenges. The sub-theme that runs through this volume concerns the changing nature of cross-border sharing. In particular, the provision of technical assistance by more industrialized countries to lower and middle income countries has given way to collaborations that place the latter's participating institutions on a more equal footing. At the same time, there is a greater number of partnerships that link higher education systems in the East Asian region to one another. Even as boundaries become more porous and permeable, there is growing acceptance of the view that cross border collaboration, if done well, can offer mutually beneficial advantages on multiple levels. There is a new recognition that the intensified international sharing of ideas, strategies of learning, and students is not only of enormous value to systems and institutions but essential to their long term survival. To this end, the chapters in this volume examine various motivations, goals, mechanisms, outcomes and challenges associated with cross-border collaboration in higher education.

David W. CHAPMAN is the Birkmaier Professor of Educational Leadership in the Department of Organizational Leadership, Policy, and Development in the College of Education and Human Development at the University of Minnesota. **William K. CUMMINGS** is Professor of International Education and International Affairs at George Washington University. **Gerard A. POSTIGLIONE** is Professor and Head, Division of Policy, Administration and Social Sciences, and Director of the Wah Ching Centre of Research on Education in China, Faculty of Education, the University of Hong Kong.

More details: www.hku.hk/cerc/Publications/publications.htm

CERC Studies in Comparative Education 25

Revisiting The Chinese Learner
Changing Contexts,
Changing Education

Edited by
Carol K.K. Chan & Nirmala Rao

Publishers: Comparative Education Research
Centre and Springer
ISBN 978-962-8093-16-8
June 2009; 360 pages
Price: HK$250 / US$38

This book, which extends pioneering work on Chinese learners in two previous volumes, examines teaching and learning in Chinese societies and advances understanding of 'the Chinese learner' in changing global contexts. Given the burgeoning research in this area, pedagogical shifts from knowledge transmission to knowledge construction to knowledge creation, wide-ranging social, economic and technological advances, and changes in educational policy, *Revisiting the Chinese Learner* is a timely endeavor.

The book revisits the paradox of the Chinese learner against the background of these educational changes; considers how Chinese cultural beliefs and contemporary change influence learning; and examines how Chinese teachers and learners respond to new educational goals, interweaving new and old beliefs and practices. Contributors focus on both continuity and change in analyzing student learning, pedagogical practice, teacher learning and professional development in Chinese societies. Key emerging themes emphasize transcending dichotomies and transforming pedagogy in understanding and teaching Chinese learners. The book has implications for theories of learning, development and educational innovation and will therefore be of interest to scholars and educators around the world who are changing education in their changing contexts.

Carol K.K. Chan is an Associate Professor in the Faculty of Education at The University of Hong Kong. Her research areas include learning, cognition and instruction, computer-supported knowledge building and teacher communities for classroom innovation. She has published in leading journals in these areas and won international research awards on knowledge building conducted in Chinese classrooms. Dr Chan has received Outstanding Teaching Awards from both her Faculty and University. She is currently Co-Director of a Strategic Research Theme on Sciences of Learning at The University of Hong Kong.

Nirmala Rao is a Professor in the Faculty of Education at The University of Hong Kong. She is a Developmental and Educational Psychologist whose research focuses on early childhood development and education. She has published widely in these areas and has engaged in policy relevant child development research in several countries in the region. She has also been actively involved, at the international level, in several professional organizations concerned both with the well-being of young children and research on early child development.

More details: www.hku.hk/cerc/Publications/publications.htm

CERC Studies in Comparative Education 19

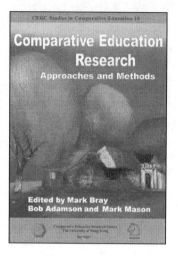

Comparative Education Research
Approaches and Methods

Edited by
Mark Bray
Bob Adamson
Mark Mason

Publishers: Comparative Education Research Centre and Springer
ISBN: 978-962-8093-53-3
Date: 2007; 444 pages
Price: HK$250 / US$38

Approaches and methods in comparative education research are of obvious importance, but do not always receive adequate attention. This book contributes new insights within the longstanding traditions of the field.

A particular feature is the focus on different units of analysis. Individual chapters compare places, systems, times, cultures, values, policies, curricula and other units. These chapters are contextualised within broader analytical frameworks which identify the purposes and strengths of the field. The book includes a focus on intra-national as well as cross-national comparisons, and highlights the value of approaching themes from different angles. The book will be of great value not only to producers of comparative education research but also to consumers who wish to understand more thoroughly the parameters and value of the field.

The editors: *Mark Bray* is Director of the UNESCO International Institute for Educational Planning, in Paris; *Bob Adamson* is Associate Professor in the Hong Kong Institute of Education; and *Mark Mason* is Associate Professor in the Faculty of Education at the University of Hong Kong. They have all been Presidents of the Comparative Education Society of Hong Kong (CESHK), and Directors of the Comparative Education Research Centre (CERC) at the University of Hong Kong. They have also written extensively in the field of comparative education with reference to multiple domains and cultures.

More details: www.hku.hk/cerc/Publications/publications.htm